Politics and Economics of the Middle East

Afghanistan National Development Strategies and Plans

POLITICS AND ECONOMICS OF THE MIDDLE EAST

Additional books in this series can be found on Nova's website
under the Series tab.

Additional E-books in this series can be found on Nova's website
under the E-books tab.

POLITICS AND ECONOMICS OF THE MIDDLE EAST

AFGHANISTAN NATIONAL DEVELOPMENT STRATEGIES AND PLANS

JENNIFER L. BROWN
EDITOR

Nova Science Publishers, Inc.
New York

Copyright © 2011 by Nova Science Publishers, Inc.

All rights reserved. No part of this book may be reproduced, stored in a retrieval system or transmitted in any form or by any means: electronic, electrostatic, magnetic, tape, mechanical photocopying, recording or otherwise without the written permission of the Publisher.

For permission to use material from this book please contact us:
Telephone 631-231-7269; Fax 631-231-8175
Web Site: http://www.novapublishers.com

NOTICE TO THE READER

The Publisher has taken reasonable care in the preparation of this book, but makes no expressed or implied warranty of any kind and assumes no responsibility for any errors or omissions. No liability is assumed for incidental or consequential damages in connection with or arising out of information contained in this book. The Publisher shall not be liable for any special, consequential, or exemplary damages resulting, in whole or in part, from the readers' use of, or reliance upon, this material. Any parts of this book based on government reports are so indicated and copyright is claimed for those parts to the extent applicable to compilations of such works.

Independent verification should be sought for any data, advice or recommendations contained in this book. In addition, no responsibility is assumed by the publisher for any injury and/or damage to persons or property arising from any methods, products, instructions, ideas or otherwise contained in this publication.

This publication is designed to provide accurate and authoritative information with regard to the subject matter covered herein. It is sold with the clear understanding that the Publisher is not engaged in rendering legal or any other professional services. If legal or any other expert assistance is required, the services of a competent person should be sought. FROM A DECLARATION OF PARTICIPANTS JOINTLY ADOPTED BY A COMMITTEE OF THE AMERICAN BAR ASSOCIATION AND A COMMITTEE OF PUBLISHERS.

Additional color graphics may be available in the e-book version of this book.

LIBRARY OF CONGRESS CATALOGING-IN-PUBLICATION DATA

Afghanistan national development strategies and plans / editor, Jennifer L. Brown.
　　p. cm.
　Includes index.
　ISBN 978-1-61209-637-7 (hbk.)
　1. Afghanistan--Economic policy. 2. Afghanistan--Social policy. 3. Afghanistan--Politics and government--2001- 4. Afghanistan National Development Strategy. I. Brown, Jennifer L., 1950-
　　HC417.A3195 2011
　　338.9581--dc22
　　　　　　　　　　　2010054072

Published by Nova Science Publishers, Inc. † New York

CONTENTS

Preface		vii
Chapter 1	Afghanistan National Development Strategy *Islamic Republic of Afghanistan*	1
Chapter 2	Prioritization and Implementation Plan (Mid 2010-Mid 2013) *Afghanistan National Development Strategy*	309
Chapter 3	National Justice Sector Strategy *Islamic Republic of Afghanistan*	373
Chapter Sources		415
Index		417

PREFACE

Following almost three decades of war, the challenges facing Afghanistan's development remain immense. By 2001, the ravages of conflict had bestowed upon Afghan citizens and the incumbent administration an inheritance of debt not wealth. Following six years of reconstruction, at a cost of billions of dollars, the path to prosperity from extreme poverty remains as distant as ever. Insecurity, poverty, corruption and the expanding narcotics industry signify that while the challenges facing Afghanistan have changed in nature, they have not necessarily changed in magnitude. This new book explores the Afghanistan National Development strategies and plans for the future.

Chapter 1 Following almost three decades of war, the challenges facing Afghanistan's development remain immense. By 1380 (2001), the ravages of conflict had bestowed upon Afghan citizens and the incumbent administration an inheritance of debt not wealth. With the Taliban dominating the political landscape from 1375 (1996) onwards, Afghanistan had been moving backwards in all aspects. The results of war, the destruction of core institutions of state and a heavily war torn economy led to unrivaled levels of absolute poverty, national ill health, large scale illiteracy and the almost complete disintegration of gender equity. And yet, following six years of reconstruction, at a cost of billions of dollars, the path to prosperity from extreme poverty remains as distant as ever. Insecurity, poverty, corruption and the expanding narcotics industry signify that while the challenges facing Afghanistan have changed in nature, they have not necessarily changed in magnitude. Yet, the price of securing peace and freedom at this pivotal moment in history will be nothing compared to the long term costs of failure both for Afghanistan and the international community. Averting failure and establishing Afghanistan on a virtuous path towards peace, stability and prosperity are therefore the cornerstones of the new Afghan National Development Strategy (ANDS). At the core of the ANDS is a policy of Afghanization, meaning that ANDS has been fully developed and owned by Afghanistan.

Chapter 2- On July 20, 2010, the Government of the Islamic Republic of Afghanistan and the international community met in Kabul to deliberate on and endorse an Afghan-led action plan to improve governance, social and economic development, and security. Demonstrating a renewed commitment to the People of Afghanistan within the framework of the *Afghanistan National Development Strategy*, the new generation of National Priority Programs presented at the Kabul International Conference on Afghanistan aim to empower all Afghan citizens and government and non-governmental institutions to contribute to improved service delivery, job creation, equitable economic growth, the protection of all Afghan citizens' rights, and a durable and inclusive peace. In essence, these programs define the *Kabul Process*.

Chapter 3- Over the last six years, the Supreme Court (SC), Ministry of Justice (MOJ) and Attorney General's Office (AGO) have worked assiduously to lay solid foundations for the sustainable development of the justice sector. The National Justice Sector Strategy (NJSS) is designed to enhance performance, integrity, transparency, efficiency and independence of justice institutions.

The NJSS is based on a vision of an Islamic society in which an impartial, fair and accessible justice system delivers safety and security for life, religion, property, family and reputation with respect for liberty, equality before the law and access to justice for all.

NJSS builds upon prior reform efforts and in particular the individual strategies of the SC, MOJ and AGO.

In: Afghanistan National Development Strategies and Plans
Editor: Jennifer L. Brown

ISBN: 978-1-61209-637-7
© 2011 Nova Science Publishers, Inc.

Chapter 1

AFGHANISTAN NATIONAL DEVELOPMENT STRATEGY

Islamic Republic of Afghanistan

FOREWORD

In the name of Allah, the most Merciful, the most Compassionate

Six and one-half years ago, the people of Afghanistan and the international community joined hands to liberate Afghanistan from the grip of international terrorism and to begin the journey of rebuilding a nation from a past of violence, destruction and terror. We have come a long way in this shared journey.

In a few short years, as a result of the partnership between Afghanistan and the international community, we were able to create a new, democratic Constitution, embracing the freedom of speech and equal rights for women. Afghans voted in their first-ever presidential elections and elected a new parliament. Today close to five million Afghan refugees have returned home, one of the largest movements of people to their homeland in history.

Thousands of schools have been built, welcoming over six million boys and girls, the highest level ever for Afghanistan. Hundreds of health clinics have been established boosting our basic health coverage from a depressing 9 percent six years ago to over 85 percent today. Access to diagnostic and curative services has increased from almost none in 2002 to more than forty percent. We have rehabilitated 12,200 km of roads, over the past six years. Our rapid economic growth, with double digit growth almost every year, has led to higher income and better living conditions for our people. With a developing road network and a state-of-the-art communications infrastructure, Afghanistan is better placed to serve as an economic land-bridge in our region.

These achievements would not have been possible without the unwavering support of the international community and the strong determination of the Afghan people. I hasten to point out that our achievements must not distract us from the enormity of the tasks that are still ahead. The threat of terrorism and the menace of narcotics are still affecting Afghanistan and the broader region and hampering our development. Our progress is still undermined by the betrayal of public trust by some functionaries of the state and uncoordinated and inefficient aid delivery mechanisms. Strengthening national and sub-national governance and rebuilding our judiciary are also among our most difficult tasks.

To meet these challenges, I am pleased to present Afghanistan's National Development Strategy (ANDS). This strategy has been completed after two years of hard work and extensive consultations around the country. As an Afghan-owned blueprint for the development of Afghanistan in all spheres of human endeavor, the ANDS will serve as our nation's Poverty Reduction Strategy Paper. I am confident that the ANDS will help us in achieving the Afghanistan Compact benchmarks and Millennium Development Goals. I also consider this document as our roadmap for the long-desired objective of Afghanization, as we transition towards less reliance on aid and an increase in self-sustaining economic growth.

I thank the international community for their invaluable support. With this Afghan-owned strategy, I ask all of our partners to fully support our national development efforts. I am strongly encouraged to see the participation of the Afghan people and appreciate the efforts of all those in the international community and Afghan society who have contributed to the development of this strategy. Finally, I thank the members of the Oversight Committee and the ANDS Secretariat for the preparation of this document.

Hamid Karzai
President of the Islamic Republic of Afghanistan

ACKNOWLEDGMENTS

In the name of Allah, the most Merciful, the most Compassionate

The Afghanistan National Development Strategy (ANDS) could not have been developed without the generous contribution of many individuals and organizations. The ANDS was finalized under the guidance of the Oversight Committee, appointed by HE President Hamid Karzai and chaired by H.E. Professor Ishaq Nadiri, Senior Economic Advisor to the President and Chair of the ANDS Oversight Committee. The committee included: H.E. Rangeen Dadfar

Spanta, Minister of Foreign Affairs; Anwar-ul-Haq Ahady, Minister of Finance; H.E. Jalil Shams, Minister of Economy; H.E. Sarwar Danish, Minister of Justice; H.E. Haneef Atmar, Minister of Education; H.E. Amin Farhang, Minister of Commerce; and H.E. Zalmai Rassoul, National Security Advisor.

We would like to sincerely thank the First Vice-President and Chair of the Economic Council, H.E. Ahmad Zia Massoud. Special thanks are also due to H.E. Hedayat Amin Arsala, Senior Minister and H.E. Waheedulah Shah- rani, Deputy Minister of Finance and the Ministry of Finance team. In addition, we would like to thank the Supreme Court, the National Assembly, Government Ministries and Agencies, Provincial Authorities, Afghan Embassies abroad, national Commissions, the Office of the President, Civil Society Organizations, and International Community.

All Ministers, deputy ministers and their focal points, religious leaders, tribal elders, civil society leaders, all Ambassadors and representatives of the international community in Afghanistan; and all Afghan citizens. National and international agencies participated actively in the ANDS consultations. Their contributions, comments and suggestions strengthened the sectoral strategies, ensuring their practical implementation. Thanks are also due to the Ministry of Rural Rehabilitation for their significant contributions to the subnational consultations. Special thanks are further due to the Presidents Advisors, Daud Saba and Noorullah Delawari for their contributions, as well as Mahmoud Saikal for his inputs. We are also indebted to the Provincial Governors and their staff for their contributions, support and hospitality to the ANDS preparations.

Special thanks go to Wahidullah Waissi, ANDS/PRS Development Process Manager, for his invaluable contribution and for the efforts of his team of young Afghan professionals who dedicated themselves tirelessly to completing the I-ANDS, Afghanistan Compact and the full ANDS in consultation with both national and international partners. The Sector Coordinators included Rahatullah Naeem, Farzana Rashid Rahimi, Shakir Majeedi, Attaullah Asim, Mohammad Ismail Rahimi, Zalmai Allawdin, Hedayatullah Ashrafi, Shukria Kazemi, Saifurahman Ahmadzai, and; the Sub-National Consultations Team consisted of Mohammad Yousuf Ghaznavi, Mohammad Fahim Mehry, Shahenshah Sherzai, Hekmatullah Latifi, Sayed Rohani and Osman Fahim; and Prof. Malik Sharaf, Naim Hamdard, Saleem Alkozai, Mir Ahmad Tayeb Waizy, Sayed Shah Aminzai, Khwaga Kakar and Mohammad Kazim. Thanks to Nematullah Bizhan for his special contribution from the JCMB Secretariat. We are also indebted to the many national and international advisers who supported this effort. In particular, we would like to thank Zlatko Hurtic, Paul O'Brien, Jim Robertson, Barnett Rubin, Peter Middlebrook, Richard Ponzio, Anita Nirody, Shakti Sinha, Ashok Nigam, Christopher Alexander and Ameerah Haq.

Finally, I would like to thank all who contributed towards this endeavor in preparation of the first Afghanistan National Development Strategy, a milestone in our country's history and a national commitment towards economic growth and poverty reduction in Afghanistan.

Adib Farhadi,
Director, Afghanistan National Development Strategy, and Joint Coordination and Monitoring Board Secretariat

ACRONYMS AND ABBREVIATIONS

AC	Afghanistan Compact	DAB	Da Afghanistan Bank (Central Bank of Afghanistan)
ACBAR	Agency Coordinating Body for Afghan Relief	DABM	Da Afghanistan Breshna Moassessa (the Afghan electric utility)
ADB	Asian Development Bank	DAC	District Advisory Committee
ADC	Area Development Councils	DCN	District Communication Network
AfCERT	Afghanistan Cyber Emergency Response Team	EC	European Commission
AFMIS	Afghanistan Financial Management System	ECOTA	Economic Cooperation Organization Trade Agreement
AGO	Attorney General's Office	EPAA	Export Promotion Agency of Afghanistan
AIHRC	Afghanistan Independent Human Rights Commission	EPHS	Essential package of hospital services
AISA	Afghanistan Investment Support Agency	EU	European Union
ANA	Afghanistan National Army	FCCS	Foundation for Culture and Civil Society
ANDMA	Afghanistan National Disaster Manage ment Authority	FDI	Foreign Direct Investment
ANP	Afghan National Police	FSMS	Food Security Monitoring Survey
ANSA	Afghanistan National Standards Author ity	GDP	Gross Domestic Product
ANSF	Afghan National Security Forces	GIAAC	General and Independent Administration
ANWP	Afghanistan National Welfare Program		Against Corruption and Bribery
APPPA	Afghanistan Participatory Poverty As sessment	GIS	Geographical Information System
ARCSC	Administrative Reform and Civil Service Commission	GoA	Government of Afghanistan
ARDS	Afghan Reconstruction & Development Services	GSM	Global System Mobile
ARDZ	Agriculture and Rural Development Zones	Ha	Hectare
ARTF	Afghanistan Reconstruction Trust Fund	HCS	Health Care Service
ASYCUDA	Automated System for Customs Data	HIPC	Heavily Indebted Poor Countries
ATRA	Afghanistan Telecommunication Regulation Authority	HIV	Human immunodeficiency virus

AUWSSC	Afghanistan Urban Water Supply and Sewerage Corporation	HIV/AIDS	Human Immune-deficiency Virus/ Acquired Immune Deficiency Syndrome
BPFA	Beijing Platform for Action	HNS	Health and Nutrition Sector
BPHS	basic package of health services	HNSS	Health and Nutrition Sector Strategy
CAO	Control and Audit Office	IAGs	Illegal Armed Groups
CAR	Central Asian Republics	I-ANDS	Interim Afghanistan National Development Strategy
CARD	Comprehensive Agriculture and Rural Development	IARCSC	Independent Administrative Reform and Civil Service Commission
CAREC	Central Asian Regional Economic Cooperation	IATA	International Air Transport Association
CASA	Central and South Asia	ICAO	International Civil Aviation Organization
CBN	Cost of Basic Needs	ICCD	Inter-ministerial Commission for Capacity Development
CCCG	Cross Cutting Consultative Group	ICE	Inter-Ministerial Commission on Energy
CDCs	Community Development Councils	ICT	Information and Communications Technology
CEDAW	Convention on the Elimination of all forms of Discrimination against Women	IDLG	The Independent Directorate for Local Governance
CG	Consultative Group	IDP	Internally Displaced Persons
CIS	Commonwealth of Independent States	IDPs	Internally Displaced Persons
CMRS	Central Monitoring and Reporting System	IEC	Independent Electoral Commission
CN	counter narcotics	ILO	International Labor Organization
CNPA	Counter Narcotics Police of Afghanistan	IMF	International Monetary Fund
CNTF	Counter Narcotics Trust Fund	ISAF	International Security Assistance Force Air Command
CSO	Central Statistics Office	IT	Information Technology
CSTI	Civil Services Training Institute	IWRM	Integrated Water Resources Management
MEAs	Multilateral Environmental Agreements	JCMB	Joint Monitoring and Coordination Board
MIS	Management Information Systems	Km	Kilometer
MoD	Ministry of Defense	KWH	Kilowatt-Hour (Unit of electric energy)

Acronyms and Abbreviations (Continued)

MoE	Ministry of Economy	LOTFA	Law and Order Trust Fund
MoE	Ministry of Education	M&E	Monitoring and Evaluation
MoF	Ministry of Finance	MoCIT	Ministry of Communications & Information Technology
MoFA	Ministry of Foreign Affairs	MCN	Ministry of Counter Narcotics
MoHE	Ministry of Higher Education	MDGs	Millennium Development Goals
MoI	Ministry of Interior	PAR	Public Administration Reform
MoJ	Ministry of Justice	PAYG	Pay-as-you-go
MoLSAMD	Ministry of Labor, Social Affairs, Martyrs and the Disabled	PDPs	Provincial Development Plans
MoM	Ministry of Mines	PFM	Public Financial Management
MoPH	Ministry of Public Health	PIO	Project Implementation Office
MoU	Memorandum of Understanding	PIP	Public Investment Program
MoUD	Ministry of Urban Development	PPA	Power Purchase Agreement
MoWA	Ministry of Women's Affairs	PRDP	Pro-active Regional Diplomacy Program
MRRD	Ministry of Rural Rehabilitation and Development	PRSP	Poverty Reduction Strategy Paper
MTFF	Medium Term Financial Framework	PRT	Provincial Reconstruction Team
MW	Megawatt	PRTs	Provincial Reconstruction Teams
NABDP	National Area-Based Development Program	RBA	River Basin Agency
NAPWA	National Action Plan for the Women of Afghanistan	RED	Rural Road Evaluation Model
NATO	North Atlantic Treaty Organization	RIMU	Reform Implementation Management Unit
NDCS	National Drug Control Strategy	SAARC	South Asian Association for Regional Cooperation
NEPA	National Environmental Protection Agency (GoA)	SCO	Shanghai Cooperation Organization
NEPS	North-East Power System	SCWAM	Supreme Council for Water Affairs Management
NGO	Non-Governmental Organization	SEPS	South-East Power System
NIRA	National Internet Registry of Afghanistan	SMEs	Small and Medium Enterprises
NRAP	National Rural Accessibility Program	SNC	Sub-National Consultation

NRVA	National Risk and Vulnerability Assessment	SOE	State Owned Enterprises
NSC	National Statistical Council	SPECA	Special Program for the Economies of Central Asia
NSDP	National Skills Development Program	SPS	Sanitary and Phyto-sanitary
NSP	National Solidarity Program	TA	Tripartite Agreement
NVETA	Proposed National Vocational Education and Training Authority	TAG	Technical Advisory Group
ODA	Official Development Assistance	TWG	Technical Working Group
OECD	Organization for Economic Cooperation and Development	TWGs	Technical Working Groups
OEF	Operation Enduring Freedom	UN	United Nations
OMO	Open Market Operations	UNAMA	United Nations' Assistance Mission to Afghanistan
OSC	Oversight Committee	UNCAC	United Nations Convention Against Corruption
OSCE	Organization for Security and Cooperation in Europe	UNDP	United Nations Development Program
P&G	Pay and grading	UNHCR	United Nations High Commission for Refugees
PAG	Policy Action Group	UNICEF	United Nations International Children's Emergency Fund
UNIFEM	United Nations Development Fund for Women	USAID	United States Agency for International Development
UNODC	United Nations Office on Drugs and Crime	WATSAN	Water and Sanitation Committees
WB	World Bank	WTO	World Trade Organization
WCS	Wildlife Conservation Society		
WB	World Bank		

GLOSSARY OF AFGHAN TERMS

Amu Darya   A river originated from Pamir mountain and flowing in the northern region of Afghanistan
Bank-e-Milli   National Bank
Darya   River
Gozar   Smallest Administrative Unit inside the Urban area
Imam   An Islamic leader, often the leader of a mosque
Jirgas   Local Consultation Meetings
Kareze   Underground canals connecting wells uses as traditional irrigation system
Kuchi   Nomad
Loya Jirga   Grand Council, "Grand Assembly of elders"

Madrassa	A school, where mostly Islamic Studies are concerned
Meshrano Jirga	Senate (Upper House of Assembly)
Mirab	A person responsible for water management in a community
Sharia	Islamic Laws
Shura	Traditional or Local Council (Shuras, pl)
Taqnin	Law making, legislation
Ulama	Religious Scholars
Wolosi Jirga	National Assembly (Lower House of Assembly
Zakat	Islamic concept of tithing and alms. It is an obligation on Muslims to pay 2.5% of their wealth to specified categories in society when their annual wealth exceeds a minimum level. In addition, Zakat is one of the basic principles of Islamic economics, based on social welfare and fair distribution of wealth.

Afghan Calendar					
1.	Hamal	March 21	7.	Meezaan	September 23
2.	Saur	April 21	8.	Aqrab	October 23
3.	Jawza	May 2	9.	Qaus	November 22
4.	Sarataan	June 22	10.	Jaddi	December 22
5.	Asad	July 23	11.	Dalwa	January 21
6.	Sunbula	Aug 23	12.	Hoot	February 20

INTRODUCTION

Background

Following almost three decades of war, the challenges facing Afghanistan's development remain immense. By 1380 (2001), the ravages of conflict had bestowed upon Afghan citizens and the incumbent administration an inheritance of debt not wealth. With the Taliban dominating the political landscape from 1375 (1996) onwards, Afghanistan had been moving backwards in all aspects. The results of war, the destruction of core institutions of state and a heavily war torn economy led to unrivaled levels of absolute poverty, national ill health, large scale illiteracy and the almost complete disintegration of gender equity. And yet, following six years of reconstruction, at a cost of billions of dollars, the path to prosperity from extreme poverty remains as distant as ever. Insecurity, poverty, corruption and the expanding narcotics industry signify that while the challenges facing Afghanistan have changed in nature, they have not necessarily changed in magnitude. Yet, the price of securing peace and freedom at this pivotal moment in history will be nothing compared to the long term costs of failure both for Afghanistan and the international community. Averting failure and establishing Afghanistan on a virtuous path towards peace, stability and prosperity are therefore the cornerstones of the new Afghan National Development Strategy (ANDS). At the core of the ANDS is a policy of Afghanization, meaning that ANDS has been fully developed and owned by Afghanistan.

Achievements since 2001

In 2001 Afghanistan was certainly a thoroughly devastated country in virtually every respect. The political, social and economic structures of the country had been severely damaged or completely destroyed. Massive numbers of Afghans had left as refugees, had died during the conflict or were severely disabled. Every family had paid a price – many had to cope with the loss of main breadwinner. For the young people that remained, their education had been disrupted and in many cases, including for all girls and women, ended. Today Afghanistan has among the highest rates of illiteracy in the world. Yet despite these desperate conditions, since 2001 the country has had some remarkable achievements. The progress that has been made should be measured against the desperate conditions that prevailed at the time of the fall of the Taliban. While Afghanistan still faces many enormous challenges, the progress that has been made gives cause for some optimism that with the determination of the Afghan people to rebuild their lives and their country, the transformation to a peaceful and prosperous can be achieved.

The goals of the ANDS for the next five years ought to be viewed against what has been accomplished during the last six years. Only some of the most significant achievements can be mentioned here.

Political Achievements:

- In 1380 (2001) the Bonn Agreement established a roadmap for the political transformation of Afghanistan to a legitimate democratic state. The targets set in the Bonn Agreement were fully met on time and included:
- The Transitional Administration was established to guide the process. It derived its authority through an Emergency Loya Jirga, the first genuinely representative Afghan national meeting in decades.
- In 1383 (2004) Afghanistan adopted its first constitution in 30 years, which laid the political and development foundation for the country and established legal protections for private property and a market economy.
- Free and fair democratic elections for President, the National Assembly and Provincial Councils were conducted. 76 percent of eligible voters participated in the presidential election. Women were elected to 27 percent of the seats in the National Assembly.
- After the successful completion of the Bonn Agreement, Afghanistan and the international community entered into a new partnership, based upon the Afghanistan Compact, which was agreed at the London Conference of 1384 (2005). The Compact set ambitious goals for comprehensive state building, setting benchmarks in all sectors of security, governance, and development, including the cross-cutting goals of counter-narcotics and regional cooperation.
- In 1385 (2006) the new National Assembly began its work, including the approval of a new cabinet; a new Chief Justice and other judges for the Supreme Court; and the National Budget. A new Attorney General with a new mission to fight corruption was appointed. New Provincial Governors were named.

- The disarmament, demobilization and reintegration of ex-combatants has been completed. Today the national army and police forces are close to full strength. Afghanistan is no longer a safe haven for terrorists.

Social and Humanitarian Achievements:

- Since 1381 (2002), more than five million Afghan refugees have returned home. In 1385 (2006) 342,925 Afghan refugees returned from Pakistan and Iran and 1,004 from other countries. More than 150,000 benefited from the assistance package provided by UNHCR.
- The Government has so far distributed 30,000 residential plots of land to needy returning refugee families.
- From under one million in 2001 the school population has grown to 5.7 million in 2007 and new enrolments into Grade 1 have ranged between 12-14 percent per annum in the last 5 years. Two million of the children (or 35 percent) enrolled are girls – a 35 percent increase in five years. The number of schools has trebled to 9,062 in 2007 including 1,337 all girls' and 4,325 coeducational schools. Similarly, the number of teachers has increased seven-fold to 142,500 of who nearly 40,000 are female. Fifty thousand of these teachers have received in-service teacher training.
- Major advances have been made in extending health care services throughout the country and rebuilding a decimated educational system. The percentage of the population living in districts where the Basic Package of Health Services is being implemented has increased from 9 percent in 2003 to 82 percent in 2006.
- Over 2.5 million people have benefited from social protection arrangements covering (i) martyr's families; (ii) disabled with war-related disabilities; (iii) orphans and children enrolled in kindergartens; (iv) victims of natural disasters; (v) pensioners; and (vi) unemployed.
- Measurable progress has been achieved since 2003 in improving rural livelihoods. Almost 20,000 km of rural access roads (i.e., all weather, village-to-village and villageto-district centre roads) have been constructed or repaired, increasing access to markets, employment and social services. More than 500,000 households (36 percent of villages) have benefited from small-scale irrigation projects. Currently, 32.5 percent of the rural population has access to safe drinking water and 4,285 improved sanitation facilities have been provided. More than 336,000 households have benefited from improved access to financial services. Some 18,000 CDCs have been established and are implementing community-led development projects. Efforts have made to assist the poorest and most vulnerable.

Economic Achievements:

- Macroeconomic stability has been maintained, based upon disciplined fiscal and monetary policies. A new unified currency was successfully introduced; inflation has remained low while the exchange rate has been stable.
- Sixteen private commercial banks have been licensed; a leasing and financing company is operating; an equity fund is underway to invest in local businesses. There

are also thirteen microfinance institutions providing services to almost 200,000 active clients in 27 provinces.
- State owned enterprises are being privatized, corporatized or liquidated.
- A lively free and privately owned media have developed and over which people are able to express political views freely – which they do daily.
- The legal and commercial infrastructure is being put in place for a market oriented economy.
- Electricity capacity has almost doubled compared to 2002.
- Over 12,000 kilometers of roads have been rehabilitated, improved, or built. This includes the ring road system, national highways, provincial roads and rural roads.
- Kabul International Airport has been expanded and extensively rehabilitated.
- Private airlines have entered the aviation sector and established air links throughout the region.
- A key bridge investment has opened up direct road links to Tajikistan and greatly reduced transportation times through to Urumqi in China, one of the fastest growing trade hubs in the world.
- Two million urban residents have benefited from investments in water supply and 12 percent from investment in sanitation in major cities between 2002 and 2007.
- About 35,000 water points 59 networks and 1,713 water reservoirs and 23,884 demonstration latrines have been constructed.
- More than three million people have benefited directly from the rural water supply and sanitation activities in the country.
- Around a third of the provinces reported some improvement in access to clean drinking water during the consultative process under the ANDS.
- Irrigation Rehabilitation has been given high priority over the past four or five years. Of some 2,100 rehabilitation projects, approximately 1,200 have been completed and have been placed back into commercial service.
- Major advances have been made in opening up the telecommunications sector to private sector investment under a 'investment friendly' regulatory framework aimed at maintaining a competitive market for services, and phone subscribers have increased from less than 20 thousand to more than 5 million in less than 6 years.
- A rapid urbanization process has seen the urban population increase to almost a quarter of the total population. Despite the pressures implied by rapid urbanization, two million urban residents (31 percent of the total urban population) have benefited from investments in water supply and 12 percent from investment in sanitation in major cities between 2002 and 2007.
- Afghanistan has world class mineral deposits that are being opened up for exploration and development. The first major investment has recently been announced for developing the Aynak copper deposits in central Logar province, an almost $3 billion investment after an extensive evaluation of tenders from nine major international mining companies.

When seen against the desperate conditions that prevailed in the country in 2001, these achievements constitute an impressive record. The ANDS sets goals for the next five years that will require even greater achievements.

Afghanistan's Challenges

Few countries have simultaneously faced the range and extent of challenges with which the people and Government of Afghanistan must now contend. After nearly three decades of continuous conflict the country emerged in late 2001 as a truly devastated state with its human, physical and institutional infrastructure destroyed or severely damaged. At that time the UN Human Development Report ranked Afghanistan as the second poorest country in the World. In addition to the widespread poverty, the Government must deal with continuing threats to security from extremists and terrorists, weak capacity of governance and corruption; a poor environment for private sector investment, the corrosive effects of a large and growing narcotics industry; and major human capacity limitations throughout the public and private sectors. Meeting these challenges and rebuilding the country will take many years and require consistent international support.

The successful transformation of Afghanistan into a secure, economically viable state that can meet the aspirations of the Afghan people, live at peace with itself and its neighbors and contribute to regional and international stability will depend upon the effective utilization of all available human, natural and financial resources. In this partnership a critical role must be played by the private sector. Significantly reducing poverty will require substantially increasing employment which depends on maintaining high rates of economic growth in the years ahead. It is not sufficient to rely on the Government and the international community to sustain the high rates of investment needed to generate the levels of employment to have a major impact on reducing poverty. As the macroeconomic projections presented in Chapter 4 indicate, a substantial increase in private investment will be essential if significant progress is to be realized in meeting the social and economic objectives of the country.

Afghanistan is a country with significant potential for economic development. It has substantial water, agricultural and mineral resources and is well positioned to become a trade and business hub linking the markets of Central Asia, the Middle East, South Asia and China. The potential exists or sustainable economic growth in the future. However, there are a number of fundamental limitations in the economic environment that must be addressed if these efforts are to succeed:

- The country's 'hard infrastructure', including roads and reliable supplies of water and power, is inadequate to support rapid and sustained economic growth.
- The corresponding 'soft infrastructure', which includes the human and institutional capacity necessary for an economy to function, is also extremely limited. Considerable emphasis is being given to developing capacity in both the public and private sectors and to institutional development, but these efforts will take time.
- Economic governance is weak. The Government is pursuing comprehensive economic reform, including the introduction of new commercial laws and regulations, but the establishment of institutions needed for effective implementation and enforcement are largely lacking and will take years to develop.[1]
- Afghanistan's commercial connections to regional and global economies were severely disrupted and must be redeveloped. The development of a competitive private sector will depend on establishing access to foreign markets and developing viable export activities.

- Critical markets for land and finance are largely undeveloped, limiting the ability of private investors to establish and operate businesses. Property rights are often contested or difficult to defend.
- Afghanistan is experiencing high population. Continued rapid population growth will substantially increase the levels of investment that will be required to substantially reduce poverty.

Both the Government and the international community recognize that prolonged aid dependency will undermine the chances of achieving sustained economic growth and poverty reduction. However, given the major limitations in the economic environment that must be addressed, the successful transition to a competitive market economy will require sustained commitment by the Government, with the support of the international community. Simply creating conditions in which the private sector can operate alone will not be sufficient. Increased efforts by both the Government and the donor community to attract Afghan and foreign investors are needed if the goals of the ANDS are to be realized.

Social and economic development will also be severely curtailed if the insecurity that prevails is not resolved. Despite the considerable efforts by the Government and the international community, security has steadily deteriorated since 2004 in some parts of the country. Ongoing cross-border activities, particularly in the southern and southeastern provinces, have resulted in several areas being effectively off limits to meaningful development assistance.

The lack of stability reduces the ability of aid agencies and the Government to operate in many areas and to effectively implement projects and programs. The impacts of these limitations typically fall most heavily on the poor. Insecurity also increases the cost of doing business and undermines private sector growth and development.[2] The difficulties in maintaining security contribute significantly to two closely related issues: increasing corruption in the public sector and the rapid growth of the narcotics industry. There is a consensus that corruption in Afghanistan is widespread and has been getting worse.[3] Public corruption represents a major disincentive for private investment, substantially increasing the costs and risks of doing business. A lack of security in some parts of the country has created conditions in which poppy cultivation has flourished, feeding a growing narcotics industry that both funds terrorist activity and feeds public corruption. Although poppy cultivation has been greatly reduced in 29 of the 34 provinces, in the remaining five it has seen explosive growth to where Afghanistan accounts for around 90 percent of the world's opium production.

International Support for Afghanistan

After the fall of the Taliban, the international community's response was not only military but also began to provide Afghanistan with the institutional and financial resources to start the state building process. In 2006, the Afghanistan Compact agreed between the Government and international community established goals for state building, setting benchmarks in core sectors of security, governance, and development, including the cross-cutting goals of counter-narcotics. To implement its obligations under the Afghanistan

Compact, the Government developed the Afghanistan National Development Strategy (ANDS) to clarify existing conditions, establish objectives and define the policies, programs and projects needed to achieve those objections. The international community made new pledges of financial and security assistance and set out to improve its coordination by renewing and upgrading the UN Assistance Mission for Afghanistan (UNAMA), headed by a Special Representative of the Secretary General with enhanced powers for coordination.[4]

The ANDS represents an important milestone in the efforts to rebuilding of Afghanistan which has been underway since late 1380 (2001). During this time there have been a number of reports, conferences and strategies developed to address Afghanistan's challenges.[5] In addition, the Government and the international community have entered into a series of agreements concerning the direction and support for the country's development efforts, including notably the Bonn Agreement, the commitment to the Millennium Development Goals (MDGs) and the Afghanistan Compact. The ANDS builds on all of these and provides a comprehensive and integrated strategy that reflects recent experience and current conditions.

The Afghanistan National Development Strategy

The Afghanistan National Development Strategy (ANDS) represents the combined efforts of the Afghan people and the Afghan Government with the support of the international community to address the major challenges facing the country. To comprehensively address the security, governance, and development needs of Afghanistan, the government has developed the ANDS. The ANDS reflects the government's vision, principles and goals for Afghanistan which builds on its commitment to achieve the Millennium Development Goals by 2020 and the implementation of the Afghanistan Compact benchmarks. The strategy is based upon an assessment of current social and economic conditions; offers clear intermediate objectives; and identifies the actions that must be taken to achieve these national goals. The ANDS largely focuses on the next five years, but reflects Afghanistan's longterm goals which include the elimination of poverty through the emergence of a vibrant middle class, an efficient and stable democratic political environment and security throughout the country.

Despite the full commitment of the Government and the considerable assistance being provided by the international community, it will not be possible to fully achieve all of these objectives during the next five years. Therefore it is essential that well defined priorities be established that reflect the relative contributions of potential policies, programs and projects towards reaching these goals. This is a difficult process. The contribution of any project to increasing economic growth is uncertain and is inevitably contingent on progress in other areas. It also requires a careful analysis of benefits versus costs with alternative allocations of resources. As a result, the prioritization of activities should be seen as an ongoing process that adapts to changing circumstances and the results of program and project appraisal work on alternative use of resources. In meeting this challenge, the ANDS aims to establish institutional mechanisms that will include the Afghan people, the Government, civil society and the international community in identifying priorities in an evolving environment.

A comprehensive 'bottom-up' approach was used in the development of the ANDS that has taken into account all aspects of social and economic life as well as fully reflecting the diversity of people in all parts of the country. Considerable efforts were made to ensure that sub- national consultations (i.e., outside of the central government in the capital Kabul) identified the priorities of the Afghan people living in each of the 34 provinces.[6] In addition, a comprehensive series of sector and ministry strategies were developed that address all aspects of social and economic development. The result of this inclusive process is a national strategy that is fully reflective of the aspirations of the Afghan people. The ANDS is the product of extensive consultations at the national, provincial and local levels. The Government is committed to programs and projects that directly target the poorest and most vulnerable groups for assistance. Well targeted poverty reductions programs are emphasized both in the strategy for social protection and integrated into the design of strategies across the other sectors of the economy.

The remainder of the ANDS is organized as follows:

- **Chapter 1:** provides an overview of the ANDS
- **Chapter 2:** explains ANDS extensive participatory process to ensure ownership
- **Chapter 3**: presents the poverty profile of the country, a key foundation for ANDS's policy based on evidence approach
- **Chapter 4**: presents the macroeconomic framework for the economy. It discusses the policies intended to maintain economic stability, the initial planning on resource allocations for the ANDS period and the total resources available for the implementation of public sector programs and projects through the external and core budgets.
- **Chapter 5**: presents the strategies and priorities relating to Security pillar
- **Chapter 6:** presents the strategies and priorities relating to Governance, Rule of Law, Justice and Human Rights pillar.
- **Chapter 7**: presents the sector strategies and priorities relating to Economic and Social Development pillar. This addresses private sector development, energy, transport, mining, education, culture, youth and media, agriculture and rural development, public health, social protection and refugees, returnees and internally displaced persons.
- **Chapter 8:** discusses critical cross-cutting issues that have impacts across all sectors. These include regional cooperation, counter-narcotics, anti-corruption, gender equality, capacity building and environmental management.
- **Chapter 9:** discusses aid effectiveness measure that needs to be taken jointly by the Government and the international community
- **Chapter 10:** discusses the integrated approach implementation framework of ANDS
- **Chapter 11:** discusses monitoring, coordination and evaluation requirements of the ANDS

Volume II: includes 17 sector strategies, 6 strategies for cross cutting issues and 38 individual ministry and agency strategies.

Volume III: discusses the participatory process used in developing the ANDS, 34 Provincial Development Plans and development priorities.

Part I. Process, Goals and Policy Directions

1. The ANDS: An Overview

The overriding objective of the ANDS is to substantially reduce poverty, improve the lives of the Afghan people, and create the foundation for a secure and stable country. This requires building a strong, rapidly expanding economy able to generate the employment opportunities and increasing incomes essential for poverty reduction. The ANDS establishes the Government's strategy and defines the policies, programs and projects that will be implemented over the next five years and the means for effectively implementing, monitoring and evaluating these actions. The goals included in the ANDS are fully consistent with the commitments entered into in previous strategies and agreements and build on the considerable progress that has been achieved since 1380 (2001). While focus of the ANDS is on the next five years, it will continue to adjust to changing circumstances – it is intended to be a 'living document'.

The ANDS serves as the country's Poverty Reduction Strategy Paper (PRSP). As such, it establishes the joint Government/international community commitment to reducing poverty; describes the extent and patterns of poverty that exist; presents the main elements of its poverty reduction strategy; summarizes the projects and programs that will assist the poor; and provide a three-year macroeconomic framework and three-year policy matrix relevant to the poverty reduction efforts. The PRSP has been prepared based on an inclusive consultative process to ensure broad participation and support, while also ensuring policies are based on evidence. A public policy dialogue with all key stakeholders was carried out across all provinces, allowing government officials, private sector representatives, NGOs, the media and ordinary citizens an opportunity to discuss local conditions and concerns. This allowed these communities to participate effectively in defining the poverty problem as they experience it. In so doing, a broader choice of poverty actions based on the specific concerns of the poor have been established for each province, as well as each district.

Key issues identified by stakeholders included: (i) the lack of access to clean drinking water in all provinces; (ii) the needed improvement in provincial roads; (iii) the poor quality of public services; (iv) poorly trained teachers and doctors; (v) the lack of alternatives to poppy cultivation; (vi) the lack of vocational training for returnees and disabled people; (vii) poor access to electricity; (viii) corruption within the public administration particularly respect to the security services. The Government has examined a range of poverty actions based on the specific concerns of the poor including vulnerability, conflict sensitivity, insecurity and governance.

The ANDS lays out the strategic priorities and the policies, programs and projects for achieving the Government's development objectives. These are organized under three pillars: (i) Security; (ii) Governance, Rule of Law and Human Rights; and (iii) Economic and Social Development.

Security

Security and stability in all parts of the country is essential for economic growth and poverty reduction. Afghanistan still faces a number of serious challenges before it can assume full responsibility for this. International terrorists and domestic extremists prevent the Government from establishing effective control in some areas, particularly in the south and southeast. The large-scale production of narcotics continues to provide funds to these groups. Unexploded ordinance remains a significant threat to Afghans, with some five thousand citizens either killed or wounded in mine explosions since 1380 (2001). Currently only two of the country's 34 provinces are completely clear of land mines. A long standing presence of illegal armed groups in different parts of the country is hindering the process of empowerment of local democratic institutions. Some of these groups have close links with police or even belong to local governments. This situation enhances corruption and is considered a key obstacle in cracking down the narcotics industry.

The Government is fully committed to, and is giving the highest priority, to successfully: (i) implementing an integrated and comprehensive national security policy and strategy; (ii) building a robust security sector reform program; (iii) strengthening civil and military operations and coordination; (iv) increasing the role of security forces in counter-narcotics activities; and (v) strengthening the civilian components of security entities. Detailed Compact benchmarks have been established to measure progress in improving capacity within the security organizations and improving security.

Significant progress has been made since 2001 in strengthening the ANA and ANP. For example, militias have been integrated into the Ministry of Defense (MoD), with the majority demobilized. A multi-sector donor support scheme has been established where individual donors are allocated responsibility for overseeing support for each of the key elements of the reform, including: disarmament, demobilization, and reintegration of ex-combatants; military reform; police reform; judicial reform; and counter-narcotics. The ANP has been receiving extensive training and equipment from the international community.

Governance, Rule of Law, Justice and Human Rights

In 2000 the World Bank assessed the 'quality' of Afghanistan's governance institutions as falling in the bottom one percent of all countries. Progress since 2001 includes the adoption of the constitution; successful parliamentary and presidential elections, and progress in improving the livelihood and welfare of women and other disenfranchised groups. Despite some progress, a number of significant issues must be addressed, including: (i) the existence of multiple and often parallel structures of state and non-state governance entities; (ii) the confusion over core centre-periphery administration and fiscal relations; (iii) weak public sector institutions and underdeveloped governance and administrative capabilities; (iv) high levels of corruption; (v) fiscal uncertainty; (vi) weak legislative development and enforcement; (vii) weak political and parliamentary oversight capacities; (viii) weak community and civil society institutions; (ix) limited capacity in a justice system; (x) gender inequality; and (xi) underdeveloped human rights enforcement capacities.

If significantly improved governance is not rapidly achieved it will be difficult to make substantial progress with respect to security and economic development. An emerging political and administrative vacuum will be filled by non-state structures driven by illegal and narcotic interests, not by the Government.

Religious affairs

The Government will focus on the following priorities: (i) to improve infrastructure for religious affairs, such as mosques, shrines, holy places, and religious schools; (ii) improve the training and capacity of Imams, preachers, religious teachers and other scholars to raise public awareness and to teach; (iii) finalize a comprehensive culture curriculum for primary and higher education; (iv) strengthen Hajj arrangement systems for Afghan pilgrims; (iv) support efforts by religious organizations to help alleviate poverty and protect vulnerable groups; (v) support efforts of the other government agencies to improve literacy, dispute resolution and to contribute to strengthening of the national solidarity. The expected results include: (i) reforms implemented in line with Islamic values; (b) improved infrastructure and financial sustainability of religious affairs, particularly of the religious education system; (iii) greater participation of Islamic scholars in raising awareness about importance of implementation of key reforms; (iv) a greatly strengthened role of the religious institutions in programs for poverty reduction.

Economic and Social Development

The economic and social development strategy, vision, objectives and expected outcomes have been prioritized within the overall macro-fiscal framework to allow a logical progression of investments that systematically overcome the core binding constraints to growth and social development. An integrated approach focuses investments through the sector strategies summarized below. The sector strategies were developed based on strategies first put forward by individual ministries and groups of ministries. Although Ministry strategies were the starting point, the sector strategies are broader than those of the ministries for several very important reasons. First, the sector strategies in many cases involve actions and programs that need to be undertaken by several ministries. Considerable attention has therefore been given to developing better coordination between ministries through Inter-Ministerial Committees. The sector strategies have also taken account of donor activities being implemented outside of ministries and informed by the Provincial Development Plans (PDPs). The success of the sector strategies will be heavily dependent on resource effectiveness, revenue enhancement and fiscal sustainability, human and natural resource development and investments in productive and trade-based infrastructure and private sector driven development.

Private sector development

The ANDS strategic objective is to enable the private sector to lead Afghanistan's development within a competitive market-based economy in which the Government is the policy maker and regulator of the economy, not its competitor. The establishment of a strong enabling environment for a competitive private sector is an on-going effort by both the Government and donors. Almost all sector strategies involve the development of new legislation. The Government will enact and implement key laws and amendments to establish the basic legal and regulatory framework that will encourage private sector involvement in social and economic development. Almost all sector strategies involve institutional strengthening that is designed to improve the ability of ministries and other agencies to administer legislation in an unbiased and predictable manner.

Privatization and corporatization of state owned enterprises is an on-going program that is on schedule. It represents an important step in expanding the scope for private sector growth and development. These steps will: (i) improve general levels of efficiency in the economy; (ii) assist in eliminating corruption; (iii) encourage better resource allocation, and (iv) generate increased government revenues.

An open trade policy will facilitate a competitive environment for private sector development, avoid the high costs incurred with protectionist policies and facilitate Afghanistan becoming better integrated as a 'trading hub' in the region. Any proposals to provide protection to particular industries will be evaluated with a proper 'economy wide' perspective that fully accounts for the costs and benefits from such actions, including the negative impacts on other firms and on the consumers who must pay higher prices. Increased priority will be given to regional economic cooperation initiatives aimed at developing regional transportation and transit infrastructure, facilitating regional trade and investment flows and developing Afghanistan as a regional business hub linking Central and East Asia with the Middle East and South Asia.

A second major component of the private sector development strategy attempts to encourage increased private sector investment by creating investor friendly regulatory frameworks for private sector operations in the development of natural resources and infrastructure. This approach has been very successful in the telecommunications sector, where phone usage went from less than 15,000 under a state monopoly to over five million subscribers as private investments in cellular communication were encouraged. Significant initiatives are included in the sector strategies for energy, mining and agriculture based on leased access to state lands to strengthen these investor friendly regulatory frameworks, and pilot projects and innovative initiatives are being investigated to allow public funding to support private sector activities in the provision of education services, vocational training and public health services.

A third and closely related component of the strategy is based on a concerted effort by the Government and the donor community to more vigorously promote private sector investment. Given the limited capacities in the public sector and in the nascent domestic private sector, much of this effort will focus on trying to encourage foreign firms with the expertise, ability to manage risk and access to financial resources to take advantage of the many opportunities that exist for investment in Afghanistan. Efforts at investment promotion will be designed to convince these investors that they are both needed in Afghanistan and that they will be able to operate profitably with full government support consistent with maintaining a competitive environment.

Energy

The ANDS strategic objective for the energy sector strategy is an energy sector that provides reliable, affordable energy increasingly based on market-based private sector investment and public sector oversight. The immediate task of the ANDS strategy, with assistance from the donor community, is to expand energy availability at a price that covers cost (for all but the poorest members of society) and to do so in the most cost effective manner. The Government will also take steps to provide the basis for the transition of the sector from public provision to private provision of electricity. As the Afghan energy sector moves from primarily state owned operations to a more private market orientation, new institutional arrangements will be established.

Until recently a focus in the energy sector has been on using donor funds and contractors to rehabilitate and expand the infrastructure of the government-owned electric company DABM, with virtually no attention being given to establishing an enabling environment that would promote increased private investment in the sector. This will change with a major effort to set up a transparent regulatory framework and a pricing system that is designed to encourage private sector investment in the sector. A new market oriented paradigm, significant institutional changes and considerable capacity development will be established under guidance from the Inter-Ministerial Commission for Energy (ICE). Streamlined government oversight and greater reliance on private sector investment is essential. As the energy line ministries shift from operating as production-based institutions to becoming policy making regulatory agencies, staff capacity and in-house functions will be reoriented to market practices. The Government will assess its sector assets and establish a plan for liquidation, restructuring and commercialization or sale. In particular the Government will provide more support for the corporatization and commercialization of national power operations. All these efforts will occur even while donor funded projects continue to work to relax the severe constraints in the energy and power sectors, but will lay the framework for a shift to a more commercial energy system in the coming years..

Mining

While geological studies of Afghanistan have been conducted over the last 50 years, due to political, social and economic factors, 90 percent of the territory of Afghanistan has not been systematically studied. However the limited results have been highly promising with over 400 mineral occurrences having been identified, including Aynak copper, coal and a number of small and medium mines such as gold, silver, platinum, zinc, nickel, emerald, lapis, ruby, canset, tourmaline, fluorite, chromate, salt, radioactive elements and numerous deposits suitable for construction materials. The availability of significant oil and gas fields in Afghanistan has been well known for almost 50 years.

The ANDS strategic objective in the mining sector is to encourage legitimate private investment in the sector so as to substantially increase government revenues, improve employment opportunities and foster ancillary development. Implementation of the strategy will help to develop effective market-based economy sector policies, promote and regulate sustainable development of minerals and ensure that the nation's geological resources are progressively investigated and developed. The Ministry of Mines is making the transition from being primarily a producer of minerals and other commodities to a policy making and regulatory institution. For mining and minerals, the emphasis is on the exploration, extraction and delivery to market; for hydrocarbons the emphasis is exploration and development. There is a great potential for the mining sector. The test will be in moving quickly from the success in attracting investment in the Aynak copper deposits to the development and exploration of the many other mineral resources of the country.

Water Resources

Agriculture accounts for 95 percent of water consumption. In the 1970s, some 3.3 million hectares were cultivated using various irrigation methods. However, because of civil conflict and drought, at present only about 1.8 million hectares of land are being irrigated. Of this, only ten percent is being irrigated using properly engineered systems with the remainder dependent on traditional irrigation methods, some of these based on run-offs from or use of aquifers that are being degraded by deep water wells and insufficient investment in recharge basins. Significant donor funded investment has gone into rehabilitating damaged or degraded irrigation systems, but little has been done in terms of making new investments the structures needed to increase efficiency in water use. There is a lack of resources needed to improve water management, including a lack of skilled human resources. Information systems are now being reconstituted, but there is a lack of reliable hydrological, meteorological, geo-technical and water quality data. The infrastructure and equipment needed to efficiently conserve and utilize water resources is insufficient. There are limited data on ground water resources and information indicating that un-regulated deep well drilling may be depleting aquifers that are essential to water supplies and traditional irrigation systems (Karezes and springs). There is a lack of economic mechanisms regulating water use and investments for water supply, sanitary systems, irrigation, and hydropower generation.

The efficient management of Afghanistan's water resources is essential for social and economic development and is an area where there is a great need for public sector involvement. Both government and donor efforts have under-invested in better water resource management that will have a major impact on the productive capacity of the economy and the lives of the people. Within the water resources sector, feasibility studies will be completed and investments will be made in the needed storage facilities, recharge basins, multi-purpose dams, irrigation systems required to improve water sector management for both agricultural and non-agricultural uses. These efforts will augment on-going efforts to rehabilitate and improve management in existing systems. Over time there will be a movement away from a project by project focus on rehabilitation to an Integrated Water Resource Management (IWRM) system geared to the five major river basins in the country, with an eventual devolution of responsibilities down to independent River Basin authorities.

Transport

The ANDS strategic goal for the transport sector is to have a safe, integrated transportation network that ensures connectivity and that enables low-cost and reliable movement of people and goods domestically as well as to and from foreign destinations. The strategy will contribute to achieving the following targets established in the Afghanistan Compact. (i) Afghanistan will have a fully upgraded and maintained ring road, as well as roads connecting the ring road to neighboring countries by end-2008 and a fiscally sustainable system for road maintenance by end-2007; (ii) By end- 2010, Kabul International Airport and Herat Airport will achieve full International Civil Aviation Organization compliance; Mazar-iSharif, Jalalabad and Kandahar will be upgraded with runway repairs, air navigation, fire and rescue and communications equipment; seven other domestic airports will be upgraded to facilitate domestic air transportation; and air transport services and costs will be increasingly competitive with international market standards and rates; and (iii) By end-2010 Afghanistan and its neighbors will achieve lower transit times through Afghanistan by means of cooperative border management and other multilateral or bilateral trade and transit agreements.

The Government continues to give high priority to rehabilitate a badly damaged road system. This includes: (i) completion of a fully upgraded and maintained ring road and connector roads to neighboring countries, (ii) improving 5,334 km of secondary (national and provincial) roads and (iii) improving and building 6,290 km of rural access roads as a key to raising rural livelihoods and reducing poverty and vulnerability in rural areas. Better rural roads will improve market access and opportunities for rural households. The actual allocation of resources amongst these three areas of planned activity will depend on the estimated rates of return from analysis of proposals put forward for funding by the international community or by the ministries involved in implementing the transport sector strategies.

A Transport Sector Inter-Ministerial Working Group will be formed that will coordinate the ministries in the sector to assure that investments are properly coordinated to obtain the highest returns and greatest impact on the poverty reduction goals. Careful consideration will be given to increasing employment opportunities, and assuring that the local resources or funds channeled through local communities are effectively used to maintain the rural roads established as part of this strategy.

Information and Communications Technology

In early 2003, Afghanistan had fewer than 15,000 functioning telephone lines for a population of approximately 25 million, one of the lowest telephone penetration rates in the world. The Government with donor assistance adopted major policy reforms for the ICT sector, moving rapidly to establish the legal framework and regulatory arrangements to promote private sector investment, resulting in a competitive environment and the rapid growth of mobile phone use from almost nothing to a present subscriber base of over five million. This development is one of the major success stories of in the implementation of the private sector based development strategy. Greater efforts will be made during ANDS period to adopt a similar investor friendly regulatory framework for development of natural resources and infrastructure. With respect to telecommunications, the ANDS strategic objective is to expand access to mobile phone service to 80 percent of the country and greatly increase access and use of the internet by consumers, the private sector and the Government.

Urban Development

The ANDS strategic objective for urban development is to greatly improve the management of urban areas through a devolution of authority and responsibilities to municipalities in a way that improves urban infrastructure and services, reduces urban poverty and allows urban residents to live safe, healthy and productive lives and cities to grow and prosper. Effective management of the rapid urbanization process will make a significant contribution to the recovery of the country. As of 2005 nearly a quarter of Afghanistan's population lived in urban areas. Outcomes will include: (i) strengthened municipal capacity to manage urban development and deliver services; (ii) improved institutional coordination and monitoring of key urban indicators; (iii) increased access to basic services for urban households; (iv) phased regularization of tenure for 50 percent of households living in informal settlements; (v) upgrading public services and facilities, including new urban area development; (vi) increased availability of affordable shelter, including a 50 percent increase in numbers of housing units and 30 percent increase in area of serviced land on the market, coupled with access to affordable finance; and (vii) improved urban environment with green areas and open spaces

More is now being done under the ANDS to devolve authority to municipalities. The urban development strategy is designed to improve urban governance through: (i) decentralization, participatory processes, market-based approaches, and improved regulations; (ii) capacity building at all levels of urban governance; (iii) establishing a clear national land policy, including urban informal settlement policy; (iv) improved revenue generation in cities through direct cost recovery for and economic pricing of urban services, property-based taxes, and use of computer systems; (v) expanding urban upgrading pilots, including phased regularization of informal settlements, and programs to meet the immediate housing, tenure security and service needs of the poor and vulnerable people; (vi) increasing the supply of serviced land by developing new urban areas, especially within the cities, to meet the present and future housing needs of the people; (vii) improving city-wide basic infrastructure and services, in particular water supply, sanitation, roads and green areas; and (viii) rehabilitation of urban heritage facilities and sites.

Education

Efforts to improve education, which started in 2002, were focused on getting 1.5 million children into the primary/secondary school system. There are now over 6 million children at primary and secondary school. In addition universities have reopened and there are increasing opportunities for vocational training. There are now 52,200 students at higher education institutions. Although the expansion of education has been impressive, there is an urgent need to improve the quality of education.

This is one area where programs designed to meet benchmarks defined in terms of enrolment or coverage fail to give adequate consideration to the quality of the service being provided. Increased priority will be given to teacher training and other mechanisms to encourage private sector investment in educational activities.

Vocational training will become an increasing focus of attention. There is an urgent need to address problems in the vocational education sector that include staff shortages, overbuilding, lack of standardization in training courses, and qualifications that are difficult for potential employers to assess. A new organization, the National Vocational Education and Training Authority (NVETA), will be established and will: (i) manage, but not operate, all vocational training institutions; (ii) set minimum core competencies for courses, carry out accreditation, and inspect vocational institutions, to ensure that they meet minimum standards; and (iii) call for tenders by ministries or by the private sector to operate vocational training facilities owned by the Government.

The potential role of the private sector has been expanded considerably in this strategy. In the primary and secondary education area there will be an expansion in private and NGO schools, encouraged by a more accommodating regulatory environment. In higher education the university cooperation plans that have already commenced will allow universities in Afghanistan to interact and be supported by recognized foreign universities. NVETA will contract with private sector groups or NGOs for provision of educational services. Some areas will be left to the private sector, including preschool education.

Culture, media and youth

The ANDS strategic objective for this sector is: (i) to create awareness and foster a sense of pride in the country's history, future, culture and achievements; (ii) to document and preserve cultural artifacts and heritage sites; (iii) to ensure an independent and pluralistic media that contributes to an open and democratic society; and (iv) to foster a sense of confidence among the young that they can contribute to and benefit from a stable and prosperous the country. An accessible and well maintained cultural artifacts data base and the cultural artifacts collection held by the Ministry will be expanded. In the longer term, museums will be established and or expanded and historical or heritage sites will be protected. Media legislation will be enacted to provide a stable and predictable environment in which a largely privately run and independent media can operate. Media will be employed as an educational tool in addition to entertainment. Key priorities include a country-wide coverage of public Afghan media (radio and television), an increased number of hours of public broadcasting, and improved quality of programming. At this stage in its post-war development, state-owned media will be used to promote and convey information on gender policies, public health and national security. Extensive reforms have been introduced within the education strategy that is designed to assist youth. These include expansion of the education system; rehabilitation programs for young people whose education may have been limited because of the security situation; and reforms to vocational education to provide youth with marketable skills and better employment opportunities.

Health and nutrition sector strategy

By all measures, the people of Afghanistan suffer from poor health. The country's health indicators are near the bottom of international indices, and fare far worse, in terms of their health, than any other country in the region. Life expectancy is low, infant, under-five and maternal mortality is very high, and there is an extremely high prevalence of chronic malnutrition and widespread occurrence of micronutrient deficiency diseases. Substantial improvements in the health system and the health status of the people of Afghanistan have been achieved in recent years, but there are a number of challenges and constraints that must be addressed if continued progress is to be made, including: (i) inadequate financing for many of the key programs; (ii) reliance on external sources of funding; (iii) inadequately trained health workers; (iv) lack of qualified female health workers in rural areas; (v) dispersed population, geographical barriers and a lack of transportation infrastructure; (vi) low levels of utilization for certain health services, especially preventive services; (viii) variable levels of service quality; (ix) insecurity in some provinces, making it difficult for program implementation, recruitment and retention of staff, expansion of service coverage and monitoring by the provincial and central levels; (x) lack of effective financial protection mechanisms for poor households to receive the care they need without experiencing financial distress; and (xi) lack of mechanisms for effective support to and regulation of for-profit private sector clinics and pharmacies.

Programs have been designed to expand and improve the system and to try and target vulnerable groups with preventive or curative programs. The Ministry of Public Health (MoPH) will review and develop relevant legal and regulatory mechanisms, such as accreditation systems, that govern health and health related work in the public and private sectors. The goal of the regulatory system will be to facilitate competitive and cost effective provision of services, carrying out its broader mandate to not only contract out service provision to civil and private groups but also to facilitate growth of the 'for profit' sector. The MoPH will review, develop and enforce relevant legal and regulatory instruments that govern health and health related work to safeguard the public and ensure service quality. The MoPH will work to identify, encourage, coordinate, and review and in some cases conduct relevant, useful research that can assist evidence-based decision making and the formulation of new policies, strategies and plans.

Agriculture and rural development

The ANDS strategic objective for the agriculture and rural development sector is to jointly use private investment and public sector support for efforts to transform agriculture into a source of growth and means of livelihood for the rural poor. The sector strategy articulates a road map for the way forward in which poverty reduction through economic regeneration is the central objective Some of the focus will be on the transformation of agriculture in a number of well defined zones where the conditions for growth are most favorable.

Agriculture has traditionally been the main activity for much of Afghanistan's population, particularly in the most remote and vulnerable areas. While non-farming activities account for large amounts of time, many of these are related to processing, transporting or marketing agricultural goods. The agriculture and rural development strategy establishes ambitious plans for a series of programs that are designed to achieve an improved quality of life for rural citizens – one in which food security is assured, basic services are provided, incomes increase with households actively engaged in legal activities, employment opportunities expand and where people live in a safe and secure environment. Activities are grouped into two main components of the strategy: a Comprehensive Agriculture and Rural Development (CARD) and the Agricultural and Rural Development Zone (ARDZ) initiative.

The CARD strategy articulates a road map for the way forward in which poverty reduction through economic regeneration is the central objective. The overall focus is to support the poorest and most vulnerable segments of rural society. Proposed interventions will provide a range of measures that will differ between groups and between regions, but all are designed to help diversify incomes, including income support, direct provision of assets, skills training and market opportunities.

The second main component of the strategy, the Agriculture and Rural Development Zones (ARDZ) program, is the Government's approach to expanding commercial activities and increasing agricultural productivity. The ARDZ recognizes that geographic priorities have to be set in support of the development of commercial agriculture. These geographic priorities will be used to target infrastructure, utilities and other support by various ministries. The Government will release publicly held land to increase private sector investment through a competitive bidding process. Further, the Government will continue to investigate and implement measures to increase financial and technical support that can be utilized by private firms to expand operations. This will ensure the process of transforming underutilized state land into commercially viable agro-processing enterprises will be as fast and efficient as possible.

Social Protection

The ANDS strategic objective for social protection is to assure that the benefits of growth reach the poor and vulnerable, either through the attention to these groups in the design of programs and projects aimed at stimulating growth or through well targeted support programs. The social protection sector has significantly improved since 2002 in all areas: social support, pension distribution and disaster preparedness. Cash transfer benefits have been established for martyr's families and the disabled as the main instrument of the social support and national solidarity with the victims of the war. The MoLSAMD has established its departments in all provinces and strengthen its capacity for targeting and cooperating with NGOs and donors. Around 2.5 million people have been covered with some type of public arrangement for social protection. Efforts will now focus on: (i) improving efficiency of public arrangements for social risk management; (ii) diversifying market-based arrangements for social risk management; (iii) strengthening informal arrangements for social risk management (iv) capacity building and restructuring in the MoLSAMD; and (vi) improving partnership with civil society and NGOs to enhance aid coordination. The main principle for future social support will be to enhance fiscal sustain- ability by focusing on the most vulnerable and supporting the "poorest of the poor". Finally, strengthening the public/NGOs/private sector partnership will support the Government's intention to remain mainly in the area of policy making and providing regulations and having the private sector and NGOs increasingly involved in service delivery.

Refugees, returnees and internally displaced persons (IDPs)

The ANDS strategic objective with respect to refugees, returnees and IDP's is to efficiently manage the voluntary return of refugees and IDPs and their reintegration into productive participation in society. World-wide experience has indicated that large, unplanned, and essentially involuntary returns which have to be managed as emergency influxes generate a range of negative consequences. Therefore the planned and voluntary return of refugees and IDPs return is the guiding principle for the sector strategy.

More than five million persons have returned to their homes since 2002. Their reintegration into society has been challenging but there has no been no pattern of discrimination against returnees. There is some evidence of secondary migration of returnees from places of origin to cities and back to the neighboring countries. The latter occur most noticeably from border provinces. Population movements have largely normalized with socio-economic factors largely replacing security and politics as the key drivers. The numbers of IDPs has also fallen significantly since 2002. Currently there are an estimated 129,000 IDPs displaced by past drought and conflict and an additional 29,000 more recently displaced by recent fighting in the southern provinces. The majority of the one million IDPs identified in 2002 have returned to their homes. During 2007 there was some rise in local internal displacement in the southern provinces of Helmand and Uruzgan due to clashes with terrorist groups. Within the region, the principle legal and operational framework governing voluntary repatriation is provided by the Tripartite Agreements (TA) signed between Afghanistan, UNHCR, Iran and Pakistan respectively. These agreements are serviced by regular meetings of Tripartite Commissions at both Ministerial and working level.

It is very probable that high levels of mass and voluntary repatriation are over. The refugees' long stay in exile, poverty, and dissuasive conditions in many parts of Afghanistan are likely to prove difficult obstacles to overcome in the future. Security, lack of economic opportunities (employment) and social services (health and education) continue to limit return and reintegration. The most significant challenges for future will be: (i) ensuring peace and security in areas of refugee origin; (ii) improving the Government's abilities to negotiate effectively with its neighbors on refugee, displacement and migration issues; (iii) improving the political, economic, social and organizational absorption capacities in key sectors and areas; and (iv) developing an implementation plan and supporting resources executed over a number of years.

Cross-Cutting Issues

Since 1383, the Government has given considerable attention to a set of issues that cut across all the sectors, motivated by the belief that the overall success of the ANDS will be in jeopardy if these issues are not effectively addressed. These cross cutting issues involve (i) regional cooperation; (ii) counter-narcotics; (iii) anticorruption; (iv) gender equality; (v) capacity development; and (vi) environmental management..

The regional cooperation initiatives are intended to increase access to power; generate revenues through transit trade; reduce impediments to trade and expand both import and export opportunities; increase investment and contribute to improved employment and business opportunities; facilitate the free flow of goods, services, and technology; allow the costs or benefits of development of common resources to be shared; reduce regional tensions and facilitate regional efforts to reduce cross border crime and terrorism; and facilitate the voluntary return of refugees.

Counter-narcotics programs are designed to; (i) disrupt the drugs trade; (ii) strengthen and diversify legal rural livelihoods; (iii) reduce the demand for illicit drugs and improve treatment for drug users; and (iv) strengthen state institutions combating the drug scourge within central and provincial governments. Provincial governors will be responsible and accountable for the process of control and management of counter narcotics intervention in their jurisdiction with support from MCN.

The National Anti-Corruption Strategy is based on the following key goals: (i) enhancing government anti-corruption commitment and leadership; (ii) raising awareness of corruption and evaluating the effectiveness of anticorruption measures; (iii) mainstreaming anticorruption into government reforms and national development; and (iv) strengthening the legal framework for fighting corruption and building an institutional capacity for effective implementation of the United Nations Convention Against Corruption (UNCAC).

The ANDS goal for gender equality is an Afghanistan where women and men enjoy security, equal rights and equal opportunities in all spheres of life. The National Action Plan for Women focuses on three main outcomes: (i) government entities embracing 'gender equality' in their employment, promotion, policy making and budgetary allocations; (ii) measurable improvements in women's status as evidenced by reduced illiteracy; higher net enrollment ratio in educational and training programs; equal wages for equal work; lower maternal mortality; increasing leadership and participation in all spheres of life; greater economic opportunities and access to and control over productive assets and income; adequate access to equal justice; reduced vulnerability to violence in public and domestic spheres; and (iii) greater social acceptance of gender equality as evidenced by increased participation by women in public affairs and policy discussions.

The ANDS capacity development objective is to assure that the skills needed to effectively implement programs and projects included in the ANDS exist or can be developed within the required time frame for implementation. The institutional responsibility will be with Inter- ministerial Commission for Capacity Development (ICCD) that will serve as a single reporting point for both government and donors. ICCD will provide a coordinated approach to support the effective management of funds and aid flows, to cut down on duplication and to ensure that critical capabilities for program and project implementation are well defined and (most importantly) that capacity development and technical assistance programs are properly focused on meeting these critical needs.

Environmental protection efforts are geared to: restoration and sustainable use of rangelands and forests; conservation of biodiversity; preservation of Natural and Cultural Heritage sites or resources; encouragement to community based natural resource management, prevention and/or abatement of pollution; and improved environmental management, education and awareness. Throughout all sectors, any environmental costs will be fully accounted for in appraisals aimed at ensuring that benefits of proposed programs or projects.

Enhancing Aid Effectiveness and Aid Coordination

The Government has implemented processes to increase the monitoring of aid-funded activities and to improve the efficiency of implementation. The Aid Coordination Unit in the Ministry of Finance has responsibility for issues related to the delivery and monitoring of external assistance. The Government would like to see increased core budget support (direct budget support), giving greater ownership and enabling a more effective allocation of resources based on needs and priorities. Channeling aid through established trust funds is also effective, with the Government able to access funds on an as needed basis. Pooling of donor funds also significantly reduces the duplication of efforts and leads to better coordination, management, and effectiveness of aid. This is especially so with technical assistance grants.

Efforts to increase capacity to implement the Core Development Budget more efficiently will result in higher donor contributions, aiding coordination. Equally important is the Government's accountability to Afghan citizens on how aid funds have been spent. The MoF's Public Expenditure Financial Accountability (PEFA) framework is crucial to this process. The ANDS provides the framework for priority aid delivery. Aid delivery will be greatly improved where Government, civil society and the international community align expenditures with the ANDS priorities. Further, the Government will work with civil society organizations and Provincial Reconstruction Teams to ensure that these activities are also aligned with the ANDS priorities and goals.

Implementation and Monitoring of the ANDS

The success of the ANDS depends on effective implementation. The National Budget is the central tool for implementing the ANDS. Given this, all line ministries will first develop or align their programs and projects with the ANDS Sector Strategies; sector program and projects will then be costed and re-prioritized against the medium-term budget ceilings. Based on this, the ANDS Public Investment Program (PIP) will be prepared to enable the full integration of the ANDS into the medium term budget in accordance with the MoF's ongoing activities to introduce program budgeting. Furthermore, the Government will improve its absorption capacity and fiduciary practices to encourage donors to implement their projects through the National (Core) Budget or, if this is not possible, to assure that programs or projects implemented through the external budget are aligned with the ANDS objectives and priorities.

At the national level, the following structures will link policy, planning, budgeting and monitoring of the ANDS: The National Assembly is responsible for legislating an enabling environment for security, economic growth and poverty reduction. The Council of Ministers headed by the President is the highest level decision-making body, providing overall policy guidance and direction under existing legislation. The ANDS Oversight Committee (OSC), composed of senior ministers, will oversee and coordinate the overall ANDS implementation process. Line ministries and other government agencies will also be responsible for implementation itself. The MoF will play an important role by making sure that the program and projects of the line ministries are costed, prioritized and integrated into the National Budget. The OSC will play a key role in coordinating overall efforts to implement the ANDS. Moreover, the Ministry of Economy will strengthen this mechanism by coordinating the work of the line ministries at the operational level. The Joint Coordination and Monitoring Board will remain the highest Government-donor mechanism in charge of coordination and monitoring, which will cover not only the Afghanistan Compact but the entire ANDS. The Consultative and Working Groups will continue to be the key forums for improving aid coordination and ensure alignment of the donor programs and projects with the ANDS.

2. THE PARTICIPATORY PROCESS AND PROVINCIAL DEVELOPMENT PLANS

Public support for the successful implementation of the ANDS is essential. Therefore, Government has developed the ANDS over the course of the past three years through a thoroughly participatory manner, to seed the emergence of a grass roots democracy, ensuring ownership from people from all corners and walks of life, civil society, the private sector, religious establishments, international community and all government institutions at the national and sub-national levels. In the course of developing the ANDS, the Government has undertaken a public policy dialogue with all key stakeholders, embarking on a provincial based planning process across all provinces to bring government closer to its people, and the people closer to government. The outcomes and lessons learned from this consultation exercise provided an opportunity to participate in discussions on the development national policy and strategy framework.

The ANDS is the product of extensive consultations at the national, provincial and local levels. National consultations involved practically all governmental and major civil society institutions including Non Governmental Organizations (NGOs), cultural associations, religious communities, the private sector, influential individuals, experts and the international community. Sub-national consultations involved discussions with provincial governors, provincial representative bodies, representative village councils, parliamentarians representing each province, local civil society, representatives of Provincial Reconstruction Teams (PRTs) and prominent individuals in all 34 provinces of Afghanistan. More than 17,000 people, 47 percent of whom were women, directly participated in the consultation process. The consultations included all pillars of ANDS. This section summarizes the participatory and consultative process and the lessons learned from it.

Organizing Principles and Participation Process[7]

The Government undertook extensive and thorough consultations, far exceeding the depth and quantity of consultations usually undertaken as part of a PRSP process. To support the comprehensive development framework of the ANDS, the aims of the consultation process were to:

- build a national consensus with respect to the Government's overall vision, development strategy, and greater understanding of the realistic pace at which national development could take place;
- ensure that citizens had a real impact on development and implementation of public policy;
- ensure ownership by the Government, which is critical for successful strategy implementation;
- be as inclusive as possible to capture the opinions and views of different groups to ensure a representative strategy would emerge capable of addressing the needs and priorities of all citizens, and in the process ensuring Government fulfillment of the participatory requirements of the PRSP;
- lay the groundwork for a sustainable process, which would last beyond the life of the development of the full ANDS, and ensure regular inputs into Government decision-making processes, thereby creating a participatory process which will be institutionalized over time; and
- Strengthen the capacity of the Government to consult widely on its strategies, as well as to facilitate wider input into its policy- making.

The consultation process was designed to reflect the structures of Government at national, provincial and district levels, guided by the programmatic structure provided in Figure 2.1.[8]

Consultations brought together central and provincial decision-making institutions. Valuable outcomes and lessons have been learned as part of this process, which are being used to strengthen the policy, planning and budget formulation. As the consultation design allowed for ministerial and cross-ministerial cooperation, some of the outcomes of the process have addressed cross-cutting issues. This is particularly so where national and subnational planning, budgeting and financing intersect. Consultations have been ongoing throughout the development of the ANDS (figure 2.2).

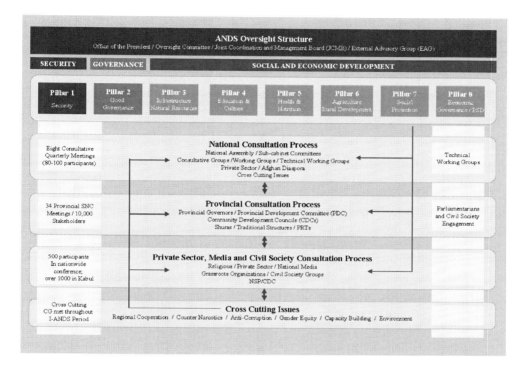

Figure 2.1. ANDS oversight structure

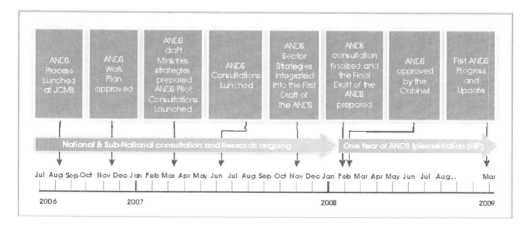

Figure 2.2. ANDS timeline 1385 – 1388 (2006-2009)

Consultation Process

Consultations were conducted with primary and secondary stakeholders from the: (i) national; (ii) sub-national; (iii) international; and (iv) private sector, civil society, religious and traditional communities. Through the consultation process the Government has aimed to connect newly formed central and provincial governance structures and ensure harmonization and co-ordination of the development process. The following section provides a very brief summary of the important strategy design process.

- **National Consultation Process**: The day to day preparation of the ANDS was managed by the ANDS Directorate, with the supervision of a Presidential Oversight Committee, chaired by the Senior Economic Advisors. The Oversight Committee (OSC) was formed to oversee the economic, policy and strategic direction for the implementation and development of the ANDS. The committee is composed of Cabinet Ministers, including the Ministers of Finance, Foreign Affairs, Economy, Commerce, Justice, Education and the National Security Advisor and meets bimonthly to monitor the progress of implementation of the Afghanistan Compact, I-ANDS and the ANDS. Within the framework of the various Consultative and Technical Working Groups, each Ministry and Agency developed its individual strategy, coordinated within the sector wide approach underpinning the ANDS. These strategies cut across the three pillars and seventeen sectors of the ANDS, including the mainstreaming of cross cutting issues, to deliver a mutually reinforcing, fully prioritized and integrated strategy. The Joint Coordination and Monitoring Board (JCMB) coordinates the efforts of all partners in the process, and reports the results to the President, the National Assembly, and the UN Secretary General as well as to the international community and the public. Between quarterly meetings, the JCMB Secretariat coordinates activities that keep the benchmarks on track. The JCMB serves as the official link between the Consultative Groups (CGs) as well as between the Technical Working Groups (TWGs) and the OSC. Moreover, key national stakeholders involved in the National Consultation Process include (a) the national assembly (b) sub-cabinet committees (c) consultative and technical working groups and (d) the private sector and members of the Afghan diaspora.
- **Sub National Consultation Process**:[9] The sub-national consultation process of the ANDS represented the first significant dialogue between the central Government and the provinces; designed to strengthen centre-periphery relations. The outcome of this consultation process included the formulation of 18,500 village based development plans, leading to 345 district development plans, which were finally consolidated into 34 Provincial Development Plans (PDPs). This process involved consultation between parliamentarians, provincial authorities, provincial development committees, village Shuras, local Ulama, the international community (including the Provincial Reconstruction Teams) and most importantly ordinary Afghan citizens. These PDPs identified needs and key development priorities for each province. Both the National (top-down) and sub-national (bottom-up) processes were developed into the sector strategies, with a move towards the formulation of Sector Wide Approach and Programmatic Budgeting.

- **International Consultation Process**: Engagement between the Government and the international community has been substantially guided by the Bonn process which set high level political goals: the Securing Afghanistan Future exercise; the Afghanistan Compact and the MDG process. The international community was involved in the ANDS consultation process through the External Advisory Group (EAG). Among other issues, this organ f ocuses on implementation of the principles of the Paris Declaration. The ANDS Secretariat provides support to these structures to enhance coordination and effectiveness and the linkage with the national consultation process. The international community was extensively involved in the development and preparation of the ANDS.
- **Consultation with the Civil Society, Private Sector and Media**: The Government carried out extensive consultation with civil society groups, including: (a) the religious establishment; (b) village shuras[10]; (c) non governmental and not for profit agencies; (d) cultural associations; (e) human rights organizations; (f) grassroots associations related to women's affairs, youth development and disability; and (g) Water and Sanitation Committees (WATSAN). Six Afghan coordination bodies and partner NGOs were extensively engaged during the development of the Sector Strategies. Moreover, throughout the process the media has been actively reporting on the ANDS, through newspapers, TV, radio and internet. The role that civil society organizations have played at different levels as facilitators, communicators, advocates and monitors has been invaluable.[11] As part of the economic diagnostic and PDP work, provincial discussions were held to discuss the private sector development strategy in the five largest commercial cities, which culminated in the 'Enabling Environment Conference' held in Kabul in 1386 (June 2007).
- **Poverty diagnostic consultations**: The Government's participatory approach to poverty diagnostics involved enabling poor communities and their institutions to participate effectively in defining, analyzing and monitoring poverty as they experience it. This work was also conducted in the most remote and conflict affected communities of Afghanistan. In so doing, a broader choice of poverty actions based on the specific concerns of the poor have been established for each province, as well as each district. Government has considered a range of poverty actions based on specific concerns of the poor including vulnerability, conflict sensitivity, insecurity and governance. As a result of provincial and district planning, different targeting of poverty reduction programs/interventions have been considered to establish a best fit between poverty profile and poverty actions.

Provincial Development Plans (PDPs)

As part of the ANDS PDPs were developed for all 34 provinces of Afghanistan to provide a coordinated framework for the Government and the international community to undertake sector programs and projects at the sub- national level. The linking of consultation to the provincial based planning process has allowed local communities to prioritize, sequence, plan and be involved in the implementation of projects. The PDPs developed through the Sub National Consultations ensure that the priorities in the ANDS reflect the best interests of the Afghan people and are the product of the three rounds of Sub-National Consultations that took place across Afghanistan March 2007- March 2008.

The PDPs have informed policy formulation, articulated goals and needs of the people and provided strategic direction to the sector strategies and the overall ANDS. During the Sub National Consultations (SNCs), preparation and input for the PDPs was based on the following inputs:

- line ministry strategies and plans;
- priorities of rural communities including those set out in Community and District Development Plans;
- priorities of urban communities, including those set out in Urban Plans;
- priorities of vulnerable social groups including Kuchis, refugees, returnees and Internally Displaced Persons (IDP) and the disabled; and
- priorities of women, who attended the consultations with an average of 47 percent participation.[12]

Development of Provincial Profiles

The PDPs contain a profile of each province using information from both the National Risk and Vulnerability Assessment (NRVA) and UNFPA's Socio-Economic and Demographic Profiles, providing a geographic, poverty-based and social picture of the province and perspectives on the state of provincial development. Opportunities for poverty alleviation have been included with the agreed goals and needs for each pillar. This provides a guide to potential development in each province; especially for the most urgent local needs.

Priority Projects

Ten projects have been prioritized for each sector and for each province aligned with the fiscal envelope of ministries within the outreach of national programs. In total, 80 priority projects were identified for each province. The SNCs served as an opportunity for these ideas in the shape of Community Development Plans (CDPs) and District Development Plans (DDPs) to be consolidated and improved and to reach consensus on them with a wider audience from the province before being incorporated into PDPs as priority projects. Priority projects from the eight sectors across the 34 provinces therefore represent a list of activities that respond to the most urgent sectoral needs in each province. These are being mapped into the national budget process.

Prioritization and Sequencing of the PDPs

Prioritization of the provincial priority projects, aligned with National Programs, forms the basis on which implementation of the ANDS will take place at the local level. Out of the eighty projects prioritized during the SNC process, the most critical projects were aligned with the five most crucial sectors and prioritized into tiers. Tier one projects represent the most urgent tasks. This has allowed for a logical resource allocation and prioritization process to be carried out. Provincial budgeting, as a component of the National Program Budgeting Reform Progress, is also informed by the provincial prioritization process. It aims to empower local authorities and increase the appropriateness of resource allocation. This is currently being piloted in ten provinces and will be extended to a further ten in 1387 (2008).

Integration of the PDPs into ANDS

The data from the SNCs and PDPs was fully incorporated into ANDS in the following ways:

- For each Sector Strategy; comments gathered from the SNCs from a provincial perspective on challenges for that particular sector have been a starting point for addressing the country's most urgent needs. Thus each sector can be seen to respond directly to the concerns raised by the people.
- Prioritized projects will be aligned with ministries' national programs. This will enable a more transparent provision of services and a more clearly defined implementation and monitoring mechanism.
- The prioritization process will assist ministries with effective resource allocation and provincial projects highlighted as the most urgent should be seen as priority action by the ministries.

Outcomes from the Provincial Development Planning Process

One of the most valuable outcomes of the sub- national consultations was the clear indication that the 34 provinces have different development priorities. As outputs, the PDPs have formed an integral part of Government policy formation, prioritization, sequencing and needs- related resource allocation. In addition, two national overriding considerations emerged as critically important to any intervention: the importance of preserving the country's Islamic religious principles, culture and lifestyle and ensuring equity of access to resources and intervention.

Security emerged as a top priority in two thirds of the PDPs; most strongly in the south and the east of the country. In these regions, security is perceived as the fundamental basis on which all other development depends.

Key issues identified by stakeholders[13] include: the (i) lack of access to clean drinking water in all provinces, for both domestic use and throughout institutions such as schools and clinics; (ii) improvement of provincial roads, 83 percent referring specifically to the need for tertiary road services, to improve communication between villages to district and provincial centers; access to basic services such as schools and clinics; (iii) improvement in the present low quality services emerged as a key priority throughout the country, especially with respect to poorly trained teachers and doctors; (iv) lack of alternative livelihoods to poppy cultivation; (v) lack of vocational training for returnees and disabled people; (vi) poor access to electricity cited in 80 percent of the PDPs; and (vii) corruption within the public administration (mentioned in 80 percent of the PDPs, particularly within the security services).

Prioritization of the Pillars

Using qualitative information from the PDPs the ANDS pillars have been prioritized. This has been illustrated in two ways. Figure 2.3 shows the proportional representation of priorities within the top five sectors across the 34 provinces. Unsurprisingly, with 80 percent of the population relying on some form of agriculture, it has appeared as a national priority. Sectors such as health and social protection are also one of people's top priorities. In order, the key priorities are:

- Agriculture
- Security
- Education
- Governance
- Health
- Private sector
- Roads
- Infrastructure (energy and water) and social protection.

Table 2.4 shows the top priorities for provinces, shown for all 34 provinces. Thus in 17 out of 34 provinces security can be seen as the absolute number one priority. Roads is shown as a sub sector since people articulated this as a separate requirement from other infrastructure development (health is not mentioned because although it appears numerous times in the top five priorities for provinces, it is not considered the top priority in any province).

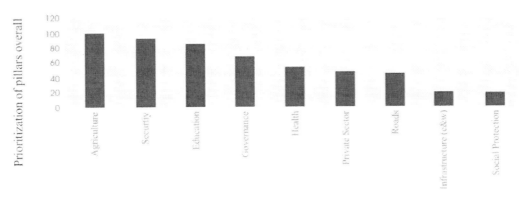

Figure 2.3. Proportional representation of sectors across all 34 provinces

Afghanistan National Development Strategy

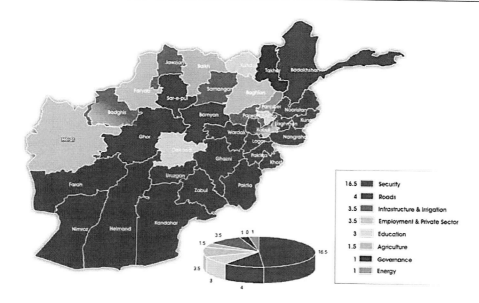

Figure 2.5. Top priorities of provinces – primary ranking.

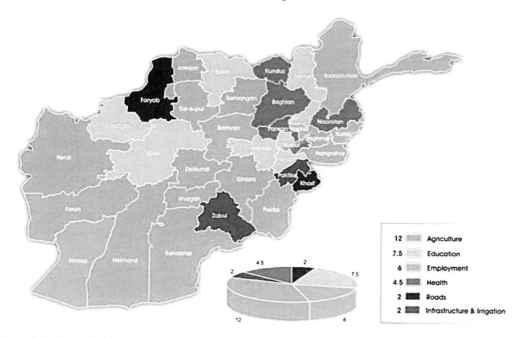

Figure 2.5. Top priorities of provinces – tertiary ranking.

Table 2.4. Sectors/pillars and the number of provinces in which they are a top priority

Sector or Pillar	No. of provinces
Security	17
Infrastructure	5
Education	4
Employment	3
Roads	3
Agriculture	2
Governance	1

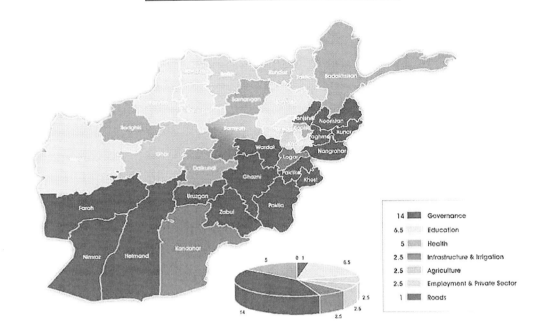

Figure 2.6. Top priorities of provinces – secondary ranking.

Regional Variation in Priorities

From a regional analysis some general similarities can also be seen from the above map:

- In the South and South East regions the major priority is security.
- In the West and Northern regions priorities are mainly employment generation and infrastructure development
- In the North East and Central Highlands areas the main priorities are provision of roads, education and agriculture.

The clearest message to be obtained form a provincial level analysis is that every province is unique in its needs, goals and priorities and this should be a major consideration within the resource allocation process.

Conclusion

The ANDS is the result of an extensive process of consultations involving key players at international, national, provincial and grassroots level. The insights provided by these consultations have served to highlight both national and local priorities to form the holistic vision of the country's development strategy, keeping in mind the vast experiences of the international community in this arena. The PDPs have enabled the prioritization of provincial sectoral goals and needs into time-bound activities. The voices of the poor have informed the overall policy framework and the poverty profile, as well as the various sectoral priorities outlined in this document. It is envisioned that participation processes will be sustained throughout implementation of the strategy. Lessons learned have been formally integrated into the policy, planning and budgeting processes, including ongoing concerns about regional cooperation, conflict management, counter-narcotics, anti-corruption, gender, the environment and capacity building. It is assumed that integration of the provincial planning, budgeting and implementation into the national development process will contribute to a relevant and accountable national development process.

3. THE POVERTY PROFILE

In the development of the ANDS Government has adopted evidence based policy making, through detailed poverty diagnostic work, within which to understand the causes and effects of poverty. Based on this analysis we have been able to develop the ANDS as a pro-poor growth strategy. By pro-poor, the Government means making investments that have a preferential impact on bringing poor people out of extreme poverty through the adoption of growth enabling policies and targeted social protection investments. This means that Afghanistan aims to achieve pro-poor growth, where the incomes and livelihoods of the poorest rise faster than the average growth of the economy. Key findings of spring 2007 National Risk and Vulnerability Assessment (NRVA) showed 42 percent of those living below poverty line with income of US $ 14 per capita per month. Moreover, food poverty was estimated to be around 45 percent of people who were therefore unable to purchase sufficient food to guarantee the world standard minimum food intake of 2,100 cal/day. Furthermore, 20 percent of people were slightly above the poverty line indicating high vulnerability.

In addition to the high incidence of consumption disparity, there is a significant difference in poverty levels between provinces, and between rural (36 percent) and urban (21 percent) communities. For example, the depth of poverty (the poverty gap) in the Northeast appears to be higher than in the South whereas the average distance between the poor and the poverty line seems to be larger in Badakhshan than in Zabul. Parwan and Logar provinces have poverty rates of less than 10 percent while Daikundi has a poverty rate of 77 percent and the lowest level of welfare among all groups, are women and Kuchis. Gender inequality is an important characteristic of poverty in Afghanistan. The vast majority of women do not participate in paid economic activities making them highly dependable on their husbands or families. The literacy rate among women being much lower (19 percent) than for men (40 percent) and, the net primary school enrolment rate for girls (6-9) is around 21 percent while much higher for boys (28 percent).

Data Collection, Poverty Measurements and Estimates

The Government has undertaken extensive assessments to improve understanding of the determinants of poverty and the impacts of growth and poverty reduction programs on different income groups. In addition to the NRVA studies, the Government has relied on information from the Participatory Poverty Assessments conducted by ACBAR (Agency Coordinating Body for Afghan Relief) and the FCCS (Foundation for Culture and Civil Society). ACBAR launched the Afghanistan Pilot Participatory Poverty Assessment (APPPA) in several provinces to enhance collective understanding of different poverty perspectives, its analysis and formulation into the ANDS poverty reduction strategy.

Data Collection: National Risk and Vulnerability Assessments

Information on the specific nature of poverty in Afghanistan is restricted by the considerable quality and quantity limitations, with the NRVA comprising the majority of information available. These have been based on limited household surveys. The 2005 NRVA covered approximately 31,000 households, allowing national and provincial poverty rates to be assessed. While the 2005 NRVA survey was a substantial improvement on previous studies, it also had several weaknesses with only one season being covered. To overcome this, a separate survey conducted in spring 2007.

Ongoing data collection includes the planned 2007/08 NRVA survey (predominantly funded by the EC). This study will cover all seasons and the consumption module includes assessment of more food items and non-food items. Moreover, stronger emphasis has been placed on survey design and the collection and computation of high quality of data.

Sub-National Consultation and the Pilot Participatory Poverty Assessment

The ANDS sub-national consultation process has contributed to a far deeper understanding of the specific nature of poverty in the Afghan context. Consultations were held in all provinces, with discussions on critical priorities for poverty reduction, such as education, health, water and sanitation, agriculture and social protection. A significant number of women (46 percent) took active part in these discussions.[14]

> **BOX 3.1. VOICES OF THE POOR**
>
> "The poor are being the ones with an empty stomach", or "the poor are being the ones who do not have enough milk to make yogurt". Furthermore, Afghan citizens states poverty 'as being an incapacity to plan the future' with the 'poor being unable to foresee what will happen tomorrow". One man in Bamiyan province defined poverty by saying: "the poor are the ones who can be sick today and be dead the next day".
> Interviews by: MoWA, 2007

Poverty measurement: cost of basic needs analysis

The Cost of Basic Needs (CBN) poverty line represents the level of per capita expenditure at which the members of a household can be expected to meet their basic needs comprised of food and non-food items. Adding the food and non-food poverty lines the poverty analysis based on NRVA 2005 yielded a CBN poverty line for Afghanistan estimated to be 593 Afghani per capita per month or around US$14 (at 2005 prices). Spring National Risk Vulnerability Assessment (NRVA) 2007 survey provides an updated CBN poverty line of 708 Afghani per capita per month (again around US$14 at the 2007 exchange rate).

Poverty Estimates

However, the latest NRVA survey (Spring 2007) indicates that 42 percent of the population lives below the CBN poverty line (figure 3.2). That is, almost half of the Afghan population is unable to purchase a basic food basket to provide 2,100 calories consumption per day.

Seasonality and poverty

Poverty levels in Afghanistan vary by season. This further compounds the understanding of poverty in Afghanistan. The Food Security Monitoring Survey (FSMS) suggests that households tend to have the richest consumption in summer following the harvest, with more restricted food consumption during winter, especially in March.[15]

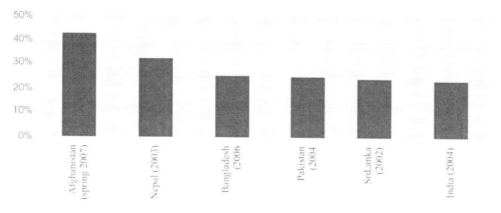

Figure 3.2. Regional poverty comparisons.

> # BOX 3.3. SEASONALITY AND POVERTY
>
> During spring we plant, in winter we harvest so in autumn and winter we have enough food. At the end of winter and the beginning of spring we do not have enough." Female participant, Shawak village, Badakhshan.
>
> Source: APPPA final report, march 2008

Vulnerability

The 2005 NRVA highlighted that 20 percent of the population are located very close to the poverty line, indicating high vulnerability. Even small consumption shocks can result in substantially higher rates of poverty. For instance, a 5 percent reduction in consumption across the board will cause the poverty headcount rate to rise from 33 to 38 percent. According to the 2005 NRVA, a 25 percent upward shift in the poverty line would result in 53 percent of the population living in poverty. Meanwhile, a 25 percent downward shift in the poverty lines would reduce the poverty rate to 14 percent. Table 3.4 highlights the potential impact of consumption shocks on poverty incidence.

Poverty in Afghanistan: Main Characteristics of Inequality

Afghanistan has the lowest level of inequality in South Asia as measured by the Gini coefficient. This however is largely due to the widespread nature of poverty across the country. However, within Afghanistan, significant inequality does exist between many segments of Afghan society. The variation in poverty between the rural, Kuchi and urban populations is significant and of great importance. Meanwhile, gender inequality is one of the highest in the world.

Table 3.4. Impact of consumption on poverty rate[16]

Sector	Base case (% poverty)	5% shock (% poverty)	10% shock (% poverty)
Kuchi	30	33	38
Rural	36	40	45
Urban	21	25	29
Total	33	38	42

Table 3.5. Share of consumption by quintile

Group	Share of total consumption (%)
Bottom 10 %	3.6
Bottom 30 %	15.6
Top 30%	47.8
Top 10%	21.1
Top 1%	3.5

Table 3.6. Estimated poverty headcount rates and food insecurity (spring 2007)[17]

Sector	Food poverty	CBN poverty	Food insecurity index
Kuchi	40	45	39
Rural	45	45	39
Urban	41	27	37
National	45	42	39

Consumption Disparity

Consumption inequality is a concern. The World Bank has estimated (based on the 2005 NRVA) the bottom 10 percent of the population accounts for 3.6 percent of total consumption while the bottom 30% account for 15.6% of total consumption. Combined with very low overall levels of consumption, this indicates that the poorest population suffers from high levels of deprivation (table 3.5).

Poverty also varies significantly between provinces. Poverty headcount rates vary from around 10 percent to more than 70 percent, with poverty more severe in the Northeast, Central Highlands and parts of the Southeast. Entire provinces like Daikundi, Badakhshan, Zabul and Paktika represent large pockets of poverty.

The 2005 NRVA indicates a significant disparity in poverty between rural people and the Kuchi population compared to urban populations. Around 45 percent of rural and Kuchi populations appear to be poor as opposed to 27 percent of those who live in urban areas. Rural populations have the highest rates of food insecurity, with 45 percent not meeting daily minimum food requirements. Moreover, it is noted that 40 percent and 41 percent of the Kuchi and of urban population respectively are also unable to meet their minimum food intake (table 3.6).

These disparities are reflected in primary school enrollment rates (table 3.7), though in this regards, the Kuchi population is particularly disadvantaged.

Table 3.7. Enrollment rates (ages 6-9)[18]

Group	Female (%)	Male (%)	All (%)
Kuchi	5.0	5.8	5.4
Rural	20.1	28.8	24.6
Urban	34.7	34.9	34.8
All	21.2	28.4	24.9

Characteristics of Rural Poverty

The rural population – who make up the majority of the poor – account for approximately 80 percent of the population. The main characteristic of the rural poverty is high food insecurity and a lack of access to infrastructure and basic public services. Illiteracy rates are prevalent among rural Afghans and the level of education is low. Rural households are highly dependable on agriculture. However, non-farm activity has started to play a bigger role in the coping strategy of the rural poor. The poorest among the rural households are those who live in remote and mountainous area, whose head is illiterate or without any education and who do not poses land or livestock.

Characteristics of Poverty among Kuchis

Kuchis are nomadic pastoralists (estimated at 1.5 million people) and are heavily dependent on livestock and migration patterns for their livelihood. In recent years, 15 percent of Kuchi families have been forced to cease migration and settle. Kuchi poverty has many of the core characteristics of rural poverty although food insecurity is not as high as in the case of rural households (table 3.6). However, the poorest Kuchis are those who have settled. Reasons for settling include loss of livestock due to recent droughts and insecurity which disrupted traditional migratory routes. Moreover, the biggest cause of being settled is growing banditry and local crime as well as conflict with settled populations over grazing areas. The failure of local authorities to deal with disputes over traditional pasture rights has already led to number of conflicts and rising poverty among Kuchis.

Characteristics of Urban Poverty

Urban poverty and food insecurity are lower amongst the rural and Kuchi populations. However, recent research regarding urban livelihoods from a European Commission funded project suggests that urban poverty is increasing, and is positively correlated with the growing urban population.[19] Many informal settlements around major cities have been built in order to accommodate migrant workers, returnees and others. For years these suburbs have been one of the largest neglected pockets of poverty. A number of recent studies have concluded that low paid employment does not guarantee that citizens live above the poverty line.[20] Due to poor daily wages many urban workers fall into the category of the "working poor".[21] Insecurity of employment leads to income irregularities and to a chronic shortage of money. Many urban poor households lack of finance to smooth consumption and are forced to take short term loans to purchase basic needs such as buy food and pay rent. Income fluctuation, job insecurity and high indebtedness are core characteristics of a typical "poverty trap" for the urban poor.

Gender Inequality

Gender inequality is an important characteristic of poverty in Afghanistan. The vast majority of women do not participate in paid economic activities making them highly dependent on their husbands or families. In spite of this women, especially in rural areas, actively contribute to the household income through employment (often unpaid) in agriculture and livestock activities. Nevertheless, the gender gap remains large with (i) the literacy rate among women is much lower (19%) than for men (40%) and, (ii) the net primary school enrolment rate for girls (6-9) is around 21 percent while much higher for boys (28%) (table 3.7).

Female headed households are closely correlated with the high poverty due to a lack of education and employment opportunities.[22]

Most Important Causes of Poverty: Poverty Correlates

A number of factors contribute to poverty, including a lack of infrastructure, limited access to markets, social inequity, historical and ongoing conflict and various productivity constraints. The APPPA found that the key determinants of poverty were: (i) a weak assets base, (ii) ineffective institutions: including the disabling economic environment; weak regional governance, service delivery and corruption; weak social protection programming; social inequalities; and (iii) vulnerability to: conflict; natural disasters; decreasing rule of law; increasing basic costs; increasing population; food insecurity; winterization; and (iv) non-diverse livelihoods. Source: APPPA Final Report, March 2008.

Literacy levels

Poverty is highly correlated with literacy skills. The 2005 NRVA highlights that poverty rates for households with illiterate heads is 37 percent, compared to 23 percent among households with literate heads. Citizens with primary education experience up to 10 percent lower poverty than families with uneducated heads.

Agriculture and livestock are positively correlated with poverty

The poorest households are found to be dependent mainly on livestock and agriculture activities. The NRVA 2005 report found that agriculture and livestock activities are the largest contributors to poor household incomes. Meanwhile, households in the top two consumption quintals earn more from trade and services. Education and literacy are also highly correlated with higher involvement in nonfarming activities as is access to major roads.

Asset ownership and crop diversification

A lack of ownership of land and livestock is associated with lower poverty.[23] Small land owners, landless families and families without livestock are in most cases poor. Moreover, ownership of non irrigated land is strongly associated with levels of poverty with families who are engaged in cultivating rain fed land much poorer than families that cultivate irrigated land. Equally, livestock ownership appears to decrease economic vulnerability. Urban families without home ownership are highly vulnerable as they have to allocate large parts of income to paying rent. Moreover, crop diversification appears to be an important spring board strategy for escaping poverty.

Access to education

Poverty reduction and economic growth are closely associated with the population's level of education. As highlighted above, a literate head of household has greater earning potential and is negatively correlated with poverty. Access to education by the bottom consumption quintile is low, resulting in a lower net primary school enrollment rate.[24] The 2005 NRVA also highlights a significant gender disparity in net primary school enrollment, especially among Kuchi and in rural areas, while the disparity in urban areas remains marginal.

Access to health facilities

A lack of access to health facilities and poverty are closely related. Higher household consumption is associated with more frequent visits to health facilities and higher vaCross Cutting Issuesnation rates of children (see box 3.8). Access to the Basic Package of Health Services (BPHS) has significantly improved, covering 85 percent of the population in 2006. This has contributed to a lowering of poverty rates in these areas.

BOX 3.8. HEALTH AND HOSPITAL SERVICES IN THE PROVINCES

"We don't have a clinic here but if you are lucky enough to be able to drive the 30 kilometers to the nearest hospital you find doctors who are not professional, who don't pay attention to you, and who tell you to go out and buy your own medicine." female participant, Papchi village, Herat.

Source: APPPA, final report march 2008

Other important causes of poverty

A number of other factors are linked with poverty in Afghanistan:

- Indebtedness: a lack of job security, irregular income, pressure to buy food and having to pay rent forces many rural and urban poor to increase borrowing.
- Remoteness: the NRVA data indicate poverty is much lower in areas that are close to the main roads (Ring Road). Topographical remoteness and the lack of access to major roads remains a major causative factor of poverty.
- Female household heads and disability: research conducted by MoWA identified female households as being linked with higher rates of poverty. Likewise, having a disabled head of household or a disabled family member is also associated with higher poverty.

The remaining causes of poverty include: (i) security; (ii) large households with small children; (iii) poor access to basic services (water and electricity), and (iv) natural disasters.

BOX 3.9. POVERTY AND NATURAL DISASTERS

"In the spring the river overflows – there is no retaining wall and our lands are damaged" male participant, Bai Sar community, Herat.

Source: APPPA final report, march 2008

Who the Poor Are: The Most Vulnerable Groups

According to the Spring 2007 survey approximately 10 million Afghans, around 42 percent of the population, live below the poverty line and do not meet their daily food and non-food requirements. While high rates of poverty exist amongst Kuchi and rural households, the incidence of poverty is increasing in urban areas and large city suburbs.

Families with a large number of small children

Afghanistan has one of the largest child populations and the smallest proportion of working age populations in the world[25] which exposes families with a large number of small children to economic shocks. Moreover, the country also has one of the highest under 5 infant mortality rates in the world. Children up to five years remain the most vulnerable because they require high quality nutrition as well as other forms of child care unaffordable to most families. Many rural and urban children are forced to work to bolster family incomes resulting in widespread child labor and school drop-outs, "trapping" the children in the endless cycle of poverty.

Female Headed Households

According to 2005 NRVA data, female-headed households comprise around 2.5% of Afghan households. These households are typically highly vulnerable to economic shocks, with a significant number not having a single able bodied income earner.

Disabled, internally displaced and extremely vulnerable poor

Afghanistan has one of the largest rates of disability in the world. According to Handicap International there are around 800,000 disabled people in Afghanistan. The unemployment rate among these groups is almost 90 percent. The country also has a large number of internally displaced persons (IDPs). The high vulnerability to natural disasters, ongoing conflict and forceful repatriation of the refugees from the neighboring countries contributes to overall poverty. Increasing migration to cities, job insecurity, indebtedness and the collapse of traditional safety nets has placed many urban poor into extreme poverty.

Policy Framework for Poverty Reduction

Poverty in Afghanistan is complex and multidimensional. The NRVA surveys reveal the severity of poverty with one in two Afghans being classified as poor. Further, a large number of people are concentrated close to the poverty line and are highly vulnerable to natural, security and price based shocks.

To address this, the policy framework for the ANDS will be premised on the following principles:

- Promoting pro-poor growth: the Government will tackle poverty first and foremost through promoting strong equitable and broad based private sector led growth. In parallel, fiscally affordable social protection safety nets will be undertaken as part of regular Government business.
- Promoting pro-poor budgeting: the most important sectors impacting on poverty and poverty reduction, including security, education, health, and social protection, will see budget allocations maintained or increased over the medium term.
- Allocating adequate resources to the poorest areas: although past expenditure allocations were in favor of the pro-poor sectors, actual spending has not always been well focused to benefit the poor and vulnerable.

- Providing the balanced support to the Kuchis, rural and the urban poor: the majority of Government and donors interventions have been aimed at supporting the rural poor. Future support to the Kuchis, rural and urban poor will need to be more balanced based on levels of poverty.
- Focusing on the poorest and most vulnerable: given the huge needs and scarce resources of the Government and the international community, the poverty reduction strategy will need to prioritize targeting the poorest of the poor.
- Improving donor coordination and aid- effectiveness: donor support as well as improved donor coordination together with the elimination of duplication in delivering assistance to the poor will be essential to the success of the ANDS poverty reduction strategy.
- Strengthening the capacity for data collection and poverty analysis: institutional capacity for data collection and poverty analysis will need to improve in order to better inform policies for poverty reduction. The Government will actively mainstream the poverty focus throughout monitoring and data collection mechanisms.
- Building partnership between the Government and NGOs: the role of NGOs in delivering services to the Afghan poor is recognized. Strengthening the Government's policy making capacity needs to be combined with a strengthening of the partnership with NGOs in the area of service delivery.

Implementation, Monitoring and institutional Strengthening

Implementation and monitoring of the ANDS poverty reduction policies will be mainstreamed through the sector strategies. However, the evaluation of the overall ANDS sector policies for poverty reduction will be evaluated separately to inform policy makers about their effectiveness. The NRVA will remain the main tool for data collection on matters of poverty. However, the introduction of the household budget survey and strengthening of the CPI and national income data will also contribute to this understanding. The forthcoming Census Survey will play an important role in enhancing the understanding of poverty. The capacity of the CSO's for data collection of key poverty and development indicators will need to be strengthened. Moreover, the Government will continue to improve its own capacity to undertake poverty analysis within the CSO and other Government agencies.

High Priority Sector Policies for Poverty Reduction

Security, Maintaining Strong Growth and Macroeconomic Stability

Maintaining steady growth rates of between 7 and 9 percent of the GDP (in real terms) through the promotion of the private sector is expected to lead to a reduction in the national headcount poverty rate of around 2 percent on an annual basis. Equitable growth distribution is the precondition for broad based poverty reduction. This will require higher (budget) expenditure in the critical sectors of health, education and social protection and higher levels of public spending in the poorest provinces and remote areas where poverty levels are high.

Maintaining macroeconomic stability including prudent fiscal policies is critical to growth as is maintaining price stability and single-digit inflation rates. Improving the security environment would significantly contribute to poverty reduction leading to increased economic activity and the preservation of human capital and household assets. Moreover, it would decrease internal displacement and reduce pressure on impoverished dwellers due to migrating impoverished rural families to the cities.

Generating employment and labor market policies

Given widespread low productivity employment and the large number of jobless, employment generation will be one of the most important policies for poverty reduction. An improved security and business environment will support stronger private sector growth, which will gradually become the main source of employment and the main instrument of poverty reduction. This requires expanding the mining and oil and gas sector. The Government, supported by the donors, will increase public work activities and their presence in the poorest provinces. The National Solidarity Program (NSP) will continue to play an important role in generating jobs and income for the rural poor. Skills development programs will expand to help the unemployed obtain in demand qualifications. Moreover, public administration will employ more women and disabled people. Labor market regulation and the pension reforms will be improved to provide protection from the employers, especially for workers engaged in the informal economy.

Education and health

Education and health will remain the priority sectors for public spending. The Government will continue the policy of providing free universal education. Increasing the literacy and net primary school enrollment rates and decreasing the number of school dropouts will be the main contribution of the education sector to poverty reduction. Higher attention will be given to supporting disabled peoples access to facilities, including specialized institutions and adjusting schools and universities to meeting their needs.

The Health sector will continue to be strengthened. Building new health centers in rural and poor urban areas will be priority for health sector public spending. The special needs of disabled will be better accounted for in the Basic Package of Health Services (BPHS).

Two major issues that contribute to women's poverty are a lack of maternal heath services and education for girls. Both issues are caused by a lack of facilities and are interlinked with the need for culturally appropriate services for women and girls. In relation to the provision of maternal health services, there is a great need for female doctors and trained midwives to offer 'culturally appropriate' health services. Afghanistan has one of the highest population growths among developing nations and despite strong cultural limitations the overall poverty reduction strategy will need to encourage family planning.

Social protection and urban development

Social protection programs will focus on supporting the most vulnerable and the poorest of the poor. This includes "children at risk", chronically poor women, poor disabled, mentally ill without family protection, neglected elders and drug edicts.

Many urban homes are built without the necessary construction permits, creating uncertainty and risk for typically poor families. To address this uncertainty, the Ministry of Urban Development will include pro-poor urban development programs. The first priority will be to legalize constructions in residential areas and develop basic infrastructure to improve public service delivery.

Malnutrition is one of the major causes of the high infant mortality under 5, with the poor the most vulnerable. The Government will consider introducing the Zakat-based tax to increase allocations for social programs to support these programs.

Agriculture and rural development

Rural development and agriculture are key sectors for improving the rural livelihoods. Access to markets has been indicated as an important determinant for rural poverty in Afghanistan. Programs to support crop diversification, targeted livestock, orchards, distribution and providing farming implements will contribute to poverty reduction among the rural poor. As will improved access to rural all- weather roads, sanitation, electricity, job opportunities and promoting rural enterprises. These programs are important tools for rural income generation and the elimination of poppy cultivation.

Water and Irrigation

Investments in water management and irrigation will significantly contribute to higher food security and poverty reduction for those currently operating on rain fed land. In addition to malnutrition, the lack of the access to clean water, poor sanitation and sewage is one of the main causes of high infant mortality. The Government will increase public spending on improving the access clean water as well as improved health protection to address this.

Disaster preparedness and community-based insurance schemes

Natural disasters, particularly droughts and floods are one of the major sources of vulnerability among the poor. The NRVA 2005 highlighted the destruction of crops due to droughts represents a higher poverty risk than sickness or loss of a working family member. Building more efficient disaster preparedness and response will decrease the risk of falling into poverty. Further, the Government will initiate the establishment of community based crop insurance schemes to enable the poor to better mitigate the risks of losing harvest.

Energy and transport

Expanding the national road network, including the construction of the rural roads, will allow poor households to diversify income generation – from low profitable crops to more profitable activates such as trade, services and small businesses. Investments in transmission lines and power generation will increase access to electricity, improving productivity.

Social protection safety nets will be strengthened to ensure the poor can cope with the planned elimination of energy subsidies, which will increase the risk of the poor and marginal households falling further into poverty, especially for the urban households.

Justice and anti-corruption

Greater access to justice, especially for women, is an important component of the ANDS to empower the poor and provide more efficient protection to victims of violence. Justice reform will also improve the business environment and increase investments and job generation. The ANDS will also reduce corruption in key sectors such as justice, health, public administration and education, which will have a significant benefit for the poor.

Empowering the poor: role of NGOs

Expanding the service delivery and policy input role of NGOs and civil society are crucial to reducing poverty. This is strengthened by the ANDS' participatory structure with Afghan society. ANDS progress reports will be publicly disseminated. Civil society and sub-national level bodies will be consulted in preparation of the ANDS updates. Participatory poverty qualitative assessments and quantitative analysis will be provided on a regular basis to obtain input from NGOs and civil society on the key priorities for the poverty reduction. The role of the NGOs in delivering the services to the poor will also increase as will their role in providing the Government with the "voices of the poor" and policy advice.

Conclusion

During the pre-harvest spring of 2007, the NRVA estimated that 42 percent of the population was below the poverty line. A great many more people remain vulnerable to falling below the poverty line as a result of rising food and fuel prices or bad weather. Great reliance is being placed on private sector-led development and growth to create sustainable employment and market opportunities. It is these opportunities that will allow the majority of Afghans to improve their lives and pull themselves out of chronic poverty. As the ANDS sector strategies are implemented, great effort is being made to use participatory and consultative processes to better understand the needs of the poorest and most vulnerable groups, to inform the design of appropriate programs to address those needs. The real needs are so enormous that substantial interventions are indeed required to provide real assistance to the neediest, particularly women who are burdened with child care responsibilities, social constraints, and the disabled who are not provided enough opportunity for full participation in society in order to take advantage of improved employment and market advantages. Special programs are suggested to be put in place to target these groups so that they too share in the benefits from economic and social development programs. This is important not only on humanitarian grounds but in terms of building the community cohesion that is the foundation of a tolerant and compassionate Islamic state.

PART II. THE NATIONAL DEVELOPMENT STRATEGY

4. MACROECONOMIC FRAMEWORK

High, sustainable, broad-based economic growth and the preparation of a viable macroeconomic framework are indispensable for poverty reduction and employment creation. The overall growth strategy of the ANDS is based on a firm policy of private sector led growth. During the last five years per capita income nearly doubled from US$147 to US$289. Comparable rapid economic growth will be needed during in the next five years if the poverty reduction goals of the ANDS are to be achieved. This will require a supportive environment for social and economic development, which will depend crucially on making significant progress toward improving security, eliminating the narcotics industry, reducing corruption and strengthening governance. Equally important will be the continued maintenance of sound and stable macroeconomic policies.

Table 4.1. Macroeconomic projections

	1385 2006/07	1386 2007/08	1387 2008/09	1388 2009/10	1389 2010/11	1390 2011/12	1391 2012/13
Real sector	(annual percent change)						
Real GDP (excluding opium)	6.1	13.5	9.0	9.0	8.0	7.7	7.0
Nominal GDP (excluding opium)	9.5	24.1	19.8	16.4	14.2	13.2	12.1
Consumer Price Index	5.1	9.8	10.2	7.2	6.0	5.4	5.0
Fiscal sector	(percent of GDP)						
Total expenditures (A)	21.55	22.6	23.0	24.2	23.5	22.6	22.0
Revenues/Financing (B) (operating and development)	20.1	21.2	21.5	22.5	22.6	21.7	21.4
Budget balance (B minus A)	-1.4	-1.4	-1.5	-1.8	-0.9	-0.9	-0.6
Fiscal sustainability indicator (domestic revenues as % of operating expenditures)	66.3	67.0	69.9	72.0	82.9	91.4	100.1
Monetary sector	(percent of GDP)						
Net foreign assets	30.1	26.7	24.0	19.3	16.5	13.9	12.4
Net domestic sales	-14.1	-12.0	-9.2	-5.5	-3.4	-1.5	-0.6
External sector	(percent of GDP)						
Merchandise trade balance	-70.1	-67.6	-64.5	-52.7	-46.3	-39.0	-33.4
Current account balance, including official transfers	-6.3	-1.4	-0.1	-0.7	-2.6	-3.6	-4.5
Foreign direct investment	3.4	3.3	3.3	3.4	3.9	4.0	4.1
Memorandum items	(percent of GDP)						
External budget (= grants)	55.4	54.5	51.6	38.0	30.8	23.6	18.0

Past high growth experience does not guarantee similar high rates of growth in the future. In recent years strong economic performance has reflected substantial public investment in reconstruction activities and large foreign assistance inflows. These factors cannot be expected to continue to contribute to economic growth to the same extent in the coming five years. While public/donor investment will undoubtedly continue to be important in the near term, there will be an increasing reliance on private economic activity for longer term growth to be sustainable and to extend the benefits of development to the entire population.

The drivers of economic growth are the rate of investment and the rate of improvement in productivity. A key strategic objective of the ANDS is to establish a secure economic environment in which it will be possible to attract sufficient levels of investment and which will encourage the employment of human, financial and natural resources in the most productive ways possible. A critical element in achieving this objective will be to substantially increase investment in the development of capacity of the workforce in order to expand employment opportunities and increase incomes.

The ability to implement the projects and programs included in the ANDS depends upon the resources that will be available. This chapter presents summaries of macroeconomic projections for the next five years on which estimates of available resources are based and projections of the domestic and donor financial resources that will be required to implement the ANDS. In order to ensure that sufficient resources will be available, a high priority for the Government is to significantly increase domestic revenues.

Fiscal policies will remain a central policy tool for macroeconomic stability, public resource allocation, and implementation of the development strategy – all of which are important ingredients for sustained robust economic growth. Foreign assistance (including core and external budget) has averaged 40 percent of GDP for the past five years. In order to best use foreign assistance for growth and development, there are two major challenges for fiscal policy. One is that distribution of financial resources (including domestic revenues and foreign assistance) must be aligned with ANDS prioritization. The other is to improve absorption capacity to improve both quantity and quality of projects and project execution.

Linking Growth with Poverty Reduction and Employment Creation

A growth strategy is the backbone of the ANDS. Poverty in Afghanistan is high by any standard. Estimated poverty incidence ranges from 34 percent around harvest season to as much as 42 percent in the leaner season. The unemployment rate hovers at around 40 percent. High annual average growth rates at 12 percent in the past few years likely have had positive impacts on reducing poverty and generating employment at the margins, which are undoubtedly hard to measure (see Poverty Profile chapter). Afghanistan's poverty and unemployment have the following key characteristics:

- **High vulnerability**: A significant number of Afghans are concentrated around the poverty line, especially among the rural population. The concentration around the poverty line implies that even small shocks could further increase national poverty figures.
- **Seasonality**: National poverty has strong seasonality and uneven dispersion across the country.
- **Working poor**: Low salaries subject many unemployed to the risk of falling below the poverty line. The poor are concentrated primarily in the informal sector, which pays very low salaries and leaves them without job protection.

The high poverty and unemployment rates as well as their characteristics suggest that there is a need to sustain high growth rates in the medium-term (sustainability) and results of high growth should reduce poverty and generate employment (quality).

High growth rates: GDP per capita nearly doubled from $147 in 1381 to $289 in 1385 (excluding opium). Nevertheless, GDP per capita is still one of the lowest in the world. Continued high rates of growth will be essential to achieve further increases in average per-capita incomes. Preliminary estimates of the elasticity of growth on poverty reduction suggest that there will be significant reductions in the poverty rate if growth remains strong in the next few years. These estimates suggest that the poverty rate could fall as much as 20 percentage points – from 42 percent of the population in 1386 to 22 percent in 1391.[26]

Sustainable growth rates: High growth rates in the past few years were mainly supported by foreign assistance and related activities (e.g. construction). Although GDP figures do not include the opium economy, this sector has nonetheless provided job opportunities and some degree of poverty reduction. However, dependence on foreign assistance and the opium economy will not be sustainable in the medium-term. A shift to private sector led economic growth will be crucial.

Quality growth rates: The results of high growth should achieve corresponding poverty reduction and employment generation. In this regard, identifying the best potential sources of growth is important. For example, while agriculture accounts for 27 percent of GDP (excluding opium), about three quarters of labor force is employed in that sector. As a sudden shift of labor force from agriculture to other sectors is unrealistic, an increase in agricultural productivity is one of the best strategies to enable higher contributions from the agriculture sector to quality growth rates.

State of the economy and constraints to growth

Economic growth has been high but volatile. Between 1381 and 1385, (2002-06) the annual average growth rate was 11.7 percent, the highest in the region. The growth rate of industry and services were either constant or accelerating, while agricultural growth has remained volatile (Figure 4.1). Sectoral breakdowns show that while growth rates of industry and services were constant or accelerating, those of agriculture have experienced high volatility. Cereal production, which accounts for approximately 75 percent of agricultural output, is susceptible to weather conditions. In industries, manufacturing and construction (heavily supported by reconstruction activities and foreign assistance) contributed equally to growth. However, in manufacturing, 'food, beverage and tobacco' is dominant with few other significant categories. Services, transportation, government services, and wholesale and retail trading also account for significant contributions to economic growth rates. This suggests that agriculture and its related sectors (manufacturing of food, beverages and tobacco along with transportation, trade, and services) are currently the dominant activities in the economy.

One of the most significant developmental achievements has been the maintenance of macroeconomic stability. Successful currency reform in January 2003, alongside prudent fiscal and monetary policy (e.g. no-overdraft policy to finance the budget deficits) have contributed to achieve macroeconomic stability reflected in the deceleration of inflation rates and stable nominal exchange rates (figure 4.3).[27]

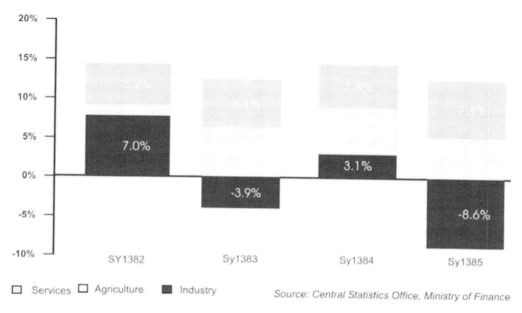

Figure 4.2. Contribution to growth rates

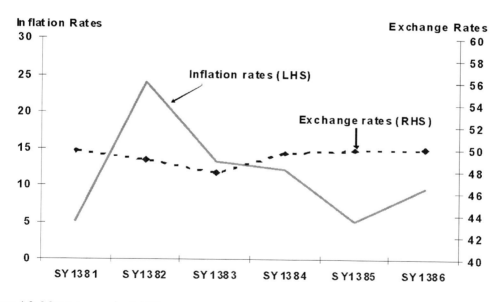

Figure 4.3. Macroeconomic stability.

Due to increasing challenges posed by insecurity in some areas of the country, opium has become Afghanistan's leading economic activity.[28] Opium production increased in 2007 by 34 percent to 8,200 tons. The impact of the opium economy on the overall economy, polity, and society is profound, including some short-term economic benefits for the rural population. However, these are vastly outweighed by its adverse effects on security, political normalization, and state building, which are key elements of high, sustainable and quality growth.

During the past five years foreign assistance has averaged about 40 percent of GDP, of which roughly one third was channeled through the core budget while the remainder was spent outside the government budget system (Figure 4.4).[29] One of the Government's key macroeconomic[30] policy objectives will be using both fiscal and monetary policy to mitigate the most detrimental effects of foreign assistance and ward off any potential "Dutch Disease" effects.

Afghanistan faces daunting challenges to achieve high, sustainable and quality growth led by the private sector. In recent years, an informal equilibrium has been evolving (figure 4.5). That is, increased informal activities negatively impact on the rule of law, weakening governance and the effectiveness of the state institutions. This suggests that some key aspects of state building and the formalization agenda are going off-track, and that overall progress is being threatened by the:

- emerging political patterns in which conflict-generated political groupings are playing an increasingly important role;
- increasing linkages between some key figures and the consolidating drug industry;
- continuing insecurity in some parts of the country; and
- modalities by which most aid is delivered coupled with disappointing results thus far despite large aid inflows.

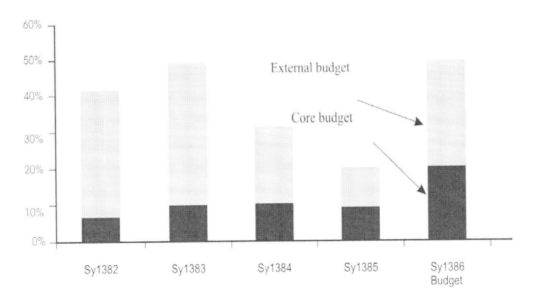

Figure 4.4. Size of foreign assistance.

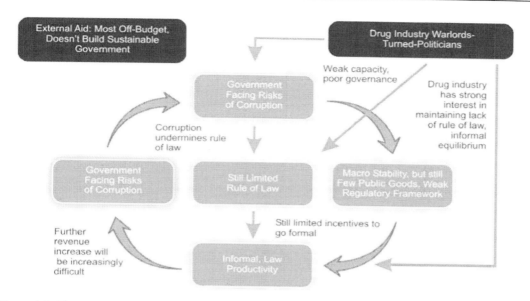

Figure 4.5. The Evolving Informal Equilibrium.

Growth Projection and Strategy

The average annual economic growth rate is projected to be 8.1 percent for 1387-1391. In subsequent years, growth rates are projected to gradually decelerate from 9.0 percent in 1387 to 7.0 percent in 1391 (Figure 4.5). This growth scenario envisages the following developments:

- **Agriculture**: Agriculture is expected to grow 5 percent per year, the same rate as the average growth rates for 1382-86.
- **Industry**: Industry is expected to grow 9 percent per year, supported by high investment (average investment is 34 percent of GDP). The main source of investment is expected to shift from public investment to private investment (including domestic and foreign direct investment) with domestic investment initially leading foreign direct investment.
- **Services**: The services sector is also expected to grow 9 percent. Although still high in absolute terms, this is lower than the previous years' average (14.5 percent).

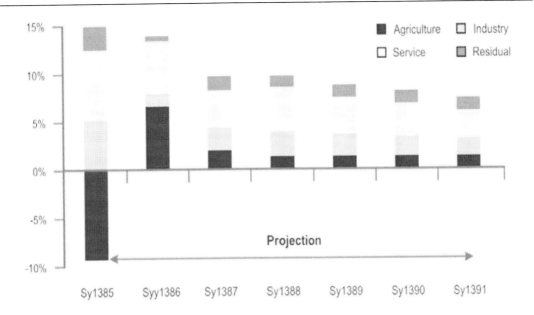

Figure 4.6. Medium term growth projections.

A key assumption underlying this ambitious growth projection is an increasing role of the private sector over the projection period. This assumption is based on the understanding that strong private sector development better contributes to creating employment and hence poverty reduction. Under the current environment (i.e. the evolving informal equilibrium), it is essential to break the informal equilibrium using the following strategies:

- **Strengthening governance**: Fighting corruption will require credible demonstrations by high-level government – including strong commitments and clarification of institutional arrangements; public administration reform including merit-based selection and appointment of civil servants; improving governance at the sub-national level; further strengthening of public financial management; and strengthening the external and public accountability mechanism (e.g. external audit, National Assembly review).
- **Responding to the challenge of the opium economy**: Past lessons have indicated that a key principle for success is focusing on those parts of the drug industry that pose the greatest danger to the nation and its development agenda – in other words, the larger drug traffickers and their sponsors. Some strategies could include:
  - Focus eradication efforts on wealthier opium poppy cultivating areas and also areas that are new to poppy cultivation;
  - Increase interdiction efforts against medium and large drug traffickers and their sponsors;
  - Actors associated with the drug industry who are discovered to hold powerful "legitimate" positions in government or private sector should be removed and prosecuted;
  - The government should focus on sensible rural development, instead of short-term alternative livelihoods programs;

- The counter-narcotics dimension should be mainstreamed into development program.
- **Improving macroeconomic policy management and aid effectiveness**: It is very important that macroeconomic policy formulation is transparent and avoids short-term ad-hoc measures. Some strategies could include:
  - Further strengthening coordination among relevant line ministries. It is important that line ministries share the same view regarding the direction of macroeconomic policy;
  - Continuing to enhance the budget process and the role of the budget as the central instrument for policy and reforms;
  - Maintaining macroeconomic stability and progressing toward fiscal sustainability together with prudent monetary policy will continue to be important.

In order to break the evolving informal equilibrium, we must also ameliorate specific private sector investment constraints. The results of World Bank's investment climate assessment in 2005 show that more than half of respondents identify: (i) electricity; (ii) access to land;(iii) corruption (discussed above); and (iv) access to finance as major constraints to private investment. As the increase in private investment is a key assumption to achieve high, sustainable and quality growth rates, the following specific strategies are suggested:[31]

- **Electricity**: Involve the private sector to expedite power generation and distribution projects in urban centers as well as in rural areas. Specific strategies include:
  - Developing the legal framework to permit and encourage power generation and distribution by the private sector;
  - Accelerating the execution of priority power generation initiatives;
  - Improving distribution system.
- **Access to land**: Implement measures to facilitate access to land by clarifying property rights, simplifying procedures for the transfer of titles, and allowing for longer-term leases. Specific strategies include:
  - Developing a strategy for industrial parks;
  - Implementing improved and simplified procedures for transfer of privately owned land;
  - Developing better legal frameworks for land registration and land adjudication.
- **Access to finance**: Strengthen the financial sector to increase access to credit and financial services, paying special attention to alleviating capacity constraints. Specific strategies include:
  - Enacting an appropriate legal framework;
  - Building capacity in the financial sector;
  - Increasing the availability of financial services in rural areas.

Scaling up of industrial parks is a possible short-term solution: Although in the medium-term the Government should tackle the abovementioned issues, in the short-term the government could work to "scale up" and maximizing the effectiveness of Industrial Parks. This could provide investors and entrepreneurs with security, access to land, infrastructure (power, water, convenient transport) and some insulation from red tape and corruption, at least on an "enclave" basis.

Opportunities and Risks: There exist several potential exogenous shocks which could seriously affect growth projections. Shocks such as drought pose a serious threat to an economy dependant on agriculture. Insecurity too can harm private sector development, investment, employment creation, and reconstruction efforts, which could have a negative impact on overall growth. Finally, global economic conditions pose serious risks for the Afghan economy. A precipitous rise in oil prices would hamper economic growth especially via the private sector. Also possible slowdowns in the global economy and donor fatigue also pose risks.

Factors which may affect this macroeconomic framework in a positive or negative way, including:

- **The political situation:** Presidential and parliamentary elections are scheduled to be held in 2009. Successful and peaceful elections provide confidence in political stability to the private sector and international community;
- **Insecurity:** Security costs can be as high as 15 percent of total revenues.32 Further insecurity would add additional costs to companies' operations and inhibit private investment;
- **Weather:** Agriculture is directly affected by weather conditions. As the sector employs about 70 percent of the total labor force, variations in agricultural production have a significant impact on poverty and employment.

Fiscal Policy

Fiscal policy remains a key policy instrument for macroeconomic stability, and the budget is an important tool to implement the ANDS and prioritize public sector activities. Prudent fiscal policy and effective budget planning and execution will support sustained robust economic growth. Proper budget allocation enables the reconstruction of basic infrastructure, supports private sector development, improves overall economic efficiency and enhances the population's standard of living, especially for the poor. Despite the increase in expenditures in absolute terms, the Government remains committed to sound expenditure management and increased revenue mobilization, as well as ensuring fiscal sustainability. Fiscal prudence remains the underlying principle, which ensures macroeconomic stability and provides the government some flexibility to respond to external shocks.

The Government continues efforts to increase revenues by improving revenue administration and enforcement and broadening the tax base. This will be essential for achieving fiscal sustainability, delivering priority development expenditures and a reduction in aid dependency. Without domestic revenue mobilization Afghanistan will remain heavily dependent on external support over the long-term. The domestic revenue to GDP ratio is expected to reach 8.2 percent in 2007, which substantially exceeds the revenue target in the Afghanistan Compact for 2010.[33] Although domestic revenue is expected to reach 10.7 percent of GDP in 1391 (Figure 4.6), Afghanistan's revenue-toGDP ratio still is among the lowest in the world, requiring sustained commitment to pursue revenue reforms. In the medium-term, a broad-based consumption tax will play an important role in domestic revenue mobilization. In order to accomplish this, broadening the tax base, improvements in tax policy, administration and enforcement will be implemented. In this regard an immediate high priority for the Government is the enactment of the amendments to the income tax law by National Assembly. Progress in domestic revenue mobilization in coming years will enable the Government to be less dependent on foreign assistance. New tax measures will focus equally on improving the revenue intake, while simultaneously reducing the cost of doing business, improving the country's investment environment and enhancing competitiveness.

Consistent with the growth strategy of the Government, the prioritization framework of budgetary allocations is expected to allocate significant resources to productive sectors such as infrastructure, health, education, agriculture and rural development, and rule of law and governance. Cumulative total public expenditures during 1387-91 in roads, energy, water and irrigation, airports, and communications technologies alone are expected to reach about $11 billion (or about one-third of the total expenditures).[34] Similarly, health and education sectors are expected to receive about 17 to 18 percent of the total resources – considerably higher than current allocations. Other priority areas include agriculture, rural development, rule of law and governance, where the Government will invest significant resources.

The Government is taking measures to improve the overall absorption capacity and execution of projects in these sectors through more effective public finance management and efficient project management methods. Key public finance management reforms include introduction of the medium term budget framework (MTBF), program and provincial budgeting. Other Government reforms are targeting project preparation and management, as well as procurement procedures. The overall development budget execution rate has been steadily increasing – the core development expenditure rate for 1385 increased to 54 percent from 31 percent in 1383. The public finance management reforms and prioritization process are expected to improve the overall fiscal situation and improve the quality of public expenditures. Significantly higher execution rates and improved quality of public expenditures in key sectors over the medium term in turn will improve the growth and development process in the country.

Government expenditure policy will focus on creating an enabling environment for the private sector; enhancing production capacity and productivity; and improving the quality of life of the population. The Government's budget allocation prioritization is expected to improve physical infrastructure, enhance human capital and build institutions necessary for private sector led growth and increased employment opportunities.

Core budget expenditures will remain constant at about 25 percent of GDP although the allocation of various expenditures changes over time to align with the Government's development priorities. Throughout the projection period, while the share of operating expenditures decreases, that of development expenditures increases. A considerable portion of expenditure goes to security, counter-narcotics, roads and social expenditures (i.e. education and health).

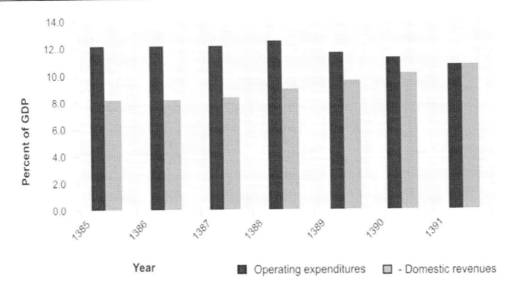

Figure 4.7. Domestic revenues and operating expenditures as a percent of GDP.

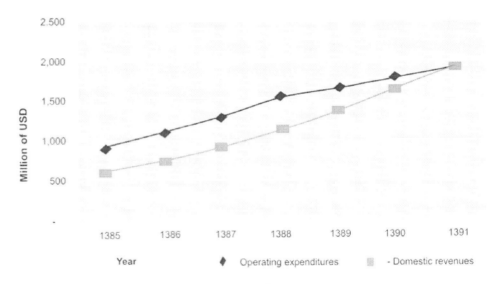

Figure 4.8. Domestic revenues versus operating expenditures.

Fiscal sustainability is essential to ensure macroeconomic stability. The operating budget balance (excluding grants) is projected to improve from a deficit of 4.4 percent of GDP in 1386 to a balanced budget 1391 (Figure 4.7). This requires that the donor grants to the operating budget (e.g. Afghanistan Reconstruction Trust Fund) will free up domestic revenues for key development expenditures after 1391.

Two key fiscal policy challenges are on the horizon: the integration of the external budget into the core budget, and improvement of the absorption capacity of line ministries. Currently, more than two thirds of foreign assistance does not go through the Government's treasury account, and thus information regarding these expenditures is often partial and difficult to obtain. This impedes the Government in its attempts to allocate scarce financial resources in line with its priorities and development objectives. Donors can greatly help by providing more information and/or shifting from the external budget to the core budget; the Government can also improve the situation by articulating clearer priorities – which should be achieved through the ANDS itself. In the past few years, the government has spent less than available financial resources, resulting in delayed investments needed for development. Improving the absorption capacity of the Government, therefore, will continue to be important.

Prudent debt management will continue to be essential as Afghanistan moves towards fiscal sustainability. As a supplement to donor funds the country expects to continue to use limited amounts of debt to finance specific projects and various program requirements. It is expected that any debt received will carry terms that are below market in nature as this is a requirement under Afghanistan's current agreements with various international financial institutions and the Paris Club group of creditors. Debt sustainability in future periods is an important goal for the Government to achieve and will continue to be a guiding principle governing the country's use of debt in the coming years.

Monetary Policy

Consistent with DAB's medium to long-term strategic objectives in conducting monetary policy, it will remain vigilant against inflation. The main goal is to maintain core inflation at single digit levels, preferably between 2.5 to 4 percent, although this will continue to be a great challenge.[35]

Nominal exchange rates are expected to remain constant at around Afs 50 against US dollar. Stable exchange rates will contribute to contain inflationary pressure from imported products as well as provide predictability to the private sector. Nevertheless, stable nominal exchange rates imply the appreciation of the real exchange rates. In the short-term, the impacts on the appreciation of the real exchange rates would not significantly hurt competitiveness as other costs associated with security and electricity seem bigger than the negative impacts on the exchange rate appreciation. However, the Government will keep its eyes on the impact of real exchange rate appreciation for competitiveness in the medium-term.

Access to finance is one of the most severe constraints to the private sector development. High interest rates, caused by high inflation rates and a high risk premium will threaten the financial sustainability of the private sector. Such high interest rates could jeopardize the growth of the nascent financial sector in the country. In the medium to long term, prudent monetary policy together with a disciplined fiscal policy will contribute to a reduction in the risk premium. Effective financial intermediation and macroeconomic stability will eventually bring down real interest rates in the long run as prospects for long term stability improve. The central bank will closely monitor the monetary developments and ensuing liquidity situation along with developments in interest rates and credit markets and will react appropriately to these developments.

To achieve price stability, DAB intends to expand the menu of instruments that have not yet been fully utilized in directing monetary policy. The Central Bank currently relies on foreign exchange auctions as the most dominant tool to maintain price stability and reduce exchange rate volatility. The use of other tools of monetary policy – such as Open Market

Operations (OMO) and Reserve Requirement Ratio (RRR) – has so far been very limited. Other monetary policy tools, such as short-term interest rates and discount rates, have not yet been introduced due to the lack of a market for such securities.

DAB will issue capital notes with various maturity periods and create a secondary market for trading of these notes. The more capital notes are traded in secondary markets, the more the need for foreign exchange auctions will be diminished. Overall, by creating a capital market and a strategic repositioning of monetary policy tools through gradual transitioning from foreign exchange auctions to utilizing other tools of the monetary policy, DAB's room for maneuverability will expand.

Banking system

Through its regulatory mandate, DAB is committed to help banking institutions to manage the risks involved in their operations. Pursuant to Paragraph 2 of Article 2, and other articles stipulated in the DAB law, the central bank is in charge of supervising all depository financial institutions that are legally authorized to take deposits from the public on a continual basis. DAB will continue to supervise banks' lending practices and encourage transparency and accountability in the entirety of their financial transactions, in order to avoid bank failures which can negatively impact the economy.

DAB will strive to encourage financial institutions to actively take part in economic developments by granting short-term, medium-term and long-term credits to small and medium enterprises (SMEs), owners of factories and construction companies and to start mortgage lending to commercial and residential customers. Consumer lending should also become available to the citizens of this country. To do so, DAB needs to remove any prevailing obstacles and unnecessary legal constraints by drafting required laws and regulations and submitting them for approval to the National Assembly as quickly as is practicable. Fortunately, DAB has already taken significant steps in drafting four laws which will facilitate medium- to long-term lending in the country.

External Sector

Exports are unlikely to increase substantially from the current very low base. Afghanistan's exports are currently dominated by low value- added agricultural exports and carpets. Scaling up the export base would require significant FDI (Foreign Direct Investment) inflows. Under the current situation, FDI is concentrated in the telecommunications sector and the financial sector, which are not export-oriented industries. Large scale exploitation of copper, natural gas, petroleum and precious minerals will help in the medium and long term, although investments in this sector are relatively lumpy.

The Current Account Balance, excluding the re-export of goods, is likely to decline over the projected phase. This is largely due to an anticipated decline in the imports-to-GDP ratio, particularly for manufacturing consumed goods. In the outer years, local products and services are expected to become a more significant factor in Afghanistan's economy.

Table 4.9. Overall Financing Envelope for the ANDS 1387-1391 (2008-2013)

	1387 2008/09 US$m	1388 2009/10 US$m	1389 2010/11 US$m	1390 2011/12 US$m	1391 2012/13 US$m	Total US$m
Core + External Budget Funding						
Domestic Revenue	887	1,104	1,351	1,611	1,911	6,864
Total Assistance from Donors*	6,513	4,960	4,814	4,398	3,908	24,593
Total Funding*	7,400	6,064	6,165	6,009	5,819	31,457
Budgeted Core + External Expenditure						
Security	3219	2585	2679	2790	2906	14179
Infrastructure	1781	3093	3681	4180	4451	17185
Agriculture and Rural Development	829	921	916	909	912	4486
Education and Culture	742	893	980	1077	1181	4872
Good Governance and Rule of Law	374	558	640	685	728	2985
Health & Nutrition	325	465	530	563	595	2478
Economic Governance & PSD	237	215	230	244	260	1186
Social Protection	192	359	394	421	449	1815
Others (Sub Codes)	205	198	185	170	157	915
Total Expenditure	7,903	9,286	10,236	11,038	11,637	50,100

* Based on discussions with donors and the 1386 (2007) financial review

Financing the ANDS

The Government has determined sectoral budget ceilings that reflect priorities established in the ANDS (see Table 4.9). This reflects the Ministry of Finance's adoption of a system of program-based budgeting that is designed to achieve the country's development needs. It is based on levels of domestic and donor financing in previous years and projections for future revenues.

This process is an integral part of the Government's Medium-Term Fiscal Framework (MTFF) and the preparation of the budget. From 1387 (2008/09) onward the MTFF and the budget will be based on the prioritization established in the ANDS and the utilization of resources for the implementation of ANDS through the budget.

These sectoral expenditure ceilings reflect the fact that security will remain the highest priority. Over the lifetime of the ANDS, security spending is expected to total $14.2 billion. The funding for this sector is expected to come primarily through international assistance. The Government estimates that in future years, the need for security assistance will decrease as the threat declines. However, given the uncertain nature of the instability facing Afghanistan, the Government envisions the possibility of potentially significant revisions to the financing envelope for the security sector.

In the short term, the Government will focus its public expenditure programs on investments in infrastructure, agriculture and rural development in recognition of the high importance of these sectors for the development of the private sector and for employment growth. Over the lifetime of the ANDS, the Government will focus progressively more resources on education, governance, health, and social protection. The Government commits to allocating sufficient resources to the key priorities of strengthening economic governance and improving the enabling environment for private sector development.

Conclusion

For Afghanistan to become a peaceful and prosperous country able to provide its people with an acceptable standard of living, it has to build a strong economic foundation that will support long term and broad-based economic growth with the private sector as its engine. With sound macroeconomic policies undertaken during the last five years, per capita income nearly doubled. For the poverty reduction goals of the ANDS to be achieved, comparable levels of economic growth will be needed in comings years. This will require a conducive environment for social and economic development, which in turn depends on the continued maintenance of sound and stable macroeconomic policies to enable the private sector to establish itself as a vigorous engine of growth and employment creation.

A key strategic objective of the ANDS is to establish a secure economic environment in which it will be possible to attract sufficient levels of private sector investments that will lead to the increased employment of human, financial and natural resources in more productive ways. A critical element in achieving this objective will be to substantially increase investment in capacity development and creating a skilled workforce in order to expand employment opportunities and increase incomes.

Average economic growth is projected at an 8.1 percent rate for 1387-1391. A key assumption underlying this ambitious goal is an increasing share of total investment will come from the private sector. To reach these goals, the Government will continue to maintain strong macroeconomic management characterized by fiscal sustainability, prudent monetary policies, and the avoidance of short-term ad hoc measures.

The ability to implement the projects and programs included in the ANDS depends upon the resources that will be available. In this regard, a major contribution of the ANDS has been the determination of budget ceilings that reflect the Government's sectoral priorities. These are being built into the MTFF and the Ministry of Finance's program-based budgeting system focused on achieving the country's development needs. Security will remain the Government's highest priority, while the public expenditure programs for investments in energy, water and irrigation, transportation infrastructure, agriculture, agro-based industry, and rural development will remain high priorities, acknowledging the high importance of these sectors for the development of the private sector and for long term and sustainable employment growth. In the coming years the Government will also devote progressively more resources on education, governance, health, and social protection.

5. SECURITY

Security in all parts of the country is essential for economic growth and poverty reduction. The ANDS long term strategic vision for the Security sector is to ensure security of state, persons and assets through the provision of a costed, integrated and sustainable national security infrastructure and law and order policy. The Government has developed the National Security Policy to be implemented through the Security Sector Reform (SSR) program. This will strengthen and improve coordination among the Afghan National Security Forces (ANSF), ISAF/NATO, CSTC-A. While continued international support is vital, the Government aims to assume an increasing share of the security burden – the Afghanization of the country's security activities. However, Afghanistan still faces a number of serious challenges before it can assume full responsibility for its own security. Terrorism, instability and weak capacity of governance are preventing the Government from establishing effective control in some areas, particularly in the south and south-east. The large-scale production of narcotics continues to provide funds to these groups. Unexploded ordinance remain a significant threat, with some five thousand citizens either killed or wounded in mine explosions since 1380 (2001). Currently only two of the country's 34 provinces are completely clear of land mines.

The "Afghanization" of the country's security will require: (i) comprehensive security sector reform; (ii) a new division of labor between the international security forces and the Afghan National Army (ANA); (iii) a reassessment of the design, composition and size of the army; (iv) accelerated training for the officers; and (v) an intensified national recruitment drive.

Current Situation

Afghanistan currently faces a whole range of security threats. To counter these threats and ensure national interests the Government plans to strengthen the military, economic and political ties with its regional and international partners. The security objectives are aimed at protecting the country's independence, establishing a democratic and economically stable society, free of corruption. Implementing development policies outlined in ANDS can only be possible if there is peace and security in the country because security and sustainable development inevitably go hand in hand.

NATO is currently the major force through which the International Community is providing security assistance to Afghanistan with the International Security Assistance Force (ISAF) in cooperation with the Afghan Government. The Government aims to secure stronger commitments from NATO whilst building the capacity of Afghanistan's national armed and other security forces. The Government is intent on building administrative capacity, investing in human resources development and justice sector, and spurring private sector development to help improve Afghanistan's internal situation. An educated and prosperous society is less likely to be influenced by concepts spread by extremist elements. A strong National Security Structure will facilitate development of Afghanistan's economy, social fabric and thus will enhance national unity and peaceful coexistence.

Terrorism and illegally armed groups

The major challenges to stability are terrorism- related, due to the revival of the Taliban in the south and southeast. The Government's security forces and their international partners will focus on fighting terrorism, illegally armed groups and neutralizing armed elements operating along the borders. Given that many of these groups receive support from foreign sources, both regional cooperation and diplomatic initiatives are vital. To defeat terrorism, new strategies attuned with political objectives of the Government are being adopted, such as strengthening the effectiveness of ISAF and Coalition Forces assistance. This includes special attention to building the professional capabilities of Afghan security forces designed to defeat terrorism and to render assistance to victims of war and avoid civilian casualties. The government aims at strengthening its ownership over law enforcement to effectively overcome internal security problems. Furthermore, combating criminal activity and increased narcotics production are integrated components of the security strategy.

Countering a terror-dominated Taliban and illegally armed groups is an extremely complex form of warfare. In many ways it is a competition for the support of the population. The active support of the Afghan people is vital to success. This demands a firm political will and substantial persistence by the Government and the Afghan people, and unwavering long term commitment and patience from the international community. Government legitimacy is a pre-requisite if we are to isolate the Taliban. The Government's support and legitimacy will increase only if we can assure the security of the people and provide them with the basic necessities of life: food, water, shelter, healthcare and the means to make a living. The use of excessive force in operations should be avoided, targets should be accurately identified, and collateral damage and especially casualties among civilians be avoided as much as possible.

Narcotics

Poppy cultivation and production of narcotics poses a serious challenge to Afghanistan's security. The high level corruption that enables the narcotics industry to thrive endangers foreign assistance to development. Huge revenues from opium and production of narcotics have drawn in terrorist elements, organized- crime groups and extremists. Revenues from opium and drug trafficking is also a considerable source of funding to remnants of illegal armed groups. The Government's strategy coordinates international efforts with Government plans and addresses issues such as the development of economic infrastructure, demand reduction, poppy eradication, countering drug trafficking and establishing alternative livelihood programs. As the police are reformed and the judicial system strengthened, a major effort will be made to reduce corruption, better policing officials involved in cultivation and interfering with eradication efforts.

Illegal Armed Groups

Wars and violence have turned Afghanistan into a fully armed society where people use guns to earn a living or to control resources. Illegally armed groups pose a direct threat to national security. The long-term presence of illegal armed groups in different parts of the country is obstructing Government control, hindering development of local democratic institutions and posing a serious threat to national unity. They are obstacles to the rule of law and stand in the way of social and economic development. Many commanders of illegal armed groups have close links with police or even belong to local governments. This situation enhances corruption and is considered a key obstacle in cracking down on the narcotics industry. Unless the Government is able to provide adequate security with police presence in every village and district, people will feel the need to keep guns for self- protection. People are now required to have a license to carry arms and this law needs to be enforced effectively.

The Disbandment of Illegal Armed Groups (DIAG) and the continuation of the Disarmament, Disintegration and Rehabilitation program (DDR), is the first step in disarming illegal armed groups. The existence of arms and ammunition caches and mines in different parts of Afghanistan also pose a threat, because opponents of the government can use them for terrorist operations. The government –in cooperation with international organizations – is trying to garner support from local communities to get rid of these arms caches.

Mines and Explosive Remnants of War (ERW)

Mines and other ERWs are major obstacles to infrastructure and economic reconstruction.The benchmark for locating and destroying all stockpiles of anti-personnel mines was reached in 1386 (October 2007). However the existence of mines and explosives still pose a threat to the lives of four million Afghans. Only two provinces have been completely cleared of mines. Statistics have shown that about 5,000 Afghans have been either killed or wounded in mine explosions since 1380 (2001). Unknown arms and ammunition caches and mines in different parts of Afghanistan pose an additional threat because opponents of the Government can use these for terrorist operations.

Policy Framework

The National Security Policy is drafted for a period of five years and reviewed annually. The policy contains two interrelated strategies: National Security Strategy and Security Sector Reforms Strategy.

The Security Sector Reforms Strategy establishes a mechanism to regulate relations between ministries and departments to ensure effective coordination. The policy encompasses the functions of other government departments including the legislative, judiciary and law enforcement. The reforms establish responsibilities and coordination in the security sector for implementation of programs and give guidelines for planning, prioritization, assessment of resources, and operations. Sustained financial support is needed to avoid compromising either development or security objectives. The OECD DAC Implementation-Framework for Security Sector Reform provides a useful framework for increasing national ownership and laying out the core elements of a 'right- financing' framework.37

The Government is committed to addressing the following strategic benchmarks to achieve the security sector strategic vision:

- **The Afghan National Army**: (i) Through Jaddi 1389 (end-2010), with the support of and in close coordination with the government, the NATO-led ISAF, Operation Enduring Freedom (OEF) and their respective Provincial Reconstruction Teams (PRTs) will promote security and stability in all regions of Afghanistan, including by strengthening Afghan capabilities. (ii) By Jaddi 1389, (end-2010): the Government will establish a nationally respected, professional, ethnically balanced ANA that is accountable, organized, trained and well equipped to meet the security needs of the country. It will be increasingly funded from Government revenue, commensurate with the nation's economic capacity. Support will continue to be provided to expand the ANA towards a ceiling of 80,000 personnel with additional 6,000 personnel, including trainers. The pace of this expansion will be adjusted on the basis of periodic joint quality assessments by the Government and the international community against agreed criteria which take into account prevailing conditions.

- **The Afghan National Police**: By Jaddi 1389 (end-2010) a fully constituted, professional, functional and ethnically balanced Afghan National Police and Afghan Border Police with a combined force of up to 82,180 will be able to effectively meet the security needs of the country and will be increasingly fiscally sustainable.
- **DIAG**: All illegal armed groups will disbanded by 20 March 2011 in all provinces. Approximately 2,000 illegal armed groups have been identified. Nearly 300 are now fully or partially disbanded and 1200 more are engaged to cooperate with DIAG.
- **Removing Unexploded Ordnance**: By Jaddi 1389 (end-2010), in line with Afghanistan MDGs, the land area contaminated by mines and unexploded ordnance will be reduced by 70%; and by end-2010 all unsafe, unserviceable, and surplus ammunition will be destroyed. The goal is to clear 90% of all known mine/ERW contaminated areas by 1391 (2012). The goal furthermore is to clear all emplaced antipersonnel mines by 1391 (1 March 2013) according to the Ottawa Convention. A capacity to remove mines and ERWs beyond the 2013 MAPA transition deadline probably will be needed.
- **Counter-Narcotics**: By 2013, the area under poppy cultivation will be reduced by half compared to 2007 levels.

The security sector expected outcomes are:

- Effectively coordinated security sector, where decisions and plans are timely made and implemented and external and internal threats are deterred, contained or eliminated;
- ANA and ANP operationally capable of performing those missions and tasks assigned;
- ANP and ABP expenditures are fiscally sustainable;
- Citizens have an enhanced level of justice with the help of Police and the Army;
- Narcotics industry is reduced in line with counter-narcotics national strategy;
- Reduction of corruption in the ANA, ANP and amongst other government officials;
- Reduced level of deaths and casualties caused by UXOs, reduce the number of affected communities and increased safety precautions;
- Enhanced public trust on government ability to deliver justice and security as illegally armed groups are disbanded and reintegrated; and
- Eventual eradication of Poppy Production and crack down on drug trafficking.

Security Institutions

Afghanistan's security sector includes a number of institutions responsible for maintaining security and enforcing laws. Increased capacity and improved coordination is necessary to achieve the strategic objectives for this sector.

The security sector includes ministries, departments and institutions that are responsible for enforcing security and laws to protect the Government and the Afghan people. These include among other: National Security Council (NSC), Office of the National Security Council (ONSC), the Policy Action Group (PAG), Ministries, National Directorate of Security (NDS), National Army and Air Forces, Afghan National Police (ANP), Presidential Guard, Parliamentary Commissions on Security and Monitoring, Public Audit and Evaluation Offices, justice and judicial institutions, Ministry of Justice, Prosecution Departments and the Human Rights Commission. To improve professional capabilities of the security institutions their duties and responsibilities need to be coordinated. This will guarantee appropriate regulations, set priorities in policy making, help forecasting financial expenses and ensure correct allocation of funds.

National Security Council

The National Security Council is the highest institution for identifying and addressing national security issues. The Council, led by the President, is responsible for developing strategies and policies, determining priorities, and is responsible for the oversight and coordination of the security sector and institutions. The National Security Advisor identifies the needs and requirements of the sector and leads the Policy Action Group (PAG) which has been established as an emergency response mechanism to address the deteriorating security conditions in the six southern provinces. The PAG directs and coordinates security, development work, reconstruction and strategic relations across all functional areas of the Government and the International Community (both civilian and military).

Ministry of Defense (MoD), and the Afghan National Army (ANA)

MoD is responsible for establishing and maintaining peace and security. The Minister of Defense is a civilian with the ministry being non-political and non-partisan. MoD stands ready to provide support to the MoI, which is responsible for border control in emergency situations. Reforms and capacity building initiatives are in process to make the MoD more transparent and accountable with a strong administration and internal discipline. The MoD is developing an ethnically balanced, nonpolitical army with a single military doctrine and operational capabilities. Education, training and equipping the national army to create a professional army with strong operational capability to fight terrorism and armed groups are top priorities. The MoD must ensure that all military units under its command observe and respect Islamic religion and Afghan values. MoD's primary responsibilities include:

- National defense against foreign military aggression;
- Fighting illegally armed groups and terrorism, and help establish the rule of law;
- Deter wars and ensure stability to secure national interests;
- Play an active part to solve crisis and control emergency situations;
- Render assistance to civilian officials to control any emerging security crisis, natural disasters and emergency situations;
- Protect and expand Afghanistan's national interests; and
- Support the National and Border Police to curb organized crime.

To achieve these goals, the MoD has established the ANA.

The National Army (ANA)

The National Army is responsible for protecting Afghanistan's territorial integrity, upholding and protecting the Constitution, defending national interests and the Islamic religion, and establishing a favorable environment for public welfare and progress. The National Army, led by civilian leadership and supported by the National Police, has a mandate to improve internal security. It also plays a role to boost regional security through military cooperation with ISAF and regional and international allies. A reassessment of the design, composition and size of the ANA has led to intensified national recruitment drive and training.

Following a presidential decree to establish a National Army in 2003 the Ministry of Defense and the Afghan National Army have achieved considerable progress. The ministry is responsible for maintaining professional cadres to design appropriate policies, manage the ANA and defense institutions, and establish necessary coordination among security institutions and international partners. The quality and quantity of the ANA is rapidly growing, and will continue to grow until the army is capable of maintaining the stability of the country, defending its sovereignty, and contributing to regional security. The National Army has a mandate to assist the civilian administration and police whenever needed. If instructed by the National Security Council, the ANA will cooperate with the National Police, Anti- Disasters Department, Afghan Red Crescent Society and other civilian charity organizations to tackle emergency situations requiring disaster response and humanitarian assistance.

Ministry of Internal Affairs (MoI), and the Afghan National Police (ANP)

The Ministry of Internal Affairs is responsible for ensuring internal security, establishing the rule of law, justice and protecting the country's international borders. MoI's responsibilities with regard to security are to ensure internal security and fight criminal activity. High priority activities include:

- Crack down on organized and international crimes including drugs and human trafficking; fight terrorism and other national security threats in cooperation with MoD, ANA, ISAF and Coalition forces;
- Establish a border police force to control cross-border movements and assist with collection of customs revenues in cooperation with MoD, ANA and Ministry of Finance (MoF);
- Enforce justice by detecting crimes, carry out investigations, and promptly handover suspects to the judicial authorities without delay in accordance with the law;
- Provide witness protection and support to victims of crime and establish detention centers;
- Implement the DIAG program: Collect unregistered arms in cooperation with other security departments and implement and enforce new regulations regarding private security companies.

The National Police (ANP)

The Police are undergoing reforms aimed enhancing efficiency by improving police training and education, upgrading staff and equipping the department adequately. The current

MoI Tashkeel allows for 82,180 uniformed personnel in the ANP. Police capacities have been increasing with extensive help from donors that has led to the expansion of government control to provinces. However, there is a need to accelerate recruitment, education and training programs to ensure not only professional performance but also to improve the reputation of the ANP. Ensuring quality police performance and accountability of police and the MoI is the key to stabilization of the society and gaining popular support for the Government.

The Border Police (BP) are responsible for border control, in cooperation with customs officials. The BP establish check points to monitor crossings, particularly in areas with suspected terrorist activity, and are responsible for preventing human trafficking, and drug smuggling. The Counter-Narcotics Police of Afghanistan (CNPA) has been especially established to work on drug related crimes.

Significant steps have been taken since 2001 to revamp and train the Afghan National Army and the Afghan National Police. Police capacities have been increasing with extensive help from the international community. Large militias have been integrated into the Ministry of Defense, with the majority demobilized. A multi-sector donor support scheme has been established where individual donors are allocated responsibility for overseeing support for each of the key elements of the reform, including: disarmament, demobilization, and reintegration of ex-combatants; military reform; police reform; judicial reform; and counter-narcotics.

National Directorate of Security (NDS)

The National Directorate of Security is responsible for lending support to the military and police in fighting terrorism, anti-government elements and narcotics. NDS fulfill its duties by collecting and analyzing information and offering specific recommendations on security. The Directorate is designed to help improve effectiveness of operations carried out by national security agencies. NDS also shares information and cooperates with international security organizations stationed in Afghanistan. NDS is non-political institutions with merit based promotion system.

Ministry of Foreign Affairs (MoFA)

The Ministry of Foreign Affairs is responsible for organizing and following Afghanistan's relations with other countries and international organizations. It is mandated to:

- Establish cordial international relations based on sovereignty and mutual trust;
- Set foreign policy objectives in line with national military strategies and activities of the National Army and border police;
- Support and promote international peace and welfare by upholding and implementing international laws, conventions and national development strategies ;
- Support development and encourage investment in Afghanistan and promote trade;
- Promote regional peace and prosperity, adopt active diplomacy to achieve regional stability and support economic programs that help in securing national interests;
- Support and promote bilateral and multilateral economic initiatives with neighbors to secure national interests.

Ministry of Counter Narcotics (MCN)

The Ministry of Counter Narcotics is responsible for the implementation of the National Drug Control Strategy (NDCS). The MCN's policies are designed to address: (i) development of projects to provide alternative livelihood opportunities in districts where poppy is grown; (ii) programs to reduce demand for drugs including addiction treatment facilities in affected provinces; (iii) development of effective mechanisms to deal with drug-related crimes; and (iv) media and public awareness campaigns to discourage people from growing poppy and producing narcotics; and (v) poppy eradication programs..

'Right-Financing' Security Sector Reform

Fiscal sustainability is essential for a sound and stable security forces. Given the limitations of the National Budget at present, additional time is needed before security sector expenditures can be included in the ordinary budget. The security sector must therefore rely on continued assistance from Afghanistan's international allies. Limited internal revenue will inevitably force the Government to make some very tough decisions when it comes to security sector spending. The Government supports the development of a 'Right-financing' approach to the security sector, within which to strike an appropriate balance between current security needs and the goal of building a fiscally sustainable security sector based on realistic resource projections.

Afghanistan has no wish to be a burden on the international community for longer than is necessary. In line with a three phased effort to develop the Afghan military, coalition allies will move progressively from carrying the major burden of combat operations to a supporting and enabling role. The First Phase, an accelerated development both in numbers and capabilities of Afghanistan's security forces that are adequately manned, equipped and trained to defeat all internal and external threats, is well advanced. The Second Phase is to transition from coalition-led, to an Afghan- led and NATO-supported security operation. Although much of the security burden remains with our coalition allies, there has been progress in combined Afghan/Coalition operations, and in independent ANA security operations. Phase Three will encompass efforts to further improve professionalism, discipline and operational cohesiveness and the ANA will conduct independent operations and lead the fight. ISAF will move to a supporting role. At the end of this final phase, a capacity to defend the country will have been established, and the partnership with allies will become one of normalized defense relations.

Sound Administration, Justice and Judicial System

Establishing a transparent and accountable judicial administration is a key in achieving durable stability in the country. The Government is committed to strengthening the justice system, incuding the Supreme Court, Attorney General's Office, Chief Prosecution Department, Ministry of Justice, and military courts in the capital and provinces. Priority programs of the Government include appointing professional cadres, coordinating law enforcement and justice sector development programs to establish a prosperous, stable, and a just society based on democratic values and international standards. An effective legal administration that ensures the rule of law is important for people to have faith in their government. The Government is implementing programs to strengthen and support reform in the Ministry of Justice, the Supreme Court, and the Attorney General's Office.

Relations with Nieghbors and International Allies

Afghanistan's security is closely linked with international developments. The country borders with six countries and inevitably has economic and political interests with these countries that are related. The Government seeks to cooperate with its neighbors by strengthening regional security linkages with intelligence sharing to tackle cross-border infiltration, terrorism and narcotics trafficking.

The Government will make every effort to ensure regional stability, security and prosperity for itself and for neighboring countries. The Kabul Declaration on Peaceful Coexistence and Good Neighborliness was signed in 1381 (2002). It obliges Afghanistan and its neighbors to respect each others' territorial integrity, establish friendly relations and cooperation, and ensure non-interference in each other's internal affairs. All of the Government's efforts to maintain security and accelerate social and economic development will not work without some degree of cooperation and support from Afghanistan's neighbors. A secure Afghanistan in a stable region is in the best interest of entire world. The Government will work with the international community and neighboring countries for an effective diplomatic solution to security challenges. This will require: (i) concerted diplomatic pressure against the safe havens enjoyed by terrorist groups outside of Afghanistan's borders; (ii) coordinated and effective measures for strengthening border and cross-border security; (iii) support for the programs agreed in recent regional economic cooperation conferences; and (iv) a further strengthening of the Tri-partite Commission to dialogue with Pakistan on substantial issues.

Conclusion

The Government is fully committed to successfully: (i) implementing an integrated and comprehensive national security policy and strategy; (ii) building a robust security sector reform program; (iii) strengthening synergies between civil and military operations; (iv) increasing the role of security forces in counter-narcotics activities; and (v) strengthening the civilian components of security entities. While international assistance is vitally necessary at the present time, the Government is planning and looking forward to taking on an increasing share of the responsibility for security in Afghanistan.

Table 5.1. Integration of the Cross Cutting Issues into the Security Sector

Anti-Corruption	Gender Equality	Counter-Narcotics	Environment	Regional Co-operation	Capacity Building
Programs within the Sector Strategy emphasize accountability and transparency. By Jaddi 1392 (end-2013), corruption in the government at all levels especially in security and, customs will be significantly reduced. A monitoring mechanism to track corruption at high places, including the security sector, will be put in place by Jaddi 1387 (end-2008). By Jaddi 1387 (end-2008), the Government will establish and implement a mechanism. This will include complaints against the security forces or the security sector. Targeting corruption is vital for security reasons: Narcotics traffickers thrive in insecurity and absence of governance; corruption at the highest levels facilitate for narcotics trade that spur anti- government elements.	Increase the number of qualified female staff throughout the security sector. Promote gender mainstreaming and gender-balance throughout the security sector. Increase awareness of gender and rights, raising women's decision-making role and ensuring that women have equal employment opportunities within the Sector. Recognize in all policies and programs that men and women have equal rights and responsibilities through the security sector. Ensure that monitoring mechanisms are in place to realize goals for gender equality. This calls for setting indicators to monitor improvements. Ensure reduction of violence and harassment against women in the workplace, by implementing specific training, units/programs (e.g. referral centers) and effective complaint and redress mechanisms.	The international forces in Afghanistan must cooperate with the Afghan National Army (ANA) to facilitate for Afghan counter-narcotics operations. Afghan security forces provide force protection and law enforcement for eradication and interdiction operations. Eradication of poppy crops needs to be enforced, in particular where those who benefit are using the profits for anti government activities. There is a need to enhance border control to crack down on drug trafficking. By Jaddi 1389 (end-2010), the Government will increase the number of arrests and prosecutions of traffickers and corrupt officials with the help of the security sector. Increased security is needed to guarantee alternative livelihoods. Capacity for eradication must similarly increase.	Improved security will ensure sustainable development with minimum negative impact to environment. Implement DIAG and mine/UXO clearance programs to enhance security that would allow for extensive land to be taken back into use for farming and development. Stability throughout the country is needed to prevent natural resources from being degraded.	Establish and develop good international relationships based on mutual respect, non-interference. Enhance Afghanistan's active position as a positive and effective member of the UN. Enhance cooperative border management with Afghanistan's neighbors to crack down on illegal border crossing and trafficking. Regional cooperation to improve security will lead to overall stability in the region. Multilateral and bilateral agreements reached with the countries of the region and further efforts to promote regional cooperation would contribute to the stability in the region and enhance the pace of economic development in Afghanistan.	Reforming defense and the security sector is a priority of the Afghan Government to strengthen Afghan capabilities and transform the Afghan security forces into effective and modern force, confirming to international standards. MoD reform and reconstruction aim to rehabilitate a strong defense sector to protect national security and to be able to begin assuming primary responsibility for Afghanistan's security with a gradual withdrawal of international security forces. Intensive field and operational training is and will continue to further enhance the capabilities of the ANA and ANP. Capacity and budget needs of the ANA and the ANP will be under constant review. There is a need for overcoming financial challenges and insufficient funds to realize capacity building of the security strategy. Specific capacity development programs will be required for preparing the security forces for counter narcotics operations. Special programs will be developed for developing gender sensitive security system internally as well for external interactions.

6. GOVERNANCE, RULE OF LAW & HUMAN RIGHTS

The goal for the Governance, Rule of Law and Human Rights is strengthen democratic processes and institutions, human rights, the rule of law, delivery of public services and government accountability.

Improving governance is essential to the attainment of the Government's national vision and the establishment of a stable and functioning society. The government's guiding principles for improving governance are openness, participation, accountability, effectiveness, efficiency, coherence, equity, inclusiveness, justice and rule of law applied at all levels of the government. The government will act as a policy maker, regulator, enabler and not a competitor, of the private sector. The main priorities for the governance sector are (i) to increase the pace and quality of public administration reform; (ii) strengthen sub-national governance structures; (iii) reform legal and courts processes; and (iv) strengthen parliamentary and legislative processes including holding free and fair elections.

While much has been achieved in strengthening the formal and informal structures of governance and rule of law, as well as extending human rights, considerable challenges still stand in the way of achieving the goals under this pillar. These include: (i) the existence of multiple, parallel structures of state and non- state governance entities; (ii) confusion over centre/sub-national governance entities; (iii) weak public sector institutions and underdeveloped governance and administration capabilities; (iv) high levels of corruption; (v) fiscal uncertainty; (vi) weak legislative development and enforcement; (vii) weak parliamentary oversight; (viii) weak community and civil society institutions; (ix) ineffective and poorly defined justice system; (x) gender inequality; and (xi) underdeveloped human rights enforcement capacities.

Three sectors are contained under this pillar: Governance, Public Administration Reform and Human Rights, Justice Sector and Religious Affairs. Sub-national consultation and the Provincial Development Plans (PDPs) were instrumental in developing the sector strategy.

Governance, Public Administration Reform and Human Rights

Role of the Sector in ANDS

In the Afghanistan Compact, the Government and the international community reaffirmed their commitment to certain benchmarks on Public Administration Reform, Anti-Corruption, The Census and Statistics, National Assembly, Elections, Gender, Land Registration, Counter- Narcotics and Human Rights within the specified timelines. Functional institutions with trained staff will be established in each province to implement appropriate legal frameworks and appointment procedures. The Government will also establish a fiscally and institutionally sustainable administration for future elections and prioritize the reform of the justice system to ensure equal, fair and transparent access to justice.

The strategy includes out efforts to reduce gender inequality. Institutional and administrative frameworks will be established at the local government level that will enable women to play an important role in decision making (such as the CDCs established under the NSP). The Constitution allows limited decentralization specifying that a Provincial Councils (PC) with elected members are to be formed in every Province and, that District, Village and

Municipal Councils and Mayors are to be elected through, free, general, secret and direct elections every three years.

Current Situation in the Sector

Afghanistan has come a long way in the last 7 years. In 2000 the World Bank assessed the 'quality' of Afghanistan's governance institutions as falling in the bottom one percent of all countries. The rule of law, adherence to good governance practices and respect for human rights in Afghanistan is weak but improving. The ANDS vision for this sector is the establishment of a stable Islamic constitutional democracy where the three branches of government function effectively and openly, are accountable, inclusive and abide by the rule of law.

Progress since 2001 includes the adoption of the constitution; successful parliamentary and presidential elections, and progress in improving the livelihood and welfare of females and other disenfranchised groups. In addition, the ANDS sets out a series of reforms to address these constraints:

- **Justice:** The Ministry of Justice (MoJ) is strengthening the review process for laws and regulations and identifying areas for reform, including instituting a code of ethics and professional standards. In March 2007, the Supreme Court, the MoJ, and he Attorney General's Office presented new comprehensive reform strategies at the Rome Conference. These include plans to restructure the institutions; develop merit-based and transparent recruitment; promotion and accountability mechanisms for improving professional standards, ethics and discipline; improving the conditions of service for justice officials; and increasing women's representation at all levels of the justice system.
- **Corruption:** The High Level Commission against Corruption has been established to assess and analyze the factors contributing to corruption. The Commission presented recommendations to prevent corruption and developed the roadmap in its document "Fighting Corruption in Afghanistan - Strategy and Action".
- **Legislative Reforms:** Progress is being made in reforming the legal framework of the country. Laws have been enacted to promote investment and trade. Measures to deal with illegal drugs, corruption and money laundering are under review and being enacted. As part of the judicial reform program a number of other important laws will soon be approved.
- **Gender:** The National Action Plan for Women of Afghanistan is being implemented to establishing greater gender equality by eliminating discrimination, building of women's human capital and promoting their participation and leadership.
- **Governance:** Public administration is generally recognized as being weak. The Government will undertake comprehensive institutional strengthening and capacity building within the ministries, provinces, districts, municipalities and villages. This will achieve improvements in the delivery of services to the people and communities living in the provinces, districts, municipalities and villages.

A number of constraints continue to face the sector: weak public sector capacity; a lack of resources and unsustainable fiscal outcomes; a restrictive legislative environment that limits private sector activity; limited legislative oversight and representational experience of public figures; extensive corruption; excessive centralization; a lack of coordinated decision-making across Government; limited female participation in the Government; limited direct accountability to clients; and state capture by illicit power-holders.

Policy Framework: Sector Strategy

The governance agenda addresses three major challenges: pervasive corruption, low public sector capacity and human rights deprivations for girls and women in Afghanistan. 80 percent of provinces identified reducing corruption in public administration as a priority during sub national consultations.

The policy framework for the proposed reform program to strengthen governance includes all national and sub-national government, parliamentary, civil society and political structures.

The mainstreaming of cross-cutting issues of anti-corruption, capacity building and gender are of particular relevance to this pillar. In summary, the policy framework for this pillar includes the following goals:

- **National Assembly Empowerment**: To enhance the capacity of the National Assembly in discharging legislative, oversight, transparency and accountability functions.
- **Public Administration Reform**: Public administration reform will focus on pay and grading reforms to increase competitive recruitment, hiring of a trained and capable public sector workforce, strengthening merit based appointments, conducting performance-based reviews.
- **Anti-corruption**: Measures to achieve a reduction of corruption in the judiciary and throughout the government will be introduced. There will be increased monitoring of corruption at senior levels. Appropriate new applications will be introduced to limit potential corruption. Public reporting and complaints mechanisms will be expanded.
- **Enhanced availability of information to public and enforcement**: Public rights to access to information will be increased. Sanctions will be enforced against those involved in the drugs trade.
- **Enhanced participation of Women in Governance**: Fulfillment of the national action plan for women's rights will be implemented and affirmative action programs made available to women.
- **Enhanced participation of Youth in Governance**: A proactive policy to expand opportunities for young people that encompasses all areas of Government activity will be adopted.
- **Effective system of disaster preparedness and response**: The national disaster management and mitigation policy will be implemented.
- **Independent Election Commission**: The capacity of the Independent Election Commission will be strengthened. A permanent voters' registry will be established. Regular national and sub-national elections will be held as mandated by the Constitution.
- **Single National Identity Document**: To enhance public accountability and transparency a single national identity document will be issued.

- **Census and Statistical Baseline Data**: The national census will be completed and the results published. National economic and poverty baselines will be established.
- **Geodesy and Cartography**: Village and Gozar boundaries will be verified and mapping exercises will be undertaken.
- **Land Administration**: A modern and community-based land administration system and establishment of a fair system for settlement of land disputes will be established.
- **Independent Directorate of Local Governance (IDLG)**: A sub-national governance policy will be developed. People's participation in sub-national governance will be increased. Provincial Councils will be empowered. Laws on District Councils, Municipal Councils, and Village Councils will be introduced. Regular elections of District Councils, Municipal Councils, Mayors and Village Councils will be held. Public administration will be reformed at the sub-national level and the capacity of the public sector workforce at sub-national level strengthened. Provincial planning and budgeting will be institutionalized.
- **Governance Administration**: Review and assessment of the facilities in all government offices will be undertaken and appropriate facilities provided.
- **Communication with and within the Government**: There will be enhanced flow of information between all government entities related to national policy, strategy and national budget procedures.
- **Human Rights**: The realization, protection, promotion and extension of human rights, including the Action Plan on Peace, Justice and Reconciliation will be implemented.

Justice

Role of the Sector in ANDS

The role of the Justice Sector in the government's development strategy is to ensure improved integrity, performance and infrastructure of Afghanistan's justice institutions in each province; to streamline administrative structures, ensure professional integrity and improve coordination and integration within the Justice system between government and civil society institutions, and improve access to the justice system for all. The government has developed the National Justice Sector Strategy (NJSS) to fully articulate these objectives. The NJSS will be implemented through the National Justice Program (NJP). This will strengthen and improve coordination among the justice institutions, and within the justice institutions and their bilateral and multilateral funding partners. In the longer term the sector will seek to increase specialization and diversification of justice practices to meet more complex demands – including the important and necessary interaction and relationship with informal justice systems, which are prevalent throughout the country, while expanding justice services. Transitional Justice is obviously an important aspect of the sector. The Government's Action Plan for Peace, Reconciliation and Justice in Afghanistan acknowledges that any mechanism for building peace and justice must be carried out with the active and meaningful participation of all national stakeholders, including the justice institutions.

Contribution to the ANDS

Economic Growth: An efficiently operating justice system will encourage investment and for economic activity to move from the informal to the formal sector, thereby strengthening the ability of the government to raise revenue internally.

Employment: Growth of the private sector, a prerequisite of which is an efficient judicial system will generate increased demand for labor. In addition, improved labor and contract laws will lower the cost of hiring labor and directly encourage increased employment, particularly in urban centers.

Poverty Reduction: Economic growth and increased employment will contribute to a reduction in poverty. In addition it should be noted that women and the poor and marginalized are most likely to be the ones to suffer the lack of access to a fair and unbiased judicial system.

Security/Stability: Poor security in certain parts of the country makes service delivery difficult or impossible and justice professionals operate at great personal risk. Police devote most of their resources to maintaining security.

Contribution of the Sector to Implementation of the Compact and MDGs

Afghanistan Compact: The Justice Sector will have met the four Rule of Law Compact benchmarks by the end of 1391 (2010).

Millennium Development Goals (MDGs): Although justice and the rule of law are not among the eight plus one MDGs, they provide the enabling environment for poverty reduction and economic development.

Current Situation in the Sector

Achievements: Afghanistan has a mixed civil law and Islamic Sharia-based formal legal system that has evolved over many years. In most non-urban areas customary legal systems continue to operate. While there is considerable variation in these customary legal systems they are usually based around traditional tribunals – jirgas, maracas shuras or mookee khans. Traditional systems usually have core principles of apology and forgiveness, followed by reconciliation. Most Afghan customary systems are based on the principle of restorative justice.

The Constitution introduced three major reforms to the judicial system:

- Art. 97 declared the judiciary an "independent organ of the State" which "discharges its duties side by side with the Legislative and Executive Organs;"
- The Constitution created a unified judicial system with an organizational structure that is headed by the Supreme Court;
- The constitution created a unified system of laws. The Constitution and statutes created under the Constitution are legally dominant, with the basic principles of the Sharia acting as a guide to the legislature.

In August 2006 a new Supreme Court was approved by National Assembly. The Supreme Court then adopted a new Code of Judicial Conduct, based on the internationally recognized Principles of Judicial Conduct and establishing ethical standards.

Donor activity in the justice sector has generally focused on building capacity of the judicial system, including police training and court construction.

Needs Assessment: the following needs have been identified at the national and provincial levels:

- Salary support: to improve performance, mitigate corruption and ensure professional qualification;
- Infrastructure and office equipment: Subject to survey of essential work to be targeted.
- Transportation: Subject to survey of essential work to be targeted;
- Operating costs need to be financed to improve performance of justice institutions;
- Capacity building and training: continuing professional development requirements;
- Information management and human resource management to be established;
- Codes of Ethics and oversight mechanisms to be established for all legal professionals;
- Financial management: budgets are inadequate and budget execution rates are low;
- Public awareness: There is a need to develop tools and instrument which ensure access at all level of society.

Challenges, Constraints, Weaknesses: Weak infrastructure; lack of trained staff; delays and backlogs of appeals; lack of information technology and capacity; uncompetitive salaries; poor education and vocational training, public confidence; resource constraints; security situation: Security constraints in certain parts of the country make service delivery difficult or impossible.

Policy framework: sector strategy

The Government's vision for justice is of an Islamic society in which an impartial and independent justice system delivers safety and security for life, religion, property, family and reputation; with respect for liberty, equality before the law and access to justice for all.

Table 6.2. Key Objectives of the National Justice Program

Public can rely on effectively organized and professionally staffed, transparent and accountable justice institutions.
A.1. Justice institutions are structured, managed and administered according to their mandate and functions
A.2. Justice institutions are professionally staffed by men and women who are equally remunerated according to their competencies and qualifications.
A.3. Justice institutions have established the organs necessary for implementation of the national justice program
A.4. Justice institutions and organizations have adopted and are enforcing codes of professional conduct and ethics
A.5. Justice institutions have developed transparent operating procedures
A.6. Justice institutions have adopted effective anti-corruption measures

Justice institutions have access to infrastructure, transportation, equipment, and supplies adequate to support effective delivery of justice services.
B.1. Justice institutions, including the central prisons directorate, are provided with buildings necessary for fulfillment of their tasks.
B.2. Justice institutions are provided with equipment and supplies necessary for their tasks
B.3. Justice institutions are provided with means of transport necessary for their tasks
Legal education and vocational training are adequate to provide justice professionals with sufficient know-how to perform their task.
C.1. Universities provide legal education which equips graduates with the intellectual skills and substantive knowledge to perform well as justice professionals.
C.2. Justice institutions equip new professionals with the practical and professional skills necessary to fulfill their duties
C.3. A system of continuing legal education for justice professionals, paying specific attention to women, is in place and operational.
Statutes are clearly drafted, constitutional and the product of effective and consultative drafting processes.
D.1. The taqnin has sufficient capacity and resources to review, amend or draft legislation.
D.2. All laws in force have been reviewed for constitutionality
D.3. Capacity for legislative drafting has been enhanced throughout other government institutions including parliament
D.4. System is in place to ensure consultation of stakeholders regarding proposed or pending legislation
Justice Institutions effectively perform their functions in a harmonized and interlinked manner.
E.1. Coordination and cooperation among justice sector institutions is enhanced, resulting in improved criminal and civil trials and case management
E.2. Adequate institutional organization structures capable of addressing cross cutting issues in rule of law are in place
E.3. Criminal justice is administered effectively, and in accordance with the law, the constitution, and international standards.
E.4. Civil justice is administered effectively, and in accordance with law, the constitution, and international standards.
E.5. Policies regarding introduction of administrative law structures are in place.
E.6. Policies are in place to ensure that the corrections system operates in accordance with international standards.
E.7. Enhance legal and policy framework related to juvenile offenders and children in conflict with the law.
Citizens are more aware of their rights and are better able to enforce them.
F.1. Practices and procedures governing trials and routine legal transactions, including registration of documents, have been streamlined and rationalized
F.2. Enhanced access to formal legal system for indigents, illiterates, women, and children
F.3. Enhanced monitoring of human rights enforcement throughout the government
F.4. Increased knowledge of laws, rights, and responsibilities through legal awareness campaigns
F.5. The role of traditional dispute resolution in the rule of law is defined, and tdr decisions consistently meet international human rights standards.
F.6. Begin the process of establishing a transitional justice system to record past human rights abuses and preserve the rights of victims consistent with the government's action plan for peace, reconciliation and justice.

Sector Priority Policies and Goals: These are all detailed in the sector strategy and further elaborated in the NJP, however a brief summary of the policy reform areas is provided below under three main goals:

- Integrity, performance and infrastructure: Administrative reform and restructuring of justice institutions; legal education; systematic records systems; enhancing administrative capacity; eradicating corruption; promulgation of ethics codes, engagement of public through complaints systems; expansion of justice services through infra- structural development, procurement of transportation assets and equipment.
- Coordination and integration with other government institutions and civil society: Improved legislation through enhanced capacity of drafting and parliamentary personnel; establishment of National Legal Training Centre for vocational education and vocational excellence; increased opportunities for external stakeholders and civil society to contribute to legal policy development in policy analysis and legislative drafting. Support the Provincial Justice Coordination Mechanism (PJCM), to improve the delivery of justice assistance in the provinces.
- Improved Justice Practices and Processes: investigation system established to determine delays in criminal justice system and lack of representation and improved case management; Sentencing Policy developed; Juvenile Justice Policy implemented; Specialization to address cross-cutting and emerging issues in criminal justice; Enhanced and improved civil court case administration and jurisdictional structures in major litigation categories; nationwide access to legal information and representation; investigating policies for improved links between formal and informal justice sectors and oversight of the informal by the formal.

Integration of the PDPs: Seventeen out of the thirty-four PDPs cited security as the main obstacle to development and stability, and cited it as the priority sector in their provinces. As a result, many of the projects requested by the people indicate the need for justice sector infrastructure and a law enforcement presence at the district level.

Sector Related Issues

Role of the Private Sector: The justice system lowers the cost of doing business and allows firms to enter into commercial enforceable contracts. Businesses in the formal sector have a strong interest in promoting an efficient judicial system

Role of Civil Society: Civil society urgently requires a judicial system at both the national and provincial level that can be trusted to administer justice and has the confidence of the general population.

Policies to improve Aid Effectiveness: An important criticism has been that the donor community has neglected provincial issues and aid has been uncoordinated. Donors should not attempt to impose an external judicial system that may not be accepted throughout the country.

Religious Affairs

Role of the Sector in ANDS

The ANDS strategic objective for this sector is to provide competent and qualified religious services and increase the public awareness of Islamic religion and values in order to promote people's participation in the poverty reduction and development programs. The Government's primary goal is to ensure that all Afghans have equal opportunities to exercise their Islamic and religious believes and that Islamic values will be embedded in the Afghan recovery and development. The religious affairs strategy intends to establish a system which ensures that religious values are reflected with every aspect to Government policy and contributes to the overall development of the country. The sector strategy was developed after extensive consultations with religious institutions, scholars and religious leaders at both national and sub-national levels.

With respect to this the Government will improve religious infrastructures including mosques, shrines and other holy places. The Government will also develop religious schools (madrassas) and will significantly strengthen the training of imams, preachers and religious teachers. The Government will provide training opportunities for Islamic teaching. In order to meet these objectives, the strategy requires the provision of religious services, poverty reduction and effective economic development of the country

Contribution of the Sector Strategy

Economic growth: The Government recognizes that Islam is contrary to many challenges that Afghanistan faces today such as corruption, poppy production and others and that by raising public awareness of the link between economic recovery, the role of the economy in strengthening Afghan society and Islamic values support of the Government's efforts to implement number of key reforms will be strengthened.

Poverty reduction: The religion of Islam requires all Muslims to support the poor and vulnerable in society, as well as promoting the idea of social solidarity and actively encouraging charity. With the establishment of the Zakat Administration within the government, as well as the possibility of a Zekat-based tax, donations can now be collected and redistributed in an organized manner among the most needy.

Stability: The religion of Islam is a religion of peace. The sacred religion of Islam calls on all Muslims to treat people with kindness and mercy and always try to forgive and avoid bad deeds. Religious scholars and leaders will play a significant role in propagating an end to the current conflict and encourage national reconciliation.

Human rights: Islam is based on human rights, including the rights of women, orphans and children. Affirmation of these basic rights, like all other Islamic values, will build support for the reform and implementation of the ANDS. Basic human rights and freedom are essential to building a strong free market economy in addition to being essential for any democracy.

Current Situation in the Sector

Achievements: A great deal of work has been done since the establishment of the transitional government of Afghanistan in terms of religious affairs including:

- Afghanistan is an Islamic Republic
- The Constitution is fully based on the principle of Islam;
- The Constitution states in Article 2: "The sacred religion of Islam is the religion of the Islamic Republic of Afghanistan. Followers of other faiths shall be free within the bounds of law in the exercise and performance of their religious rituals."
- Improved Hajj services and strengthening of Ministry of Hajj and Endowment;
- The construction and rehabilitation of hundreds of new mosques and other holy places;
- Restoration of the endowed properties extorted by individuals;
- Inclusion of Islamic subjects in the new curriculum of primary, secondary and higher education systems;
- Establishment and rehabilitation of the Islamic Madrasas and Dar-Ul-Hefazs;
- Rehabilitation of the Department of the Islamic Sciences of the Science Academy;
- Growth of the Islamic literature through public and private media, "electronic, visual and audio".

Needs assessments: The rehabilitation and construction of religious schools is the most pressing need for the sector. Additionally there is a need to improve the Islamic female education system and to hire an adequate number of imams.

Challenges and Constraints

- Lack of qualified scholars' and lack proper training for the scholars;
- Lack of qualified cadre in religious education;
- Weak coordination among the different religious government and non-government institutions;
- Low level of professional capacity: lack of adequate facilities and competent professionals which hinders the effective implementation of programs;
- Uncertain funding and the dependence of the religious institutions on private charities. A lack of adequate funding is one of the major constrain in the realization of the sector programs, which minimize the ability of the government institutions to implement their projects.
- Security problems: continued insecurity is a barrier to the implementation of the programs in some parts of the country.

Policy Framework: Sector Strategy

The vision for the sector is to provide competent religious services and raise religious awareness of the public in order to promote their participation in the development programs of the Government. This will ultimately lead to poverty reduction and the development of Afghanistan.

Table 6.1. Cross cutting issues in the Governance, Rule of Law and Human Rights Pillar

Anti-Corruption	Gender Equality	Gender Equality	Environment	Regional	Capacity Building
By Jaddi 1392 (end-2013), the corruption in the judiciary and the government at all levels especially in security, customs, civil administration and municipalities will be significantly reduced. A monitor-ing mechanism to track corruption in high places will be put in place by Jaddi 1387 (end-2008). By Jaddi 1387 (end-2008), cross-cutting electronic government applications will be launched to reduce corruption and increase efficiency. By Jaddi 1387 (end-2008), the Government will establish and implement a public complaints mechanism. The citizens have right of access to in-formation from government offices in accordance with Article 50 of the Consti-tution. This right will have no limits, unless it violates the rights of others. By Jaddi 1389 (end-2010), the legal frame-work required for exercising this right provided under the constitution will be put in place, distributed to all judicial and legislative institutions, and made available to the public and, implemented. By Jaddi 1389 (end-2010), the Govern-ment will increase the number of arrests and prosecutions of traffickers and cor-rupt officials, and improve its informa-tion base concerning those involved in the drugs trade, with a view to enhanc-ing the selection system for national and sub-national public appointments.	The Government will fully implement the National Action Plan for Women in Afghanistan by Jaddi 1389. The Government will bring legisla-tion on affirmative action providing a specific percent reservation of seats for women in the elected district, municipal and village councils as well as in the civil service. The set targets will be seen as a minimum and not, over time, as a maximum. Affirmative action on allocating seats for women will be linked to education reforms for women. Educating women will help break the gender bias and prepare women for more significant participation in gov-ernance.	By Jaddi 1389 (end-2010), the Government will increase the number of arrests and prosecutions of traffickers and corrupt officials, and will im-prove its information base concerning those involved in the drugs trade, with a view to enhancing the selection system for national and sub-national public appointments. Public officials elected and appointed to high positions will be required to declare their assets be-fore taking office and on a periodical basis during their tenure in public office. The Government will establish and support the existing Counter Narcotics units in key ministries and will es-tablish coordination mechanisms for a coor-dinated Government response. The National Assembly will organize trainings for its members on CN issues, in particular the CN Law. Youth groups are im-	National Environmental Governance: The Government will establish the following rights of the public (individuals and their associations) with regard to the environment: 1. The right of everyone to receive environmental information that is held by public authorities ("access to envi-ronmental information"); 2. The right of both women and men to participate in en-vironmental decision-making. ("public participation in envi-ronmental decision-making"); 3. The right to review procedures to challenge public decisions that have been made without respecting the two aforementioned rights or environmental law in general ("access to environmental justice"). Local Environmental Governance: Natural resources will be managed through	LOGOTRI is the Network of Local Government Train-ing and Research Institutes in Asia and the Pacific. Its members are both governmental, autonomous and private sector insti-tutions and or-ganizations in-volved primarily in local government training and research. The Inde-pendent Directorate of Local Gov-ernance (IDLG) will collaborate with the LOGOTRI with a view to or-ganizing training and study tours of	The capacity of National Assembly Members will be built in drafting and ratification of legislation, review and input to the national budget review, oversight, and representation, and on issues related to women's rights, national security, international relations, and inter-ethnic relations. The Government will strengthen the capacity of Provincial Councils, support knowledge sharing and exchange among Provincial Coun-cils. The Government will strengthen the elected sub-national representative bodies enabling them to perform their roles and fulfill their responsibilities towards their constituent citizens. By end-1389 (20 March 2011), the Government will build institutional and administrative capabilities in provincial, district and, municipal administrations to manage basic service delivery through reforming organizational structures, stream-lining management processes, de-veloping essential skills and knowl-edge of civil servants. A training policy for entire public sector workforce will be developed and implemented. Institutional arrangements shall be put in place to ensure that each member of the workforce gets trained at least once

Table 6.1. (Continued)

Anti-Corruption	Gender Equality	Gender Equality	Environment	Regional	Capacity Building
Pub-lic officials elected and appointed to high positions will be required to declare their asset before taking charge of their office. The Government will establish a single leadership and monitoring within government and parliament on anticorruption process and implementation of UNCAC. Institutional arrangements within the Government to fight corruption will be rationalized and strengthened. The Government will fight corruption with resolve and commitment and improve its capacity to do so. The actions contained in the Anti Corruption Road Map will remain priority actions for the Government in 2008 and beyond. The Government will take steps contained in the report of Inter-Institutional Commission.		portant civil society organizations. Awareness of CN issues will be incorporated into the programs developed for youth groups. Provincial level counter narcotic initiatives will be implemented with the cooperation of the Governors and the Provincial Council Members	community-based mechanisms and with the support of legitimate local governments. Natural Resource Management-related interventions will be based on broad consultations with local communities (that include marginalized groups like pastoralists or indigenous groups) and will reflect local values. These will form an essential part of a process of poverty reduction, since improved productivity will directly increase rural livelihoods, food security and market participation.	Afghan sub-national governance policy makers and Afghan offi-cials at LOGOTRI member-institutions in Asia and the Pacific.	in two years in organization specific and job specific training along with generic training. Women's participation will be ensured. The aim of T & D policy shall be to: Provide job-related education, training, and development opportunities for all Civil Servants so that they may perform their jobs competently and happily. This recognizes that when strategically planned and implemented, Training and Development is vital for strengthening Civil Servants' knowledge, capabilities, skills, gender sensitive and supportive attitudes, and values in the performance of work

Sector Priority Policies: the government will focus on the following priorities:

- Improve infrastructure for religious affairs: (mosques, shrines, holy places, religious schools);
- Improve the training and capacity of the Imams, preachers, religious teachers and other scholars to raise public awareness and to teach;
- Finalize overall cultural curriculum for primary and higher education;
- Strengthen Hajj arrangement systems for pilgrims;
- Support efforts of other government agencies to improve religious literacy.

Expected outcomes:

- All Government activities will not contradict Islamic values;
- Improved religious infrastructure;
- Financial sustainability of religious affairs sector will be achieved;
- The religious education system will be improved;
- Increased participation of Islamic scholars in rising awareness of importance of key Government reforms;
- Strengthening the role of the religious institutions in programs for poverty reduction.

Government priorities for Religious Affairs:

- Implement reforms in the education system and teaching methods in the public and private Madrasas;
- Implement administrative reform programs in the Ministry of Haj and Endowment and its provincial offices;
- Reform the Hajj and pilgrimage services systems;
- Reform and improve coordination of the Sharia faculties of Afghan Universities;
- Strengthen the support for building and maintaining mosques and other religious institutions;
- Improve self-sustainability of the religious institutions through building shops and business centers within the properties owned by mosques and other holy places and opening bank accounts for collecting donations;
- Establish Ulama Councils for settlement of local disputes and implementation of development programs in the community;
- Establish Zakat related office within the ministry of Hajj and Endowment;
- Establish effective and transparent mechanisms for collecting revenues from shrines and holy sites.

Conclusion

Good governance and adherence to the rule of law are much needed reforms that the Government of Afghanistan is committed to pursue. While the donor community can support reforms and provide technical assistance, these reforms have to be initiated by internal decisions to implement improvements in governance. Without good governance and a sustained social contract for the acceptance of the rule of law, the total development strategy that has been developed in the ANDS will fail. This is because the strategy has at its core the development of a private sector that will generate economic growth and demand for skilled labor. In this framework, the ANDS encourages the public sector to concentrate on the creation of a safe and conducive environment that encourages the smooth operation of a robust private sector. This means a much greater focus by Government on governance issues rather than involvement in the production of goods and services that can be provided by a significantly larger and more efficient private sector.

Governance and the rule of law will remain a primary concern of the Government and has directed that a considerable proportion of available resources be devoted to strengthening the institutions responsible for delivering good governance. They include the National Assembly, the judicial system, including the courts, the AGO, the police, and the Ministries that administer much of the legislation. In its early stages, strengthening of governance and the institutions that support governance has tended to concentrate on the central government level.

The Afghan 'ownership' of this strategy requires that the Government seeks donors close cooperation in capacity building and know- how transfer, but retains ultimate responsibility so that a system can evolve that allows the best parts of the functional traditional governance system to co-exist with a universal system that recognizes and supports principles of social diversity, respect for human rights and the rule of law.

7. Economic and Social Development

This chapter summarizes the sector strategies developed as part of the ANDS under Pillar 3: Economic and Social Development.[38] The ANDS strategy depends upon achieving sustained high rates of economic growth that will increasingly be based on private sector-led development.[39] A key component of the ANDS is the development of an enabling environment that encourages the private sector to play a central role in the economic development of the country. While the sector strategies cannot specify private sector investments, which are a result of private decision making, the actions and programs designed to establish an enabling environment for the private and non- government sectors are included.

Private Sector Development

The Government's economic vision has been consistent since 1381 (2002)[40] and remains the strategic objective for the private sector development strategy. The market based economy is enshrined in the Constitution, article 10, which states that:

> The State encourages and protects private capital investments and enterprises based on the market economy and guarantees their protection in accordance with the provisions of law.

As President Karzai also stated,

> We aim to "enable the private sector to lead Afghanistan's development".[41] We will build a market-based system, driven by private sector growth,[42] in which Gov-ernment is the "policy maker and regula-tor of the economy, not its competitor".[43] If the Government is to achieve its aim of significantly enhancing per capita GDP in the next five years,[44] it must complete the foundations for socially responsible pri-vate sector growth and encourage sustained high levels of foreign and domestic private investment.

The implementation of the private sector development strategy will contribute directly to the achievement of a number of objectives embodied in the Afghanistan Compact and the MDGs:

- Afghanistan Compact: Private Sector Development and Trade: "All legislation, regulations and procedures related to investment will be simplified and harmonized by end-2006 and implemented by end-1386 (2007). New business organization laws will be tabled in the National Assembly by end-2006. The Government's strategy for divestment of state-owned enterprises will be implemented by end-1388 (2009)."
- Afghanistan Compact: Regional Cooperation: "By end-1398 (2010) Afghanistan and its neighbors will achieve lower transit times through Afghanistan by means of cooperative border management and other multilateral or bilateral trade and transit agreements; Afghanistan will increase the amount of electricity available through bilateral power purchases; and Afghanistan, its neighbors and countries in the region will reach agreements to enable Afghanistan to import skilled labor, and to enable Afghans to seek work in the region and send remittances home."
- MDGs: Goal 8: "Further develop an open trading and financial system that is rule-based, predictable and non-discriminatory, which includes a commitment to good governance, development and poverty reduction. Goal 8: In cooperation with the private sector, make available the benefits of new technologies — especially information and communications technologies."

The macroeconomic framework presented in Chapter 4 makes clear that maintaining high rates of economic growth during the life of the ANDS and beyond depends on a substantial increase in the level of private investment in the economy.

Key components of the private sector development strategy

The strategy to foster private sector development and increase domestic and foreign investment consists of three main components: (i) continued efforts to build a strong and stable enabling environment that will encourage a competitive private sector; (ii) expand the scope for private investment in developing national resources and infrastructure; and (iii) strengthen efforts to promote investment from domestic sources, the Afghan diaspora and foreign investors.

Component 1: Strengthening the Enabling Environment

The main objective of an improved enabling environment is to reduce the costs of doing business. This entails the elimination of excessive or unnecessary impediments to business activity that raise costs, and improving the 'soft' and 'hard' infrastructure essential to efficient economic activity. This requires that the private sector have access to necessary inputs at reasonable cost, including land for commercial purposes, credit and imported raw materials and intermediate goods. Efficient land, labor and financial markets and a stable, open trade regime have a major impact on the ability of firms to operate competitively.

Private sector development requires macroeconomic stability and an environment where there is a general reliance on the rule of law. While it is relatively easy to introduce a suitable legal and regulatory framework, it is considerably more difficult to ensure that it is effectively implemented. This requires that all parties, both public and private, reliably abide by the legal system. It is critical that contracts can be entered into and enforced with disputes readily resolved. A high priority of the ANDS is the strengthening of the institutions, including the establishment of effective commercial courts, responsible for the implementation of commercial laws.

ANDS strategic priorities to promote private sector development involve activities in the following areas:

- A stable macroeconomic environment and supportive financial system: The Government will control inflation at low levels similar to those achieved in recent years. The growth of a supportive financial sector that is able to extend credit to viable firms will be supported through legal and regulatory reforms, including the implementation of secured transactions laws.
- Private sector investment: Attracting private investment is the responsibility of the entire Government and will be an integral part of all projects and programs implemented under the ANDS. This will require institutional strengthening of Government agencies and ministries, including AISA as the lead investment promotion agency. All ministries have the scope to expand the opportunities for private business activities and to increase their contribution to the growth and development of the economy. Donors will be encouraged to fulfill their commitments to increase the goods and services sourced within the country.
- Legislative Reform: Enact and implement key commercial laws and amendments to establish the basic legal and regulatory framework that will encourage private sector involvement in social and economic development and consistent with the Afghan conditions. ANDS priorities actions include:
  - The Government will introduce and implement the remaining commercial laws included in the Afghanistan Compact benchmark.
  - The Government will consult with representatives from private business and civil society in a meaningful and timely manner during the process of drafting policies and laws.
  - The necessary steps will be taken to establish the authority of mediation and arbitration tribunals to resolve private- private and private-public disputes, including land issues.
  - The Government will ensure that no law will be implemented unless it has been published in the newspapers, and made available electronically and in hard copy to the public. Regulations, including import tariff rates, will be made readily available on the Ministry of Finance website.

- Administrative Reform: The Government will ensure that ministries and agencies are able to competently administer commercial laws and regulations in an unbiased and predictable manner. These actions will include:
    - Invest in capacity development for National Assembly so that MPs are better informed and supported in their role and understanding of proposed laws.
    - Ensure the competency and transparency of tribunals by establishing standards and building the capacity of arbitrators, mediators and lawyers.
    - Undertake financial audits of state owned assets and corporations.
    - Implement effective programs to provide institutional strengthening and capacity development throughout the public sector.
- State owned enterprises: The Government will continue the program of privatization and corporatization of state owned enterprises, a process that is presently on schedule. This will: (i) improve the level of efficiency in the economy; (ii) assist in eliminating corruption; (iii) encourage better resource allocation; and (iv) generate increased government revenue.
- Formalizing private sector operations: The Government is encouraging firms to formalize their activities by introducing tax number identification and applying commercial laws and regulations. Consideration is being given to innovative efforts to channel some public funds now being used for vocational training through properly registered firms in compliance with tax laws for their use in financing training for their employees in properly accredited vocational training programs.
- Improve private sector access to finance: The Government will implement a well defined strategy to expand the availability and range of financial products and services, especially targeting small and medium enterprises. Priority actions include:
    - Passage and enactment of four key financial laws: Secured Transactions, Mortgage, Leasing and Negotiable Instruments Laws.
    - Establish an independent banking and business training institute as a joint commercial bank – DAB initiative.
    - A credit information bureau will be established to facilitate commercial and consumer lending.
    - The financial tribunal will be established to provide swift legal resolution of financial disputes.
- Maintain a pro-trade environment: The Government remains committed to maintaining trade policies with low barriers for imports and exports and a liberal foreign exchange system. The Government's trade policies will take into account the need to increase domestic revenues and support increased domestic production by the private sector. Pressures can be expected to arise from some groups for tariff protection, which would likely impose burdens on consumers or other producers in the economy. Such proposals will only be considered by evaluating the economy-wide costs and benefits, including the impact on consumers. The Government will undertake systematic tariff reform as part of the budget process and in consultation with the private sector and will avoid ad hoc changes. The Government will continue to vigorously seek to increase access for Afghan goods and services in foreign markets though bilateral, regional and multilateral trade agreements. The Government remains committed to WTO accession. Expanding trade with

neighboring countries will help to establish Afghanistan as an important 'trading hub' in the region.
- Firm-level technical assistance: The Government is determined to assist the private sector develop its competitiveness and to substantially increase the volume of domestic production. At present, Afghanistan's exports are very low by regional standards, dominated by dried fruit and carpets. However, in recent years a number of new manufacturing industries have begun to emerge, some with demonstrated export potential, such as production dairy products, honey, cement, sunflower products, glass, sugar beet, olive oil, cashmere, and flowers and floral essences. The Government will seek firm-level technical assistance to increase the ability of firms in these and other new industries to compete more effectively in potential export markets.
- Trade Facilitation: The Government will introduce trade facilitation measures to reduce the costs of moving goods within the country and across borders, including endeavoring to relax restrictions arising from transit agreements with neighboring countries. Institutional capacity to support the export of domestically produced goods and services will be increased, including for example the technical resources to establish that Afghan agricultural products meet sanitary and phyto-sanitary (SPS) requirements of importing countries and international product standards are met. The Government will reduce the burden of export documentation and processes will be further streamlined and essential services, including market information will be provided to the exporters by the EPAA.
- NGOs and civil society: The strategy recognizes the vital contribution that NGOs and other civil society organizations are making in implementing the social and economic goals of the ANDS. The Government will maintain an open and effective social dialogue with civil society and encourage their contributions to social and economic development.

Component 2: Expand opportunities for the private investment in infrastructure and natural resources development

The country requires enormous investment in infrastructure, including roads, power generation, water supply, and irrigation. A substantial part of these requirements could be undertaken profitably by private investors with an appropriate regulatory environment. Private investment in the development of natural resources, particularly minerals development will become viable when suitable regulations are in place.

- The Government will establish a multi- sector regulatory authority following an approach similar to that used to develop the telecommunications industry. This regulatory system will establish appropriate fees and royalties, public purchase agreements (e.g., for power), ensure transparent procedures and dispute resolution mechanisms. Its mandate will be to maximize private investment in these areas.
- Opportunities for entering into public- private partnerships for investment in infrastructure projects, such as roads and bridges, will be developed based on international best practices.

- The Government will encourage private provision of public services wherever it will be feasible, including areas such as health, education, municipal services, etc.

Opportunities to expand private investment occur in sectors where multiple ministries have responsibilities. This will require improved coordination and strengthening the capacities of most ministries and agencies. To be successful, the development and promotion of private investment opportunities cannot be the responsibility of only one or two agencies or ministries, but must entail a concerted effort by the entire Government. Efforts to encourage private sector investment also require the understanding and cooperation of the donor community.

This aspect of the private sector development strategy is reflected in many of the sector strategies set out below. For example, it represents a major reform in the energy sector designed to attract private investment into the power sector and development of energy resources. It is the basic foundation for development of the mining sector. It plays an important role with respect to the efforts to make more efficient use of state owned land to stimulate commercial agriculture. The Government will seek to attract medium and large scale agricultural producers and processors to invest in commercial agriculture in order to increase employment and market opportunities in rural areas and to develop export markets for higher value Afghan products. It is reflected in innovative efforts to try and use public funding to support and improve private provision of education and health services. There is scope for using donor funding to develop a vibrant and competitive domestic private construction industry in the projects being implemented by Government ministries.

Component 3: Concerted private sector investment promotion

The third component of the strategy involves concerted efforts to promote investment from foreign and domestic sources, including from the Afghan diaspora. After a long period of isolation, Afghanistan must rebuild commercial ties and demonstrate that there are considerable profitable opportunities for investors in the country. The Afghanistan Investment Support Agency will play a central role in this process and will be strengthened. But the responsibility for promoting increased investment will be a government-wide task and will be an integral part of all projects and programs undertaken as a part of the ANDS.

The objective is to make known to potential investors the opportunities available in Afghanistan, to ensure them that the Government recognizes the importance to the country of increased private investment and to work with potential investors to assure them that their investments will not fail due to unpredictable and unfavorable changes in the tax environment or policies towards private investors. This needs the full support of the international community. This can be done through focused efforts by donors to create conditions necessary for increased private investment in the country. It can also be done by bilateral donors using their relationships with firms in their own countries that are potential investors in Afghanistan to make known the great importance the Government is now placing on the need to expand private sector investment and operations within Afghanistan.

Energy

Role of the Sector in ANDS

Energy is a critical input to economic growth. The ANDS strategic vision and goal for the energy sector strategy is: "An energy sector that provides drivers of growth in the economy with long term reliable, affordable energy based on market-based private sector investment and public sector oversight". This strategy supports (1) commercially and technically efficient energy delivery as a priority; (2) reformed sector governance that will safeguard consumers, workers and resources; (3) the establishment of a market-based enabling environment where legitimate private investment will be facilitated; (4) the diversification of energy resources for long term low cost energy, energy security and clean energy use; and (5) identifying and supporting inter-sectoral supporting linkages including comprehensive system-based planning not limited to projects, energy for industry and vehicles. The Government puts great emphasis on expanding domestic capacity for electricity generation and will take steps to provide the basis for a transition of the sector from public to private provision of electricity. As the Afghan energy sector moves from primarily state owned operations to a more private market orientation, new institutional arrangements will be established.

The Afghanistan Compact benchmarks that specifically deal with the energy sector include:

- "By end 2010, electricity will reach at least 65 percent of households and 90 percent of non-residential establishments in major urban areas and at least 25percent of households in rural areas."
- "By end 2010, at least 75 percent of the costs will be recovered from users connected to the national power grid", a benchmark that the Government now intends to exceed for all but the poorest members of society.[45]

These are ambitious goals. Meeting these objectives will require the transformation of the sector similar to the changes that took place in the telecommunications industry with the reorganization and commercialization of public sector activities and with a greater role being played by the private sector.

Current Situation in the Sector

The energy sector suffered considerable damage due to war and operational neglect. The country has never had high rates of electrification. Today it is estimated that 20 percent of the population have access to public power (grid-supplied) on certain days for a limited number of hours. Nationally seven grids distribute power, with supply coming from domestic hydro generation; imported power and thermal generation. Isolated diesel generation has dramatically increased since 2002 and will continue to play a large role in power supplies. Rural populations use local waste, solar panels, batteries and small wood, coal, kerosene supplies for basic cooking and heat.

Over the past five years, the Government has worked with the international community to increase the availability of electricity and other energy resources and to carry out the planning necessary to make the transition to a more sustainable and efficient private sector led energy sector. A power sector master plan (2003-04); a gas sector master plan (2004-05), and a renewable energy plan (2006) were developed and/or updated. Considerable Investment in expanding domestic generation capacity has been undertaken, including the rehabilitation of the damaged power infrastructure. To a lesser extent, repairs at gas, coal and other energy infrastructure have taken place while millions of dollars have been spent for diesel fuel and support of more than 1,700 small renewable energy projects. Since 2006, there has been an on-going program for commercialization of operations in power operations by the state owned power company, DABM.

The Inter-Ministerial Commission for Energy (ICE) was established in 2006 to coordinate Government policy in energy; to leverage donor resources; and integrate sector planning. Cadastre and Inspectorate functions are now located at the Ministry of Mines to support oil, natural gas and coal contracts.

The efforts mentioned above have resulted in a significant improvement in the availability of electricity and other energy sources compared to the devastated conditions prior to 2002. Electricity capacity compared to 2002 has almost doubled, largely due to imported supply, which was non-existent prior to 2002 (see Table 7.1). However, on a per capita basis, the electricity generating capacity is well below what it was in 1978. The present goal of electricity availability set for 2010 is below 40 kwh per capita, (compared to a present availability in, for instance, Tajikistan of over 2,200 kwh per capita). Technical standards of operations remain antiquated and do not appropriately reflect the new technologies or modern safety measures.

Despite progress and efforts to date, the existing governance arrangements and policy framework for the sector are still insufficient to support a market-based energy system. Some of the obstacles to making the desired transition include:

- **Dispersed institutional support**: Seven ministries include energy as part of their portfolio.
- **Lack of regulatory framework**: No legal or regulatory regime (though an energy law is under preparation) is in place to guide sector operations. There are no legal professionals trained in commercial energy law or regulatory processes.
- **No divesting or meaningful commercialization of state energy assets**: The Government and energy enterprise operations are overstaffed and highly inefficient, lacking fundamental tools and capacity to support technically and commercially viable operations. This includes power, natural gas, coal and liquid fuels. Some of the state owned enterprises and budgetary units operate with considerable government support with virtually no audit, fiscal or legal oversight.

Table 7.1. Electricity supply sources and operating capacity

Year	Hydro (MW)	Thermal (MW)	Imported (MW)	Other: diesel, micro hydro & renewable (MW)	Total supply (MW)
1357 (1978)	259	137	0	0	396
1381 (2002)	141	16	87	0	243
1386 (2007)	262	90	167	133	652

- **A drain on budgetary resources**: A sector that could be generating revenues for government with normal rates of taxation applied to sector activities is, under present arrangements, a major drain on government resources.
- **Inefficient and wasteful use of electricity**: Underpriced electricity is used inefficiently. Appropriate cost recovery will provide incentives to cut down on this wasteful use.
- **Limited opportunities for private participation**: There are no legal impediments to private investment in the energy sector. In practice, there is a weak legal and regulatory infrastructure in place to support and monitor investments. Potential investors cite unclear policies and corruption as a barrier to investment. In a well developed market, the majority of services now provided by the 11 SOE and three budgetary units that support energy operations could be implemented by the private sector in ways that are more cost-effective and technically efficient. Areas where private sector engagement has immediate potential with appropriate regulatory include independent power production and oil and gas concessions.

In the Provincial Development Plan consultations, a number of issues were frequently highlighted across a range of sectors and in a majority of provinces, and therefore emerge as overarching development priorities. Access to electricity, both for domestic use through the extension of availability of electricity to more remote villages, and for productive purposes such as factories and businesses was mentioned in 80 percent of the PDPs.

Policy Framework: Sector Strategy

Substantial new investment is required in the sector to increase domestic generating capacity and ensure adequate supplies. A central thrust in the strategy will be increased investment in energy related infrastructure. The three key hydro power projects (described above) will substantially add to generating capacity, but also support agricultural growth and improved management of water resources. Substantial additional private investment is also required. The Government will leverage currently available donor funds to ensure longer term access to private investment and capital. Policies to support private investments will be established. Improved procurement, accounting functions, contracting and reporting at the government level will be put in place.

A new market oriented paradigm will be developed, supported by significant institutional strengthening and capacity development. As the energy line ministries shift over time from operating as production-based entities to become policy-making regulatory agencies, staff capacity and in-house functions will be reoriented to market practices. The key programs of the sector are: (i) efficient operation of infrastructure; (ii) market based sector governance; (iii) rural electrification and renewable energy; (iv) expand supplies, (for additional detail refer to the full sector strategy in ANDS Volume II).

The Priority Polices and Projects include:

- *Implementation of key power infrastructure projects:* The Government will give priority to the implementation of four major infrastructure projects that will substantially increase power supplies, but also contribute to expanded irrigation and rural development: (i) the Kokcha-e-Ulia Hydro Power Plant, which will generate a total of 1,900 MW and add 57,000 hectares of irrigated agricultural land; (ii) the Baghdara Hydro Power Plant, which will generate 210 MW, benefit more than 105,000 families, increasing irrigation coverage; (iii) the Irrigation and Power Project of Kokcha-eSofla, which will generate 100 MW of power, benefiting more than 950,000 families in the area; and (iv) the Sorobi II Hydro Power Plant, which will generate 180MW and help meet electricity needs in Kabul. Other key projects include expansion of the public power grid through the rehabilitation and upgrading of Kabul and other key infrastructure areas (i.e., distribution − lines, substations, meters); the development of the North East Power System (NEPS) to be followed by the South East Power System (SEPS), Western and Eastern Power Systems; the development of the Sheberghan gas and oil fields; construction of new transmission and related distribution for power imports; installation of a dispatch and control system as well as a reactive power system.

- **Restructured energy sector governance:** The Government will consolidate energy planning and policy-making functions through the Inter-Ministerial Commission for Energy (ICE). This may involve some regrouping of Ministerial functions as well as improved line ministry staff capacity to plan and budget. Use of the ICE mechanism as well as improved public information will be essential for improved government coordination in the energy sector. Related or duplicated energy functions at various ministries will be consolidated and appropriate line ministry terms of references will be introduced. It is essential that the donors themselves improve the way in which they are engaged with the energy sector. At present there are 25 donors engaged in the sector; in addition there are 15 different US agencies. Afghan counterpart resources are limited and stretched to the limit. Improved governance will mobilize investment, mitigate corrupt practices and improve the technical quality of energy supply. A viable legal and regulatory framework will be established that includes the development of market-based power purchase and production sharing agreements.

- **Legal reform and Regulatory standards.** Finalization of primary legislative and regulatory tools is essential. These include mining regulations, the Hydrocarbons Upstream Law and drafting legislation for the electricity sector. There are no meaningful technical standards or financial standards for operation in place; these need to be urgently developed as well as staff capacity to implement them. The Government is working with the international community to draft a revised Hydrocarbons Law as well as mining and hydrocarbons regulations). Drafting of regulation for hydrocarbons is underway in the strengthening of the cadastre and inspectorate functions and more focus on grid and off-grid regulation of electricity as well as liquid fuels is required.

- **Commercialization and/or divestiture of state and "quasi-state" assets:** The Government will assess its sector assets and a plan for liquidation, restructuring and commercialization or sale. In particular the Government will provide more support for the corporatization and commercialization of national power operations. Commercialization and increasing the efficiency of the state power company DABM includes, for example, the installation of international accounting and procurement practices that will follow in other energy sub-sectors.

- ***Improve the enabling environment for private sector investment*** As new energy developments emerge including new power import transmission, gas-fired power, coal- fired power and new hydro generation, the introduction of the private sector to finance and operate these assets will be important. In most instances no local capacity is in place to support these market operations and private investments. A market- friendly enabling environment to facilitate private investment must be developed that is sufficiently flexible to entice private investment but effective in how these investments are monitored to safeguard Afghan resources, workers, consumers and environment. The ANDS energy sector strategy calls for the establishment of a sector regulator, which will adopt a transparent licensing regime and establish conditions that will attract private investment in electricity generation and in the related fields of mining, natural gas and hydropower. A market-friendly enabling environment to facilitate private investment will be developed. Key areas for investment in the near term include: (i) increased domestic power generation that includes new hydro power, natural gas and coal- fired power facilities; (ii) power distribution including lines, substations and metering; (iii) power construction and services (i.e., outsourcing); (iv) exploration and exploitation of coal, natural gas and oil; (v) installation and operation of rural energy services.
- ***Expanded Public Power Grid:*** The Government is committed to improving energy access for people across the country. A high priority in this area is the rehabilitation and expansion of grid-supplied power, including investment in new generation, distribution and transmission. The Government is also implementing a series of large and small infrastructure improvements, generation, transmission and improved distribution of electricity throughout the country. Future actions include: (i) rehabilitation and upgrading of Kabul and other key infrastructure areas (i.e., distribution – lines, substations, meters); (ii) development of the North East Power System (NEPS); to be followed by the South East Power System (SEPS), Western and Eastern Power Systems; (iii) construction of new transmission and related distribution for power imports. Installation of a dispatch and control system as well as a reactive power system will be underway in 2008. These on-going donor funded activities to expand the power grids will be adjusted to be compatible with the move to a more market based system.
- ***Increase Access to rural energy services:*** Micro-hydro, solar, waste and even small diesel power and energy generating sources will be promoted to improve rural access. Commercial operation of these services will be encouraged and technical standards will be established to ensure cost-recovery, sustainability and safety. High levels of cost recovery will avoid preempting potentially more efficient provision of such services by the private sector. Several private firms are involved in the development of off-grid power supplies based on wind or solar power and efforts will be made to encourage the development of these activities, or at least not undermine their viability with subsidized public sector activities.
- **Increase Regional Cooperation and Trade in Energy Products:** Afghanistan is geographically well positioned to import additional resources from neighboring countries. Afghanistan joined as a full member the Central Asia South Asia (CASA) 1300mw project in November 2007. Power purchase agreements (PPA) are being finalized for regular power imports from neighboring countries and new PPAs are

being negotiated for increased power imports. Afghanistan is also participating in ongoing planning for a TurkmenistanAfghanistan-Pakistan-India (TAPI) natural gas pipeline. A number of regional energy trade and import arrangements have commenced and will contribute to long-term energy security.
- ***Poverty Reduction Initiatives:*** The energy sector will provide essential power supplies needed for private sector development, job creation and poverty reduction. Investments in the sector will create direct employment opportunities in the development of power plants, oil, gas and coal fields, the construction of grid systems and the commercial operations of the sector. The development of small energy installations will contribute to local economic development particularly in rural areas. Subsidies for electricity will be maintained for the poorest households. Micro-hydro, solar, waste and even small diesel power and energy generating sources will be promoted to improve increased rural access to power. Commercial operation of these services will be encouraged and technical standards will be established to ensure cost-recovery, sustainability and safety. A number of private firms are currently involved in the development of off-grid power supplies based on wind or solar power and efforts will be made to encourage the development of these activities.
- ***Environmental Protection:*** The environmental implications of the expansion of the energy sector will be fully accounted for. These will be both positive, such as reduced pressure for deforestation, while others may be potentially negative, such as increased green house gas emissions. There will be scope for using wind and solar energy, particularly in areas away from the regional grids, and the relative benefits of this type of energy should be recognized in policies to support their use.

The energy sector strategy therefore combines efforts supported by donor funding to expand public sector operations while laying the groundwork for much greater involvement by the private sector investors. The relative weight given to these two components will be dependent on the relative effectiveness of the two efforts over the implementation period for the ANDS (for details refer to ANDS Volume II).

Integration of the Provincial Development Plans (PDPs)

Access to electricity, both for domestic use through the extension of availability of electricity to more remote villages, and for productive purposes such as factories and businesses was cited in 80 percent of Provincial Development Plans. PDPs in eight provinces, principally in the center, south and south east of the country report progress in access to electricity since 2005, however, provinces in the center and south also most frequently mentioned the need for improvement. Little mention or understanding was cited with respect to the non- electricity use of energy, i.e., for heating, fuel for small equipment, vehicle fuel, etc.

Expected Outcomes

The key outcomes of the sector strategy are:
- Improved Governance and Commercialization
- Expanded Public Power Grid
- Increased Access to Rural Energy Services
- Enabling environment for private sector investment in energy sector. (For detail information refer to Appendixes 3-National Action Plan and 4-Monitoring Matrix.)

Water and Irrigation

Role of the Sector in ANDS

The ANDS strategic vision and goal of the water sector can be summarized as follows: to manage and develop the water resources in the country so as to reduce poverty, increase sustainable economic and social development, and improve the quality of life for all Afghans and ensure an adequate supply of water for future generations.

There are significant water resources in Afghanistan. Average annual precipitation is equivalent to about 165,000 million m^3, yielding an annual surface runoff water volume of about 57,000 million m^3. This amounts to approximately 2,280 m^3/year per capita. This would be an adequate amount, except: precipitation is primarily in the form of snowfall and the resulting snowmelt runs off in a matter of a few months without adequate catchment systems; and precipitation in not evenly distributed geographically. Reliance is therefore placed on groundwater extraction that is not sustainable and currently only an insignificant amount of surface water storage exists. Deep water drilling without adequate investment in recharge basins or storage structures is degrading the aquifers on which much of traditional irrigation systems depend. Despite considerable assistance in rehabilitating irrigation systems, progress towards establishing a comprehensive plan with prioritized and costed investments is still in the formative stage.

The Afghanistan Compact Benchmarks for Water Management commit both the Government and the donors to the development of sustainable water resource management strategies and plans covering irrigation and drinking water supply, and irrigation investments will result in at least 30 percent of water coming from large waterworks by end 2010. Other Compact Benchmarks under Urban Development, Environment, Agriculture and Rural Development directly address and contribute to the water sector, as follows:

- **Urban Development**: Investment in water supply and sanitation will ensure that 50 percent of households in Kabul and 30 percent of households in other major urban areas will have access to piped water and improved sanitation.
- **Environment:** Environmental regulatory frameworks and management services will be established for the protection of air and water quality, waste management and natural resources.
- **Agriculture:** The necessary institutional, regulatory and incentive framework will be established for securing access to irrigation, water management systems and food security.

- **Rural Development:** Rural development will be enhanced for 90 percent of villages through the provision of safe drinking water, sanitation (50 percent) and small scale irrigation (47 percent) by the end of 2010.

Millennium Development Goals: The MDGs state that: "access to water and sanitation, electricity, and livelihoods sources have been negatively impacted through the decades of war. Drinking water supplies reach only 23 percent of Afghanistan's total population – 43 percent in urban areas and 18 percent in rural areas. The country's total sanitation coverage of only 12 percent deserves attention. While around 28 percent of the urban population is covered, only 8 percent of rural population had access to improved sanitation in 2006.[46]

Target 10 of the MDGs is to halve by 2020 the proportion of people without sustainable access to safe drinking water and ensure environmental sustainability.

The sector strategy incorporates feedback and comments from the sub-national consultations. Access to clean drinking water has been identified as a priority in the Provincial Development Plans in all provinces. Participants generally voiced concern that unsafe drinking water is a cause of disease, and the provision of safe drinking water is therefore seen to be as much a public health issue as an issue of infrastructure, rural and urban development. In over a quarter of PDPs, the need for access to clean drinking water is specifically raised by women who often have the responsibility of collecting water for the household. However, this issue is not confined to the domestic context and the PDPs in six provinces highlighted the need for access to safe drinking water in public institutions such as schools.

Current Situation in the Sector

Given the importance of water resources, the Government has made improved water management a high priority. Steps are being taken to address shortcomings in governance as well as meeting some of the most pressing needs through donor funded projects. Some key achievements have been:

- The formulation of the Supreme Council for Water Affairs Management (SCWAM) to coordinate and overcome the problems of diverse ministerial responsibilities for water management. A Technical Secretariat has been established to develop new water laws and develop a consistent set of policies for water management. New environmental laws were recently enacted by the National Assembly.
- Steps have been undertaken to re-organize water resource management on the basis of an Integrated Water Resource Management System based on the five main river basins. Development will still be planned and implemented centrally, but in the future individual river basin organizations or authorities will be established. Feasibility studies have been completed or are underway for small, medium and large water infrastructure projects. The rehabilitation and modernization of hydrological stations have been started. Research and modeling of the availability of allocation of safe drinking water supplies in Kabul are being developed.
- Significant progress has been made in providing increased access to safe drinking water and sanitation. The Afghanistan Urban Water Supply and Sewerage Corporation (AUWSSC) has been established. Some 80 water supply and sanitation

projects have been implemented around the country. Research and assessment of the underground water resources available to Kabul is on-going. The urban water supply systems will be transformed into quasi- public agencies. Two million urban residents (31 percent) have benefited from investments in water supply and 12 percent from investment in sanitation in major cities between 2002 and 2007. About 35,000 water points 59 networks and 1,713 water reservoirs and 23,884 demonstration latrines have been constructed. More than three million people have benefited directly from the rural water supply and sanitation activities in the country. Around a third of the provinces reported some improvement in access to clean drinking water since 2005 during the consultative process under the ANDS.
- Irrigation Rehabilitation has been given high priority over the past four or five years. An estimated 1.8 million hectares of land is under irrigation; 10 percent gets water from engineered systems and large works, the remaining through traditional irrigation methods. Of some 2,100 rehabilitation projects, approximately 1,200 have been completed and have been placed back into commercial service. The Government will continue to work with the mirabs that manage these systems. [47]

Despite some progress in establishing better governance in the sector and in rehabilitating existing assets, a lot more needs to be done. Prior to 1979, some 3.3 million hectares were cultivated under various irrigation methods, compared to the 1.8 million hectares now being irrigated. The remaining amount employs traditional irrigation methods. Out of 7.9 million hectares arable land, 5.3 million hectares is irrigable. Irrigation water management is a high priority of the Government.

There is a lack of skilled human resources with experience in water management. Information systems are only now being reconstituted and there is a lack of reliable hydrological, meteorological, geo-technical and water quality data. There is a lack of the infrastructure and equipment needed to efficiently conserve and utilize water resources that result from seasonal runoff with the snow melt. There is limited data on ground water resources and information indicating that un-regulated deep well drilling may be depleting aquifers that are essential to water supplies and traditional irrigation systems (Karezes and springs). There is a lack of economic mechanisms regulating water use and investments for water supply, sanitary systems, irrigation, and hydropower generation.

Unclear delineation of responsibilities between ministries complicates planning. Some donors are focused on emergency projects that are not integrated into an integrated system of water use. Access to drinking water and sanitation, while improved, is still not in compliance with the Millennium Development Goals. There is a lack of hydro geological investment in urban areas. A significant risk exists for underground water contamination. A major river basin water supply master plan with good information on water balances, that is, supply versus demand for water for drinking, irrigation, hydro power and environment purposes is not yet available. There is a pressing need to enhance the ground water resource recharge capacity. Coordination among water related institutions and agencies remains weak.

This sector strategy incorporates feedback and comments from the sub-national consultations. The projects identified and prioritized during the SNC process are included in the Water Sector Strategy. Access to clean drinking water has been identified as a priority in the Provincial Development Plan in all provinces. Participants generally voiced concern that unsafe drinking water is a cause of disease, and the provision of safe drinking water is therefore seen to be as much a public health issue as an issue of infrastructure, rural and urban development. In over a quarter of PDPs, the need for access to clean drinking water is specifically raised by women who often have the responsibility of collecting water for the household. However, this issue is not confined to the domestic context and the PDPs of six provinces highlight the need for access to safe drinking water in public institutions such as schools. Around a third of the provinces spread across the country report some improvement in access to clean drinking water since 2005.

Policy Framework: Sector Strategy

For the immediate future, the Government centrally will play the dominant role in setting policy priorities and decisions pertaining to development and management of water resources at the national level. The Government, acting through its operating entities, can influence the necessary international cooperation relating to several international water bodies. This extends to coverage provided by policy frameworks, appropriate legislation, and institutional structures under which water management can over time be devolved to the river basin and/or river sub-basin levels. Groundwater on the other hand seldom has aquifer boundaries coinciding with river basins. Management of groundwater aquifers may necessitate collaboration with special inter-basin entities established for that purpose. (For additional details refer to ANDS Volume II).

Towards an Integrated Water Resource Management System (IWRM)

The water sector is extremely diverse. The responsibilities for supply management and use of water are distributed among a number of line ministries. The sector's governance mechanisms (organizational structure, policies and legislation) are in the process of reformulation and implementation. Adoption and implementation of an effective IWRM program will take into consideration all activities and development requirements influencing water resources. This will include sociological and ecological considerations, in addition to water supply, irrigation, hydroelectric power, sanitation, land use, fisheries, and forestry. The program will prioritize a series of specific activities required to effectively implement IWRM policy framework.

The river basin approach to water management will lead to improvements in capturing surface water using storage reservoir and recharge basins. By devolving authority to the RBA and thus encouraging more effective use of water resources, the water resource strategy (when integrated with programs in the transport, agriculture, health, education, power sectors, along with counter narcotics programs, private sector development programs) will contribute to sustainable development and poverty reduction.

Key Components of the Water Sector Strategy

While an IWRM approach has major benefits, supplementary comprehensive river basin data management programs are needed to support this approach. It is important to improve mechanisms regulating water use and to attract investment to rehabilitate and construct irrigation, water supply and sanitary systems, as well as hydropower generation. Essential legislation and a new policy framework governing the water sector have been prepared. The sector is in the process of transitioning from a project-by-project approach to a sector-wide approach, using an integrated water resources management (IWRM) system. Improved governance mechanisms were identified and are being implemented. Foremost among them was the formation of the Supreme Council for Water Affairs' Management (SCWAM), and its associated Technical Secretariat.

Until the IWRM comes into effect, considerable reliance will have to be put on a project-byproject approach for continued investments in rehabilitation of existing systems. New projects need to be assessed relative to the returns from rehabilitation efforts and returns in other sectors.

Responsibilities for a number of water related activities are distributed among a number of line ministries and agencies. Each of these entities have prepared sector specific strategies f ocusing on their particular sector mandate, often underemphasizing water related programs and/or activities. Development of a water sector strategy therefore requires coordinating all relevant water sub-sector strategies being administered by individual government entities into one single unified water sector strategy document. The following sub-sectors have been included in this unification: (i) urban and rural water supply and sanitation; (ii) irrigation and drainage; (iii) hydro power; (iv) industrial water supply and wastewater disposal; (v) flood protection and preparedness; (vi) drought mitigation measures; and (vii) environmental requirements, including forestry, fisheries, and bio-diversity. Facilitating related development of each of these sub-sectors will require institution building, enhancement of legal frameworks, capacity development, enlisting economic mechanisms, and intensive rehabilitation of infrastructure.

The Strategic Policy Framework for the Water Sector approved by SCWAM recommended that the following policies, laws, regulations and procedures should be developed in order to move forward in the development of the water sector. Under this policy framework, the Water Law of 1991 will be revised; water resources and irrigation policies and regulations will be established along with an institutional framework for water resources management; regulations for Water User Associations will be developed; plans will be developed and steps taken to preserve surface and underground water resources; national urban and rural water supply and sanitation policies and institutional development will be implemented; access to safe drinking water and improved drainage and sanitation systems will be established; and key groundwater and hydropower development plans and policies will be established.

For the immediate future, the Government will play the dominant role in setting policy priorities and decisions pertaining to the development and management of water resources. This extends to policies, legislation, and institutions under which water management can in time be devolved to the river basin and/or river sub-basin levels. (Management of groundwater aquifers may sometime necessitate collaboration with special inter-basin entities established for that purpose.) Ongoing and planned water sector projects have been structured into eight programs (i) Institutional Setup and Capacity Building (ii) National Water Resources Development (iii) National River Basin Management (iv) Irrigation Rehabilitation (v) Urban Water Supply and Sanitation (vi) Rural Water Supply and Sanitation (vii) Riverbank Protection (viii) Agriculture "Food Security for All". For detail on all of the programs refer to ANDS volume II. The highest priority programs are:

- **Institutional Building and Capacity Development Program**: Activities in this program focus on the institutional and human capacity development of water resources management as well as infrastructure development at national, river basin

- **National Water Resources Development Program**: Under the Water Law the Ministry of Energy and Water is responsible for the preparation of a national water resources development plan. This plan will cover the development of water resources for the social, environmental and economic needs of the country as well as: (i) elaborating river basin development and management plans, fostering ministry and water users' capacity for on-farm and off-farm water management; (ii) preparing for discussions on trans-boundary water issues with some neighbor countries; (iii) supporting analytical capacity and research; (iv) enabling private investments in the water sector; and (v) proper planning and implementation of infrastructure for rain and flood water harvesting, supplementary irrigation, groundwater recharge and soil stabilization. As a first step in the development of this national development plan, a Master Plan for the Kabul River Basin has been prepared. In addition, the Ministry has prepared a list of water resources development projects in the five river basins.
- **Irrigation Rehabilitation Program**: Several projects to address the immediate needs in irrigation infrastructure have been developed.[48] Although these projects mainly focus on the infrastructure, they contribute to the development of water resources and address related issues like the rehabilitation of the hydro-metric network for data collection on river flows and weather. Components of the emergency irrigation rehabilitation program for the period 2008 to 2013 include the rehabilitation of the National Hydrological Stations to aid in the undertaking of national hydrological surveys to aid in planning and building irrigation infrastructure; and rehabilitation of nationwide small, medium and large traditional irrigation schemes, such as the 'Emergency Irrigation Rehabilitation Project' – a three year country-wide project for the rehabilitation of infrastructure and capacity building.

These programs respond to the dual tasks of remodeling and modernizing institutions while at the same time rehabilitating and improving infrastructure. They consider short term emergency water infrastructure rehabilitation and income generation needs as well as the long term goal of sustainable development of institutions and creation of new multifunctional infrastructure.

The development of the country's water resources will continue to be heavily influenced by programs and projects implemented by donors. It is essential that these activities be effectively coordinated and aligned with the priorities in the ANDS. SCWAM will undertake a leadership role among government organizations in providing coordination with the international community. The ANDS water sector goals are achievable with the implementation of an effective integrated water resource development strategy. Some of the benefits will be realized only over the long term, while others will be realized within a very short time span.

Expected Outcomes

The key expected outcomes of the Water Sector Strategy are:

- Improved water sector legal and governance structures and institutions in place

- Sustainable water resource management strategies and plans covering drinking and irrigation water supply developed and implemented.
- Water resources for drinking and irrigation purposes improved as well as poverty reduction and employment creation.
- Infant mortality decreased and life expectancy increased as result of higher access to clean water. (For more detailed information refer to Appendixes 3-National Action Plan and 4-Monitoring Matrix.)

Agriculture and Rural Development

Role of the Sector

The ANDS long term strategic vision for agriculture and rural development is to ensure the social, economic and political well-being of rural communities, especially poor and vulnerable people, while stimulating the integration of rural communities within the national economy. This will require transforming agricultural production so that it is more productive and increasingly commercially oriented and expanding off-farm employment opportunities as the basis for increasing incomes among the rural population. This sector strategy articulates a road map for the way forward in which poverty reduction through economic regeneration is the central objective. A central focus is on supporting the poorest and most vulnerable segments of rural society and promoting the development of medium and large scale commercial agricultural activities. Advancements in the sector will improve the quality of life for rural citizens, increase food security, improve the delivery of basic services, increase incomes and contribute to establishing a safe and secure environment.

The Afghanistan Compact Benchmarks related directly to agriculture and rural development call for measurable improvements in:

Compact Benchmark 6.1

- The necessary institutional, regulatory and incentive framework to increase production and productivity will be established to create an enabling environment for legal agriculture and agriculture-based rural industries.
- Public investment in agriculture will increase by 30 percent. Particular consideration will be given to perennial horticulture, animal health, and food security by: instituting specialized support agencies and financial service delivery mechanisms, supporting farmers' associations, branding national products, disseminating timely price and weather-related information and statistics, providing strategic research and technical assistance, and securing access to irrigation and water management systems.

Compact Benchmark 6.2

- assistance to and rehabilitation and integration of refugees and internally displaced persons; and
- assistance to female-headed households that are chronically poor and increases in their employment rates.

Other major Government goals relating to agriculture and rural development should be noted, including:

- creating the necessary policy and regulatory framework to support the establishment of micro, small and medium-size rural enterprises;
- creating the enabling environment for sustainable management and use of Afghanistan's natural resources;
- access to safe drinking water will be extended to 90 percent of villages, and sanitation to 50 percent;
- road connectivity will reach 40 percent of all villages.
- 47 percent of villages will benefit from small-scale irrigation. (See ANDS Volume Two for more details)

Current Situation

Agriculture has traditionally been the major activity for a large proportion of the population, particularly in the most remote areas. The years of turmoil left much of the country's agriculture and rural infrastructure in a serious state of disrepair and led to a significant reduction of cultivatable land and degradation of the environment. Between 1978 and 2004, agricultural production declined by an average of 3.5 percent a year; 50 percent of the livestock herd was lost between 1997 and 2004.

Recent performance in the sector has been positive. Measurable progress has been achieved since 2003 in improving rural livelihoods. Through a variety programs, almost 20,000 km of rural access roads (i.e., all weather, villageto-village and village-to-district center roads) have been constructed or repaired, increasing access to markets, employment and social services. More than 500,000 households (36 percent of villages) have benefited from small-scale irrigation projects. Currently, 32.5 percent of the rural population has access to safe drinking water and 4,285 improved sanitation facilities have been provided. More than 336,000 households have benefited from improved access to financial services. Some 18,000 CDCs have been established and are implementing community-led development projects.

The contribution of agriculture to GDP increased from 48 percent in 2006 to 53 percent in 2007, although the longer run trend (not including opium) is down due mainly due to rapid growth in construction and other activities. Other achievements include: 5.5 million metric tons of wheat and other grains produced in 2007 compared to 3.7 million metric tons in 2002; 0.9 million metric tons of horticulture and industrial crops produced in 2007 compared to 0.4 million metric tons in 2002; 3.2 million animals received veterinary and health services; 5,000 metric tons of improved wheat seed was produced and distributed to farmers in 28 provinces; $120 million is to be invested in commercial agriculture; more than 3,000 cooperatives and farmers organization have been created and strengthened; and 20,000 cooperative members trained.

However, significant improvements are still to be made. With a few notable exceptions, all rural citizens are poor in relative and absolute terms, lacking both physical and social assets. 80 percent of the Afghan population live in rural areas, most of whom are engaged in agriculture to some degree, although many are also heavily engaged in processing, trading or marketing activities of agricultural products; 12-15 percent of total land area is suitable for cultivation; water constraints inhibit cultivation of up to one third of irrigated land; three million hectares of land are rain-fed, in a country of repeated droughts; 58 percent of villages have limited seasonal or no access roads (the average distance to the nearest road is 4.6 km); 13 percent of rural Afghans have access to electricity at some point during the year; more than 70 percent of rural Afghans do not have access to safe drinking water; 96 percent of rural Afghans do not have access to safe toilets/sanitation (28 percent have no toilets at all). The continued high population growth projected for Afghanistan will imply continued decline in per capita levels of agricultural resources unless major investments are made in improved water management.

Ongoing instability, widespread poverty and lack of governance resulted in a dramatic upsurge in opium poppy cultivation, involving 3.3 million people (14 percent of the population). Poppy production is now highly concentrated in five southern and eastern provinces, whereas production in the other 29 provinces has fallen and is half 2004 levels.

Further, the unstable security situation coupled with capacity constraints presents major obstacles to program implementation, including community mobilization, survey and design of projects, service and input provision, selection of qualified contractors and NGOs willing to work in high-risk areas, and the ability to monitor projects for quality assurance and financial control purposes. These constraints affect the pace, cost and quality of development activities.

Most farmers are engaged in subsistence or near-subsistence agriculture, and many farming families lack food security with risky livelihoods often combined with chronic debt. Further, many rural households are involved in down-stream agricultural activities, including processing, transporting and marketing. As a result, the country's vulnerability to natural disasters and food shortages is high. The ability to engage in agricultural pursuits is central to improving wellbeing of the rural poor.

Limited coordination between ministries and between the Government and the international community has impeded progress. Government funds have been channeled through highly centralized ministries, with many national programs and donor-funded projects working independently of each other. The role of provincial administration units has been and remains unclear, especially in the areas of economic planning, budget execution and service delivery. Provincial governments have limited authority, budgetary resources or technical skills to facilitate development. Ministries which deliver services to the rural population are still struggling with the legal structures of past administrations and over-centralization of administrative processes has impeded the timely and effective delivery of services to local communities.

The Government recognizes that to meet these enormous challenges nationwide, progress may be slow, incremental and uneven; it may take a generation or more to adequately meet the needs of all rural Afghans. Nevertheless, the Government is committed to providing a proper enabling environment for the rural economy and working to address the needs and articulated priorities of the rural population. This long term effort requires a considered and cohesive policy framework.

Policy and Strategic Framework

The Government is committed to working to address the needs and articulated priorities of the rural population. This long term effort requires a considered and cohesive policy framework across ministries and sectors. The following are the key components of this policy framework of this sector:

- Comprehensive and strategically cohesive poverty reduction programs
- Public/Private sector responsibilities
- Assurance of food security
- The restoration and expansion of Afghanistan's licit economy through the promotion of livelihoods free from dependency on poppy cultivation
- Land tenure security
- Assistance to farmers to increase production and productivity
- Environmental protection and assistance to communities to manage and protect Afghanistan's natural resource base for sustainable growth
- Improvements in agricultural and rural physical infrastructure and irrigation systems providing services to meet basic human rights
- Development of human resource capital
- The strengthening of local governance
- Institutional coordination
- Cross sector policy development
- Strengthening of national capacities
- Mitigation of natural and man-made disasters

The strategy intent focuses on five thematic areas of programming. The following five thematic areas are loosely sequenced, based upon their level of interdependence

- Local Governance
- Agricultural Production
- Agricultural and Rural Infrastructure
- Economic Regeneration
- Disaster and Emergency Preparedness (See ANDS Volume Two for more details)

The key priorities of this program are the:

- Development of a comprehensive set of programs and projects – the Comprehensive Agriculture Rural Development program – designed to improve rural livelihoods and reduce rural poverty; and
- Support of commercialized agriculture, leading to an improvement in agricultural productivity throughout the rural economy.

Comprehensive Agriculture and Rural Development program: The Comprehensive Agriculture and Rural Development program (CARD) is a series of programs designed to support the poorest and most vulnerable segments of rural society. The CARD represents the Government's approach to providing diversified income sources, through income support, direct provision of assets, skills training and market opportunities, and is crucial to providing alternatives to producing narcotics. Interventions will be targeted and tailored to specific regions and groups.

In implementing the CARD, the Government will ensure that efforts to promote activity in the sector will stimulate and not displace spontaneous viable private sector development. The devolution of authority will be undertaken over a number of years to ensure the capacities at all levels of government exist. The Government will work to reconcile the introduction of sub-national governance measures down to the village level with existing community organizations. In particular, the role between proposed Village Councils and the existing Community Development Councils set up under the National Solidarity Program and which have been given legal status will be clarified. Strengthening sub-national governance structures in line with the newly-formed Independent Directorate for Local Governance will also be undertaken.

The Government will work with NGOs, civil society and the international community on the prioritization of the sub-components of the overall CARD program and to develop the funding requirements in some detail within a log frame matrix, identifying what will be done by when. This will allow a cooperative effort by the international community and the Government to reallocate resources towards those efforts that appear most effective in improving rural livelihoods. Ongoing monitoring and evaluation will be essential to address identified constraints and successes and alter the programs as necessary.

The principal program among the 15 programs of the CARD is the **National Solidarity Program** (NSP), the Government's main community development program. Implemented by the Community Development Councils (CDC), the more than 50,000 projects benefit approximately 2 million people in rural areas. The NSP is developing the capacity of CDCs to identify community needs and transfer funding and necessary support resources to fund localized small scale activities of importance to rural communities, such as roads, irrigation, water wells and school. It is a successful and popular program used to empower these communities. It is a major contributor to meeting a number of the Compact benchmarks and is a successful example of country-wide Government, donor and NGO coordination. It establishes the framework for future programs that provide greater control to local communities, including the private sector, over development funds.

The other 14 programs of the CARD include:

- **The National Food Security Program** will promote and implement food security opportunities at the household level, benefiting over 1.2 million households by 2010. This will decrease malnourishment rate from 57 percent to 35 percent. A key component of this program is the support to improve local governance in 38,000 villages.
- **The National Area Based Development Program** will support all District Development Assemblies to develop district level development plans which will support comprehensive rural development and regeneration.
- **The Horticulture Program** will support horticulture development and supply farmers with saplings, provide equipment for trellises and establish pest control systems leading to a 20 percent increase in perennial crop production and significant exports through public private sector partnerships.
- **The Livestock Program** will support livestock production by importing purebred sheep, establishing commercial dairy plants and poultry units for women farmers, increasing productivity and output.
- **The National Rural Access Program** will support rural road construction and rehabilitation that will provide all weather road access to 65 percent of villages by 2013.

- **The Rural Water Supply and Sanitation Program** will assure that by 2013 98 percent of villages will have access to safe drinking water and 50 percent of villages will have improved sanitation facilities. This will substantially improve health, hygiene and welfare in rural communities.
- **The Irrigation Program** will establish irrigation infrastructure on an additional 105,000 ha of new irrigated land by 2018 and improve on-farm water use efficiency.
- **The National Resource Program** will establish National Resource Management committees and develop national resource management plans for forests, rangeland, wildlife and desertification control.
- **The National Surveillance System Project** will assist MRRD and CSO in the development of a national poverty, vulnerability and food security surveillance system and enable the government to provide credible and timely information to all government and non-government agencies.
- **The Rural Electrification Program** will result in over 4,000 villages being connected to local electrical facilities.
- **The Rural Enterprise Program** will provide training and finance to establish rural enterprises across 70 percent of all CDCs and create an estimated 2.1 million jobs, better integrate the rural economy with the national economy and reduce poppy cultivation.
- **The Research and Extension System** will establish a research and extension capability; provide access to credit, support farmers organization and private sector market development through cooperatives, leading to agricultural growth and diversification.
- **The Emergency Response System** will provide a mechanism for humanitarian and disaster response that will provide emergency assistance, assure access to areas affected by snow and disasters and protect vulnerable people and assets.
- **The Capacity Building Program** will provide the institutional and organizational capacity at the national, provincial and district levels needed to successfully implement the other CARD programs. (See ANDS Volume Two and Appendix "National Action Plan/Policy Matrix" for more details)

Support for Commercial Agriculture: There is virtually no large scale commercial agricultural activity currently undertaken in Afghanistan. This has not always been the case. Earlier turmoil destroyed much of the country's agricultural and physical infrastructure, halting commercial activities. There has been limited recovery since 2002. This includes ongoing efforts to increase the international community's, including ISAF, procurement of agricultural products from local producers, promoting large scale production and supply chain processes.

The Agriculture and Rural Development Zones (ARDZ) program is the Government's approach to expanding commercial activities and increasing agricultural productivity. This is necessary to increasing incomes and employment opportunities in rural areas and to develop potential agro-based export potential.

The ARDZ recognizes that geographic priorities have to be set in support of the development of commercial agriculture. These geographic priorities will be used to target infrastructure, utilities and other support by various ministries. The Government will release publicly held land to increase private investment. Competitive bidding for the rights to lease these lands will be similar to the competitive bidding to lease development rights for mineral resources and the competitive bidding for the rights to use the telecommunications spectrum. Further, the Government will continue to investigate, implement and monitor key steps necessary to increasing financial and technical support so that private firms are able to expand operations. This will ensure the process of transforming underutilized state land into commercially viable agro-processing enterprises will be as fast and efficient as possible.

The Government's objective is to largely rely on private investment and public sector support to transform agriculture in some well defined zones where the conditions for growth are most favorable and high value added commercial agricultural activities can flourish.

This requires integrating and upgrading existing private and public sector networks and investing in essential infrastructure projects that shorten trade distances, reduce costs and increase productivity, encouraging entrepreneurs to expand private sector activity.

In implementing the ARDZ, the Government will:

- identify and map agricultural growth zones;
- quantify the necessary factors required for accelerated growth within each zone;
- identify key competitive product value chains and the connector firms that drive these value chains;
- develop plans to extend the reach of agricultural zones into more remote rural areas;
- ensure rural development activities are national in scope and linked to the agricultural growth zone plans; and
- mobilize private sector investment and operations as the key element in the success of the agricultural growth zone initiative.

To date, five distinct agricultural growth zones have been identified:

- a North Western Zone centered on the primary market town of Mazar-i-Sharif that includes ten secondary market towns and which is well positioned to take advantage of trade linkages with the Central Asian Republics;
- a North Eastern Zone centered on the primary market town of Kunduz that includes seven secondary market towns and which, with the new bridge at Shirkhan, is well positioned for trade with Tajikistan and, with good road connections to Urumqi, with China;
- a Central Zone centered on the primary market town of Kabul that includes thirteen secondary towns and which is linked with the important market center in Jalalabad and the regional market in Peshawar, Pakistan;
- a South Eastern Zone centered on the primary market town of Kandahar and which includes four secondary towns (one of which is the important agricultural production town in Lashkargah) and which is linked to the regional market in Quetta, Pakistan; and
- a Western Zone which is centered on the primary market town of Herat and which includes four secondary market towns and which has linkages to markets in and through Iran.

As part of the ARDZ, the Government has begun the process of establishing the Executive Management Unit with Presidential authority to coordinate and develop a five year action plan and organize the necessary funding and commitment from line Ministries and donors so as to establish a program implementation plan. This unit will ensure critical infrastructure, such as power, water, transportation links, telecommunications, financial services and vocational programs are available. The Unit will work with relevant Ministries to ensure priority is given to providing services in these zones. (See ANDS Volume Two for more details)

Expected Outcomes

The Agriculture and Rural Development expected outcomes are as follows:

- **Strengthened Local Governance**: Functioning formal and informal local governance, including social and economic activities implemented and maintained by communities that contribute to the human capital development and improved livelihoods. Improved management of local natural resources including clarifying the legal status of natural resources, roles of both communities and institutions in governance and management will help ensure food security, contribute to poverty alleviation and improve both ecological integrity and the natural resource base.
- **Poverty Reduction and Food Security**: The National Food Security Program (NFSP) will increase household food security and nutritional status while contributing to national food security and economic growth in rural areas.
- **Increased Agricultural Production and Productivity**: Public and private sector partnerships strengthen horticulture industry. Increased livestock production and productivity will improve food security and incomes that will lead to a reduction of illicit agriculture and a decline in livestock imports. Agriculture diversification through various value-added activities, research, extension, access to credit, market development, establishing/strengthening farmers' organization, private sector development, trainings, will improve the rural economy. (See ANDS Volume Two for more details)
- **Provision, and maintenance of Agriculture and Rural Infrastructure**: Successful crop production requires: technical irrigation management (e.g., availability of irrigation water supply, improving water efficiency and productivity, building effective and efficient irrigation and village based irrigation infrastructures, utilize modern irrigation technologies and human resource water management (e.g., organizing and strengthening mirabs, farmers associations, irrigation associations, decentralization of irrigation management at basin and sub- basin levels, water allocation. etc.).

Transport

Role of the Sector in ANDS

The ANDS strategic vision and goal for the transport sector is to have a safe, integrated transportation network that ensures connectivity and that enables low-cost and reliable movement of people and goods domestically as well as to and from foreign destinations. This will give impetus to economic growth and employment generation and help integrate Afghanistan into the global economy. A high priority is to have in place an efficient and viable road transportation network for achieving economic growth and poverty reduction, particularly in rural areas.

In the 1960s and 1970s, a large portion of the 'ring road' and connecting roads to neighboring countries were constructed. This network was subsequently largely destroyed during three decades of war and political strife. The Government has continued to give high priority to completing the rehabilitation and extension of this system over the past six years. Due to the significant impact of the road system on economic activity and the impact on poverty reduction, this will continue to be a high priority under the ANDS strategy.

The Transport Sector Strategy will achieve the following targets established in the Afghanistan Compact. (i) Roads: Afghanistan will have a fully upgraded and maintained ring road, as well as roads connecting the ring road to neighboring countries by end-2008 and a fiscally sustainable system for road maintenance; (ii) Air Transport: By end-2010, Kabul International Airport and Herat Airport will achieve full International Civil Aviation Organization compliance; Mazar-i-Sharif, Jalalabad and Kandahar will be upgraded with runway repairs, air navigation, fire and rescue and communications equipment; seven other domestic airports will be upgraded to facilitate domestic air transportation; and air transport services and costs will be increasingly competitive with international market standards and rates. (iii) Regional Cooperation: By end-2010 Afghanistan and its neighbors will achieve lower transit times through Afghanistan by means of cooperative border management and other multilateral or bilateral trade and transit agreements.

Current situation in the sector

Since 2001, significant achievements have been made in the transport sector as donors contributed over $3.3 billion to rebuilding the transport system between 2002 and 2007. Some of the main achievements include:

- An estimated 12,200 kilometers of roads have been rehabilitated, improved, or built including segments of the ring road system, national highways, provincial roads and rural roads.
- Kabul International Airport has been expanded and extensively rehabilitated.
- Four major airports (at Herat, Mazar-i-Sharif, Jalalabad, and Kandahar) as well as seven other regional airports are either slated for, or currently undergoing, extensive rehabilitation and expansion.
- In July 2007, trade and transit agreements with Uzbekistan and Turkmenistan were reached. A transit agreement is currently being drafted with Tajikistan. These agreements will help reduce transit time for shippers moving goods trans- nationally.
- The introduction of the automated customs and data systems (ASYCUDA) has been initiated which will reduce transit times and encourage promote trade, and aid in tracking customs collections.

Much remains to be done to expand and improve the transportation system. Road, air and rail links all require significant investment. Some of the most pressing needs include:

- A system for road maintenance and rehabilitation urgently needs to be put into place and made operational. Roads that have been reconstructed will begin to deteriorate unless maintenance is done in a systematic way.
- Approximately 85 percent of the total 130,000 km road network (some 43,000 km of national, regional, urban and provincial roads and an estimated 87,000 km of rural roads) is significantly degraded, with a major portion not passable by motor vehicles. Most bridges and culverts are in bad condition and at risk of collapse.
- A limited number of airports are available for commercial use and all are in need of infrastructure improvements. None of the civil air services meet the international standards and practices required by the International Civil Aviation Organization (ICAO) and the International Air Transport Association (IATA). While there has been private entry into the civil aviation sector and regional connections have expanded, much must still be done to create a truly 'open skies' regulatory framework that both encourages new entry but maintains international standards for safety.
- The country has no internal rail links, but relies on rail heads in neighboring countries for trade. The railhead transfer stations are inefficient, increasing the costs of rail transportation. Mines cannot be developed and potential resources cannot be explored and utilized without having a railway links to the neighboring/regional countries.
- Transport sector ministries and institutions are weak in the human capacity and organization to carry out budgeting; procurement and contract administration; and adequate management of transport-related assets. The institutions lack the necessary regulatory and enforcement frameworks and personnel management systems. There are overlapping ministerial responsibilities in the sector. There is a lack of coordination and communication within the transport sector governance institutions and with other sectors. For detail refer to ANDS Volume II.

The Transport Sector Strategy incorporates feedback, proposed projects and comments which emerged from the Sub-National Consultations process. The construction of roads was among the top five most prioritized sectors in the PDPs. In areas such as Badakhshan, Bamyan, Ghor and Sari Pul, road construction was listed as the number one priority.

Policy framework: sector strategy

The Government continues to give high priority to rehabilitate a badly damaged road system. This includes: (i) completion of a fully upgraded and maintained ring road and connector roads to neighboring countries, (ii) improving 5,334 km of secondary (national, urban and provincial) roads and (iii) improving and building 6,290 km of rural access roads as a key to raising rural livelihoods and reducing poverty and vulnerability in rural areas.[49] Better rural roads will improve market access and opportunities for rural households. The actual allocation of resources amongst these three areas of planned activity will depend on the estimated rates of return from analysis of concrete proposals put forward for funding by the international community or by the Ministries involved in implementing the Transport sector strategies. A Transport Sector Inter-Ministerial Working Group has been formed to coordinate the work of the ministries in the sector to assure that projects are properly designed to obtain the highest returns and greatest impact on the poverty reduction goals. Careful consideration will be given to increasing employment opportunities, and assuring that the local resources or funds channeled through local communities are effectively used to maintain the rural roads established as part of this strategy. The main programs of the strategy are (i) Regional, National Highways and Provincial Roads (ii) Rural Road (iii) Urban Transport (iv) Civil Aviation (v) Transport Sector Maintenance (vi) Pubic Transport (vii) Railway Program. (For further details refer to ANDS Volume II.)

In addition to the above work on the road transportation system, there are many areas that need to be addressed to both increase returns from an improved network but also to improve other aspects of the total transportation system. These include:

- **Transportation Services and Trade Facilitation**: Improved transportation services, customs, and logistics management will require new investment and coordinated multilateral efforts, including work with the Economic Cooperation Trade Agreement (ECOTA), the Central Asian Region Economic Cooperation (CAREC), and the Shanghai Cooperation Organization. The Government will undertake feasibility studies to assess the economic viability of railway development within Afghanistan and links with neighboring countries.
- **Air transport links**: The Government gives high priority to the development of a new airport in Kabul. In addition, the Government will implement programs to ensure that the principal airports and the civil aviation authorities conform to the requirements of the ICAO and IATA, including establishing a new Civil Aviation Authority to promote air transport in a competitive environment. A regulatory framework will be introduced to encourage private investment under an 'open skies' policy.
- **Regional Transportation and Transit**: Regional transportation investments will be coordinated by the Inter-ministerial Working Group for Transport to assure that investments are designed in such a way as to best serve the development goals of Afghanistan. Relevant investments include the rail links that will be constructed under the agreement for developing the Aynak copper fields in Logar province and the energy transmission lines developed under transit arrangements.
- **Urban Road Networks**: Under the urban sector strategy, much greater authority and responsibility is being given to municipalities. The development of the national and regional road networks will be coordinated with municipal authorities with responsibilities for the urban road networks. Municipal transportation management will be strengthened to improve urban road quality, road network maintenance, road network planning, and transportation facilities and services.
- **Railways**: The Government will pursue the Afghanistan Railway Project which will include 1,824 km rail links to connect Kabul, in the East with Islam Qala in the West through Kandahar and Hirat. The Government will also undertake feasibility studies to assess the economic viability of railway links with neighboring countries.
- **Aviation:** The Government will seek investment in a new international airport in the Kabul area to provide Afghanistan with a modern international airport and implement programs to ensure that the principal airports and the civil aviation authorities conform to the requirements of the ICAO and IATA, including establishing a new Civil Aviation Authority to promote air transport in a competitive

environment. A regulatory framework will be introduced to encourage private sector investment under an 'open skies' policy.
- **Interaction with vulnerable groups**: Use an integrated participatory regional development approach in rural areas, combining improved roads with agriculture, water, education, health, and counter-narcotics initiatives so that the poor derive the benefit from roads. Undertake transport development through investments in secondary and rural roads to significantly increase provincial and village access to the national road system.

Expected Outcomes

The key expected outcomes of the transport sector strategy are:

- An efficient and safe road transportation system, through:
  - improved connectivity throughout Afghanistan;
  - lower road user costs;
  - improved business environment for private sector development, creating jobs and reducing poverty;
  - lower accident and fatality rates, measured by personal injuries per million vehicle kilometers; and
  - reduced journey times due to congestion.

- A viable civil aviation sector that provides efficient access to the country and region:
  - increased domestic and international passengers and freight traffic;
  - improved stakeholder information on the viability of air transport systems;
  - improved governance within the civil aviation sector; and
  - overall improvement in urban air quality from reduced congestion, better fuel quality and improved fuel efficiency. (For more detailed information refer to Appendixes 3, National Action Plan and 4, Monitoring Matrix.) Information and Communication Technology

Information and Communications Technology

Role of the Sector in ANDS

The ANDS strategic vision and goal for the Information and Communication Technology (ICT) sector is to make affordable communication services available in every district and village of Afghanistan through an improved enabling environment for private sector investment. ICT will contribute to the Government's efforts for a broad-based reconstruction effort. A modern telecommunications sector, incorporating e-government initiatives will enhance the effectiveness, efficiency and transparency of the public sector and the provision of social services. All Afghans, men and women alike, will in time be able to access ICT to access information and social services, foster the rebuilding process, increase employment, create a vibrant private sector, reduce poverty and support underprivileged groups.

ICT provides an opportunity to bridge the communications gap that exists within the country. Women in particular face movement restrictions due to security concerns and local traditions. To establish greater national unity, it is important that all 365 districts, major villages and rural areas should be able to communicate with Kabul, with each other, and with the rest of the world. ICT is a basic enabler of informal social and economic discourse necessary in the strengthening of civil society and the promotion of economic activity (e.g. access to markets and pricing). Despite its importance, there are no explicit AC benchmarks or MDG goals for this sector. The ICT Sector Strategy will achieve the following targets established in the I-ANDS: By end-2010, a national telecommunications network to be put in place so that more than 80 percent of Afghans will have access to affordable telecommunications; and more than $100 million dollars per year will be generated in public revenues.

Current Situation in the Sector
In early 2003, Afghanistan had fewer than 15,000 functioning telephone lines – a telephone penetration rate of 0.06 percent, among the lowest in the world. In addition to a shortage of basic telephone switching capacity, the local transmission network delivering last mile services, presented an even more difficult bottleneck. The cabling conduit, trunk cables and copper wires were old or completely destroyed. Afghanistan did not have a functioning long distance network to provide national or international connectivity. The absence of transmission and switching facilities meant that citizens could only complete calls within their own cities and were unable to reach any other parts of the country or the outside world.

The Government adopted major policy reforms for the ICT sector in October 2002, which was immediately posted to one of the first government websites. This initial broad policy statement was further refined and divided into two separate policies – one for basic telecom infrastructure and regulatory principles, and a second for ICT applications and a vision for the Information Society. These policies have remained the basis for the reforms over the last five years. The basic principles have been given a statutory basis, in the form of the Telecom Law that was promulgated in December 2005. The telecom infrastructure aspects are being implemented by ATRA, which was established in June 2006. The ICT applications aspects are being implemented via the ICT Council, which was established in May 2007.

The transparent approach taken to the adoption of the policies and the consistency of the vision from design to implementation has produced rapid results. The fact that most of the existing infrastructure was either antiquated or broken meant that the industry was free to essentially start again with a clean slate. In 2003, the obvious choice for personal communications was wireless. Accepted global standards meant that the equipment was reliable, cheap and could be deployed rapidly. In July 2003, two nationwide mobile (GSM) networks began operation, following an international competitive tender. The licenses required commercial service to be offered in Kabul within six months of the effective date, with nationwide service within 18 months. Pursuant to the original Telecom Policy, these first two licenses also were provided a legal duopoly for three years. In October 2005 and May 2006, two additional nationwide mobile (GSM) licenses were awarded, with identical terms and conditions. There was immediate strong demand for mobile services, with over 5 million Afghans now having access.

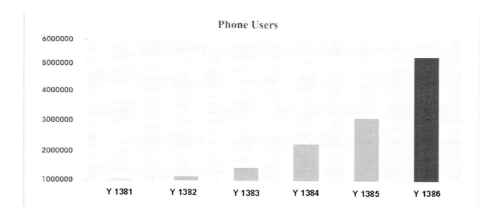

Figure 7.2. Growth in phone use.

The 2003 ICT sector strategy has been the reference template for subsequent reform policies, procedures and activities. The Telecom Law was promulgated by President Karzai on 18th December 2005. The law is compliant with the World Trade Organization Basic Telecom Agreement framework requirements in that it separates the three basic functions and assigns responsibilities to three independent sector elements, as follows (i) Policy – MoCIT; (ii) regulation – ATRA; and (iii) operations – Licensed Service Providers. The Telecom Law has led to the establishment of the independent sector regulator, ATRA. The legal authority of ATRA rests with its five member board appointed by the President.

Despite the considerable progress in expanding the use of mobile phones, much more needs to be done to take advantage of the telecommunications revolution in both the private and public sectors. Impediments to the growth of ICT sector include:

- Lack of Security represents an impediment to construction and maintenance of ICT infrastructure in remote areas. Lack of clear property rights adds to construction times.
- Government bureaucracy (length of time for simple decisions) adds time and costs to development and operation of the system.
- Lack of electricity and high cost of diesel fuel for generators raises construction and maintenance costs.
- The high level of illiteracy reduces the immediate impact of many internet applications, especially limiting the access of women to internet services.
- The numbers and skills within ICT work force is a constraint to the adoption and promotion of ICT.
- The limited awareness and acceptance of ICT within Government leadership

Policy Framework: Sector Strategy

The immediate goal of the sector is to increase access to telecom services to cover 80 percent of the country. Most populated areas will be covered by 2010. A key component of this effort will be the completion of the Fibre Optic Cable and Copper Cable Network, allowing an expansion of high-speed data services and extending mobile phone coverage. The private- sector is expected to make additional major investments in the telecommunication sector. With the establishment of a national data center by end of 2008, and implementation of e- Government, e-Commerce, e-Health (telemedicine) towards the end of 2010 Afghan citizens will be able to more fully participate in the information age. For the next five years, MoCIT policies, working through ATRA will also deploy satellite-based services to the less populated areas where personal mobile facilities are too costly. The current program is to reach at least 3,000 villages by 2010. Plans are also underway to issue new licenses for the provision of fixed wireless access for broadband internet.

There will be a $100 million revenue contribution to Government revenue by 2010. The ICT sector is already the most heavily taxed, primarily because it is comprised of the largest formal enterprises in the country. A major study is currently being prepared that will provide guidance to the ICT Council, and the Government on improving governance and increasing public sector capacity for the industry.

The key programs of the ICT sector are (i) Enabling Environment (ii) Infrastructure Development (iii) E-Afghanistan (iv) ICT Literacy. For detail refer to volume II. In addition to the investment in the cable network, the policy priority for the Government is the passage and implementation of ICT legislation that will create an appropriate environment for further growth and development. MoCIT has commenced drafting the ICT Law, which will address infrastructure and services, including issues such as legal recognition of electronic/digital signatures and formation of electronic contracts (affecting transactions both in public and private sectors), content regulation, competition regulation, electronic evidence, data privacy protection, consumer protection and rights, domain name registration and regulation, intellectual property rights, encryption and security, financial and banking sector law and regulation relating to electronic transfers and settlements, taxation of transfers, customs, jurisdiction, dispute resolution and civil and criminal offences, limitations of liability of internet service providers, cyber piracy and digital rights management, facilitation of e-government and cross border interoperability of e-commerce frameworks affecting trade.

The sector priority policy is passage and implementation of ICT legislation that will create an appropriate environment for further development. MoCIT has commenced drafting the ICT Law. The telecom law addresses the telecom infrastructure and services, but the law doesn't cover the content of the services. The ICT law will address issues such as legal recognition of electronic/digital signatures and formation of electronic contracts (affecting transactions both in public and private sectors), content regulation, competition regulation, electronic evidence, data privacy protection, consumer protection and rights, domain name registration and regulation, intellectual property rights, encryption and security, financial and banking sector law and regulation relating to electronic transfers and settlements, taxation of transfers, customs, jurisdiction, dispute resolution and civil and criminal offences, limitations of liability of internet service providers, cyber piracy and digital rights management, facilitation of e-government and cross border interoperability of e-commerce frameworks affecting trade.

The ICT Council, through the MoCIT, will work to achieve the following:

- By end-2008, actions designed to promote transparency and citizen access to public information will be implemented. This will include adopting Rules and Procedures to require all Government institutions to publish documents on their official websites (as a supplement to the Official Gazette). Actions designed to promote Government efficiency, reduce costly waste and ensure information system inter-operability will be implemented. This will involve adopting a full set of Rules and Procedures that will govern the competitive procurement and utilization of ICT by all Government institutions. An e-Government resource center will be established for the design and implementation of projects. MoCIT will promote private investment for Afghan Telecom to reduce the financial burden on the Government, and adopt the legal instruments for private investment in the sector. Afghan Post offices will be modernized using ICT to ensure reliable collection and distribution of mail. The infrastructure of mobile networks will be adapted to enable mobile commerce, meaning the use of phones to transfer funds and conduct other financial transactions (pay utility bills and taxes, make retail purchases). MoCIT will submit draft ICT legislation governing e- transactions, electronic commerce, electronic signatures and cyber crimes to the National Assembly. The Afghanistan National Data Center will be ready to host the e-government applications.

- A unified curriculum and regulatory framework for private ICT training centers will be drafted in cooperation with Ministry of Education. MoCIT will have established an IT Training center in all provincial capitals where security permits.
- By end-2009, further efforts will be made to reduce corruption by reviewing all Government services and making recommendations for the adoption of ICT to streamline and automate (for example, customs processing, procurement and licensing).
- An ICT Village will be established in Kabul, this facility will attract foreign and local investments in ICT. Efforts will be made to ensure that all schools have access to internet and multimedia resources, together with a basic curriculum that includes browsing, searching and messaging.
- By end-2010, the ICT sector will contribute five billion Afs ($100 million) annually to the treasury by broadening the tax base (attracting additional investors to the market, rather than over-burdening the existing ones). ATRA will foster a transparent legal-regulatory regime that attracts a further 37.5 billion Afs ($750 million) in private investment, and adds 50,000 jobs.
- National ICT networks will be expanded and interconnected so that at least 80 percent of Afghans will have access to affordable telecom services.
- By end-2018, all pupils should be digitally literate by the time they leave school. Digital literacy will be adopted as one of the basic skills of all young Afghans.

The ICT sector strategy incorporates feedback, proposed projects and comments from the Sub National Consultations. The ministry actively utilized its video conferencing capabilities to reach out to all 34 provincial capitals and many of the 240 district capitals that are presently served by the District Communications Network (DCN) infrastructure. MoCIT has also worked with National Assembly to reach all communities. The Ministry has furthermore conducted planning sessions by bringing together representatives from all 34 provinces for workshops in Kabul. ATRA is in the process of instituting greater responsiveness to the needs of remote communities, by making available financial support from the Telecom Development Fund (TDF) upon request from community leaders.

Policy framework: key initiatives and issues

The MoCIT is responsible for providing the institutional leadership for the ICT sector. It has the primary responsibility for developing policy and supervises the implementation of a number of key ICT projects, such as the National Data Center, the Optical Fiber Cable and the Copper Cable Network projects.

Afghan Telecom is presently a corporation that is 100 percent owned by MoCIT however it is being privatized (an 80 percent share is to be sold), reflecting the Government's 2003 Telecom and Internet Policy. This will lead to the further expansion of the mobile phone network.

The Ministry's Information Communication Technology Institute (ICTI) provides specialized technical training and certification has launched a four year ICT bachelors program (the first class of 50 students have recently commenced studies). Since 2003, it is also in the process of considering a transformation to public-private partnership in order to ensure that its curriculum meets the needs of the private sector (which has a huge demand for properly skilled workers).

The ICT Council is the primary forum for all stakeholders in the ICT sector. It consists of all of government institutions that have ICT activities and is open to all other institutions as they acquire ICT infrastructure and applications. The ICT Council is chaired by the First Vice President and its total membership is fully inclusive of all interested parties, including the private sector, civil society organizations, and academia. The National Assembly has become an important institutional player in the ICT sector, both in terms of policy and utilization.

The role of the private sector is central to this strategy. A modern telecommunications sector, incorporating e-government initiatives wherever possible, will enhance the effectiveness and efficiency of the public sector. By mobilizing resources to build up the ICT sector within the public sector institutions, MoCIT will also be accelerating the development of ICT support capabilities of the private sector in Afghanistan, both through contracts and via participation in the policy processes of the ICT Council.

The ICT sector is Afghanistan's biggest success story in terms of attracting private sector investment, $925 million as of the end of 2007. This is expected to reach $1.5 billion by end 2010. According to numerous studies this is by far the largest investment in the licit economy.

Expected Outcomes

The key expected outcomes in the Information and Communications Technology sector are;

- Improved Enabling Environment
- Improved Infrastructure with Fiber Optic and Copper.
- E-Afghanistan created
- ICT Literacy improved

It is expected there will be wide community acceptance of ICT facilities. Access to facilities will be expanded. Government administration will be predictable and unbiased, in accord with all legislation. The role of the private sector will be increased. ICT access will be generally available in education institutions, including many primary and secondary schools.

For detail information regarding outcomes refer to action plan and M&E matrices. For detail information refer to Appendixes 3-National Action Plan and 4-Monitoring Matrix.

Urban Development

Role of the Sector in ANDS

The ANDS strategic vision and goal for urban development sector is to ensure increased access to improved services, and affordable shelter while promoting sustainable economic development as part of efforts to reduce urban poverty through encouragement of private investment. The urban areas in the country will become hubs for economic growth with all basic infrastructure and services. The management of urban areas will be improved through the devolution of authority and responsibility to municipalities in ways that improve urban infrastructure and services, reduce urban poverty and allow urban residents to live safe, healthy and productive lives and cities to grow and prosper. Effective management of the rapid urbanization process will make a significant contribution to the recovery of the country. Cities contribute to economic growth through their high productivity as a result of economies of scale and agglomeration, and by providing opportunities for the accumulation of capital, investment, trade and production. Urban investments create employment opportunities and urban jobs account for a disproportionate share of GDP. Urban growth can stimulate rural development through increase demand for food, markets for rural products, off-season employment for farmers, and remittances and provide opportunities to move goods and services in the region. However, cities are often linked to increased violence, crime and insecurity. Improving the urban environment, the supply of urban services, providing employment opportunities, utilizing the potential resources and improving the livelihoods of the population will lead to improvements in security.

The importance of effective management of the urban development process has been recognized in the Afghanistan Compact benchmarks:

- Urban Development: By the end of 2010; Municipal Governments will have strengthened capacity to manage urban development and to ensure that municipal services are delivered effectively, efficiently and transparently; in line with MDG investments in water supply and sanitation will have ensured that 50 percent of households in Kabul and 30 percent of households in other major urban areas will have access to piped water.
- Energy: By end-2010: electricity will reach at least 65 percent of households and 90 percent of non-residential establishments in major urban areas, at least 75 percent of the costs will be recovered from users connected to the national power grid.

The Millennium Development Goals most relevant to the urban sector development include:

- Goal 7: By 2020 halve the proportion without access to safe drinking water and sanitation. Significantly improve the lives of all slum-dwellers by 2020. Sustainable development to reverse the loss of environmental resources

Current situation in the sector

Achievements: While investments in the urban sector continue to lag far behind actual needs across the country, there have been some achievements. The most important are as follows:

- Water supply and sanitation: 2 million urban residents (31 percent of the total urban population) have benefited from investments in water supply and 12 percent from investment in sanitation in major cities between 2002 and 2007.
- Up to 1.4 million people (20 percent of urban population) have benefited from rehabilitation of public works, with 250,000 (4 percent) benefiting from upgrading programs
- In addition to legislative reforms, a pilot land tenure security project is underway in Kabul
- The Dehsabz City Development Authority has been established to facilitate the development of new city housing for up to 3 million people north of Kabul. Additionally, new small settlements (satellite townships) have been planned for 1 million people.
- Regional and city planning: strategic development plans are being prepared for 7 regional cities, while a city development plan for three major cities (Mazar, Jalalalabad, Kabul) and existing-Kabul plan is due for completion by mid 2008.
- Urban policy: initiatives include a comprehensive National Urban Program (NUP), a draft National Land Policy was submitted in 2007 for approval to the Ministry of Justice. And a draft of national building codes for construction has been developed.
- Institutional reforms within MoUD, KM & IDLG (established in 2007) continue, along with investments in strengthening institutional capacity.
- Almost 5 percent of vulnerable families has been provided improved shelter in major cities. Private sector so far has made little contribution to the development of housing sector.
- Three conservation initiatives are under way in historic quarters of Kabul, Herat and Tashqurghan.
- The Afghan Urban Water Supply and Sanitation Corporation has been established as a quasi independent public entity.

As of 2005 nearly a quarter of Afghanistan's population lived in urban areas. By 2015 it is estimated that almost a third of Afghans will be living in urban areas. Current needs include:

- Urban Poverty: In 2002, one fifth of the urban population was living below the poverty line. The NRVA (2005) study found that 28 percent of urban households perceive themselves to be food insecure, 31 percent fall below the minimum level of dietary energy consumption, 45 percent borrow money to purchase food, and 48 percent sometimes have problems satisfying their food needs. It is estimated that 4.95 million people inhabited informal settlements in 2006, suggesting that 68.5 percent of the urban population is living without security of tenure.

- Water and Sanitary Conditions: In 2005, about 20-22 percent of urban households had access to safe drinking water, although the percentage varies significantly between urban areas. The country's total sanitation coverage is only 8 percent, (16 percent urban and 5 percent rural as of 2002). Few places in the world face such scarce and alarming water supply and sanitation coverage levels. The percentage of urban households using: (i) traditional covered latrines and (ii) improved latrines, and (iii) flush toilets are about 67 percent and 15 percent, and 9 percent, respectively. In Kabul city, 14 percent use a flush latrine, 2 percent are covered by a sewerage system.
- Roads: About 61 percent of urban dwellers access homes through unpaved roads and about 25 percent through footpaths, including in Kabul.

There are a number of challenges and constraints facing the Sector:

- Low coverage of basic services and inadequate public resources to meet growing needs
- A rapid pace of urbanization partly due to returning refugees and rural-urban migrants, leading to high population density
- Widespread urban poverty and limited access to productive employment
- A high proportion of informal settlements and associated problems
- Lack of capacity and coordination among urban sector institutions
- Limited scale of private sector investment in urban enterprises, facilities or services
- Lack of accurate data on which to base critical policy decisions
- Land security and titling: Absence of proper land registration system, Land grabbing, inadequate legal instruments and institutions
- Lack of available financial funds due to limited interest of donors in the urban sector.

The Urban Sector Strategy incorporates feedback, proposed projects and comments from the Sub National Consultations (SNCs) and is a response to the people's needs and development goals. Key urban infrastructure needs emerged from City Development Pland (CDPs) and PDPs-related consultations as well as CAP (City Action Plans based on the city profiles report) have been integrated into the strategy, reflecting the range of sub-national development needs

Key components of the urban sector strategy

The objective is to ensure increased access to improved basic infrastructure and services, and affordable shelter while promoting sustainable economic growth. The key to the urban sector development strategy is a national urban policy that decentralizes decision making to the local level, encourages participatory processes based on urban community councils or other neighborhood organizations, adopts a market based approach that encourages private sector activity and that establishes a regulatory framework focused narrowly on environmental protection and the rationalization of land use. The main programs of the sector strategy are (i) Urban Governance, Finance and Management (ii) Land Development & Housing (iii) Urban Infrastructure & Services (for details of program refer to volume II).

Urban Governance: The Ministry and Municipalities will be restructured and jointly work to prepare city action strategies and structure plans for Kabul and the 34 major urban areas, with special attention to local area plans for selected, fast growing areas, strengthen urban and municipal governance, finance and management. This involves establishing an enabling environment where stakeholders participate in municipal elections and residents can have a say in policy formulation and the design of implementation activities. This will be done through democratically elected Community Development Councils (CDC) at the neighborhood level, comprising clusters of households, and Area Development Councils (ADC) at the sub-urban district level.

Finance and Management: Steps will be taken to increase revenue generation capacity and improve management by upgrading accounting and budgetary practices and linking the capital budget to the planning process. Review existing revenue base and assets and develop action plans for revenue improvement plans to include widening revenue base, improved collection rates, user charges, cofinancing or co-production with users, property or sales taxes, intergovernmental transfers, municipal borrowing, mobilization of local government resources through loan guarantees. Develop mechanisms to increase local revenues to finance part of the costs of improved urban service. Promote public partnerships with the private sector and NGOs to more efficiently provide urban services or meet urban needs. The draft Public Finance and Expenditure Management Law will be enacted.

Urban Development and Land Management: The Government will prepare a national spatial development plan. The plan will provide (i) a framework for balanced urbanization, urban-rural links, and greater regional coherence; (ii) a town planning policy, processes, laws, standards, and guidelines as well as development regulations; (iii) effective land management and information systems and a national settlements plan will be put in place; (iv) improve tenure security gradually through improving infrastructure and services; (v) clarify property rights, providing temporary certificates, addressing environmental and planning concerns; (vi) land management laws will be passed with the objective of preventing unlawful occupation of government and private land for economic (and political) gains; facilitating land registration and adjudication; and enabling government acquisition of private land for public purposes; (vii) improve land management through steps to register land titles; (viii) develop a system for settlement of land disputes; (ix) develop a computerized (GIS) land management system; (x) cadastral surveys and reconciliation of cadastre with actual conditions; (xi) linkage of cadastre to a municipal property tax system and with the land registration data; (xii) linkage to a planning and development control system; (xiii) create new serviced and un-serviced land in connection with new urban plans that identify real demand for serviced land at specific locations within individual towns and cities and in all urban areas.

Standards of servicing will be based on affordability of target groups. Priority will be given to sites and service schemes, an approach that has proven effective in many countries. The strengths of these schemes are that they can: cater to various household affordability levels and needs through various planning, servicing and technical standards; provide basic infrastructure and services relatively efficiently; permit progressive development through provision of a sanitary core (known as an "embryo" housing unit). Sectoral agencies will consider other options for providing developable land including: land-sharing, land readjustment, land pooling, and infill development.

Land security will be improved through mapping and land surveying of communities, tenure formalization, and land registration. If informal settlements are recognized and provided with tenure security, they are more willing to invest their own financial and other resources in improving the community and their houses. Moreover, they can use the title as collateral. Security of tenure may include formal and informal arrangements, from full land title to customary rights. Although the tenure legalization approach is popular, it is also possible to regularize without any policy intervention to legalize tenure. The regularization strategy focuses on physical interventions, such as infrastructure, amenities provision, and health and education services.

The Government, through the Dehsabz City Development Authority, will continue to examine the potential for the development of a new city on the Dehsabz plain north of the existing Kabul City. As part of the Dehsabz project, the Barikab area located to the north of the new city will become a private commercial agricultural zone designed to not only supply many of the needs of Dehsabz, but to become a center for the cultivation of exportable agricultural products. The development of this urban center will be undertaken primarily by the private sector. The extent of the Government's direct role will generally be limited to planning, investment in some of the basic urban infrastructure and facilitating private commercial investment. This project will be largely financially self-sustainable and become a center for new investment in private agro-based and service industries. Most of the land in Dehsabz belongs to the Government hence, the sale and lease of land will generate revenues needed for investment in the new city and for the pressing reconstruction and infrastructure development needs of Kabul.

Housing: New housing will be produced and improved through: (i) public sector housing production (ii) support to informal and small scale housing producers – the 'peoples housing process'; (iii) support to research and development of appropriate building materials and technologies; (iv) upgrading the skills of contractors and laborers; (v) supporting entrepreneurs to upgrade or set up building components manufacturing units; (vi) support to private sector production, particularly of rental housing.

Housing programs will consider the particular needs of various groups such as civil servants, returnees, Kuchis, IDPs, widows and other vulnerable groups. Housing finance will be provide – for purchase, rehabilitation, and construction of new housing – through: integrating housing finance; stimulating private banks to increase mortgage lending to low-income households, through, for example, mortgage guarantees; initiating community mortgage schemes; lowering mortgage interest rates; reducing collateral and down payment requirements; introducing flexible repayment schemes. This will enhance purchasing power of urban inhabitants and attract private investment in housing programs. This will lead to a system of affordable land and housing and assured cost recovery for the investors.

Housing subsidy programs will be provided for very low income households, including both owners and renters. The following options will be examined: direct loans to purchase an existing or construct a new house; government guarantees of loans made by private sector lenders, thus enabling households to purchase houses without a down payment; mutual self-help housing programs which makes homes affordable to groups of households by valuing to work, or "sweat equity", by each homeowner; portable rent subsidies that give eligible households a choice about where to live, including market rate rentals subsidies directly to the property owner who then applies the subsidies to the rents that are charged to low-income tenants.

Urban Infrastructure and Services: A concerted effort will be made to improve infrastructure including roads, footpaths, storm drainage, water supply, electricity, street lights, sanitation, and solid waste collection. Social infrastructure will be improved, including open space, children's' parks, community and health centers, schools, and markets. Support will be provided to house construction and rehabilitation, but only in line with an approved plan and with careful consideration given to levels of cost recovery. Steps will be taken to rehabilitate and extend water supply and sanitation services, giving priority to rehabilitating existing areas to an adequate level of service before extending service to new areas. Extensions to new areas will be done in connection with an approved plan for new settlement development. Improve solid waste management through waste minimization (reduce, reuse, and recycle) and improved collection, transport and transfer, and disposal alternatives. Consideration will be given to privatization, community management, affordability and cost recovery. Improve urban transportation management through improvements to circulation and road networks, transportation facilities and services by function, type, capacity, and condition, bus system, bicycles and pedestrians, transportation demand management including on- and off-street parking system management.

The most significant heritage areas will be identified and a detailed inventory of heritage assets will be undertaken. This will be done in coordination with NGOs already working on the preservation of heritage areas. Conservation plans for each heritage area (rehabilitation and preservation) will be developed and implemented through efforts to raise public awareness, economic incentives to private owners, tourism development, legal protection, public investment, and outreach to international bodies.

Key steps to improve and monitor progress with urban development will include the identification of indicators on which strategic, tactical, and operational decisions will be based; the establishment of GIS and databases to manage information; and the improvement of analytical routines and creation of the creation of web- based information systems. The priority focus will be on the establishment of land information and registration systems in municipalities.

Expected Outcomes

The following outcomes are expected to be achieved in this Urban Sector Strategy in coming five years:

- Strengthened municipal capacity to manage urban development and deliver services.
- Improved institutional coordination and monitoring of key urban indicators
- Increased access to basic services for urban households[50]:
  - Kabul: 50 percent of households with piped water, sanitation, drainage and waste collection; 30 percent coverage for programs of hygiene promotion
  - 30 provincial towns/cities: 30 percent of households with piped water, sanitation, drainage and waste collection; 10 percent coverage of hygiene promotion programs.

- Phased regularization of tenure for 50 percent of households in informal settlements, in parallel with upgrading of public services and facilities, as well as new urban area development.
- Increased availability of affordable shelter, with 50 percent increase in numbers of housing units and 30 percent increase in area of serviced land on the market, coupled with access to affordable finance.
- Improved urban environment with green areas and open spaces.

For detail information, refer to Appendix 3- National Action Plan and 4-Monitoring Matrix.

Mining

Role of the Sector in ANDS

The ANDS strategic vision and goal of the mining sector is to establish Afghanistan as an attractive destination for investment in survey, exploration and development of mineral resources. The intention is to encourage legitimate private investment in the sector so as to substantially increase government revenues, improve employment opportunities and foster ancillary development centered on mining activity. Implementation of the strategy will help to develop effective market-based economic policies, promote and regulate sustainable development of minerals and ensure that the nation's geological resources are progressively investigated and properly documented. This strategy supports large and small scale mining for immediate and sustainable economic gains. For mining and minerals, the emphasis is on the exploration, extraction and delivery to market; for hydrocarbons the emphasis is exploration and exploitation.

Experience during the period 1987 to 2000 has demonstrated that if governments address issues such as: up-dating the mineral policy and strategy; amending the mining legislation (particularly in respect of mining rights); up-dating the mining taxation regime; reinforcing government supervisory institutions; building greater capacity (including good governance) within institutions; and developing a reliable and comprehensive scientific database; the country can attract significant amounts of investment in this sector. Employment and benefits from opportunities for skill improvement will be substantial. Most mining related activity is expected to occur in isolated areas where unemployment is high. In addition, the large contribution that the mining sector will make to government revenues will increase the availability of social services, such as education and health services, which will contribute to increased security and stability.

The Afghanistan Compact Benchmark calls for an enabling regulatory environment for profitable extraction of Afghanistan's mineral and natural resources to be created and for the investment environment and infrastructure to be enhanced so as to attract significant domestic and foreign direct investment by end 2010.

Table 7.3. Mining sector reform and its effect on economic growth

	Exploration (US$m)		Production (US$m)		Exports (US$m)	
Country	Before Reform	After Reform	Before Reform	After Reform	Before Reform	After Reform
Argentina	<3	150	340	1,310	70	700
Chile	15	250	2,400	7,500	2,300	6,900
Peru	10	200	2,000	3,900	1,900	3,600
Tanzania	<1	35	53	350	53	350

Current Situation

While geological studies of Afghanistan have been conducted over the last 50 years, 90 percent of the territory of Afghanistan has not been systematically studied despite highly promising findings. A geological map of Afghanistan has been prepared and over 400 mineral deposits have been identified including copper, coal and a number of small and medium deposits including gold, silver, platinum, zinc, nickel, emerald, lapis, ruby, kuznite, tourmaline, fluorite, chromite, salt, radioactive elements and numerous deposits suitable for construction materials.

The availability of oil and gas fields in Afghanistan has been well known for almost 50 years. Russian equipment was used to explore the first fields. Subsequently, gas fields in Yateem Taq, Khwaja Gogerdak, Khwaja Bolan, Zigdeli and Bayan of Ghor province as well as outskirts of Sheberghan district of Jowzjan province have been identified. Afghan and Russian experts identified a total of 500 structures of which 67 were extended with exploratory approaches. Known gas reserves have a capacity of 180 billion cubic meters and an exploitation capacity of 120 billion cubic meters. Sar-e-pul oil reserves have been identified (44.5) million tons with the extractable reserves of 14.5 million metric tons. During the past few years, five oil and gas fields have been identified. More work has been carried out in the vicinity of Amu Darya, and Afghan-Tajik basins.

The first major investment has recently been announced for developing the Aynak copper deposits in central Logar province, an almost $3 billion investment. The selection of the company was made after an extensive evaluation of tenders from nine major international mining companies. There will be important indirect benefits from this investment. The company will establish a power station with 400 mega watt capacity at a cost of over $400 million and will construct a town for the workers of the company. The company will also establish a railway route from Hairatan port in northern Afghanistan to Torkham in eastern Afghanistan. Ongoing and planned activities include the: (i) fertilizer and power plants at Balkh with capacity of 110,000 tons of urea each year, and 48 mega watt power per hour; (ii) Ghori cement factory with capacity of 100,000 tons per year; (iii) Jabal Seraj cement factory with maximum capacity of 30,000 tons per year; and (iv) Herat cement factory and Ghori 2 with capacity reaching 200,000 annually.

In July 2005 a Minerals Law was approved by the Government. In December 2005, a Hydrocarbons Law was also approved. Regulations are being drafted which may be finalized during 2008.

Some of the most immediate needs of the sector are being addressed as part of a $30 million project supporting sustainable development of natural resources. The main purpose of this project is to assist the Ministry of Mines to improve its capacity to effectively transform the sector so that it is primarily operated by the private sector and contributes to sustainable economic growth through tax revenues, employment, rural development and economic spin-offs. The major institutional strengthening objective of the project will be to assist MoM to make the transition from a producer of minerals and other commodities to a policy making institution that will facilitate the operation of private firms within the industry. It will also strengthen financial and budgetary procedures in the ministry, assist with the internal geological survey work being done, assist in identifying unlicensed mining operations, and attempt to enforce improved and safer work mining work practices.

The landlocked nature of Afghanistan and the current lack of rail links represent a barrier to the movement of large bulk commodities. Security difficulties limit mining in some areas, principally in the south. Roads, energy and water are all lacking. The danger of unexploded ordnance makes mining difficult. There is a shortage of trained labor. Most of the state-owned mining enterprises are not operating on a commercial basis. The North Coal Enterprise has been privatized and is operating successfully while Mineral Exploitation Enterprise and Afghan Gas are about to be privatized.

This Sector Strategy incorporates feedback and comments from the Sub National Consultations (SNCs). A key finding was the lack of information available to local communities on mine opportunities. There is also reflected a lack of market-based thinking and considerable expectation for the Government to provide sector support. It should be noted that investments in the mining sector are primarily commercial decisions that should be taken by the private sector. Projects identified and prioritized during the SNC process include the extraction of marbles, precious and semi precious stone mines in Anaba and Shotol districts of Panjshir province. The Ministry of Mines has been identified as the responsible agency for enabling this development.

Policy framework: sector strategy

The sector strategy is geared to supporting development through private firms engaged in a mix of large and small operations. The private sector will operate within a legislative and regulatory framework designed to facilitate investment and maintain a competitive sector. While there will be some public sector activity, these will be required to operate under the same legislative and regulatory framework as the private sector. The focus will be on using Government projects or competitive bidding for exploration contracts to better determine the extent of natural resources in Afghanistan; on the establishment of an improved, transparent and capable management system for the effective extraction of mines and natural resources; and the establishment of a regulatory environment that facilitates local and international investment in the mining sector.

The key reform will involve the refocusing of the Ministry of Mines from one involved in production to one that is primarily concerned with the creation of an enabling environment that requires mining companies to operate effectively and responsibly in accordance with the law. Mining legislation will be passed and implemented. Planned actions include exploration and exploitation of mineral resources by the private sector or MoM; capacity building programs; successful implementation of the Aynak project; development of long term geoscience projects; and a reconstruction program including equipping the laboratory and technical sections of the ministry. Steps will also be taken to raise the production level of gas and increase utilization of mineral and gas resources; encourage expansion of the cement industry and increase power supplies by raising the production of mineral resources, oil, gas and underground water; and increase the production of urea. The main programs of the sector are (i) Implementing PRR (ii) Legislative affairs completion (iii) A comprehensive geological study follow- up program in the country (iv) Exploration and exploitation of mineral resources by private sector or geology survey of MoM (v) Exploration, extraction and exploitation program of gas and oil fields in the country by the government or private sector (vi) Capacity building (vii) Long term geo science research (viii) Reconstruction program, equipping of laboratory and technical section of the ministry (for detail refer to ANDS Volume II).

Priority Projects: Top priority projects, in order of priority are:

- completing and implementing the hydrocarbons regulations by Ministry of Justice;
- finalizing of Afghanistan gas law (downstream);
- completing the second round of PRR in the MoM;
- providing background information and invite bidding for three blocks of oil and gas in the northern provinces aimed at exploration and exploitation.

Expected Outcomes

Given the known mining resources that are available, implementation of this strategy will lead to considerable investment in small and large projects. Mining will play a major role in achieving the high rates of economic growth envisioned in the ANDS and increased government revenues. Increased revenues will be derived from mining royalties, taxes and customs revenues on largely private operations as well as through licenses, permits and other taxes charged as part of the bidding process. Mining projects will generate employment opportunities for thousands of citizens, in remote areas where alternative legal productive opportunities are few. Mining firms will increasingly enter into the formal part of the economy. They will operate within a legislative framework that is accepted and impartially administered by MoM. Mining will bring with it access to advanced technology that can be of benefit in many areas of the economy. There will also be major indirect benefits from mining, including the construction of roads, bridges, housings, health clinics, mosques, playgrounds, schools and parks (for detail information refer to Appendixes 3-National Action Plan and 4-Monitoring Matrix).

Health and Nutrition

The ANDS strategic objective for this sector is to improve the health and nutrition of the people of Afghanistan through quality health care service provision and the promotion of healthy life styles. Afghanistan ranks towards the bottom on global measures of health and nutrition. Improving health and nutrition is vital to improving the livelihood and well being of the Afghan people and to achieving the goals of the MDGS and the Compact which include:

- By end-2010 the Basic Package of Health Services will be extended to cover at least 90 percent of the population;
- By end-2010 maternal mortality will be reduced;

- By end-2010 full immunization coverage for infants under-5 for vaccine-preventable diseases will be achieved and their mortality rates reduced by 20 percent;
- Between 2003 and 2015 reduce the under- five mortality rate by 50 percent, and further reduce it to one third of the 2003 level by 2020;
- Between 2002 and 2015 reduce the maternal mortality ratio by 50 percent, and further reduce it to 25 percent of the 2002 level by 2020;
- To have halted and begun the reverse the spread of HIV/AIDS by 2020;
- To have halted by 2020 and begun to reverse the incidence of malaria and other major diseases.

For more details refer to the Appendices I and II (National Action Plan and Monitoring Matrices).

Current Situation

Afghanistan's health indicators are near the bottom of international indices, and are far worse, in terms of their health, than any other country in the region. Life expectancy is low, infant, under-five and maternal mortality is very high, and there is an extremely high prevalence of chronic malnutrition and widespread occurrence of micronutrient deficiency diseases. For more information refer to volume II.

Achievements: Substantial improvements in the health system and the health status of the people of Afghanistan have been achieved in recent years.

- Expansion of primary health care services. The percentage of the population living in districts where the Basic Package of Health Services is being implemented has increased from 9 percent in 2003 to 82 percent in 2006. The percentage of people in Afghanistan who live within two hours walking distance from a primary health care facility was approximately 66 percent in 2006.
- Increased access to female health care workers. The percentage of primary health care facilities with at least one female doctor, nurse or midwife has increased from 26 percent in 2004 to 81 percent in 2007.
- Increased use of reproductive health services in rural areas. Between 2003 and 2006, use of a modern family planning method among married women in rural Afghanistan increased from 5 percent to 16 percent, receipt of skilled antenatal care by pregnant women increased from 5 percent to 32 percent and use of skilled birth attendants for assistance with delivery increased from 6 percent to 19 percent.
- Increased coverage of child immunization in rural areas. Between 2003 and 2006, coverage of BCG vaccine among children 12-23 months of age to protect against tuberculosis increased from 57 percent to 70 percent and receipt of three doses of oral polio vaaccine increased from 30 percent to 70 percent.
- The Afghan Compact High Level Benchmark for reduction of infant mortality has been reached ahead of schedule. From a high baseline level of 165 infant deaths per 1000 live births, a 20 percent reduction in infant mortality was targeted by 2010. With the infant mortality rate estimated by the 2006 Afghanistan Health Survey to be 129 per 1000 live births, a 22 percent reduction from the baseline level has already been achieved.

- The Afghan Compact High Level Benchmark for reduction of under-five mortality has been reached ahead of the schedule. From a high baseline level of 257 under-five deaths per 1000 live births, a 20 percent reduction in under-five mortality was targeted by 2010. With the under-five mortality rate estimated by the 2006 Afghanistan Health Survey to be 191 per 1000 live births, a 26 percent reduction from the baseline level has already been achieved.

There are a number of challenges and constraints that must be addressed if continued progress is to be made, including:

- Inadequate financing for many of the key programs;
- Reliance on external sources of funding;
- Inadequately trained health workers;
- Lack of qualified female health workers in rural areas;
- Dispersed population, geographical barriers and a lack of transportation infrastructure
- Low levels of utilization for certain health services, especially preventive services;
- Variable levels of service quality;
- Insecurity which makes program implementation difficult, recruitment and retention of staff, expansion of service coverage and monitoring by the provincial and central levels;
- Lack of effective financial protection mechanisms for poor households to receive the care they need without experiencing financial distress;
- Lack of mechanisms for effective regulation of for-profit private sector clinics and pharmacies.

Policy framework: sector strategy

The strategy is for the MoPH to maintain and strengthen its stewardship role for the Health and Nutrition Sector. For that purpose, a new organizational chart and programmatic structure have been defined, enabling a comprehensive approach to health service delivery, with primary health care services, hospital services, disease control, nutrition and reproductive and child health integrated under the same Health Care Services Provision General Directorate. The overarching priority policy of the MoPH has been to obtain nearly universal coverage of a standard Basic Package of Health Services (BPHS) through a 'contracting out' initiative, to create strong linkages with the hospital sector through an effective referral mechanism. However, the MoPH will also be responsible for creating an enabling environment for expansion of the Health Care System beyond the provision of the BPHS.

The MoPH will focus on the following policy areas:

- Leadership at all levels in policy formulation and translating policies into concrete actions to ensure that actions are geared toward attaining the specified goals;
- Conducting monitoring and evaluation of the implementation of health care services in order to ensure quality, equity and efficiency of the health system;

- Coordinating the contributions of all national and international agencies involved in the Health and Nutrition Sector, upholding standards and mapping services to avoid duplication and gaps;
- Decentralization of appropriate responsibility and managerial autonomy to the provincial level;
- Increase the active participation of communities in the management of their local health care services through developing strong, active participatory links with shura (community committees) and training and supporting community health workers;
- Developing legislation and regulations to facilitate growth and assure quality in the private sector provision or civil service provision of health care services. For more information refer to the Volume II.

The Government will give high priority to the following projects in this sector for the next five years:
CDC and Non-CDC Program
Primary Health Care Program
Hospital Care Program
Reproductive Health and MCH Program
Policy and Planning Support Program
Human Resource Development and Research
Pharmaceutical Management Support Program

The Health and Nutrition Strategy comprises eight core programs (Refer Appendix I) – four related to the Health Care Services Programs (Primary Health Care Program; Hospital Care Program; Disease Control and Nutrition Program; and RH and Child Health Program) and four related to the Institutional Development program (Policy and Planning Support Program; HRD and Research Program; Pharmaceutical Management Support Program; and Administrative Program). In addition, the efforts to stimulate the development of 'for profit' private sector provision of health care services can be considered a third priority component of the Health and Nutrition Strategy.

Health Care Services Programs: Primary Health Care and Hospital Care Programs: The MoPH will ensure the provision of a comprehensive referral network of secondary and tertiary hospitals that provide, as a minimum, the Essential Package of Hospital Services and do so within a framework of agreed upon, to set standards to improve clinical and managerial performance.

Pharmaceutical Management Support Program: MoPH will also act to ensure the accessibility, availability, safety, efficiency, effectiveness and affordability of medicines, through several means, including establishment of a functional drug quality control laboratory at the central level. Establish and use standard international level procurement, stocking and logistics systems to enable international contracting, bidding, stocking and transportation. MoPH will also establish, maintain and further develop an affordable, useful and functioning communications network using modern information and technology systems at both national and provincial levels.

Disease Control and Nutrition Program: MoPH will establish and maintain a surveillance system (Disease Early Warning System) to respond to epidemics and other risks to human health as well as responding to health emergencies in a timely manner. This will involve implementing actions needed to better control communicable diseases through strengthened management of integrated, cost- effective interventions for prevention, control and treatment. The prevention and management of outbreaks will also be strengthened further through raising public awareness and responding more rapidly through the Disease Early Warning System. A key action will be the development and institutionalization of a Comprehensive Health Preparedness Plan at the national and provincial levels and allocate appropriate resources for responding to natural and man-made emergencies in an effective and timely manner. This plan will set out the programs needed to address key emerging public health problems, such as illicit drugs and their use, smoking, HIV/AIDS, blindness, and road traffic accidents.

MoPH will also work to increase awareness and understanding of potential adverse health consequences of environmental factors, such as poor water supplies; lack of adequate sanitation facilities; inadequate rubbish disposal and collection; health facility waste; poor food handling and hygiene; and high levels of air pollution. MoPH will also oversee programs to reduce malnutrition of all types, including reduction of micronutrient deficiency diseases, through integrated and coordinated programming and promotion of food and nutrition security for all by adopting a public nutrition approach involving multi-sectoral interventions that address the underlying causes of malnutrition, including food insecurity, poor social environment, and inadequate access to health care services.

This program will also develop a flexible range of integrated mental health support and care services at all levels of the health system. Particular attention will be given to post-traumatic counseling through the training of more community health care workers and psychologists and their placement in accessible community health facilities; and ensure that people with temporary or permanent disabilities have access to both general health services and specialized services, and detect and treat disabilities early through more appropriate diagnosis of newborn and small children with disabilities.

Reproductive and Child Health Program: High priority will be given to ensuring that development partners deliver the different components of reproductive health as an integrated package, and increase accessibility to, and utilization of, quality reproductive health care services, including antenatal care, intrapartum care, routine and emergency obstetric care and post partum care, counseling and modern family planning services. This will focus on reducing child mortality, morbidity and disabilities and improve child growth and development by promoting exclusive breast feeding, expanding implementation of integrated management of childhood illnesses, enhancing the control of vaccine preventable diseases and addressing adolescent health through school health programs. For more information refer to the Volume II

Institutional Development Programs: Policy and Planning Support Program: The national health care system will be organized and managed to reduce inequity and improve efficiency and accountability at all levels. Steps will be taken to improve capacity at the provincial level and to decentralize responsibilities as provincial capacity is established. In addition, efforts will be made to enhance evidence- based, bottom-up and participatory strategic planning in all levels of the health system through development of annual, business plans with costs in all departments, strengthened links between the different levels of the health system, implementation of the National Monitoring and Evaluation Strategy and translation of recommendations from research and practical experiences to policy formulation and health planning.

MoPH will enhance coordination between the MoPH and partner organizations through formal and informal mechanisms and facilitate stronger donor coordination, especially when undertaking assessment and planning missions and in supporting health priorities. MoPH will also work with both donors, partners and the private sector to coordinate the delivery of health care services by setting and distributing policies, standards and guidelines, convening the Consultative Group on Health and Nutrition and task forces to work on specific technical issues under the leadership of the MoPH and further develop Provincial Public Health Coordination Committees within each province.

MoPH will also review and develop relevant legal and regulatory mechanisms, such as accreditation systems, that govern health and health related work in the public and private sectors. The goal of the regulatory system will be to facilitate competitive and cost effective provision of services, carrying out its broader mandate to not only contract out service provision to civil and private groups but also to facilitate growth of the 'for profit' sector. This being said, MoPH will also review, develop and enforce relevant legal and regulatory instruments that govern health and health related work to safeguard the public and ensure service quality. MoPH will work to identify, encourage, coordinate, and review and in some cases conduct relevant, useful research that can assist evidence-based decision making and the formulation of new policies, strategies and plans. One area of resource is with respect to facilitating the growth of the private sector providers operating on their own outside the framework of contracts from MoPH.

Human Resource Development, Research and Administration Programs: The MoPH will work closely with the Civil Service Commission to implement the National Priority Reform and Restructuring competitive recruitment processes for placing the most highly qualified Afghan health professionals in established posts throughout all levels of the health system. Efforts will be made to promote a culture of quality throughout the Health and Nutrition Sector, especially in health facilities, through leadership and good examples set in day-to-day work, strengthen the use of quality standards, and promote frequent supportive-supervision. A Quality Assurance Committee has been established to promote improvements in service within public sector facilities. Once effective regulatory mechanisms are developed and can be enforced, the MoPH will address quality issues in the private-for-profit sector, especially pharmacies and drug sellers. A comprehensive approach to human resource development will be developed to produce, deploy and retain where they are needed an appropriately trained health workforce possessing the variety of skills needed to deliver affordable, equitable and quality health care services. Further develop and maintain a health care worker registration system and a national testing and certification examination process (in collaboration with the Ministry of Higher Education) will be established standards for accreditation of training institutes and programs. There will be a significant Expansion of the community midwife training program model to other cadres of health workers, with particular emphasis on recruiting, training and deploying couples to work together in health facilities in their community after graduation. For more information refer to the Volume II and Appendix II, National Action Plan Matrix.

Health Care Financing: The MoPH will undertake health advocacy to increase funds and resources to the health sector, ensure spending is in line with priorities and coordinated across sectors, strengthen transparency in the allocation of financial resources and financial management, strengthen coordination of different sources of funding, and monitor different mechanisms of financing the delivery of services for their cost-efficiency and acceptability. MoPH will also coordinate closely with the Ministry of Finance on the National Development Budget, the development of mechanisms to improve total public expenditure from internal and external resources, the development of alternative health care financing. Work undertaken on facilitating private sector growth in the sector will also be used to explore the potential costs or savings from efforts to facilitate such growth or from the budget savings because of such growth

Rule of Private Sector and Civil Society: Through the Basic Package of Health Services, the contracting out initiative, and the focused development of the MoPH's ability to exercise the stewardship function, highly effective partnerships with non-profit private sector agencies have been achieved. Strategic actions related to the private sector include: (i) continuing the effective partnership with non-governmental organizations in the health sector (ii) further developing the MoPH's capacity to establish policies, strategies and plans, monitor performance in delivery of health services and coordinate diverse actors from the public and private sectors working within health and nutrition; and (iii) developing regulatory mechanisms for engaging the for-profit private sector. Many of the later issues have been discussed in describing earlier programs.

Civil society plays a role in the delivery of health services and in the interaction between government and the population in determining health needs and priority areas. This strategy has been designed to specifically target the health and nutritional needs of the most vulnerable groups in Afghanistan. Civil Society groups will play a key role interacting between all players to ensure this happens. Recognizing that transparency and accountability are essential in order to attract resources, and aware that in a post-conflict environment many well-intentioned governmental and nongovernmental partners tend to impose and arrange for the implementation of programs of their own design, the MoPH has pursued a strategy of close coordination with all actors in the health sector. A Consultative Group for Health and Nutrition that includes donors, major NGOs, ISAF, UN agencies, and other line ministries meets regularly to review recent developments in the health sector and to contribute to making policies and suggesting programs for the future. For more information refer to the volume II

The Sub-national Consultation (SNC) process of the ANDS has successfully involved the sub- national administration of the sector. It has strengthened the sense of cohesion between the central MoPH and the provincial public health departments. The MoPH's evaluation criteria for the SNC proposals seek equity by looking at the depth of poverty and vulnerability of the population to be served. It takes into account health indicators of mothers and children, utilization and availability of the health services in the area of concern, and availability of funds:[51]

- the proposals that are on-going and/or to be implemented with the current funds;
- the proposals that are included in the MoPH Construction Plan and to be implemented when fund is available;
- the proposals that are considered in the HNSS timeframe and implemented when fund is available; and
- the proposals that have to be discussed in detail with the MoPH because they are not adhering to the evaluation criteria, colliding with the HNSS strategies and/or duplicating the efforts and inputs of the MoPH and its partners.

The MoPH acknowledges that the SNC is an opportunity for all the stakeholders in the sector to create more dialogue and thus refine the route towards the accomplishment of the HNSS.

Private Sector 'For Profit' Health Care Provision: In addition to the contractual arrangements with NGOs and Private Sector groups to provide MoPH service packages, mechanisms will be developed by which 'for profit' private sector providers of medical and hospital services can be supported by Government. This reflects the realization that while public funding for many social services such as education and health is necessary, 'for profit' private sector provision may be more efficient. In many countries, private sector provision has developed to cover the needs of a significant proportion of the population seeking quality education and health care. These 'for profit' private sector providers have emerged despite not have any access to public funding. As part of the ANDS, an effort will be made to foster competition between public sector providers, public sector contractors and 'for profit' private sector operations. Communities or individual consumers who feel they can get better service from the 'for profit' private sector providers should not lose their claim on public funds just because they make this choice. Voucher schemes and/or direct public sector payments for approved services provided by accredited 'for profit' private sector providers will be used to encourage this competition.

Expected Outcomes

The key expected outcomes in the Health and Nutrition sector are:

- Increased quality of health care services;
- Increased access to health care services;
- Effective Reproductive and Child health system; and
- Increased competition amongst health care providers.

Education

Role of the Sector in ANDS

The ANDS strategic vision for this sector is that regardless of gender, ethnicity, socio-economic status or religious affiliation, all Afghans will have equal access to quality education to enable them to develop their knowledge and skills and thereby maximize their potential. An education sector that engenders a healthy workforce with relevant skills and knowledge is a key to long-term economic growth.

Over the last six years the sector has experienced a number of major achievements, notably in terms of enrollment rates. There are today more than six million children, youth and adults receiving education. Communities have demonstrated their desire for a better future for their children by sending them to school in their millions. Tens of thousands of youth and adults, both female and male attend literacy classes and vocational training programs. Households are making large personal and financial sacrifices to provide an education for their children. However, much remains to be done. This strategy outlines the Government's priorities for education that will facilitate the development of an education sector from which students will emerge literate, numerate and technologically proficient.

Access to education is enshrined in the constitution, which states that:

> education "is the right of all citizens and offered free of charge in State institutions... .and that the State is obliged to devise and implement effective programs for a balanced expansion of education all over Afghanistan" (article 43).

The education sector in Afghanistan comprises three sub-sectors: (i) Primary and Secondary Education, which includes general, Islamic and technical/vocational education, from Grades 1 to 14; (ii) Higher Education for all tertiary education; and (iii) Skills Development that encompasses literacy and technical vocational education/training

The Millennium Development Goal for the sector is that by 2020 all children in the country – boys and girls alike – will be able to complete a full course of primary education. A set of medium term benchmarks (to be met by the end of 2010) identified in the Afghanistan Compact has guided the development of strategies for each of the sub-sectors.

The Afghanistan Compact Benchmarks for the sector is net enrolment in primary schools for girls and boys will be at least 60 percent and 75 percent respectively; a new curriculum will be operational in all secondary schools; the numbers of female teachers will be increased by 50 percent; 70 percent of Afghanistan's teachers will have passed a competency test and a system for assessing learning achievement will be in place". The total number of students enrolled in universities will be 100,000 of which at least 35 percent will be female".150, 000 men and women will be trained in marketable skills through public and private means,

The Government has set itself a target to enable at least 1.8 million Afghans to attain demonstrated literacy by 2010, and ensure that at least 60 percent of the learners are females, members of minority groups, nomads or persons with disabilities.

Expected Outcomes: The overall education system agreed outcomes include an increase in the literacy rate, improved quality of education, an expansion in the capacity of the education system to absorb more students (particularly female students), equal access to education for all, improvement in opportunities and quality for Higher Education, expanded capacity and improved quality of vocational education and skill development, improved conditions for sport, improved and expanded capacity of the Academy of Science, and mainstreaming of cross-cutting issues. For detail information refer to Appendix 3 National Action Plan and Monitoring Matrix

Sector Priority Policies: Priority short term policies over the next four years involve retraining 70 percent of teachers in primary and secondary school and coping with increased demand for education by increasing enrolments from 6.1 million to 7.7 million. Other priority policies include an increase in the quality and independence of the Higher Education system and a move to place vocational educational on a more sustainable basis that can better contribute to emerging demands for skills.

Current Situation in the Sector

After decades of disruption to education and the near total destruction of the education system, one of the Government's top social priorities was to get children to return to school. Data from the sub-sector[52] indicate unparalleled success giving a clear indication of the aspirations of the people that reflects a social transformation taking place (see box 7.4).

BOX 7.4. SUCCESS IN THE EDUCATION SECTOR: INCREASED PRIMARY EDUCATION

The Back to School campaign launched in 2002 aimed to get 1.5 million children enrolled in primary and secondary education. From under one million in 2001 the school population has grown to 5.7 million in 2007 and new enrolments into Grade 1 have ranged between 12-14 percent per annum in the last five years. Two million of the children (or 35 percent) enrolled are girls – a 35 percent increase in five years. In keeping with the exponential increase in enrolment, the number of schools has trebled to 9,062 in 2007 including 1,337 all girls' and 4,325 co-educational schools. Similarly, the number of teachers has increased seven-fold to 142,500 of who nearly 40,000 are female. Fifty thousand of these teachers have received in-service teacher training. Islamic education in Afghanistan has been reviewed and a broad-based curriculum has been developed through a national consultative process. The number of reformed religious schools that teach a broad-based Islamic education curriculum has increased to 336 and the National Islamic Education Council has been established to oversee and monitor the delivery of Islamic education across the country.

In Higher Education, universities have reopened. There are now 52,200 students in higher education institutions taught by 2,713 lecturers. Demand for higher education is currently four times greater than the available places in tertiary education institutions. The next stage of rehabilitation involves improving the quality of education in existing institutions and expanding the number of places available. Partnerships with foreign universities and other educational institutions have been introduced in about half the universities. Such partnerships foster and provide support to develop and enhance the capacity of these universities.

Skills development – through technical and vocational education and training as well as focused functional literacy – has also seen significant growth in the last five years. The Government established the National Skills Development Program in 2005 as a national priority program. Technical/vocational education at the secondary level through public institutions has seen a 10-fold increase in the last five years with nearly 10,500 students enrolled in 44 schools. Short-term technical/vocational training courses that focus on specific skills set are conducted by the non-government and the private sectors. Similarly, functional literacy for youth and young adults are carried out by both the public and non-government sectors. In the public sector alone nearly 320,000 persons undertook a 9-month literacy course in 2007, 75 percent of whom were female students.

The key achievements noted above are commendable but are by no means the whole picture. While the Government is satisfied with the progress made so far, it recognizes the many challenges that lie ahead in achieving its long-term vision and medium term objectives. These challenges pertain to meeting the growing demand for access to quality and relevant education.

The demand for education far outstrips the supply across the sector in Afghanistan today. Only half of all school-age children[53] are enrolled in schools and there are huge provincial, gender and rural/urban disparities. Eight-two percent of children enrolled in schools are in primary grades.

BOX 7.5. PROGRESS IS STILL REQUIRED IN THE EDUCATION SECTOR

Half of all schools today do not have adequate, safe or appropriate learning spaces that are conducive to parents allowing their girls, particularly at the secondary level, to enroll in schools. This together with a severe shortage of female teachers in rural areas – 80 percent of rural districts do not have a girls' high school because there are no female teachers available locally to teach in them (there are only 216 girls' high schools across the country, a majority of them located in regional and provincial capitals). Only 28 percent of all teachers are women and eighty percent of them are found in urban schools. Schools for children with special needs are woefully lacking while those for Kuchi children are inadequate. Every year between 40,000-70,000 youth graduate from high schools across the country but only 25-30 percent of them are able to enter tertiary education due to the severe shortage of places in higher education institutions. In 2006 there were 58,300 applicants for entry into tertiary education institutions. Only 17,700 were successful. Most of the universities have buildings that require rehabilitation and there is a drastic shortage of qualified lecturers.

The lack of access to education in the recent past has resulted in a massive backlog of illiterate people in Afghanistan. Based on recent national surveys[54] it is estimated that only 28 percent of the population in the country can read. Disaggregated by gender this statistic reveals that only 18 percent of females and 36 percent of males are able to read, a female to male ratio of 0.5. Based on population projections developed specifically for this work and literacy rates by the Afghan Institute for Rural Development it is estimated that there are 11.2 million illiterate persons in the country today, half of whom are out-of-school children primarily above the age of thirteen.

Other quality constraints revolve around teaching spaces, teacher and trainer qualifications, skills and motivation, outdated curricula and poor teaching and learning materials. Add to this weak assessment and accreditation systems. Only half the teachers employed in the primary and secondary sub-sector meet the minimum qualification which is set at Grade 12 for primary school teachers. But this is hampered by the numbers of high schools graduates available and/or willing to train as teachers. There is major shortage of qualified master trainers in the vocational training.

Primary school curriculum has been reviewed and revised and new textbooks developed; production and distribution of these textbooks is still ongoing. However, secondary school students are still being taught from an outdated curriculum developed more than 20 years ago. While a new curriculum has been developed over the last 12 months, the development, production and distribution of textbooks, teachers' guides and learning materials will take a further 12-18 month period. Teacher training in the use and teaching of the new curriculum still needs to be addressed. Libraries and laboratories are singularly lacking even in most urban schools and higher education institutions as are trained librarians, technicians and science teachers. In higher education there is a need to transform the monolithic system into a modern system of independent, well managed universities that operate in the interests of their students. Technical/vocational education and training are overloaded with academic subjects, have poor laboratory environments for practical training, are short of teaching aids and lack adequate training materials. These programs provide limited exposure to students on the practical application of their training.

The relevance of education as it applies to the content, proper articulation from elementary to high school level and appropriateness for student learning and teachers teaching are a challenge that is still being defined in the sector today. Skills development is rarely linked to market relevance and weak job linkages. There is no minimum qualification standards imposed particularly in course content or assessment procedures for technical/vocational training. Similarly, there is no uniformity in course length across various training programs and courses are often not sub-divided into levels of competency. The quality of student input is low and consequently the quality of students entering formal higher secondary or tertiary education do not possess adequate literacy and numeracy skills needed to cope with higher level theory and practical courses. In the case of vocational training the problem is further compounded by the lack of prior academic training.

Throughout the education sector there is a general lack of engagement with the private sector and the use of private sector resources that would generate competitiveness and thereby encourage and enhance quality of the education services. Benefits to delivery of relevant education services would be greatly enhanced through market linkages and the private sector.

Perhaps the most daunting challenge facing the sector today is that which is posed by terrorism. Educational institutions, students and teachers have become the soft targets through which terrorists are depriving the population their basic rights. Threats to schools, destruction of school buildings, killing and maiming of students and teachers is increasing, particularly in the southern provinces. Despite the bravery of communities and school authorities in keeping schools open when threatened or reopening them as soon as possible after an incident or threat, the terrorists continue their campaign of intimidation. In 2007 alone 117 schools were burned down or destroyed, 207 schools had to be closed due to severe threats, 157 students and teachers lost their lives and over 200 others have been injured or maimed. For detail information refer to Volume II

Policy Framework: Sector Strategy

Three dominant policy goals drive the education sector strategy; equity, quality and relevance:

Equity: Access to education for all is enshrined in the Constitution which makes it illegal to deny or refuse access to schools for any reason. Although there has been significant progress in the past five years at the national level, boys' enrolment in primary schools is still nearly twice that of girls, while at the secondary levels it is three to four times higher. In urban areas girls are approaching gender equity but only at the primary level. In rural areas, girls are much less likely to be enrolled at any level but after the primary years boys are more than ten times as likely to be enrolled. The shortage of girls' schools and female teachers, especially at post- primary levels, are the greatest risk factors for achieving higher participation rates and gender equity in rural areas. Access to education for nomadic children, those with learning disabilities, pre-school children and older children who have missed the first years of basic education and now want to enter the system is also generally low.

Equity in access to primary and secondary education will provide a firm base for equity in higher education. In order to improve and increase access, the government plans to pursue an aggressive building and equipment program in addition to assessing the potential for distance learning strategies. This will include assessing the optimal role for government and identifying strategies for achieving national coverage relatively quickly through the use of existing national facilities. As part of the aggressive building program, efforts will be made to include improved security, comfort and hygiene in the building designs in order to improve the physical learning environment. Improvement in equitable access to education will be indicated through increased net enrolment in the various sub-sectors, by gender and special needs; additional physical infrastructure and facilities for that caters to all including females, special needs and nomadic communities in suitable locations.

Quality: The quality of education in Afghanistan is quite low across the sector. There are multiple reasons for this including teachers who do not have a thorough knowledge of either the subjects taught or effective teaching methods; the lack of adequate learning spaces, as well as the lack of quality teaching and learning materials. The classroom environment and the quality of education are critically dependent on the quality of teaching. Teacher- centered classrooms and rote learning are the norm in Afghanistan's classrooms across the sector. Existing classroom-based methods do no deliver basic literacy and numeracy and they do not develop critical thinking and analytical skills of students. Teachers either do not know how to implement more student- centered methods or are not motivated to change their teaching style.

Although improving the pedagogical skills of teachers is a contributor to improving the quality of education in Afghanistan, recent surveys indicate that the knowledge level of teachers is also extremely low. This indicates the need for a teacher training program that consists of both subject-content training as well as pedagogical training. The quality of education will also be improved by continued updating and revision of the curriculum and by increased community involvement in the management of education delivery. Enhanced quality of education will be measured by the progression rates of students through the system and the numbers of teachers who have successfully completed competency tests and the systems put in place to monitor and coach teachers on a regular basis.

Relevance: For education to contribute to poverty reduction and economic growth it is important that the skills and knowledge acquired in the education system are relevant to present day needs and market demands. The content of education in Afghanistan has not evolved with the times and not for want of good reasons. However, it is opportune now to leapfrog in time and adopt relevant methodologies, content and appropriateness that suit both the individual and the people at large to better contribute to and benefit from economic growth.

The review and revision of curriculum to make Islamic education broad-based to allow multiple career paths for graduates, the teaching and learning of technical and vocational skills that are in demand and will lead to jobs, adult literacy that is linked to productive skills, are some examples of how government is attempting to make education more relevant to present day Afghanistan. For detail information refer to Volume II.

Strategic approaches

The underlying principle of government in ensuring equal access to education for all is to develop a strategy that is national in scope but local in focus and delivery. Different measures will be required to overcome constraints to access and supply due to geography and thereby promote the diversity of Afghanistan.

Government will work towards strengthening partnerships, clarifying responsibility and transferring skills. The value and contribution of partners to the education sector will be enhanced through improved understanding and collaborative implementation.

A government-led education sector needs to be supported through building an accountable and transparent system of education financing and administration. The underpinning strategy that the government will employ to achieve its policy goals, therefore, is the reform and restructuring of the management systems in place that facilitate the delivery of education services. At the primary and secondary school level, a major policy shift seeks to devolve greater authority to the school level for minor operating expenses, planning and execution. This is part of the overall intention to improve governance and management standards.

Recruitment processes will be reviewed and be part of the overall public administration reforms. Registration of all teaching professionals across the sector, implementation of public administration reform, teacher salaries and other incentives are being reviewed as part of the pay and grading process, including appropriate career development of teaching professionals based on merit and performance to increase retention, in conjunction with the Civil Service Commission.

Strategies

Primary and Secondary Education: A comprehensive five-year strategic plan[55] for the delivery of education services has been developed by the Ministry of Education to meet the medium-term benchmarks for primary and secondary education set in the Afghanistan Compact by 2010. Based on the overarching policy of attaining national and gender equity in access to quality and relevant education, including affirmative action initiatives, the Strategic Plan encompasses the National Education Program that comprises two subsets of priority programs. The first set comprises service delivery programs and the second set quality assurance and support programs. The service delivery programs are General Education, Islamic Education, Technical/Vocational Education and Literacy,[56] while the quality of education is assured through the Teacher Education & Working Conditions, Curriculum

Development & Learning Materials, Education Infrastructure Rehabilitation and Development, and Education Administration Reform and Management. Each of these programs has a set of costed projects that are prioritized and sequenced for implementation. For detail information refer to Volume II.

Higher Education: The Higher Education strategy involves improving quantity and quality aspects to satisfy the demand for the market based economy with skilled professionals. This will involve increasing the capacity to accommodate more qualified students, together with an improvement in the quality of higher education by improving the number and quality of lecturers and offering a greater variety of courses. There are plans to provide universities with greater autonomy. A key component of the strategy is to encourage universities to enter into cooperative arrangements with other universities, both domestic and foreign, so that there can be an exchange of lecturers. Implementation of this strategy has already commenced. Eleven cooperative partnerships between individual universities in the country with well qualified foreign universities are in various stages of finalization.

In 2007 a Higher Education Law has been passed by Cabinet. A Master's course has already begun as part of the objective to offer a greater variety of courses. Ministry of Higher Education has started to introduce accreditation through the Academic Coordination Committee. This body, whilst still in the early stages will also be involved in quality assurance and control, which is an integral component of the accreditation procedures. This component of the strategy will be monitored by the structure that has been established through an agreement and Memorandum of Understanding (MoU) signed with the World Bank on establishment of Afghanistan National Qualification Authority. In its efforts to improve the quality of Higher Education, most funds available to the Ministry will be used to refurbish the existing university campuses and carry out construction of buildings for libraries and laboratories in the existing universities. It is also important as part of the strategy to conduct a review of university funding so that universities have greater autonomy. For detail information refer to Volume II.

Skills Development and Training: Many of the courses delivered by mandated institutions suffer from the similar problems: lack of modern equipment that can be used by students to acquire trade-relevant skills and lack of adequately trained and motivated staff. Issues that need to be addressed include the need to clearly identify administrative responsibility for delivering and setting standards in the area of vocational education. There are problems of staff shortages, overbuilding, lack of standardization in training courses, and qualifications that are difficult for potential employers to access. These problems are being addressed through the MoU mentioned above.

The strategy that has been proposed to address this is to establish a new organization, National Vocational Education and Training Board (NVETB) that would manage, but not operate, all vocational training institutions. The NVETB would set minimum core competencies for courses, carry out accreditation, and inspect vocational institutions, to ensure that they meet minimum standards. They would be responsible for calling tenders to operate vocational training facilities owned by the state. Tenders to operate training centers that comply with NVETB standards could be accepted from both the public and private sectors. The proposed approach using NVETB would address the problems of lack of modern equipment that can be used by students to acquire trade-relevant skills, lack of adequately-trained and motivated staff, and lack of standardization in courses. It would provide for sustainability of the sector, which is currently lacking. Part of the strategy would involve the development of an accreditation system for NGO and private sector providers who provide the bulk of vocational training. By 2008 there would be a plan to formalize existing apprenticeship arrangements and expand the system. The approach will ensure that a recognized qualification is provided to people undertaking apprenticeships who have achieved specified basic competencies.

Technical/vocational education, as part of the formal secondary education, is included under the National Education Strategic Plan as is Literacy and Non-formal education. These two programs address all three policy goals of the sector. Under the former a National Institute of Administration and Management is being established to address the lack of capacity in both the public and private sectors in basic project management, accountancy and booking and information and communication technology. A nation-wide literacy and productive skills program is being launched that is envisaged making at least half a million people literate and numerate with skills that will enable them to find employment. This would be in addition to numerous other literacy service providers who coordinate their activities and interventions under the leadership of the National Literacy Centre.

There are now firm proposals agreed to by relevant institutions to the establishment of regulatory bodies to operate across the whole of the education spectrum in order to improve educational standards. These include a Board of Secondary Education, a National Vocational Education and training Board, the Islamic Education Board and Higher Education Board. It has been agreed to establish the necessary legislation for these Boards and for the implementation of the Afghanistan National Qualifications Framework. In order to oversee these components of the strategy a committee on education and skills policy has been established. This committee covers the entire education sector. It is chaired by the Vice-President. There are four Government members representing MoE, MoHE, MoLSAMD and MoF, two members representing the private sector and two members representing the donor community. A committee to monitor Capacity Utilization, headed by the Minister of economy will also be established. This committee will monitor individual projects where there is potential for capacity utilization issues to present implementation problems. The private sector will be represented on this Committee. For detail information refer to Volume II.

In some countries, heavy investments in higher education have resulted in low returns because of low absorption capacity for these skills in the economy, with unemployment rates high for graduates unwilling to take jobs considered beneath their skill level. If the quality of education can be improved, this is not expected to be a problem in Afghanistan where there is a dearth of well qualified individuals. Increased investment is crucial for the demand for labor to increase. This requires higher rates of growth, broad investment to increase and productivity to be higher. With increased investment in many areas of the economy, there will be high demand for well qualified Afghans.

There is an urgent need for qualified teachers, trainers, doctors, professors, for those with the requisite skills for planning and implementing improved water management practices, for qualified professionals in the Civil Service, for skills needed in the management and development of mineral resources, for meeting the management and safety needs of a growing civil aviation sector, for managing and maintaining an expanding road system, for work in regional trading enterprises centered in Afghanistan, in developing, energy resources, working in Independent Power Producers, and in managing and improving electricity transmission and distribution systems, developing commercial agriculture, and working in operations to assist the poor and most vulnerable either within or outside government. If the ANDS educational strategy is successful in addressing the quality shortcomings in the public education system and expanding the scope for private education, the expected growth of the economy will create the demand for well qualified Afghans emerging from the educational system. Care will need to be taken to assure that existing but less qualified employees in the public sector do not block the way of better qualified applicants for these jobs, although these existing employees should also be given the opportunity to develop the needed skills through in house capacity development programs and through 'educational leaves' to upgrade their skills.

There are other sub-sector policies covering areas such as Sport and the Afghan Academy of Science.

- In sports policy there will be an effort made to encourage private sector support. Provided funds are available, there is a program to build sports complexes and strengthen sports through provincial sports departments and sports improvement programs in capital and provinces. The anti- narcotics message will be promoted strongly through sports activities.
- The Academy of Science will be strengthened and supported so as to use the resources and talents of the academy to assist with the restoration and development of Afghanistan society

Integration of the PDPs: At the provincial and district level Provincial and Development Plans (PDPs), have been developed through a sub- national consultation process. These Plans ensure that the priorities in the ANDS reflect the best interests and most urgent needs of the people. The most urgent provincial needs in education, health, and transport have been identified and will be integrated in the sector strategies. A problem in the education sector has been direct provincial infrastructure aid by country donors, such as construction of provincial agricultural colleges, that is not sustainable because the provincial recipient does not have the funds to finance the running costs, including as salaries and equipment, which are essential to enable this type of infrastructure aid to make a contribution to provincial development. For detail information refer to Volume III Provincial Development Plans.

Institutional Arrangements: Education services are delivered by a number of government institutions. The Ministry of Education is mandated to deliver primary and secondary education, including general education, Islamic education, teacher education, technical/vocational education and literacy. The Ministry of Higher Education is responsible for all tertiary education while the Ministry of Labor and Social Affairs is mandated to deliver vocational training.

Culture, Youth and Media

Role of the Sector in ANDS

The ANDS strategic vision for this sector is to preserve and protect the cultural heritage of Afghanistan and hand it on to new generations to foster cultural creativity and to establish media that are independent, pluralistic and accessible to women and men throughout the country thereby promoting an open and democratic society, young people (male and female) to be confident that they have a stable, prosperous and productive future in the country.

Culture provides the social basis that allows for stimulating creativity, innovation, human progress and well-being. In this sense, culture can be seen as a driving force for human development, in respect of economic growth and also as a means of leading a more fulfilling intellectual, emotional, moral and spiritual life.

The Afghanistan Constitution article 47 articulates that the state shall devise effective programs for fostering knowledge, culture, literature and arts. The state shall guarantee the copyrights of authors, inventors and discoverers, and, shall encourage and protect scientific research in all fields, publicizing their results for effective use in accordance with the provisions of the law. Freedom of expression shall be inviolable according to Article 34 and every Afghan shall have the right to express thoughts through speech, writing, and illustration

The Afghanistan Compact Benchmarks targets comprehensive inventory of Afghan cultural treasures by end-2007 and measures will be taken to revive the Afghan cultural heritage, to stop the illegal removal of cultural material and to restore damaged monuments and artifacts by end-2010.

Current Situation in the Sector

Achievements: Considerable progress has been made in the past six years. From virtually no public debate, there are now over 130 independent television and radio stations covering the entire country. In Kabul alone there are 11 independent television stations, while access to cable television is increasing. There are large numbers of independent newspapers. Many of these outlets are managed and target youth, female and minority groups. This provides avenues for vulnerable and marginalized groups to have a voice in society.

These advancements have created an environment in which the caliber of public debate is high and lively. Criticism as well as praise for public programs and figures are common and encourage the public's involvement in government actions and the development process. This debate filters down through society and is responsible for increased questioning and analysis of Government activities more broadly.

The Government is committed to furthering this public debate and independence of media. The Government recognizes that public debate is crucial for allowing the needs of the Afghan people to be fed into development activities. Independent media report development activities and programs and are critically important to increasing public awareness on the Government and international community's efforts.

At the same time, local independent entertainment programs have been developed and are highly popular. Regional television shows are also broadcasted meeting the needs of the Afghan people.

Many historical and valuable artifacts that were believed lost or stolen have been accounted for and returned. There is now a need for a comprehensive inventory to determine the extent of holdings.

In Media, a large number of media outlets, television, radio and newspapers have been started in the last six years. These stations produce considerable local Afghan content and are popular within the country. The media law is drafted and is under debate.

In Youth a Joint National Youth Program is being implemented. This program is designed to increase the participation of youth in governance, recovery, development and peace- building of the country. It has been produced from inputs by eight Ministries and seven United Nations agencies.

Challenges and constraints

- There is an urgent need to take action to prevent the looting of valuable cultural artifacts and to encourage other countries to return them.
- The inability of the Ministry to reach assigned targets is due to the lack of resources, both human and financial. This is the basic cause of the weaknesses in the Sector. Institutional strengthening should look not only at the resource needs of the Ministry but also look at the way resources are organized.
- In the area of culture, legal and policy frameworks, such as those guaranteeing respect of cultural rights for all Afghans, are weak and not comprehensive.
- Most media infrastructure and equipment for both print and broadcast media are out-of-date or have been damaged or deliberately destroyed. State-owned media needs to be reformed in order to ensure that it promotes democratic values and is editorially independent of influences from various interested factions.
- Media legislation that will provide an environment in which a free, independent and responsible media can operate has been drafted. It will be passed through Parliament in 2008. Despite some setbacks, the Government is determined that the freedoms that have been introduced will remain and will be protected by appropriate legislation.

Policy framework: sector strategy

Culture

The objective of this sub-sector to the ANDS will be to establish a system that documents and safeguards Afghanistan's history and culture for the benefit of future generations. Major goals include:

- Establish an accessible and well maintained cultural artifacts data base;
- Plans will be accepted, and donors will be identified, to establish regional museums;
- Maintain Kabul museum and take measures to establish thematic museums such as ethnology, anthropology, science and technology, handicrafts and community museums;
- The cultural artifacts collection held by the Ministry will be expanded;
- Take appropriate measures to promote live culture (Music, Poetry, Arts, Theater & Dance)

In the longer term goals will include the establishment and expansion of museums as well as the protection of historical and heritage sites. For detail information refer to volume 2

Media

The contribution of this sub-sector to the ANDS will be to ensure an independent, pluralistic and accessible media for Afghan men and women throughout the country which it is hoped will promote an open and democratic society. The objectives with respect to media are:

- To establish legislation that will provide a stable and predictable environment in which a largely private sector, independent media can operate;
- Media will be employed as an educational tool in addition to entertainment.

Expected outcomes for the media sub-sector in the short term will include:

- New Media legislation will have been passed and Government and the Ministry will successfully administer this legislation in an open manner;
- A country-wide coverage of public Afghan media (radio and television);
- An increased number of hours of public broadcasting, and improved quality of programming;
- Press freedom has been declining drastically in Afghanistan over the past 4 years and so the need to promote and protect the independence of the media as well as ensure press freedom is extremely important;
- Press freedom is a fundamental aspect of a democratic society therefore the Government will work to reverse setbacks and ensure that press freedom be protected both in legislation and in practice. For detail information refer to volume 2

Youth

The contribution of this sub-sector to the ANDS will be to instill in young people a sense of confidence in a stable, prosperous and productive future in the country. In addition a Joint National Youth Program is now in the process of being implemented. This program has been produced with inputs from eight Ministries of the Government of Afghanistan and seven United Nations agencies is designed to increase the participation of youth in governance, recovery, and peaceful development of the country. It provides young women and men with enhanced capacities, education, and recreation and employment opportunities.

The Joint National Youth Program contains four main components:

- Strengthening the capacity of the Government to respond to the needs of the youth of the country;
- Promoting non-formal education, increasing awareness and developing skills (literacy, leadership, strategic planning, conflict resolution, peace-building, etc.) in young people so to provide better quality of life and livelihood opportunities;
- Engaging youth in governance, development and social-political processes at local, district, municipal, provincial and national level, ensuring the participation of young women and men in democracy and advocacy; and

- Promoting voluntary efforts for peace and development and establishing a youth volunteer corps for the country. For detail information refer to volume 2

The most important projects to support the sub-sector strategies included the development, maintenance and expansion of the database that documents the collection of artifacts held by the Ministry; and the passage of the new Media legislation and its implementation as well as the implementation of the Joint National Youth Program.

Social Protection

Current Situation

Improving social protection is vital to reducing poverty and increasing the livelihood of the Afghan people, particularly the poor and most vulnerable. This sector strategy is critical to the Government's ongoing poverty reduction efforts. The programs highlighted below form a key part Government's approach to achieving this; alleviating the impacts of poverty and improving the welfare of the country.

The Afghan Constitution defines the role of social protection and obliges the Government to take necessary measures to support the most vulnerable. Since 2001 progress has been achieved in number of areas: cash transfer benefits have been established (martyr's families and disabled) as the main instrument of social support for the victims of the war; regular support to orphanages has been provided from the Core Budget; the MoLSAMD has established departments in all provinces and strengthened its capacity for targeting and cooperating with the NGOs and the donors. In total, some 2.5 million people have been covered with some type of public arrangement for social protection.

The pension system has been strengthened: Although highly dependent on budget transfers, the basic pension scheme for civil servants and military personal has been established. The number of pensions paid has steadily increased from around 10,000 to more than 50,000 (in 2006). The MoLSAMD's Pension Department receives technical assistance for further improvements and the MoF has intensified its effort on collecting pension contributions.

The capacity of ANDMA to coordinate disaster preparedness and response has improved as well. Basic risk vulnerability studies have been either completed or initiated. The links with sub-national structures have been established. The Emergency Budget for Disastrous Situations has been established under the President's authority and a number of interventions for risk mitigation have been made.

Despite the progress in the strengthening of social protection, important challenges and constraints remain, including security issues and low mobilization of the domestic revenues. A further constraint is limited coordination within the Government and with the donors, which leads to duplication of efforts and inefficient targeting.

The ANDS Risk and Vulnerability Assessments indicate that the Afghan people are vulnerable to number of risks:

Table 7.6. Reach of social protection programs

Social protection program	Number of recipients
Martyrs' families	224,850
Disabled	87,717
Orphans	10,500
Children enrolled in kindergartens	25,000
Pensioners	54,000
Public works	1,700,000
Microfinance	340,000
Total	2,442,067

Security and economic risks: The continued insecurity has led to the loss of lives and forced people to migrate. Afghanistan is one of the most heavily land-mined countries. In 2006, landmines killed or injured an average of 61 people per month. The latest survey (NRVA Spring 2007) estimated that 42 percent of the total population was estimated to be poor and living below the CBN poverty line. The incidence of food poverty has been estimated to be even higher. Afghanistan has one of the largest child populations and the smallest proportion of working age populations in the world. Almost 40 percent of the adult population is unemployed.

Health and natural risks: Afghanistan has one of the lowest life expectancies in the world with the life expectancy of 43 years for women and 44 years for men. Unlike in most countries, the life expectancy of women is shorter than for men. Faced with natural disasters, many vulnerable families sold the assets, children were taken out of school to work, many pre-pubescent girls were married and many young men migrated in search for work.

Life-cycle and social risks: Despite legislation prohibiting this practice, around 57 percent of girls are married before the age of sixteen. The early marriage of girls, and consequently, early pregnancy, puts women in high risk. Widespread poverty and the nonexistence of an effective safety net or pension system leaves a high proportion of elderly people vulnerable. According to a study conducted by UNIFEM, out of the 1,327 registered cases of violence against women 30.7 percent were related to physical violence.

Environmental risks and seasonality: People's high dependence on natural resources has increased with rising poverty resulting in serious devastation of the environment. Forests have been seriously depleted. This adversely affects soil stability and weakens flood protection. According to the NRVA 2005 the consumption of the poorest is the highest in summer while it typically falls to critical levels in winter.

A rough estimate shows that half of the Afghan population (12 million) requires public support. They are either poor or concentrated very close to the poverty line and are vulnerable to falling into poverty. In 2006 only around 2.5 million people benefited from social protection arrangements. Currently social protection interventions cover several groups: (i) martyr's families; (ii) disabled with war-related disabilities; (iii) orphans and children enrolled in kindergartens; (iv) victims of natural disasters; (v) pensioners; and (vi) unemployed. A rough calculation shows that the Government would require annually around $2 billion just to keep the poorest and most vulnerable above the poverty line.

Sector targets and expected results

The implementation the strategy will aim to achieve the following targets in line with the Afghanistan Compact and MDGs:

- By end-2012/13 the spring national poverty headcount rate (42 percent) will decrease by 2 percent per year; by end-2010 proportion of people who suffer from hunger will decrease by 5 percent per year;
- By end-2012/13 prevalence of underweight children under five in urban and rural areas will decrease by 2 percent per year; by end-2012/13 proportion of the population below minimum level of dietary energy consumption (urban and rural areas) will decrease by 2 percent per year;
- By March-2011, the number of female- headed households that are chronically poor will be reduced by 20 percent and their employment rate will increase by 20 percent;
- By end-2010 increased assistance will be provided to meet the special needs of all disabled people, including their integration into society through opportunities for education and gainful employment;
- By end-2010 skill development training will be provided for 150,000 unemployed of which women will comprise 35 percent and the disabled will comprise minimum 10 percent;
- By end-2012/13 the Government will employ 3 percent of disabled persons within its administration;
- By end-2012/13 the Government will employ 20 percent of women within its administration;
- By end-2015 reduce gender disparity in access to justice by 50 percent, and completely by 2020;
- By end-2010 the number of treated drug users will increase by 20 percent;
- By 2012/13 pension reforms will be implemented;
- By end-2010 an effective system of disaster preparedness will be in place; by end-2010 an effective system of disaster response will be in place.

Implementation of these strategic objectives and priority policies will lead to visible progress in implementation of the following major outcomes: (i) poverty and vulnerability reduction; (ii) improved social inclusion: (iii) lower infant and maternal mortality; (iv) reduction in harmful child labor; (v) reduction in drug demand within the country; (vi) improved employment; (vii) reduction in vulnerability to natural disasters; (viii) improved aid effectiveness.

Policy framework: sector strategy

Fiscally sound and well targeted social protection interventions are of critical importance for improving the poverty outcomes. The Government is committed to pursuing sustainable interventions through social support, pension system and by strengthening disaster preparedness and response. Given the scarce donor and public funds the focus will be put on supporting the most vulnerable (i.e., the poorest of the poor) by allocating adequate resources to the poorest areas through nationwide targeted programs and transfers and by phasing out non-targeted subsidies (such as energy subsidies) and building the planning and administrative capacity of the MoLSAMD (and other line ministries) to deliver coordinated programs and improve social protection.

The ANDS strategic objectives for the social protection sector are to decrease vulnerability of large number of Afghans and to help the poor to climb out of poverty. It is also to empower the poor and make their voices heard – to decrease inequality, especially among women, and to enhance social inclusion of the neglected such as minorities and disabled. The ultimate objective is to build a country of social justice in line with Islamic values and Afghan traditions. Other important objectives are to support economic growth by improving human capital accumulation; and to support the stability of the country by reducing poverty and increasing social inclusion.

To achieve these objectives the Government will pursue the following priority policies: (i) maintain macroeconomic stability, ensure equitable growth and increase mobilization of domestic revenues; (ii) build fiscally sustainable social support and pension systems; and (iii) improve disaster preparedness and response capacity.

Social support: Reform in this area will focus on the following priority policies: (i) to improve efficiency of the public arrangements for social risk management; (ii) to diversify market based arrangements; (iii) to strengthen informal arrangements; (iv) to improve targeting; (v) to strengthen the capacity and restructure the MoLSAMD; and (vi) to improve partnership with the civil society (NGOs) and enhance aid coordination.

In the future social protection will target two main groups: the population "at risk" and war survivors.

BOX 7.7. GREATER SUPPORT TO POOR FAMILIES WITH SMALL CHILDREN: ZAKAT-BASED TAX

Limited resources are impediment for more substantial support to the poor families with small children. Introduction of the Zakatbased tax and establishment of the Afghanistan Social Protection Fund to attract charity contributions in line with the Islamic values could mobilize significant resources to support vulnerable families. Larger support to poor families with small children would decrease prevalence of underweight children and infant mortality. Given this, the MoLSAMD will initiate public debate about prospects and modalities for introduction of the Zakat-based tax.

The population "at risk" includes: (i) chronically poor female headed households with small children; (ii) children "at risk"(orphans, street working children, children in begging and exploitative work; children in conflict with law; children with mothers in detention; children with severe disability); (iii) poor persons with disability; (iv) victims of violence, such as women and children victims of violence, abuse and victims of human trafficking; (v) extremely vulnerable individuals, including mentally ill persons, and drug addicts, and (vi) unemployed, underemployed and victims of natural disaster.

The target group of "war survivors" includes:(i) martyr's families from the previous and ongoing conflict; (ii) disable individuals with war related disability, and (iii) civilian victims of the ongoing conflict.

The civilian victims of the ongoing conflict includes the following vulnerable groups: (i) families who lost the breadwinner or members as result of military operations; (ii) families who lost their breadwinner or members as result of suicide bombing that targeted international or Government troops; (iii) families that lost the breadwinner or members as result of military attack at the international or Government troops; (iv) individuals which became disabled as result of military operations; (e) individuals that became disabled as result of suicide or military attacks on international or Government troops; and (vi) families or individuals whose property was destroyed or damaged as result of military operations, suicide and military attack at the international and the Government troops. Social support to this group will be coordinated with the support from the MoD and MoI.

Implementation of this will be through the National Social Protection Sector Program and will consist of: (i) public arrangements; (ii) market-based arrangements; (iii) informal arrangements; and (iv) capacity building. Preliminary costing of the program indicated that around $500 million will be required for the next five years which will need to be met through the Core and the External Budgets.

Public arrangements to enhance social support reform: Future social support systems will include most of the existing public arrangements such as: (i) direct cash payments;(ii) payments in kind; (iii) public works; (iv) skills development; (v) lump sum payments; (vi) support to orphanages; and (vii) land distribution. However, given the insufficient impact on the poor some arrangements like subsidies (for fuel, pensions, and kindergartens) will gradually be eliminated. Support to orphanages will remain part of the social support system; however, they will be reorganized to provide day care services for other children "at risk".

The current cash transfers to the martyr's families and individuals with war related disabilities will be integrated into the pension system and will cease to be part of the social support system. However, this will occur only in the medium term and after completion of pension reforms. The new direct cash transfers will be gradually introduced for the poor disabled with non-war related disability. The inclusion of the poorest families with small children into direct cash transfers will depend on mobilization of domestic revenues and possible introduction of the Zakat-based tax.

Payment in kind, through distribution of humanitarian assistance, will continue to be used to support higher children's enrolment in schools (e.g., food for education) and training of teachers (e.g., food for training). According to the NRVA 2005 the poorest households have critically low consumption during winter, especially in March. Therefore, a new system of payments in kind will be introduced for the poorest families with small children (winterization). The parcels with basic food and nonfood items will be distributed through Afghan Red Crescent Society to support the poorest households in the most difficult period of year. Given the high incidence of rural poverty the new program will be developed to provide free distribution of livestock, orchards and tools for farming helping the poor to diversify agriculture production. Both, direct cash transfers and payments in kind will be made conditional: poor families will have to enroll children in school and take them to regular health checkups.

Given the extent of unemployment, skills development will remain one of the high priority public arrangements in the social support system. However, the terms of reference of the NSDP will be changed to introduce the most vulnerable as the highest priority group for skills development training. Public works programs, such as NSP, NABDP and NRAP will continue to provide job opportunities for the poor. Moreover, the new public work program to re-forest Afghanistan (i.e., "Greening of Afghanistan") will be introduced to supply additional jobs to decrease deforestation of the country. All programs will be redesigned to reach the most isolated and remote areas. In addition to other public arrangements, targeted land distribution and lump sum payments will continue to be used to help the poorest war victims and victims of natural disaster.

Diversification of the market based arrangements: In Afghanistan, market based arrangements for social protection are dominated by microfinance schemes. These will be further developed and strengthened. However, efforts will be made to develop other market-based arrangements such as increasing financial market literacy and the introduction of community-based insurance schemes. Loss of women's inheritance entitlements to male relatives and denial of their property rights prevents women from using collateral and limits access loans for creating employment opportunities. Therefore, future Government policies will introduce measures to enforce women's rights to inheritance.

Strengthening informal arrangements for social risk management: Migration to work in neighboring countries and remitting funds will remain as a key informal arrangement for the poor. The Government will ensure that Afghan migrant workers are not subject to abuse in the countries of their destination. In this regard, the Government will conclude international agreements with the neighboring and other countries to regulate the rights of the Afghanistan's migrant workers.

Priority measures to provide social include:

- Integrate the current direct cash transfers to martyr's families and people with disabilities into the pension system;
- Develop projects for the distribution of livestock, orchards and tools for farming;
- Develop projects for the distribution of food parcels in winter (winterization);
- Develop a new public works program: "Greening of Afghanistan"
- Develop mechanisms for distributing direct cash entitlements to poor disabled individuals with non-war related disabilities and include rehabilitation of the disabled in the BHP in all provinces;
- Develop programs for community-based rehabilitation of drug-addicts;
- In cooperation with NGOs implement pilot projects to support extremely vulnerable groups which will include options for reintegration into families;
- Conduct surveys to collect data on civilian victims of conflict and develop policies to support civilian victims;
- Conduct reviews of the MoLSAMD and prepare plans for capacity building and restructuring, including the establishment of the Child Secretariat within MoLSAMD.

Strengthening the capacity and restructuring the MoLSAMD: Implementation of effective social protection reform will require significant capacity building of the MoLSAMD. The main objectives of this will be to improve policy/strategy/elaboration of standards of care, monitoring, targeting and project preparation/implementation in partnership with NGOs in charge of service delivery; and to increase absorption capacity. Enhanced roles of the private sector and NGOs in providing the services will support timely implementation of the projects. Finally, developing courses to enable university graduates to obtain qualification for social workers will be important for capacity building.

Pension reform: The main objective of pension reform will be to improve old-age protection (especially for civil servants and military) and establish fiscally sustainable pension schemes. Priorities will include the enhancement of fiscal sustainability by increasing collection of the pension contributions, and building the capacity of the Pension Department

Design of the pension reform: Coverage: The future pension system will cover the same groups of employees that are covered in the current system (civil servants and military personal). The system will remain a defined benefit system based on a formula that will take into account age, years of service, and a specified accrual rate. The average benefit for an employee with 25 years of service will equal 50 percent of final pay after Pay and Grading reform. The benefit accrual rate will be 2 percent for each year of service. This formula will be adjusted to increase equity, reduce cost, and address human resource needs of the Government. Pension benefits will be increased in absolute terms (as a result of Pay and Grading reform), but reduced as a percentage of last drawn pay of an employee. They will be automatically indexed for increases in cost of living to preserve the value of pensions. Employees will be eligible for a pension at age 65 if they have ten years of service and will be able to retire at age 55 if they have accumulated 25 years of service. In addition to regular pensions benefits will be provided to pre- retirement and post-retirement war survivors. The existing direct cash transfers to martyr's families and individuals with war related disability will be integrated into the future pension system.

Financing and transition: The pension system will be self-financed from government and employee contributions on wages (payroll tax). Direct budget subsidies will be gradually eliminated. The overall contribution, however, will increase from 11 percent of pay to 16 percent to ensure fiscal sustainability. Around 2 percent (of the 16 percent) will be used to fund post-retirement survivors' benefits. Both, the Government and employees will contribute 8 percent of the payroll amount. The employee's contribution will gradually increase while the Government's will gradually be reduced. Employees retiring before implementation of the Pay and Grading reform will earn pension based on the current pension system rules.

The implementation of pension reforms will also be supported through the National Social Protection Sector Program. The specific components of the pension reform will include: (i) budget subsidies to the pensions system (which will gradually be eliminated); (ii) capacity building, and (iii) modernization of equipment. Preliminary costing of the funding needs have identified the cost of around $150 million which will mainly be covered through the Core Budget (mainly budget subsidies for payments of the pensions which will be eliminated in five years).

Priority measures to support implementation of pension reform:

- Promulgate pension reform by the Government decree;
- Conduct capacity building and training for the staff and managers of the Pension Department, and develop new IT system and processes;
- Modernize accounting and internal operational procedures in harmony with the IT system implementation and improve record keeping and processes;
- Improve collection of the pension payroll taxes and establish a central database to store and process the details on pensioners and their bank accounts; and
- Introduce payments of pensions through banks in Kabul by mid-2009, and throughout the country by end 2010 subject to availability of banking services.

Strengthening the capacity of the Pension Department: Employees of the current pension department, including management, will be required to go through comprehensive training. The staff will be trained in the use of new automated systems. Managers will be required to acquire new skills in program supervision and project management. The most significant attribute of the new pension scheme will be introduction of the payment of pensions through authorized banks.

Disaster preparedness: The main objectives of the sub-sector strategy for disaster preparedness will be to decrease risks from natural disasters and improve disaster preparedness and response with the aim of protecting human lives, assets, public infrastructure and the environment. This objectives will be achieved through implementation of the following priority policies: (i) to strengthen the capacity of ANDMA, not only for coordination and policy making, but also for implementation of programs and projects; (ii) to strengthen the capacity of line ministries for disaster preparedness and disaster response; (iii) to enhance the provincial and community mechanisms for disaster preparedness and response; (iv) to improve coordination within the Government for disaster preparedness and response; (v) to improve aid coordination in the area of delivering the humanitarian assistance, and (vi) to address long-term needs for rehabilitation.

ANDMA: Under existing legislation, the prime responsibility of ANDMA is to coordinate the Government's efforts and to provide policy making. However, lack of the responsibility for implementation of key projects for disaster preparedness/response and overreliance on the line ministries is a weakness. Therefore, the existing legislation will be amended to reflect the need to strengthen the ANDMA's role in implementing key projects. It is important to stress that line ministries will remain responsible for the implementation of most projects for disaster preparedness/response.

Disaster preparedness will also be supported by the National Social Protection Sector Program and will include: (i) finalization of risk vulnerability assessments and disaster preparedness plans at the national and sub-national level; (ii) strengthening the capacity and the role of the ANDMA; (iii) establishing the emergency operation centers at the provincial level and regional warehouses; and (iv) modernization of equipment.

Priority measures to support sub-sector strategy for disaster preparedness:

- Amend the legislation to clearly reflect the leading role of the ANDMA in coordinating the national efforts but also for implementing of key programs and projects;
- Approve annual plans for disaster preparedness, finalize disaster risk analyses and guidelines for disaster response, and develop the provincial disaster management plans;
- Develop standardized operating procedures for quick assessment and response, reporting, and for rapid mobilization of international assistance;
- Establish Emergency Operation Centers at provincial level, response centers and teams at the regional level and effective early warning systems and develop the community emergency response system and develop back-up communication system based on Codan;
- Construct 12 regional storage facilities for aid assistance and equipment and improve public awareness activities and raise national awareness about disaster risks and vulnerabilities

Strengthening capacity and improving coordination: The ANDMA, and to a lesser extent the line ministries, require strong capacity building and equipment modernization. Having rescue equipment, management tools and operational centers at the provincial level will provide the necessary facilities to respond to disasters. Strengthening disaster preparedness and response at the community level through CDCs will be required. Maintaining access to modern technology, such as with alarm systems, is important for reducing casualties and damages that occur during disasters. Finally, given the existing legal ambiguities, the role of the ANDMA in leading and coordinating the national efforts for disaster preparedness and response will need to be clearly defined and this will require adjustment of the current legislative framework.

Refuges, Returnees and Internally Displaced Persons

The ANDS strategic objective for the Refugee, Returnee and Internally Displaced Persons (IDPs) strategy is to facilitate the planned and voluntary return of refugees and IDPs and the reintegration of returnees and IDPs into society. This strategy establishes the Governments efforts in coordinating and reintegrating refugees and the IDPs into society. The planned and voluntary return of refugees and IDPs will contribute to economic growth, the reduction of poverty and the strengthening of security and stability of the country and the region. World-wide experience has indicated that large, unplanned, and essentially involuntary returns generate a range of negative consequences as they are managed as emergency influxes.

Situation in the Sector

More than five million persons have returned to their homes since 2002. Yet over three million Afghan refugees remain in Iran and Pakistan. Several hundred thousand others are present in former Soviet Union countries (CIS, CAR) and Europe.

The majority of those that remain in Pakistan (2.1 million) and Iran (0.9 million) have been in exile for over twenty years remain a serious constraint for voluntary repatriation. The presence of these communities places strains on both the Government and neighboring country governments. The desire of the neighboring countries to engineer large scale return is a challenge to the principle of voluntary repatriation. Experience indicates that such pressures will not produce sustainable or humane outcomes. This is particularly the case for extremely vulnerable individuals: unaccompanied women, unaccompanied minors, women at risk, the elderly, the very poor, those in need of medical care and drug addicted individuals.

Economic and social reintegration faces many constrains and challenges. Since 2005 repatriation of refugees has slowed down considerably. This is attributable to a number of factors: (i) the deterioration in the security situation; (ii) limited economic opportunities, including employment, upon arrival; (iii) access to housing; (iv) limited access to basic health and education facilities; and (v) the length of time in exile. Lower return figures have led to an increase in the pressures from the neighboring countries to stem the continuing trend of out-migration from Afghanistan. The most visible indication has been the deportation of over 350,000 unregistered Afghans from Iran.

It is very probable that high levels of mass and voluntary repatriation are over. The refugees' long stay in exile, poverty, and dissuasive conditions in many parts of Afghanistan are likely to prove difficult obstacles to overcome in future.

Internal displacement remains a significant problem facing the same constrains and challenges as do refugees: (i) ongoing conflict; (ii) natural disasters (drought, floods); and (iii) lack of livelihoods. As a consequence, there are approximately 160,000 internally displaced persons, mostly in southern Afghanistan. There is also evidence of secondary migration of returnees from places of origin to cities and back to the neighboring countries.

Further, many of those that return face significant hardships and difficulties re integrating into life in Afghanistan. Drug abuse and its socio-economic repercussions on families and communities are aggravated by the large numbers of refugees returning. These groups have often been exposed to drugs during their stay abroad. The difficulties of economic and social reintegration also place them at particular risk of drug abuse on their return. Ensuring that they do not contribute to drug production or become drug uses requires viable and visible employment prospects.

The sector strategy provides policies for voluntary, planned and sustainable return of the refugees and IDPs that will support stability of Afghanistan, its economic development and poverty reduction. The strategic vision of the sector strategy is to provide safe, voluntary, gradual and sustainable reintegration possibilities for all Afghan refugees, returnees and IDPs choosing to return. This vision supports the rights of all Afghans to return to their homes, reposes property and enjoy all constitutional and human rights. Greater attention to protection of the vulnerable groups among refugees and IDPs, including children and women is an important part of this vision.

The main strategic objective of the sector is to transition out of a purely refugee and humanitarian framework for managing population movements to a more comprehensive set of policy arrangements that, will advance durable solutions for the remaining 3 million Afghans in the neighboring countries, for returnees, and for Internally Displaced Persons (IDPs) including the most vulnerable populations, and which will not rely solely on voluntary returns. Overall strategic goals and objectives have been divided in three categories:

The Government's expected outcomes from the sector strategy are to:

- support the safe, voluntary, an gradual return of refugees from Pakistan, Iran and elsewhere;
- prepare and implement more visible and effective, sustainable reintegration programs and interventions;
- improve social protection and disaster preparedness;
- strengthen the management of cross border movements and economic migration;
- prepare plans to improve the response to internal displacement crisis; and
- give greater attention to the protection of the vulnerable groups among refugees and IDPs, including children and women.
- improve the facilitation for gradual return of all Afghans who wish to return voluntarily from Pakistan, Iran and other host countries through policy negotiation and coordination;
- strengthen the Government's capacity to plan, manage, and assist the reintegration of returning Afghans and IDPs;
- improve the capacity of the Government to plan for and respond to internal displacement;
- improve the terms of stay and conditions for Afghans in neighboring countries;
- make progress towards the implementation of the bilateral agreements on temporary labor migration; and
- improve access to land for the refugee and the IDP population.

Further, the strategy will support the implementation of the following Afghanistan Compact benchmarks:

- By end-2010, all refugees opting to return and internally displaced persons will be provided assistance for rehabilitation and integration in their local communities; their integration will be supported by national development programs, particularly in key areas of return
- Afghanistan, its neighbors and countries in the region will reach agreements to enable Afghanistan to import skilled labor, and to enable Afghans to seek work in the region and send remittances home.
- Human rights monitoring will be carried out by the Government and independently by the AIHRC, and the UN will track the effectiveness of measures aimed at the protection of human rights; the AIHRC will be supported in the fulfillment of its objectives with regard to monitoring, investigation, protection and promotion of human rights.

Depending on the success of the implementation of the ANDS and the specific sector programs, some broad scenarios for the return and reintegration sector could be envisaged for the period (2008-13). These assume that current trends will be unlikely to deviate dramatically (positively or negatively) from the present situation and that therefore there will still be a substantial number of Afghans remaining outside their country in 2013:

- **Scenario One**: progress towards peace and security, political stability, economic and social development improves on current trend lines. There are no changes to current legal and operational frameworks governing repatriation. Support for reintegration through national programs benefits from increased and better targeted investments. Afghans continue to enjoy international legal protection as refugees. Internal displacement continues as a consequence of localized conflict. Under these conditions, it may be envisaged that a projected figure of between 800,000 and 1,000,000 Afghans return home voluntarily and sustainably, predominantly to the west, north and central regions of the country.
- **Scenario Two**: progress towards peace and security, political stability, economic and social development follows current trends. The number of Afghans returning outside the Tripartite Framework increases as a result of new measures introduced by the neighboring countries. Support for reintegration through national programs benefits from increased and better targeted investments and improved response capabilities. The terms and conditions for registered Afghans to remain in the neighboring countries deteriorate. Conflict induced internal displacement persists, especially in southern Afghanistan. Under these conditions it may be envisaged that a projected overall figure of 600,000 – 800,000 returns voluntarily or are returned.
- **Scenario Three**: progress towards peace and security, political stability, economic and social development deteriorate. There are no changes to current legal and operational frameworks governing repatriation. Support for reintegration through national programs benefits from increased and better targeted investments but implementation is weak due to poor operating conditions (security). Afghans continue to enjoy a measure of international legal protection as refugees though less than before. Internal displacement continues as a consequence of localized conflict. Under these conditions, it may be envisaged that a projected figure of between 400,000 and 600,000 Afghans return home voluntarily and sustainably, predominantly to the west, north and central regions of the country.

The Government will implement the following priority policies to achieve the sector objective:

- prepare and implement more visible and effective reintegration programs and interventions and to improve mechanism for delivering immediate reintegration assistance to returning refugees and IDPs;
- improve social protection and disaster preparedness;
- address concerns of long-staying Afghans that prefer to remain in exile;
- develop broader policy responses to population movements;
- retain the Tripartite Agreements is an important tool to ensure policy coordination and respect for refugee law and humanitarian principles;
- improve access to land for the refugee and the IDP population;
- improve inter-ministerial coordination; and
- improve aid coordination and increase aid effectiveness.

Specific activities the Government will undertake are detailed below.

Maintaining frameworks to manage repatriations

Within the region, the principle legal and operational framework governing voluntary repatriation is provided by the Tripartite Agreements signed between Afghanistan, UNHCR, Iran and Pakistan respectively. These agreements are serviced by regular meetings of Tripartite Commissions at both Ministerial and working level.

The Tripartite Agreement with Iran was renewed for a further year in February 2007; an extension of the agreement with Pakistan for three years was signed in August 2007. Afghanistan has signed similar agreements with Denmark, France, the Netherlands, Norway, the United Kingdom, Sweden and Switzerland.

The Government is committed to continue working with Iran, Pakistan and the UNHCR on the implementation of the Tripartite Agreement and the Tripartite Commission.

Specifically, the most important measures to be taken to support implementation of the strategy are to:

- fully reflect the principles of voluntary, dignified and gradual return in the Tripartite agreements between countries of asylum, Afghanistan, and UNHCR;
- discuss and agree the annual return planning figures with the Governments of Pakistan and Iran within the Tri-Partite Commissions;
- strengthen the management of cross border movements and economic migration; and
- promote a national framework and policy guideline for the protection of IDPs as well as the IDP mapping exercise.

The Government's policy supports the voluntary, planned and sustainable repatriation movements. At the same time, the Government is committed to increasing the overall rate of returns. This requires improving the livelihoods and welfare opportunities in the country, increasing the attractiveness of the country to displaced persons.

The Government will work to address the constraints returnees face on returning, including increasing economic opportunities (employment) and social services (health and education).

The Government, with support from the international community, will develop a range of political and practical solutions to work with and address the concerns of neighbors on the recent slowing of repatriation rates. This will assist in reducing bilateral tensions on this issue.

The retention of the Tripartite Agreements is an important tool to ensure policy coordination and respect for refugee law and humanitarian principles. Ensuring the voluntariness of return is critically important in improving sustainability and minimizing humanitarian distress. In view of the potential political and humanitarian consequences of large induced returns, and taking into account the need to develop broader policy responses to population movements, future policy actions will benefit from the active involvement of a wider cross section of Government ministries.

Table 13.0.1. Cross Cutting Issues in Social and Economic Development Pillar

Sector	Anti-Corruption	Gender	Counter-Narcotics	Environment	Regional Cooperation	Capacity Development
Energy	The high priority on improved sector governance and the development of improved procurement, tender and contracting processes will mitigate corruption. By promoting increased private sector participation, international operating standards and government as sector regulator, a new paradigm for sector operations can improve transparency, service quality and compliance with the law.	Improved local energy can reduce traditional women's household burdens through efficient stoves, water pumping and agro-processing that also improve women's and other household residents' (i.e., young children, older relatives) health conditions.	Improved supply of power can have an immediate impact on local communities by increasing employment and drawing labor from poppy productions Energy as a business itself— power generation, supply and fuel supply - can provide alternative employment to those presently without employment in many communities.	Improved sector governance includes environmental regulation as well as meaningful measures for enforcement of standards. Emphasis on energy efficiency, renewable energy, and improved cooking fuels will have measurable impact on improved environmental conditions; The current energy law provides for environmental protections that are now being developed.	Regional cooperation in the trade and transmission of energy products plays an important part in the expansion of power supplies in Afghanistan.	Improved technical, commercial and regulatory skills are essential in all energy sub-sectors. This strategy supports (1) the development of vocational training for power and energy sector workers to become familiar with installation, health and safety and monitoring of operations; (2) improved university and other academic training to instill project finance, project management, legal skills and overall commercial capacity; (3) professional training for government officials to implement important regulatory and oversight functions; (4) commercial skills to manage and operate the sector.
Transport	The strategy provides a framework to improve governance in Transportation Ministry. This includes expanding merit-based selection and performance based contracts for key staff. Penalties for	Government Transport agencies will increase female participation through dditional training and new	Support enforcement activities of the MoI and police against narcotics smuggling. Checkpoints for narcotics smuggling will be built into border customs clearance stations, truck pull-offs for permanent and roving	Environmental impact assessments and management plans will be prepared and implemented in accordance with Afghan Law for all works. Better quality roads improve the efficiency of vehicles, reducing per km fuel usage. Fuel and other petroleum products must	Improved transportation links will significantly improve Afghanistan's links with regional and international markets. This will strengthen Afghanistan's role and links with a number of trading groups, including	A Transportation Training Institute will be established to boost capacity of sector ministries and institutions. This will help strengthen the planning capacity of staff for all transport modes for feasibility studies and infrastructure planning. Capacity will be increased so

Table 13.0.1. (Continued)

Sector	Anti-Corruption	Gender	Counter-Narcotics	Environment	Regional Cooperation	Capacity Development
	corrupt practices are also specified.	opportunities Greater consultation with women. Also implement the National Action Plan for the Women of Afghanistan.	weigh stations, and urban bypasses. As civil airports will be secured against narcotics smuggling.	be clean in order to meet Afghan environmental standards.	SAARC, CAREC, SCO and ECOTA	that Ministry staff are able to conduct drivers' licensing tests, vehicle safety inspections and enforce traffic flow regulations. Capacity will also be increased in the Civil Aviation Authority in order to take over control of civilian airspace from international forces
Water Resource Management	Adoption of a River Basin administrative structure should decentralize traditional mechanisms which have been prone to foster corruption.	Access to clean water and improved sanitation facilities will improve health in households, thereby benefiting all household members but particularly women who often are caretakers and who face threats to health during child birth.	Implementing strong water strategy programs having extensive user participation should infuse effective anti-narcotics sentiments into the populace. Control of water allocations could be sued to discourage the poppy cultivation and encourage production of other high value crops.	Environment Law establishes a framework for the conservation and productive use of natural resources, including water, granting enforcement and permitting rights to the government to be implemented through NEPA. Water sector strategy programs and the sector's institutional structure will be used to support environmental policies, regulations and laws.	Since water resources require the rationalization of use by different countries, regional cooperation is required for effective management of water resources shared by different countries. It is an important factor in developing effective management of several key river basins.	Water sector capacity building programs are essentially targeted at the three principal development components: Institutional, organizational, and individual. And, each component is further sub-divided amongst various relevant sub sectors comprising water resources management, rural and urban water supply, and irrigation.
Information and Communications Technology (ICT)	E-Governance and other E-Enabled services will reduce the scope for corruption because it provides better record sand more information	Mobile and Electronic commerce will make it possible to work at home and be commercially viable without offending cultural sensitivities.	Better communications Will improve enforcement and detection	Telephone services and the internet reduce the need for physical travel. It reduces congestion costs and pollution from vehicles. Emissions.	Better communications assists regional cooperation	Communications is at the forefront of skills development. It encourages computer literacy which is a key capacity constraint in Afghanistan. Because it is based on English, it encourages key language skills.

Sector	Anti-Corruption	Gender	Counter-Narcotics	Environment	Regional Cooperation	Capacity Development
Urban Development	More effective scrutiny of tendering for public sector projects. Monitoring of sources of finance for private urban development, where appropriate.	Women will benefit from improved living conditions as a result of upgrading. Improved living conditions could enhance levels of female education. Women could enjoy access to housing finance and economic development initiatives. Roles and responsibilities of female professionals in government will be enhanced.	Contributions could be made to demand-reduction through sustainable employment and vocational training.	Introduction of an environmental focus in planning processes and new regulatory frameworks, to cover water/waste management, pollution control, etc. Enforcement of environmental impact assessments for all urban projects.	Focus on the specific situation of frontier cities, including Herat, Mazar, Jalalabad. Take account of the potential for regional business in development of new cities. There could be RC for urban planning?	The strategy includes a strong focus on reform and strengthening of key urban institutions, both at the central and regional level, as a precondition of effective urban governance.
Mining	There will be improved sector governance aimed at increased legitimate private investment. Reforms include improved tender and contracting functions of Government, and drafting of fundamental legal and regulatory documents, and also include the establishment of legal, financial and monitoring institutions.	There have been virtually no women entering the sector in recent years. A targeted initiative for "Women in Mining" to improve female employment will be supported.	Mining will be an alternative source of employment in some poppy growing regions in the South.	Inspectorate and Cadastre to be established at the Ministry Mines. This includes environmental inspection and regulation. Regulations will be specifically drafted that address environmental requirements for public and private investment.	There is already considerable cross-border trade in this sector. Opportunities to formalize these arrangements and enhance government revenues exist. Government will consider opportunities to work with cross-border countries where improved transport (i.e., select light rail) and infrastructure may have mutual benefit.	The Ministry proposes capacity building for its staff members. Capacity building will be required to implement the hydrocarbon and mineral legislation, and bidding and tendering processes, including tender evaluation.

Table 13.0.1. (Continued)

Sector	Anti-Corruption	Gender	Counter-Narcotics	Environment	Regional Cooperation	Capacity Development
Education	This issue has been addressed with institutional strengthening programs in all Ministries. There are also improved accounting procedures and support with procurement that will lower the probability of corruption.	The strategy reduces barriers for women to enter the education sector both as students and teaching staff.	There will be specific counter narcotics programs introduced into primary and secondary school curricula. In addition an anti narcotics message will be built into the sports program	Environmental issues will be incorporated into the primary and secondary curriculum	The education system is regionally dispersed. The primary and secondary strategy has a component to support remote and disadvantage communities. The universities both in Kabul and in the provinces are to be considerably upgraded, and each university will be supported by a recognized external university.	Lack of capacity development in the past has resulted in a failure to spend allocated funds. An inter-ministerial committee with the education Ministries and Ministry of Finance has been established to solve this problem. Capacity building projects have been included in MoE ad MoHE.
Culture, Media and Youth	There will be institutional strengthening program at the Ministry. As part of this, an internal audit department and a computing department will be established and there will be a review of security procedures. Legal and diplomatic efforts to retrieve missing artifacts will also be made	Gender will be a core issue covered in all state owned media.	The Ministry will work closely with the Ministry of Counter Narcotics and seek advice from them about the incorporation of an anti drugs message in all forms of media. The National Youth Program, through all its components will promote a drug-free society.	Preservation and rehabilitation of historical sites and artifacts makes an important contribution to the environment. Under the Youth Program, youth will be encouraged to become invoved in environmental programs	Tourism, culture and media can be further developed through an effective and fruitful cooperation with regional partners. Regional cooperation can also support and ensure the efforts of MoIC by strengthening the legal framework and the enforcement of the law in relation to archaeological sites to stop illicit traffic at the borders, and awareness-raising at both the national and the international level.	The major capacity weakness is the lack of qualified staff at the Ministry. The Ministry requires a computer department with trained staff ,software and hardware, an internal audit department with accountancy skills, and officials with legal skills to deal with drafting legislation and retrieval of artifacts

Sector	Anti-Corruption	Gender	Counter-Narcotics	Environment	Regional Cooperation	Capacity Development
Agriculture and Rural Development	All programs within the Sector Strategy emphasize accountability and transparency. Local governance programs reduce corruption, since the act of community ownership and participation promotes a sense of obligation and accountability which is continually reinforced through all functions of project management.	The focus on community level development promotes gender mainstreaming and gender-balanced development. Strategy is designed to ensure that women have community representation and to promote gender-sensitive development planning, implementation and monitoring of all projects. Involvement in income-producing activities. Skills development and other capacity building programs will contribute further to both women's empowerment and increasing household income levels.	The Sector Strategy focuses on providing viable income-generating alternatives by raising the profitability of licit crops, promoting market linkages and creating off-farm employment. Rural communities are closely knit. Those communities isolated from government are more prone to grow poppy and other illicit crops. Those benefiting from integrated rural development programs are less likely to grow poppy. Improved governance can influence entrenched attitudes and is therefore vital to the enabling environment to tackle drugs production.	The Government will provide capacity development to assist communities to be able to manage their natural resources and implement projects based on sustainable use. Government is currently developing the regulatory environment in such areas as environmental impact assessments, protected areas management and compliance and enforcement.	Strategy is to develop institutional linkages in the areas of collaborative research, technology transfers and training/skills enhancement, and the exchange of scientific information with regard to Afghanistan's disaster preparedness program. AREDP will require a high level of regional interaction, particularly in the area of current imports and potential future exports. Afghanistan's membership in the South Asian Association for Regional Cooperation (SAARC) will operationalize a Regional Food Security Reserve and proposed Regional Food Bank. The Center on Integrated Rural Development for Asia and the Pacific (CIRDAP) is a regional intergovernmental autonomous	Capacity development is an integral part of the ARD Sector Strategy. In addition to internal capacity building and institutional reform both at the central and local levels, every program intervention in agriculture and rural development has a significant capacity development component.

Table 13.0.1. (Continued)

Sector	Anti-Corruption	Gender	Counter-Narcotics	Environment	Regional Cooperation	Capacity Development
					organization established for the promotion of integrated rural development in the region.	
Health & Nutrition	Strategic actions related to anti-corruption include: Establish Health Service Ombudsmen unit as a fully autonomous entity. Promote public awareness campaign related to the Health Service Ombudsmen Raise professional standards in key MoPH entities Promote Civil Service Commission Code of Conduct Establish permanent MoPH transparency working group.	The Basic Package of Health Services is aimed at women and children. The MoPH has placed emphasis on having female health staff employed at every health facility. Increased number of qualified female health workers at local facilities Increase awareness of gender and health and rights, raising women's decision-making role in relation to health seeking practices. Ensuring that women have equal employment opportunities within the Sector Monitor equity issues.	The MoPH is the line Government of Afghanistan agency with primary responsibility for delivery of treatment and rehabilitation services to drug users throughout Afghanistan and implementation of HIV prevention programs. Strategic actions related to counter-narcotics include the: implementation of the National Drug Control Strategy; and implementation of the Counter-Narcotics Implementation Plan.	Environmental health, including water and sanitation, indoor and outdoor air quality and proper housing is an important pillar of public health. Strategic actions related to the environment include the: enforcement of existing laws, by-laws and regulations; strengthening human resource expertise in the field of environmental protection; raising awareness of environmental issues with the public; formulating a National Environmental Action Plan for Afghanistan; and monitoring the progress toward the achievement of a clean and safe environment.	Afghanistan is fully committed to the implementation of International Health Regulations 2005, through which the MoPH is responsible for detecting, reporting and responding to all public health emergencies of international concern. Afghanistan has increasingly become a full participant in health activities in the South Asia region and its role in international organizations, including WHO and UNICEF, has strengthened over the past few years. Strategic actions include: implementing the Kabul Declaration on Regional Collaboration in	The strategy provides a framework for increasing the capacity of staff in the sector to better deliver health and nutrition services. Strategic actions include: undertaking a Training Needs Assessment of MoPH staff; building the core skills of MoPH staff in English, report writing, basic computer skills, basic management and introductory public health; establishing different levels of training courses suited to the Afghan situation; improving the coordination between MoPH and its partners in the implementation and revision of the MoPH training plan; and determining the unmet training needs based on the job description of the employees

Sector	Anti-Corruption	Gender	Counter-Narcotics	Environment	Regional Cooperation	Capacity Development
					Health; and fostering a stronger partnership with Iran and Pakistan that will provide a platform for dialogue and ensure joint actions for ad-dressing critical cross-border health issues.	
Social Protection	to improve management of the direct cash transfers and eliminate irregularities to ensure that distribution of the land plots will be free of corruption	to introduce benefits for chronically poor female headed households, victims of violence and other cate-gories of women "at risk" to improve legislation to ensure women's rights to inherit to improve "Food for Schooll" programs to increase pri-mary school enrolment of girls to introduce free legal ad-vise benefit for women "at risk" and improve women's access to justice	to improve treat-ment of the drug addicts to improve rehabilitation of drug ad-dicts and their access to education, skill development and job opportunities to contribute to re-duction in domestic drug demand and poppy cultivation by improving the social support system	to prepare and implement new public work program (Greening of Afghanistan) to reduce de-forestation of the country and miti-gate environment risk	to support implementa-tion of the SAARC's Social Protection Chart to establish the Na-tional Coordination Committee in line with the SAARC's recom-mendations	to improve MoLSAMD's capacity for vulnerability analysis, targeting and project preparation and implementation To improve the capacity of the Pension Department for implementation of the pension reform To improve ANDMA's capacity for co-ordinating the disaster preparedness process within the Government, with sub-national level and with donors and humanitarian agencies To modernize ANDMA's equipment and build regional warehouses
Refugee, Returnee & IDP's	In the design of reintegration program components such as land allocation, shelter and housing, attention will be paid to	Special attention will be paid to protect children, women and the elderly during the return proc-ess.	To improve re-habilitation and reintegration into society large number of drug users will be among the returnees.	Environmental issues will merit greater focus, especially in view of the additional strains on urban and municipal infrastructure and services occasioned by possible	The Government will aim to conclude and implement regional and bilateral agreement on population movements and migration;	The capacity for Inter-ministerial cooperation will need to be improved. The refugee return is not responsibility of MoRR only. Capacity for program

Table 13.0.1. (Continued)

Sector	Anti-Corruption	Gender	Counter-Narcotics	Environment	Regional Cooperation	Capacity Development
	anti-corruption measures by providing full transparency on beneficiary selection processes.			return of further 3 million persons which will put additional pressure on natural resources; As the refugee return increases, the Government will need to pay particular attention to the poten-tial for conflicts over land and access to natural resources (land, pasture, water, forests) especially in ethnically mixed provinces	Plan to better communicate to the neighboring countries the Government policies and programs for repatriation of the refugees	preparation and implementation will also need to be improved, especially for im-mediate response to IDPs crisis. The draw down of funds from Ministry of Finance has been slow. A program/project implementation unit (PIU) has been established within MORR to assist with the Land Allocation Scheme.
Private Sector Development	Removal of nuisance procedures, licenses and taxes will reduce corruption. Making admini-stration more predictable so that laws are followed and administrative discre-tion is reduced will also help.	Economic growth will pro-vide a strong base for increasing demand for female labor and increasing their role in all aspects of the economic life of the country. Also programs that will provide women with greater access to training and credit facilities and will encourage the women-owned and operated businesses.	Increased demand for labor and increased investment opportunities in legal private sector activity provides an alterna-tive to the incomes they are now making in the illicit narcot-ics trade.	Increasedr formalization of firms increases the likelihood that environmental regulations are ad-hered to.	Efforts at developing closer regional cooperation with neighboring countries will help expand markets for the private sector and contribute to the success of the private sector development strategy. Open domestic markets with a strong private sector will further in-crease integration as trade, transport, communication and other links are made with neighboring countries.	Government, donors, the private sector and NGOs will provide additional support to increase the skills of the Afghan workforce. This will help assist both government and the private sector.

Provide housing, facilities and social services to returnees

The Government will continue to provide housing facilities, land plots and infrastructure to returnees to encourage voluntary returns.

Key programs and projects to support implementation of the strategy will be implemented by several line ministries. These projects will support the reintegration of the returnees by providing housing, public services and income generation opportunities. Distribution of land plots to solve the housing problem will remain an important public arrangement. Public works programs will provide job opportunities together with skill development training. These projects will be developed, costed and integrated into the National Budget by the end of 2008.

Since 2002 over a million returnees have benefited from a rural housing program implemented in all regions of the country. Approximately 170,000 houses have been built. Over 10,000 water points have been constructed in key returnee destinations.

A Land Allocation Scheme was launched in 2005 to address the needs of landless returnees and IDPs for land for housing. These settlements have the necessary infrastructure including schools, clinics, roads, mosques, potable water, parks and sanitation.

Priority has been given to those who have already applied for land (those that returned between 2002 and 2006) and the most vulnerable (for example the disabled and widowed). Presently over 520,000 applications have been registered, approximately 100,000 beneficiaries have been selected, 23,000 plots have been distributed and 5,500 families have moved into houses on site.

The Government will also increase the provision of social services available to returnees, refugees and IDPs. These programs include:

- providing legal aid and vocational training for Afghan refugees and support to the host communities in Pakistan;
- improving primary and secondary health care for Afghan refugees in Mashhad and Zahedan, Iran;
- enhancing emergency preparedness for IDPs to ensure the timely and necessary support is provided to minimize hardship and suffering; and
- providing public works programs will provide job opportunities together with skill development training.

Enhance government capacity to encourage voluntary returns

Ongoing efforts to increase Government capacity to manage returns will continue. Specifically, the Government will work to:

- improve internal Government coordination mechanisms, intern-ministerial cooperation and capacity for refugee and IDPs return;
- enhance policy advice, data collection, analysis, research, knowledge generation and advocacy;
- provide policy advice to provincial authorities;
- promote a national framework and policy guideline for the protection of IDPs and an IDP mapping exercise;

- identify and implement programs and interventions to support voluntary refugee and IDPs return;
- incorporate IDPs and returnees into development and national programs and to provide for a national framework for their protection;
- ensure greater access to land for the refugee and IDP population;
- ensure refugees and IDPs have greater access to microfinance loans; and
- improve the capacity of the Ministry for Refugees and Returnees.

Conclusion

The sector strategies summarized here identify the ANDS strategic objectives, principal output targets and the projects and programs that will be required to reach these goals. More detailed sector and ministry strategies are presented in ANDS Volume II.

The objective of the ANDS with respect to economic and social development is to provide effective support to the mobilization of the country's resources through the private sector, including efficiently providing the needed physical, legal and commercial infrastructure and institutional frameworks, while taking action to meet the pressing needs of the poor and most vulnerable members of the society. This strategy recognizes the need to highlight the lessons learned over the past six years. These have been reflected in common themes that run throughout the ANDS.

The ANDS provides a renewed emphasis on mobilizing private sector investment, both because of the limited resources available relative to the tasks at hand, and also because of the much greater efficiency evident with private sector operations compared to either state owned enterprises, Ministry implementation efforts, and donor funded and implemented activities. This principle is reflected in most of the sector strategies under this pillar. A model for these efforts to be considered is what has been accomplished in the telecommunications sector. Of course, for many reasons, it is easier to establish a good enabling environment and regulatory framework for telecommunications services than it is to bring private investment into the development of natural resources, infrastructure and public utilities or even provision of educational and health care services. A number of the approaches set out in the ANDS are either built on enabling private investment to play a greater role in sectors presently dominated by state operations (e.g., power, mining) or to carrying out pilot projects to test the potential for doing so (e.g., education and commercial agriculture utilizing state owned land).

An attempt has been made to create more f ocused ministries and government agencies. based on well defined mandates, in line with their capabilities within the appropriate role of the public sector activities, and with mechanisms in place to efficiently monitor and evaluate their performance. In some cases, past attempts to establish the role of government in the economic and social development process, for state building purposes, left Ministries and government agencies with very broad and unrealistic mandates and objectives.

Efforts are also being made to devolve responsibilities for narrower tasks to result-oriented departments or authorities, and providing the managers of these institutions with sufficient authority to achieve results. Thus, responsibility for Urban Development is being devolved down to Municipalities, where municipal leaders are expected to be more responsive to realistic needs of their cities and more accountable to their residents for municipal services. Similar devolution of both operational control and responsibility is at the heart of the National Solidarity Program's efforts to enable Community Development Councils implement projects to the benefit of their communities. Accordingly, independent regulatory authorities will be established with well defined mandates to encourage private sector investment and put in place regulatory frameworks needed to assure effective competition. For example, river basin authorities will eventually be given greater autonomy and responsibility for development of the five major river basins in the country; a Civil Aviation Authority will be given greater responsibility for civil aviation development and safety. Various regulatory authorities are already being given a mandate to create the conditions necessary for attracting private investment while maintaining a competitive market place. At the same time, provincial governors are being given greater responsibility to oversee development activities in their relevant provinces, to be coordinated by the Independent Department for Local Governance under the supervision of the President for more efficiency.

8. CROSS-CUTTING ISSUES

The ANDS has pursued a proactive policy with regard to the treatment of cross-cutting issues. In terms of importance, Government views cross-cutting issues as being of equal significance to the sector strategies themselves. The Government recognizes the development vision of the ANDS cannot be met without addressing the presence of large scale illegal narcotics activities, high levels of corruption, gender inequity, limited public and private capacities, a degraded environment and weak regional cooperation. For this reason, the Government has fully integrated six crosscutting issues into the ANDS: (i) regional cooperation; (ii) counter-narcotics; (iii) anti-corruption; (iv) gender equality; (v) capacity building; and (vi) environmental management. The strategic objectives and mainstreaming of the outcomes of these six issues are outlined below.

Regional Cooperation

Background and Context

The strategic vision of regional cooperation is to contribute to regional stability and prosperity, and to enhance the conditions for Afghanistan to resume its central role as a land bridge between Central Asia and South Asia, and the Middle East and the Far East, as the best way of benefiting from increased trade and export opportunities.

The reestablishment of trade allows for the reconnection of Central Asia with South Asia, and also the development of potentially important trade links between China and the Middle East and Europe. This will contribute substantially to the economic growth and integration of the countries in the region and foster cooperation on mutual interests. Access to Chinese markets and its rapidly developing business hub of Urumqi has expanded with the completion of a bridge at the border with Tajikistan.

The central goal of the Regional Cooperation issue is to contribute to regional stability and prosperity, and to enhance the conditions for Afghanistan to resume its central role as a land bridge between Central Asia and South Asia, and the Middle East and the Far East, as the best way of benefiting from increased trade and export opportunities.

Strategic outcomes are detailed below.

- Enhanced regional cooperation provides Afghanistan an opportunity to connect land locked energy rich Central Asia with warm water ports and energy deficient South Asia. As a result of this expanded trade Afghanistan would be able to meet part of its energy demand.
- As a transit country, Afghanistan will realize increased revenue and enhanced economic activity, enabling it to better meet its main development challenges.
- The removal of trade impediments and lower trade barriers will create a freer market and enhance the flow of goods, services, investment, and technology and support Afghan economic development.
- Regional cooperation facilitates harmonization of standards and regulations to enhance cross border initiatives, such as greater regional trade and investment, the exploitation of hydro-power, hydrocarbons, infrastructure development, and social development.
- Improved border management and customs cooperation at regional level increases security and helps to fight organized cross- border crime such as trafficking in arms and drugs.
- Improved access for women to wider political and economical participation at national and regional levels.
- Improved economic conditions for facilitating the return of refugees and reduce migration.

Implementation framework

The re-establishment of Afghanistan as a major trading hub at the heart of Asia will require the support of the key international players, namely the U.S., E.U., and the big economies of South Asia and the Far East. Since early 2002, Afghanistan has signed at least 21 agreements in trade, transit, transport and investment with countries and organization in the region. The December 2002 Kabul Conference on Good Neighborly Relations, the December 2005 Regional Economic Cooperation Conference, held in Kabul, and its subsequent follow up conferences in New Delhi, and the more recent Pak- Afghan Regional Peace Jirga, held in Kabul on 9-12 August 2007, are all important regional initiatives.

Efforts to strengthen regional cooperation are based on mutual benefit. Improving bilateral, regional and international trade relationships, for example, benefits all countries involved. Likewise, improving security benefits all countries. Part of the Government's efforts will be to work with regional partners on implementing practical project based activities. This includes and emphasis on increasing the transfer of knowledge with regional partners. Increasing the human interaction between Afghanistan and it's neighbors, at the government, diplomatic, social and local level will lead to improved relationships.

The Government is implementing a multifaceted Pro-active Regional Diplomacy Program (PRDP). The PRDP will encompass security, political, economic and social aspects. Under the PRDP, the Government, through relevant Ministries, will commit the necessary human and technical resources towards regional cooperation capacity building programs, including the mobilization of Afghan Missions in the regional countries

Improving security, governance, justice and the rule of law continue to remain a central focus of the Government's reform efforts. The Declaration of the cross-border Pak-Afghan Regional Peace Jirga, , recommends further expansion of economic, social, and cultural relations between the two countries. It identifies the implementation of infrastructure, economic and social sector projects in the affected areas (in the south-east) as a key part of bringing security to the country. There is still some tension still prevalent in the region but the Government gives the highest priority to the development of projects to strengthen regional cooperation. In security, the Government will seek better intelligence sharing and cooperation in counter terrorism measures.

From late 2002, the Government has adopted a policy of joining effective regional groupings. Afghanistan is now the only country enjoying membership or affiliation of all the major regional economic groupings of the surrounding region. In addition to the Government's ongoing efforts to accede to the World Trade Organization (WTO), it is also actively pursuing the expansion of bilateral and regional trade agreements with the countries of the region. While Afghanistan already has in place bilateral trade agreements with India and Pakistan, the two largest members of the South Asia Association for Regional Cooperation (SAARC), there is considerable scope to increase trade with South Asia now that Afghanistan has become a full member of SAARC in April 2007. Since November 2005, Afghanistan has been serving on the Contact Group of the Shanghai Cooperation Organization (SCO). In April 2003, Afghanistan became a Partner of the Organization for Security and Cooperation in Europe (OSCE). Afghanistan also attended the Special session of the Regional Advisory Committee of the United Nations Program for the Economies of Central Asia (SPECA), held in Astana on 27 May 2005.

Afghanistan is a signatory to a number of regional consultative processes that focus on developing frameworks to manage migration. The Government continues to make all possible efforts to integrate politically, socially and economically with its regional neighbors.

Counter Narcotics

Background and Context

The continuing expansion of the narcotics industry represents the single greatest threat to Afghanistan's stability, especially since the narcotics trade is inextricably linked to insecurity and terrorist activities. According to the United Nations Office on Drugs and Crime (UNODC) Afghanistan Opium Survey 2007, the cultivation of poppy in the country broke all records in 2007 and the trend is likely to continue in 2008. The number of domestic drug users in Afghanistan has also increased significantly and illicit drugs and the corruption surrounding it is threatening to destroy the next generation of Afghan youth. The explosive growth of poppy production has taken place in five southern provinces. In the other 29 provinces, poppy production has been cut in half over the past four years.

In 2006 the Government adopted the National Drug Control Strategy (NDCS) that remains the overall policy and strategy for CN activities and the Government is moving immediately to accelerate and improve strategy implementation through:

- Provision of force protection for eradication in targeted areas;
- Restructure and reform of the Counter- Narcotics Trust Fund (CNTF)
- Provincial based planning for CN policy implementation based on the Provincial Development Plans;
- Expansion and effective delivery of programs to promote licit development, including economic support for licit cash crops and rural industries;
- Strengthening of justice, other legal institutions and interdiction efforts;
- Further strengthening of cross-border, regional, and international cooperation for CN activities; and,
- Mainstreaming CN into all government policies.

Counter Narcotics is a core crosscutting issue in the ANDS and will be the responsibility of all sectors; while the MCN will take the leadership role. The goal is to ensure a rapid and sustainable decrease in cultivation, production, trafficking and consumption of illicit drugs with a view to complete and sustainable elimination of narcotics by providing a conducive development environment and opportunities while taking requisite direct action. Progress will be measured against four priorities set out in NDCS to: (i) disrupt the drugs trade; (ii) strengthen and diversify legal rural livelihoods; (iii) reduce the demand for illicit drugs and expand the treatment of drug users; and (iv) strengthen state institutions both at centre and in the provinces.

Implementation framework

The implementation of the strategy will rely on a provincial based approach to counter-narcotics, which will provide the provinces requisite responsibility for developing counter narcotics action-plans aligned with the Provincial Development Plans (PDPs). Governors will be consulted in developing local CN implementation plans ultimately consolidated and prioritized into a national implementation plan. The Governors will coordinate the local planning process involving line departments, international organizations, districts, and communities. At the national level the Ministry of Counter Narcotics, in conjunction with provincial Governors, line ministries, the IDLG, and ANDS must help identify provincial CN priorities and support the design of comprehensive provincial counter narcotics plans in line with Provincial Development Plans (PDPs) within the framework of the national budget.

The Government will increase its eradication efforts. The JCMB has established a goal of eradicating 50,000 ha of the opium cultivation in 2008. A robust system of eradication will be introduced together with state capacity, minimizing the level of corruption and improving the access of the eradication teams to less secure areas. As the NDCS states that "targeted and verified eradication will be carried out where access to alternative livelihoods is available," targeting will be made more accurate through mechanisms to monitor and evaluate the availability of alternative development.

Articles 52 and 54 of the Law on Drug Control as well as chapter 3 of the NDCS articulate the roles and responsibilities of ministries for implementing counter narcotics activities. Provincial-based planning will identify further roles line ministries and other organizations. NDCS Chapter 3 also specifies, by the eight pillars, the ministries and organizations that are expected to be involved in the evaluation and implementation of CN plans. The Government will mitigate weaknesses in the ministries, agencies and provinces charged with implementing the CN plans by drawing on the resources of international donors and contracting expert staff. The other key institutional capacity that needs to be addressed by the international community is the lack of sufficient CN expertise. The international community will be asked to provide sustained CN specific technical assistance to Afghan counterparts.

The new NDCS implementation plan has to include a commitment by the international community to fund and support efforts to:

- Integrate CN into operations of ISAF/NATO (this is suggested but will required to be dealt with in a combined as well as bilateral manner in consideration with the the individual partners capacity and sensitivity);
- Adequate financing of CNTF and adjust alternative development programs to the priorities of PDPs, subject to reform and improved functioning;
- Increase funding of the Good Performance Initiative;
- Prevent the import of precursors into Afghanistan;
- Create markets for Afghan products through trade preferences and investment in infrastructure for export;
- Arrest and prosecute international drug dealers/traffickers;
- Procure supplies and services for international military forces and organization in Afghanistan from Afghan sources, as envisaged in the "Afghan First" policy;
- Improve intelligence sharing on counter- narcotics activities;
- Provide large scale assistance to follow up eradication and reduction in cultivation;
- Production and market development programs for cash crops in certain areas; and,
- Reduce global demand for illicit drugs.

Anti-Corruption

Background and Context

Corruption, the misuse of public office for private gain, undermines the authority and accountability of the Government, lessening public trust and reducing the legitimacy of state institutions. Corruption is a significant and growing problem in Afghanistan. According to one of the most widely-used international indexes, 'Worldwide Governance Indicators, 1996-2006 published by the World Bank Institute (2007), Afghanistan is close to the bottom among the 212 countries in terms of its ability to control corruption – ranking in lowest percentile alongside Bangladesh, Somalia and Zimbabwe.

The Government is fully committed to controlling corruption, promoting transparency and accountability through establishing new and effective preventative mechanisms and implementing the Afghanistan Compact Anti- Corruption Benchmarks. The chronic poverty conditions in Afghanistan are seen as natural breeding grounds for systemic corruption due to social and income inequalities and perverse economic incentives. A key ANDS strategic objective is to establish a state administration that operates with integrity and accountability to provide an enabling environment for economic and social development, based upon the rule of law, impartiality in political decision- making, the proper management of public resources, the provision of efficient administrative systems and the active engagement of civil society.

The National Anti-Corruption Strategy and Roadmap developed as part of the ANDS will be implemented in support of the following strategic aims: (i) enhancing Government anticorruption commitment and leadership; (ii) raising awareness of corruption and evaluating the effectiveness of anti-corruption measures;(iii) mainstreaming anti corruption into Government reforms and national development; strengthening the enforcement of anticorruption aimed to strengthen the legal framework for anti-corruption and build a coherent and fully capacitated system of enforcement institutions required to support the effective implementation of the UNCAC; (v) reinforcing counter-narcotics integrity; (vi) reinforcing the integrity of public and business sector relationships; and, (vii) increasing political accountability.

Implementation framework

The mainstreaming process will be driven primarily by the three complementary and interdependent areas of public administration, financial management and legal reform:

- **Improving Public Sector Management**: aimed at the creation and consolidation of a motivated, knowledgeable, skilled, efficient and effective public service.
- **Strengthening Public Accountability**: aimed at increasing the transparency and accountability of procedures and controls for the management of public resources and thereby deterring corrupt practices, or increasing the likelihood of detection of those practices and generating systemic improvement to prevent their future reoccurrence.
- **Reinforcing the Legal Framework and Judicial System**: aimed at ensuring the comprehensiveness and robustness of the legal and regulatory framework in order to support activities and measures of Afghanistan's anti corruption institutions and measures.

The anti-corruption mainstreaming process will be applied jointly with the security sector strategy and the economic and social development sector strategies to guide their completion in order to ensure that anti-corruption measures are explicitly included and implicitly reflected in their development proposals. Implementation will draw upon the diagnostic efforts for institutional arrangements for combating corruption concluded by UNDP's Accountability and Transparency project. However the key partner institutions on anticorruption are the ministries and agencies with responsibilities for delivering the Government's reform agenda comprising:

- The IARCSC, responsible for the Government-wide PAR program, directed at improving public service management and public service delivery by addressing administrative structures and systems; human resource management policies, procedures and practices and institutional capacity building.
- The Control and Audit Office and the Ministry of Finance, responsible for strengthening the Government's financial control systems and practices.

- The Ministry of Justice and Supreme Court, responsible for strengthening the legislative framework and improving the efficiency and effectiveness of the justice and rule of law sector.
- The AGO, the GIAAC, and Ministry of Interior responsible for policing anti-corruption measures via inspection and investigation of corrupt practices in the public and private sectors.
- The AIHRC and the National Assembly representative oversight bodies such as the National Assembly and Provincial Councils, responsible for promoting links between civil society and the political decision-making processes.

The Government is firmly committed to fully and effectively implementing these anticorruption measures.

Gender Equity

Background and context

The Gender Equity Cross Cutting Strategy is the basis for the ANDS to address and reverse women's historical disadvantage. The strategy provides a roadmap for various sectors to bring about changes in women's position in society, their socio-economic condition and access to development opportunities. This strategy is an overarching framework that synthesizes the critical measures to be pursued through all ANDS sectors to fulfill the Government's commitments to women's development as embodied in the Constitution, Afghanistan MDGs, Afghanistan Compact, I-ANDS, and international treaties such as the Convention on the Elimination of all forms of Discrimination against Women (CEDAW) and the Beijing Platform for Action (BPFA).

The ultimate goal is 'gender equality'; a condition where women and men fully enjoy their rights, equally contribute to and enjoy the benefits of development and neither is prevented from pursuing what is fair, good and necessary to live a full and satisfying life, Three immediate goals have been prioritized, namely: (i) to attain the 13 gender-specific benchmarks of the Afghanistan Compact/I-ANDS, including the five-year priorities of NAPWA; (ii) to realize the gender commitments that are mainstreamed in each of the ANDS sectors; and (iii) to develop basic institutional capacities of ministries and government agencies on gender mainstreaming.[57]

This strategy targets three main outcomes:

- a significant number of government entities embracing and implementing gender equity efforts, as indicated by gender sensitive policies, strategies, budgets and programs; increased expenditures on gender equity; increasing number of ministries with functional gender equity-promoting mechanisms and technically capable professionals; and indicators that will be agreed upon for Gender Equity in the ANDS;
- measurable improvements in women's status as evidenced by reduced illiteracy; higher net enrollment ratio; control over income; equal wages for equal work; lower

maternal mortality; increasing leadership and participation in all spheres of life; greater economic opportunities and access to and control over productive assets and income; adequate access to justice systems that are gender sensitive; and reduced vulnerability to violence in public and domestic spheres; and

- greater social acceptance of gender equality as manifested in support for women's participation in public affairs, increased appreciation of the value of women and girls' education, increasing number of influential men and institutions promoting gender equity; and participation of women in policy discussions.

Implementation framework

The implementation of strategy for gender equity is a shared responsibility among government entities at the national and sub-national levels. MoWA's status as lead ministry for women's advancement will be maintained and strengthened. All government entities will: (i) foster a work environment that supports egalitarian relationships between women and men; (ii) establish internal enabling mechanisms for gender equity; and (iii) support women's shuras. ANDS consultative and working groups will be provided with capacity to pursue gender mainstreaming. Gender capacities of sector professionals will be strengthened and Gender Studies Institutes will be established in selected universities beginning with Kabul University. The informal network of gender advisers will be tapped for a 'gender mentoring program' that will transfer gender expertise to nationals. A technical support program for women managers in the civil service will also be created. Local chief executives are mandated to ensure that gender equity theme is incorporated into the local development plan and into the overall work of the local government. Pilot provinces on gender mainstreaming will be developed. DOWAs will build a network of gender advocates and their capacity to oversee sub-national gender mainstreaming will be strengthened.

International organizations are encouraged to adopt gender equity in their development cooperation and technical assistance and directly support ministries in implementing gender equity strategy. The NGO Coordination Council will be strengthened as a major link of government to the NGO community in promoting gender equity. NGOs will be encouraged to target women as project participants and beneficiaries and to increase the participation of women in the management of their organizations. An advocacy and public communication strategy that will transform negative perceptions and attitudes toward women will be implemented nationwide, with particular attention to women, men, media, religious leaders, and institutions and influential decision makers in society. Non-traditional, culturally-sensitive forms of mass communication will be explored for remote and tribal communities to address cultural obstacles to women's education, leadership and participation in public life, reproductive rights, property ownership and inheritance.

The Government will establish mechanisms to effectively facilitate, monitor, and coordinate activities on gender. The Government will also adopt a monitoring scorecard that ministries will use to track their own performance on gender equity. All sectors will be required to collect and use sex disaggregated data, adopt gender sensitive indicators, and include gender related performance in their regular reports. Performance of sectors on gender will be monitored by the Oversight Committee and the JCMB. The gender indicators and statistical framework of MoWA will be elaborated to contain indicators on the performance of government on the promotion of women's status. The monitoring and evaluation system of every ministry will:

- Include gender in the terms of reference of the monitoring and evaluation unit and job description of its chiefs;
- Provide training on gender sensitive monitoring and reporting;
- Adopt gender sensitive indicators;
- Collect and process sex disaggregated data; and,
- Highlight gender achievements in ministry and sector reports. Surveys that will set the baseline data for monitoring will be conducted.

The baseline statistics on women and men in Afghanistan will be updated annually and disseminated to strategic users, and NRVA data collection process will be further strengthened to support greater gender desegregation. Evaluation will be undertaken periodically to take stock of achievements, correct gaps and adjust strategies as necessary. A mid-term evaluation will be conducted in 2008 and another on 2011. Insights from the evaluation will be used to inform future planning, including the updating of the National Action Plan for the Women of Afghanistan.

Capacity Development

Background and context

It has become increasingly evident that technical and financial support will remain underutilized or poorly utilized unless adequate systemic capacities are built. Years of strife and outmoded methods of governance and management, without accountability and transparency has weakened the capabilities of the public sector, particularly at provincial and district levels. There are, however, indications that the capacity of the public sector has been increasing over time. In 2004 ministries were only able to spend about 31 percent of their development budget allocations. In 2005 this figure had risen to 44 percent and in 2006 the corresponding figure was about 49 percent; in real terms this represents an average growth rate of around 60 percent as budget allocations are increasing quite fast. There are no clear indicators on whether or not the effectiveness of these expenditures have also been increasing. There are indicators that lack of capacity remains a serious problem within the public sector. The Government, through specific institution building will take the lead in directing capacity development to where it is most needed and to evaluating the impact of capacity development and technical assistance programs. This institutional responsibility will be with Inter-ministerial Commission for Capacity Development (ICCD) that will serve as a single reporting point for both the Government and donors. ICCD will work out detailed goals for capacity development that will serve crosssectoral purposes.

The Government encourages donors to donor- funded projects to engage to the maximum extent possible qualified Afghan expatriates and to make greater use of technical experts from the region. These people bring greater understanding of the historic and cultural environment in which development activities are being implemented. Development projects that focus on capacity building should increasingly be designed to build on regional human resource capacity. The Government also recognizes that increasing reliance on building managerial capacity in both the public and private sectors will be necessary to effectively implement the goals of the ANDS.

Implementation framework

There is a limited capacity to effectively implement such extensive and intensive capacity development programs in all areas and this will require a well structured institutional mechanism which has to be built and constantly strengthened. The institutional arrangements for capacity development, in addition to the ICCD, include the Capacity Development Working Group (CDWGs), Independent Administrative Reforms and Civil Service Commission (IARCSC) and the Reform Implementation Management Units (RIMUs). ICCD will seek the assistance of the international community to establish and staff a technical secretariat, to provide the administrative and technical support to ICCD.

ICCD has undertaken a survey of capacity development and technical assistance programs. At the ministerial level, under the guidance of the Independent Administrative Reforms and Civil Service Commission (IARCSC), Reform Implementation Management Units (RIMU) have been established primarily to restructure ministries so that they could move ahead on pay and grading reform – this process of restructuring requires clarifying roles and responsibilities, and laying down very clear reporting lines, and assessing whether individuals are fit to hold the job they are holding. Capacity development is not the primary role of the RIMUs, but the RIMUs will identify capacity development needs, coordinate programs and initiatives to meet those needs, while monitoring and evaluate the impact. The ICCD will monitor the progress of the capacity development projects and programs. The President and Cabinet will receive regular reports on performance of all projects. Those that are under-performing will be required to provide explanation for their underperformance and their recommendations for bringing the performance back on target. Persistent underperformance will result in a major redesign or closure.

Under the auspices of ICCD the IARCSC will be empowered to encourage RIMUs to work together along the lines of the ANDS/ sectoral groupings, to identify common needs and solutions as well as assist to articulate specific needs and formulate outline proposals as appropriate. Where needed, the IARCSC with donors' assistance will provide training on capacity needs assessments, capacity development activities and monitoring and evaluation. Actions include:

- Agreement on specific terms of reference for RIMU;
- Identify any short term technical assistance requirements;
- Conduct capacity assessments with RIMUs, establish and implement training programs;
- Empower and train RIMUs in capacity assessments, capacity development, monitoring and evaluation;
- Agreement on reporting protocol through capacity development unit to Inter-ministerial capacity development committee; and
- Empower RIMUs to undertake a department by department capacity assessment until all ministries have been assessed and capacity development plans drawn up to meet needs.

Once the basic institutions required for capacity development, program implementation mechanism and priority sectors have been agreed upon, there will be a need to set up a number of training projects. This will include Core Public Sector Training, Financial

Management training, Procurement Training, Policy Formulation, Project Development and management, priority capacity development in the private sector, priority capacity development to increase skills in work force and to make more effective use of Diaspora Afghans.

It will take some time to get results from the capacity development efforts. In the meantime, more efforts will be made to attract:

- Afghan Expats in country with their diff skills and knowledge;
- Technical assistance from the region, given the many qualified people fully familiar with regional issues; and
- good managers with management skills for variety of managerial positions.

Environment

Background and Context

The National Environment Strategy recognizes the need to give greater attention to environmental protections as development occurs. In May 2005, an independent National Environmental Protection Agency was established, being elevated from a department previously established in the Ministry of Irrigation, Water Resources and Environment. The organizational transition of the environment function since 2002 has precluded the consistent development of technical and managerial skills within both NEPA and other governmental authorities involved in environmental management. Therefore the ANDS focuses on developing National Environment Protection Agency's (NEPA) capacity to perform its regulatory, coordination and policy-making duties.

The ANDS strategic vision is to improve the quality of life of the people of Afghanistan through conservation of the nation's resources and protection of the environment. Goals include: (i) secure a clean and healthy environment; (ii) attain sustainable economic and social development while protecting the natural resource base and the environment of the country; and (iii) ensure effective management of the country's environment through participation of all stakeholders. The strategy elaborates priority programs areas for environmental management based on thematic strategies including: restoration and sustainable use of rangelands and forests, conservation of biodiversity, accession to/ signing and enforcement of MEAs, preservation of natural and cultural heritage sites, encouragement to community- based natural resource management, prevention and abatement of pollution, urban environmental management; environmental education and awareness.

Implementation framework

Strengthening EIA awareness and institu-tional capacity of NEPA and the line ministries will be accorded priority. Short term and long term outcomes linked to the the-matic objectives (eg. conservation of biodiversity, abatement of pollution, environmental awareness, etc.) will also be prioritized based on assessment of the expected environmental, social, and health impacts and the institutional, economic and political constraints.

Strategic coordination of the ANDS is to take place on a sector-by-sector basis through a inter-ministerial and consultative group (CG) mechanisms. Under the CG mechanism, environment features as a cross-cutting issue and is also a sectoral issue in its own right. Environment as a cross-cutting issue, must be mainstreamed across all sectors and in each program area through the development of policy benchmarks to ensure that the Government, donors and implementing agencies follow established norms with respect to the incorporation of environmental considerations into the design and implementation of projects, and provide adequate oversight and monitoring of the environmental impacts of economic and social development projects.

There is a defined institutional arrangement for implementation and monitoring of environment themes. The groups engaged in the implementation of the ANDS will play a crucial role in ensuring issues encountered in the implementation of programs and ministerial/ sectoral strategies are effectively addressed. Their assessment must be frank, identifying the problems encountered in the implementation of these activities. This will allow the Government to more effectively address the issues and meet their obligation of reporting to the Oversight Committee (OSC) and the JCMB on progress in fulfilling these objectives.

Conclusion

The ANDS consolidates critical crosscutting issues and integrates them into sector strategies. These are issues that will have a decisive impact on the achievement of all ANDS goals.

Greater regional cooperation will contribute significantly to establishing security in a volatile region and improve the prospects for economic growth and development in Afghanistan. A key objective in the regional cooperation strategy is to remove barriers to investment and trade so that regional investors will be better able to do business in Afghanistan and Afghan firms will have greater access to regional markets.

The elimination of the narcotics industry is essential for increasing security, improving governance and strengthen formal economy if the country. The large amount of money derived from narcotics supports terrorism and creates opportunities for corruption in public institutions. The narcotics produced in Afghanistan not only destroy the lives of Afghans, but impose enormous social costs on people in other countries. The Government, with the active support of the international community is determined to eliminate this menace from the country.

Establishing gender equality is essential so that the country is able to make use of a major human resource that is not significantly under-utilized – Afghan women. Removing barriers that prevent women from fully participating in all aspects of public and private life requires comprehensive efforts by the Government, donors and throughout the private sector.

Developing the capacity of the Afghan people to effectively govern this country and to engage in productive employment is necessary if poverty is to be substantially reduced. The Government has established mechanisms to ensure that the enormous resources being devoted to developing capacity in the public and private sectors are utilized in the most effective ways possible.

Achieving these goals require a long term vision. All of the cross-cutting issues will have significant impacts on core national objectives such as poverty reduction, economic growth, people's participation in the development process, human rights, reducing social vulnerability, enhancing the role of civil society, effective public administrative reforms, developing a sound legal system and expanding financial resources.

PART III.

9. AID EFFECTIVENESS AND COORDINATION

The Government will continue to maintain the principles of the Paris Declaration as the cornerstone of the ANDS. Since 2001, Afghanistan has received more than $15 billion in Official Development Assistance (ODA), not including off-budget security spending which is not formally reported as part of the OECD DAC aid reporting system. Current estimates for total assistance, ODA and security-related expenditures, are $40 to $50 billion. This chapter lays out the Government's approach to increased effectiveness and efficiency as a vital element in the successful implementation of the Afghanistan Compact and ANDS. Moreover, and in spite of considerable gains in recent years, the Government remains concerned about the urgent need to strengthen the aid delivery framework (management, coordination, mobilization, and effectiveness) to improve results, particularly at the sub-national level. The Government is aware that donor funds are limited. The main principle of the Government's aid effectiveness policy is to ensure that donors' funds will be spent in the most productive way and in line with the ANDS priorities.

The other core principles relevant to this strategy include: Afghanistazation (ownership); alignment; coordination and harmonization; managing for results; and mutual accountability.

Paris Declaration and Afghanistan Compact

Afghanistan and the international community agreed on the Afghanistan Compact and signed the Paris Declaration on Aid Effectiveness in 2006 to improve the delivery and impact of external assistance. The Government's aid strategy is in line with the major principles of the Paris Declaration whereby (i) partner countries own and exercise leadership over their development policies (ii) donors align their overall support on partner countries' national development strategies (iii) donor actions are more harmonized, transparent and collectively effective (iv) resource management and decision-making are more results-oriented; and (v) donors and partners are accountable for development results. In addition to this the Government's aid effectiveness policies are also in line with the Afghanistan Compact, MDGs and ANDS poverty reduction targets.

The effectiveness of aid can be measured against progress towards the attainment of MDG, Compact and ANDS poverty reduction and development targets. Much has been achieved over the course of the past six years, but a great deal more needs to be done. Afghanistan's current heavy reliance on aid is a reflection of the extent of the devastation following years of turmoil.

Current Situation : Assessment of Aid Effectiveness

The effectiveness of aid can be measured against attainment of MDG, Compact and ANDS poverty reduction targets. While much has undoubtedly been achieved over the course of the past six years, lack of services, high poverty incidence and a lack of security in some parts of the country continue to undermine reconstruction and development efforts. Afghanistan's current reliance on aid can be attributed to the fact that most of Afghanistan's institutions, infrastructure and human capacity were destroyed or depleted during the threedecade-long war. Despite this and since 2001 there has been noticeable progress in improving the peoples' lives: the average per capita income almost double from 2001 to 2007 from US$147 to US$289, Afghanistan averted major humanitarian catastrophe in 2001; 6.0 million children have enrolled in primary and secondary education, with 35% being female; the basic package of health services is now at 87% national coverage with immunization at 80% coverage; more than 5 million Afghans have returned home; more than 12,200 km of road have been rehabilitated and rebuilt including the ring road; and in urban areas especially, professional opportunities for women are beginning to increase.

Aid Effectiveness Strategy Framework

Experience in other countries has shown that external aid has in many cases, contributed to economic growth, private sector development, and poverty reduction. The Government is strongly committed to making aid more effective by working with donors to achieve the benchmarks set out in the Paris Declaration and the Afghanistan Compact. The Government will continue to work on to deepen the ownership and successful implementation of the ANDS. This will require the full cooperation and assistance of the donor community. The motivation behind this commitment is simple: the realization that making aid more effective by reducing overlap, duplication and the administrative cost of aid in the short run will have an even greater impact on increasing the benefits of aid in the longer term.

The Government will continue to provide strong political backing for economic reforms through support to the conditions attached to programs and projects undertaken by donors. This will be strongly supported by the Government where institutions and policies are weak and the policy environment is distorted. The Government encourages program and project designs that focus on creating and transmitting knowledge and building capacity. Over the ANDS period, post evaluation of all development projects will be undertaken which will provide valuable information on the lessons learned and improve the future design of development programs and projects. The Government's aid policies will be based on the following principles:

- **Maintaining Macroeconomic Stability**: sustainable growth and reducing poverty both require a sound and stable macroeconomic framework. The Government will continue to improve its overall macroeconomic framework by identifying and removing structural rigidities and market distortions to permit higher levels of economic growth.

- **A performance/results-based approach**: with improved monitoring, coordination and evaluation of development programs and projects by both the Government and the international community;
- **Good governance**: good governance provides the broad setting for development and the quality of that governance will have a profound effect on development success and aid effectiveness.
- **Building capacity**: enhanced capacity—in public and private sectors—is also critical to sustainable development. Past aid programming often failed because it focused on resource transfers by donors but did not provide enough support for local capacity development efforts to sustain these investments once donors had withdrawn support.
- **Engaging civil society**: participatory processes, particularly those engaging civil society, are essential to establishing clear, locally owned priorities so that aid is demand driven and has maximum impact. This will also ensure that aid meets the needs of the poorest and most marginalized people in society.

Aid Effectiveness Objectives: Key objectives are to increase aid effectiveness and maximize the impact of international assistance and achieve the following objectives: (i) improved security and stability; (ii) reduced poverty; (iii) enhanced environment for private sector development; (iv) further democratization of Afghan society in accordance with the Islamic values; and (v) increased social inclusion and equality. For the Government aid is one of most important tools in implementing the ANDS.

Excepted Outcomes: The Government's aid effectiveness policies will achieve the following outcomes: (i) improved security and poverty reduction (ii) higher participation of the private sector in the GDP and employment (iii) higher school enrolment and literacy (iv) better social inclusion (v) lower infant and maternal mortality (vi) improved access to a higher quality of public services and (vii) improved human rights.

Developing Priority Policies: Increasing aid effectiveness is a joint effort between Government, donors and agencies involved in the implementation of programs and projects. The Government will implement reforms that will lead to higher transparency and absorption capacities. Donors will be expected to undertake measures to improve aid delivery in line with the Paris Declaration.

Building Greater Ownership: The Government has demonstrated a genuine commitment to lead the development process and make aid more effective by establishing the Afghanistan Compact and signing the Paris Declaration in 2006. Afghanistan's long-term development vision as set out in the ANDS, identifies and articulates national priorities in the medium term. All assistance should be aligned with ANDS priorities as presented in the sector strategies. To this end, the Ministry of Finance will monitor the Government's total aid portfolio and it will, in collaboration with line ministries, encourage donors to channel their resources in a manner that is consistent with the principles of Islam, the Government's Aid Policy and the ANDS priorities.

Improving Public Finance Management: Although the tax system does not directly relate to aid effectiveness, its further strengthening will increase domestic revenues and the Government's potential to allocate more resources to fund recurrent costs of donor- funded projects. The tax system is in the process of being strengthened. Institutional capacity for efficient tax collection will improve tax administration at all levels. The Government's domestic revenue collection has significantly improved to the point where today it covers as much as 64 percent of recurrent expenditures.

Even though the Government is putting in place increasingly effective public financial management systems, it still faces major challenges. The Government seeks cooperation from its development partners to channel more funds through the Core Budget, an important step for enhancing financial management systems. The capacity to implement the Development Budget more efficiently will improve, resulting in a higher donor contribution to the overall Core Budget. The Government's target is for 75 percent of aid to be channeled through the core budget.

Major public administration reforms being implemented or planned—such as the introduction of a merit-based civil service system, and professional management of government ministries and departments, or the creation of a more formalized budget, procurement, and audit processes and agencies—had their roots in the desire of the Government to avoid earlier abuses of graft and political patronage. Equally important will be the Government's accountability to the Afghan people with regard to the expenditure of aid money, which will be supported by the ongoing efforts of the MoF to develop the Public Expenditure Financial Accountability (PEFA) framework.

This process will be strengthened by: (i) deepening the linkages between the ANDS, MTFF, MTB and in the future with the MTEF; (ii) enhancing the 'budget literacy' of citizens and civil society organizations through engagement in budget processes; (iii) support to civil society organizations and downward accountability in the context of decentralized service delivery; (iv) assessing the experience gained under the National Solidarity Program and the National Rural Access Program and disseminating these lessons; (v) regular reporting to National Assembly and other public entities in how budgetary resources (core and external) are being spent; (vi) better communication with the public using the ANDS framework on plans, aid received, disbursed, outcomes and impact and (vi) supporting civil society organizations and non-governmental organizations to ensure that local governments are held accountable on how aid money is being spent to improve the people's welfare.

Curbing Corruption: The drug trade, porous borders, and informal markets have led to increased corruption in public institutions. The Government is conscious of the fact that corruption and aid effectiveness are inversely correlated and is therefore committed to significantly reducing corruption. Some mitigating measures to improve anti-corruption in the area of aid delivery will be as follows: (i) increase publicly available information about donor aid provision at the national and provincial levels; (ii) harmonization of donor support around the Government's anti-corruption strategy as prescribed in the ANDS; (iii) increase donor support for preventive action based on corruption vulnerability assessments of specific processes and actions practiced by government departments and agencies and (iv) eliminate the narcotics industry in a manner that provides alternative sources of income to the farmers.

The Government has also passed the Public Finance Management, Procurement, and Auditing and Accounting Laws and will ensure that these laws and regulations are implemented and enforced diligently. As corruption and other rent seeking activities are one of the main causes of ineffective aid delivery, the Government will address this issue in an affirmative manner to win the trust, confidence and continued support of the donor community.

Improve information on aid flows and predictability: Incomplete reporting of Official Development Assistance (ODA), including reporting on the activities of Provincial Reconstruction Teams (PRTs), civil society organizations and the international NGOs to the Government has limited transparency and hindered the ability of the Government to monitor and manage external assistance. This information is critical to planning and budgeting processes as well as the execution of the development budget. The MoF expects that the ongoing Paris Declaration Survey will improve information about the aid flows.

Additionally, a lack of multi-year commitments by development partners has made it difficult for the Government to plan for the medium to long-term allocation of resources to national priorities. Consequently, it has been difficult to obtain a complete picture of external assistance to Afghanistan.

The conduct of the Financial Reviews and the implementation of the Harmonized Reporting Format since October 2007 will enable the Government to access comprehensive and coordinated information on aid flows as well as highlight the problems and issues impeding project implementation, improving aid management.

Reducing High Transaction Costs and Parallel Funding Mechanisms: Even though significant progress has been made in terms of aligning external resources and priorities of the ANDS a number of challenges still remain. For instance, a significant proportion of external resources provided are still being routed directly to projects by donors. Funds channeled through the Core Budget, by means of pooled funding modalities, including the Afghanistan Reconstruction Trust Fund (ARTF), Law and Order Trust Fund for Afghanistan (LOTFA) and Counter Narcotics Trust Fund (CNFT) will be fully integrated into national planning and resource accountability systems across the different layers of Government.

Funds disbursed through the external budget often have high transaction costs, particularly those funds disbursed to stand alone projects. As highlighted in the Afghan Economic Impact study, the greatest local economic impact is obtained when resources are provided directly to the Government (local impact around 85 percent) compared to funds provided to international companies (less than 20 percent) to carry out projects. Where funds are disbursed through the external budget their economic impact is maximized when spending is on locally procured goods and services.

To manage its own resource allocation in an effective manner in the annual budget process and ensure maximum alignment with national priorities, the Government will require that information on all activities financed under parallel funding mechanisms is communicated to the MoF in a timely manner. Donors who are implementing parallel funds are encouraged to show flexibility in aligning their projects with sector strategies of ANDS and having definite time-lines for eventually bringing such assistance on-budget.

Prior to the allocation of resources for parallel funding, there should be consultation with the Government through existing consultation mechanisms (CGs, WGs, Aid Effectiveness CG and JCMB). This will help improve aid coordination, management, mobilization and effectiveness. The Government's aid policy calls for the reduction of parallel funding mechanisms through the gradual integration of these mechanisms with the Government's budget and a "no pinching of staff" policy from Government agencies by other stakeholders.

Reducing Tied Aid: A significant proportion of aid provided to Afghanistan is still tied. That is, many donors procure imported goods, mostly from their own countries, and import their own labor force rather than hire local workers to work on their projects. According to the 2006 Baseline Survey of the Paris Declaration on Aid Effectiveness, 56 percent of aid is tied in Afghanistan. This indicates that a large percentage of aid is effectively contracted to technical assistance from donor countries, and is not necessarily consistent with or aligned to the ANDS. Rebuilding Afghanistan, creating jobs, and reducing poverty requires strong local economies and untied aid. One of the main reasons behind the slow revival of the economy is the conditions attached to external assistance. In order to help Afghanistan achieve its development goals, there is a need to increase the local impact of aid. The Government would like to encourage donors to use more locally produced goods as well as local implementing agencies so as to promote greater private sector development and employment.

Simplifying Aid Management Procedures and introducing More Flexible Conditionality: Both the Government and donors should aim to further simplify their processes and procedures for implementation of programs and projects, to avoid unnecessary delays in implementation. Simplification of processes and procedures, albeit, with safeguards in place to minimize corruption and other rent seeking activities would enable the Government to manage the development process in a smoother manner and for donors to allocate more resources to the reconstruction of Afghanistan. Excessive conditionality attached to foreign assistance should be avoided at all costs. At the same time, simplification of processes and procedures must also ensure that there is no corresponding increase in fiduciary risk. Safeguards for donor funds have often involved special implementation arrangements that bypass mainstream government systems. However, the fiduciary security derived from separate controls and "ring-fencing" of aid funds has limits. Earmarking of funds is not a guarantee against fungiblility; separate controls do not address (and may worsen) the underlying weaknesses of public finance management; and the costs of complying with such safeguards may reduce the value for money of aid.

Improving inter-government cooperation: Inter-government coordination is an important precondition for increasing the impact of the international assistance. The ANDS will provide the basis for improved inter-ministerial cooperation. Based on the sector strategies inter-ministerial committees will be established to support implementation of the ANDS, which will work to create an enabling environment. Finally, Government agencies will be responsible for implementation of the ANDS and arbitrary priority setting by ministries outside of the agreed ANDS service delivery framework will be heavily discouraged. In terms of federal - provincial relations, central CGs will work closely with provincial coordination offices to enhance co-ordination between national and sub-national priorities.

Improving donor coordination: The ANDS sets the framework for improving donor coordination in line with the Paris Declaration which recommends greater alignment between ODA and the ANDS. Based on this, the Government will strongly recommend to donors the harmonization of their programs and the development of their Country Assistance Strategies and Joint Donors Response (JDR) with ANDS priorities to minimize the risk of duplication, poor alignment, coordination and harmonization.

The donor implementing agencies (NGOs) will need to increase their cooperation with line ministries to ensure that the future donor- funded programs and projects will support implementation of the ANDS. The JCMB, CGs and the WGs will remain the primary mechanisms for Government-donor dialogue and consultation.

Future Government /donor cooperation needs to be based on the basic principle of mutual accountability. Furthermore, benchmarks will be developed to measure progress against commitments on both sides. For its part, the Government remains committed to (i) improving existing coordination mechanisms; to (ii) increasing collection of domestic revenues, and to (iii) increasing absorption capacity, allowing for higher migration of the donor resources from the External to the Core Budgets (especially in dealing with large sums of external funds). From the donor side the Government expects that the donor external funding will be in line with the ANDS priorities.

Increasing the volume and concessionality of donor assistance

Significant investments are required to achieve the MDGs and benchmarks, leading to the effective implementation of the ANDS. The amount of money pledged per head for Afghanistan's reconstruction is still low in comparison to pledges made previously for other post-conflict countries such as Bosnia and Herzegovina. Thus there is a need for more appropriate levels of aid reflecting the needs of Afghanistan.

Even though Afghanistan received debt relief under the Paris Club initiative, the challenge will be ensuring that Afghanistan's external debt will be maintained at sustainable levels by reaching the completion point for the Heavily Indebted Poor Countries (HIPC). Despite this the majority of all future donor aid should be delivered in the form of grants with very limited amount of lending which should continue to be under favorable concessional terms.

In order to increase investment, while maintaining debt at sustainable levels, the Government needs to mobilize significant additional resources. At the same time, it is also important to address the Government's absorptive capacity constraints through well coordinated and executed TA/Capacity Building programs. If these constraints are not simultaneously addressed, it will be futile to seek increases in the level of development assistance, even though the development needs of Afghanistan remains large. In parallel with this the Government will implement reforms that will lead to higher mobilization of domestic revenues in order to ensure fiscal sustainability in the long run and decrease aid dependence.

Improving the management of the technical assistance (TA)

Afghanistan is a large recipient of technical assistance. Over the ANDS period, the Government will ensure that technical assistance will be demand-driven and aimed at building Government capacity. In addition, it will ensure that it is delivered in a coordinated manner. All technical assistance channeled outside the Core Budget should have capacity building components and require Afghan counterparts. Technical Assistance also must focus on developing systems and procedures the local staff can utilize to perform their daily duties. Furthermore, each TA should have an exit strategy. All terms of reference for TA must recognize this as the ultimate objective of such assistance. The Government will develop a policy for dealing with the TA to ensure higher coordination and delivery of assistance in line with the Government priorities and improved effectiveness. The selection process needs to favor foreign advisers that have proven record in capacity building. Finally, international advisers should always encourage local ownership and despite the weak capacity, should avoid being involved in decision making processes.

Improved communication with the general public

The perception of aid effectiveness has been hampered because of a failure to meet the public's expectations and meet the high demand for resources. The Government will improve communication in order to better manage expectations of the public and provide transparent information about aid delivery.

Ensuring proper coverage of maintenance costs

A number of development projects already suffer from lack of planning in terms of maintenance cost. This has already become a high risk for project sustainability and aid effectiveness. Both the Government and donors will improve planning to ensure that required maintenance cost funding will be included in project implementation.

Implementation and Monitoring

The MoF is the leading government institution for aid effectiveness issues. The Aid Coordination Unit (ACU), within the Budget Department, is responsible for most issues surrounding the delivery and monitoring of external assistance. The Government's aid policies lay out preferred aid modalities on the delivery of development assistance, how it views the role of the other stakeholders such as the nongovernmental organizations (NGOs) and the provincial reconstruction teams (PRTs) in the aid delivery process, its external debt policy and how it proposes to enhance its partnership with all donors.

Preferred aid modalities

The Government prefers core budget support (direct budget support). This modality gives the Government greater ownership and enables it to more effectively allocate resources based on needs and priorities. Direct budget support also strengthens the Government's financial management systems by providing hands-on experience to those involved in managing and monitoring the core budget. More aid in the form of budget support would also simplify administration and reduce overheads.

The Government is aware that the External Budget, as well as PRTs budget lines will continue to exist, however it will seek to the transfer of more funds to the Core Budget. In addition, the Government expects that the future implementation of the programs and projects from the donor-funded External Budget and the PRTs budget lines will be strictly in line with the ANDS priorities.

Channeling aid through already established trust funds (ARTF, LOFTA, CNTF) would be the second preferred option as this would mean that the Government would be able to access these funds on an as-needed basis. The Government also prefers to see a progressive decline in non-discretionary budget support, which distorts the allocation of Government spending across sectors, and in turn weakens the Government's role in determining its financing priorities. However, for this to happen, the Government is aware that continuous progress will need to be made in fighting corruption and implementing public administration reforms. Finally, the Government prefers that donor funds be pooled rather than earmarked for individual projects. Pooling of donor funds also significantly reduces the duplication of effort and leads to better coordination, management, and effectiveness of aid, especially with respect to technical assistance grants.

The Government will not support provision of assistance in the form of donor preferred and designed projects based on needs assessment done solely by donors with little or no consultation with the Government. The approval of the ANDS provides the framework for priority aid delivery for Government ministries and agencies and donors.

Improving Cooperation with Civil Society Organizations (CSOs)

Both local and international CSOs active in Afghanistan play crucial and diverse roles in delivering development assistance to the Afghan public. Generally, the CSOs mobilize public support and voluntary contributions for aid; they often have strong links with community groups and often work in areas where government-to-government aid is not possible. Given their important contribution to the improvement of the welfare of rural and remote communities, the Government will ensure that it adopts a supportive approach vis-à-vis the work of the CSOs. The Government however, will encourage the CSOs to align their assistance with ANDS priorities and conduct their business according to the NGO Law and other relevant legislation covering CSOs.

The NGOs and the CSOs will be required to improve their reporting systems and provide accurate and timely information on their development activities through the Harmonized Reporting Form. However, the Government remains committed to improving the reporting mechanism by introducing more simplicity and increasing compliance as well as removing unnecessary barriers to their effective operation.

Improving cooperation with provincial reconstruction teams (PRTs)

The Government recognizes the important role that the PRTs play in supporting the sub-national governments. Given this the Government would encourage the PRTs to assist in the implementation of priority projects through the Provincial Development Plans (PDPs) in line with national priorities (ANDS). In order to avoid duplication, all PRTs will need to report their activities to the Government through the Harmonized Reporting Form.

Securing debt relief under the HIPC initiative

After receiving debt relief under the Paris Club negotiations, Afghanistan has become eligible for additional debt relief under the HIPC. The Government will continue with the implementation of the PRGF. Moreover, the successful implementation of the ANDS will be one of the main drivers in achieving the HIPC requirements and securing debt relief.

Enhancing strategic partnership

The Government's aid policy aims to strengthen the partnership with the donors by encouraging information sharing and policy dialogue, at both sectoral and program levels. In addition, the Government's policy will encourage the launching of joint analytical projects between the Government and donors. That is, the Government will develop agreements — in the form of Memoranda of Understanding with all donors in which rights; mutual obligations; and accountabilities are clearly identified.

The following lessons learned will be implemented across all consultative structures and platforms to ensure an effective dialogue:

- All CG's Working Groups will remain focused on results, with time-bound action plans and clearly defined targets and milestones;
- Government and donors will improve their representation to ensure that only representatives with adequate technical expertise will take part in consultations;
- Maximize the efficiency of the Consultative Group meetings. The ministries and agencies chairing the meetings will establish secretariats including the participation of technical people from the leading donor agencies;
- Helping the Government achieve development objectives and implementing the ANDS will be main priorities for donors rather than a donor-driven policy agenda.
- Where necessary, joint Government/Donor sub-groups should be formed on specific issues to improve efficiency of development work.

Conclusion

The Government and people of Afghanistan are grateful to international community for their timely and much needed assistance. For Afghanistan to shift from recovery-related growth to long-term sustainable development, additional continued and efficient donor support will be required. Of course, building a more prosperous Afghanistan is a joint task between the people, the Government and the international community. This joint effort should be viewed in the context of the common benefits that will accrue to the Afghan people and the international community from overcoming the threats of terrorism and drugs. With proper support, Afghanistan will emerge as stable and growing economy in the region, cooperating with its neighbors for mutual prosperity, and finally at peace with its self, the region and the world.

The successful implementation of the ANDS will remain dependent on securing the required levels of the donor assistance. It has been widely acknowledged that achievement of the Afghanistan MDGs cannot be accomplished with current levels of international support. At the same time, it is known that success of the ANDS also depends on the Government and donors' ability to increase aid effectiveness and efficiency. Government policies based on the ANDS provide a good framework for achieving this goal. However, both the Government and donors will have to do more to improve aid delivery mechanism and efficiency to bring more tangible changes to the life of ordinary Afghans. The Government is accountable to Afghan people and National Assembly on how aid is spent. The Government is committed to do its part to ensuring the successful implementation of Paris Declaration and their support of the Government's policies and strategies.

PART IV.

10. IMPLEMENTATION FRAMEWORK

The implementation framework for the ANDS is based on an integrated approach that will be structured to address the three interdependent pillars of security; governance, rule of law and human rights; and economic and social development, and five cross-cutting issues. Stabilizing conditions in Afghanistan will require continuing security operations combined with the implementation of the rule of law and credible sub-national governance. It will require equality of access to the delivery of basic services, in particular education, road infrastructure and health throughout the country.

The implementation of the ANDS will be based on an integrated approach to these challenges, uniting government, international community, civil society and private sector effort in support of common goals, shared policies and joint programs. The integrated approach takes as its point of departure the requirement for all actors, not only to accept a shared vision of development and stabilization outcomes, as expressed in the Afghanistan Compact and the ANDS, but also to plan and deliver jointly in order to maximize impact and aid effectiveness. This process must take place on the basis of the National Budget approval process and the national programs that are at its core. In practical terms, any identified national priority (e.g. CNTF, food and agriculture, governance) should be given policy attention at the Oversight Committee prior to obtaining overall approval and direction from the cabinet. This process would then lead to the development of a national program, which would be introduced both to the National Assembly and to donors as part of the national budget process.

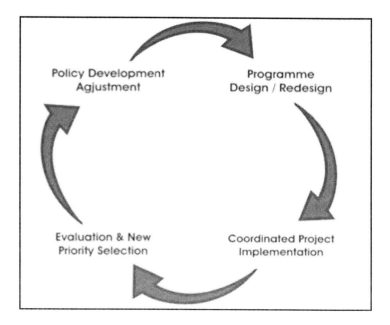

Figure 10.1. Implementation cycle.

An integrated approach makes it easier for the Government to meet challenges in a dynamic political context with multiple stakeholders, internal and external risks, and evolving security challenges. A major key to success is to ensure effective coordination with international community. However, the functioning of these institutions needs to be improved and their capacity further developed. This chapter outlines: (i) lessons learned; (ii) the principles of an integrated approach; (iii) budget management; (iv) the necessary institutional framework arrangements; (iv) the coordination framework; and (v) integrating Conflict Management into Sector Strategies.

Lessons Learned during the Interim ANDS

The country's development efforts in recent years have highlighted the following constraints facing effective implementation:

Fiscal Sustainability: Recurrent financing needs now met by donors must increasingly be offset by strong growth in the formal taxable economy.

Lack of Capacity: The ANDS must focus more efforts at the sub-national level, where the capacity of government, private sector and civil society remains weak.

Low Aid Volume and Low Disbursement: Despite generous pledges, Afghanistan has not received the same per capita commitment as other post-conflict states.

Weak Aid Coordination and Effectiveness: Despite the Afghanistan Compact and JCMB, the external budget has remained dominant, limiting coordination.

Enhancing Provincial Equity and Poverty Targeting: Unequal provincial development and a failure to target vulnerability using NRVA data remain endemic.

Private Sector Capacities: Inadequate attention has been given by the Government and donors alike to the enabling environment for private sector growth.

Donor Alignment: Despite sector strategies and national programs, donor efforts have remained fragmented, and there has been poor coordination and reporting; as well as programmatic and provincial biases.

Conflict Sensitivity: It is essential that a system be put in place to ensure that conflict sensitivity is mainstreamed into all development programs.

Management of Complexity: Both the Government and donors are faced with complex policy and delivery challenges that require a concerted and coordinated effort.

Implementation Framework and Integrated Approach

The Government will integrate the national budgetary process, legislative agenda and program delivery simultaneously. This will require development partners and donors to align their efforts with ANDS priorities and activities through joint planning and evaluation. The Government will concentrate on integrating and delivering donor-supported programs that achieve the ANDS goals of (i) stability, (ii) delivery of basic services and infrastructure and (iii) enabling a vibrant national economy.

This integration will require a strengthening of government machinery both at the centre (OAA, NSC, Ministry of Finance, IARCSC and JCMB Secretariat) and at sub- national level (through the Ministry of Interior, MCN, IDLG and Ministry of Economy). This new capacity will itself require a program approach.

The sector strategies and the implementation framework are premised on the application of the following principles:

- Enhance the Medium Term Budget Framework, maintain fiscal sustainability, adopt sector-wide approaches and build upon Provincial Development Planning;
- Strengthen links between Kabul and the provinces and support the resolution of conflicts;
- Targeting basic and essential services and social protection through national programs;
- Enhance budget prioritization, sequencing, aid effectiveness and provincial equity;
- Enhance private sector engagement to enhance competitiveness;
- Focus on productive infrastructure development;
- Improve security through governance, rule of law and regional cooperation;
- Meeting PRGF and HIPC requirements;
- Improve government and civil society capacity through a human capital strategy;
- Enhance poverty and economic growth diagnostic monitoring and impact evaluation.

The proposed implementation and coordination framework, outlined below, balances the need for coordination between the Government and donors as well as provincial based formulation and execution capacities to enhance service delivery. This will require improved coordination between the Government and various stakeholders.

Implementation Plan and the ANDS Implementation Cycle

Implementation Mechanism

The ANDS sector strategies will be implemented through national programs which will generate results at the local level, as well as being synchronized with national and provincial budgeting and legislative and evaluation cycles. The main instruments for the implementation will be the Budget and private sector.

The medium term budget expenditures of the Core Budget will support implementation of the national programs that will be aligned with the ANDS priorities. This will be reflected in the MTFF. Based on the Paris Declaration, the donors will be asked to implement programs and projects from the External and the PRT's budgets in line with the ANDS. The existing JCMB coordination mechanism will be used to ensure this. The ongoing activities of the MoF to cost sector strategies and develop the program and provincial budgeting will enhance entire process of implementation of the ANDS through the Government and donor funded budgets.

Apart from the Budget, the private sector is expected to play important role in the implementation of the ANDS contributing to job creation, infrastructure development and revenue mobilization. The private sector contribution to development of the country was one of the criteria for the Government's expenditure prioritization framework (see Table 10.5). It is expected that the private sector will play leading role in implementation of the ANDS priorities in number of sectors such as: ICT, mining and natural resources, agriculture, private sector development and others.

Together these processes comprise the integrated ANDS implementation process. To support this process, institutions will be strengthened and capacity build within the central government and at the sub-national level. Apart from this the high priority will be given to skill development programs to meet the needs of the private sector and increase employment. This sequencing of priorities in framework is illustrated in Figure 10.2.

Implementation Cycle

Following the approval of the Government, the ANDS will be submitted to the World Bank and International Monetary Fund and presented to the international community, outlining the ANDS funding requirements.

Because the Budget is the central tool for implementing the ANDS, all line ministries and agencies will develop and align their national programs and projects with the ANDS Sector Strategies, which will then be costed and prioritized against the fiscal framework which itself has already been prioritized and sequenced.

Based on the costing and prioritization of sector strategies, the Public Investment Program (PIP) will be prepared to enable (i) full integration of the ANDS into the Medium-Term Fiscal Framework and the Budget; and (ii) presentation to the National Assembly. This will be accomplished by by Jaddi 1387 (end-2008).

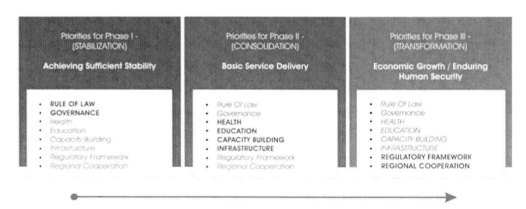

Figure 10.2. Sequencing of priorities for an integrated approach.

The first ANDS Progress Report will be prepared by end-1387 (March 2009). Following the Government's approval of the Progress Report, it will be presented to the World Bank and IMF (within the context of reaching the HIPC completion point). This review process will also be used to continually strengthen and adjust policy and program delivery throughout the period of implementation.

Based on the progress and evaluation reports the ANDS Review/Update will be completed by mid-1389 (September 2010). This will allow for policy correction and adjustments following the completion of the period envisaged for the implementation of the Afghanistan Compact.

The implementation of the ANDS is summarized in Figure 10.3.

Role of the National Budget and the MTFF

The Budget is the funding mechanism through which ANDS policy will be implemented. High levels of insecurity have meant that the costs of many development and reconstruction activities have been dramatically increased. This has led to fragmentation of the policy development process, lower levels of aid effectiveness and a failure to effectively utilize the national budgetary process as an effective tool for coordination and prioritization.

Strengthening the role of the Budget as the instrument of national policy making is critical to the implementation of the ANDS. An integrated approach will rely on the Budget as its principal vehicle for delivering stabilization and development results. All public expenditures aimed at enhancing economic growth and reducing poverty are formulated and executed through the budget formulation and execution process, as outlined in Figure 10.4 below.[58]

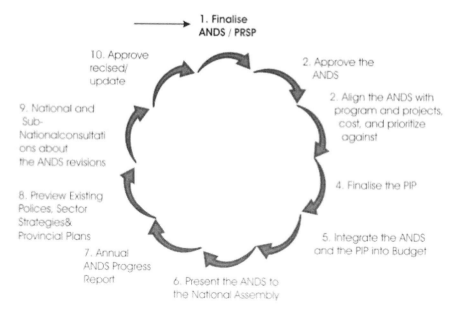

Figure 10.3. ANDS Implementation Cycle.

By committing themselves to funding national programs according to ANDS priorities, international community will ensure that their assistance is leveraged to bring stability to the government planning cycle. The integrated approach to planning and implementation will ensure that priorities and potential synergies (across national programs as well as across the public/private sector divide) are identified at the planning stage and utilised to develop context-specific approaches. The integrated approach will also set the conditions for external budget funds to be more easily aligned to the ANDS; if the capacity to design and deliver national programs is successfully increased, the proportion of assistance delivered through the external budget will begin to decline.

A forward-looking partnership between Afghanistan and the international community is needed to ensure external aid is managed in line with the ANDS and recommendations of the Paris Declaration. The implementation of the ANDS will depend upon the donors to implement more programs and projects through the Core Budget. As afore-mentioned , effective implementation will require that those programs and projects funded through the External Budgets and the PRTs be aligned with ANDS priorities. Finally, this approach will also require: (i) enhanced Government ownership of the development process; (ii) more effective public expenditure management; (iii) an increased focus on outcomes and service delivery; (iv) greater harmonization between Government and donor policies, and (v) more mutual accountability between the Government and the international community.

The Government's current approach is based on programmatic budgeting. This will help ensure the Budget is realistic; based on sector strategies; has measured and unambiguous budget management guidelines that reflect improving government capacities; involves key stakeholders (including sub-national bodies based on provincial development plans); is transparent, with relevant, accurate and timely information provided to decision makers, including the National Assembly and the public at large; and accountable through internal and external audits.

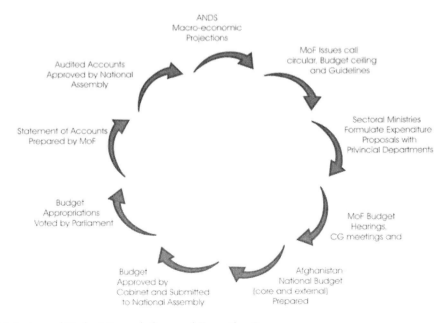

Figure 10.4. Annual Budget Formulations and Execution Process.

Control of on-budget resources is being strengthened through fundamental reforms of the Public Finance Management (PFM) system, including procurement, accounting, reporting, auditing, and other systems of accountability. The ANDS presents the strategic orientation within which future resource utilization will be determined. Specific emphasis will include:

Strengthening aggregate fiscal discipline: Government will aim to (i) increase the revenue to GDP ratio; (ii) reduce the ratio of operating expenditures to revenues, and (iii) make progress according to fiscal targets established through the MTFF.

Enhancing resource allocation and utilization based on strategic priorities: Currently, the Ministry of Finance uses program budgeting in key sectors and ministries. This activity will expand to include all ministries, which will significantly support the integrated approach. Budgetary proposals will be examined on the basis of their alignment to the ANDS policies. Specific criteria to the following elements will need to be met:

- **Rationale**: Does this project require public sector finance? Does the project directly address poverty reduction, economic growth or contribute to easing tensions in the communities? Does the project address cross-cutting issues such as gender?
- **Cost-effectiveness**: Have multi-year cost implications (sustainability) and the least-cost alternative been identified, including through competitive bidding?
- **Benefit-cost**: Have the benefits (including economic, social and environmental) been quantified and do they exceed the costs? Is the rate of return on expenses sufficient to justify expenditure?
- **Risk mitigation**: Do project management capacities exist to allow successful project implementation within the time frames? Have risks been identified and are they acceptable?

Supporting greater efficiency and effectiveness in the delivery of services: The Government will expedite the procurement of services, labor and supplies.

Implement Sector Wide Approaches and National Programs[59]: The success of these sectoral frameworks will depend on an appropriate enabling legal frameworks, institutional capacity, infrastructure, human resources, technical assistance, finance, baseline data and data management systems, risk management strategies, and standard audit and PFM procedures.

Further integrate existing trust funds and PRTs into the budgetary process: Efforts will continue to incorporate the Afghan Reconstruction Trust Fund (ARTF), Law and Order Trust Fund (LOTFA) and the Counter Narcotics Trust Fund (CNTF) into the budgetary process. This will ensure these trust funds contribute to the effectiveness of broader sector wide approaches. To the maximum extent possible, appropriations will be made through the treasury system.

Integrate budgetary processes with cabinet- level policy-making and legislative planning: The linkages among policy-making, planning and budgeting will be strengthened to promote more results-based performance management. Medium-term expenditure priorities will receive expedited treatment in the cabinet policy- making and legislative processes.

Program and provincial budgeting will provide multi-year budget proposals which integrate recurrent and capital expenditures. These processes will also integrate the Provincial Development Plans (PDPs) and address any provincial or regional imbalances.

Tracking of poverty related spending: Evaluating the effects of public spending on poverty reduction will be enhanced by introducing the system of tracking of poverty related spending within the framework of the future monitoring mechanism. The JCMB Secretariat will take lead on this in cooperation with the MoF, CSO and line ministries.

Role of the MTFF

The three year Medium Term Fiscal Framework (MTFF) will continue to provide the resource framework. The MTFF allows the Government to put in place an affordable, realistic and sustainable medium-term fiscal framework to ensure (i) transparency in setting fiscal objectives; (ii) stability in fiscal policy-making process; and (iii) efficiency in design and implementation of fiscal policies.

The MTFF will be essential planning tool to implement ANDS and evaluate impacts of its policies. Through the MTFF the ANDS priorities will be considered in yearly budgeting: within the limits of the capacity, the MTFF will ensure that the ANDS implementation will be coordinated with the budget preparations. Based on this the MoF plans to embark on the process of developing the Medium-Term Expenditure Framework (MTEF) to strengthen the Governments capacity for expenditure planning.

Role of the Control and Audit Office (CAO)

The role of the Control and Audit Office (CAO) will be strengthened to provide oversight of the expenditure functions of core spending ministries. However, given the CAO's current weak capacity, the MoF will assume these responsibilities in the short term.

Budget management framework, prioritization and funding requirements for the implementation of the ANDS

The Medium Term Fiscal Framework and sector wide programming and costing will (i) strengthen realistic resource projections; (ii) sectoral prioritization; (iii) support fiscal sustainability, and (iv) develop budget ceilings for all budget entities. Table 10.5 below provides a high level sectoral overview of the projected sectoral costs for the period 1386 to 1391 (2007- 2012).

As afore-mentioned, the implementation of the ANDS will be aligned with the Government's commitments toward the PRGF and HIPC. The Government expenditure prioritization framework will ensure that proper resource allocation will be made to support implementation of these commitments and if necessary appropriate adjustments will be done.

Table 10.5. Projected Operating and Development Spending (US$ m) 1387-1391[60]

Sector	1387 US$m	1388 US$m	1389 US$m	1390 US$m	1391 US$m	Total US$m
Security	3219	2585	2679	2790	2906	14179
Infrastructure & Natural Resources	1781	3093	3681	4180	4451	17185
Agriculture and Rural Development	829	921	916	909	912	4486
Education and Culture	742	893	980	1077	1181	4872
Good Governance, Rule of Law and Human Rights	374	558	640	685	728	2985
Health and Nutrition	325	465	530	563	595	2478
Economic Governance & PSD	237	215	230	244	260	1186
Social Protection	192	359	394	421	449	1815
Others	205	198	185	170	157	915
Total	**7,903**	**9,286**	**10,236**	**11,038**	**11,637**	**50,100**

The total estimated cost of the ANDS over the next five years (1387-1391) is $50.1 billion. Of this amount the Government will contribute $6.8 billion and external assistance is expected to be $43.2 billion.

National Implementation Structures

At the national level, the following structures link policy, planning, budgeting and monitoring of the ANDS:

To facilitate coordination, 17 Inter-Ministerial Committees (IMCs) will be established, each responsible for overseeing the implementation of an ANDS sector strategies. The membership of these bodies will include the ministers from those ministries with responsibility in the particular sector. The IMCs will report regularly to the President and Cabinet and to the JCMB through the Oversight Committee. The IMCs will be coordinated by the ANDS Oversight Committee and supported by the JCMB Secretariat.

The line ministries and other government agencies will be responsible for the implementation of the ANDS (program and projects) with support from the Ministry of Finance, Independent Administrative Reform and Civil Service Commission (IARCSC) and international partners.

The National Assembly will be responsible for legislating an enabling environment for security, economic growth and poverty reduction. Parliamentarians and committees are already actively engaged in the formulation of the ANDS

The Council of Ministers headed by the President as the highest level decision-making body, will oversee the progress and provide overall policy guidance and direction under existing legislation.

The ANDS Oversight Committee as high level body comprised of senior ministers will oversee the implementation of the ANDS and report about the progress directly to the President and the Cabinet.[61]

MoF will be responsible to ensure that the programs and projects of the line ministries will be costed, prioritized against the fiscal framework, sequenced and integrated into the MTFF and the Budget.

Sub-National Implementation Structures

At the sub-national level, the following structures are to be established to enhance the link between policy making, planning, and implementation of the PDPs, budgeting and monitoring:

The Independent Department for Local Governance (IDLG), under the President's Office, will be responsible for the overall coordination of local governance and all provincial governors will report to it on the progress of the implementation of the ANDS.

At the provincial level, the Provincial Councils, Provincial Development Committees and Provincial Governors will be directly involved in the implementation of the ANDS. The provincial departments of the line ministries will be responsible for implementation of the sub- national projects. At district and community levels the District and Community Development Councils (DDCs, CDCs) will continue to play key role in implementation of the community level projects under the overall leadership of the Wuluswal..

Coordination Structures

The Government and the international community have established the Joint Coordination and Monitoring Board (JCMB), with responsibility for overall strategic coordination and monitoring of the implementation of the Afghanistan Compact.

Consultative Groups (CGs) will continue to play important role in coordinating the efforts of the Government and donors in implementation of the development programs and projects. The CGs will be important forum for improving aid coordination, policy and implementation dialogue, and ensuring alignment of the donor programs with the ANDS. Each CG is co-chaired by the Minister of Finance and a relevant member of the Oversight Committee. Line ministry representatives and other representatives selected by the co-chairs are responsible for the substantive work of the CGs, assisted by the Secretariat.

Working Groups (WGs) have been established for each sector, and where necessary are supported by sub-working groups. They will remain to be the key forum through which line ministries and international partners can develop programs, align efforts and monitor results.

The Policy Action Group (PAG) will provide overall direction to key Afghan and international actors to ensure that the interdependence of security, governance and development objectives guide operations and programs in order to achieve the conditions for basic service delivery, development programs and private sector-led growth, especially in conflict affected areas.

At the sub-national level, the Provincial Development Committees (PDCs), chaired by the Governors, will ensure coordination within the provincial administration and with the donors, PRTs and civil society.

Integrating Conflict Management into Sector Strategies

There are deep concerns about the feasibility of initiating development and reconstruction programs due to the ongoing conflict in some provinces, as well as increasing attacks countrywide. This insecurity is preventing the implementation of development projects in several areas of the country. The impacts of conflict and violence on development efforts will be more comprehensively addressed in implementation of the programs and projects. The conflict evaluation mechanism will be established within the existing monitoring structures with aim to sensitizing development and aid to conflict and risks. However, a proper diagnosis will be part of program and project preparations.

The Central Monitoring and Reporting System (CMRS)[62] will conduct specific assessment and analysis which will subsequently mainstream and integrate conflict awareness and sensitivity into all areas of development assistance (based on criteria to be developed in cooperation with the donors) to ensure that development programs will not erode stability or increase conflict. Finally, conflict awareness and peace- promoting initiatives will be incorporated into reconstruction and development assistance and special attention will be paid to ensure that development programs do not upset cultural values or beliefs.

Conclusion

Implementation of the ANDS under the Integrated Approach will require synchronization of budgetary, cabinet, legislative, program and stabilization cycles. In particular, it will require measures to further strengthen the capacity of state bodies responsible for these processes (Office of Administrative Affairs, Ministry of Parliamentary Affairs, Ministry of Finance, IARCSC, IDLG, NSC) and Inter-Ministerial Committees, as well as those responsible for program delivery (line ministries, provincial and district administrations). It will require strengthened coordination and alignment by international partners under the overall authority of the JCMB, delivered through CGs, WGs and the PAG.

The implementation framework conceived in this strategy requires an ongoing evaluation and monitoring, and an enhanced risk management mechanism, as there are continuing significant risks to stability which may yet undermine the underlying assumptions. The main risk for successful implementation of the ANDS will continue to be security. Domestic and donor resource mobilization remains an extremely demanding challenge, which will not yield reliable long-term predictability for the budget process for some time to come. Implementation of donor commitments will be highly dependent on implementation of the ANDS reforms. There is also a risk that domestic support for the ANDS will weakens, thus, further consultative processes will be undertaken to overcome this. However, these risks can only be mitigated rather than being eliminated.

The Integrated Approach reflects a recognition that building on achievements to date will require an unprecedented number of actors to come together to support institutional structures in order to overcome complex challenges.

Figure 11.1. Formulations, Implementation and Monitoring and Evaluation Process.

By focusing on agreed programs and building coherence and synergy among activities at the local level, stability can be achieved in all parts of Afghanistan and a genuine national development process can begin. In the framework of such a strategy, the Integrated Approach in ANDS implementation aims to bring visible improvements to the lives of all Afghans.

11. MONITORING FRAMEWORK

The ANDS, as the country's PRSP, consists of (i) formulation (ii) implementation and (iii) monitoring and evaluation phases. The monitoring and evaluation phase (see Figure 11.1 below) runs parallel to implementation, allowing actions and measures taken to be monitored, providing an indication of their efficiency and effectiveness in meeting poverty reduction and development targets. The Government has already begun establishing a Central Monitoring and Reporting System (CMRS) to fulfill both internal and PRSP reporting functions. While the CMRS will take some time to establish, this chapter outlines the core approach adopted to measuring development outcomes and impacts in line with ANDS priorities, Compact benchmarks and the MDGs. As the ANDS has an increasingly provincial focus, with public spending linked to provincial development plans, an effective monitoring and evaluation system will need to be established in both the provinces and by the Government in Kabul.

The Afghanistan Compact benchmarks and the MDGs have been integrated into the ANDS Sector Strategies. The JCMB Secretariat, as the body responsible for high-level co-ordination, together with the line ministries, will play a key role in high-level, strategic monitoring of the implementation of the Afghanistan Compact and the MDGs.

It will be important to distinguish between two levels of monitoring and oversight: (a) input/output or program monitoring of the implementation of the ANDS, and (b) outcome/impact monitoring for high level Government institutions (OSC, Cabinet) and the JCMB to ensure that the strategic priorities of the ANDS are met.

ANDS Monitoring and Evaluation Principles

In developing a responsive, manageable and outcome oriented monitoring and evaluation system, the Government commits to:

- Establishing a centralized and eventually provincial based monitoring and reporting system;

- Adopting a comprehensive approach to poverty measurement and economic diagnostic work through determination of baselines and benchmarks;
- Adopting evidence-based systems for monitoring and evaluating policy and implementation;
- Increasingly not only measuring inputs and processes, but outcomes, performance and development and poverty impacts (positive and negative);
- Strengthening the management of knowledge and information access around the M&E system;
- Increasingly, over the course of the ANDS, seeking to strengthen linkages between the M&E system and the provincial planning process;
- Maintaining transparency and accountability and encouraging support from NGOs, the Central Statistics Office and citizens in the provision of data and analysis of findings;
- Building the core institutional capacities needed to sustain M&E processes, both within the CMRS, as well as the CSO, NRVA and line ministry systems;
- Setting service delivery benchmarks will utilize accepted international specific, measurable, achievable, realistic and timely outcome indicators for poverty measurement; and,
- Integrating the M&E system across the entire national budget cycle, to support the setting of multi-annual and annual performance targets.

Institutional Structure

The institutional structure for monitoring will include a number of government, donor and non-government intuitions, however; the JCMB, line ministries and the CSO will play the most important roles.

The Role of the ANDS Oversight Committee
The OSC will remain the key high-level government body coordinating and monitoring the implementation of the ANDS. It will approve bi-annual and annual progress on ANDS implementation reports as well as the reports prepared for the Cabinet and the JCMB. The OSC makes up the Government part of the JCMB.

The Role of the JCMB
The JCMB is the strategic level coordination mechanism between the Government and the international community. It will focus on resolving the strategic problems arising from the implementation, coordination and monitoring not only of the Afghanistan Compact but also the entire ANDS. Co-chaired by the Government and the United Nations it will provide (i) high level oversight, ensuring an integrated approach to delivery of the Compact and ANDS; (ii) directions to address any obstacles or bottlenecks surrounding implementation, coordination and monitoring of the ANDS; and (iii) report on the implementation of the Afghanistan Compact and ANDS to the President, National Assembly, the UN Secretary General, the international community and the public.

The Role of the JCMB Secretariat

The JCMB secretariat will provide policy and strategy analysis/assessment, monitoring and evaluation reports to JCMB on the overall implementation of ANDS and Afghanistan Compact Benchmarks as well as supporting the work of the standing committees. It will strengthen its capacity to provide independent analysis to enhance the high level oversight and problem solving role of the JCMB. The capacity of the JCMB Secretariat must be significantly strengthened to perform these tasks.

The Role of the Central Monitoring and Reporting System (CMRS)

The CMRS will be developed within the JCMB Secretariat and Ministry of Economy as the central machinery of government to support the monitoring and reporting process. Alongside the CSO, it will provide the central hub for all national monitoring as an apex monitoring body, with a particular focus on monitoring and evaluating the impact of the Compact and the ANDS. It will not function in isolation but will bring together existing information from the CSO, consumer price indices, the NRVA, Afghanistan Financial Monitoring Information System, Afghanistan Country Stability Picture (for ISAF), Afghanistan Information Management Service, Donor Assistance Database and GeoBase, the Project and Activity Tracking system of USAID/Afghanistan as well as sectoral ministries.

The CMRS will focus on data analysis and reporting of outputs, outcomes and impacts. There will be no conflict between the roles of the CMRS and the CSO, as they will be at two opposite ends of the data systems. While the CSO will concentrate on data collection through various means including surveys and their reporting, the CMRS will be collating the filtered data produced by the CSO and will facilitate various monitoring processes and disseminate information. They will in fact complement each other. Finally, the CMRS will be responsible for gathering information on programs for conflict sensitivity, and to mainstream conflict sensitivity into programs based on criteria to be developed within the JCMB Secretariat in cooperation with the Government and line ministries.

The Role of the Central Statistics Office (CSO)

The CSO will remain the main provider of primary and secondary information in relation to national statistics, as an input to the CMRS. The CSO is currently compiling statistics on national accounts, prices, external trade, population and demographics for monitoring economic, financial, and structural policies as well as other operations that will provide lots of quality information for improving the monitoring framework. The capacity of the CSO will be strengthened so that a meaningful statistical system be put in place for providing useful data on various macro-economic processes and important sectors. It is necessary for this purpose to strengthen the collection of operational data in various sectors through respective agencies. The CSO will coordinate data collection systems in various ministries and organizations.

The Role of NRVA and Other Surveys

One of the most important data-capturing exer-cises has been the NRVA surveys, from which the current poverty line has been calculated. Three surveys have already been conducted and provide critical information on poverty, as well as other important sectors. The role of these surveys will be further expanded so that they can meet the immediate data needs of the other sectors. The multi-purpose household surveys will be conducted under the supervision and guidance of the Central Statistics Office (CSO). To monitor the impact on poverty, the NRVA and the future household budget surveys will serve as the key source for monitoring for critical poverty and social outcome indicators and completion of the reports on poverty situation (see appendix III).

The Role of the Line Ministries

Line departments will continue to collect sector relevant information to monitor the output and sectoral outcome of national spending through the ANDS. The CMRS and CSO will work closely with line ministries to standardize methodological approaches to monitoring National Programs. The Ministry of Economy will be responsible for the wider inter-ministerial coordination.

The Role of Provincial Offices

The line ministries will strengthen their provincial offices to collect disaggregated data on all indicators to monitor progress on individual projects at provincial, district and village level. The provincial offices and institutions of sub- national governance will utilize monitoring, support and reporting mechanisms to feed data to the line ministries which will assist in provincial budgeting, planning and monitoring of the overall implementation of the ANDS. The Governor will report to the Provincial Councils on the progress of implementation of the sub- national ANDS priorities and other parts of the PDPs.

The Role of the National Budget

The Budget remains the central tool of government policy. The close day-to-day working relationship between the MoF (AFMIS), the various budget entities, the CMRS and CSO will provide vital information in setting and costing sectoral priorities and targets to be funded through the medium term budget framework. Annual targets will be reported against the agreed sectoral baselines and the budget hearing sessions will increasingly move towards reportage of budget outcomes, not just financial and input reporting.

The Role Of Donors, IFIs and the UN

The Government will continue to request support from international partners in (a) developing analysis of the main obstacles to more rapid growth and poverty reduction; (b) discussing the quality, coverage and timeliness of key data, including possible final and intermediate indicators; (c) assessing the main policy issues confronting the Government in the macroeconomic, structural, and social areas, given the core objectives of promoting growth and reducing poverty; (d) assessing the current 'resource envelope' and, within this, the possible scale of expenditures for poverty reduction; and (e) discussing current levels and nature of external assistance, and prospects for increased aid over the medium-term.

The Role of NGOs and Civil Society

Independent monitoring and reporting by NGOs, CSOs, the media and other civilian bodies will be a vital part of the overall monitoring and reporting system. Their participation will be encouraged and actively supported. They will play an important role in the external monitoring of the implementation of the ANDS which will be carried out in continuing consultations with NGOs and the civil society, sub- national representatives and the international community.

Monitoring and Evaluation Reporting

For the purposes of the Compact and the ANDS, the JCMB Secretariat will provide ad hoc, periodic impact evaluation reports to the Government, the public and international partners. The JCMB Secretariat will produce and the Government will approve annual progress reports on ANDS implementation, to serve as the basis for reporting. The Annual ANDS report will be presented to the Board of Directors of the WB and the IMF. This report will indicate to what extent outside views are sought and incorporated into the report, particularly of the IMF, World Bank and UN.

Based on annual progress and evaluation reports every two years, a full update of the ANDS/PRSP, developed with broad participation will be constituted as an impact evaluation. This update, which will be publicly disseminated, will provide an opportunity for all stakeholders to assess progress on implementation and adjust policies to achieve higher efficiency.

In order to evaluate effects of implementation of the ANDS on poverty reduction, the JCMB Secretariat will be producing reports on poverty situation on three year basis to coincide with the completion of the NRVA surveys, which will continue to be most important instrument for collection of the poverty related data and produce annual MDG progress reports.

Finally, public expenditure reviews will be conducted and integrated into the ANDS monitoring process. In line with the budget cycle, ad hoc and periodic sectoral monitoring and reporting will be conducted.

Indicators for Monitoring

The measurement and analysis of poverty, inequality, and vulnerability are crucial for various reasons: The Government has developed poverty and vulnerability surveys largely based on income and consumption data, disaggregated by province, household, agro-economic zone, gender and household size, among other factors. Against these a new poverty line has been developed. The process of data collection and analysis has led to a far deeper understanding of the causes of poverty, and these constraints are being addressed within the various sector strategies. Figure 11.2 outlines the overall poverty monitoring and strategy design process undertaken in formulating and implementing the ANDS. The CMRS will play a pivotal role in providing information to decision-makers as part of this process.

In establishing an effective monitoring and evaluation systems for the ANDS, based on relevant national statistics (CSO/NRVA), the Government has already determined the following: (i) goals, indicators and targets (ii) levels of data desegregation including by province and gender; (iii) appropriate targets, for example through the MDGs, Compact and ANDS sectoral levels; (iv) data requirements to meet the minimum standards of a PRSP; and (v) the frequency of data collection and monitoring.

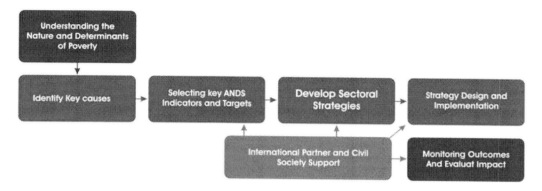

Figure 11.2. ANDS Poverty Monitoring and Strategy Design Process.

In developing the ANDS, the sectoral strategies and the provincial development plans, the Government has established a core set of monitoring and evaluation indicators for monitoring outcomes and impact for security, law and order and human rights, governance, social and economic development and poverty programs. In addition to standard sector strategies such as education and health, social protection and welfare programs have also been developed, within which the needs of particularly vulnerable groups can be targeted. Appendix III outlines the main indicators to be used in measuring the progress of the ANDS on reducing poverty and improving economic development. Monitoring matrices have been developed within all sector strategies, which provide important outcomes, indicators, targets and baselines (where available). The various sectoral strategies outline targets for each reporting period on an annual and three-yearly basis.

Data requirements to feed into the input, output, outcome and impact assessment process are gradually being established. Sources of data to feed into the CMRS include, government administrative records, donor project status reports, ministry MIS systems data, CSO household listings, NRVA data and other forms of data (i.e. AIMS, AFMIS), sector specific survey data, IMF Enterprise Survey results, consumer price information, budget and expenditure data, the ACSP database and existing databases (e.g., AFMIS, DAD, DevInfo, GeoBase.). Indicators for the cross-cutting issues of, regional cooperation, counter-narcotics, corruption, capacity building, gender and the environment have been mainstreamed across the sectoral strategies.

However, due to weak statistical data, the baselines for a number of key development and poverty indicators are yet to be established. This is going to be an important priority for the first two years of implementation of the ANDS. Strengthening of the CSO and the capacity of the line ministries will be essential for establishing clear baselines. These efforts will include mapping intermediate indicators with final outcomes. In cases where actual indicators are difficult to measure or cannot be provided with sufficient frequency, proxy indicators will be used.

Since early development stages will not yield measurable outcomes in the short run, a series of process indicators are used in order to measure immediate results. These indicators are part of the overall monitoring framework both for the Compact and the ANDS that identifies progress on reaching key milestones. The indicators are measured in index format which contain multiple components that also ensure strict monitoring to take action on various areas of reform. For example, they are built into the ANDS Action Plan to improve legislation, institutional building and policy making.

Finally, working together will the MoF and the line ministries, the JCMB Secretariat will ensure that the budgets will be aligned with the indicators and costing priorities. However, the Government is aware that this activity will also require a significant capacity building.

Monitoring and Evaluation Framework

Based on the development of the sector strategies, initial Sector Monitoring and Evaluation Frameworks have been prepared to identify needs with regard to existing and planned policies, and developing the programs/projects and indicators. These Frameworks have identified: (i) the milestones in implementation of the M&E plans; (ii) activities required to build on existing monitoring structures; and (iii) reporting requirements for the multilateral agencies on the progress of the implementation of the ANDS. The monitoring and evaluation plan will also identify data requirements and additional surveys, where required, to establish sectoral baselines. The M&E plans will furthermore be developed and monitored to capture progress on the achievement of benchmarks. An exercise to rationalize and adjust the Compact benchmarks to the Government's implementation capacity has already been addressed at JCMB meetings.

Table 13.1. Monitoring and Evaluation Indicators

No.	Indicators	Collection Frequency	Data Source	Responsible Agency
	Poverty and Hunger			
1	Proportion of population below national poverty line (National/ Prov/ Urb/Rur/Kuchi)	3-years	NRVA	CSO
2	Poverty gap ratio [incidence x depth of poverty]	3-years	NRVA	CSO
3	Share of poorest quintile in national consumption	3-years	NRVA	CSO
4	Proportion of population below minimum level of dietary energy consumption (National/Prov/ Urb/Rur/Kuchi)	3-years	NRVA	CSO
	Economic Indicators			
5	GDP (US$ billions)	Annual	National Accounts	DAB
6	Gross domestic investment/GDP	Annual	National Accounts	DAB
7	Exports of goods and services/GDP	Quarterly	National Accounts	DAB
8	Gross domestic savings/GDP	Quarterly	National Accounts	DAB
9	Gross national savings/GDP	Quarterly	National Accounts	DAB

No.	Indicators	Collection Frequency	Data Source	Responsible Agency
10	Current account balance/GDP.	Quarterly	National Accounts	DAB
11	Interest payments/GDP	Quarterly	National Accounts	DAB
12	Budget balance	Quarterly	National Accounts	MoF
13	Revenue/GDP	Quarterly	National Accounts	MoF
14	Public Expenditure/GDP	Quarterly	National Accounts	MoF
15	Total debt/GDP	Annual	National Accounts	DAB
16	Gross national reserves	Annual	National Accounts	DAB
17	Total debt service/exports	Quarterly	National Accounts	DAB
18	Present value of debt/GDP	Annual	National Accounts	DAB
19	Present value of debt/exports	Annual	National Accounts	DAB
	Other Social Indicators			
20	Population *(millions)*	Annual	National Survey	CSO
21	Labor force (%)	3-years	National Survey	CSO
22	Urban/Rural/Kuchi population (% of total population)	Annual	National Survey	CSO
23	Life expectancy at birth (years)	Annual	National Survey	CSO
	Governance			
24	Index on progress of empowering the National Assembly.	Six Months	Admin Data	OoP
25	Index on progress of Reforming Public Administration.	Annual	Admin Data	IARCSC
26	Index on progress of building capacity of Public Sector Work-force.	Annual	Admin Data	IARCSC
27	Index on progress of Implementing systems, mechanisms and procedures to implement merit based appointments and peformance-based reviews.	Six Months	Admin Data	IARCSC
28	Index on progress of introducing systems, mechanisms and procedures to reduce and monitor corruption at different levels in the government and the judiciary.	Six Months	Admin Data	IARCSC
29	Index on progress of putting plans, systems and mechanisms in place for improved participation of women in governance.	Annual	Admin Data	IARCSC

Table 13.1. (Continued)

No.	Indicators	Collection Frequency	Data Source	Responsible Agency
30	Index on progress of creating a strong and capable Independent Election Commission to hold regular Elections as mandated by the Constitution.	Six Months	Admin Data	OoP
31	Index on progress of putting in place legal, policy, institutions and other systems and procedures for strengthening the sub-national governance.	Annual	Admin Data	IDLG
32	Index on progress of putting in place legal, policy, institu-tional and other systems in place to realize, protect, promote and extend human rights in the country.	Six Months	Admin Data	MoJ, MoFA
	Justice			
33	Index on progress of putting in place legal framework and systems so that Criminal and Civil justice is administered effectively, and in accordance with law, the Constitution, and international standards.	Six Months	Admin Data	MoJ
34	Index on progress of making justice institutions transparent and accountable.	Six Months	Admin Data	MoJ
35	# of functioning and adequately resourced, judicial institutions in each province	Six Months	Admin Data	MoJ
	Religious Affairs			
36	Index on the progress of enhancing the impact of religious affairs for socio-economic development	Six Months	Admin Data	MoHRA
	Energy			
37	Index on progress of putting in place an enabling environment for private sector investment in energy sector.	Six Months	Admin Data	MoEW
38	% of households electrified (National/Urban/Rural)	3-years	NRVA	CSO
39	Index on progress of expanding public power grid (National/Urban/Rural)	Six Months	Admin Data	MoEW
40	Index on progress of increasing access to rural energy	Six Months	Admin Data	MoEW
41	Index on Progress of restructuring energy sector governance and commercialized operations	Six Months	Admin Data	MoEW
	Transport			
42	Index on progress of putting in place institutional mechanisms for better governance of the Transport Sector.	Six Months	Admin Data	MoT
43	Index on progress of enabling legislations and regulations for efficient working of the transport sector and various players therein.	Six Months	Admin Data	MoT
44	% of target Km of ring road or roads to the neighboring countries fully upgraded and rehabilitated.	Annual	Admin Data	MoPW

No.	Indicators	Collection Frequency	Data Source	Responsible Agency
45	% of all villages connected by all-weather roads	Annual	Admin Data	MRRD, MoPW
46	Index on the progress of the process of completion of International Civil Aviation Organization (ICAO) compliance for Kabul and Herat Airports.	Six Months	Admin Data	MoT
	Urban Development			
47	Index on the progress of providing improved to basic services by urban household	Six Months	Admin Data	MoUDH
48	Index on the progress of providing increased availability of affordable shelter	Six Months	Admin Data	MoUDH
49	% completion of city development plans for 34 provinces	Six Months	Admin Data	MoUDH
	Water Resources			
50	Index on the progress of putting in place improved water sector legal and governance structures and institutions in place	Six Months	Admin Data	MoEW
51	Index on the progress of developing and implementing sustainable water resources management strategies and plans covering irrigation and drinking water	Six Months	Admin Data	MoEW
52	# of Hydrometric stations installed and equipped	Annual	Admin Data	MoEW
	Information and Communication Technologies (ICT)			
53	Index on the progress of creation of E-Afghanistan	Six Months	Admin Data	MoCIT
54	% increase in annual revenue generated from the ICT Sector	Annual	Admin Data	MoF
55	% of population access to mobile phones	3-years	NRVA	CSO
56	number of internet users	3-years	NRVA	CSO
	Mining			
57	Index on progress of creation of enabling and regulatory environment for increased investment in mining sector	Six Months	Admin Data	MoM, MoCI
58	% of increase in revenue generated from mining sector	Six Months	National Accounts	DAB
	Education			
59	Literacy rate of population (National/Urban/Rural)	5-years	MoE Survey	MoE
60	Net enrolment ratio in primary education (Na-tional/Urban/Rural)	Annual	MoE Survey	MoE
61	Attendance Rate (National/Urban/Rural)	Annual	MoE Survey	MoE
62	Proportion of pupils starting grade 1 who reach grade 5 (Na-tional/Urban/Rural)	Annual	MoE Survey	MoE
63	Literacy rate of 15-24 year-olds (National/Urban/Rural)	5-years	MoE Survey	MoE

Table 13.1. (Continued)

No.	Indicators	Collection Frequency	Data Source	Responsible Agency
64	Index of improving quality of education including higher and vocational education	Six Months	Admin Data	MoE, MoHE
	Media and Culture			
65	Index on progress of protecting and preserving Afghan culture and heritage	Six Months	Admin Data	MoC
66	Index on progress of promoting independent and free media	Six Months	Admin Data	MoC
	Health			
67	Under-five mortality rate (National/Urban/Rural)	3-years	NRVA	CSO
68	Infant mortality rate (National/Urban/Rural)	3-years	NRVA	CSO
69	Proportion of 1 year-old children immunized against measles (National/Urban/Rural)	3-years	NRVA	CSO
70	Prevalence of underweight children under-five years of age (National/Urban/Rural)	3-years	MoPH Survey	MoPH
71	Maternal mortality ratio (National/Urban/Rural)	3-years	MoPH Survey	MoPH
72	Proportion of births attended by skilled health personnel (National/Urban/Rural)	3-years	NRVA	CSO
73	Condom use rate of the contraceptive prevalence rate (National/Urban/Rural)	3-years	NRVA	CSO
74	% of population within two hours walking distance from PHC services (National/Urban/Rural)	3-years	NRVA	CSO
75	% of population access to clean water (National/Urban/Rural)	3-years	NRVA	CSO
76	% of children under 1 year receiving three doses of DPT vaccine	3-years	NRVA	CSO
77	% of children under 1 year received measles antigen.	3-years	NRVA	CSO
78	TB case detection rate	3-years	MoPH Survey	MoPH
79	Malaria incidence	3-years	MoPH Survey	MoPH
80	HIV prevalence	3-years	MoPH Survey	MoPH
	Agriculture and Rural Development			
81	Index on the progress of facilitating economic regeneration	SixMonths	Admin Data	MRRD, MAIL
82	Index on progress of Strengthened Local Governance	Six Months	Admin Data	MRRD, IDLG
83	Index on progress of Reduced Poppy cultivation through Alternative Livelihoods	Six Months	Admin Data	MRRD, MAIL
84	Index on the progress of increasing agriculture production and productivity.	Six Months	Admin Data	MRRD, MAIL
85	Index on the progress of improving agriculture and rural infrastructure	Six Months	Admin Data	MRRD, MAIL
	Social Protection			
86	Index on progress of a social protection system for vulnerable sections of society	Six Months	Admin Data	MoLSA

No.	Indicators	Collection Frequency	Data Source	Responsible Agency
87	Percentage of poor female headed households (National/Urban/Rural)	3-years	NRVA	CSO
88	Number of employed poor women who are heads of their households (National/Urban/Rural)	3-years	NRVA	CSO
89	Percentage of poor persons with disability (National/Urban/Rural)	3-years	NRVA	CSO
	Refugees and Internally Displaced Persons			
90	Index on progress of strengthening government's capacity to manage and assist refugees and displaced persons	Six Months	Admin Data	MoRR
	Private Sector Development			
91	Index on progress of development of enabling legal and regulatory framework for private sector and trade	Six Months	Admin Data	MoCI
92	Nominal value of the annual actual investment of the private sector	Annual	Admin Data	DAB
93	Number of registered company to AISA	Annual	Admin Data	AISA
	Gender			
94	Ratios of girls to boys in primary, secondary and tertiary education	Annual	Ministry Data	MoE, MoHE
95	Ratio of literate women to men, 15-24 years old	3-years	NRVA	CSO
96	Share of women in wage employment in the non-agricultural sector	3-years	NRVA	CSO
	Environment Sustainability			
97	Proportion of population with sustainable access to an improved water source (National/Urban/Rural)	3-years	NRVA	CSO
98	Proportion of population with access to improved sanitation (National/Urban/Rural)	3-years	NRVA	CSO
99	Proportion of households with access to secure tenure (Ur-	3-years	NRVA	CSO

Conclusion

The ANDS monitoring and evaluation system being developed will track the progress of implementation of the ANDS towards the achievement of its objectives in poverty reduction and overall development in the country. It also provides valuable inputs for further policy-streamlining, planning and implementation fine-tuning. The monitoring and evaluation institutions, especially the JCMB and CMRS, and capacity created in the country will produce a strengthened and sustainable development process. The availability of relevant information produced by this system, will promote constructive public debate on the challenges, solutions and progress in poverty reduction and economic development. The central role that the CMRS will eventually play within the implementation framework of the PRSP will enable the development of a poverty monitoring and analysis system, based on accepted international criteria. Given the existing weak capacity in the Government, it is important to stress that the strengthening of the monitoring framework will require a staged approach that will eventually develop into a more sophisticated monitoring and evaluation system.

12. CONCLUSION

While significant gains have been made in the reconstruction and development efforts over the course of the past six years, it seems that at the beginning of state building process in 2002, Afghanistan and the international community severely underestimated the depth and the extent of the calamity this country has gone through, and the time and costs that would be required to redress these. While the challenges facing Afghanistan have evolved in nature, they have not necessarily changed in magnitude. The deteriorating security in the past two years has definitely altered the path of development that the country has been pursuing since 2002, thus, substantially changing the assumptions on which the Afghanistan Compact was based. In many respects, the immense progress that has been made during these years has struggled to keep pace with the rapid growth of new problems and challenges. Despite that, the people of Afghanistan still believe that the path to prosperity from extreme poverty is on track.

Sustaining the nascent Afghan democracy will require the emergence of a prosperous Afghanistan in which poverty reduction and economic growth are able to raise the potential of the Afghan people for a better future. Success will require the emergence of a productive private sector active that plays a major role in most areas of the economy with public sector resources primarily focused on providing the needed physical, commercial and legal infrastructure and ensuring that the results of development benefit all citizens.

The ANDS represents an important milestone in the rebuilding and development of Afghanistan and serves as the country's Poverty Reduction Strategy Paper (PRSP). Through the ANDS, the Government is firmly committed to continuing state building efforts. It includes a realistic and comprehensive assessment of the enormous constraints and challenges facing the country and plans for addressing security, governance, rule of law, human rights, and social and economic development issues in an integrated approach. The primary goal of the ANDS is to establish a framework in which the Government and international community can work jointly to substantially reduce poverty based on a foundation of a private sector led sustained economic growth. This requires simultaneous progress on improving security, strengthening governance, increasing the effectiveness in delivering basic social services and taking the actions necessary to ensure that the private sector can invest and operate competitively. Achieving substantial progress in all of these areas is a complex task that will require commitment and coordination by all parts of the Government and the donor community. As such, the ANDS will help to coordinate and guide the joint activities of the Government and donors.

The development of the ANDS has been a genuinely Afghan 'owned' exercise, based on a broad consultative process, engaging donor community and stakeholders at national, provincial and grassroots levels to define the development of national and local priorities. This enabled men and women from all provinces to participate in defining national development objectives and to express their priorities. The voices of the poor have informed the policy framework, the poverty profile, as well as the orientation of the sectoral strategies that form the foundation of the ANDS. Important insights have been gained in security and conflict management, regional cooperation, counter- narcotics, anti-corruption, gender, the environment, and capacity development. Within the Government, the ANDS was developed based on strategies prepared by all ministries and broader sector strategies that were discussed extensively in ministries, Inter-Ministerial Committees, and with donors, NGOs, and the private sector. This inclusive participatory process will be maintained throughout the life of the ANDS.

The effectiveness of the ANDS will depend crucially on building a strong economic foundation that will support long term, broad-based economic growth, with the private sector being its driving engine. With proper policies undertaken during the last five years, per capita income nearly doubled. To achieve the poverty reduction goals of the ANDS comparable levels of economic growth will be needed in comings years. This will require a supportive enabling environment for social and economic development, which in turn depends on the continued maintenance of sound and stable macroeconomic policies to enable the private sector to establish itself as a vigorous engine of growth and employment creation.

A key strategic objective of the ANDS is to establish a secure economic environment in which it will be possible to attract sufficient levels of private sector investments that could in trun encourage the employment of human, financial and natural resources in the most productive ways possible. A critical element in achieving this objective will be to substantially increase investment in human capacity development and creating a skilled workforce in order to expand employment opportunities and increase incomes.

The ability to implement the projects and programs included in the ANDS depends upon the resources that will be available. Average economic growth is projected at an 8.1 percent rate for 1387-1391. A key assumption underlying this ambitious goal is an increasing role of the private sector in the economy. To reach these goals the Government will maintain strong macroeconomic management characterized by fiscal sustainability, prudent monetary policies, and the avoidance of short-term ad hoc measures.

A major contribution of the ANDS has been the determination of budget ceilings that reflect the Government's sectoral priorities. These are being built into the MTFF and the Ministry of Finance's program-based budgeting system focused on achieving the country's development needs. Security will remain the Government's highest priority, while the public expenditure programs for investments in energy, water and irrigation, transportation infrastructure, agriculture, agro-based industry, and rural development will remain high priorities, acknowledging the high importance of these sectors for the development of the private sector and for long term and sustainable employment growth. In the coming years the Government will also devote progressively more resources on education, governance, health, and social protection.

Acknowledging that in the near future, security sector development remains the country's highest priority, the Government is fully committed to successfully: (i) implementing an integrated and comprehensive national security policy and strategy; (ii) building a robust security sector reform program; (iii) strengthening civil and military operations; (iv) increasing the role of security forces in counter-narcotics activities; and (v) strengthening the civilian components of security entities. While international assistance is vitally necessary at the present time, the Government is planning and looking forward to taking on an increasing share of the responsibility for security-related activities in Afghanistan. This requires sufficient resources to enhance the capabilities of the country's armed forces, including the ANA, ANP and NSD, which is only possible through joint efforts and long-term commitments of the international community to Afghanistan.

Good governance and adherence to the rule of law are much needed reforms that the Government is committed to pursue. Whilst the donor community can support reforms and provide technical assistance, these reforms have to be initiated by internal decisions to implement improvements in governance. Without good governance and a sustained social contract for the acceptance of the rule of law, the total development strategy that has been developed will fail. This is because the strategy has at its core, the development of a private sector that will provide economic growth and demand for skilled labor. In this framework, the ANDS approach has been to encourage the public sector to concentrate on the creation of a safe and conducive environment that encourages the smooth operation of a robust private sector. This means a much greater focus by Government on governance issues rather than involvement in the production of goods and services that can be provided by a significantly larger and more efficient private sector. The Afghan 'ownership' of the strategy requires that the Government seeks donors close cooperation in capacity building and know-how transfer, so that a system can evolve that allows the best parts of the functional traditional governance system to co-exist with a universal system that recognizes and supports principles of social diversity, respect for human rights and the rule of law.

The successful implementation of the ANDS strategies for social and economic development is expected to contribute substantially to the long term transformation of Afghanistan. At the center of these strategies is the creation of conditions for accelerated private sector development. The Afghan private sector is now quite weak after years of isolation and an almost total lack of investment. The limited foreign investment that has taken place has been largely in the telecommunications industry. The Government is taking steps to establish an enabling environment, based on sound market-oriented policies and an adherence to the rule of law. There is great potential to attract private investment in the critical areas of infrastructure and natural resource development – including power generation, commercial agriculture and agro-based industry, development of water resources, and mining. To realize this enormous potential, the Government is developing the legal and regulatory structures required to enable private investment to operate profitably.

Given the devastated condition of much of the country's 'hard' and 'soft' infrastructures, huge public investments, particularly in agriculture, energy and water resources development, and transportation infrastructures will be necessary to create conditions in which the private sector can be competitive and successful. With donor assistance, considerable investment in essential infrastructure is currently being undertaken, particularly in roads, power, commercial agriculture, healthcare, and education and vocational skills. The Government intends to undertake public investment in infrastructure in ways that complement private investment in these areas or using public-private partnership arrangements whenever feasible.

It will take many years for a large competitive private sector to emerge in Afghanistan. An immediate goal of the ANDS is to put the pieces in place for this process to realize quickly and effectively. It is expected that in five years substantial progress will at least be made towards providing reliable access to electricity and water; the ability to efficiently transport goods throughout the country and to markets in neighboring countries; the implementation of major investments in commercial agriculture and minerals development to be underway; and for all Afghan businesses to operate formally with reliable legal protections.

The central objective of the ANDS is the reduction in poverty. Afghanistan is afflicted with extreme poverty for a large part of its population. As much as 42 percent of the population lives below the poverty line, while a significant number of people live precariously, where even relatively small increases in the cost of living will have the potential to greatly increase the numbers living in absolute poverty. And today, like much of the rest of the world, the Afghan people are facing substantial increases in the prices for food and fuel, which are having a disproportionate impact on the poor. The Government puts heavy emphasis on increasing employment as the most effective means for reducing poverty. Unemployment and under-employment are high – the unemployment rate is estimated to be near 40 percent. It is recognized that a high proportion of the growth in employment must come through the growth of a robust private sector.

The Government and people of Afghanistan remain grateful to the international community for their considerable and timely assistance in overcoming the enormous security and development challenges. The ANDS addresses the questions of the amounts and distribution of aid that will be required in the coming five years and the most effective modes of delivery. The Government expects that donors will align their support to reflect the priorities established in the ANDS. The successful implementation of the ANDS under the Integrated Approach will require greater coordination and increased responsiveness on the part of the Government and donors. Achieving alignment between the country's priorities and aid programs, and effectively adjusting priorities and programs as conditions change require a continued strong partnership between Afghanistan and the international community embodied in the JCMB.

Afghanistan faces extremely difficult challenges that will take many years to fully overcome. The successful transformation of Afghanistan to a secure and developing country is vital not only for the Afghan people, but to neighboring countries in a volatile region and to the entire world. The ANDS represents an important step towards achieving these objectives shared by the country and its international partners.

APPENDICES

APPENDIX I. NATIONAL ACTION PLAN (2009 – 2013)I

PILLAR : SECURITY
SECTOR : SECURITY

Expected Outcomes	Policy Actions and Activities	Category	Timeframe	Responsible Agency
Effectively coordinated security sector	Monitor and coordinate security issues between ministries and departments and establish 13 coordination centers	Institution Development	2008 - 2013	NSC, MoD, MoI, NDS, MCN, MoFA
ANA operationally capable of performing those missions and tasks assigned	Recruit additional personnel to reach the newly agreed 80,000 army ceiling with additional 6000 staff of mentors, trainers etc	Institution Building	ongoing - end 2009	MoD
	Revise Operations and tactical structures and new weaponry to be provided then accordingly	Institution Building	2007 - 2013	MoD
	Equip the ANA with technical and administrative support	Institution Building	2008 - 2013	MoD
	Equip the ANA by Land and Air force	Development	2008 - 2013	MoD
	Establish new ANA training centers	Development	2008 - 2013	MoD
	Equip existing ANA training centers/Academies	Development	2008 - 2013	MoD
	Reform and capacity building of the ANA to a sustainable level	Development	2008 - 2013	MoD
	Strengthen logistical support to the Army in regional and provincial battalions	Institution Building	2008 - 2013	MoD
	Establish computerized system in MoD to strengthen human resource, financial and program management	Institution Building	2008 - 2013	MoD
	Extensive training schemes to equip national units to fight terrorism and anti gov-ernment elements	Development	2008 - 2013	MoD
	Focus on conflict prevention programs in areas where anti government activities are ripe	Development	2008 - 2013	MoD
	Information campaigns about the benefits of peaceful processes	Development	2008 - 2013	MoD
ANA expenditures are fiscally sustainable	Develop a 'Right-financing' approach to the security sector	Institution Building	2008 - 2013	MoD
ANP operationally capable of performing those missions and tasks assigned and crime rates reduced	Recruit Personnel to reach the Benchmark of 82,000	Institution Building	ongoing - End 2010	MoI

Expected Outcomes	Policy Actions and Activities	Category	Timeframe	Responsible Agency
	Equip the Police with technical and administrative support	Institution Building	2008 - 2013	MoI
	Reform and capacity building of the ANP and ABP to a sustainable level	Development	2008 -2013	MoI
	Strengthen logistical support to ANP and ABP in regional and provincial centers	Institution Building	2008 - 2013	MoI
	Construct new Stations and Substations for Police in Provinces	Institution Building	2008 - 2013	MoI
	Establish/Equip Fire Brigade Departments	Institution Building	2008 - 2013	MoI
	Restore Traffic signals structure in Urban areas and highways	Development	2008 - 2013	MoI
	Establish/Equip Health care centers/facilities for Police in center and provinces	Development	2008 - 2013	MoI
	Extensive training schemes to equip national units to fight terrorism and anti gov-ernment elements	Institution Building	2008 - 2013	MoI
	Focus on conflict prevention programs in areas where anti government activities are ripe	Development	2008 - 2013	MoI
	Information campaigns about the benefits of peaceful processes	Development	2008 - 2013	MoI
	Conduct training to increase the capacity of Afghan National Police forces to en-force the law against poppy cultivation and drug trafficking	Institution Building	2008 - 2013	MoI
	MoI reform to support the transformation of police	Institution Building	2008 - 2013	MoI
	Establish computerized system in MoI to strengthen human resource, financial and program management	Institution Building	2008 - 2013	MoI
Operational border posts able to protect national sovereignty, levy and collect custom duties and process those collections to the central government.	Reform, train and equip the Border Police	Institution Building	2008 - 2013	MoI
	Establish/Rehabilitate and equip Border Posts	Institution Building	2008 - 2013	MoI
ANP and ABP expenditures are fiscally sustainable	Develop a 'Right-financing' approach to the security sector	Institution Building	2008 - 2013	MoI
	Improve revenues and finance security sector spending; this includes licenses to private security companies	Institution Building	2008 - 2013	MoI
Reduced level of deaths and casualties caused by UXOs, reduce the number of	Clear 90% of all known mine/ERW contaminated areas by 1391 (2012). The goal furthermore is to clear all emplaced antipersonnel mines by 1391 (1 March 2013)	Development	2008-2013	MoFA

Appendix I. (Continued)

Expected Outcomes	Policy Actions and Activities	Category	Timeframe	Responsible Agency
affected communities and increased safety precautions				
	All unsafe unserviceable and surplus ammunition will be destroyed	Development	2008-2013	MoFA, MoI
Enhanced public trust on govern-ment ability to deliver justice and security as IAGs are disbanded and reintegrated	DIAG plans need to be instated and properly implemented	Development	ongoing - (by end of 2011)	DDR/DIAG, MoD
Eventual eradication of Poppy Production and crack down on drug trafficking	Coordinate and target poppy eradication, in particluar where the beneficiaries are supporting anti government activities	Institution Building	2008 - 2013	MCN, MoD, MoI
	Conduct training to increase the capacity of Afghan Security forces to enforce the law against poppy cultivation and drug trafficking	Institution Building	2008 - 2013	MCN, MoI
	Cooperate and coordinate with neighboring countries with intelligence sharing, particular with regard to drug smuggling across borders.	Institution Building	2008 - 2013	MCN, MoI
	Conduct effective information campaigns against poppy production and drug trading	Development	2008 - 2013	MCN, MoI

PILLAR : GOOD GOVERNANCE
SECTOR : GOVERNANCE AND HUMAN RIGHTS

Expected Outcomes	Policy Actions and Activities	Category	Timeframe	Responsible Agency
Empowered National Assembly	Technical and Administrative Support Training	Institutional Development	Jaddi 1392 (end-2013)	Meshrano Jirga, Wolosi Jirga
	Capacity Building	Institutional Development	Jaddi 1392 (end-2013)	Meshrano Jirga, Wolosi Jirga
Reformed Public Administration	Public Administration Reform	Institutional Development	Jaddi 1392 (end-2013)	IARCSC
	Oversee/Implement/Monitor Training and Capacity Building of Public Sector Workforce	Institutional Development	Jaddi 1392 (end-2013)	IARCSC
	Appoint civil servants based on Merit	Institutional Development	Jaddi 1392 (end-2013)	IARCSC
	Oversee/Implement/Monitor Performance-based Reviews	Institutional Development	Jaddi 1389 (end-2010)	IARCSC

Expected Outcomes	Policy Actions and Activities	Category	Timeframe	Responsible Agency
Corruption Reduced	Take effective measures to Reduce Corruption	Institutional Development	Jaddi 1392 (end-2013)	GIAAC, President's Office, other Ministries
	Monitor Corruption at high places of Government	Institutional Development	Jaddi 1387 (end-2008)	GIAAC, President's Office, other Ministries
	Launch E-Government Applications	Institutional Development	Jaddi 1387 (end-2008)	President's Office, MoICT
	Implement Public Complaints Mechanism	Institutional Development	Jaddi 1387 (end-2008)	President's office, GIAAC, MoJ etc
	Mid-term plans formulated and implemented	Development/ Gender Cross Cutting Issues	Jaddi 1387 (end-2008)	Inter-ministerial Consulta-tive group
	Credible institutional infrastructure established	Institutional Development	Jaddi 1387 (end-2008)	All relevant ministries
	Enhance Research & Data management Capacity	Development/ AC Cross Cutting Issues	Jaddi 1387 (end-2008)	IARCSC, all ministries
	Public sector reforms instituted incorporating anti-corruption issues	Institutional/ AC Cross Cut-ting Issues	Jaddi 1387 (end-2008)	IARCSC, all Ministries and Agencies
	Regulations and monitoring mechanism for the private sector development developed and implemented	Institutional/ AC Cross Cut-ting Issues	Jaddi 1387 (end-2008)	Consultative group
	Implement Public awareness programs on anti-corruption issues	Development/ AC Cross Cutting Issues	Jaddi 1387 (end-2008)	All Ministries and Agencies along with their sub national units
Enhanced Availability of Information to Public and Enforcement	Right to Information Available to People	Legislation	Jaddi 1389 (end-2010)	IDLG, GIAAC, OoP, MoJ, Cabinet, National Assembly
	Enforce Sanctions against those involved in the drugs trade	Institutional Development	Jaddi 1389 (end-2010)	MoI (Police), MCN, AGO, IARCSC
	Productivity Commission advising the Cabinet	Institutional Development	Jaddi 1389 (end-2010)	GIAAC, MoJ, Cabinet, Na-tional Assembly

Appendix I. (Continued)

Expected Outcomes	Policy Actions and Activities	Category	Timeframe	Responsible Agency
Improved Participation of Women in Governance	Implement National Action Plan for Women	Institutional Development	Jaddi 1389 (end-2010)	MoWA, All other ministries & Agencies
	Affirmative action available to women	Legislation	Jaddi 1389 (end-2010)	MoJ, Cabinet, National As-sembly, Office of President
	Piloting of a Regional Leadership Institute for Women in 2 areas	Institutional Development/ Gender Cross Cutting Issues	Jaddi 1387 (end-2010)	IARCSC
	Capacity Building Program for Women in Government at the level of National Assembly, provincial council and women laid off by the PRR processes Capacity Building for Ministries and LGUs on Gender Sensitive Budgeting	Development/ Gender Cross Cutting Issues	Jaddi 1389 (end-2010)	IARCSC
	Establishment of Women's Councils at the District Level	Institutional Development/ Gender Cross Cutting Issues	Jaddi 1389 (end-2010)	IDLG
	Gender awareness raising of senior officials of government	Development/ Gender Cross Cutting Issues	Jaddi 1389 (end-2010)	IARCSC
Nation Prepared for Disaster Management	Establish an effective system of disaster preparedness and response	Institutional Development	Jaddi 1389 (end-2010)	ANDMA, IDLG
Strong and Capable Independent Election Commis-sion holding regular national and sub national Elections as mandated by the Constitution	Independent Election Commission Capable to fulfill its Role	Institutional Development	Jaddi 1388 (end-2009)	Election Commision, IDLG, Police
	Permanent Voters Registry Available	Institutional Development	Jaddi 1388 (end-2009)	Election Commision, IDLG, MoI
	Sub National Elections Regularly held	Institutional Development	in the year 1389 (2010) and 1392 (2013)	Election Commision, IDLG, Police
Single National Identity Document	Establish civil registry with a single national identity document	Institutional Development	Jaddi 1392 (end-2013)	MoI, IDLG

Expected Outcomes	Policy Actions and Activities	Category	Timeframe	Responsible Agency
Census and Statistical Base line Data available for use of the nation	Census Completed and Results Published	Institutional Development	Jaddi 1387 (end-2008)	CSO
	Statistical Baselines Established and the Statistical Capacity Built		Jaddi 1392 (end-2013)	CSO, MoF
Villages and Gozars Mapped	Village and Gozar Boundaries Reviewed	Institutional Development	Jaddi 1387 (end-2008)	AGCHO, IDLG, MUD, MRRD
	Mapping of Villages and Gozars	Institutional Development	Jaddi 1388 (end-2009)	AGCHO, IDLG, MUD, MRRD
Modern Land Administration System	Establish Modern Land Administration System	Institutional Development	Jaddi 1387 (end-2008)	SC, MUD, MAIL, MoJ, AGCHO
Established and A fair System for Settlement of Land Disputes Available	Establish A fair System for Settlement of Land Disputes		Jaddi 1386 (end-2007)	SC, MUD, MAIL, MoJ, AGCHO, IDLG
Government Connected to People and Increased reach of the Government by strengthening sub-national governance	Develop Sub National Governance Policy	Legislation	end-1389 (20 March 2011)	IDLG, MoJ, OoP, National Assembly
	Ensure Peoples' Participation in Sub National Governance	Institutional Development	end-1389 (20 March 2011)	IDLG, Election Commission, Prov. Councils, MoJ
	Empower Provincial Councils	Institutional Development	end-1389 (20 March 2011)	IDLG, MoJ, Offfice of President, National Assem-bly
	Law on District Councils, Municipal Councils, and Village Councils	Legislation		The President, IDLG
	Regular Elections of District Councils, Municipal Councils, Mayors and Vil-lage Councils	Institutional Development		Election Commision, Prov. Councils
	Empowered District Councils, Municipal Councils, Elected Mayors and Vilage Councils	Institutional Development		Office of President, IDLG
	Capacity built, the structures reformed, the processes streamlined in the provinces, districts and municipalities	Institutional Development	end-1389 (20 March 2011)	IDLG, IARCSC
	Reform Sub National Public Administration	Institutional Development	end-1389 (20 March 2011)	IDLG, IARCSC, Office of President
	Institutionalize Provincial Planning and Provincial Budgeting	Institutional Development	end-1389 (20 March 2011)	IDLG, MoF, All ministries

Appendix I. (Continued)

Expected Outcomes	Policy Actions and Activities	Category	Timeframe	Responsible Agency
	Empower Municipalities	Institutional Development	Jaddi 1392 (end-2013)	IDLG, KM, MoF, IARCSC
Government Offices physi-cally equipped to fulfill their Role	Facility and Amenities to the Government Offices Reviewed	Institutional Development	Jaddi 1387 (end-2008)	All ministries and agencies
	Basic Facility and Amenities Provided to all Government Offices	Institutional Development	end-1392 (20 March 2013)	All ministries and agencies, MoF
Free Flow of Information from all the District Centers	Free Flow of Information from all the District Centers	Institutional Development	end-1389 (20 March 2011)	Ministries, MoICT, IDLG, Office of President
Communication with the Government made Easy	Communication with the Government made Easy through the websites	Institutional Development	end-1389 (20 March 2011)	All the Ministries and Agen-cies, MoICT
Youth Involved in Govern-ance	Provide Definite Mechanisms for youth involvement	Institutional Development	end-1389 (20 March 2011)	IDLG, Dept of Youth
Human Rights Realized, Protected, Promoted and Extended	Human Rights Realized, Protected, Promoted and Extended	Institutional Development	Jaddi 1389 (end-2010)	IDLG, National Assembly, MoI, MoJ, MoUD, MoCI, MoWA, MoD, MoLSAMD, MoRR, MoE, AIHRC, and all relevant
	Action Plan on Peace, Justice and Reconciliation Implemented	Institutional Development	Jaddi 1387 (end-2008)	AIHRC, Office of President, NA, SC, MoJ, IARCSC, others

PILLAR : GOOD GOVERNANCE
SECTOR : JUSTICE AND THE RULE OF LAW

Expected Outcomes	Policy Actions and Activities	Category	Timeframe	Responsible Agency
Public can rely on effectively organized and professionally staffed justice insti-tutions	Analyze and develop recommendations regarding justice institutions' record-keeping practices in order to improve accuracy and irretrievability and to avoid redundant pro-esses	Institution Building	By year 2	SC,MoJ,AGO
	Analyze and make recommendations for improving existing remuneration and human resources systems in justice institutions.	Institution Building	By year 1	SC,MoJ,AGO

Expected Outcomes	Policy Actions and Activities	Category	Timeframe	Responsible Agency
	Support development and introduction of institution-specific remuneration and human resources schemes, such as pay and grading and performance evaluation measures	Institution Building	By Year 2	Program Oversight Committee
	Justice institutions to establish links with universities for recruiting candidates (e.g., job fairs and short internships).	Institution Building	Year 3 and on	MoJ, AOG, SC, MoHE
	Survey, develop and implement recommendations to improve existing career development practices in each institution with particular attention to complying with gender benchmarks.	Institution Building	Year 3 and on	SC,MoJ,AGO, MoWA, MoHE
	Develop institutional capacity to train professionals	Institution Building	Year 2 and on	SC,MoJ,AGO, ICCD
	Analyze and, in consultation with stakeholders, develop recommendations for improving the organizational, management and administrative structures of justice institutions to enable them to fulfill their respective mandates and functions at headquarters and at provincial and district level offices	Development	By year 2	SC,MoJ,AGO
	Implement recommendations	Development	Year 3 and on	SC,MoJ,AGO
	Implement security measure for Judges safety	Development	By end year 4	SC, MoJ, MoI
	Public information system improved	Development	Year 2 on	MoJ
	Enhanced awareness of public in general and women in particular of women's legal rights	Development r	Year 2 on	MoWA
	Public demands Sexual Harassment and grievance handling laws/policy to be enacted		Year 2 on	
	Justice institutions construct, acquire or make functional on a priority basis infrastructure necessary to expand delivery of justice services throughout provincial and district areas outside of regional centers.	Development	Year 3 and on	SC,MoJ,AGO
	Assess and priorities equipment and supply needs of justice institutions and establish effective and accountable procurement systems.	Development	By end year 2	SC,MoJ,AGO
	Provide equipment and supplies in accordance with needs assessment.	Development	Year 2 and on	SC,MoJ,AGO
	Conduct comprehensive inventory of all transportation assets, indicating condition and expected lifespan.	Development	By end year 2	SC,MoJ,AGO
	Survey existing asset management capacity and make recommendations for improvement	Development	By end year 1	SC,MoJ,AGO
	Justice institutions acquire and maintain transportation assets sufficient to fulfill their tasks.	Development	Year 3 and on	SC,MoJ,AGO
	Increased and improved facilities to deal with female offenders	Institution Building	Year 2 on	MoJ

Appendix I. (Continued)

Expected Outcomes	Policy Actions and Activities	Category	Timeframe	Responsible Agency
Legal education and vocational training are adequate to provide justice professionals with sufficient know-how to perform their task	Create and launch agreed core subject curriculum for Sharia, law and political science faculties.	Development	By end Year 2	SC,MoJ,AGO
	Create and launch agreed core subject curriculum for Sharia, law and political science faculties.	Development		SC,MoJ,AGO
	Survey and make recommendations for enhancement of legal research facilities, including a feasibility study of the establishment of an advanced legal research institute.	Development	Year 3 to 4	SC,MoJ,AGO
	Create stakeholder consultations to develop policy and planning mechanisms for enhancing legal research capacity.	Development	Year3 to 4	SC,MoJ,AGO
	Law and Sharia faculties establish links with foreign legal educational institutions to enhance research capacity, in-cluding foreign study programs for both students and staff.	Development	Year 2 and on	MoHE, MoFA
	Universities identify and enhance infrastructure so as to accommodate female students and staff	Development	By year 2	MHE, MoJ
	Universities develop and implement policies to raise per-centage of female students and staff to at least 30 percent	Development	By end year 2	MHE, MoJ
	Justice institutions, in coordination with the Independent National Legal Training Center, develop appropriate voca-tional training courses for justice professionals, paying specific attention to the needs of female professionals.	Development	By end year 2	INLTC
	Justice institutions, in coordination with the Independent National Legal Training Center, develop and implement specialized programs for continuing legal education, paying specific attention to the needs of female professionals.	Development	Year 3 and on	SC,MoJ,AGO, INLTC
Statutes are clearly drafted, constitutional and the prod-uct of effective and consulta-tive drafting processes	Perform comprehensive needs assessment of Taqnin and make recommendations for technical assistance and capacity building	Institution Building	By end Year 1	MoJ, National Assembly
	Provide technical assistance and capacity building for Taqnin in line with recommendations.	Institution Building	Year 2 and on	MoJ
	Establish a working body to promote greater cooperation and enhance the efficiency of the legislative drafting pro ess.	Institution Building	Year 2 and on	MoJ, National Assembly

Expected Outcomes	Policy Actions and Activities	Category	Timeframe	Responsible Agency
	An indexed compilation of all laws in force is assembled and updated regularly.	Development	By end Year 3 and on	MoJ
	Taqnin conducts a review of the constitutionality of all laws in force, and recommends amendments to ensure constitutionality.	Development	By end Year 3 and on	SC, MoJ, AGO, MoI
	Unconstitutional laws are amended to ensure constitutionality	Development	Year 3 and on	National Assembly, MoJ, AOG
	Assess capacity of government institutions and entities to draft laws and make recommendations for enhancing that capacity	Development	By end year 2	MoJ
	Implement recommendations for enhancing legislative drafting capacity in justice institutions.	Development	commencing year 3	MoJ
	Establish a Taqnin working group to make recommenda-tions for inclusion of civil society stakeholders in legislative deliberations.	Development	Year 2	MoJ
	Implement recommendations	Development	Year 3 and on	MoJ
	Develop and implement procedures to safeguard and further the role and function of defense attorneys in criminal investigations and trials	Legislation	Year 1 and on	AGO, MoJ
	Update and implement court regulations in order to facilitate filing and tracking of civil and criminal cases (including AGO Information System).	Legislation	By end Year 4	SC, AGO
Justice institutions effectively perform their functions in a harmonized and interlinked manner	Create and establish the Program Oversight Committee, together with requisite administrative and logistical support	Institution Building	By commencement Year 1	SC, MoJ, AGO
	Create and establish the Program Implementation Unit	Institution Building	By commencement Year 1	Oversight Committee
	Design and administer a baseline survey of legal system performance	Institution Building	By end Year 1	MoJ
	Improve information sharing between justice institutions, and coordinate information management and interfacing.	Institution Building	Year 3 and on	SC, MoJ, AGO
	Develop, establish, and implement measures and mecha-nisms to improve police prosecutor coordination in criminal matters; and addressing the cross-cutting issues	Institution Building	Year 1 and on	AGO, MoJ, MoJ
	Introduce effective "one-stop" complaints system covering all justice institutions.	Institution Building	Year 2 and on	SC, MoJ, AGO
	Enhance capacity of police and prosecutors to conduct pro-active criminal investigations.	Institution Building	Year 2 and on	AGO, MoI
	Enhance capacity for managing corruption issues.	Institution Building	Year 2 on	SC, MoJ, AGO, MoI
	Train judges, lawyers and prosecutors in trial practices and trial management.	Institution Building	Year 2 and on	SC, MoJ, AGO

Appendix I. (Continued)

Expected Outcomes	Policy Actions and Activities	Category	Timeframe	Responsible Agency
	Assessment of information interfacing needs of AGO, MoJ, MoJ, courts, and other specialized agencies.	Institution Building	By end Year 1	SC,MoJ,AGO
	Assessment and improvement of paper-based case file and case tracking systems.	Institution Building	By end Year 1	SC,MoJ,AGO
	Evaluate the viability of converting paper-based file systems to combined paper and electronic file systems	Institution Building	Year 2 and 3	Program Oversight Committee
	Justice institutions develop plans and implement coordination mechanisms for specialized units addressing cross-cutting issues	Institution Building	Year 2 and on	Program Oversight Committee
	Recruit qualified professionals with specialized knowledge of cross-cutting issues	Institution Building	Year 2 and on	Program Oversight Committee
	Justice mitigation measures are developed	Institution Building		MoJ
	Build capacity of judges, prosecutors, and investigators by training on cross-cutting issues.	Institution Building	Year 2 and on	Program Oversight Committee
Citizens are more aware of their rights and justice institutions are better able to enforce them.	Assess the needs of the justice institutions and citizens for legal materials. Compile and distribute legal materials in response to needs and establish system for routine updating of legal resources.	Development Development	By end Year 1 By end Year 3	MoJ MoJ
	Develop and distribute judicial and procedural manuals for legal professionals, including judges, prosecutors and defense advocates.	Development	From Year 2 on	MoJ
	Survey and standardize routine legal documents (e.g., bonds, title deeds, marriage certificates and certificates of the courts) and the existing systems for registering, indexing and retrieving them.	Development	By Year 4 and on	MoJ
	Distribute forms to relevant justice facilities nationwide and train staff to use them and make them available to the public for standardized nominal fees.	Development	By Year 4 and on	MoJ
	Pilot an electronic storage and retrieval system for legal registration documents	Development	Year 2 to 3	SC,MoJ,AGO
	Design legal awareness programs paying particular attention to: • Successes and lessons learned from previous campaigns • Human rights and Islamic values • The rights of women and children • The needs of illiterate persons • Transitional justice • The roles of each justice institution in promoting access to justice for all.	Development	Years 1 - 3	MoJ
	Implement legal awareness programs, in coordination with activities expanding formal justice systems to provinces.	Development	Commence end Year 2 on	MoJ, IDLG

Expected Outcomes	Policy Actions and Activities	Category	Timeframe	Responsible Agency
	Conduct baseline survey legal aid service provision	Development	Commence end Year 2 on	MoJ
	Consider options and costs of various models for legal aid delivery, and draw up recommendations for a legal aid sys tem.	Development	By Year 2	MoJ
	Implement legal aid recommendations	Development	Year 2 and on	MoJ
	Conduct needs assessment and survey of obstacles to access to and use of formal legal system.	Development	By end Year 1	MoJ
	Draw up recommendations to increase access to and use of formal legal system	Development	By end Year 1	MoJ
	Survey of legal gateways to justice services.	Development	By end Year 1	MoJ
	Consider options and costs of various models for improving access to formal system, and draw up recommendations	Development	By end Year 1	MoJ
	Implement recommendations to improve access	Development	Year 2 and on	SC,MoJ,AGO
	Generate public awareness about corruption and anti-corruption issues	Development	Year 2 on	SC,MoJ,AGO
	strengthened institutional response to stop violence against women	Institution Building	Year 2 on	SC,MoJ,AGO
	improved capacity of the provincial govt to address and deal with VAW	Development	Year 3 and on	SC, SGO, MoJ
Civil justice is administered effectively, and in accordance with law, the Constitution, and international standards	Review existing civil justice processes and practices, in-cluding enforcement of judgments, and develop recommen-dations based on the findings.	Institution Building	Year 2	MoJ, AOG,, SC
	Public demands Sexual Harassment and grievance handling laws/policy to be enacted	Legislation	Year 2 and on	National Assembly, MoJ, AOG
Criminal justice is administered effectively, and in ac-cordance with law, the Constitution, and international norms and standards	Strengthen the legal framework so as to improve respon-siveness to the needs of juvenile offenders and children in conflict with the law	Legislation	From Year 2 on	MoJ
	Strengthen the legal and institutional framework for chil-dren accompanying their parents in prison.	Legislation	From Year 2 on	MoJ
	Develop and implement policy recommendations for im-proving sentencing, detention, and conditions of prisoners.	Legislation	From Year 2 on	MoJ
	Promote practices within the justice institutions that are supportive of the rights of victims, witnesses, the accused, and those convicted of crimes	Institution Building	From Year 2 on	SC,MoJ,AGO

Appendix I. (Continued)

Expected Outcomes	Policy Actions and Activities	Category	Timeframe	Responsible Agency
	Family Response Units, staffed by all female police officers, are functional in all provinces, and are effectively linked with Special Victims Units in the AGO.	Institution Building	Starting Year 2 and on	SC, MoJ, AGO
	Develop and implement training programs for corrections officials incorporating recommendations based on analysis.	Institution Building	By end year 4	MoJ
	Rationalize and update civil justice process and practices, including enforcement of judgments, in accordance with the developed recommendations	Institution Building	Starting Year 3	PAR (MoJ)
	Review and analyze existing assistance, programs and activities for juvenile offenders and children in conflict with the law.	Development	By Year 1	MoJ, MOLSA
	Develop information campaigns to enhance the public's knowledge of the rights of victims, witnesses, and the accused in the criminal justice system	Development	Starting Year 2 and on	MoJ, MOLSA
	Procedural code is amended to address specific needs of witnesses, including women and other vulnerable groups	Development	By Year 3	MoJ, MOLSA
	Establish a system to record past human rights abuses and to preserve the rights of victims	Development	Year 2 and on	MoJ, MOLSA
	Carry out a baseline survey of prosecution efficiency and number of criminal complaints proceeding to trial.	Development	By end year 1	SC
	Develop a program for prioritizing prosecution resources according to seriousness of the offense.	Development	By end year 2	AGO
	Review and analyze existing assistance, programs and activities relating to sentencing practices, detention practices, and prisoner conditioners.	Development	By Year 2	MoJ
	Regulatory reforms, procedures and protocols established	Institution Building	Year 2 and on	MoJ
	Counter Narcotic Laws implemented	Legislation	Year 2 and on	MCN, AGO, SC, MoI
Justice institutions are transparent and accountable	Develop, finalize and disseminate codes of ethics for professionals in justice institutions.	Institution Building	By end Year 1	SC, MoJ, AGO
	Performance evaluation with special focus on corruption incorporated as part of the system transparency and accountability	Institution Building	Year 2 and on	SC, MoJ, AGO
	Train justice professionals on ethics code.	Institution Building	Year 2 on	SC, MoJ, AGO
	Design and establish dedicated and effective institutional units and procedures to advice on and enforce codes of ethics.	Institution Building	Year 2 and on	SC, MoJ, AGO
	Improve the professional and ethic standards of attorneys at law through an Independent Bar Association.	Institution Building	Year 2 and on	SC

Expected Outcomes	Policy Actions and Activities	Category	Timeframe	Responsible Agency
	Develop and standardize informational materials on the mission, the function and the operating procedures of each justice institution and make it available to the public.	Institution Building	By end year 3	MoJ
	Establish a dedicated office within each justice institution and organization capable of acting as a focal point for public inquiries.	Institution Building	By end Year 3	SC,MoJ,AGO
	3 Justice institutions participate in a commissioned study of the feasibility of introducing administrative law structures and procedures to enhance accountability of government institutions	Institution Building	Year 4 and on	MoJ
	Implement the activities related to operations of the justice sector contained in the National Anti Corruption Strategy.	Institution	Year 2 and on	SC,MoJ,AGO

PILLAR : ECONOMIC GOVERNANCE AND PRIVATE SECTOR DEVELOPMENT
SECTOR : PRIVATE SECTOR DEVELOPMENT AND TRADE

Expected Outcomes	Policy Actions and Activities	Category	Timeframe	Responsible Agency
The legal framework for the business sector is improved	Enact the required laws (Corporations, Partnerships, Commercial Arbitration, Commercial Mediation, Contracts, Agency, Standards, Copyrights, Trade marks, and Patents) to complete and update the basic legal and regulatory framework governing private sector activity in social and economic development. Government, business and the international community to make a stronger effort in lobbying National Assembly regarding the urgency of enacting laws.	Legislation	Mid-1389	Cabinet, DAB and National Assembly
	Invest in capacity building for National Assembly so that MPs are better informed and supported in their role and understanding of the rationale, use and content of proposed laws.	Institution Building	Mid-1388	National Assembly and donors
	Establish the principle and formalize and standardize processes to consult with the private sector (business and civil society) in a meaningful and timely manner during the process of drafting policies and laws	Legislation	End-1386	Cabinet, DAB and National Assembly
	Establish the principle that no law can be implemented unless it has been gazetted, published in the newspapers, and made available electronically and in hard copies at no cost. Explore the option of using the Afghanistan National Development Strategy (ANDS) website as an interim solution for publishing laws after their enactment. Publish the tariff structures on the Ministry of Fi-nance website.	Legislation	End-1386	Ministry of Justice, Ministry of Finance, ANDS
	Amend the tariff legislation to facilitate ROZ (Reconstruction Opportunity Zone) trade along the border with Pakistan	legislation/ RC Cross Cutting Issues		MoCI, MoJ, MoFA, MoF
	Endorse the authority of mediation and arbitration tribunals to resolve private-private and private-public disputes, including land issues.	Institution Building	Mid-1389	MoJ

Appendix I. (Continued)

Expected Outcomes	Policy Actions and Activities	Category	Timeframe	Responsible Agency
	Ensure the competency and transparency of tribunals by establishing standards and building the capacity of arbitrators, mediators and lawyers.	Institution Building	Mid-1389	MoJ
	Undertake financial audits of State Owned Enterprises	Other Measures	Mid-1388	MoCI, MoF
	Privatize and corporatize state owned assets	Other Measures	Mid-1389	MoCI, MoF
	Implement an adequate insurance law.	Legislation	Mid-1389	MoF, DAB, FIs
	Encourage the development of an appropriately regulated private insurance sector.	Other Measures	Mid-1388	MoF, DAB, FIs
	Work with donors to create risk management tools for domestic and foreign investors, appropriate to the specific risks of investing in Afghanistan.	Other Measures	End-1389	AISA/MIGA
Private sector access to finance is increased	Lay out a concrete strategy with time-bound actions to significantly expand the outreach and range of financial products and services, especially targeting small and medium enterprises.	Other Measures	Mid-1388	DAB, Afghanistan Bankers' Association, Microfinance Investment
	Enact an appropriate legal framework including passage of four financial laws: Secured Transactions, Mortgage, Leasing and Negotiable Instruments.	Legislation	End-1388	DAB, Ministry of Justice
	Build capacity in the financial sector by establishing an independent banking and business training institute as a joint commercial bank – DAB initiative.	Institution Building	Mid-1388	DAB together with Afghanistan Bankers' Association
	Establish a credit information bureau to facilitate commercial and consumer lending.	Institution Building	End-1388	DAB, Afghanistan Bankers' Association
	Establish a financial tribunal to provide swift legal decisions on financial disputes.	Institution Building	End-1388	DAB, Ministry of Justice
	Expand provision of donor and private sector micro and SME finance	Other Measures	End-1388	MoF, MoCI, DAB, Afg Bankers' Association
	Establish an office in DAB in conjunction with Ministry of Interior to provide security for cash in transit between banks and bank branches in Kabul.	Institution Building	Mid-1389	DAB in cooperation with Ministry of Interior
	Increase the offering of financial services in rural areas through the further	Other Measures	Mid-1389	Ministry of Agriculture, DAB,
	development of effective and sustainable delivery mechanisms with special consideration to women.			MISFA

Expected Outcomes	Policy Actions and Activities	Category	Timeframe	Responsible Agency
	Implement the agreed upon privatization strategies in Bank-e-Milli and Pash-tany Bank, including the placement of professional management and board to restructure the banks free of government interference.	Institution Building	Mid-1387	Ministry of Finance and DAB
The government uses Public-Private Partnerships to expand infrastructure	Ensure the evolving legal framework to permit and encourage power generation and distribution by the private sector, including through the establishment of Public-Private Partnerships (PPPs).	Legislation	Mid-1387	Ministry of Energy and Water
	Accelerate the execution of priority power generation initiatives: (a) Sheberghan natural gas generation project; (b) the high voltage transmission line from Tajikistan.	Other Measures	End-1386	Ministry of Energy and Water
	Improve distribution system, beginning with Kabul, including through out-sourcing of billing and collections and by providing information to the private sector on opportunities to invest in electricity supply.	Other Measures	Mid-1387	Ministry of Energy and Water, DABM
	Corporatize DABM (national electricity company) with qualified management team selected through transparent process.	Institution Building	Mid-1387	Ministry of Energy and Water, DABM
	Launch pilot initiatives in non-grid small and medium-scale provision in smaller cities and in community-based rural power, including micro-hydro power.	Other Measures	Mid-1387	Ministry of Energy and Water
	Negotiate competitive terms for reliable power supply from Central Asia.	Other Measures	Mid-1387	Ministry of Energy and Water
	Establish a liaison mechanism for joint forums with Business/Trade/Employers' association.	Institution Building/ RC Cross Cutting Issues		MoCI, AISA
	Trade Facilitation Zones (TFZ) in key areas of Afghanistan that will connect district and provisional level production to regional and international markets by providing the basic infrastructure for processing, packaging and storage.	Other Measures/ RC Cross Cutting Issues		MoCI, others
Surplus land is used by the private sector to increase economic activity	Draft legislation based on the recommendations of the land policy that com-prises legal frameworks for land registration; land adjudication, including community-based systems; and the formalization of informal land holdings, including legislation for adverse possession.	Legislation	End-1387	Ministry of Justice, Ministry of Agriculture
	Implement improved simplified procedures for transfer of privately owned land.	Other Measures	End-1387	Ministry of Justice, Office of the President
	Clarify and simplify the procedures associated with the transfer of publicly-owned and privately-owned land.	Institution Building	Mid-1387	Ministry of Justice

Appendix I. (Continued)

Expected Outcomes	Policy Actions and Activities	Category	Timeframe	Responsible Agency
	Permit foreign investors to obtain access to land through 90-year leases.	Other Measures	Mid-1387	Ministry of Justice
	Extend the duration of leases for government land and ensure that they are either wholly or partly transferable.	Other Measures	Mid-1387	Ministry of Justice
	Develop a strategy for industrial parks, including the creation of an industrial park development department as an independent authority.	Other Measures	End-1387	Ministry of Commerce and Industry, AISA
Regulations, taxes and licenses are streamlined and better enforced	Consolidate the registration of private sector entities and the issuance of tax identification numbers into a single platform, extending the service to smaller businesses.	Institution Building	End-1387	Ministry of Commerce and Industry
	Remove licensing requirements except for reasons of health, safety, environ-mental protection, land use and access to natural resources.	Other Measures	Mid-1387	Ministry of Commerce and Industry
	Make necessary business licenses more effective by re-engineerinrg and streamlining them	Institution Building	12 months	Ministry of Commerce and Industry
	Adopt the principles of regulatory best practice (RBP) to ensure that new regu-lations are appropriate and minimize compliance cost	Legislation	18 months	Ministry of Commerce and Industry, Ministry of Justice
	Minimize compliance costs for SMEs by introducing appropriate administra-tive and reporting exemptions for SMEs	Other Measures	12 months	Ministry of Finance
	Publish comprehensive information on licensing requirements and procedures	Other Measures	12 months	Ministry of Commerce and Industry
	Educate private sector stakeholders' (investors, employers, employees and consumers) to increase awareness and understanding of their legal and regula-tory rights and responsibilities.	Other Measures	12 months	Ministry of Commerce and Industry
	Establish and enforce "one-stop collection points" for tax payment and other government revenue collection in every district centre.	Institution Building	Mid-1387	Ministry of Finance
	Continue to eliminate nuisance taxes and reform the tax system to make it simpler, fairer, more competitive and easier to comply with	Institution Building	12 months	Ministry of Finance
		Institution Building	End-1386	High Commission on Investment, AISA

Expected Outcomes	Policy Actions and Activities	Category	Timeframe	Responsible Agency
	Reform and revitalize the High Commission on Investment (HCI). Ensure that AISA is an effective secretariat; ensure that it meets regularly (starting in the next 14 days); focus it on policy issues; introduce increased private sector representation; improve member selection process to focus on competence and experience; extend access to SMEs throughout the country. Report results of HCI reform to the private sector.	Institution Building	End-1387	Ministry of Finance
	Apply customs regulations consistently across the country and commit to achieving an average time for importing and exporting goods in line with best practice in the region (reduced by at least half of current levels).			
	Examine the merits of outsourcing custom services	Other Measures	Mid-1388	Ministry of Finance
Civil society groups are able to operate effectively to aid in the development process.	Revise, clarify and update the legal framework governing civil society organi-zations, including the NGO Law and Social Organizations Law, to cover civil society more comprehensively, easing the establishment/ registration of CSOs and ensuring adequate (not burdensome) oversight.	Legislation	End-1387	Ministry of Economy, Ministry of Justice with Civil Society stakeholders
	Develop self-regulatory mechanisms with clearly defined quality standards or a "code of conduct" to ensure that civil society organizations are well managed, accountable and their activities are well conceived, effective and attuned to the needs of Afghans, with governance models drawn from international best practice.	Legislation	Mid-1387	Civil Society with the endorsement of the Ministry of Economy
	Establish independent certification bodies for civil society organizations that are recognized by Government, the private sector, donor agencies and civil society while introducing the associated capacity building services required to achieve certification.	Institution Building	End 1387	Civil Society with the endorsement of the Ministry of Economy
Economic activity increases in response to increased human capacity and skill sets and business services	Facilitate private sector involvement to offer short-cycle certificate-level education for school leavers to rapidly develop the skills of young people and adults that are crucial to economic development.	Other Measures	End-1386	Civil Society with Business
	Establish the modality for public-private partnerships in the provision of education from basic education through to tertiary levels, including provision of professional and vocational education.	Other Measures	Mid-1387	Ministry of Education

Appendix I. (Continued)

Expected Outcomes	Policy Actions and Activities	Category	Timeframe	Responsible Agency
	Computerize all HRM and project activities in MoCI to strengthen Human Resource and Program Management	Institution Building/ AC Cross Cutting Issues		MoCI
	Establish a coherent national policy framework to guide professional and vocational education, linked to the overall higher education strategy that will ensure coordination, assign clear accountability and set world-class standards (including the process for licensing, certification and accreditation).	Other Measures	End-1387	MoEC, MoE, MoHE, MoLSA, Business Community, Civil Society
	Border Management Initiative to focus on the establishment of effective and efficient Border Crossing Points/Facilities at each Border Control Zone of Afghanistan.	Other Measures/ RC Cross Cutting Issues	Ongoing	MoCI
	Consider quickly piloting specific market-based vocational and professional training initiatives through coalition of Government, industry groups and training institutions with special consideration to women.	Institution Building	Mid-1387	MoEC, MoE, MoHE, MoLSA, MoWA, Business Community, Civil Society
	Create incentives for private sector to invest in education specific to skills training, mentoring and on-the-job training.	Other Measures	End-1387	Ministry of Economy, Ministry of Finance
	Conceptualization of Private Sector Employment Strategy for Women that will yield to pro-women employment strategies in the private sector	Other Measures/ Gender Cross Cutting Issues		MoCI, MoWA
	Invest urgently in vocational and professional education to meet current needs, while simultaneously making parallel investments in reform of basic and higher education systems that will yield longer term results.	Other Measures	Mid-1387	Ministry of Labor and Social Affairs, Ministry of Education, Ministry of Economy
	Strengthen chambers of commerce and business membership organizations	Institution Building	Immediate	Ministry of Commerce and Industry
	Co-ordinate public and private sector approaches to increasing access to essential business services	Other Measures	Mid-1388	Ministry of Commerce and Industry
	Increase access to information on current business development services	Other Measures	Mid 1387	Ministry of Commerce and Industry

Expected Outcomes	Policy Actions and Activities	Category	Timeframe	Responsible Agency
	Support the establishment of accounting, auditing and other professional associations and the adoption of related professional standards	Institution Building	Mid-1388	Ministry of Commerce and Industry
Increased and more effective competition	Create the legal framework for and ensure the rapid development of the Afghanistan National Standards Authority (ANSA)	Legislation	Immediate	ANSA
	Establish a consumer protection agency to define, communicate and protect consumer rights	Institution Building	End-1389	ANSA
Public-Private Partnerships are used to aid social and economic development	Identify and implement three pilot projects to test new approaches in areas such as power, water supply, transportation infrastructure and social development.	Other Measures	Mid-1387	MoEW, MRRD, MoT, MOLSA
	Catalogue best practices drawn from across ministries (especially of Ministry of Health) of genuine partnerships between public and private sectors. Attention on increased women participation	Other Measures	Mid-1387	MoPH, MoE, MoLSA
	Develop programs of public-private partnership that would improve health, education, drug demand reduction	Other Measures/ CN Cross Cutting Issues	End-1387	MoPH, MoE, MoLSA, MCN
Increased levels of formalization	Develop a formalization strategy grounded in an understanding of the incentives and disincentives facing business, which reduces entry costs to, and operating costs within, the formal sector and increases the benefits of formalization	Other Measures	End-1387	MoCI, MoF
	Effectively communicate the nature and benefits of operating in the formal economy	Other Measures	Mid-1388	Ministry of Labor, Ministry of Commerce and Industry
	The new Afghanistan Pakistan Transit Agreement (APTA), the revised version of Afghan Trade and Transit Agreement (ATTA) signed with Pakistan in 1965	Other Measures/ RC Cross Cutting Issues		MoCI, MoFA, MoF
Increased provincial economic growth	Work with provincial public sector institutions to increase the consistency of application of commercial laws and regulations	Institution Building	End-1389	Ministry of Commerce and Industry
	Develop and implement economic growth strategies for provinces, based on private sector development	Other Measures	Mid 1388	Ministry of Commerce and Industry

Appendix I. (Continued)

Expected Outcomes	Policy Actions and Activities	Category	Timeframe	Responsible Agency
Civil society helps drive economic and social development	Create the necessary legal and fiscal incentives that actively encourage individual and corporate support for social and economic development.	Legislation	Mid-1387	Ministry of Finance
	Improve the legal framework governing corporate social responsibility (CSR) and philanthropy including creating a Foundation law; revising NGO law to allow CSOs to generate (non-commercial) revenue to ensure self-sustainability; creating tax deductions for giving; and developing new mechanisms for private giving such as Zakat funds, a Diaspora fund and community foundations.	Legislation	End-1387	Ministry of Finance, Ministry of Justice, Ministry of Economy
	Form a business donor's group to share best practices in corporate social responsibility and philanthropy to create more flexibility, risk-taking and imaginative practices in approaches to corporate giving, including lending good business practices to civil society.	Institution Building	Mid-1387	Business community
	Increase trust and credibility of the civil society sector by establishing a system to vet CSOs through standards that the businesses would work with, publicizing CSO successes, and educating businesses to increase understanding of the concept of CSR.	Other Measures	End-1387	Ministry of Economy; Civil Society
The Private Sector and Trade sector strategy is implemented	Create a Council for the Private Sector, reporting on progress against this matrix to the President.	Institution Building	Immediate	Office of the President
	Develop a list of the private sector's most urgent priorities that would support an enabling environment, developed through a process of sub-national consultation and engagement with the private sector to be presented to the Government within three to six months.	Other Measures	Immediate	Business community
	Establish a system of stocktaking at six-month intervals to monitor implementation of the Conference Road Map, with public dissemination of results.	Institution Building	Mid-1387	Proposed Council for the Private Sector, Conference Steering Committee

PILLAR : INFRASTRUCTURE
SECTOR : ENERGY

Expected Outcomes	Policy Actions and Activities	Category	Timeframe	Responsible Agency
An enabling environment for private sector investment in energy sector created	Issuance of tenders for exploration and exploitation in northern country notably for power	Development	2008	MoM MEW MoF
	Develop private sector opportunities to take on long-term production, transport, supply of CNG	Development	2009-2010	MoM, MEW
	Outsourcing operations at DABM (audit, billing)	Development	2007-2009	MEW
	Implement Private distribution projects	Development	2008	MEW, MoM

Expected Outcomes	Policy Actions and Activities	Category	Timeframe	Responsible Agency
	Private sector promotion in renewable energy	Development	Immediately	MRRD, MEW, AISA
	Divestiture of the Liquid Fuels Enterprise	Development	Program not in place	MoF
	Assess and revitalize oil refinery	Development		MoCI, MoM
	Development of Sheberghan Gas Fields and Power Plant	Development	2008	MoM
	Promotion of regional cooperation to facilitate various projects under the energy sector	Institution Building / RC Cross Cutting Issues	2008-2010	MEW, MoFA
	To mainstream into all administrative reform programs measures required to address the systems and incentives promoting anti-corruption within the public administration system and Development Activities.	Institution Building/ AC Cross Cutting Issues	2008-2009	MEW, MoM
	To maintain the highest level of transparency, accountability and integrity in the relationship between the public and private sector.	Institution Building / AC Cross Cutting Issues	2008-2009	MEW
	Gender mainstreaming in the policies in the energy sector.	Development / Gender Cross Cutting Issues	Continue	MEW, MoWA
	Encouragement to Community Based Natural Resource Management for meeting energy needs of the people.	Institution Building / Env. Cross Cutting Issues	TBD	MoM, MEW
	Awareness generation of policy makers on the environmental issues so that they are taken care of in all projects in the energy sector.	Institution Building / Env. Cross Cutting Issues	Continue	MEW, MoM
	Leveraging available donor assistance, pilot CNG for public vehicles (i.e., buses) and taxis; conversion of engines, fitting gas pump stations.	Development	No action at this time.	MEW, MoCI, MoM
Expanded public power grid	Procure spare parts and fuel for thermal generation	Development	2008	MEW
	Repair existing transmission and distribution systems including rehabilitating and/or upgrading substations and distribution networks	Development	2008-2010	MEW
	Install meters for cross border transmission	Development	2008-2010	MEW
	Repair existing thermal plants	Development	2008-2009	MEW
	Starting National Energy Conservation Program (NECP)	Development	2009	MEW
	Implement ICE technical assistance (ADB)	Development	Commenced, ongoing through 2009	MEW MoM MoCI MoF MRRD MoE
	Take appropriate measures to reduce electricity loss	Development	2008-2010	DABM MEW MoF

Appendix I. (Continued)

Expected Outcomes	Policy Actions and Activities	Category	Timeframe	Responsible Agency
	Promotion of energy efficiency	Development	2008	MEW DABM
	Kabul distribution procurement	Development	Commence work February 2008	MEW MoF DABM/S
	Completion of NEPS transmission	Development	Oct 08-Mar 09	MEW MoF
	Complete Turkmen assessment	Development	March 2008	DABM/S
	Assessments of South, East and West Transmission needs	Development	2008-2009	
	Procurement for meters	Development	Partially conducted now under distribution tender; more needed.	MEW MoF DABM
	Installation of Dispatch and Control System	Development	End 2009	MEW DABM
	Motion detectors	Development	2008 commence and ongoing	DABM/S
	Line inspections (regular protocols)	Development	Jul-05	MEW
	Health & Safety protocols	Development	2008	MEW, MoM
	Operation & Maintenance protocols	Development		
	Priority to providing energy in areas having substantial narcotics cultivation to promote economic activity to generate alternate livelihoods	Development/ CN Cross Cutting Issues	Continue	MEW
Increased Access to Rural Energy Services	Link rural energy with micro and small finance programs	Development	Commencing 2008	MRRD
	Develop a comprehensive and appropriate rural energy program	Development	TBD	MEW
	Public awareness on rural energy opportunities, benefits, funding	Development	2009	MEW, MRRD
	Assessment of priority areas based on income-generation opportunities	Development	2008	MEW, MRRD
	Special attention to gender issues in providing energy for rural areas.	Development	TBD	MEW, MRRD, MoWA
Promotion of Private sector	Private Sector promotion in close as formalization of existing operator rights; tender for new rights (i.e., to support power generation)	Legislation	End 2008	MoM MEW MoF
	Private power generation policy	Legislation	End 2008	DABM/S
	In collaboration with National Regulation Utility Commission (NURC), develop Rural-remote Energy Policy	Legislation	2008	MRRD, MEW
	Power Purchase Agreements for Power Imports	Legislation	2008	MEW
Restructured Energy Sector Governance and Commercialized	Revise 2 laws and 2 regulations related to Hydrocarbons, minerals and Market Cadastre & Inspectorate	Legislation	End 2008	MoM
	Corporatization and ongoing commercialization of DABS	Legislation	March 2008	MEW, MoF

Expected Outcomes	Policy Actions and Activities	Category	Timeframe	Responsible Agency
	Power tariff reform	Legislation	Assess in 2008	MoJ, MEW
	Establishment of viable ICE working groups	Institution Building	Feb 2008	MoE MEW
	Improved GoA, Donor & NGO Coordination	Institution Building	2008	Energy Sector Ministries and Institutions
	Build Afghan capacity to operate and maintain system	Institution Building	2009	Energy Sector Ministries and Institutions
	Needs Assessment and Data Base	Institution Building	2009	Energy Sector Ministries and Institutions
	Establish Project Management Unit	Institution Building	Jun-05	MEW
	Establish Pricing regime for natural gas	Institution Building	End 2008	MoM, MoF
	Define Government roles in clearly defining TORs for MRRD and MEW on rural energy aspects	Institution Building	Apr 2008	MRRD MEW
	Development of basic technical standards based on MRRD materials	Institution Building	Immediately	MRRD
	Annual audit of all operations	Institution Building	Power – March 2008; others TBD	MoM, MEW
	Develop and implement the organizational structure and staffing plan for Rural Livelihoods and Energy Department (RLED)	Institution Building	2008	MRRD, MEW
PILLAR : INFRASTRUCTURE **SECTOR : TRANSPORT**				
Improved connectivity through out Afghanistan and to the foreign destinations within the region.	Massive road rehabilitation, improvement and maintenance programs. (Ring Roads/Regional highways)	Development/ RC Cross Cutting Issues	March 2009	MPW
	Massive road rehabilitation, improvement and maintenance programs. (Prior-ity: 5,335 km) (National Highways/Provincial Roads)	Development	End of 2010	MRRD, MPW
	Massive road rehabilitation, improvement and maintenance programs (with its entire infrastructure including drainage, walkways and street lighting system for urban roads). (Rural Roads and Urban Roads) (Priority: 6,290km Rural roads)	Development	End of 2010	MRRD, MPW, MoUD, Municipalities
	The road and air infrastructure will be built and maintained to a higher quality, giving road users lower costs. Whereas, the Feasibility Study of the railway links will be done.	Development	March 2009	MPW, MRRD

Appendix I. (Continued)

Expected Outcomes	Policy Actions and Activities	Category	Timeframe	Responsible Agency
Lower road user costs	Rationalize road user fees (one fee) and use funds to establish a road fund that manages all road improvement programs.	Institution Building	End 2009	MPW, MoF
	Lower road user fees by 75% by end 2008.	Development	End 2008	MPW, MoTCA, MoF, MoFA, MoCI
	Subsidy to private bus operators to implement the policy on promoting equitable access to transportation	Development/ Gender Cross Cutting Issues	End 2008	MoTCA
Less journey time lost due to congestion	Massive road rehabilitation, improvement and maintenance programs (with its entire infrastructure including drainage, walkways and street lighting system for urban roads). (Urban Roads)	Development	End 2010	MUD, Provincial Municipali-ties, MPW, MRRD
	Improve Public Transport Provision in Urban and inter-provincial (34 prov-inces) (with having bus and truck terminals in all the provincial centers)	Development	2010	MoTCA, MPW, KM, MoUD, Provincial Municipalities
Improved air quality.	Pass enabling legislation so that the environmental law has regulations that can be enforced	Legislation	By end-2008	Transport sector line ministries and institutions
CIVIL AVIATION				
Increased domestic and in-ternational passengers and freight traffic.	Massive reconstruction program (Kabul Int'l Airport, Herat in compliance with ICAO and IATA requirements)	Development	By March 2011	MoTCA
	Massive reconstruction program (Mazar-i-Sharif, Jalalabad, Kandahar airports)	Development	By March 2011	MoTCA
	Massive reconstruction program (Seven Other Domestic airports)	Development	By March 2011	MoTCA
All stakeholders are well informed about the viability of air transport systems.	More air transport service providers enter the Afghan market—requires an enabling environment for businesses	Legislation	By March 2011	MoTCA
Improved governance of civil aviation sector.	Institutional reform programs and a reduction in the requirement of ISAF to use air facilities (Create a new Civil Aviation Authority (CAA), and restore control of Afghan airspace to the Civil Aviation Authority.)	Institution Building	By end 2009	MoTCA, MoF
	Massive capacity building programs		End 2008	MoTCA
OVERALL TRANSPORT SECTOR				
Improved governance structure of the structure	Capacity building specially in the areas of project monitoring and contract management • Completing the regulatory framework- developing the regulatory framework for the implementation of the Procurement law, developing	Institution Building/ AC Cross Cutting Issues	End 2010	MoTCA

Expected Outcomes	Policy Actions and Activities	Category	Timeframe	Responsible Agency
	roads standards and codes, land acquisition; • Establishing an effective external scrutiny system; • Conducting VCA and developing mitigation plans in the sector; • Targeted anti corruption training for the responsible anti-corruption agencies to effectively investigate and report on corruption; • Developing code of conducts and enforcement mechanisms • Increasing wages of the civil service			
Improved connectivity through out Afghanistan and to the foreign destinations within the region.	After a study of international standards, adopt a set of standards that are compatible with Afghanistan's neighbors.	Institution Building	End 2008	MPW, MRRD, KM, MoUD, IDLG
	Establish a Transport Sector Inter-ministerial Working Group to determine the lines of authority between the transportation-related governance institutions and the roles and responsibilities of each institution.	Institution Building	End 2008	MPW, MoTCA, MRRD, MoUD, MoF, IDLG, MoI, KM
	Create an inter-ministerial costing committee to work with the Ministry of Finance to cost out annually programs that take five to fifteen years to implement	Institution Building	End 2008	MPW, MoTCA, MRRD, KM, MoI, IDLG, MoF
	Institute a substantial capacity building program, including a road safety program. (Improve the MoI's capacity to conduct drivers' licensing tests, vehicle safety inspections and enforce traffic flow regulations.)	Institution Building	End 2008	MoI
	Develop the Traffic Management Bureau form the MoI to the Provinces and Municipalities through the new Independent Directorate of Local Governance	Institution Building	End 2009	MoI, IDLG
	Institutional reforms put in place to simplify governance of the sector, including devolution of authority to the Provinces and Municipalities.	Institution Building	End of 2010	Transport sector line ministries and institutions
	Cost savings will be realized by the governing institutions and thus there will be Government budget savings.	Institution Building	2009	Transport sector line ministries and institutions
	Put in place systems to improve transparency in all functions of the government in the transport sector	Institution Building	2010	Transport sector line ministries and institutions
	Give more autonomy to local communities and the Provincial Governments to determine how and when rural roads are improved, as well as provincial roads	Institution Building	End 2009	MRRD, IDLG

Appendix I. (Continued)

Expected Outcomes	Policy Actions and Activities	Category	Timeframe	Responsible Agency
	Increase public sector salaries in tandem with increases in capacity	Institution Building	End 2008	GoA and Transport sector line ministries and institutions
	Annual assessment of data collected and databases maintained and updated in all planning departments, including municipalities, mapping progress against the goal of "best practices" data collection and databases for transport sector planning, with necessary funding mechanisms and capacity building programs in place and operational	Institution Building	2009	Transport sector line ministries and institutions
	Strengthening the planning capacity of ministry staff for road transport, airports, and rail functions so that the ministry staff can perform feasibility studies, Master planning, and multi-modal planning, as well as asset management planning, to international standards	Institution Building	2010	Transport sector line ministries and institutions
Business environment for private sector development improved to create jobs and reduce poverty.	Pass legislation and enabling regulations to allow transport sector governing institutions to competitively engage and manage private contractors, private contract supervision engineers to maintain roads, airports and other transport infrastructure, also regulations that protect the normal market rights of those contractors.	Legislation	2013	Office of the President, the National Assembly, MoTCA, MPW, MoI, MoF, MRRD, IDLG and MoUD
	Pass required legislation and enabling regulations so that the Mortgage law is passed and enforced.	Legislation	End 2008	Office of the President, the National Assembly, MoUD, MoJ, and MoF
	Pass any required legislation and enabling regulations so that private and public sector rights are protected in contract law, enforcement, and penalties for violation.	Legislation	End 2008	Office of the President, the National Assembly, MoCI, MoJ and MoF
	Reform laws relating to determining "fair market value" of lands purchased for transport sector improvements	Legislation	2010	MPW, MoF, MRRD, MoUD, IDLG, Office of President, National Assembly, MoJ
	Develop and put in place an axle-load limit violation fees and an enforcement system	Legislation	End 2008	MPW, MoF

Expected Outcomes	Policy Actions and Activities	Category	Timeframe	Responsible Agency
	Pass any required legislation and enabling regulations so that private sector insurance, auditing, and bonding industries can develop, and foreign insurance firms can operate in Afghanistan, protecting rights of the companies and the public, with penalties for violations.	Legislation	End 2008	Office of the President, the National Assembly, MoCI, MoJ and MoF
	Improved trade, transit documentation procedures	Legislation/ RC Cross Cutting Issues	End 2009	National Assembly, MoTCA
	Introduce and checks and balances for illicit transpiration of human and commodities like precursors, drugs, etc.	Legislation and Development/ CN Cross Cutting Issues	Mid 2009	National Assembly, MoTCA. MCN, MoI, MoJ

PILLAR : INFRASTRUCTURE
SECTOR : URBAN DEVELOPMENT

Outcomes	Policy Actions and Activities	Category	Timeframe	Responsible Agency
Access to secure tenure and improved services and public facilities for inhabitants of informal settlements	Review of relevant legislation to facilitate regularization, followed by program of investments in basic infrastructure and public facilities with drawing from best practices in the region	Legislation/ RC Cross Cutting Issues	End 2013	KM/IDLG/MUD
Improved institutional coordination and monitoring of key urban indicators	Institutional reform and enforcement of administrative processes; introduction of effective systems of monitoring and evaluation for the implementation phase for transparent urban development processes	Institution Building	Mid 2009	KM/IDLG/MUD
Increased and inclusive access for urban households to basic services	Investments in piped water systems and drainage networks (improved sanitation).	Development	March 2011 End 2009	KM/IDLG/MUD IDLG, MoUD
	Urban Property registration and mapping in major municipalities	Development		
	Feasibility studies for building new roads	Development	End 2008	IDLG, MoUD, MPW
	Implementation of Traffic Management Strategies	Development	2009	MoUD, IDLG, KM, MoI
	Increase reconstruction of asphalt roads in major and secondary cities	Development	2010	IDLG, MoUD, KM, MPW
	Rehabilitation of existing damaged roads	Development	2009	IDLG, MoUD, KM, MPW
	Design and build (asphalted) new roads	Development	2010	IDLG, MoUD, KM, MPW

Appendix I. (Continued)

Outcomes	Policy Actions and Activities	Category	Timeframe	Responsible Agency
Increased availability of affordable shelter	Investments by public and private sector in land and housing development, coupled with development of systems of housing finance	Development	End 2013	KM/IDLG/MUD
	Most needy households receive a housing subsidy	Development	2009	KM/IDLG/MUD
	City Development Plans for 40 major municipalities	Development	2010	MoUD, KM, IDLG
	Regional Development Plans for all 8 zones of the country	Development	2010	MoUD, IDLG,
	Detailed development plans for major 10 cities	Development	2010	MoUD, IDLG,
	Provide land tenure to the inhabitants in informal settlements	Development	2009	MoUD, KM, IDLG
	Upgrade the basic infrastructure and urban services in the informal area	Development	2010	MoUD, KM, IDLG
	Establish Dehsabz New City and turn Kabul into a business hub of the surrounding regions	Development	2007 - 2025	DCDA
Strengthened institutional capacity to plan and manage urban development in a systematic and transparent manner	Review and update policies, regulations and implementation plans that will consider crosscutting issues gender, environment, ant-corruption and counter narcotics.	Legislation/ Cross Cut-ting Issues	End 2009	KM/IDLG/MUD
	Comprehensive and gender sensitive reform of institutions, review and update of relevant legislations, policies and administrative processes	Institution Building/ Gender Cross Cutting Issues	End 2009	KM/IDLG/MUD, MoWA
	Institutional Reform Action Plans in 34 municipalities/ministerial departments	Institution Building	End 2009	KM/IDLG/MUD
	Computerize HRM/Finance and program activities to strengthen Human Resource, Financial and Program Management	Institution Building/AC Cross Cutting Issues		MUD, KM
	Improved financial management in 30 major municipalities	Institution Building	End 2009	KM/IDLG/MUD
	Property tax implementation	Institution Building		IDLG, KM
	Preparation of economic data base for revenue administration	Institution Building		MoUD, IDLG, KM
	Establish Uni- urban Data collection unit (encourage disaggregated data col-lection)	Institution Building/ Gender Cross Cutting Issues		MoUD, IDLG, KM
	Training and capacity building of the key staff in the process of monitoring and evaluation and re-planning	Institution Building	End 2009	KM/IDLG/MUD
	Capacity building of technical and managerial staff of provincial municipalities	Institution Building		IDLG,

Outcomes	Policy Actions and Activities	Category	Timeframe	Responsible Agency
Improved environment friendly programs and policies	Management Plans and Implementation of management plans initiated for protected areas and national parks, including game reserves, wetlands and bird sanctuaries	Development/ Environment Cross Cutting Issues		MUD, KM, NEPA
	Ensure environment sustainability of all urban development programs	Development/ Environment Cross Cutting Is sues		MUD, IDLG, KM, NEPA
	Develop national settlement and regional strategic plans and through them provide a framework for balanced urbanization and greater regional coherence, from which the border cities of Afghanistan and neighboring countries shall benefit.	Institution Building/ RC Cross Cutting Issues	End 2009	MUD, IDLG,

PILLAR : INFRASTRUCTURE
SECTOR : MINES AND NATURAL RESOURCES

Objectives or Outcomes	Policy Actions and Activities	Category	Timeframe	Responsible Agency
Geophysical and geological information available	Planning exploration activities, mapping, survey of minerals, oil and gas, collection of geophysical and geological information	Development	Continued	MoM
	Conducting geological research studies	Development	Continued	MoM
Increased access to water resources	Master plan on underground water development	Development	End 2014	MoM, other line ministries
	Manual for underground water management	Development	End 2008	MoM
	Rehabilitation of the Hydrological and Geo-engineering research sections	Development	End 2010	MoM
	Issuance of permit to Private Sector who work on underground water	Development	TBD	MoM
	Rehabilitation and establishment of new Hydrological Stations for collection of the necessary information and figures	Development	Continued	MoM
	Enhancement of working relationships with related line ministries for water	Development	Continued	MoM
Increased Private Sector Investment in mining sector	Design and implementation of Mineral policy	Legislation	2008-2013	MoM
	Preparation of Gas Law and Manual	Legislation	End 2009	MoM
	Analysis study of loss and damages in mines extraction	Development	Continued	MoM
	Categorizing oil and gas fields to gas blocks for better management	Development	Continued	MoM
	Leasing of oil and gas blocks to privates sector for research and study	Development	Continued	MoM
	Establishment of new organizational structure for gas and oil management	Institution Building	End 2008	MoM
Public access to natural gas	Design of plan for gas pipeline grid to provinces	Development	Continued	MoM

Appendix I. (Continued)

Objectives or Outcomes	Policy Actions and Activities	Category	Timeframe	Responsible Agency
Strong regulatory framework in place	PRR Implementation Capacity building of Survey and Geological staff	Institution Building Institution Building	End 2009 Continued	MoM MoM
	Equipping labs of GSD	Institution Building	First Phase will be done by 2008 and then Continued	MoM
	Standardizing working a capacity of Geology staff	Institution Building	Continued	MoM
	Coordination with different countries in raising capacity of the public sector	Institution Building	Continued	MoM
	Introduction of measures to ensure environmental concerns taken care of.	Institution Building/ Env. Cross Cutting Issues	Continued	MoM
	Conservation of Biodiversity in implementing mining projects	Development/ Env. Cross Cutting Issues	Continued	MoM
	Promotion of regional cooperation to facilitate various projects under the mining sector	Development/ RC Cross Cutting Issues	Continued	MoM
	To mainstream into all administrative reform programs measures required to address the systems and incentives promoting anti-corruption within the public administration system and Development Activities.	Institution Building / AC Cross Cutting Issues	Continued	MoM
	To maintain the highest level of transparency, accountability and integrity in the relationship between the public and private sector.	Institution Building / AC Cross Cutting Issues	Continued	MoM
	Gender mainstreaming in the policies in the mining sector.	Development/ Gender Cross Cutting Issues	2008-2013	MoM
	Priority to areas having substantial narcotics cultivation to promote economic activity to generate alternate livelihoods	Development/ CN Cross Cutting Issues	2008-2010	MoM

PILLAR : INFRASTRUCTURE
SECTOR : WATER RESOURCES

Objectives or Outcomes	Policy Actions and Activities	Category	Timeframe	Responsible Agency
Improved water sector legal and governance structures and institutions in place	Assess, identify, draft, review, debate, resolve, finalize water law and supple-mentary regulations	Legislation	2008-2009	MEW, MAIL, MoM, MoUD, MRRD, NEPA, MoPH
	Conduct appropriate studies, identify specific pilot programs, experimentation, and customize river basin institutional structures.	Institution Building	by 2010	MEW, MAIL, MRRD, MoM, MoUD, NEPA

Expected Outcomes	Policy Actions and Activities	Category	Timeframe	Responsible Agency
	Establishment of institutions for hydrometric network in the country	Institution Building	by 2010	MEW
	National urban and rural water supply institutions in place	Institution Building	by 2011	MoUD, MRRD
	Training of staff from various sector ministries on integrated water resources management	Institution Building	Continue	MEW, MAIL, MoM, MoUD, MRRD, NEPA, MoPH
	Establishment of organization and capacity building of River Basin Agencies and Sub-agencies (RBA/ SBA) and River Basin and Sub-basin Councils (RBC/SBC)	Institution Building	2008-2009	MEW
	Training of SCWAM Technical Secretariat staff	Institution Building	Continue	MEW, MAIL, MoM, MoUD, MRRD, NEPA, MoPH
	Gathering of data socio-economics, geology/groundwater, environment, hydrological, meteorological and others for project development	Institution Building	by end 2010	MEW, MAIL, MoM, MoUD, MRRD, NEPA, MoPH
	Development of curriculum in water resources management at local universities/technical colleges	Institution Building	by end 2009	MEW, MAIL, MoHE, MRRD, MoM
	Assessment studies for project	Institution Building	Continue	MEW,MAIL, MRRD, MoUD, NEPA, MoPH
	Institute training in HEC RAS and other appropriate modeling techniques	Institution Building	2010	MEW, MAIL, MoM, MoUD, MRRD
	Assignment of staff/personnel to consultancy contracts for training	Institution Building	end 2009	MEW, MAIL, MRRD,MoUD, MoM
	Gender discrepancies in various laws systematically uncovered	Legislation/ Gender Cross Cutting Issues	2008-2009	National Assembly, MoUD, MoJ
	Regional water issues dialogues initiated	Legislation/ RC Cross Cutting Issues	TBD	MoFA, MEW, MAIL, SCWAM

Appendix I. (Continued)

Expected Outcomes	Policy Actions and Activities	Category	Timeframe	Responsible Agency
Sustainable water resources management strategies and plans covering irrigation and drinking water supply devel oped and implemented.	Initiate appropriate inventory studies, water resources planning studies and basin master plans	Development	end 2010	MEW, MAIL, MoM, MoUD, MRRD, NEPA
	Complete master plan investigations	Development	2010	MEW, MAIL, MRRD,MoUD, MoM, SCWAM,NEPA
	Identify, study, design, procure and implement projects	Development	Continue	MEW, MAIL, MRRD,MoUD, MoM,NEPA
	Identify, prioritize, and implement rehabilitation program	Development	Continue	MEW, MAIL, MRRD,MoUD, MoM,NEPA
Water resources for irrigation and Drinking purposes improved	Enhance achievement tracking procedures and augment NSP resources WUA implementation programming	Development Development	by 2010 Continue	MRRD MEW, MAIL, MRRD, MoUD
	Strengthen required resources and monitor programs	Development	Continue	MEW, MAIL,MoUD, MRRD, NEPA
	Improve existing drinking water supply systems and build new systems in villages and cities, including Kabul	Development	by 2010	MoUD, MRRD, MoM, MEW
	Rehabilitation of National Hydro-meteorological network	Development	by 2010	MEW
	Development of technical plans, management plans, and implementation strategies for Amu Darya River Basin, Northern River Basin, Western River Basin, Helmand River basin, and Kabul River Basins,	Development	by 2011	MEW
	Rehabilitation of all small, medium, and large traditional irrigation schemes and strengthen water users association	Development	Continue	MEW, MAIL, MRRD
	Provision of access to water and sanitation facilities to rural people	Development	Continue	MRRD
	Undertake riverbank protection and erosion control works and implement long-term flood control program	Development	Continue	MEW
	Community based natural resource management established	Development/Env. Cross Cutting Issues	Continue	MEW, NEPA, MRRD, MAIL
	Water resources for irrigation utilized for non-poppy farming	Development/ CN Cross Cutting Issues	by 2010	MEW, MCN, MAIL, MRRD

PILLAR : INFRASTRUCTURE
SECTOR : INFORMATION & COMMUNICATION TECHNOLOGY

Expected Outcomes	Policy Actions and Activities	Category	Timeframe	Responsible Agency
E-Afghanistan created	Internet Exchange point	Development	2008-2010	MoCIT
	ICT Village	Development	2008-2010	MoCIT
	E-Government	Development	2008-2013	MoCIT
	National Internet Registry of Afghanistan (NIRA)	Development	2008-2011	MoCIT
	Afghanistan Cyber Emergency Response Team (AfCERT)	Development	2008-2011	MoCIT
	National Identity Management Initiative (NIMI)	Development	2008-2013	MoCIT
Enabling Environment	Development of policies, laws, regulations procedures and other normative acts to accelerate the role of telecom services to citizens	Legislation	2008-2010	MoCIT
	Establish Telecom Development Fund (TDF)	Legislation	2008-2013	MoCIT
	Drafting the ICT Law	Legislation	2008-2009	MoCIT
	Develop CIO (Chief Information Officer) culture in government organizations	Institution Building	2008-2009	MoCIT
	Movement of the government institution to a modern level of services to the citizens	Institution Building	2008-2013	MoCIT
	Developing Curriculum and Regulatory Framework for ICT Training Centers in the Private Sector	Institution Building	2008-2011	MoCIT
	Develop rules and regulations to require all government institutions to publish documents on their official websites (as a supplement to the Official Gazette)	Institution Building	end 2008	MoCIT
	Adopt a full set of Rules and Procedures that will govern the competitive procurement and utilization of ICT by all government institutions	Institution Building	end 2008	MoCIT
	Reduce corruption by reviewing all government services and making recommendations for the adoption of ICT to streamline and automate (for example, customs processing, procurement and licensing	Institution Building	end 2009	MoCIT
	Pilot home based ICT related work for women	Development/ Gender Cross Cutting Issues	3nd 2008	MoCIT
ICT Literacy improved	Establishment of ICT centers in 34 Provincial capitals	Development	2008-2011	MoCIT
Improved ICT coverage and Infrastructure	Optical fiber backbone	Development	End 2008	MoCIT
	Government online (web presence)	Development	2008-2013	MoCIT

Appendix I. (Continued)

Expected Outcomes	Policy Actions and Activities	Category	Timeframe	Responsible Agency
	E-government Resource Centre	Development	2008-2013	MoCIT
	Copper Cable Network	Development	2008-2013	MoCIT
	Expansion of District Communication Network (DCN)	Development	2008-2013	MoCIT
	Expansion of Microwave System	Development	2008-2013	MoCIT
	Village Communications Network (VCN)	Development	2008-2013	MoCIT
	Modernization of Postal Services	Development	2008-2013	MoCIT
	National Data Centre (The electronic data of the government will be securely hosted and will be available to all entities upon request and level of access)	Development	2008-2013	MoCIT
	The National Data Centre will have information on crosscutting issues like anti-corruption, counter narcotics, and environment.	Development/ Cross Cutting Issues	2008-2013	MoCIT

PILLAR : HEALTH AND NUTRITION
SECTOR : HEALTH AND NUTRITION

Expected Outcomes	Policy Actions and Activities	Category	Timeframe	Responsible Agency
Increased quality of health care services	Develop an effective organization and management system to coordinate all services of NHCS	Institution Building	2008 - 2013	MoPH
	Strengthen HRD unit to oversee the HR and R&D issues, Computerize all HRM activities to strengthen Human resource management	Institution Building/ AC Cross Cutting Issues	2009 - 2013	MoPH
	Develop a suitable regulatory framework to encourage private sector invest-ment	Legislation	2009 - 2013	MoPH
	Strengthen policy and planning support unit in the Ministry	Legislation	2008 - 2013	MoPH
	Effective monitoring and reporting of quality of services provided by different agencies	Institution Building	2008 - 2013	MoPH
	Establishment of a quality support program	Institution Building	2008 - 2013	MoPH
	Making service delivery performance based through incentives and contract monitoring and exploring options for implementing results based financing of health service delivery in Afghanistan.	Institution Building	2009 - 2013	MoPH
	To mainstream into all administrative reform programs measures required to address the systems and incentives promoting anti-corruption within the public administration system and Development Activities.	Institution Building/ Cross Cutting Issues	2008 - 2013	MoPH
Increased access to health care services	Implement the Primary Health Care Program	Development	Ongoing	MoPH
	Develop a comprehensive referral system integrated with BPHS to improve the service delivery level	Development	2008 - 2013	MoPH

Expected Outcomes	Policy Actions and Activities	Category	Timeframe	Responsible Agency
	Harmonize the system of procurement and disbursement of essential medicines	Institution Building	2008 - 2013	MoPH
	Develop a comprehensive care system for communicable diseases like TB, HIV and malaria	Development	Ongoing-2013	MoPH
	Establish and maintain required number of Health Facilities providing diagnos-tic and treatment TB services	Development	Ongoing-2013	MoPH
	Establish number of Health Facilities providing diagnostic and treatment Malaria services	Development	Ongoing-2013	MoPH
	Establishing effective surveillance system and Volunteer Confidential Counseling and Testing Center for HIV cases in each province	Development	2008 - 2013	MoPH
	Awareness generation against ills of drug usage and environmental issues affecting health	Development/ CN Env. Cross Cutting Issues	Ongoing-2013	MoPH
	Establishing centers for treatment and rehabilitation of Drugs users.	Development/ CN Cross Cutting Issues	Ongoing-2013	MoPH
	Promotion of regional cooperation to make health facilities available to the people of Afghanistan if such facilities are not available in the country.	Development/ RC Cross Cutting Issues	Ongoing-2013	MoPH
Effective Reproductive and Child health system	Develop an integrated reproductive and child health care system with the support of development partners	Development	Ongoing-2013	MoPH, MoE, MoWA, MoHE
	Develop effective immunization coverage system with adequate doses of DPT vaCross Cutting Issuesne & Hepatitis, measles and polio in all provinces	Development	Ongoing-2013	MoPH
	A Special Cell be created to take care and promote all gender issues especially health of females and mothers	Development/ Gender Cross Cutting Issues	Ongoing-2013	MoPH

PILLAR : EDUCATION AND CULTURE
SECTOR : EDUCATION

Objectives or Outcomes	Policy Actions and Activities	Category	Timeframe	Responsible Agency
	PRIMARY AND SECONDRY EDUCATION			
Improved quality of education	Approval of laws for setting up of Independent Boards for secondary education, vocational education and for national standards of accreditation and regulatory framework for quality assurance of education services	Legislation	1386	MoE
	Develop policies to encourage the non-government sector to offer services	Legislation	1386	MoE

Appendix I. (Continued)

Objectives or Outcomes	Policy Actions and Activities	Category	Timeframe	Responsible Agency
	Establish School Advisory and Support Councils (SASC) in all schools	Institution Building	1385-1389	MoE
	Establish Independent Boards for secondary education, NESA and National Institute of Management and Administration	Institution Building	1387-1389	MoE
	Establish a National Institute of Curriculum Development incorporating national standards benchmarks	Institution Building	1387-1389	MoE
	Strengthen institutional and staff capacities in curriculum development with special focus on gender, counter-narcotics, environment and anti-corruption.	Institution Building/ Cross Cutting Issues	1387-1389	MoE
	Create a sustainable, transparent and accountable financial management system at central, provincial and district level	Institution Building	1386-89	MoE
	Create a computerized HRM system to strengthen human resource management	Institution Building/ AC Cross Cutting Issues	1387-1388	MoE
	Monitor the activities of sector administrative units to confirm adherence to ethical standards, professional service and staff integrity, based upon relevant laws, codes of conduct and standardized procedures and protocols	Institution Building/ AC Cross Cutting Issues	1387	MoE
	Implement PRR and Pay and Grading of all approved positions within the ministry including teaching staff	Institution Building	PRR1385-1386 Approved position 1387-1389	MoE
	Build a national partnership program of literacy and non-formal education	Institution Building	1387	MoE
	Increase the number of female primary and secondary teachers including re-training all female teachers who were separated from service during the PRR process and re-employing them.	Development / Gender Cross Cutting Issues	1389	MoE, MoWA
	Establish/strengthen teacher training colleges in all provinces	Development / Gender Cross Cutting Issues	1386-1389	MoE, MoWA
	Train 17,000 teachers and 3,500 mullahs in the delivery of literacy courses with at least 30% of them being female teachers.	Development	1386-89	MoE
	Improve the quality of primary and secondary teaching (training teachers, school principals)	Development	1387-1389	MoE
	Improve teaching material and new curricula for secondary schools	Development	1386-1389	MoE
	Student Competency tests prepared and implement testing	Development	1387-1389	MoE
	Adopt an enabling policy to implement the Constitutional provision of compul-sory education up to intermediate level	Legislation / Gender Cross Cutting Issues	1387	MoE

Objectives or Outcomes	Policy Actions and Activities	Category	Timeframe	Responsible Agency
	Reduce dropout level by	Development	1389	MoE
	Adopt a system to follow up female drop outs and provide incentives to return them to school	Institution Building / Gender Cross Cutting Issues	1387-1389	MoE; MoWA
Literacy rate increased	Increase enrolment rates at primary and secondary school	Development	1386-1389	MoE
	Implement parent-oriented campaign to promote support to girls' enrolment	Development/ Gender Cross Cutting Issues	1386-89	MoE; MoWA
	Conduct review class for girls who graduate from secondary schools to prepare for college entrance examinations	Development/ Gender Cross Cutting Issues	1386-89	MoE
	Have a program of remedial education to address literacy rates	Development	1387-1389	MoE
Equal opportunity for all	Construction and School Rehabilitation	Development	1389	MoE
	Construct dormitories and pro-women facilities, especially in the secondary level schools	Development/ Gender Cross Cutting Issues	1386-89	MoE
	Produce new textbooks and teacher guides	Development	1386-89	MoE
	Establish National Institute of Management and Administration at MoE /TVET Department. Operation of the Institute to be contracted out	Development	1387	MoE
	Disaggregate by sex all human related statistics	Institution Building/ Gender Cross Cutting Issues	1386-89	MoE
HIGHER EDUCATION				
Improved quality of academic teaching and research	Policies that require new university professors and lecturers to be hired on the basis of academic merit and gender balance.	Legislation	1386-1389	MoHE; MoWA
	Upgraded qualifications of faculty through university partnership programs	Institution Building	Already commenced. This is a continuing program (1386-1389)	MoHE
	Recruit foreign residing Afghan and regional Professors through regional agreements	Institution Building/ RC Cross Cutting Issues	TBD	MoHE, MoFA
	Institutional strengthening at MoHE	Institution Building	Commence 1389- continuing	MoHE

Appendix I. (Continued)

Objectives or Outcomes	Policy Actions and Activities	Category	Timeframe	Responsible Agency
	Create a computerized HRM system to strengthen human resource management	Institution Building/ AC Cross Cutting Issues	TBD	MoHE
	Monitor the activities of sector administrative units to confirm adherence to ethical standards, professional service and staff integrity, based upon relevant laws, codes of conduct and standardized procedures and protocols	Institution Building/ AC Cross Cutting Issues	TBD	MoHE
	Investigate possible funding models that would provide greater autonomy	Institution Building	1386-1389	MoHE
	A reorganized and streamlined recruitment and hiring process (PRR) at the MoHE within its departments and at the 19 institutions of higher learning	Institution Building	1385-88	MoHE
	Adopt strategy to hire more women professionals; re-train female teachers who were dismissed during the PRR process and re-employ them	Institution Building/ Gender Cross Cutting Issues	1385-89	MoHE; MoWA
	Establish a separate body responsible for standards and accreditation all degree granting institutions and professional programs, public and private, in Afghan stan.	Institution Building	1387-TBD it is a conti-	MoHE
	Monitor standards and ensure consistency between institutions	Institution Building	1387	MoHE
	Revised and approved curricula and related teaching materials; training for professors and lecturers in use of these	Institution Building	1388	MoHE
	Identify and evaluate existing research capacity in higher education institutions and non-governmental organizations in Afghanistan.	Institution Building/ AC Cross Cutting Issues	TBD	MoHE
Improved access to Higher Education	Rehabilitate existing universities and build new library and laboratory facilities at existing universities.	Development	1381-1389	MoHE
	Construction of 24 new dormitories 12 for men and 12 for women	Development	1385-1389	MoHE
	Recruit 3000 new professors, including qualified Afghan professors from the region (India, Pakistan, Tajikistan, and Iran).	Development	1387-1389	MoHE
	Increased number of research centers at higher education institutions.	Development	1389	MoHE
	New MA programs at departments of languages and literature at Kabul University, and new programs for the faculties of social science, law, economics, geology, engineering, agriculture, and Islamic law.	Development	Already Commenced	MoHE
	Strengthen security in the campus	Institution Building / Gender Cross Cutting Issues	1386-89	MoHE

Objectives or Outcomes	Policy Actions and Activities	Category	Timeframe	Responsible Agency
	Conduct review class for girls to prepare them for college entrance examina-tions	Institution Building / Gender Cross Cutting Issues	1386-89	MoHE
	Disaggregate by sex all human related statistics	Institution Building / Gender Cross Cutting Issues	1386-89	MoHE
VOCATIONAL EDUCATION				
Improved quality of vocational education	Proposal to formalize existing apprenticeship arrangements and expand the system. Ensure that a recognized qualification is provided to people undertak-ing apprenticeships who have achieved specified basic competencies.	Legislation	1387	NSDP
	Expand the capacity and improve the quality of Vocational Education and Skill Development	Institution Building	1389	NSDP
	Improve the capacity of the national VET system to manage and deliver market-driven skills training and linkages to micro-credit and business development support services is planned to have increased.	Institution Building	1389	MoL/NSDP
	Within the next 12 months, establish an independent National Vocational Education and Training Authority with the responsibility for managing and co-coordinating national VET policy will be established. Teaching and operation of individual VET institutions to be contracted out.	Institution Building	1387-TBD it is a contin-ued Program	NSDP
	Target the most vulnerable women and youth in the selection of training and provision of employment opportunities	Institution Building/ Gender Cross Cutting Issues	1386-89	NSDP
Improved access to vocational education	Develop an accessible, regional network of TVET schools and training centers, including 17 new schools and a school for those with special needs	Development	1387-1388	MoE/TVET Dept
	Establishment of job-placement centers in all 34 provinces	Development	1387-1389 (2010)	NSDP
	The NSDP will procure the services of a variety of training providers (pri-vate/public) for the provision of training to 150,000 unemployed Afghan women and men through competitive bidding procedures	Development	1385-1389 (2010)	MoL/NSDP
	Disaggregate by sex all human related statistics	Institution Building/ Gender Cross Cutting Issues	1386-89	MoL/NSDP
SPORTS				

Appendix I. (Continued)

Objectives or Outcomes	Policy Actions and Activities	Category	Timeframe	Responsible Agency
Improved sports facilities	Delegate the overall authority to coordinating sports services in the country to the Olympic Committee	Legislation	1389	MoE/NOC
	Build capacity of professional staff of the National Olympic Committee for quality programming of administration and service delivery	Institution Building	1389	MoE/NOC
	Approach countries and foreign sporting agencies with facilities for advanced athletes to allow Afghan sports people to train and compete in foreign countries	Development	1387	MoE/NOC
	Adopt and implement a strategy to realize the benchmark of increasing women's access, leadership and participation in sports	Institution Building/ Gender Cross Cutting Issues	1386-89	MoE/NOC; MoWA
	Improve Infrastructure (build sports complexes and strengthen sports through provincial sports departments, sports improvement programs in capital and provinces)	Development	1389	MoE/NOC
	Sex-disaggregate all human related statistics	Institution Building/ Gender Cross Cutting Issues	1386-89	MoE/NOC;MoWA
SCIENCE ACADEMY				
Enhanced contribution of the Academy in Science	Establish advisory committees consisting of academy members and MoE and MoHE officials. To advise on training and curriculum issues.	Institution Building	1388	Science Academy
	Complete Encyclopedia Project	Institution Building	1386-1389	Science Academy
	Consider publication of an academic journal edited by the academy	Institution Building	1389	Science Academy
	Construct a 7-story building for use by the academy (note: this building could also be used for higher education teaching and seminars)	Institution Building	1385-1389	Science Academy
	Rehabilitate the Centre for Literature and Language at the academy	Institution Building	1385-1389	Science Academy
	Provide laboratory facilities for the academy	Institution Building	1387-1389	Science Academy
PILLAR : EDUCATION AND CULTURE				
SECTOR : MEDIA AND CULTURE				
Afghanistan's cultural Heritage Protected and Preserved	Rehabilitation of Kabul theater, Ministry complex, 20 historical monuments, building for MoIC provinces Dept. libraries in provinces, music institute in Kabul construction of museum in Nangarhar, Bamyan etc...	Development	2010	MoIC
	Comprehensive inventory of Afghan cultural treasures	Development	2007	MoIC

Objectives or Outcomes	Policy Actions and Activities	Category	Timeframe	Responsible Agency
	Measures to be taken to revive the Afghan cultural heritage, to stop the illegal removal of cultural material and to restore damaged monuments and artifacts	Legislation	2010	MoIC
	Registration, conservation and restoration of sites and monuments	Development	2010	MoIC
	The MoIC will continue registration and conservation of monuments, repair and preservation of museum, archeology items and historical monuments	Development	Continue	MoIC
Free and independent media	Pass Media Law	Legislation	2008	MoIC
	Inventory of intangible cultural heritage (music)	Development	2008	MoIC
	Take appropriate measures to promote Live Culture (Music, Cinema and Arts)	Development	2013	MoIC
	Development of a truly editorially independent public service broadcasting of a high standard educational radio-TV production centre	Development	2010	MoIC
	Renovation of the existing Radio Studios (National) equipments	Development	1385	MoIC
	Sensitizing media about the issues related to gender, anti-corruption, counter-narcotics, environment and regional cooperation	Development/ Cross Cutting Issues	2010	MoIC (Youth Affairs Deputy Ministry)
Empowerment of Youth	Promoting non-formal education, increasing awareness and developing skills (literacy, leadership, strategic planning, conflict resolution, peace-building, etc.) in young people so to provide better quality of life and livelihood opportunities.	Development	2010	MoIC (Youth Affairs Deputy Ministry)
	Engaging youth in governance, development and social-political processes at local, district, municipal, provincial and national level, ensuring the participation of young women and men in democracy and advocacy.	Development	2010	MoIC (Youth Affairs Deputy
	Promoting voluntary efforts for peace and development and establishing a youth volunteer corps for Afghanistan and also in the fields of gender, anti-corruption, counter-narcotics, environment and regional cooperation.	Development	2010	MoIC (Youth Affairs Deputy Ministry)
	Sensitizing youth about the issues related to gender, anti-corruption, counter-narcotics, environment and regional cooperation.	Development/ Cross Cutting Issues	2010	MoIC (Youth Affairs Deputy Ministry)

PILLAR : AGRICULTURE AND RURAL DEVELOPMENT
SECTOR : AGRICULTURE AND RURAL DEVELOPMENT

Expected Outcomes	Policy Actions and Activities	Category	Timeframe	Responsible Agency
Improved service delivery within the Agriculture & Rural Development sector	Review of the legal framework governing ARD sector, including governmental institutional reforms	Legislation/ Policy/Plan	1387 - 1389	MAIL, MRRD, MCN and IDLG CARD Inter-ministerial
	Develop 5 years action plan which quantifies all 8 functions of ARD zones	Legislation/ Policy/Plan	1387 - 1388	

Appendix I. (Continued)

Expected Outcomes	Policy Actions and Activities	Category	Timeframe	Responsible Agency
	including budget requirements, roles and responsibilities and appropriate M&E systems			Committee Inter-ministerial Committee
	To mainstream into all administrative reform programs measures required to address the systems and incentives promoting anti-corruption within the public administration system and Development Activities.	Legislation/ Policy/Plan / AC Cross Cutting Issues	1387 - 1389	MAIL, MRRD
	To maintain the highest level of transparency, accountability and integrity in the relationship between the public and private sector.	Legislation/ Policy/Plan / AC Cross Cutting Issues	1387 - 1391	MAIL, MRRD
Poverty Reduced in line with MDG targets	Align ARD Programs to promote sustainable growth and distribute wealth through CRD	Legislation/ Policy/Plan	1387 - 1391	MAIL, MRRD and MCN
	Develop and implement poverty baseline and survey database in addition to NRVA	Legislation/ Policy/Plan	1387 - 1391	MAIL, MRRD and MCN
Improved Local Governance	Review and update legislation concerning sub-national governance formal and informal structures, roles and responsibilities	Legislation/ Policy/Plan	1387-1389	MRRD, IDLG, MAIL
	Formulate and implement policy imperatives requiring all development actors to carry out their activities through the established sub-national structures	Legislation/ Policy/Plan	1387-1389	MRRD, IDLG, MAIL
Increased Agriculture Pro-duction and Productivity	Review, revise and formulate land use and government owned land for lease Review, revise and formulate Natural Resources laws (wetlands, forests, range	Legislation/ Policy/Plan Legislation/ Policy/Plan	1387-1389 1387-1391	MAIL MAIL
	lands, arid lands, watershed)			
	Review, revise and formulate Food laws and regulations (Quality and Safety, CODEX standards, quarantine)	Legislation/ Policy/Plan	1387-1390	MAIL
	Review, revise and formulate laws and regulations on Livestock rand Horticulture	Legislation/ Policy/Plan	1387-1390	MAIL
	Review, revise and formulate laws and regulation on Pesticides Use, plant and animal protection	Legislation/ Policy/Plan	1387-1390	MAIL
	Review, revise and formulate laws and regulations on agricultural imports and exports	Legislation/ Policy/Plan	1387-1391	MAIL
	Formulation of laws on concerning forests, food safety and control, strategic food reserves, agricultural imports, horticulture and improved seeds.	Legislation/ Policy/Plan	1387-1390	MAIL

Expected Outcomes	Policy Actions and Activities	Category	Timeframe	Responsible Agency
	Restoration and Sustainable Use of Rangelands and forests, conservation of bio-diversity, and encouragement to Community Based Natural Resource Management	Other Measures / Env. Cross Cutting Issues	1387 - 1391	MAIL
	Special focus on gender in polices and plans and their implementation	Legislation / Policy/Plan / Gender Cross Cutting Issues	1387 - 1391	MAIL, MRRD
Improved agriculture and rural infrastructure	Develop and implement policy on infrastructure investment and maintenance	Legislation/ Policy/Plan	1387-1389	MRRD, MAIL
	Develop and implement sub-sector policies on rural roads, water, irrigation and rural energy	Legislation/ Policy/Plan	1387-1389	MRRD, MAIL
	Devise and implement appropriate labor-intensive approach and technologies for investment and maintenance of infrastructure	Legislation/ Policy/Plan	1387-1389	MRRD, MAIL
	Review, revise and formulate laws and regulations on Water Management and utilization	Legislation/ Policy/Plan	1387-1389	MAIL, MRRD, MoE&W
	Establish standards including social and environmental safeguards	Legislation/ Policy/Plan	1387-1389	MRRD, MAIL
	Enhance public and private sectors capacities to effectively and efficiently manage and deliver infrastructure programs	Institution Building	1387-1391	MRRD, MAIL
Facilitated Economic Re-generation	Review current and formulate new policies, legal and regulatory for establish-ing, stimulating and sustaining rural enterprises and credit	Legislation/ Policy/Plan	1387-1389	MRRD, MAIL
	Establish rural enterprise support services network	Institution Building	1387-1389	MRRD, MAIL
	Establish Agriculture and Rural Development Zones	Institution Building	1387-1389	CARD Inter-ministerial Committee
	Develop national and international markets for agriculture and non-agriculture produce and products	Other Measures	1387-1391	MRRD, MAIL, MoCom
	Promote regional cooperation to help generate economic growth through tech-nologies, exchange of knowledge etc.	Other Measures / RC Cross Cutting Issues	1387 - 1391	MAIL, MRRD, MoFA
Improved service delivery within the sector	Strengthen line ministries capacities at national and sub-national levels	Institution Building	1387-1389	MRRD, MAIL, MCN, IDLG
	Establish an Executive Management Unit with presidential authority and clear mandate to implement CARD	Institution Building	1387	CARD Inter-ministerial Committee
Improved Local Governance	Develop mechanism to ensure integration and linkage of local level planning with the national ARD investment planning	Institution Building	1387-1388	MRRD, IDLG, MoEc

Appendix I. (Continued)

Expected Outcomes	Policy Actions and Activities	Category	Timeframe	Responsible Agency
	Continue capacity development of the sub-national governance structures to enable them to play a greater role in the development process	Institution Building	1387-1391	MRRD, IDLG
	Strengthen the sub-national governance structures through sustainable financial mechanisms	Other Measures	1387-1389	MRRD, MAIL, IDLG
	Continue the establishment of the local governance informal and formal structures and village and district levels	Other Measures	1387-1389	MRRD, MAIL
	Sensitization of functionaries of local governance on gender, environmental, counter-narcotics and anti-corruption issues	Legislation / Policy/Plan / Cross Cutting Issues	1387 - 1389	MRRD
Improved disaster and emergency preparedness	Support the establishment of disaster early warning system	Institution Building	1387-1389	MAIL, MRRD, IDLG MAIL, MRRD MAIL, MRRD
	Establish and operationalise a system for mitigation, preparedness and response to natural disasters and plant/animal diseases and epidemics	Institution Building Institution Building	1387-1389 1387-1389	
	Special focus to gender issues in polices and plans and their implementation	Legislation / Policy/Plan / Gender Cross Cutting Issues	1387 - 1388	MAIL, MRRD
Reduced poppy cultivation through Alternative Liveli-hood	Design and implement programs to strengthen and diversify licit livelihood Mainstream CN strategy in ARD programs and projects	Institution Building Other Measures / CN Cross Cutting Issues	1387-1391 1387-1391	MRRD, MAIL, MCN MRRD, MAIL, MCN
	Interventions for promoting legal agriculture livelihood options through inputs like seeds, irrigation, fertilizers, credit and crop insurance	Other Measures/ CN Cross Cutting Issues	1387 - 1391	MAIL, MCN
	Training for self employment and micro enterprise and development of micro credit facilities	Institution Building/ CN Cross Cutting Issues	1387 - 1391	MAIL, MCN
	Development of private sector especially promotion of small and medium enterprise	Other Measures/ CN Cross Cutting Issues	1387 - 1391	MAIL, MCN

PILLAR: SOCIAL PROTECTION & REFUGEES
SECTOR: SOCIAL PROTECTION

A) SOCIAL PROTECTION

Poverty and vulnerability reduction	Initiate and complete the public debate about establishment of the Afghanistan Welfare Fund and introduction of the Zakat-based tax	Other Measures	by mid-2008	MoLSAMD, MoF, MoHaj
	Introduce the Zakat-based tax in line with the recommendations from the public debate and consultations that will take place in 2008	Legislation	by mid-2009	MoF, MoHaj, GoA

Expected Outcomes	Policy Actions and Activities	Category	Timeframe	Responsible Agency
	Approve the new National Law on Rights and Privileges of the Persons with Disability	Legislation	by mid-2008	National Assembly
	Ratifying the UN Convention for the Rights of Persons with Disabilities	Legislation	by mid-2009	MoLSAMD, MoFA, MoJ, National Assembly
	Develop and circulate the National Disability Terms Book	Legislation	by mid-2008	MoLSAMD
	Develop and circulate National Disability Referral Guide	other Measures	by end-2008	MoLSAMD
	Improve labor market regulations to eliminate employer's abuses and to decrease informal economy	Legislation	by mid-2009	MoLSAMD, GoA, National Assembly
	Develop the policy and criteria for providing comprehensive support to the female headed chronically poor households with small children	Other Measures/ Gender Cross Cutting Issues	TBD	MoLSAMD
	In cooperation with the NGOs develop the programs for reunifying the orphans with their living parent/parents. Other Measures	Other Measures	TBD	MoLSAMD
	Develop and approve policy and standards for establishing day care center within orphanages and by the NGOs	Other Measures	by end - 2009	MoLSAMD
	In cooperation with the NGOs develop the network of day care centers throughout the country	Institution Building	by end-2009	MoLSAMD
	Provide support to the Afghan Red Crescent Society for building the new shelters/marastoons	Institution Building	continuously	MoLSAMD, ARCS
	Develop the project and criteria for free distribution of the livestock, orchards and tools for farming	Other Measures	by end-2008	MoLSAMD, MAIL
	In cooperation with the NGOs develop the programs for reunifying the orphans with their living parent/parents.	Other Measures	by mid-2008	MoLSAMD
	Develop and approve policy and standards for establishing day care center within orphanages and by the NGOs	Other Measures	by mid-2009	MoLSAMD, MoJ
	In cooperation with the NGOs develop the policy and standards for dealing with the children in conflict with law and with children who live with mothers in detention	Other Measures	by-mid 2009	MoLSAMD
	In cooperation with the NGOs implement the pilot project for supporting the children that are living with mothers in detention and for children in conflict with law	Other Measures	by end-2009	MoLSAMD, MoJ
	Ensure that the most vulnerable groups will be priority for participation in the public work programs	Other Measures	continuously	respective line ministries

Appendix I. (Continued)

Expected Outcomes	Policy Actions and Activities	Category	Timeframe	Responsible Agency
	Implement awareness campaigns to increase the financial market literacy of the poor and issues, laws and regulations against corruption	Other Measures/ AC Cross Cutting Issues	continuously	MoF
	Change the NSDP terms of references to introduce the most vulnerable categories as priority group for receiving the skill development trainings	Other Measures	Ongoing	MoLSAMD
	Cost, reprioritize and integrate The ANDS Social Protection Strategy into the Core Budget	Other Measures	by end-2008	MoLSAMD, MoF
	Reach the agreement with the ISAF/NATO on long term direct support to civilian victims of conflict	Other Measures	by mid-2008	Government, ISAF/NATO
	Develop the project and criteria for free distribution of the parcels with food and non-food items in winter period (winterization)	Other Measures	by end-2008	ANDMA, ARCS
	Approve poverty-targeted criteria for channeling social protection	Other Measures	Ongoing	MoLSAMD
	Conclude international agreements with the neighboring and other countries to regulate the rights of the Afghanistan's migrant workers	Other Measures	by end-2009	MoFA, MoLSAMD
	Develop the policy and criteria for supporting the civilian victims of conflict	Other Measures	by mid-2008	MoLSAMD, ISAF/NATO
Increased employment	Establish the institutional framework for accrediting service providers for skills development training and for issuing the certificates	Institution Building	by end-2008	MoLSAMD. MoE, GoA
Poverty reduction and improved natural disaster pre-paredness/response	Develop the project for establishing community based insurance scheme	Institution Building	by end-2008 by end-2008	MoLSAMD, MoF
	Develop the new public work program (Greening of Afghanistan) to support re-foresting	Other Measures		MAIL
	Develop the Policy and criteria for supporting the victims of natural disasters	Other Measures	by mid-2008	Presidents' Office, ANDMA
	Establish, on a pilot basis, the Crop Insurance Scheme at least in two provinces	Institution Building	by mid 2009	MoF, MoLSAMD
Poverty and vulnerability reduction and capacity strengthening	Establish the Afghanistan Welfare Fund in line with recommendations from the consultations that will take place in 2008	Institution Building	by mid-2009	MoLSAMD
Poverty and vulnerability reduction, improved employment	Redesign the NSP and the NRAP to ensure their presence in remote and poorest provinces	Other Measures	by end-2008	MRRD, MOPW, MoLSAMD
	Improve the communication campaigns to better inform the poor about opportunities to participate in the public work program	Other Measures	continuously	respective line ministries

Expected Outcomes	Policy Actions and Activities	Category	Timeframe	Responsible Agency
	Cost, reprioritize and integrate The ANDS Social Protection Strategy into the Core Budget	Other Measures	by end-2008	MoLSAMD, MoF
	Reach the agreement with the ISAF/NATO on long term direct support to civilian victims of conflict	Other Measures	by mid-2008	Government, ISAF/NATO
	Develop the project and criteria for free distribution of the parcels with food and non-food items in winter period (winterization)	Other Measures	by end-2008	ANDMA, ARCS
	Approve poverty-targeted criteria for channeling social protection	Other Measures	Ongoing	MoLSAMD
	Conclude international agreements with the neighboring and other countries to regulate the rights of the Afghanistan's migrant workers	Other Measures	by end-2009	MoFA, MoLSAMD
	Develop the policy and criteria for supporting the civilian victims of conflict	Other Measures	by mid-2008	MoLSAMD, ISAF/NATO
	Cost, reprioritize and integrate The ANDS Social Protection Strategy into the Core Budget	Other Measures	by end-2008	MoLSAMD, MoF
Improved social inclusion	Develop the program for evening classes and skill development training for street working children	Other Measures	by mid-2009	MoLSAMD, MoE
	Adjust the National Action Plan on Disability with the ANDS Social Protection Sector Strategy	Other Measures	by mid-2009	MoLSAMD
	Conduct the survey to collect data on poor persons with disability	Other Measures	by mid-2009	MoLSAMD
	Develop the criteria and mechanisms for distributing direct cash entitlements to the poor disabled individuals with the non-war related disability	Other Measures	by end-2008	MoLSAMD
	Develop and approve the policy and standards for establishing the community based rehabilitation centers by the NGOs to support integration of disabled, drug users and other vulnerable groups	Other Measures	by mid-2009	MoLSAMD, MCN
	Include rehabilitation of disabled in the BHP in all provinces	Other Measures	by end-2009	MoPH
	Develop the policy and criteria for supporting the victims of violence to include the program for reintegration into families, schools and society, as well as developing the criteria for establishing the NGOs-run shelters for women "at risk" and vulnerable children	Other Measures	by mid-2008	MoLSAMD
	Develop and approve the guidance for providing the free legal advice and mediation services (for reintegration into families) to all vulnerable groups	Other Measures	by mid-2009	MoLSAMD, MoJ
	Develop and approve the policy, program and criteria for community based rehabilitation of drug-addicts and their reintegration into society	Other Measures	by mid-2009	MoLSAMD in cooperation with MoPH, MCN, MoI, and NGOs

Appendix I. (Continued)

Expected Outcomes	Policy Actions and Activities	Category	Timeframe	Responsible Agency
	In cooperation with NGOs implement the pilot project to support extremely vulnerable groups (homeless, mentally imperiled, elders without family support) to include options for reintegration into families	Other Measures	by end-2009	MoLSAMD
	Women's capacity building, and establishment of economic centers for better economic opportunities	Other Measures/ Gender Cross Cutting Issues	TBD	MoWA, MoLSAMD
	Develop the project to support the poor Kuchi	Other Measures/ Gender Cross Cutting Issues	by mid-2009	MoLSAMD, MoE, MoPH
	Regulate rights of the Kuchi and other population to use traditional summer pastures	Other Measures	by-mid 2008	GoA
Improved social protection system	Eliminate all existing misuses and irregularities in distributing the direct cash transfers	Other Measures	continuously	MoLSAMD
	Implement the new schedule for payments of the direct cash transfers (twice a year) in order to decrease cost of collecting the payments for vulnerable martyr's families and individuals with war related disability who are living in re-mote areas	Other Measures	by mid-2009	MoLSAMD
	Develop the strategy for privatization of kindergartens	Other Measures	by mid-2008	MoLSAMD, MoF
	Gradually privatize kindergartens	Other Measures	by end-2012	MoLSAMD, MoCI
	Conduct the survey and collect data on civilian victims of conflict	Other Measures	by-mid-2009	MoLSAMD, MoI, MoD
	Map the NGOs activities in social protection sector	Other Measures	by mid-2009	MOSAMD
	Develop the standards for the NGOs involvement in implementation of the social protection projects and set up recognized and publish referral system	Other Measures	by end-2008	MoLSAMD
	Ensure that social protection programs of line ministries will be in line with the SAARC Social Chapter	Other Measures	continuously	MoLSAMD
	Establish the qualitative baseline indicators for monitoring of the Social Protec-tion Sector Strategy	Other Measures	by end-2008	CSO, line ministries
	Prepare and disseminate regular progress and evaluation report on implementa-tion of the Social Protection Sector Strategy	Other Measures	continuously	ANDS..MoLSAMD, ANDMA
Decreased domestic drug demand	Implement Drug Prevention Awareness Campaign through media, schools and religious leaders	Other Measures	continuously	MoE, MCN, MoRA
Improved aid coordination system	Develop the database of all Government and donor-funded projects in the area of social protection.	Other Measures	by mid-2009	MoLSAMD

Expected Outcomes	Policy Actions and Activities	Category	Timeframe	Responsible Agency
Reduction in harmful child labor	Implement the awareness campaign against harmful child labor	Other Measures	continuously	MoLSAMD
B) PENSION REFORM				
Improved old age protection	Promulgate the pension reform by the Government decree	Legislation	by mid-2008	MoLSAMD
	Modernize accounting as well as internal operational procedures of the Pension Department	Institution Building	by end-2012	MoLSAMD
	Develop the new IT system and processes of the Pension Department	Other Measures	2008-2012	MoLSAMD
	Improve collection of the pension contributions (payroll taxes)	Other Measures	continuously	MoF
	Establish a central database to store and process the details on pensioners and their bank accounts	Other Measures	by end-2012	MoLSAMD
	Introduce payments of pensions through banks	Other Measures	by end-2012	MoLSAMD
Capacity building	Improve the capacity of the Pension Department of MoLSAMD	Institution Building	continuously	MoLSAMD
	Improve record keeping and processes of the Pension Department and minimize any corrupt practices	Other Measures/ AC Cross Cutting Issues	by end-2012	MoLSAMD
	Conduct the capacity building and training for the staff and managers of the Pension Department	Other Measures	by end-2010	MoLSAMD
C) DISASTER PREPAREDNESS				
Improved disaster preparedness /response	Adjust the legislation to clearly reflect the leading role of the ANDMA in co-ordinating the national efforts for disaster preparedness and response but also for implementing of key programs and projects. Improved disaster prepared-ness /response	Legislation	by end-2008	GoA, ANDMA
	Establish a coordination network of NGO's which are working in the field of disaster risk reduction by creating department of NGO in ANDMA structure		by end-2008	ANDMA
	Establish academic consultation network with academy of science, faculty of Engineering and Polytechnic University for designing, prevention & mitigation projects		by end-2008	ANDMA
	Establish Emergency Operation Centers (EOCs) at the provincial level	Institution Building	by end-2009	ANDMA, Governors
	Establish response centers and teams at the regional level	Institution Building	by end-2009	ANDMA
	Establish community emergency response system	Institution Building	by end-2010	ANDMA
	Establish effective early warning system	Institution Building	by end-2009	ANDMA
	Develop back-up communication system based on Codan	Institution Building	by end-2008	ANDMA
	Establish ANDMA's offices along with the operational centers	Institution Building	by end-2009	ANDMA

Appendix I. (Continued)

Expected Outcomes	Policy Actions and Activities	Category	Timeframe	Responsible Agency
	Construct 12 regional storages for aid assistance and equipment	Institution Building	by end-2009	ANDMA
	Approve regular annual plans for disaster preparedness and response	Other Measures	continuously	GoA
	Complete collecting information related to risks and vulnerabilities at the na-tional and sub-national level and finalizes disaster risk analysis	Other Measures	by end-2009	ANDMA
	Develop a guideline for disaster preparedness and response planning	Other Measures	by end-2008	ANDMA
	Develop Standardized Operational Procedures(SPO) for quick assessment and response, reporting, and for rapid mobilization of international assistance	Other Measures	by end-2008	ANDMA, line ministries
	Develop and operationalize the provincial disaster management plans	Other Measures	by end-2009	ANDMA, Governors
	Improve public awareness activities and raise national awareness about disaster risks and vulnerabilities	Other Measures	continuously	ANDMA
	Integrate disaster risk reduction in national and sub-national policies and plans' – responsible all line ministries	Other Measures	by end-2010	ANDMA & All Ministries

PILLAR: SOCIAL PROTECTION & REFUGEES
SECTOR: REFUGEES AND INTERNALLY DISPLACES PERSONS

Objectives or Outcomes	Policy Actions and Activities	Category	Timeframe	Responsible Agency
Refugees and Internally Dis-placed Persons (IDPs) return voluntarily according to agreed principles and proce-dures	Identify bottlenecks (political, security, economic, social and legal) facing re-turnees (refugees and IDPs) and promote sustainable solutions for them with special focus on chronically poor women, disabled and widows. (dispute settle-ment mechanisms land tenure, pasture management, rehabilitated livestock, productive infrastructure, vocational skills, shelters and etc	Legislation/ Gender Cross Cutting Issues	2008 – 2013	MoRR, MoFA
	Civil registry law with regards to the Kuchis implemented in close cooperation with Ministry of Interior, Border and Tribal Affairs	Legislation	2008 – 2013	MoRR, MoFA
	Tri-partite agreements are concluded between countries of asylum, Afghanistan, and UNHCR, fully reflecting the principles of voluntary, dignified and gradual return, continue to guide the conduct of the voluntary repatriation operation.	Legislation	2008 – 2013	MoRR, MoFA
	Tripartite Commissions are convened as the key policy arena within which deci-sions on the conduct of voluntary repatriation operations are taken	Other Measures	2008 – 2013	MoRR, MoFA
	Annual return planning figures, taking into account Afghanistan's absorption capacities are discussed and agreed upon in Tri-Partite Commissions, especially with the Governments of Pakistan and Iran.	Other Measures	2008 – 2013	MoRR, MoFA

Objectives or Outcomes	Policy Actions and Activities	Category	Timeframe	Responsible Agency
	Monitor border movements, interview returnees and document violations of articles of agreements, due attention to be given to counter narcotics issues	Other Measures/ CN Cross Cutting Issues	2008 – 2013	MoRR, MoFA, MCN, MoI
	Ensure continued donor support for initial reintegration assistance in critical areas like housing, water/sanitation, and financial support	Other Measures	2008 – 2013	MoRR, MoFA, MRRD
	Continued emphasis on social protection (e.g. establishment of referral systems, centers, networks for vulnerable groups and individuals with focus on women)	Other Measures	2008 – 2013	MoRR, MoFA, MoLSAMD, MRRD, MD, UNHCR, ILO, IOM and partners
	Implement programs for improved employment opportunities, skill development, basic literacy and numeracy, access to health care	Other measures	2008-2013	MoRR, MRRD, MoUD, MoE, MoPH, MoLSA
Government's capacity to manage and support return and reintegration prgrammes is strengthened	Policies adjusted to make provisions for returning refugees and IDPs in national programs Enhance capacity to prepare and reach out information to Afghans either in or outside of the country.	Legislation Institution Building	2008-2009 2008 – 2013	MoRR, MoFA, MRRD, UNHCR MoRR, MoFA
	Computerize all HRM and project activities to strengthen Human Resource and Project Management	Institution Building/ AC Cross Cutting Issues	2008-10	MoRR
	Strengthened public management capacity to develop policy and negotiate agreements and strengthen ant-corruption measures	Institution Building/ AC Cross Cutting Issues	2008-10	
	Management and implementation of Land Allocation Scheme is improved and supported to increase number of sites (5-10) in key returnee provinces. Land allocation and registration monitored for anti-corrupt practices	Institution Building/ AC Cross Cutting Issues	2008 – 2013	MoRR, MoFA
	Reforms to the structure, organization and work processes of the Ministry and provincial Departments of Refugees and Repatriation are completed.	Insitution building	2008-210	MoRR, Civil Service Commi-ssion
	Capacity building and technical assistance	Institution Building	2008-2013	MoRR, Civil Service Commi-ssion
	Enhance communications and interactions between Kabul and provinces	Institution Building	2008-2010	MoRR, Civil Service commi-ssion
	Data collection, analysis (disaggregated by gender) and knowledge generation	Institution Building/ Gender Cross Cutting Issues	2008-2010	MoRR
	Policy advice to provincial authorities,	Institution Building	2008-2013	MoRR, MoFA, UNHCR

Appendix I. (Continued)

Objectives or Outcomes	Policy Actions and Activities	Category	Timeframe	Responsible Agency
	Coordination of interventions and material assistance support.	Institution Building	TBD	MoRR, MRRD, MHUD, MoLSA
	Improved internal coordination mechanisms by establishing joint committee (ministries and related agencies) for policy and operational planning and development on land Allocation program	Other Measures	TBD	MoRR, UNHCR
	Data on Afghans in neighboring countries (Iran and Pakistan) is analyzed and Afghanistan's absorption capacity is assessed Analysis to be gender and children sensitive	Other Measures/ Gender Cross Cutting Issues	2008-2009	MoRR, MoF
	Budget allocations to sectors and provinces takes account of population expansion as a result of returns	Other Measures	2007-2010	MoRR, MoUD, MoFA, MRRD, MoE, MoPH
	National initiatives addressing returnee needs (both Male and Female) and local host communities developed and enhanced in housing, area-based and community development programs with particular emphasis on employment, livelihoods, and skill development.	Other Measures	By end-first half of 2009	MoRR, ANDMA, MRRD, pro-vincial authorities
	Monitoring and evaluation mechanisms for tracking the reintegration process are established	Other Measures	By end of 2009	MoRR, MoFA MoFA, MoRR, MoLSA
Improved terms of stay and conditions for Afghans in neighboring countries	Research and analysis to support policy advocacy Negotiations with neighboring countries led by Ministry of Foreign Affairs and Ministry of Refugees and Repatriation for more predictable and clearer legal status and renewable documentation	Other Measures Other Measures	By end of 2013 2009-2013	
	Identification of program interventions to support policy objectives	Other Measures		
Bilateral agreements on temporary labor migration progress	Research and analysis to support policy and public advocacy (Labor migration flows identified and quantified, cross border commuting assessed)	Other Measures	TBD	MoRR, MoISAMD, MoFA, MoI
	Negotiations with neighboring countries led by Ministry of foreign Affairs and Ministry of Labor and Social Affairs (Agreements with neighboring and countries in the region that accept laborers)	Other Measures	End of 2013	MoRR, MoFA, MoLSA
	Strengthened public management capacity to develop policy and negotiate agreements	Other Measures	End of 2013	MoRR, MoFA, MoLSAMD, MRRD, MD, UNHCR, ILO, IOM and partners
	International conference on "Return and reintegration in Afghanistan"	Other Measures	2008	MoRR, MoFA, MoLSAMD, MRRD, MD, UNHCR, ILO, IOM and partners

Objectives or Outcomes	Policy Actions and Activities	Category	Timeframe	Responsible Agency
	Tripartite commissions with Pakistan and Iran meet four times a year	Other Measures	2008-20013	MoRR, MoFA UNHCR
	Tripartite agreement renewed with Iran on Annual basis and signed with Paki-stan for three years	Other Measures	2008	MoRR, UNHCR

APPENDIX II. MONITORING MATRIX

PILLAR: SECURITY
SECTOR: SECURITY

Expected Outcomes	Indicators	Baselines	Targets
Effectively coordinated security sector	Index on progress of establishing joint coordination centers for the ANA and ANP	Under Assessment, 13 Coordination centers proposed	Ehanced coordination amongst security setor ministry/ departments (2013)
	# of recruited ANA personnel	64, 996 (Apr 2008)	80,000 (end 2009)
	% completion of PAR process in MoD	80% (Apr 2008)	100% (end 2009)
ANA operationally capable of performing those missions and tasks assigned	Index on progress of equipping the ANA with technical and administrative support Index on progress of equipping the ANA by Land and Air Force	Under Assessment Under Assessment	TBD TBD
	Index on equipping the ANA training centers	Under Assessment	TBD
	% of ANA personnel trained	77% (2008)	100% (2013)
ANA expenditures are fiscally sustainable	% of ANA expenditure funded from Government Revenue	21% (2008) (core budget)	TBD
	# of recruited ANP personnel	80,426 (Apr 2008)	82,000 (end 2008)
ANP operationally capable of performing those missions and tasks assigned and crime rates reduced	% completion of PAR process in MoI % of ANP received logistical support	60% (Apr 2008) 85% (Apr 2008)	100% (end 2009) 100% (2010)
	% of ANP personnel trained	55% (Apr 2008)	100% (2010)
Operational border posts able to protect national sover-eignty	Index on equipping the border posts	Under Assessment	100% (2013)
ANP and ABP expenditures are fiscally sustainable	% of ANP and ABP expenditure funded from Government Revenue	8.9% (2008) (core budget)	TBD

Appendix II. (Continued)

Expected Outcomes	Indicators	Baselines	Targets
Reduced level of deaths and casualties caused by UXOs, reduce the number of affected communities and increased safety precautions	# square meters cleared of UXOs	128,478,929 square meters of land	Clearance of 540 million square meters before end 2010
Enhanced public trust on government ability to deliver justice and security as IAGs are disbanded and reintegrated	# of districts cleared from IAGs	21 Districts complied so far	51 Districts targeted
Eventual eradication of Poppy Production and crack down on drug trafficking	# ha of poppy cultivated land area	193,000 ha	By 2013, the area under poppy cultivation will be reduced by half compared to 2007 levels

PILLAR: GOVERNANCE, RULE OF LAW AND HUMAN RIGHTS
SECTOR: GOVERNANCE

Expected Outcomes	Indicators	Baselines	Targets
Empowered National Assembly	Index on the progress of empowering the National Assembly.	Under Assessment	Empowered National Assembly to fulfill effectively its constitutionally man-dated roles (2013)
Reformed Public Administration	Index on the progress of reforming Public Administration.	Under Assessment	Reformed Public Administration (2013)
Trained and Capable Public Sector Workforce	Index on the progress of building capacity of Public Sector Workforce.	Under Assessment	By Jaddi 1392 (end-2013), a training policy for the entire public sector work-force shall be developed and implemented. Institutional arrangements shall be put in place to ensure that each member of the workforce gets trained at least once in two years in organization specific and job specific training along with the generic training.
Merit Based Appointments and Performance-based Re-views	Index on the progress of implementing systems, mecha-nisms and procedures to implement merit based ap-pointments and performance-based reviews.	Under Assessment	By March 2011, in furtherance of the work of the Civil Service Commission, merit-based appointments, vetting procedures and performance-based re-views will be undertaken for civil service positions at all levels of government

Expected Outcomes	Indicators	Baselines	Targets
Corruption Reduced	Index on the progress of introducing systems, mechanisms and procedures to reduce and monitor corruption at different levels in the government and the judiciary.	Under Assessment	By Jaddi 1392 (end-2013), the corruption in the judiciary and the government at all levels especially in security, customs, civil administration and municipalities will be significantly reduced.
Enhanced Availability of Information to Public and Enforcement	Index on the progress on enhanced availability of Information to Public and Enforcement.	Under Assessment	By Jaddi 1389 (end-2010), the legal framework required for exercise of this right provided under the constitution will be put in place, distributed to all judicial and legislative institutions, and made available to the public and, implemented.
Improved Participation of Women in Governance	Index on the progress of putting plans, systems and mechanisms in place for improved participation of women in governance.	Under Assessment	By Jaddi 1389 (end-2010) In line with Afghanistan's MDGs, female participation in all Afghan governance institutions, including elected and appointed bodies and the civil service, will be strengthened by providing a specific per-cent reservation of seats by enacting a law of affirmative action.
Nation Prepared for Disaster Management	Index on the progress of putting plans, systems and mechanisms in place at all levels for Disaster Management.	Under Assessment	By Jaddi 1389 (end-2010), an effective system of disaster preparedness and response will be in place.
Strong and Capable Independent Election Commission holding regular national and sub national Elections as mandated by the Constitution	Index on the progress of creating a strong and capable Independent Election Commission holding regular national and sub national Elections as mandated by the Constitution.	Under Assessment	The Afghanistan Independent Electoral Commission will have the high integrity, capacity and resources to undertake elections in an increasingly fiscally sustainable manner by Jaddi 1388 (end-2009), with the Government of Afghanistan contributing to

Appendix II. (Continued)

Expected Outcomes	Indicators	Baselines	Targets
			the extent possible to the cost of future elections from its own resources.
Single National Identity Document	Index on the progress of providing single national iden-tity to all citizens in the country.	Under Assessment	By Jaddi 1392 (end-2013), civil registry with a single national identity docu-ment will be established
Census Completed and Re-sults Published	Index on the progress of Census operations and publishing of results.	Under Assessment	Census enumeration fully completed during summer of 2008 in all districts. Publishing the full results of census in 2010
Statistical Baselines Estab-lished and the Statistical Ca-pacity Built	Index on the progress of building statistical capacity in the country and establishing statistical baselines.	Under Assessment	By Jaddi 1392 (end-2013), Reliable statistical baselines will be established for all quantitative benchmarks and statistical capacity built to track progress against them.
Mapping of Villages and Go-zars and reviewing their boundaries	Index on the progress of mapping and reviewing the boundaries of Villages and Gozars.	Under Assessment	By Jaddi 1388 (end-2009), Government will carry out political and adminis-trative mapping of the country with villages and gozars as basic units and, the political and administrative maps will be made available at all levels for the purpose of elections, socio-economic planning and implementation of sub-national governance policy.
Modern Land Administration System Established	Index on the progress of establishing a modern land administration system including settlement of land disputes.	Under Assessment	A community based process for registration of land in all administrative units and the registration of titles will be started for all urban areas and rural areas by Jaddi 1387 (end-2008). A fair system for settlement of land disputes will

Expected Outcomes	Indicators	Baselines	Targets
			be in place by Jaddi 1386 (end-2007).
Sub National Governance Policy Developed	Index on the progress of putting in place legal, policy, institutions and other systems and procedures for strengthening the sub-national governance.	Under Assessment	By end-1389 (20 March 2011), the Government will ensure formulation and implementation of sub-national governance policy and, its legal and regulatory framework. This will be done through a national dialogue on sub-national governance and, with technical support of international community.
Government Offices physically equipped to fulfill their Role	Index on the progress of providing basic facilities and amenities to all government offices.	Under Assessment	By end-1392 (20 March 2013), all the councils and offices including munici-palities will have basic facilities and amenities including adequate built up space, computers, communication facility and furniture. The key officials at national and sub national level will have adequate means of mobility to make connection with the communities they are serving
Free Flow of Information from all the District Centers	Index on the progress of development of a comprehensive MIS for free flow of information from all the District Centers	Under Assessment	By end-1389 (20 March 2011), all the district centers of the country will have internet facility to facilitate the flow of information between the districts, municipalities, provinces and, the centre i.e. Kabul.
Human Rights Realized, Pro-tected, Promoted and Ex-tended	Index on the progress of putting in place legal, policy, institutional and other systems in place to realize, protect, promote and extend human rights in the country.	Under Assessment	By Jaddi 1389 (end-2010), the Government's capacity to comply with and report on its human rights treaty obligations will be strengthened

Appendix II. (Continued)

Expected Outcomes	Indicators	Baselines	Targets
PILLAR: GOVERNANCE, RULE OF LAW AND HUMAN RIGHTS **SECTOR: JUSTICE AND THE RULE OF LAW**			
Public can rely on effectively organized and professionally staffed justice institutions	Index on the progress of putting in place systems so that public can rely on effectively organized and professionally staffed justice institutions.	Under Assessment	by end 2010 (1391), reforms will strengthen the professionalism, credibility and integrity of key institutions of the justice system (the Ministry of Justice, the Judiciary, the Attorney-General's Office, the Ministry of the Interior and the National Directorate of Security)
	# of oversight and disciplinary mechanism developed and implemented by AGO, MoJ and Supreme Court	Under Assessment	TBD
	Index on the progress of providing Justice institutions access to infrastructure, transportation, equipment, and supplies adequate to support effective delivery of justice services	Under Assessment	By the end of 2010 (1391), justice institutions will be fully functional and operational in each province of Afghanistan, and the average time to resolve contract disputes will be reduced as much as possible
Justice institutions have access to infrastructure, transportation, equip-ment, and supplies adequate to sup-port effective delivery of justice services	# of functioning and adequately resourced, judicial institutions in each province	Under Assessment	TBD
	# of functional prisons (Detention Centers, DC)	33 Provincial DC 184 District DC	TBD
	# of Adequate detention and correction facilities for women	2 (Kabul, Herat) 18 Provinces with no facilities	TBD
Legal education and vocational train-ing are adequate to provide justice professionals with sufficient know-how to perform their task	Index on the progress of improving legal education and vocational training to provide justice professionals with sufficient know-how to perform their task	Under Assessment	By end-2013 the Justice Institutions will Have recruited and promoted justice profes-sionals on merit, based on established policies and procedures, including meeting the target of 30% of the professional staff being female

Expected Outcomes	Indicators	Baselines	Targets
Statutes are clearly drafted, constitutional and the product of effective and consultative drafting processes	Index on the progress of making Statues clearly drafted, constitutional and the product of effective and consultative drafting processes.	Under Assessment	TBD
Justice institutions effectively perform their functions in a harmonized and interlinked manner	Index on Progress of enacting and implementing new criminal procedure Index on the progress of putting in place systems so that Justice institutions effectively perform their functions in a harmonized and interlinked manner.	Under Assessment Under Assessment	By end-2013 the Justice Institutions will have mapped in detail the processes linking all justice institutions, and have streamlined them to improve information systems and business processes, with the aim of reducing delays in processing of cases, administrative costs and vulnerability to corruption
Citizens are more aware of their rights and justice institutions are better able to enforce them.	Index on the progress of making citizens more aware of their rights and justice institutions being better able to enforce them.	Under Assessment	By end-2013, the Justice Institutions will encourage press coverage of justice pro-ceedings, public attendance at those proceedings, and general public understanding of the process at each stage of such proceedings. The justice institutions should encour-age and participate in the development of outreach programs within civil society in-cluding curriculum for public education at all levels
Criminal and Civil justice is admin-istered effectively, and in accordance with law, the Constitution, and inter-national standards	Index on the progress of putting in place systems so that Criminal and Civil justice is administered effectively, and in accordance with law, the Constitution, and inter-national standards.	Under Assessment	By end-2013, the Justice Institutions will have established an easily accessible and functioning public complaints system in at least eight major provincial capitals with clear processes for handling complaints

Appendix II. (Continued)

Expected Outcomes	Indicators	Baselines	Targets
Justice institutions are transparent and accountable	Index on the progress of making justice institutions transparent and accountable.	Under Assessment	By end-2013, the Justice Institutions will have determined their vulnerabilities to corruption and established policies and procedures to eliminate such vulnerabilities

PILLAR: INFRASTRUCTURE SECTOR: ENERGY

Expected Outcomes	Indicators	Baselines	Targets
An enabling environment for private sector in-vestment in energy sector created	Index on the progress of creating an enabling environment for private sector invest-ment in energy sector.	TBD	Enabling Environment for Private Sector by 2009
	% of households electrified in urban areas	30%	65% (2011)
Expanded public power grid	% of households electrified in rural areas.	10%	25% (2011)
	% of non-residential consumers provided electricity.	35%	90% (2011)
	Index on the progress of expanding public power grid.	TBD	TBD
Increased Access to Rural Energy Services	Index on the progress of increasing access to rural energy	6%	A strategy for the development and use of renew-able energies will be developed by March 2008
Promotion of Private sector	Index on the progress of promotion of private sector in energy sector	TBD	TBD
Restructured Energy Sector Governance and Commercialized operations	Index on the progress of restructuring energy sector governance and commercialized operations	60% 60%	Energy sector governance restructuring and commercialized operations by 2010
	% of recovery of cost of supply		75% of the costs will be recovered from users by March 2011

PILLAR: INFRASTRUCTURE SECTOR: TRANSPORT

ROAD TRANSPORT

Expected Outcomes	Indicators	Baselines	Targets
	% of target 3263 Km of regional highways or roads to the neighboring countries fully upgraded and rehabilitated.	2236 km has been rehabilitated	Fully upgraded and maintained ring road and roads to neighboring countries by March 2009.
	% of all villages connected by all-weather roads	Target has achieved 65% (Out of 38,000 villages 9,954 villages have access to rural roads)	40 % of all villages to be connected by all-weather roads to

Expected Outcomes	Indicators	Baselines	Targets
			the national road system by the end of 2010.
	Having updated transport policies/regulation and improved transport management system to enforce and implement the states law and regulations related to the transport sector	Outdated policies and regulations which need to be improved / Although that some management improvement have been in place	Improved and updated transport management by 2011
Improved connectivity through out Afghanistan and to the foreign destinations within the region.	% of all roads in municipalities (i.e. cities) improved to a good standard (with having bus and truck terminals in all the provincial centers).	15-20 % roads are in good condition with some improved services	70% of all roads in municipalities (i.e., cities) are improved to a good standard by the end of 2011.
	% of roads in maintainable condition that receive regular maintenance	out of 2236 km of rehabilitated regional highways, 860 km receives regular maintenance	Fiscally sustainable system for roads maintenance by June 2008
	Index on the progress of putting a fiscally sustainable road maintenance system in place by March 2008 and its cover-age	40%	A fiscally sustainable road maintenance system by June 2008.
	Improved sidewalks and shoulders (km) (along with improved and connected drainage system)	15-20 % roads are in good condition with some improved services	Improved sidewalks and shoulders by 2010
Lower road user costs	Index on the rationalization of road user costs.	0%	Lower road user fees by 75% by end 2008.
Less journey time lost due to congestion	Index on the improvement of Public Transport Provision and roads in urban areas and inter-provinces.	TBD	Less journey time by end 2012
Improved air quality.	Index on the progress of the process of enforcing the environmental law in transport sector.	TBD	Environmental protection from air pollution by End of 2009
CIVIL AVIATION			
	Index on the progress of the process of completion of In-ternational Civil Aviation Organization (ICAO) compli-ance for Kabul and Herat Airports.	40% Kabul 0% Heart	Kabul International Airport and Herat Airport are in compliance with the International Civil Aviation Organization's (ICAO) and the International Air Transport Association's (IATA's) requirements by March 2011.
	Index on the progress of the process of up gradation of Kandhar, Jalalabad and Mazar-e-Sharif Airports with	50% (KDH) 10% (JBD) 0% (MZR)	Mazar-i-Sharif, Jalalabad and Kandahar will be up-graded with

Appendix II. (Continued)

Expected Outcomes	Indicators	Baselines	Targets
	run-way repairs, air navigation, fire and rescue and communication equipment.		runway repairs, air navigation, fire and rescue, and communications equipment by March 2011.
Increased domestic and international passengers and freight traffic by air.	Index on the progress of the process of up gradation of 7 airports to facilitate domestic air transportation.	50% Qalainaw 30% Maimana 0% Faizabad 0% Chaghcharan 0% Zaranj 0% Lashkar Gah 0% Tarin Kowt	Seven other domestic airports will be upgraded to facilitate domestic air transportation by March 2011.
	# of International airports constructed /rehabilitated		2 (End 2010)
	# of domestic airports constructed/rehabilitated	The feasibility studies for the 10 domestic airports have been done.	10 (2013)
	Air travel price index comparable to international standards.	For have Airport services cost comparable with international standards ,ICAO person-nel is developing a tariff plan for various component of airport services on the basis of the Airport master Planning study report of 2004.	Air transport services and costs will be increasingly competitive with international market standards and rates by March 2011.
Improved governance of civil aviation sector.	Index on the progress of Institutional reform programs and a reduction in the requirement of ISAF to use air facilities (Create a new Civil Aviation Authority (CAA), and restore control of Afghan airspace to the Civil Aviation Authority.) Index on the progress of massive capacity building pro-grams in the civil aviation sector.	5% To enhance capacity of the Ministry, a training program has been finalized to the tune of 640000. ADB is funding the project.40 students will be trained under the program.	Improved governance in civil aviation sector by end 2011 By end-2013, transport sector capacity will be enhanced
		All the programs will be conducted in 2008. 30 Fire Fighter have been trained in Oman and another 17 other personnel will be trained in 2008. Under the Transition Plan also for key functions such as ATC, CNS and Fire Fighting on the job trainings will be provided by ICAO experts. The identifica-tion & the number of the	

Expected Outcomes	Indicators	Baselines	Targets
		beneficiaries will be finalized by March 2008. Further 200 students was sent to FAA academy in U.S.A and 20 others will be sent by end of 2008.	
OVERALL TRANSPORT SECTOR			
Improved Governance in the Transport Sector	Index on the progress of putting institutional mechanisms in place for better governance of the Transport Sector.	Inter-Ministerial Working Group established. TOR under review	Governance of Road Transport sector progressively improved by by 2013
Business environment for private sector development improved to create jobs and reduce poverty.	Index on the progress of passing enabling legislations and enabling regulations for efficient working of the transport sector and various players therein.	TBD	Improved business environment for private sector by 2012
	% increase in amount of taxes and duties collected through cross border trade	TBD	TBD
Access to secure tenure and improved services and public facilities for inhabitants of informal settlements	Index on the progress of providing access to secured tenure and improved services and public facilities for inhabitants of informal settlements % of informal settlements having access to basic services	0% 10-15 %	The registration of titles will be started for all major urban areas and a fair system for settlement of land disputes will be in place. 50 % by 2013
	% of informal settlements have access to secure tenure	0%	90% by 2013
Improved institutional coordination and monitoring of key urban indicators	Index on the progress of improving institutional arrangements for coordination and monitoring of key urban indicators.	In principals all the key institutions have agreed upon on but details and actions have been to prepared	Improved institutional coordination by end 2008
Increased access for urban households to basic services	Index on the progress of providing improved to basic services by urban households.	Due to capacity limitation within municipalities; the urban services delivering are very low and aren't sufficient and efficient	By March 2011, Municipal Governments will have strengthened capacity to manage urban development and to ensure that municipal services are delivered effectively, efficiently and transparently;
	% of investment in urban road networks	10-15 % urban roads are improved with some improved services.	70% by 2013
	% of households having access to safe water supply in Kabul.	18-21 % h/h has access to safe piped water	in line with MDG investment in water supply and sanitation will ensure that 50% of households

Appendix II. (Continued)

Expected Outcomes	Indicators	Baselines	Targets
	% of households having access to piped water supply in other major urban areas except Kabul.	15-18% h/h has access to safe piped water	(h/h) in Kabul will have access to piped water by March 2011 30% of households (h/h) in other major urban areas will have access to piped water"; by March 2011
	% of households having access to sanitation facilities in Kabul.	5-8% h/h have access to improved sanitation	50 % by March 2011
	% of households having access to sanitation facilities in other major urban areas except Kabul.	10-12% h/h have access to improved sanita-tion	30% by March 2011
	Proportion of open green spaces per developed urban area	less than 5%	30% By 2013
	Index on the progress of providing increased availability of affordable shelter.	less than 5%	60% by 2013
Increased availability of affordable shelter	% of urban residents having access to affordable finance % of urban residents having access to housing subsidy	0% The process is underway to implement mort-gage system	TBD 50% by 2013
	% completion of city development plans for 34 provinces	20%	90% by 2013
Strengthened institutional capacity to plan and manage urban develop-ment	Index on the progress of building strengthened institutional capacity to plan and manage urban development.	The process is under way has been recently initiated	by 2013 Sustainable water resource management strategies and plans covering drinking water supply will be developed along with improved sanitation. Municipalities will be operating under updated laws and polices and effectively and transparently delivering urban services, with better customer service system
PILLAR: INFRASTRUCTURE SECTOR: WATER RESOURCES			
Improved water sector legal and governance structures and institutions in place	Index on the progress of putting in place improved water sector legal and governance structures and institutions in place.	Partially good (improving)	Improved water sector governance by 2013

Expected Outcomes	Indicators	Baselines	Targets
Sustainable water resources management strategies and plans covering irrigation and drinking water supply developed and implemented.	Index on the progress of developing and implementing sustainable water resources management strategies and plans covering irrigation and drinking water.	Strategies 70% completed Feasibilities studies for large projects are continue	Sustainable water resource management strategies and plans covering irrigation and drinking water supply will be developed by end-2008, and irrigation invest-ments will result in at least 30% of water coming from large waterworks by March, 2011.
	% of water coming from large waterworks.	10%	TBD
	Index on the improvement of water resources for irrigation and drink-ing water purposes.	25-30%	Improved water resources for drinking and irrigation purpose by 2013
	# of Hydrometric stations installed and equipped	3 out of 177	TBD
	% of lands irrigated through rehabilitated and new water works	1.8 Million Ha	Additional 450,000 ha (2013)
	% of sites where 90% of tail-enders receive enough water on time	TBD	TBD
Water resources for irrigation and Drinking purposes improved	# of sites reserved as suitable drinking water resource	Based on recent surveys 20 % of the sites have been reserved	By 2013 sites reserved as suitable drinking water re-source
	% of beneficiaries, by gender, whose technical knowledge and skills for managing irrigation assets have increased considerably	TBD	TBD
	% of households in other urban areas except Kabul have access to piped water	15-18%	30% by end of 2011
	% of households in Kabul have access to piped water	18-21%	50% (2010)
	# of water points available for rural households	TBD	TBD

PILLAR: INFRASTRUCTURE
SECTOR: INFORMATION AND COMMUNICATION TECHNOLOGY

Expected Outcomes	Indicators	Baselines	Targets
E-Afghanistan created	Index on the progress of creation of E-Afghanistan	E-Government policies, strategies and pilot projects are already launched.	E-Afghanistan created by 2013
	# of government offices having official web presence # of provincial government offices having official web presence	15 3	All Government Offices (2013) All Prov. Government Offices (2013)

Appendix II. (Continued)

Expected Outcomes	Indicators	Baselines	Targets
	# of government offices having Chief Information Officer (CIO)	0	All Government Offices (2013)
	# of government offices connected through the fiber optic	20	All Government Offices (2013)
Enabling Environment	Index on the progress of putting legal enabling environment for the ICT Sector in place.	At present telecom law, An independent regula-tor ATRA and open telecom market is the guar-antor of the enabling environment.	Enabling Environment by 2013
	Index on the progress of building institutions for the ICT Sector.	Ministry of Communications and IT and Na-tional ICT Council are the existing.	ICT Sector institutions will be built (2013)
ICT Literacy improved	Index on the progress of establishment of ICT centers in 34 Provincial capitals	15	Improved ICT Literacy, 34 provinces 2013
	Index on the progress of putting in place improved infrastructure for the ICT Sector.	GCN, DCN, VCN, CCN, OFC and NDC pro-jects are brought, implemented at present.	By end-2010, a national telecommunications network to be put in place so that more than 80% of Afghans will have access to affordable telecommunications.
	% of Afghans having access to affordable telecommunications	70%	80% (2010)
Improved ICT coverage and Infrastructure	% increase in annual revenue generated from the ICT Sector	US$ 75 million	More than US$ 100 million dollars per year are gener-ated in public revenues by end 2010
	% of population access to mobile phones	20%	Increased Access to mobile phones
	number of internet users	500,000	Increased Access to internet
	# of Post Offices connected to a well-functioning communication network and equipped	44	Increased number of post offices connected
PILLAR: INFRASTRUCTURE **SECTOR: MINES AND NATURAL RESOURCES**			
Strong regulatory framework in place	Approval of Gas Law Approval of Mineral Regulations Approval of Hydrocarbons Regulations	Minerals and Hydrocarbons law has been passed	Creating enabling environment including legal one for increased investment in mining sector (2013)

Expected Outcomes	Indicators	Baselines	Targets
Increased Private Sector Investment in mining sector	Increase in net revenue of ministry of Mines	In current year (1386) net revenue of ministry of mines is US$ 32 million	Increase net revenue of ministry of mines after seven years to US$ 1 billion
Geophysical and geological information available	Survey of Minerals and Hydrocarbons	Surveys conducted in this regard cover only 10% and 4% of country's total hydrocarbons and minerals respectively	Survey of 5% area of country's natural resources (minerals and hydrocarbons)
Increased access to Gas resources	Renovation of Shaberghan gas network and extension of Mazar-e-sharif gas pipeline and its network	Currently consumers of Afghan gas is less than 1% of total population	Increasing gas consumers to 5% of total popula-tion
Increased access to water resources	Increased access to safe drinking water	Partial study of water in Kabul river basin has been done, but the water studied do not fulfill the need of Kabul population. Recently assessment study in Kabul river basin has been started through research and Geo engineering enterprises with support of JICA and USGS	Availability of under ground water with quality and quantity

PILLAR: EDUCATION
SECTOR: EDUCATION AND MEDIA, CULTURE AND YOUTH
PRIMARY AND SECONDRY EDUCATION

	Index on the progress of putting systems, institutions, procedures and legal framework in place for improving the quality of educa-tion.	Started in 1386 and will con-tinued till 1389 (% TBD)	EMIS is completed, NIMA, NCB are on going, Education Law's draft is completed, Law for private Schools are completed.
	Index on the process of designing and conducting competency test for teachers including principals.	Started in 1387 (% TBD)	70% of teachers pass competency test (minimum of 40% women)
	No. of competent teachers (male and female).	54,093 male (2002) 20,508 female (2002) EMIS	At least 140,000 competent teachers Increase Female teachers by 50%
	No. of competent principals (male and female)	Under Assessment	26,000 school principals
Improved quality of education	Primary Student/Teacher ratio	43 (2002)	TBD
	Government Expenditure per student	$12.1 (2002)	TBD
	Index on the progress of designing and conducting competency test for students.	Started in 1387	Competency Test for students prepared and implemented.

Appendix II. (Continued)

Expected Outcomes	Indicators	Baselines	Targets
	Index on the progress of preparation and implementation of new curriculum for primary and secondary schools.	1-6 Class Book developed and 7-12 Class under developing	New curriculum for primary and secondary schools pre-pared and implemented.
	Index on the progress of establishment of separate body responsi-ble for standards and accreditation of all primary and secondary schools.	On progress and WB is sup-porting this part	Established separate body responsible for standards and accreditation of all primary and secondary schools.
	Adult Literacy rate	28% (2000)	TBD
	Total enrolment level (millions)	5.9 million enrolled at schools (1386)	7.7 m children enrolled (1389)
Literacy rates improved	% of boys and girls enrolled.	35% and 35% respectively	Enrolment Rates (Boys 75%, Girls 60%) (1389)
	No. of illiterates in the country (male and female)	11.2 million illiterate (1386)	Separate program for non-formal education in place
	Primary Completion Rate (Percentage of all children that com-pleted primary schooling)	32.3% (2005)	TBD
Equal opportunity for all	Percentage of children having access to schools	55%	75% of school-age children to be within reach of a school with significantly reduced gender and provincial disparity
	Total number of learning spaces (formal/informal)	7,027 (2002)	TBD
	ratio of boys and girls enrolled	70% boys (2002) 30% girls (2002)	50% each
	No. of new school buildings constructed with basic amenities for both male and female	692 1386	At least 90% schools and buildings have male and female facilities by 1389
	Index on the progress of providing equal opportunity for all for education	establishment of (1,200 new schools and 1,200 CBS)and construction of 692 new schools, recruitment of 149,000 teachers (40,000 Female)	Established and constructed new schools, recruitment of teachers, especially female teachers.
HIGHER EDUCATION			
	Index on the progress of putting in place policies, institutions and systems for improving quality of academic teaching and research.	To be determined	Improved quality of academic teaching and research by 2013

Expected Outcomes	Indicators	Baselines	Targets
Improved quality of academic teaching and research	No. of faculty members benefited from such programs No. of degree or PG courses where curriculum has been revised	To be determined To be determined	Capacity building of faculty members through partnership programs New Curriculum for all courses in place by 1388
	No. of faculty members appointed (male and female)	To be determined	3000 new faculty members to be recruited from the region by 1389
	No. of students enrolled in the universities (male and female).	52200 enrolled male and female (1386)	100,000 students enrolled in universities by 1389
Improved access to higher education	No. of new facilities constructed at universities across the country. No. of new dormitories constructed for males. No. of new dormitories constructed for females.	7 facilities constructed 2 Female dormitories constructed	Construct 41 new facilities at universities across the country. Construction of 24 new dormitories (12 for women and 12 for men)
	Index on the progress of improving the quality of higher education.		
VOCATIONAL EDUCATION			
Improved quality of vocational education	Index on the progress of improving the quality of vocational education.	To be determined	Quality of vocational Education will considerably be improved (2013)
Improved access to vocational education	Index on the progress of improving access to vocational education. No. of persons trained through NSDP (male and female))	To be determined To be determined	Improved access to vocational education will be available (2013) The NSDP will provide training to 150,000 unemployed Afghan women and men through competitive bidding procedures
SPORTS			
Improved sports facilities	Index on the progress to provide improved sports facilities.	To be determined	Sport facilities will be improved in all provinces of Afghanistan (2013)
SCIENCE ACADEMY			
Enhanced contribution of the Academy in Science	Index on the progress to provide enhanced contribution of the Academy in Science.	To be determined	By 1388 make the Academy competent enough to promote the cause of science

Appendix II. (Continued)

Expected Outcomes	Indicators	Baselines	Targets
PILLAR: EDUCATION			
SECTOR: MEDIA, CULTURE AND YOUTH			
Afghanistan's cultural Heritage Protected and Preserved	% completion of cultural heritage inventory/registration	(1385) 41000 artifacts registered	Inventory of Afghan cultural artifacts prepared by 2010
	# of rehabilitated historical monuments	(up to 1386) 1271 archeological sites	All historical monuments rehabilitated and protected by 2010
	# of rehabilitated/constructed museums	4 Reconstructed	TBD
	Index on progress of taking measures to revive the Afghan cultural heritage, to stop the illegal removal	TBD	Measures will be taken to revive the Afghan cultural heri-tage, to stop the illegal removal of cultural material and to restore damaged monuments and artifacts by end-2010
Free and independent media	Index on progress of creating an environment for free and independent media	Media law is drafted, needs amendments	Media Law to be passed and implemented by 2008
	# of youths registered as volunteer corps for welfare activi-ties like rural health care campaigns etc.	TBD	TBD
Empowerment of Youth	# of youth clubs registered	60 LYC (Local Youth Councils) established in 60 Villages of 6 Provinces	TBD
	Index on the progress of providing legal, policy, institutional and systemic framework for empowerment of youth.	34925 both Male and female re-ceived training	Legal and Institutional framework for youth empowerment will be in place (2013)
Increased quality of health care services	Number of functional public and private hospitals set up	Under Assessment	Functional regulatory framework for quality health services in place by 2013
	No. of provinces where organized structure is in place	Under Assessment	Functional organization structure for quality health services in place by 2013
	Index on the progress of putting in place quality health care services	Under Assessment	Increased quality of health care services will be avail able throughout Afghanistan by 2013
	Overall score on the Balanced Scorecard	TBD	TBD

Expected Outcomes	Indicators	Baselines	Targets
Increased access to health care services	% of population within two hours walking distance from PHC services	ii) 66% - of population with nearby access to PHCs (2006)	90% of population with access to PHC services (2010)
	No. of health facilities, district, provincial and regional hospitals equipped with standard package of defined clini-cal and diagnostic services	Under Assessment	Comprehensive referral system integrated with BPHS & EPHS in place by 2013
	% of TB cases detected and treated	68% (2006)	Increase of 12% from the baseline
	% of Malaria cases detected and using preventive treatment	To be assessed	Reduction by 60% from baseline
	% of children under 1 year having received measles anti-gen, DPT & hepatitis dosage and polio drops	77%(2006)	Achieve and sustain above 90% national coverage (2013).
	% of children under 1 year received measles antigen	35% (2000)	Achieve above 90% coverage by 2010.
Effective Reproductive and Child health system	Maternal mortality ratio	1600 deaths /100,000 live births (2000)	Reduce by 50% between 2002 and 2013
	Under 5 mortality rate in the country (%)	257 deaths/1000 live births (2000)	Reduce by 50% between 2003 and 2013
	Infant mortality rate (IMR) in the country (%)	165 deaths per 1000 live births(2000)	Reduce infant mortality rate by 30% by 2013 from the baseline of 2000

PILLAR: AGRICULTURE & RURAL DEVELOPMENT
SECTOR: AGRICULTURE & RURAL DEVELOPMENT

Expected Outcomes	Indicators	Baselines	Targets
Improved service delivery within the Agriculture & Rural Development sector	Index on the progress of improving service delivery within the sector.	To be Assessed	Service Delivery will be improved within the Agriculture and Rural Development sector (2013)
Poverty Reduced in line with MDG targets	Index on the progress of aligning ARD Programs to promote sustainable growth and distribute wealth through CRD	TBD	ARD programs will be aligned to promote sustainable growth (2013)
	# of provinces, districts, villages covered by NFSP	10 provinces, 20 dis-tricts, 200 villages (2008)	34 Provinces (2013)
	# household beneficiaries covered by NFSP	20,000 households (2008)	To be Assessed

Appendix II. (Continued)

Expected Outcomes	Indicators	Baselines	Targets
	% reduction in malnourished population	57% reduction of population malnourished. (2008)	TBD
Improved Local Governance	Index on the progress of strengthening local governance.	TBD	Local Governance will be strengthened (2013)
	# CDCs established	16,502 (2007)	TBD
	# CDPs completed	16,263 (2007)	TBD
	# DDAs Established	256 (2007)	TBD
	# DDPs incorporated into provincial plans	# (2007)	TBD
	Index on the progress of increasing agriculture production and productivity.	TBD	Increased Agriculture Productivity (2013)
Increased Agriculture Production and Productivity Improved agriculture and rural infrastructure	# of increased irrigated areas	4500 hectares irrigated (2008)	TBD
	# hectares with new water efficiency techniques (2008)	1,000 hectares are water efrficient (2008)	TBD
	# hectares with new mgt techniques	1400 hectares (2008)	TBD
	Index on the progress of improving agriculture and rural infrastructure.	TBD	Improved Agriculture and Rural Infrastructure (2013)
	# of increased irrigated areas	4500 hectares irri-gated (2008)	TBD
	# hectares with new water efficiency techniques	1,000 hectares are water efficient (2008)	100% (2013)
	# hectares with new management techniques	1400 hectares (2008)	TBD
	% of rural population have access improved sanitation facilities	3% (2007)	70% (2013)
	Km of rural roads constructed and rehabilitated	13,500 km (2007)	To be assessed
	# Villages connected by road to the district centers or major service cen-ters.	4743 (2007)	56% of all villages (2013)
	% of rural population receiving income through participation in short-term employment generation activities (non-agrarian)	15% (2007)	TBD
	# of labor days generated	24.5m (2007)	110m (2013)
	# of villages benefiting from different sources of electricity	7665 (2007)	TBD

Expected Outcomes	Indicators	Baselines	Targets
	% of villages that will benefit from new/ rehabilitated small scale irrigation schemes	36% (2007)	68% (2013)
	# (hectares) of New irrigated areas increase	1.5 ha (2007)	TBD
	Improved water efficiency in existing irrigation	25% (2006)	TBD
Facilitated Economic Regeneration	Index on the progress of facilitating economic regeneration.	TBD	By end-2010, a policy and regulatory framework will be developed to support the establishment of small and medium rural en-terprises, and institutional support will be established in all 34 provinces to facilitate new entrepreneurial initiatives by rural communities and organisations
	# of rural households receiving services from formal financial institutions	219,000 (2007)	950,000 (2013)
	# of agri and non-agri-businesses established	TBD	TBD
	# of poor and vulnerable rural households supported through economic regeneration activities	TBD	TBD
Reduced poppy cultivation through Alternative Livelihood	Index on the progress of reducing poppy cultivation through alternative livelihoods.	TBD	By end-2010, decrease in the absolute and relative size of the drug economy in line with the Government's Millennium Development Goal target
PILLAR: SOCIAL PROTECTION **SECTOR: SOCIAL PROTECTION**			
Poverty and Vulnerability Reduction	Percentage of people living on less than US$1 a day	TBD	By end-2011 and in line with the MDGs the proportion of people living on less than US$1 a day will decrease by 3 percent per year.
	Percentage of people living below the poverty line (based on Spring data)	42% (2007)	By end-2012/13 the proportion of the people living below the poverty line will decline by 2 percent on annual basis (based on Spring poverty data)

Appendix II. (Continued)

Expected Outcomes	Indicators	Baselines	Targets
	Percentage of people who suffer from hunger	TBD	By end-2010 proportion of people who suffer from hunger will decrease by 5 percent
	Percentage of population below the minimum level of dietary energy consumption	45%	By end-2012/13 the proportion of the population below the minimum level of dietary energy consumption will decrease by 2 per-cent on annual basis
	Percentage of poor female headed households	TBD	By end-2010 number of female headed households that are chronically poor will be reduced by 20 percent and their employment rate will increase by 20 percent
	Percentage of employed females that on the head of the poor households	TBD	TBD
	Number of persons with disabilities received micro credit	TBD	
	Number of persons with disabilities received pension	TBD	
	Number of people received training	TBD	By end-2010 increased assistance will be provided to meet the special needs of all disabled people, including their integration into society through opportunities for education, skill development and gainful employment
	Number Persons with Disabilities received Inclusive and Exclusive Education Services	TBD	
	Number of Persons with Disabilities received Physical Rehabilitation Services	TBD	
	Number of Persons with Disability received other services	TBD	
Reduction in infant mortality	Percentage of underweight children in urban and rural; areas	TBD	By end-2012/13 prevalence of underweight children in rural and urban areas will decrease by 2 percent on annual basis
	Number of disabled that have gone trough skill development program	TBD	By end-2010 provide training for 150 000 people of which women should be 35 percent and disabled 10 percent

Expected Outcomes	Indicators	Baselines	Targets
	Number of women that have gone through skill development program	TBD	TBD
Improved Social Inclusion	Percentage of disabled in the public administration	TBD	By end-2012/13 the Government will employ at least 3 percent of disabled and 30 percent of women within its administration
	Percentage of women in the public administration	TBD	TBD
	Number of treated drug users	TBD	By end-2010 number of treated drug users will increase by 20 percent
Improved old age protection	Percentage of collected pension contribution of total pension payments	2%	By 2012/13 implement the pension reform and increase collection of the pension contributions
Improved disaster preparedness and response	Number of the people affected by the natural disaster	TBD	By end-2010 an effective system of disaster preparedness and response will be in place
	Monetary value of the destroyed assets as result of natural disaster	TBD	TBD
PILLAR: SOCIAL PROTECTION **SECTOR: REFUGEES & IDPS**			
Refugees and Internally Displaced Persons (IDPs) return voluntarily according to agreed principles and procedures	# of returnees (male, female)	3 million refugees (Pakistan 2.1 million, Iran 900,000), 140,000 IDPs (estimated)	**Scenario One** Present trend lines improve permitting 800,000 – 1 mill returns **Scenario Two** Current trends continue permitting 600,000-800,000 returns **Scenario Three** Current trends deteriorate permitting 400,000-600,000 returns
Government's capacity to manage and support return and reintegration programs is strengthened	The index on the progress of the process of strengthening government's capacity to manage and assist them	No measurable indicators currently available, existing capabilities are	By 2010, the first phase of reform within the Ministry of Refugees

Appendix II. (Continued)

Expected Outcomes	Indicators	Baselines	Targets
		varied but generally extremely limited countrywide	and Re-patriation should have been completed and inter-ministerial mechanisms for reintegration assistance should have been established and operating
Improved terms of stay and con-ditions for Afghans in neighbor-ing countries	# of tri-partite agreements signed	TPA signed with Iran Feb 2007 for one year. TPA signed with Pakistan in Aug 2007 for three years	Agreement with Iran to be renewed annually during the period 2008-2013. Agreement with Pakistan to be extended from 2009-2103
Bilateral agreements on tempo-rary labor migration progress	# of Bilateral Agreements	Currently there are no bilateral agreements covering temporary labor migration	Agreement reached with Iran on temporary labor migration by 2013, Agreement reached with Pakistan on management of cross border move- ments by 2013
PILLAR: ECONOMIC GOVERNANCE & PRIVATE SECTOR DEVELOPMENT SECTOR: PRIVATE SECTOR DEVELOPMENT AND TRADE			
The legal framework for the busi-ness sector is developed	Index on the progress of putting in place the legal, regulatory and facilitating framework for the business sector.	10 draft commercial laws	4 laws passed by mid-1387. Additional 6 laws passed by end-1388
Private sector access to finance is increased	Index on the progress of providing increased access of finance to private sector.	TBD	Number of providers increases by 25% by end-1389
	% increase in private sector investment	TBD	TBD
	% of GDP increase as investment levels increases	TBD	TBD
Public-Private Partnerships	Index on the progress of putting in place an enabling environment for Public-Private Partnerships. number of projects undertaken with PPP	PPPs underway at the end of 1386	Number of PPPs increases by 100% by end-1390
Surplus land is used by the private sector to increase economic activity	Index on the progress of creating enabling environment for use of surplus land by the private sector to increase economic activity.	Area of unused government land at the end of 1386	Area of additional government land used by the private sector increases by minimum 100ha per year
	Index on the progress of putting in place legal, regulatory and facilitating framework for registration and regulation of private sector.	TBD	TBD

Expected Outcomes	Indicators	Baselines	Targets
	% increase in firms formalizing their operations	0% of economic activity is in the informal sector	60% of economic activity is in the informal sector by the end of 1390
Regulations are streamlined and better enforced	% increase in tax revenue from the increased number of formalized firms	% of tax revenue from businesses	TBD
Civil society groups are able to op-erate effectively to aid in the devel-opment process.	Index on the progress of putting necessary legal, regulatory and facilitat-ing frameworks in place so that civil society groups are able to operate effectively to aid in the development process.	TBD	TBD
	Number of NGOs and Civil Society organizations registered	TBD	TBD
Economic activity increases in re-sponse to increased human capacity and skill sets	Number of people employed in the private sector	Data for formal sector employment at the end of 1386	Increase in formal sector employment of 10% per annum in absolute numbers Increase in number of courses by 50% by the end of 1389
Increased provincial economic growth	Index on the progress of promoting increased provincial economic growth.	TBD	TBD
Increased and more effective com-petition	Index on the progress of putting in place a legal framework to facilitate increased and more effective competition	TBD	TBD
The Private Sector Development and Trade sector strategy is implemented	Index on the progress of implementation of the Private Sector Develop-ment and Trade Sector Strategies.	2008 World Bank data in Doing Business data Indicators	Afghanistan improves its overall Doing Business ranking by a minimum of five places each year 60% of economic activity is in the informal sector by the end of 1390

Map of Afghanistan

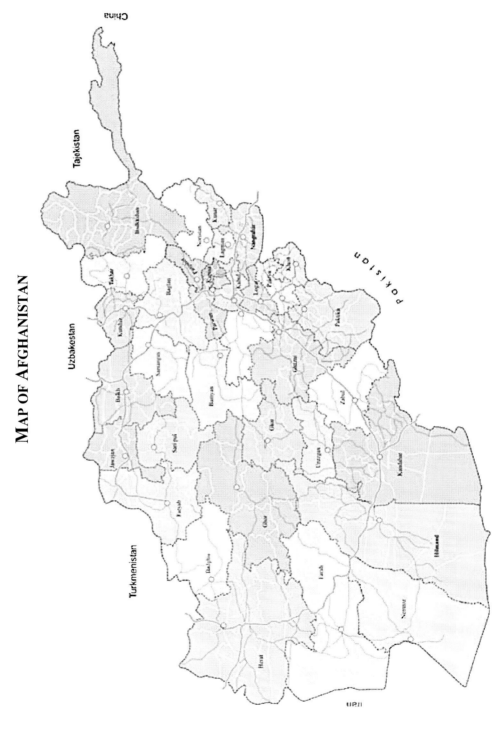

Afghanistan National Development Strategy (ANDS).

End Notes

[1] Many of the government's initiatives in this area are described in "A Policy for Private Sector Growth and Development" pre-sented at the Enabling Environment Conference, Kabul, June 2007.

[2] For example, the World Bank "Investment Climate Assess-ment" reported that companies are typically spending as much as 15 percent of total sales on security costs.

[3] For example, in the 2005 Transparency International "Corrup-tion Perceptions Index" Afghanistan ranked 117th (of 158); two years later the country was ranked 172nd (of 179).

[4] Afghanistan has also placed special emphasis on good relations with its neighbors, particularly Pakistan. The two countries con-vened a joint Peace Jirga in August 2006, and Afghanistan looks forward with hope and optimism to enhanced cooperation with Pakistan.

[5] Details for many of the key documents can be found in the bibliography.

[6] The Provincial Development Plans (PDPs) that were developed as part of this process are presented in ANDS Volume III.

[7] Participation is the process by which stakeholders influence and share control over priority setting, policymaking, resource alloca-tions, and/or program implementation. While there is no blueprint for participation, because it plays a role in many different con-texts and for different purposes, the Government has worked hard to design a meaningful participatory process as part of the future ANDS.

[8] Paris Declaration on Aid Effectiveness, 2005 (http://www.oecd.org/dataoecd/11/41/34428351.pdf).

[9] The sub-national consultation process and how the PDPs were developed and informed policy will be discussed in greater detail in the next section.

[10] Traditional village councils.

[11] In addition to the feedback, comments and support of a number of CSOs, the Agency Coordinating Body for Afghan Relief (ACBAR) and the Foundation for Culture and Civil Society (FCCS) undertook extensive research in 12 provinces, contribut-ing invaluable poverty data for the ANDS, as teams were sent to remote, poverty stricken areas in both rural and urban settings, in order to inform the sector strategies. This information was used in conjunction with findings from the National Risk and Vulnerabil-ity Assessment surveys over the past five years, to ensure that the ANDS policies are pro-poor and representative of the more dis-advantaged segments of society.

[12] A nomad woman from Balkh province stated that this was the first time she had attended the meeting on behalf of nomad women of this province in order to present her opinions for the welfare and prosperity of the country. "We would be glad if the government continues to pursue such policy. Nomads like any other people in the society would also benefit from this process". Farida Kochi, representative of Balkh' Source: ANDS Sub-national Consultation, 1386 (2007

[13] For a detailed breakdown and analysis of provincial priorities, sequencing and integration into Sector Strategies see Volume iii of the ANDS.

[14] 'A nomad woman from Balkh province stated that this was the first time she had attended the meeting on behalf of nomad women of this province in order to present her opinions for the welfare and prosperity of the country. "We would be glad if the government continues to pursue such policy. Nomads like any other people in the society would also benefit from this process". Farida Kochi, representative of Balkh' Source: ANDS Sub-national Consultation, 2007

[15] Source: Understanding Poverty in Afghanistan, Analysis and recommendations using National Risk & Vulnerability Assess-ment (NRVA) 2005 and Spring 2007, WB, October 30, 2007.

[16] Source: NRVA, 2005, WB Staff Estimation

[17] Source: The World Bank based on Spring 2007survey.

[18] Source: World Bank Staff Estimates based on 2005 NRVA.

[19] Urban Livelihoods in Afghanistan, Jo Beall and Stefan Cshutte, August 2006.

[20] Study on Chronically Poor Women in Afghanistan (Draft), March 2007.

[21] Working poor is a term used to describe individuals and fami-lies who maintain regular employment but remain in relative poverty due to low levels of pay and dependent expenses.

[22] As a recent APPPA Final Report stated, "We women have no rights or decision-making power. The men make decisions inside and outside the house. This is normal for us." Female participant, Bai Sar Community, Herat. Source: APPPA, Final Report, March 2008.

[23] According to the WB analysis based on NRVA 2005 more than 70 percent of households in Afghanistan are engaged in agricul-ture livestock activities.

[24] Net primary enrolment rate is the proportion of primary school age children (6-9) who enrolled in primary grades.

[25] Working age group is 15-64 years.

[26] Preliminary work done by World Bank, based on NRVA 2005 data. Elasticity of growth on poverty reduction calculated using Bourguinon's method.

[27] SY1386 inflation rates are likely to increase to around 10 per-cent due to higher fuel prices and subsequent increases in basic commodity prices. Stable nominal exchange rates (with combina-tion of higher than US

inflation) mean appreciation of real ex-change rates. This leads to an issue of "Dutch Disease" and competitiveness.

[28] Data is taken from "Afghanistan: Opium Survey 2007" (UNODC, October 2007).

[29] There is a possibility of significant underreport-ing/underestimates of external assistance (especially on security) in recent few years.

[30] This cited is directly from "Responding to Afghanistan's De-velopment Challenge: An Assessment of Experience During 2002-2007 and Issues and Priorities for the Future" (William Byrd, World Bank South Asia PREM Working Paper Series, Report No. SASPR-11, October 2007).

[31] See the Government's "Policy for Private Sector Growth and Development", presented at the Enabling Environment Confer-ence, June 2007.

[32] The Investment Climate in Afghanistan: Exploiting Opportuni-ties in an Uncertain Environment (World Bank, 2005).

[33] In the Afghanistan Compact, revenues are projected to exceed 8 percent of GDP in 1389.

[34] Figures in the macroeconomic framework (see tables) are based on projected execution rates of the core development budget. As a result, the original total budgeted figures for the core development budget can be higher than those in the macroeco-nomic framework of the ANDS.

[35] Note, the recent rapid increase in global prices could poten-tially create a challenge for the Government and DAB to main-tain core inflation between 2.5 and 4 percent in the short term.

[36] The level of expenditure in Table 4.9 is based on an assumption regarding the amount of financing which will be made available at the forthcoming ANDS donor conference in Paris. The macroeconomic framework which currently underpins the ANDS does not assume a similar scaling-up of donor assistance and is therefore not entirely consistent with Table 4.8. Following the donor conference, the macro-economic framework and the ANDS expenditure ceilings will be updated to reflect the actual level of donor assistance.

[37] See http://www.oecd.org/dataoecd/43/25/38406485.pdf

[38] The full sector strategies are included in the Volume II of the ANDS.

[39] See for example "A Policy for Private Sector Growth and De-velopment" presented by the Government at the Enabling Envi-ronment Conference, June 2007.

[40] See generally, National Development Framework, (2002), ANDS Volume II, and Securing Afghanistan's Future, Chapter 5 (2004).

[41] President Karzai, Opening Address at the ADF, April 2005, page 9.

[42] Minister of Finance Anwar Ahady, The Budget as a Tool for Accelerating Economic Development and Poverty Reduction, ADF, April 2005. Senior Economic Advisor to the President, Professor Ishaq Nadiri, The National Development Strategy & Key Challenges, Presentation at the Afghanistan Development Forum, April 2005.

[43] Senior Economic Advisor to the President, Professor Ishaq Nadiri, The National Development Strategy & Key Challenges, Presentation at the Afghanistan Development Forum, April 2005.

[44] Statement of Dr. M. M. Amin Farhang, Minister of Economy, at the ADF, April 2005.

[45] The poorest members of society rarely have access to electric-ity service.

[46] According to the best estimates of social indicators for children in Afghanistan, UNICEF, few places in the world face such scarce and alarming water supply and sanitation coverage levels.

[47] The mirabs are community level organizations that manage traditional irrigation systems. A similar effort has been made under the National Solidarity Program to establish Community Development Councils with a broader mandate for local funding. These organizations have different mandates, representatively and are based on a totally different geographical unit.

[48] See the discussion on hydro power projects for the energy sector.

[49] More detailed information on road construction projects can be found in the Transportation Sector Strategy and in the

[50] Note, these targets are also identified in the Water Sector Strategy.

[51] While maximizing the number of beneficiaries, the MoPH seeks equity by looking at the scientific data on topography, depth of poverty and vulnerability of the population to be served for, health indicators of mothers and children in particular, utili-zation and availability of the health services in the area of con-cern, availability of funds and so forth. By doing so, the propos-als are categorized according to four criteria.

[52] School Surveys Summary Report, 1386 (February 2008), Min-istry of Education, Islamic Republic of Afghanistan.

[53] School age refers to children between 6-18 years of age; 6-13 years = primary school which is Grades 1-6; 14-18 years = sec-ondary school from Grades 7 to 12. Basic education is described as Grades 1-9 (6-15 years of age), which is also compulsory as stated in the Constitution.

[54] NRVA 2005 and projected population projections specifically developed for this report.

[55] National Education Strategic Plan (1385-1389), Ministry of Education, Islamic Republic of Afghanistan.

[56] Outputs of these programs contribute to the development and delivery of the Skills Development sub-sector.

[57] Constraints and challenges have been addressed in detail in sector strategy paper as well as the NAPWA.

[58] The budget is currently divided into two major components; the Core Budget, controlled by the Government; and, the External Budget, which includes Provincial Reconstruction Team Civil and Military Cooperation funds,

provided and controlled by each donor individually. The Core Budget includes both Operational and Development components, 60% of which is donor provided and the remaining 40% of which comes from National revenues. The Government is committed to getting to the stage where the total Budget is Core, and is funded from nationally generated revenues, but acknowledges that it will take some time to accom-plish this goal. The near-term objectives therefore are to gain Core Operational Budget self sufficiency as soon as possible, and in the mean time to move as much External budget into the Core Budget Management Framework as practicable.

[59] In particular, a well-defined and operational PRS is a prerequi-site for the development for the proposed Sector Wide Ap-proaches (SWAPs). SWAPs involve all stakeholders (including Government, donors and NGOs) committing to using their re-sources in the sector only through the Sector Investment Program (SIP). SWAPs are considered by Government to be a tool for donor co-ordination, to reduce the administrative burden of the individual project approach to donor funding and ensure that there is a unified strategy for the sector, with no overlapping or contradictory activities by different actors.

[60] Source: Ministry of Finance, April 2008

[61] This mechanism has been very effective for formulation of Millennium Development Goals (MDGs) for Afghanistan, devel-opment of Afghanistan Compact and Interim Afghanistan Na-tional Development Strategy (I-ANDS), prioritization of various programs and projects, and approval of policies and decisions. The effectiveness of this mechanism is supplemented by the fact that the Senior Economic Advisor to the President is also a co- chair of the Joint Coordination and Monitoring Board (JCMB), which is mainly responsible for coordination between the gov-ernment and the international community. The members of the Oversight Committee are also members of JCMB. This mechanism will be a very important implementation mechanism for ANDS because of its past experience, criticality and positioning

[62] See text in the Monitoring Framework for information on the CMRS

In: Afghanistan National Development…
Editor: Jennifer L. Brown

ISBN: 978-1-61209-637-7
© 2011 Nova Science Publishers, Inc.

Chapter 2

PRIORITIZATION AND IMPLEMENTATION PLAN (MID 2010-MID 2013)

Afghanistan National Development Strategy
Kabul International Conference of Afghanistan

ACRONYMS AND ABBREVIATIONS

ALPT	Accelerated Learning Program for Teachers
AEIC	Afghan Energy Information Center
AGS	Afghan Geological Survey
ASMEDA	Afghan Small to Medium Enterprise Development Agency/Authority
ACCI	Afghanistan Chamber of Commerce and Industry
AGCHO	Afghanistan Geodesy and Cartography Head Office
ALA	Afghanistan Land Authority
AMDGs	Afghanistan Millennium Development Goals
ANQA	Afghanistan National Qualifications Authority
A-NIC	Afghanistan Network Information Center
AREDP	Afghanistan Rural Enterprise Development Program
ASDP	Afghanistan Skills Development Project
ADF	Agricultural Development Fund
GIAAC	Anti-Corruption Commission
BDS	Business Development Services
CSC	Civil Service Commission
CBNRM	Community-Based Management of Natural Resources
CBHC	Community-Based Heath Care
CARDF	Comprehensive Agriculture and Rural Development Facility
CEDAW	Convention on the Elimination of All Forms of Discrimination Against Women
DABS	Da Afghanistan Breshna Sherkat
DDA	District Development Assembly

DOWA	Department of Women's Affairs
DMTVET	Deputy Ministry of Technical and Vocational Education and Training
DCN	District Communications Network
DEO	District Education Office
EDP	Economic Development Package
EMIS	Education Management Information System
EQUIP	Education Quality Improvement Program
ESC	Employment Service Center
ERDA	Energy for Rural Development in Afghanistan
EG	Enterprise Group
ESMF	Environmental and Social Management Framework
EMS	Express Mail Services
FP	Facilitating Partners
GMU	Grant Management Unit
HEMIS	Higher Education Management Information System
IDLG	Independent Directorate of Local Government
IMCI	Integrated Management of Childhood Illness
ITSSF	Integrated Trade and SME Support Facility
IMU	Interim Management Unit
ICE	Inter-ministerial Commission for Energy
IFI	International Finance Institution
LMIAU	Labor Market Information and Analysis Unit
LBAT	Labor Based Appropriate Technology
LEFMA	Long-term Extractive industries Fiscal Model for Afghanistan
MIS	Management Information System
MMC	Metallurgical Construction Company
MEW	Ministry of Energy and Water
MPW	Ministry of Public Works
MRRD	Ministry of Rural Rehabilitation and Development
NRRCI	National Regional Resource Corridor Initiative
NREN	National Research and Education Network
NADF	National Agricultural Development Framework
NESP	National Education Strategic Plan
NEPDG	National Energy Policy Development Group
NESP	National Energy Supply Program
NEIEP	National Extractives Industry Excellence Program
NICTCA	National Information and Communications Technology Council of Afghanistan
NPP	National Priority Program
NPITT	National Program of In-service Teacher Training
NQA	National Qualifications Authority
NQF	National Qualifications Framework
NRAP	National Rural Access Program
NSDP	National Skills Development Program
NADF	National Agricultural Development Framework
OFC	Optical Fiber Cable

PACEA	Partnership for Advancing Community-based Education in Afghanistan
PRR	Priority Reconstructing and Reform
PA	Producer Association
PMO	Project Management Office
PSB	Project Steering Board
PSDD	Private Sector Development Directorate
REED	Rural Enterprise and Energy Department
RITS	Rural Infrastructure Technical Services
SG	Savings Group
SIP	School Improvement Plan
SMC	School Management Committee
SMT	School Management Training
SDNRP	Sustainable Development of Natural Resources Project
TTC	Teacher Training College
TVETB	Technical and Vocational Education and Training Board
TOT	Training Of Trainers
TVET	Technical Vocational Education and Training
UPTAF	Urban Planning Technical Assistance Facility
VSLA	Village Savings and Loan Association
WUA	Water User Association

EXECUTIVE SUMMARY

On July 20, 2010, the Government of the Islamic Republic of Afghanistan and the international community met in Kabul to deliberate on and endorse an Afghan-led action plan to improve governance, social and economic development, and security. Demonstrating a renewed commitment to the People of Afghanistan within the framework of the *Afghanistan National Development Strategy*, the new generation of National Priority Programs presented at the Kabul International Conference on Afghanistan aim to empower all Afghan citizens and government and non-governmental institutions to contribute to improved service delivery, job creation, equitable economic growth, the protection of all Afghan citizens' rights, and a durable and inclusive peace. In essence, these programs define the *Kabul Process*.

The start of the *Kabul Process* represents a turning point for the People of Afghanistan and their international partners. Unlike the past, when programs were largely prepared and implemented by international cooperation partners, now the Afghan Government and its many development partners across civil society and the private sector have the leadership and institutional capabilities to realize the full benefits of a National Priority Program approach. With the prevalence of violent extremism, pervasive poverty, and perceived high-levels of corruption across many State institutions, adopting a prioritized programmatic approach is a practical and moral imperative for three main reasons:

i. *First*, the Afghan Government must improve the lives of all Afghan citizens. Only through providing poverty reducing social services, establishing law and order, and fostering economic activity nationwide can the Afghan Government garner confidence and legitimacy in the eyes of its constituents. Further, Afghan- led programs with a national reach, that provide for the unique circumstances of different provinces and districts, can build loyalty for the central government, unifying the country and ensuring greater national, as well as provincial, stability. Ongoing peace and reconciliation efforts are based on this commitment to inclusivity and equity for all Afghan citizens.
ii. *Second*, the Afghan Government recognizes its current limited capacity to design and undertake overly-ambitious programs, and the often-unrelated proliferationof poorly integrated projects. By concentrating on the delivery of a smaller number of large-scale National Priority Programs focused on delivery over the course of the next three years, returns to growth, revenues, and employment will be increased, as will national capacities in self- governance and service delivery.
iii. Third, it is only through the provision of a clear, prioritized agenda that international partners can align behind Afghan leadership. This transfer of responsibility is critical to increase aid effectiveness. And it enables international partners to fulfill their pledge to increase the percentage of their aid aligned behind Afghan priorities through Afghan systems.

The main storyline of the Kabul International Conference on Afghanistan is a story of hope, determination, pragmatism, and peace.[1] Since late 2001, Afghanistan has witnessed significant advances in school enrollment, improved access to essential health services, huge investments in roads and telecommunications coverage from an extremely low base, increased reach of the police force and State courts, and many other areas critical to expanding people's choices and capabilities for a meaningful life with dignity. The National Priority Programs, outlined herein, have been designed to expand social and economic horizons and opportunities for all Afghans (including those living in often remote and isolated rural communities), while also ensuring that Afghanistan emerges as a country with a skilled labor force, capable of driving the economic transition to prosperity. As H.E. President Hamid Karzai expresses in his Foreword to this plan, *"With the introduction of the National Priority Programs, this ambitious action plan symbolizes my Government's renewed commitment to a secure, prosperous, and democratic future."*

As a cohesive and integrated set of priority national investment programs, these proposed investments represent the backbone of the Government of Afghanistan's transition strategy, meeting urgent and essential requirements that the Afghan State must both fulfill and be seen fulfilling. They outline specific steps to overcome the myriad complex governance and security related challenges that continue to impede socioeconomic recovery, and they acknowledge that transition requires a comprehensive approach – not a military solution only. They also seek to create an enabling economic environment to attract investment and create high-value industries that will form a strong revenue base, ensuring the continuation of government programs as foreign development assistance declines. The overall strategy is, therefore, one of increased regional and global integration, alongside targeted investment to maximize returns to growth, revenues, and sustained employment creation. For the next three years, it is estimated that these National Priority Programs will generate some 600,000 direct job opportunities and 1.84 million indirect job opportunities, plus 58.8 million additional labor days.

Each of the programs presented here have emerged as a result of a series of consultation exercises – to deepen public policy dialogue – with leading members of Parliament, Afghan civil society, the private sector, and academia, including their collective participation in Standing Committees on Governance, Economic and Social Development, and Security held in June with Afghan Government and international community participation. International cooperation partners have also been extensively engaged in the formulation process, providing guidance and feedback on issues related to fiscal forecasting, resource flows, and policy and institutional enabling reforms.

The growth storyline that underpins the entire set of proposed priority programs is also an important element. Clearly, with Government still unable to finance large parts of its operating costs, a focus on sustained and high level formal growth as a result of investments in resource corridors, extractive industries, transport, energy, and small-to-medium –sized enterprises is vital not just to secure the key functions of government, but also to allow government to finance programs through broad- based growth. At the heart of the entire Kabul Conference storyline is a shift towards growth, revenues, and employment driven investments to secure transition to a virtuous macro-economic and fiscal future. Once financed, the investments outlined here secure the transition to fiscal sovereignty, as a foundation for concluding the political, security, and socio-economic transition. The new approach, therefore, also includes a focus on improved economic governance, as well as initiatives that address social exclusion, transparency, and accountability. Finally, the programs presented here will benefit from improved absorption capacities and ever-improving fiduciary standards in public finance.

The National Priority Programs and related Government initiatives are presented in two volumes. This volume (*Volume I*) contains a synthesis of the consultation process, alongside analytical and diagnostic findings that provide direction for public investment aimed at achieving visible results over the next six month, twelve month, and three year periods in the areas of governance, socio-economic development and security. *Volume II*, found in an accompanying CD-ROM and at http://www.fa.gov.af/kabul-conference and http://www.ands.gov.af/, contains the detailed National Priority Program summaries in the various clusters (including projected medium-term outcomes for the next three-to-five years), as well as the following three initiatives: "*Joint Framework for Inteqal: A Process for Strengthening Peace and Stability in Afghanistan and the Region*", "*Regional Cooperation*", and the "*Afghanistan Peace and Reintegration Program*". Delivering success will also require a focus on the following core elements:

- Understanding and tackling the challenges of implementation;
- Building Good Democratic Governance and the Rule of Law;
- Unleashing Investments in Economic and Infrastructure Development;
- Accelerating Agricultural and Rural Development;
- Facilitating Human Resource Development;
- Transitioning to Afghan-Led Security;
- Reconciliation and Reintegration through a new Peace Initiative;
- Curbing the Trade and Harmful Effects of Narcotics;

- Expanding Regional Cooperation;
- Meeting Resource Requirements and Measuring for Results; and,
- Strengthening Leadership and Accountability.

Understanding and Tackling the Challenges to Implementation

Difficult conditions for national program implementation are caused by continued violence across Afghanistan, particularly in the South and Southeastern regions. Additional organizational, regulatory, and capacity supply-related constraints challenge Afghan Government ministries and agencies, international development partners, the private sector, and civil society organizations. These constraints have been examined in the context of the (re)-design of National Priority Programs presented at the Kabul International Conference on Afghanistan. The Government of Afghanistan recognizes these constraints and the fact that its capacity to absorb foreign assistance, while improving rapidly, remains limited. Overly optimistic planning by Government, ministries and agencies is exacerbated by a limited capacity to implement programs by both government and donors, which contributes to low budget execution. The government also appreciates that, while fund management is relatively strong, there are still risks to implementation that the Government plans to tackle within new clusters designed programs.

A concerted effort to build public financial management capacity in line ministries will be undertaken. The Government will focus on: (i) Improving procurement and project management systems; (ii) Streamlining and simplifying government and donor delivery systems; (iii) Increasing the creation and use of effective management information for all programs; and (iv) Unleashing the capacity of the private sector and civil society service-provider organizations to implement programs. This will build the confidence necessary for donors to follow through with pledges made at the London Conference to increase aid alignment with government priorities and increase aid delivered through the Afghan national budget.

This is a challenging agenda and will take time. However, the early 2010 establishment of Five Cluster Groupings of ministries (covering Governance, Economic and Infrastructure Development, Agriculture and Rural Development, Human Resource Development, and Security) to improve coordination, program delivery, and prioritization in support of ANDS implementation is a positive step forward. As demonstrated through the preparations for the Kabul Conference, this innovative arrangement for enhanced Government leadership in all major areas of recovery and rehabilitation is realizing results. The high quality of inter-ministerial and official level coordination towards setting program priorities is a major achievement in its own right, as is the identification of strong linkages between governance and socio-economic development programming. But it does not end here. These National Priority Programs begin an iterative and consultative process for setting out a short-, medium-, and long-term plan for ANDS implementation, and they lay a solid foundation for more robust prioritization and budget realism in the future.

Building Good Democratic Governance and the Rule of Law

Advanced through six National Priority Programs, the Government's goal in this area, as presented in the *Afghanistan National Development Strategy, is to: "strengthen democratic processes and institutions, human rights, the rule of law, delivery of public services, and government accountability."* Its *National Priority Program for Financial and Economic Reforms* introduces a comprehensive set of reforms to strengthen a more fiscally sustainable Afghan economy and to ensure that public (including donor) funds are used in a responsible and efficient manner, leading to effective development outcomes. Seeking to counter rising perceptions of corruption by increasing the transparency and accountability of procedures and controls, the *National Transparency and Accountability Program will* build effective and independent oversight institutions for monitoring and evaluating the performance of Government institutions and officials. The *Afghanistan Program for Efficient and Effective Government* aims to improve civil service management by: (i) Introducing and implementing broad-based policy, legal, and structural reforms in public administration; (ii) Improving public service delivery through a simplification of procedures; and (iii) Developing comprehensive training and improving working conditions of the civil service. In bringing government closer to the people by ensuring that local government is both empowered and accountable, the *National Program for Local Governance* will focus on implementing the Sub- National Governance Policy, as well as strengthening institutional development and democratic representation at the sub-national level. *The National Program for Law and Justice for All* targets those parts of the legal system that are most relevant to the way citizens experience the legal system and the rule of law, by providing legal aid, revising laws, simplifying the operations of State Courts, and facilitating linkages between informal and formal justice systems. Finally, the *Afghanistan Program for Human Rights and Civic Responsibilities* responds to the challenges of violent extremism and limited capacities to guarantee the basic freedoms of the Afghan people, by strengthening Afghan state institutions to protect human rights and raise awareness among the general population about their inherent rights and responsibilities as Afghan citizens, including through civic education.

Unleashing Investments in Economic and Infrastructure Development

To be realized through six National Priority Programs, the Government's goal in this area is to: *"support Afghanistan's transition to financial independence and develop a business climate that enables private investment."* Its flagship transport- oriented program, *National-Regional Resource Corridor Initiative*, is focused on developing the critical infrastructure needed to reap benefits directly from large-scale, environmentally friendly exploitation of Afghanistan's substantial mineral resources and, indirectly, from increased trade flows and labor mobility. The *Extractive Industries Excellence Program* will spearhead the rapid scaling-up of major and artisanal extractive industries (providing resources for the regional resource corridors) for all major mineral groups, leading to a surge in domestic revenues that will secure resources for broad-based growth in other areas. Building on gains made in both power generation and distribution, the *National Energy Supply Program* will meet increasing demand through a combination of domestic generation and imports, and through alternative sources such as solar photovoltaic and small-scale hydro- generation. The *Urban Planning Technical Assistance Facility* recognizes that good urban planning supports the development of the private sector and contributes significantly to social and security stabilization objectives, including protecting the most vulnerable and supporting the delivery of cost-effective public services. The *Integrated Trade and SME Support Facility* aims, among other objectives, to reform the Small and Medium-sized Enterprise legal and regulatory environment, achieving real gains in the international competitiveness of Afghanistan's existing and emerging SMEs. Finally, *E-Afghanistan* intends to bridge the communications gap that exists within Afghanistan, while also creating new systems of data and information management within a new model of public management. To this end, newly established authorities will benefit from improved automated management information systems to promote efficiency, effectiveness, and improved fiduciary management. Authorities and agencies, following deliberation, will be established under the Advanced Reform and Restructuring (ARR) Program.

Accelerating Agricultural and Rural Development

Guided through the implementation of four National Priority Programs in the Agricultural and Rural Development Cluster, the Government's goal is to: "*develop prosperous rural and pastoral communities.*" Achieving this goal stands or falls on whether the government, civil society, and the private sector can trigger dramatic increases in job creation, rural employment, and rural growth. Responding to damaged irrigation and other water systems, soil, rangeland, and forests, the Government's *National Water and Natural Resources Development Program* introduces large- scale natural resource projects in the areas of irrigation development and management, land management, and rural energy development. The National Comprehensive *Agriculture Production and Market Development Program* provides research and extension services, agriculture infrastructure development, rural credit, improved agricultural production methods, and market development to strengthen the value chains between production, the factory, and the domestic and export markets. The further scaling-up of the *National Rural Access Program* will link farmers and communities to the growing national road network by developing a system for nationwide labor-intensive road construction and maintenance. Finally, the *National Strengthening of Local Institutions Program* will expand the reach of Community Development Councils to all of Afghanistan's villages, providing resources for critical village infrastructure. It will also strengthen capacity and sustainability through the clustering of villages for economies of scale and stronger linkages to Government.

Facilitating Human Resource Development

To be achieved through five National Priority Programs, the Government's goal in this area is to: "*produce quality human resources and promote and sustain economic development which will, in turn, foster stability and security for its citizens.*" Its *Facilitation of Sustainable Decent Work through Skills-Development and Market-Friendly Labor Regulation Program* aims to address the skills gap in Afghanistan by enhancing the employability of Afghan youth and young adults and identifying market-demanded skills and offering literacy, skills training, and technical and vocational education in partnership with the private sector. *The Education for All Program* seeks to improve equitable access, quality, and enrollment in primary and secondary education (especially for girls) and to strengthen community ownership, especially in the most remote, less secure, and disadvantaged areas. The *Expanding Opportunities for Higher Education Program* aims to increase access and the quality of higher education, especially in fields that directly contribute to economic growth, in partnership with the private sector. The objective of *the Capacity Development to Accelerate National Action Plan for Women of Afghanistan Implementation Program* is to implement gender mainstreaming across all sectors by strengthening the Ministry of Women's Affairs and other ministries' capacity to address the needs of females in all National Priority Programs. Through the *Human Resources for Health Program,* strengthened quality and access both to education for health care workers and to health education in the school curriculum will improve the health and well-being of Afghan families. Finally, *the Increase Access and Improve the Quality of Higher Education Program* will increase access to quality higher education, especially in fields that contribute to private sector partnerships and equitable economic growth.

Transitioning to Afghan-Led Security

In accordance with the London Conference Communiqué, the Government of Afghanistan, along with international partners, has introduced a Joint Framework for *Inteqal* (transition) to: "*facilitate a phased transfer, province-by-province, to an Afghan security lead.*" It involves two main stages: (i) An assessment leading to a conditions- based joint decision and an announcement by the Afghan Government that *Inteqal* will be initiated in a province or set of provinces; and (ii) Phased implementation, which requires provincial administrations to achieve specific milestones to complete the transition to full Afghan ownership across all functions of government throughout Afghanistan. To ensure a sustainable transition, the Government and the international community will underpin security efforts with sufficient governance and development resources and approaches, including balanced local representation and inclusive access to the rule of law and economic and social development opportunities. In addition, the Government will reinforce this initiative by properly training, equipping, and increasing the size of the Afghanistan National Army to 171,000 and the Afghanistan National Police to 134,000 personnel; it will also strengthen the Ministries of Interior and Defense, including through institutional reform and leadership development.

Reconciliation and Reintegration through a New Peace Initiative

The *Consultative Peace Jirga*, held from 2-4 June 2010, demonstrated that a representative cross- section of Afghan society is ready to accept a political reconciliation process to end the conflict, provided that opposition forces accept the laws and Constitution of Afghanistan, including respect for the equal rights of men and women, and renounce violence and ties to terrorist organizations. In support of this goal, the *Afghanistan Peace and Reintegration Program* is designed to promote peace through a political approach. It will encourage regional and international cooperation, help create the political and judicial conditions for peace and reconciliation, and encourage combatant soldiers and their commanders, previously siding with armed opposition and extremist groups, to renounce violence and terrorism and to join in the constructive processes of reintegration and peacebuilding. Requiring robust civilian-military cooperation and coordination on the ground to achieve progress, the program will be led by the High Peace Council, comprised of respected Government and civil society leaders. It aims to reintegrate thousands of former combatants and stabilize 4000 communities in 220 districts over five years through, among other initiatives, a Community Recovery Program, an Agricultural Conservation Corps, and a Public Works Corps.

Curbing the Trade and Harmful Effects of Narcotics

Counter-narcotics, as a cross-cutting issue, must be integrated into the programming and initiatives of all Five Government Clusters. The Kabul Conference provides an opportunity to introduce an Afghan counter-narcotics perspective viewed as a "*new beginning*" in Afghanistan's transition away from narcotics production and trade towards alternative and sustainable livelihoods. Specifically, the Government, with support from its international and national partners, will review, integrate, and implement a more effective, coherent, and pragmatic National Drug Control Strategy (NDCS) to address narcotics issues comprehensively and in a sustainable manner. In particular, all National Priority Programs should be aligned with the following counter-narcotics strategic priorities of the Government of Afghanistan: (i) Step up the effective disruption of the drugs trade by targeting traffickers and their supporters; (ii) Facilitate the strengthening and diversification of legal rural livelihoods, with a particular focus on the needs of communities that abandon illicit cultivation; (iii) Ensure the reduction of demand for illicit drugs and the treatment of drug users; and (iv) In support of these three priorities, ensure the required strengthening of institutions both at the central Government level and in the provinces.

Expanding Regional Cooperation

Addressing regional problems requires coordinated and coherent regional approaches. Among the Government's chief priority actions for tapping the immense benefits from regional cooperation include: (i) Greater inter-security agency coordination and intelligence sharing, including identifying and eliminating terrorist sanctuaries and support bases; (ii) Combating narcotics in the framework of the Rainbow Strategy, including increased responsibility by transit countries to prevent the trafficking of chemical precursors to Afghanistan and by drug consumer countries to curb demand; (iii) Implementing the tri-partite agreement on the return and reintegration of Afghan refugees and internally displaced persons between the Islamic Republics of Iran and Pakistan; (iv) Investing in strategic regional infrastructure, including "regional resource corridors" and improving institutional capacity for identification, preparation and execution of priority integration projects; and (v) Cooperation with neighbouring and regional countries, especially in the Gulf region, on Afghan labour migration which contributes to an important source of revenue through remittances.

Meeting Resource Requirements and Measuring for Results

Based on consultation with donors, the Government of Afghanistan estimates that approximately $10 billion will be available to support core socio-economic development initiatives over the coming three years, with additional resources available to support current governance and security sector strengthening priorities. The Government has stated its desire that the international community direct 80% of its total socio-economic development assistance in support of its fifteen socio-economic development National Priority Programs. In this regard, an overall budget ceiling of $8 billion was assigned, with the Agriculture and Rural Development Cluster accounting for around 26% of the total (US$2 billion), the Human Resource Development Cluster around 25% (US$1.9 billion), and Economic and Infrastructure Development Cluster around 49% (US$3.8 billion). These funds were judged to be incremental and could be added to existing high-performing programs with committed funds and additional absorptive capacity. Draft budgets for the Economics and Social Development and Governance Clusters National Priority Programs are outlined in the Intended Results and Budget Matrices in this volume, as well as further elaborated in Volume II. In addition, the projected budget for the Afghanistan Peace and Reconciliation Program is nearly US$800 million.

In terms of measuring performance in the implementation of the *ANDS Prioritization and Implementation Plan,* the Ministry of Economy is chiefly responsible for coordinating monitoring and evaluation, with the Central Statistics Organization responsible for data collection. A major weakness in the past has been the lack of data systems to support monitoring. Through the introduction of cluster groupings of ministries, monitoring and evaluation are given renewed emphasis. Intended results – in the form of both outcomes and outputs – have been defined for all National Priority Programs individually, and in some cases for clusters as a whole. The total number of intended results has been kept manageable, and each are elaborated in easy-toreview matrices, allowing for the monitoring of different program components that contribute to the achievement of specific program and cluster outcomes and outputs. Moreover, an integrated monitoring and evaluation system, with impact indicators, will be designed as part of the ANDS results-based management system to inform decision-making on a frequent basis in the Cabinet, Parliament, Joint Coordination and Monitoring Board, and other forums.

Strengthening Leadership and Accountability

In support of the Cabinet and National Assembly, the Five Cluster Groupings of ministries mentioned above have contributed to improved coordination across Government and the prioritization of *Afghanistan National Development Strategy* implementation.

Immediately after the Kabul Conference, they will initiate work on operational action plans to facilitate delivery towards the six and twelve month targets presented in the Intended Results and Budget Matrices for the National Priority Programs and related Government priority initiatives, giving emphasis to urgent government reforms critical to the delivery of the socio-economic development related National Priority Programs. Measures were also recently introduced to strengthen the periodic ANDS review meetings of the Joint Coordination and Monitoring Board and associated Standing Committees and cluster- specific working groups. The Government of Afghanistan further welcomed representatives of the international community to meet at the Foreign Ministers level, on an annual basis, to review mutual progress on commitments and to consider new Afghan priorities, as part of a three-year *Kabul Process* towards the implementation of the first five-year *Afghanistan National Development Strategy* (mid-2008 to mid-2013).

As a key milestone towards more effective Afghan-led ANDS implementation, the Government of Afghanistan is pleased that its international partners agreed in January at the London Conference, to work together to increase assistance through the Government's central budget to 50% over the next two years.

However, the Government recognizes that off- budget programs will remain a key part of the development portfolio for the foreseeable future. To ensure accountability for all development assistance, the Afghan Government pledges to support its international partners in fulfilling the principles outlined in the 2010 "Operational Guide: Criteria for Effective Off-Budget Development Finance". In particular, international partners must ensure that all governance, development, and security sector programs undertaken in Afghanistan are designed, reported on regularly, and evaluated with meaningful input by the Government and respond directly to Afghan priorities. In addition, for every off-budget project supported, international partners must remain committed to guaranteeing that sustainability and building both Afghan private and public-sector capacities are critical steps in the design, implementation, and evaluation of every off- budget project.

Though a significant step forward, the *ANDS Prioritization and Implementation Plan* should be qualified:

i. *First*, the Kabul International Conference on Afghanistan represents only the start of the process of transition. The roadmap will need to be reviewed and updated regularly.
ii. *Second*, a balance should be struck between necessary, long-term structural reforms and a more pragmatic set of near-term reforms over the next one-to-three years, whose main purpose is to facilitate National Priority Program implementation.
iii. *Third*, as the Government takes on more responsibility for managingnational development through its budget, donor assistance will need to provide adequate resources for operating and maintaining the assets and services to be transferred to Afghan authorities.

To support the transition to greater Afghan ownership and responsibility, the Government plans to strengthen its bi-annual Donor Financial Review, Medium-Term Financial Framework (MTFF), and introduce other mechanisms to: (i) Consider long-term financing needs and gaps; (ii) Explore how the Government budget can become the main policy instrument used by donors and the Government to manage transition; (iii) Facilitate "handover strategies" from internationally-led programs; (iv) Monitor the progress of national programs in achieving agreed upon short and medium-term outcomes; and (v) Propose recommendations for overcoming implementation bottlenecks for consideration by the Cabinet, Parliament, JCMB, and other decision-making fora.

This prioritization and implementation plan for the *Afghanistan National Development Strategy* should be reviewed and discussed alongside the companion Kabul International Conference on Afghanistan Communiqué. Drawing directly on near-term targets presented in the National Priority Programs introduced at the Kabul Conference, the Communiqué emphasizes major short-term commitments by the Government of Afghanistan, to be monitored closely, updated, and renewed every twelve months. With continued direct engagement by Afghanistan's international partners - and their corresponding concrete and time-bound commitments - both of these instruments can serve as key vehicles for enhanced leadership and mutual accountability in a common effort to bring stability to Afghanistan's region and to increase the socioeconomic development and governance empowerment opportunities of its citizens.

INTRODUCTION: REAFFIRMING THE GOVERNMENT'S VISION FOR GOVERNANCE, DEVELOPMENT, AND SECURITY

On 20 July 2010, world leaders convened in Kabul with their Afghan counterparts to consider and endorse an Afghan Government-led action plan for improved governance, economic and social development, and security. The gathering, the first of its kind at the Foreign Ministerial level in Afghanistan, marks the culmination of several months of intensive study and rigorous policy debate on Government priorities implemented through national programs to achieve *Afghanistan National Development Strategy* objectives.

The *ANDS Prioritization and Implementation Plan* presented to the Kabul International Conference on Afghanistan remains committed to the *Afghanistan National Development Strategy* vision, by solar year 1400 (2020), of:

- *A stable Islamic constitutional democracy at peace with itself and its neighbors, standing with full dignity in the international family.*
- *A tolerant, united, and pluralistic nation that honors its Islamic heritage and the deep seated aspiration toward participation, justice, and equal rights for all.*
- *A society of hope and prosperity based on a strong, private-sector led market economy, social equity, and environmental sustainability.*

At the same time, the prioritization and implementation plan for the ANDS, presented in this and an accompanying volume, recognizes the central importance of achieving marked progress, over the next one-to-three years, in the critical areas of service delivery, job creation, economic growth, public revenue generation, the protection of the rights of all Afghan citizens, and stabilizing all provinces and districts. For the Afghan people and their international partners, the next twelve months, in particular, can represent a turning point in the country's transition away from violent conflict and aid dependence to an Afghan-led era of peace, justice, and equitable development.

Moving beyond a list of prioritized projects (i.e., simply a "re-prioritized budget-making process"), the Kabul Conference is distinguished by introducing truly integrated National Priority Programs, consisting of inter-connected components that address the combined needs for service delivery, governance reform and strengthening, national policy and regulatory development, resource mobilization, and establishing the conditions for sustainable economic growth and job creation. For instance, it is insufficient to provide Afghan farmers with new irrigation infrastructure and other tools for increased productivity, if they continue to lack a policy and regulatory framework that encourages access to both domestic and international markets. Rather, to provide farmers with a living wage and reliable, sustained returns on investment, a fully integrated programmatic approach is required.

In building durable foundations – in the next one to three years – for stability, broad-based development, and financial independence over the medium to longer-term in Afghanistan, the focus of future international development partner and private sector investment in the country will shift to returns to growth, revenues, and sustainable employment. Returns to revenue require formal economic growth and effective systems of governance, and formal growth is best achieved along well governed trade corridors around which transit, trade facilitation, extraction, storage, and processing capabilities can be maximized. Historically a land bridge connecting people, ideas, and commercial activities across three distinct regions of Asia, Afghanistan is poised to exploit economically its geographical location and industrious culture.

How the ANDS Prioritization and Implementation Plan was Conceived and Prepared

In response to implementation challenges presented in the next section and the perceived need to prioritize the broad *Afghanistan National Development Strategy* agenda (with its 17 sector- wide and 6 cross-cutting strategies) and to enhance By mid-February, the Government initiated Kabul Conference preparations through the three major development cluster groupings, beginning with a comprehensive situation analysis of all major development programs and projects. In March, consultations with the international community commenced, followed by a Joint Coordination and Monitoring Board Standing Committee on 13 April 2010, where the three development clusters unveiled their agreed goal, objectives, and situation analyses. Around the same time, public consultations were convened with key stakeholders from Afghan civil society, the private sector, and the Afghanistan research and academic communities.

From 10-22 May, an unprecedented gathering of Ministers from the three development clusters was leadership capabilities for coordination and implementation, the Government of Afghanistan proposed at the London Conference on Afghanistan (28 January 2010) a realignment of related Ministries around clusters to facilitate progress in the areas of Agricultural and Rural Development, Human Resource Development, Economic and Infrastructure Development, Governance, and Security. With an innovative focus on developing new and strengthening existing national programs, these Ministerial-level Clusters were requested in London to prioritize the implementation of the *Afghanistan National*

Development Strategy to further the pivotal goals of national stability, job creation, economic growth, and representative and accountable governance.

Organized in Bamyan to arrive at a select number of National Priority Programs to empower and provide social and economic opportunities to all Afghan citizens. A similar Ministerial-level meeting on related governance reform and strengthening issues took place, from 24-26 June, in Herat. Engaging local citizens in the national dialogue, each of these meetings was followed Standing Committees on Development (12 June), Security (27 June), and Governance (30 June). Discussed at the 8 July Joint Coordination and Monitoring Board gathering, summaries of twenty- one National Priority Programs were integrated, along with commitments on regional cooperation as well as from both the *Consultative Peace Jirga* (2-4 June) and a Joint Framework for *Inteqal* (transition), into one coherent action plan for ANDS prioritization and implementation.

UNDERSTANDING AND TACKLING THE CHALLENGES TO IMPLEMENTATION

With a view to ensuring that implementation is "doable", an external technical specialist team assessed the proposed National Priority Programs, the capacity of ministries to administer the programs, and steps needed for sound execution. Key findings from their evaluation, further elaborated by cluster and by program elsewhere, include:

1. *Focus in the short-term on existing programs that are being scaled-up or extended and can leverage existing systems for early results.* In the case of Afghanistan, past achievements are good predictors of future achievement. Existing programs need to learn the lessons of the past and to incorporate better processes into their operations.
2. *Programs based on significant analytical and feasibility work have a higher chance of success in the shorter term and also merit attention.* This is especially so where they are leveraging the successes of existing programs.
3. *Budgeting and planning needs to be strengthened for both on and off-budget programs.* Arrangements for multi-year budgeting, multi-year obligations, and annual appropriation and commitment controls remain inadequate. There remain a number of inefficiencies that contribute to low budget execution performance, including limited capacity for planning and project management, fragmented budgeting between Government and donors (and even amongst donors), and weaknesses in medium-term fiscal forecasting (such as grant forecasting from donors). More rigorous budget planning and program costing, and a more flexible approach to the reprioritization of both on and off-budget funds from poor performing programs to high performing programs, will contribute to improved budget execution rates.
4. *Implementation arrangements for all National Priority Programs need to be in line with broader improvements to the public financial management system, but in the short-term, management of fiduciary and development risks are paramount.* A number of existing programs have what might be termed "work arounds", such as the use of contract employees in the Ministries. While these need to be integrated into

government systems in the long- run, where they pose small fiduciary risks now but are supporting good budget-execution, they should not be removed. Removing them would severely affect the implementation of a number of key National Priority Programs. If the risks are not known, then a rapid independent assessment needs to be undertaken.

5. *Resources concentrate on key implementing Ministries.* Ministry capacity remains low, and a certain amount of "projectizing" of the National Priority Programs is needed to ensure the timely execution of these activities. Project implementation units need to be located within Ministry structures, and financial control must remain with the Ministry. However, broader capacity to manage the financial aspects of the National Priority Programs will take several years. Therefore, broader capacity-building of Ministries needs to be undertaken in parallel to executing the programs agreed at the Kabul Conference. Emphasis needs to be on increasing capacity in budget planning, procurement, treasury functions, and, in particular, budget execution.

6. *Action and time-based outputs (milestones) should be used to support implementation, but not as the primary basis to assess performance.* Intended results from program activities, in terms of outcomes, are based on high level assumptions, including good implementation performance. It needs to be understood that outcome targets are indicative and will have to be updated through an iterative process over time. Good use of available financial and non-financial information in the management of programs is lacking and should be improved.

Absorptive Capacity, Fiduciary, and Development Risks

Afghanistan's absorptive capacity - its ability to do more - is expanding (see figure one below), and inherent fiduciary and development risks are falling rapidly. But there remain significant challenges in these areas, with limited capacity in some line ministries to plan the continued perception of financial misuse amongst the public and international community. Governance Cluster programs will contribute to increased Government capacity and transparency and accountability, which will further reduce absorptive capacity, fiduciary, and development risks in the future. However, these areas require sustained and consistent support if they are to achieve positive results.

Analysis reveals that weak absorptive capacity is associated with high aid levels; constrained levels of private sector capacity; and low levels of institutional capacity. *Analysis also suggests that Afghanistan is receiving arguably sufficient levels of aid* in aggregate, given the quality of governance and public financial management. There may, however, be a case for some additional aid or reallocation of current resources to priorities that are "owned" by the Government to emphasize development effectiveness.

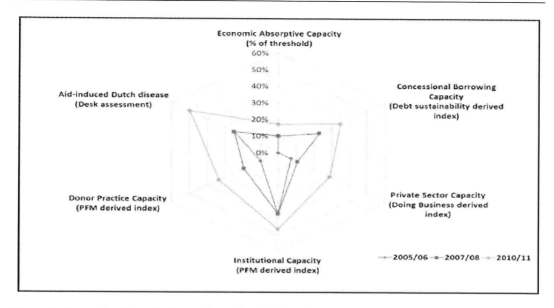

Figure 1. Absorptive Capacity Space Expanding (2005-10).

Weaknesses in the current coordination of on- and off-budget spending limit the overall credibility of the budget. While both Government and donor practices have improved significantly, development risks remain high as a result of incomplete and untimely financial information provided to the Government on off-budget project and program aid. However, behind the seemingly low rates of execution for donor funding lie some more complex issues related to the slowing effect of additional donor fiduciary controls, as well as over-ambitious appropriations for large expenditures.

Overview of the ANDS Prioritization and Implementation Process

The process of setting national priorities through Ministerial Clusters has achieved several useful outcomes likely to lead to better programs with more effective implementation. Core characteristics of the process include consultation and ownership by the Government. This process also lays the foundation for an integrated approach to budget policy. However, overall prioritization (both across and within major sectors of Government activity) can still improve, as can the quality and realism of the proposals which vary somewhat between programs. Some build on existing programs, where we maintain considerable evidence of past success; others seek to scale-up pilot programs, while many are new ideas requiring careful planning in order to produce results. By providing a forum for discussion on a wide number of proposals, the process is a practical step in operationalizing the ANDS by identifying short, medium, and long-term priorities.

Overall, there is scope to move some funds on- budget, but in some cases, large and complex projects that require detailed planning, procurement and monitoring may need to be executed primarily by international partners. Better reporting by donors of these off-budget activities (in line with the principles shared at the conclusion of this plan, and elaborated further in Volume II) is critical. At the same time, the Government must participate in some form in the governance arrangements for all programs and projects. A move by international partners to report on the same regular and detailed basis as Government-led programs and projects would be a major step towards monitoring overall budget and aid effectiveness.

BUILDING GOOD DEMOCRATIC GOVERNANCE AND THE RULE OF LAW

Governance Cluster Members: The Supreme Court, Ministry of Justice, Office of the Attorney General, Independent Administrative Reform and Civil Service Commission, Independent Directorate of Local Governance, High Office of Oversight for Implementation of Anti-Corruption Strategy, Office of Administrative Affairs, Afghanistan Independent Human Rights Commission, and Ministry of Finance. The Ministry of Rural Rehabilitation and Development, the Ministry of Interior and the Controller and Audit Office are also represented in working groups.

Situation Analysis: The government of Afghanistan has made significant strides in recent years in establishing and developing modern institutions of democratic governance. At the same time, ongoing democracy-building efforts face multiple challenges. The absence of adequate channels for Afghan citizens to voice their needs and aspirations, continued bottlenecks to the delivery of essential public services, poor reach and unclear relationships between sub-national and central government institutions, corruption and the subversion of public finance rules, the limited presence of the State judiciary and the timely dispensation of justice, and neglect of human rights and civic responsibilities promotion all erode the legitimate authority of Afghan State institutions. Countering these effects requires an integrated approach and a leadership team committed to immediate action. Ultimately, the true measure of success will be whether the Afghan people begin to accept their government as service-oriented, credible, and legitimate.

Needed Response: The Goal of Governance as presented in the *Afghanistan National Development Strategy* is to: "Strengthen democratic processes and institutions, human rights, the rule of law, delivery of public services and government accountability." The Afghan Ministries and institutions in the Governance Cluster are focused on a "whole-of-government effort" to prioritize key actions that demonstrate immediate results to the people. The Governance Cluster has defined the following set of Strategic Objectives to guide its work at both central and local levels: (i) A focus on governance reforms and capacities; (ii) Access to and delivery of justice; (iii) Human rights and civic responsibilities for the population; (iv) Strengthening governance systems at all levels; and (v) Transparency, accountability, and integrity of government and democratic processes and institutions. In support of these objectives, the following National Priority Programs are proposed:

1. *National Priority Program for Financial and Economic Reforms*: A comprehensive program of reforms to strengthen the Afghan economy and ensure that public funds are used in a transparent and responsible manner is necessary for effective governance. The public financial management reform agenda is proposed as a series

of five interrelated activities that together aim to achieve more than the sum of their parts: (i) A move toward fiscal sustainability through gradual increases of domestic revenue; (ii) Strengthening the budget as an instrument of government policy; (iii) Improving budget execution; (iv) Developing capacity to implement effective programming; and (v) Increasing accountability and transparency in public finances.

2. *National Transparency and Accountability Program*: The program aims at countering rising perceptions of corruption by increasing the transparency and accountability of procedures and controls through specific projects devoted to: (i) Building effective and independent oversight institutions; (ii) Monitoring and evaluating the performance of Government institutions and officials; (iii) Facilitating systems and process re- engineering of central and local government finance; (iv) Creating effective mechanisms to prevent corruption and the misuse of public office for private gain; (v) Reinforcing the integrity of public and business sector relationships; (vi) Promoting transparency and providing citizens with information in an easily accessible and understandable manner; and (vi) Increasing political accountability.

3. *Afghanistan Program for Efficient and Effective Government*: This program recognizes the need to improve effective public expenditure and civil service management. It will maximize public resources and foreign aid by: (i) Introducing and implementing broad-based policy, legal, and structural reforms in public administration; (ii) Improving public service delivery by Government through the simplification of procedures; (iii) Developing comprehensive training activities and improving the working conditions of the civil service; (iv) Developing measures to change the ability and capacity of the civil service to better carry out its responsibilities; and (v) Enabling the development of core economic functions of government as independent authorities.

4. *The National Program for Local Governance*: The Government is committed to bringing the public sector closer to the people by ensuring that local government is both empowered and accountable. It will achieve this by: (i) Implementing the recently approved Sub-National Governance Policy, which must now be rapidly implemented at local levels. Specific efforts will focus on the alignment of all relevant laws and regulations with the Sub-National Governance Policy, developing a new framework for sub- national finance and planning, and building consensus around official administrative procedures; (ii) Furthering institutional development through public administrative reform implementation at the sub-national level, as well as organizational and institutional development of participating agencies and municipal institutions; and (iii) Ensuring democratic representation by rationalizing political representation at the sub- national level, strengthening the organization of sub-national elections, and increasing public participation in decision-making (including through the budgeting process).

5. *National Program for Law and Justice for All*: The four components of this program target those parts of the legal system that are directly and immediately relevant to the way citizens experience the legal system and the rule of law. The first three components are concerned with the ability of justice institutions to deliver justice services to the people, including through: (i) Improving physical infrastructure and equipment, and conducting administrative and organizational reform to improve

service delivery; (ii) finalizing commentaries for Civil and Penal Codes, reviewing and revising laws and optimizing the law-making processes, and the simplification of operational processes; and (iii) Creating a dedicated police force tasked with providing security to judges and other justice personnel. The fourth component aims at improving access to justice to the Afghan people through a range of initiatives, including: (i) Addressing the urgent need to link informal and formal justice systems; (ii) Creating legal awareness; (iii) Promoting legal aid; and (iv) Improving criminal punishments.

6. *Afghanistan Program for Human Rights and Civic Responsibilities*: Human rights and civic responsibilities are fundamental to the functioning of responsive governing institutions and industrious societies, and they are also cornerstones for establishing sustainable peace and development. Violent extremism, underdevelopment, and limited capacities across the public sector continue to undermine efforts to guarantee the basic freedoms of the Afghan people. This program aims to respond to these challenges by: (i) Strengthening Afghan state institutions to protect human rights and to ensure the civic responsibilities of governing institutions; (ii) Raising awareness among the general Afghan population of their inherent rights and responsibilities, including through civic education; (iii) Strengthening the independence and sustainability of Afghanistan's national constitutional and other specialized institutions; (iv) Supporting the contributions of Afghanistan's traditional and local institutions to promote human rights and civic responsibilities; and (v) Ensuring effective measures to establish justice and end impunity.

Challenges to Implementation

First, leadership needs to remain committed over multiple years to an agenda for positive and systemic governance change. Second, instability in major regions of the country presents a significant obstacle to implementation of governance reform and strengthening efforts at the sub-national level. The ability to overcome this last challenge is a pivotal concern of all Government Clusters.

UNLEASHING INVESTMENTS IN ECONOMIC AND INFRASTRUCTURE DEVELOPMENT

Economic and Infrastructure Development (EID) Cluster Members: Ministry of Mines, Ministry of Transportation and Civil Aviation, Ministry of Public Works, Ministry of Energy and Water, Ministry of Commerce and Industry, Ministry of Communications and Information Technology, Ministry of Urban Development, and Kabul Municipality.

SUMMARY MATRIX PROGRAM 1: NATIONAL PRIORITY PROGRAM FOR FINANCIAL & ECONOMIC REFORMS

Intended Outcome: A more fiscally sustainable Afghan economy, where public (including donor) funds are used in a responsible and efficient manner – US$5.6 million

Intended Results 6-months	Intended Results 12-months	Intended Results 1-3 years
Working towards fiscal sustainability, Government will achieve increases in domestic revenues through expanding the tax base and support to the private sector.		
• Domestic revenues will increase to 9.4% of GDP at the end of 1389 (75.3bn AFS). • The Medium-Term Fiscal Framework (MTFF more accurate and practical tool as a basis for policy analysis and planning, and includes more robust expenditure and revenue projections (incl. line ministries' three year forward estimates of baseline spending, future projections of maintenance costs and cross-cutting reforms, and mining revenues).	• Government will confirm its commitment to gradually take over security financing, for example by allocating additional revenue annually to security spending. • Broadening the tax base in provinces, the share of revenue collected by Large Tax Payer Offices (LTOs) and Medium-Tax Payer Offices (MTOs) will increase to 85 percent of revenue department's tax collection, as per IMF targets.	• Domestic revenues will increase by around 0.7 percent of GDP annually for the next two years. • Based on robust financial viability analysis by Ministry of Finance, plans will be made to corporatize, privatize or liquidate SOEs. FLGE, Afghan Gas, North Power, Fertilizer and Azadi Printing Enterprise are expected to be considered for corporatization.
Government will improve the transparency and efficiency of its public spending that meets effective development outcomes		
• Budget process will result in a more realistic, performance-based budget in 1390, through consideration of performance against financial and non-financial targets and presentation of robust project plans. • Gaps in Line-Ministry PFM capacity will be addressed in seven critical Ministries in 1389 through standardized assessments and designing targeted capacity building programs. • External Audit, independent both in reporting and mandate, will be established in the Control and Audit Office (CAO) by a new Audit Law according to international standards. • The effectiveness of off-budget development assistance improves, as off-budget programs that meet the effectiveness criteria are included in the comprehensive budget.	• As a measure of improved PFM standards (in particular procurement), the ratio of eligible expenditures as monitored by the Afghanistan Reconstruction Trust Fund (ARTF) Monitoring Agent improves in a sustained manner, by at least 2% annually from 1389 to 1390 onwards. • Risk-based internal audits will be conducted in 7 Line Ministries by the Ministry of Finance Internal Audit, whilst assessing and building the capacity of their internal audit departments.	• Budget execution increases by 10-20% annually over the -medium-term (compared to the amount of executed budget for previous year). • Afghanistan's score in the Open Budget Index increases to 30% for 1390. • Effective internal audit function is undertaken across the Government on a risk-management basis, aiming to gradually cover all key Line-Ministries. The National Assembly is encouraged to examine a significant portion of the Auditor General's reports. • 50% of development assistance will be channeled through the Government budget, increasing Government ownership and capacity.

SUMMARY MATRIX PROGRAM 2: NATIOANAL TRANSPARENCY AND ACCOUNTABILITY PROGRAM

Intended Outcome: Public trust in and legitimacy of, the Government and an enabling environment for social and economic development – US$36 million

Intended Results 6-months	Intended Results 12-months	Intended Results 1-3 years
Component 1: Further legal and institutional development		
Legal Reform: Anti-corruption law and audit law amended and enacted. Independence of HOO and CAO is ensured.	Legal basis for MCTF established; Penal code drafted; access to information law enacted; UNCAC related laws prioritized. The panel provisions with UNCAC e.g. illicit enrichment, false assets declaration are harmonized. Anti-Corruption Tribunal (ACT) legislation is enacted.	Amendment to the Penal Code & UNCAC related laws are ratified.
Component 2: Strengthening accountability mechanisms		
Joint Monitoring and Evaluation Committee: The MEC & its secretariat are established & the first visit takes place.	Reports are published & recommendations for setting up new benchmarks for effective anti-corruption efforts are made.	The MEC continues its M&E activities.
Complaints mechanisms and regional expansion: Hotline established mechanism for protecting whistleblower/informant developed & 4 HOO regional offices established.	Triangular complaints initiatives (civil society, IPO, complaints) established; significant complaints acted upon & 3 remaining regional offices of HOO established.	Complaints followed up; HOO's operations expanded & CAO's regional offices established.
Three anti-corruption priorities for ministries: Implementation & oversight of anti-corruption priorities launched and continued.	Results are reviewed and reported upon; priorities revised, implementation & oversight continued.	Results reviewed & new priorities identified.
Internal audit mechanism strengthened in ministries: in the interim, MOF to conduct four risk based internal audits.	• Internal audit reports are acted upon by the ministries • Internal audit capacity strengthened in ministries.	Effective internal audit is established across the ministries.
Component 3: Introducing transparency initiatives		
Asset registration and verification: Assets of a certain number of officials registered & declared.	Assets registration, verification, investigation & updating performed.	Publication & preliminary verification of declarations performed.

SUMMARY MATRIX PROGRAM 2: NATIOANAL TRANSPARENCY AND ACCOUNTABILITY PROGRAM

Intended Outcome: Public trust in and legitimacy of, the Government and an enabling environment for social and economic development – US$36 million

Intended Results 6-months	Intended Results 12-months	Intended Results 1-3 years
Simplification of processes and procedures: Mapping of the processes of procurement, contracting, issue of construction permit & Hajj affairs.	Procedures for mapped processes reformed & mapping of the processes of passport & driving license completed.	Driving license and passport procedures reformed; business, evaluation of education certificate & pension processes mapped.
Oversight mechanism for monitoring the trial processes of corruption cases: mechanism established.	Effectiveness and efficiency of the mechanism is monitored and evaluated. Necessary changes made/ the mechanism is improved and Implementation continued.	Implementation continued.
Oversight Mechanism for Elections – mechanism within election institutions ensured.	Monitoring of the campaign process was conducted in accordance to the set mechanism.	Transparency in the elections campaign process is ensured.

SUMMARY MATRIX PROGRAM 3: AFGHANISTAN EFFICIENT & EFFECTIVE GOVERNMENT

Intended Outcome: Increased ability by the government to protect and to serve the population, and to improve the delivery of services – US$368 million

Component 1: Broad-based Policy, Legal, and Structural Reform in Public Administration

• Cabinet has direct oversight of PAR • Policy development by SPDU for more comprehensive PAR initiated • Drafting of new law "Code" to replace civil service law and civil servants law initiated • Scaling up of CSRP in line with strategy of new PAR • 20% of senior appointments with civil society/university scrutiny • Scaling up of CSRP initiated with inclusion of the strategic objectives of more comprehensive PAR • To promote transparency, civil society & university representation in appointment of 20% of senior civil servants	• Code drafted:ambiguities/contradictions; international standards met • Civil service appointment & grievance processes reformed, with strict de-politicization, transparency & integrity standards • Work of 10 service line ministries reviewed for misalignment of mandates • Begin deconcentration of recruitment: benefits subnational levels/DDP • 50% of senior appointments under civil society/university scrutiny	• Boards of appointment & appeals separated from CSMD • with work subject to further scrutiny • By 2013 P&G introduced to all under new rubrics • work of 10 service line ministries realigned/rationalized • Continue deconcentration of recruitment process • Achieved 100% of senior appointments under new rules

SUMMARY MATRIX PROGRAM 3: AFGHANISTAN EFFICIENT & EFFECTIVE GOVERNMENT

Intended Outcome: Increased ability by the government to protect and to serve the population, and to improve the delivery of services – US$368 million

Intended Results 6-months	Intended Results 12-months	Intended Results 1-3 years
- Cabinet has direct oversight of PAR - SPDU established within IARCSC - Policy development for more comprehensive PAR - Drafting of new law "Code" initiated to replace Civil service law and civil servants law - Scaling up of CSRP initiate - Scaling up of CSRP initiated		

Component 2: Improved Public Service Delivery by Government

- MoF (revenue generating areas) and IARCSC (business practices of ministries) establish corruption free, low cost, less time consuming mechanisms for transaction of public services.	- MoF: Approximately 5 candidates for reforms identified and agreed with Line ministries/agencies - IARCSC: Dedicated BPS Unit in place, reform of 3 ministries	- Minimum of 5 critical service areas reformed per year, - Public confidence in Government improves - IARCSC: BPS introduced to 5 ministries/agencies

Component 3: Comprehensive Training and Capacity Development and Improvement of Working Conditions

- CSI: Needs of educationally disadvantaged/specialized subjects met, mentoring added, performance-based management & leadership development integrated, and begin new training locations and training, including in security challenged & distant provinces/districts - Internship program instituted to address recruitment needs of aging cohort - Re-structuring of MCP initiated	- CSI completes five common functions for 16,000 civil servants - Continue establishing new civil service training centers - Begin capacity strengthening of IARCSC - With special focus on subnational level, injection of staff and staff capacity through MCP and ACSS - Begin capacity building of boards of appointment and appeals and their regional components; - Establishment of 6 RIMUs to 6 in key ministries/agencies	- Capacity building completed of: IARCSC, Boards - Continue injection of staff and staff capacity - Linkages with colleges and graduate level educational institutions to promote masters level degrees in public administration/ management and E-Learning

SUMMARY MATRIX PROGRAM 3: AFGHANISTAN EFFICIENT & EFFECTIVE GOVERNMENT

Intended Outcome: Increased ability by the government to protect and to serve the population, and to improve the delivery of services – US$368 million

Intended Results 6-months	Intended Results 12-months	Intended Results 1-3 years
Component 4: Improvement in the Operational Framework		
• 40 line management positions established, subject to MCP • Increase of women recruitment; gender units in 13 ministries • Introduction of HRMIS in select ministries.	• 80 line management positions established, subject to MCP • Gender Units established in 20 ministries • RMIS expanded to 5 ministries. agencies • M&E, performance appraisal of individuals/institutions	• 300 line management positions established, subject to MCP • Gender units established in all ministries and significant advances made in gender parity in government
Component 5: Advanced Restructuring and Reform		
• IARCSC, MoF with EID Cluster: initiate design of road map, advanced restructuring and functional review	• Complete road map; cabinet approval for ARR program • MoF: draft enabling legislation/subsidiary legislation • Initiate functional reviews of: MoTCA, MoM, MoPW, MoUD	• Complete functional reviews • Reforms achieved: authorities for civil aviation, mines, roads, railways, industrial parks

SUMMARY MATRIX PROGRAM 4: NATIONAL PRIORITY PROGRAM FOR LOCAL GOVERNANCE

Intended Outcome: Increased confidence of the population in government's ability to protect and to serve the population; improved delivery of services – US$285 million

Intended Results 6-months	Intended Results 12-month	Intended Results 1-3 years
Component 1: Sub-National Governance Policy		
• SNG Legal framework and mechanisms established and draft legal strategy developed. • High priority municipal, district and village legal frameworks and other priority SNG laws drafted and sent to CoM and onto Parliament. • Cabinet Committee established, SNG finance strategy agreed, and Provincial budgeting and strategic planning pilots underway.	• All priority 6 laws more laws drafted on SNG, Affirmative Action for Women and CSOs. • New Municipal laws drafted incl. priority regulatory frameworks. • SNG financial framework and medium-term strategy (3 years) in place. Guidance drafted on Provincial Planning	• Completion of SN Governance Legal Framework – 6 new priority laws, 11 existing laws and 22 regulations amended and approved. • Evaluation of SNG framework. • Municipal Laws and Provincial levels plans fully established and execution under way. • Provincial strategic plans in place.

SUMMARY MATRIX PROGRAM 4: NATIONAL PRIORITY PROGRAM FOR LOCAL GOVERNANCE

Intended Outcome: Increased confidence of the population in government's ability to protect and to serve the population; improved delivery of services – US$285 million

Intended Results 6-months	Intended Results 12-months	Intended Results 1-3 years
	(PDPs and Provincial Strategic Plans PSPs), the roles of govt departments and incorporation and management of NGO projects and local needs. • Financial frameworks, budgets operationalized through pilots. Monitoring/checks and balances system in place	• Provincial budgeting and execution in place.
• Administrative Boundary mapping and cadastral exercise commenced	• Methodology agreed. Basic administrative boundary data and boundary dispute mechanism developed and agreed upon.	• Full framework under execution; resources mobilized. Spatial data infrastructure in place.
• Local government opinion survey pilots launched	• Local government opinion surveys assessed and plans for rollout made.	• Local government opinion surveys rolled out, survey results utilized.
Component 2: Institutional Development and Service Delivery		
• MoU agreed with IARCSC and capacity building priorities and target setting for PAR in local government completed. • Priority appointments of Deputy Provincial Governors (DPGs) and District Governors (DGs) approved. • Approval of IDLG interim structures. IDLG program portfolio management aligned with SNG Policy Implementation. IDLG commences drafting of Local Govt Guidance. • Strategy developed and agreed to introduce performance and accountability measures in the PGOs, combined/ incorporated with development of civ-mil approach/	• 2nd round of DPGs and DGs Appointments in place. • Capacity building in IDLG, PGOs, DGOs and Provincial Councils underway • SN Appointments trained and practicing outreach, Transition of PRTs to PSTs, pilot projects underway and M&E tested. • Procurement and construction underway for priority SNG buildings/offices. • Municipalities assessed, training tailored to improve service delivery. Service	• All Programs aligned with SN Governance Policy. • Priority public admin reforms completed in all PGOs and DGOs. • PRT to PST transition completed eligible/priority provinces. • Building in all priority PGOs and DGOs constructed and fully equipped. • Municipalities' capacity improved and Councils fully established and functional and mayor elections conducted. • 80 Districts covered by DDP.

SUMMARY MATRIX PROGRAM 4: NATIONAL PRIORITY PROGRAM FOR LOCAL GOVERNANCE

Intended Outcome: Increased confidence of the population in government's ability to protect and to serve the population; improved delivery of services – US$285 million

Intended Results 6-months	Intended Results 12-months	Intended Results 1-3 years
strategy and PAR. • SNG Physical infrastructure assessments undertaken, some building works underway. • 15 Districts targeted by DDP; Municipal Structure and new models assessed. Priority projects commenced.	delivery and cost recovery plans ready. • DDP extended to further 20 Districts; *Tashkeel* filled, 1st phase basic service delivery projects completed. • Provincial Relation and Coordination Unit (PR&CU) fully functional, clear strategies and guidelines developed with Governors and local councils for, *inter alia*, having an efficient role in support of Afghanistan Peace and Reconciliation Program (APRP).	

Component 3: Democratic Representation & Civic Education

• Plan for Civil Register agreed. • Inter-ministerial working group established to start evaluating the status of CDCs, DDAs and ASOP Shuras to be transformed into DCs and VCs.	• Plans developed for transition of CDCs, DDAs and ASOP Shuras into District Councils (DCs) and Village Councils (VCs) with legal status.	• DCs and VCs established. Full democratic participation targets set and transition done.

SUMMARY MATRIX PROGRAM 5: LAW & JUSTICE FOR ALL

Intended Outcome: Improved capacity of government to deliver justice; increased trust by population in government's ability to administer justice in fair and equitable manner – US$381 million

Component 1: Simplification of Operational Procedures; Commentaries for Civil and Penal Codes; Revision and Drafting of Laws; Optimization of Law-making Processes

• Identification of shortcomings in existing operational procedures.	• Design of new simplified procedures • Launch of Pilot Scheme.	• Implementation of new operational procedures.
• Production of Commentaries of Civil and Penal Codes initiated • Strategy for review, analysis and revision of existing laws is designed, legislative processes simplified and	• Commentaries of Civil and Penal Codes completed and launched. • Translation Unit in MoJ is established and enhanced in SC.	• Civil, commercial and penal statutes are reviewed; • Existing Afghan laws and legal resources are made accessible in coherent, rationalized,

SUMMARY MATRIX PROGRAM 5: LAW & JUSTICE FOR ALL

Intended Outcome: Improved capacity of government to deliver justice; increased trust by population in government's ability to administer justice in fair and equitable manner – US$381 million

Intended Results 6-months	Intended Results 12-months	Intended Results 1-3 years
• legislative requirements of GC cluster addressed • Penal sanctions for land grabbing reviewed • Laws and regulations governing sub-standard goods are designed.	• Strategy for review and revision of legislation is implemented and defective laws identified and amended.	classified and digitized format.

Component 2: Institutional Development (Capacity Building, Physical Infrastructure, Transportation & Equipments)

• Training needs assessment of all JSI's personnel is conducted. • JSIs Organizational Structures are reviewed (PRR and P&G). • Anti Corruption Tribunals (ACT) and National Ministers Court (NMC) established. • A National Ministers Court is established and functional.	• Dedicated training programs for JSI's are designed. • ACT fully functional in 8 regions. • NMC fully functional.	• Training programs are rolled out and implemented. • JSI's PRR and P&G completed. • JSI's are linked with E-Governance program. • SC PRR is completed and implemented • Continuation of RIMUs for P&G and PRR; • Establishment of Legal Resource Centers.
• National Justice Programs (NJP) Capital Investment Plan (CIP) is completed (infrastructure, transport and equipment needs assessment).	• NJP-CIP prioritized implementation started.	• NJP-CIP implementation completed and JSI's infrastructure, transport and equipment needs met.

Component 3: Security of JSIs personnel

• Needs assessment and plan for judicial police carried out.	• Judicial and justice sector police established.	• JSIs Staff's security ensured.

Component 4: Access to Justice

• National legal awareness strategy is designed and programs are harmonized with new strategy.	• Legal awareness materials are being produced. • Legal awareness program is expanded to all provinces.	• Roll out of legal awareness strategy has commenced.
• Formulation of national informal justice policy is completed.	• Informal justice strategy is designed and law on informal justice drafted and ready for adoption.	• Nationwide implementation of informal justice strategy commenced and law implemented.

SUMMARY MATRIX PROGRAM 5: LAW & JUSTICE FOR ALL

Intended Outcome: Improved capacity of government to deliver justice; increased trust by population in government's ability to administer justice in fair and equitable manner – US$381 million

Intended Results 6-months	Intended Results 12-months	Intended Results 1-3 years
• Design of national legal aid strategy is completed; mechanism and systems for the provision of legal aid services are designed.	• Legal aid offices are expanded to all provinces.	
• Vocational training programs for prisons and juvenile detention centers are designed • Program for non-custodial punishments, like community service, is designed	• Programs for vocational training, non-custodial punishments and de-radicalization are operational.	• Medical and mental health services in prisons are enhanced and expanded.

SUMMARY MATRIX PROGRAM 6: AFGHANISTAN PROGRAM FOR HUMAN RIGHTS & CIVIC RESPONSIBILITY

Intended Outcome: Increased awareness across the State and general population about human rights and civic responsibilities – US$170 million

Component 1: Strengthen Afghan State institutions

Design strategy, identify implementing partners, and mobilize resources for government-wide human rights and civic education programs.	Pilot human rights and civic education workshops, study tours, and individualized mentoring in a select number (e.g., 5-6) of ministries and agencies.	Increased capacity of State institutions through HR promotion and civic education activities.
Establish a Human Rights Support Unit (HRSU) in the Ministry of Justice (MoJ) and further develop the capacity of existing human rights units within the Government to strengthen human rights protection across Afghanistan.	Develop an action plan for oversight and management of human rights units across the Government to improve their effectiveness in the protection of human rights across Afghanistan.	Establish human rights units in the Attorney-General's Office (AGO) and Ministry of Education (MoE) to strengthen human rights protection across Afghanistan.

Component 2: Raise awareness among the general Afghan population

Design comprehensive Civic Education and Human Rights Action Plan, identify implementing partners, and mobilize resources for human rights and civic education programs that target communities across Afghanistan.	Citizen awareness raised in at least five provinces about human rights, pro-poor development planning, gender, elections, rule of law, disaster preparedness, peace, reconciliation, security, local development, culture, environment, etc.	Enhanced public awareness in at least twenty provinces about human rights and civic responsibilities and improved Government accountability.

Component 3: Strengthen the independence and sustainability of Afghanistan's national constitutional and other specialized institutions

SUMMARY MATRIX PROGRAM 6: AFGHANISTAN PROGRAM FOR HUMAN RIGHTS & CIVIC RESPONSIBILITY

Intended Outcome: Increased awareness across the State and general population about human rights and civic responsibilities – US$170 million

Intended Results 6-months	Intended Results 12-months	Intended Results 1-3 years
Improved effectiveness of AIHRC, IEC, ECC, and PSABSA in managing their programs and resources through staff skills development in planning and operations.	Increased ability of AIHRC, IEC, ECC, and PSABSA to perform their mandated functions in an independent manner through high-level Government and broader civil society support.	Sustainable financing strategy introduced for the AIHRC, IEC, ECC, and PSABSA; improved staff skills-base, networks, and morale.

Component 4: *Support the contribution of Afghanistan's traditional and local institutions*

Design strategy, identify implementing partners, and mobilize resources for a Comprehensive Public Communication Strategy for traditional and local bodies.	Development of baseline data (for future progress reports) on the general understanding of human rights and civic responsibilities for traditional and local bodies.	Measurable improvements in the quality and quantity of traditional and local institutions' focus on human rights and civic responsibility issues.

Component 5: *Ensure effective measures are in place to establish justice and end impunity*

Raise awareness to prioritize the Action Plan on Peace, Reconciliation, and Justice across the general population through workshops and a media outreach campaign.	Reintroduce an updated version of the Action Plan by the Government	Advance peace, justice, and reconciliation goals of the Government through the Action Plan implementation.

Situation Analysis

For the first time in Afghanistan's long and eventful history, Afghanistan has the opportunity to transform its vast mineral and hydrocarbon resources into great wealth for all its current and future generations. Never before has a set of opportunities for the environmentally friendly exploitation of Afghanistan's vast mineral resources for the benefit of all Afghans presented itself to the country's leadership. While this unique set of opportunities is now in place, there are key conditions that need to be established to ensure that Afghanistan's growth prospects are realized and the country avoids all the worst effects of the resource curse. The EID Cluster has been designed to serve as the engine of formal growth and revenue mobilization. It not only requires substantial long-term investment, but is also contingent on progress being made around a set of advanced policy and institutional reforms deemed essential to attaining the EID Cluster and overall ANDS objectives.

Needed Response

The overall program is designed with a long-term vision, while delivering a number of immediate and short-term wins, as part of an overall improved economic governance framework. Moreover, given the focus on "narrow" growth, with generated revenues providing resources for broad-based inclusive growth delivered through the ARD and HRD Clusters, and the Program for Advanced Reform and Restructuring under the Governance Cluster, the EID program is designed as an integrated national economic development program.

Results emerging from the EID Cluster that directly impact on growth prospects, revenue potential and employment opportunities are considerable. Possible impacts include:

- *Growth effects.* Preliminary estimates of successful implementation of EID and Governance Cluster programs indicated that, by 2025, contribution to GDP from related components of the services sector (c20%) and industry (c25%) could represent an increase from 18% to almost 50% of GDP, with GDP potentially increasing to US$80 billion from the 2009 level of US$13 billion. A further decade could possibly see GDP reach a quarter trillion US dollars.[2]
- *Revenue Effects* include increasing net revenue earning potential to US$1b by 2017 and US$3b by 2025. Second round tax revenues would also increase exponentially up to 2025 followed by diminishing increases.[1]
- *Employment effects* are derived from a variety of sources, including: (i) 10 million labor days derived from construction related activity in the EID Cluster's flagship program: the National- Regional Resource Corridor Initiative (NRRCI); (ii) 1 million sustainable jobs from supporting the Small and Medium-sized Enterprises (SME) from increased export opportunities and import substitution; with iii) further substantial increases with successful implementation of SME support and good urban planning to build communities including around resource corridors hubs. Second round employment opportunities through growth impacts are enormous.

The overall objective of the EID Cluster is to "*support Afghanistan's transition to financial independence and developing a business climate that enables private investment.*" The six supporting National Priority Program objectives follow: (i) Connecting Afghanistan to the region, and the rest of the world; (ii) Progressing Afghanistan's financial independence through strategic partnerships with extractive industries; (iii) Delivering cost-effective energy to industries/communitie; (iv) Improving urban livelihoods; (v) Facilitating private sector led inclusive growth including increasing employment and trading opportunities; and, (vi) Fostering an open information society.

1. *National-Regional Resource Corridor Initiative* is the flagship transport oriented program focused on developing the critical infrastructure needed to reap benefits directly from large scale, environmentally friendly exploitation of Afghanistan's mineral resources and indirectly from increased trade flows and labor mobility. It aims to deliver shared-use road, rail, aviation, power and water systems in order to, *inter alia*, establish Afghanistan as a strategic land bridge that connects the East to the Middle East through to Western Europe and to Central and South Asia.

2. *Extractive Industries Excellence Program* will spearhead the rapid scaling up of major and artisanal extractive industries, as well as resource corridors, for all major mineral groups. It aims to build a stronger and modernized Ministry that delivers and implements good sector policies and support an enabled environment for private extractive industry related investment.

3. *National Energy Supply Program* will build on gains made in both power generation and distribution in order to meet increasing demand through a combination of domestic generation and imports, and through alternative sources for rural electrification. It will foster a broad approach to generation and distribution that reflects the context of Afghanistan, prioritizing private and domestic sectors in the process.

4. *Urban Planning Technical Assistance Facility* recognizes that good urban planning supports development of the private sector and contributes significantly to social and security stabilization objectives, including protecting the most vulnerable and supporting the delivery of cost- effective public services. Effective integration of land use and transportation planning is critical to enabling successful improvements in the infrastructure and economic and social environments of communities, especially in support of resource corridor hubs.

5. *Integrated Trade And SME Support Facility* objectives include reforming the Small and Medium-sized Enterprises legal and regulatory environment, achieving real gains in international competitiveness of Afghanistan's existing and emerging SMEs, and delivering highly valued business services to SMEs are key objectives. The program has important linkages with industrial parks, emerging transport and trade hubs, and in the trade, construction, agricultural and service industries.

6. *E-Afghanistan* intends to bridge the communications gap that exists within Afghanistan whilst also creating new systems of data and information management within a model of new public management. To establish greater national unity, it is important that in time all districts, major villages, and even remote rural areas can communicate with Kabul, with one another, and the rest of the world.

Illustrative Matrix for Economic and Infrastructure Development (Eid) Cluster

Intended Results: Over 3 years, 158643 direct jobs and 1.09 million indirect jobs created; 33.4 million labor-days of work generated; Government Revenue of Afs1,933,93 7,500 from transport user fees and taxes; Revenue growth of up to US$ $500 million – US$800 billion each year over the medium term achieved from extractive industries; US$50-1 00 million USD revenue generated by new SMEs; Total energy supply increased to 1800 megawatt with 1200 megawatt of domestic production; 75 % population connected through phones and 25% population through internet; Capacity of urban development ministry built to service urban populations.

Budget US$ Million 3 Yr	Expected Results		
	Immediate Term (6-months)	Immediate Term (12-months)	Short Term Intended Results (1-3 years)
1,150	**Program 1: National Regional Resources Corridor Initiative (80,710 jobs and 18 million labor days created)**		
	• Cluster Program Implementation Management Team operational • Design options for regional connecting network initiated • Design options for extractive industry hubs substantially initiated • • Options paper initiated for establishment of independent authorities tasked with delivery	• 15% of planned connectivity to the region and the rest of the world achieved • Government revenue of Afs1,333,750,000 generated from transport user fees and taxes • Adoption and publication of sector policies in transport, mining, energy and railways. • Enhanced management reporting institutionalized	• Regional resource corridor connecting network plan approved • Plan for extractive industry hubs approved • 25% of planned connectivity to the region and the rest of the world achieved • Government Revenue of Afs1,933,937,500 from transport user fees and taxes • Enhanced management follow-up institutionalized
300	**Program 2: Extractive Industries Excellence Program (8,684 jobs and 1.9 million labor days created)**		
	• Cluster Program Implementation Management Team operational • Tendered various mining sector projects on transparent manner • New structure and business plan developed and approved • Cluster programs integrated into the national budget process	• Subordinate implementing legislation for Mineral and Hydrocarbons Laws of drafted • 10% of minerals and 25% hydrocarbons surveyed • EITI validation progressing • Extractive Industry Revenue forecasting model operational	• A strong and capable ministry built including supporting good sector policies • Revenue growth of up to US$ $500 million – US$800 billion each year over the medium term achieved from extractive industries • EITI validation completed successfully • 30% of minerals and 40% hydrocarbons surveyed

Budget US$ Million 3 Yr	Expected Results		
	Immediate Term (6-months)	Immediate Term (12-months)	Short Term Intended Results (1-3 years)
	• Options developed for establishment of independent authorities tasked with delivery • Cluster programs integrated into the national budget process • Drafting instructions for subordinate legislation initiated	• National Mining Policy under Preparation • Economic criteria in program design institutionalized • Enhanced management reporting institutionalized	• Shiberghan Gas Project brought online • Centre of excellence of Extractive Industry PPP policies operational • Business Plan Implemented (continuous)
	Program 3: National Energy Supply Program (NESP) - (42,822 jobs and 9.4 million labor days created)		
1,501	• Cluster Program Implementation Management Team operational • Options developed for establishment of independent authorities tasked with delivery • Cluster programs integrated into the national budget process	• National Energy Policy under preparation • Economic criteria in program design institutionalized • Enhanced management reporting institutionalized	• National Energy Policy prepared and operationalized • 75% collection rate, 65% urban coverage, 25% rural and 90% non-residential coverage achieved • 30 per cent reduction in technical losses.
	Program 4: Integrated Trade and SME Support Facility - (2,857 direct and 1,000,000 indirect jobs and 0.6 million labor days created)		
250	• Cluster Program Implementation Management Team • Options developed for establishment of independent authorities tasked with delivery • Cluster programs integrated into the national budget process • Subordinate SME related policy and legislative drafting instructions initiated • Publication of Tax and Tariff Policy	• Subordinate SME related legislation drafted • Afghanistan-Pakistan Trade and Transit Agreement operationalized • Enhanced management reporting institutionalized	• .... new SMEs registered and assisted under the program and ...... of them became operational • % of regulatory framework in place and ASMEDA established • US$50-100 million USD revenue generated by new SMEs institutionalized • Enhanced management follow-up

Budget US$ Million 3 Yr	Expected Results		
	Immediate Term (6-months)	**Immediate Term (12-months)**	**Short Term Intended Results (1-3 years)**
	Program 5: National Urban Delivery Program: To improve urban livelihoods – (13570 jobs and 3 million labor days created)		
405	• Cluster Program Implementation Management Team operational • Cluster programs integrated into the national budget process • Commencement of drafting of an options paper for resource corridor urban plans • Commencement of sustainable social housing options linked to wider social protection policy	• Resource corridor urban proposals submitted to Cabinet • Sustainable social housing options linked to wider social protection policy submitted to Cabinet • Review of urban Planning Guidelines and Building Codes initiated • Enhanced management reporting institutionalized	• ……% of urban people below poverty line • ……% of urban population covered under safe drinking water, sanitation, electricity • ……. No. vulnerable families provided shelter through safety net • Enhanced management follow-up institutionalized
	Program 6: E-Afghanistan Program: To foster and open information society – (10000 direct and 90000 indirect jobs and 0.5 million labor days created)		
194	• Cluster Program Implementation Management Team operational • Drafting commended of medium-term policy options on access to telecommunications including phone and internet in rural and urban areas	• Publication of Government medium-term policy on access to telecommunications including phone and internet in rural (x%) and urban (x%) areas with (currently 3.3m connections) • Enhanced management reporting institutionalized • Good progress of roll-out of fiber optic and copper cable network complete	• US$100 million additional revenue generated • 15 million Afghans hold Smart Card (National ID) • 25,000 residents covered under one post office • 75% of the population connected through phones • 25% of the population connected through internet • 4,000 km National Backbone Network completed • E-Governance and national ID card project under preparation • Fiber optic and copper cable network complete
	Total Budget US$3,800 million		

Challenges to Implementation

There are five principle challenges that need to be overcome within the EID Cluster, to secure progress: i) Strengthening the economic policy environment by formulating sound sector policies in year one; ii) Enhancing economic governance and the regulatory environment through the creation of dedicated authorities (including merit based staffing arrangements) and new regulatory standards and oversight measures also in Year 1: iii) Attracting donor and regional financing through new priority program formulation linked operational investment strategies; iv) Delivering better implementation management, which requires both on and off-budget financing, built around an expedited model of project management and continuing improvements in the credibility of EID Cluster ministry budgets and risk management; and v) Increasing improvements in monitoring and sustainability through strong designs and supervision and a dedicated monitoring framework.

ACCELERATING AGRICULTURAL AND RURAL DEVELOPMENT

The Agriculture and Rural Development Cluster (ARD) Members: the Ministry of Agriculture, Irrigation and Livestock, the Ministry of Rural Rehabilitation and Development, the Ministry of Energy and Water, and the Ministry of Counter- Narcotics.

Situation Analysis

Afghanistan's rural areas are producing only a fraction of their potential. The country has more than enough water resources, but has yet to harness them fully. Improved wheat seed, coupled with fertilizer and irrigation, can increase yields by 50 percent. Less than 10% of water resources have been developed, even though irrigation can double or triple farm yields, as well as make possible the production of higher-value crops. With Government support, rural communities are pulling together to implement community-level projects that foster economic growth and productivity. Afghanistan's rural road network has also steadily expanded, providing isolated farm communities with access to inputs, markets, and basic services. Rural communications have improved dramatically with most parts of the country now having access to mobile phones and modern communications. Yet much remains to be done.

Afghanistan remains one of the poorest countries in the world, and much of its poverty is situated in rural areas. About 80% of the population depends on agriculture and associated forms of rural production. Seasonal and chronic unemployment are common and increasing. The result is a high degree of food insecurity, a socioeconomic environment that is conducive to instability, an illicit economy, and extreme poverty. Without significant, visible change to living conditions in the countryside, insurgents and narcotics traffickers will continue to find willing clients among Afghanistan's impoverished villages.

Needed Response

The Agriculture and Rural Development Cluster Goal is the *"development of prosperous rural and pastoral communities."* Achieving this goal stands or falls on whether the government, civil society, and the private sector can trigger dramatic increases in job creation, rural employment, and rural growth. To this end, five objectives are defined that taken together can transform the rural economy:

First, Afghanistan must develop a *basic information framework to* inform government policies for rural development. Second, it must improve both the *production quality and quantity* of agriculture outputs where small interventions can have an enormous impact. Third, global experience in developing countries shows that all-year road access is among the top drivers of rural transformation. Thus, *linkages to markets as well as access to credit* must be improved. Fourth, Afghanistan must i*mprove food security and services* to create a healthy population able to contribute to productive growth, and fifth, it must establish a *better regulatory and enabling environment* to counter the effects of conflict, corruption, and the deterioration of Afghanistan's natural resources.

Finally, rural development has traditionally split between large programs carried out by a central government and highly localized communities that largely bypass government activity. This must change. New partnerships between the Afghan Government, communities, and the private sector are now guiding planning for the country's Agricultural and Rural Development Cluster.

The National Priority Programs presented below together form a set of activities whose purpose is to develop an enabling framework that communities need to build up their productive assets, reduce insecurity, and improve household incomes across the countryside. They will also be the main short and medium-term means to create jobs, stabilize rural areas, and facilitate people's recovery from conflict. Two national labor intensive programs outlined below are already operational. Over time, rising production and increased economic activity stemming from water resources projects and improved production technology will come on-stream, creating more permanent jobs and, ultimately, accelerating economic growth and recovery.

1. *National Water and Natural Resources Development:* Damage to irrigation and other water systems, soil, rangeland and forests must be reversed for the agricultural economic sector to grow. At the same time, under-utilized land must be made productive, and alternative energy sources must conserve traditional fuel sources, such as timber. The first phase of this program focuses on large-scale natural resource projects in irrigation development and management, Afghanistan land management, and rural energy development.
2. *National Comprehensive Agriculture Production and Market Development:* From improved production and productivity on the farm, to the market, to the factory and finally to exports, agricultural economic growth requires the strengthening or development of new "value chains". To this end, this program focuses on research and extension services, agriculture infrastructure development, rural credit, improved agricultural production methods, and market development.
3. *National Rural Access*: Capacity to purchase inputs and sell products competitively is a prerequisite for successful rural development. Reducing transport costs, as well

as providing year-round access to markets, is fundamental for better farming and rural growth. This program, which is already operational and expected to scaleup nationally, will concentrate on linking farmers and communities to the growing national road network by developing a system for nationwide labor-intensive road construction and maintenance.

4. *National Strengthening of Local Institutions*: Partnerships with communities have also proven to be an efficient way to construct large quantities of small-scale, yet economically productive, assets for poor villagers. This program will build upon existing work to increase rural growth potential. It will expand Community Development Councils to cover all of Afghanistan's villages, and it will provide additional resources to build simple village infrastructure. This program will also strengthen capacity and sustainability potential through a clustering of villages for better efficiency and stronger linkages to formal government institutions.

Challenges to Implementation

For years, ministry staff fulfilled both public and private sector roles. Today, the single greatest challenge facing ministries in the Agriculture and Rural Development Cluster is the identification of their true public role, inclusive of transitioning contract staff into civil servants positions. Second, these same ministries require significant internal reforms to improve their efficiency and accountability. Each has carried out a review of its systems for fiduciary oversight and management, and programs will ultimately include an action plan to improve cash management and payment scheduling procedures, the capacity of internal audits, and public procurement. Third, much of the economic growth agenda embedded in these programs rests on a rigorous analysis of value chains and how the Government can remove constraints to private sector investment, rather than enhance direct Government action. This effort must be addressed in concert with other Government of Afghanistan clusters.

FACILITATING HUMAN RESOURCE DEVELOPMENT

The Human Resource Development (HRD) Cluster Members: Minister of Education (MoE), Ministry of Higher Education (MoHE), Ministry of Women's Affairs (MoWA), Ministry of Labor, Social Affairs, Martyrs and Disabled (MoLSAMD), and Ministry of Public Health (MoPH).

Illustrative Matrix for Agriculture and Rural Development (Ard) Cluster

Intended Results: Over 3 years, 337,000 direct jobs created; 16.47 million man-days of work generated through programs; Improved access to irrigation for 100,000 hectares; Agricultural Production growth increased by 10%; Sustained growth in legal rural incomes and employment by 28%; Safe drinking water coverage improved by 5 percentage points; Agriculture inputs supply and extension networks established; Access to markets improved by building 3,398 km of secondary and tertiary roads; 3.9 million Direct and 21 million indirect beneficiaries of access to basic and infrastructure services projects; 28,400 Community Development Councils (CDCs) received block grants and 21,833 CDCs implementing at least one infrastructure development sub-project of their own.

Budget (US$ million)	Immediate (6 months)	Immediate (6-12 months)	Short Term (1- 3 years)
		PRIORITY PROGRAMS	
	1. National Water and Natural Resource Development Program – (388,000 direct and indirect jobs created.)		
782	1. Full prioritization and semi-detailed budgeting completed for water priority projects. 2. Recruitment of 4 design engineers and 4 implementation engineers. 3. National Implementation plan prepared for Community-Based Natural Resources Management (CBNRM) based on priority provinces and districts. 4. 50% of NRM MAIL staff trained in national CBNRM strategy. 5. 60% preparation for implementation of Afghanistan Land Management Authority (ALMA) completed and Land Management Department of MAIL merged with ALMA.	1. Identification and Establishment of database and matrix system for water sector. 2. Identification of 50% of targeted districts for potable water. 3. National Water and Irrigation Program developed for implementation. 4. CBNRM implemented in all current projects. 5. 75% of NRM MAIL staff trained in national CBNRM strategy. 6. Afghanistan Land Management Authority established and made operational. 7. Establishment of operating and maintenance procedures for Energy for Rural Development.	1. Improved access to irrigation for 100,000 ha and safe drinking water by 5%. 2. All new projects adopt CBNRM strategy and community management of natural resources increased to over 25,000 ha. 3. All NRM MAIL staff trained in national CBNRM strategy. 4. Legal access to government land for commercial purposes by 62,500 ha. 5. Increased rural access to reliable and affordable services reducing pressures on natural resources.
	2. National Comprehensive Agriculture Production and Market Development – (515,000 direct and indirect jobs created.)		

Budget (US$ million)	Immediate (6 months)	Immediate (6-12 months)	Short Term (1-3 years)
		PRIORITY PROGRAMS	
489	1. Gap assessment for input supply (including legislative and regulatory) and knowledge transfer determined and implementation plan to address future needs completed. 2. Agro-ecological zones identified and priorities established. 3. Recruitment of specialist staff for development of the Strategic Grain Reserve Policy. 4. Technical team and general processes for delivery of credit to farmers established. 5. Establishment of implementation team and baseline survey initiated. 6. Establishment of 2 additional provincial offices and 3 Economic Development Package's approved. 7. All CARD-F manuals revised in line with lessons learnt for enabling rapid rollout.	1. Using assessments full inputs supply program for implementation developed. 2. US$50 million of credit delivered to private sector organizations and individual farmers. 3. Initial distribution and implementation areas identified. 4. Assessment document completed for Strategic Grain Reserves 3 years.	1. Sustained growth in legal rural incomes and employment by 28%. 2. US$ 150 million credit delivered to private sector organizations and individual farmers. 3. Improved access to services and resources by 20%. 4. System for supply and quality inputs established and made operational country wide. 5. Research and extension network established and operational country wide. 6. Procurement and storage capacity for 200,000 mt of wheat for Afghanistan Strategic Grain Reserve established.
3. National Rural Access Program – (16.47 million labor days generated.)			
250	1. Up-scaling of 200 KM secondary road in targeted districts completed. 2. 135 km of tertiary road improved. 3. Routine maintenance checking for 300 KM road completed 4. Implementation methodology and establishment of operational guidelines for working with community-based labor refined.	1. Up-scaling of 290 KM secondary road in targeted district completed. 2. 315 km of tertiary road improved. 3. Routine maintenance checking for 840 KM road completed. 4. Draft of operational guidelines for working with community has been prepared for review and approval.	1. Increase access to District Centre services by 10% in target areas. 2. Effective maintenance of 7,000 km of roads 3. 3,398 km of secondary and tertiary roads built or rehabilitated. 4. Rural Road Research Unit established.

Budget (US$ million)	Immediate (6 months)	Immediate (6-12 months)	Short Term (1-3 years)
		PRIORITY PROGRAMS	
	5. Selection for road establishment, mobilizing resources and initial procurement process rolled out.		5. Decrease travel times by 10%. 6. local market prices within 15% of the price in the nearest town
	4. National Strengthening of Local Institutions		
537	1. Completion of identification and initial process of establishment of CDCs in 1,697 new communities. 2. Follow up process of registration for 5,000 CDCs. 3. Completion of at least 50% of Community Development Plans (CDP) from newly established CDCs. 4. Recruitment of at least 15 civil service workers in the provinces. 5. Rolling out procurement process for technical advisor in management department, and Monitoring and Evaluation.	1. Completion of at least 5,000 new community development councils establishment 2. Completion of block grants disbursement to at least 1,800 CDCs. 3. 1,056 CDCs have utilized at least 70% of disbursed block grants. 4. Around 7,000 community sub projects have been reviewed, designed and approved. 5. Development of process for independent evaluation and monitoring, with support from technical advisor(s)	1. 3.9 million Direct and 21 million indirect beneficiaries of access to basic and infrastructure services projects created. 2. Completion of block grants disbursement to 11,000 new and 17,400 existing CDCs. 3. 9,000 kms of new or repaired farm-to-market roads. 4. 8,100 new sources of safe drinking water. 5. 6,000 new or repaired community irrigation systems. 6. 4,500 renewable village energy projects (i.e. micro-hydro); and 7. 3,900 new or fully rehabilitated village schools.
		Total Budget US$2,058 million	

Introduction

Human resources are the backbone of a nation's economy, reflecting national capacity to supply needed skills for economic growth and productivity. Without a strong, equitable, and appropriate approach to human resource development, sustainable economic growth remains elusive. Education and skills development are the vehicles by which human resource development occurs.

Despite significant improvements over the past nine years, human resource development in Afghanistan continues to face a number of challenges. One of the most significant is the skills gap between labor supply and market demands. Despite a wide range of educational initiatives, including formal and informal education, literacy programs, technical and vocational skills-building programs, neither recent graduates nor the labor force as a whole are meeting the skill demands of the market. According to recent estimates, 35% of Afghans are not employed (2008 est.). This has perpetuated a continued reliance on foreign aid and dependency on foreign labor.

Further challenges to human resource development pertain to equity, quality and access to education initiatives, issues that are particularly acute for girls and women. Gender disparities exist across all sectors, but are most evident in education and health, where few service providers and service beneficiaries are female. Of the estimated 42% of Afghanistan's school-aged population which do not have access to basic education, the majority (approximately 70%) are girls. Educational gender disparities are even greater in the poorest, less secure, and remote areas.

The issues of access, relevance, and quality also extend to higher education where opportunities for enrollment are severely constrained and formal educational offerings are few. Not surprisingly, universities are unable to provide the quality or quantity of professionals needed for the labor market, particularly in the management and technical fields where demands are critical. Finally, the energy, ideas, initiatives and market savvy of the private sector remain largely untapped in the development of labor-driven human resources, which in part, contributes to the wide skills gap and the high unemployment rate.

Needed Response

The Human Resource Development (HRD) Cluster was established with the objective of producing quality human resources and of promoting and sustaining economic development, which will, in turn, foster stability and security for its citizens. The HRD Cluster provides an inter-ministerial forum for instituting systematic improvements and is working at the policy level to find effective and creative ways to enable Afghans – both men and women – to more fully contribute to society, both socially and economically. The Cluster is organized around the shared belief that the government, private sector, and civil society should work together to form a coherent approach to the development of human resource capacity to maximize benefits for all Afghan citizens. In response to the identified challenges and needs, five main areas of focus for National Priority Programs in the HRD Cluster were identified:

1. *Facilitation of Sustainable Decent Work Through Skills-Development and Market-Friendly Labor Regulation Program* aims to diminish the skills gap by providing Afghan youth and young adults technical and vocational education which is high quality, market-relevant, demand-driven and certified. For those who have been left behind from the formal educational system, this program provides literacy training in combination with the development of marketable skills, thus enhancing employability of a broad spectrum of the population.
2. *Education for All Program* aims to improve equitable access, quality and enrollment in basic education, with a particular focus on girls. Educational service delivery in the remote, less secure, and disadvantaged areas of the country will be facilitated by providing incentives for teacher relocation and strengthening community ownership. The initiative will also strengthen the academic foundations of Islamic education through curriculum reform, teacher training, and other measures to increase opportunities for Islamic schools' graduates to find gainful employment.
3. *Expanding Opportunities for Higher Education Program* aims to increase access and the quality of higher education, especially in fields that directly contribute to economic growth, in partnership with the private sector.
4. *Capacity Development to Accelerate NAPWA Implementation Program* aims to enable the Government to more effectively implement the gender commitments espoused in the National Action Plan for Women of Afghanistan (NAPWA). This will be achieved by developing the capacities of all relevant government entities to mainstream the commitments and goals of NAP WA into their policy, planning, programming, budgeting, implementation, and monitoring and evaluation processes. The program will also build the capacity of MoWA as policy body and responsible entity for NAPWA oversight and compliance reporting.
5. *Human Resources for Health Program* aims to support the Afghan health system to deliver its management and stewardship responsibilities at all levels by strengthening institutional development, meeting the human resource needs of the health sector, and providing employment opportunities.

The National Priority Programs outlined above represent collective efforts of all five ministries in the HRD Cluster. A number of programs involve close inter-Ministerial collaboration, including: cooperative efforts on curriculum reform by MoE, MoHE and MoLSAMD, encompassing both teacher education and technical and vocational education; joint efforts by all ministries to improve the quality and effectiveness of monitoring and evaluation; cooperation on quality assurance between MoE and MoHE in developing the National Qualifications Framework.

Challenges to Implementation

A major challenge to HRD Cluster program implementation is executive capacity at both the central and provincial levels of governance. In terms of the latter, there is an acute need to ensure effective programmatic performance in insecure and remote areas. Stronger public financial management is needed to promote healthy budget execution and to curb corruption.

Monitoring and evaluation needs to be strengthened across all ministries and policy revision is required to facilitate gender mainstreaming and to promote environmental protection.

Apart from these overarching constraints, policy modifications and additional provisions are required to facilitate a productive partnership with the private sector. Further policy revisions will also be necessary to set standards for – and to receive inter-institutional recognition of – the various learning modules and skills development programs undertaken, as well as for measuring the competencies of both students and teachers. Finally, more effective linkages need to be established between training programs and job opportunities, and between ministries, to establish the required number of inter-ministerial training programs and to achieve curricula reforms.

TRANSITIONING TO AFGHAN-LED SECURITY
JOINT FRAMEWORK FOR INTEQAL

The Underlying Principles:

- *Inteqal* (transition) must underpin Afghanistan's independence, national sovereignty, territorial integrity, and effective defense of the rights and liberties of the people of Afghanistan; and consolidate the position of Afghanistan in the region and in the world as a free, proud and peaceful nation.
- *Inteqal* must provide and garner the functional capabilities, resources, and regional conditions so that the Afghan National Security Forces (ANSF) are enabled to ensure and maintain peace and stability in the country, and definitively prevent Afghanistan from once again being occupied by international terrorist forces.
- *Inteqal* must maintain and strengthen the achievements of the last nine years in Afghanistan, including democracy and human freedoms.
- Prior to the beginning of the transition process, conditions will be put in place for the reconstruction and maintenance of the country's democratic system.

Illustrative Matrix For Human Resource Development (Hrd) Cluster

Intended Results: Over three years, 116478 jobs created; 240000 students made employable through demand-driven training; Capacity created in the country to train more than 200000 students per year in skills, technical and vocational education; Access to Formal Education increased by 1.8 million to 9 million; 32000 additional seats created for higher education; 2 million people acquired functional literacy; 100000 teachers improve their qualifications to improve overall quality of education; Increase in enrolment in Islamic education by 1 70000; Gender awareness and mainstreaming achieved in all ministries and local governments; Critical human resources gaps of health sector filled.

Budget by Program USD Millions	Expected Results		
	Immediate Term (6- months)	**Immediate Term (12 months)**	**Short Term (3 years)**
	Program 1: Facilitation of Decent Work through Skills Development and Labor-friendly Market Regulation – *(15732 direct jobs create)*		
Program Budget: 445.3	1. Mapping, Assessment and Registration of TVET Providers completed across the Country. 2. 10% of the process of Establishment and Execution of Training Of Trainers (TOT) Centers plus Toolkits completed. 3. 5% of the process of Establishment of 34 new Technical, Vocational, Education Training (TVET) Facilities completed. 4. 10% of the process of Development of Competency based Occupational Standards and Capacity Development of Training Providers completed. 5. Planning completed for the conduct of the labor force survey 6. Establishment of scopes of work for construction and establishment of 200 district TVET schools	1. Capacity for skills development increased from 26000 to 60000 per year and that many students made employable through demand-driven skills development. 2. Results of the TVET mapping analyzed & skills in demand (occupations) identified 3. 50 % of the process of Establishment and Execution of Training Of Trainers (TOT) Centers plus Toolkits completed. 4. 20% of the process of Establishment of 34 new TVET Facilities completed. 5. 28% of the process of Development of Competency based Occupational Standards and Capacity Development of Training Providers completed. 6. Employment Strategy developed. 7. 22,000 literacy courses established and 500000 people acquired functional literacy.	1. Capacity for skills development increased from 60,000 to 80,000 in year 1 and to 100,000 in year 2 2. 240,000 students made employable through demand-driven skills development. 3. Establishment and Execution of Training Of Trainers (TOT) Centers plus Toolkits completed. 4. Establishment of 34 new Technical, Vocational, Education Training (TVET) Facilities completed. 5. Development of Competency based Occupational Standards and Capacity Development of Training Providers completed. 6. 81,600 literacy courses established, 23 community learning centers constructed and 2 million people acquired functional literacy.

Budget by Program USD Millions	Expected Results		
	Immediate Term (6- months)	Immediate Term (12 months)	Short Term (3 years)
	7. Needs assessment conducted for DM-TVET; capacity-building strategy & activities designed for strengthening institutional capacity of DM; TA assistance identified	8. Labor Force Survey initiated. 9. Construction contracts awarded and construction initiated on a percentage (depending on funding) of the 200 TVET schools.	7. DM TVET effectively able to provide training for 100,000 students/year. 8. 34 provincial TVETs and 200 regional schools established. 9. Labor Force Survey completed. 10. National Qualification Authority and Framework established.
Program 2. Education for all – (94,840 direct jobs and 8.93 million labor days generated)			
Program Budget: 1,005	1. Over-arching plan for national school mapping developed, including operational modalities & selection criteria for NGO partners. 2. Identification of areas where schools are most needed, particularly those districts which do not have any girls' secondary schools; 3. Identification of new NGO partners (particularly local NGOs which are currently operating in insecure, remote & under-served areas) which have the capacity & desire to implement CBE schools in these areas	1. No of general schools increased to 12,800 2. Enrolment in basic education increased to 7.6 million students 3. Enrolment in upper secondary education increased to 0.7 million students. 4. 96000 over-aged children provided accelerated learning 5. Qualifications of 43000 existing teachers improved. 6. Terms of agreement with new NGOs which will implement CBEs agreed upon, training & resources to implementers provided, CBEs inaugurated 7. New formal and CBE schools established in areas which are insecure, remote, hard to reach;	1. No of general schools increased to 14800 2. Enrolment in basic education increased to 8.1 million students (40 % girls) 3. Enrolment in upper secondary education increased to 0.9 million students (37% girls). 4. Nearly 90,000 children previously deprived of education provided with accelerated learning and integrated into normal classes (70% girls). 5. 45,000 new female teachers trained. 6. Qualifications of 100000 existing teachers improved. 7. Increase in enrolment in Islamic education by 170000 (42500 girls)
Program 3. Increase Access and Improve the Quality of Higher Education – (2600 additional jobs create)			
Program Budget:	1. Competitive bidding process for construction of dormitories underway.	1. Increase in faculty by 10%	1. 32,000 additional seats created for higher education in 23 different universities/

Budget by Program USD Millions	Expected Results		
	Immediate Term (6- months)	Immediate Term (12 months)	Short Term (3 years)
209.1	2. Needs assessment for determining curricula revision completed. 3. Comprehensive assessment initiated to identify needs for repairs, upgrades and new constructions in infrastructure.	2. Establish and implement merit-based guidelines on appointment, promotion and retirement of faculty members. 3. 225 existing faculty sent for PhD. And Masters abroad. 4. Comprehensive assessment conducted to identify needs for repairs, upgrades and new constructions in infrastructure. 5. Dormitory construction in process with some completed. 6. Curriculum revision in process with focus on subjects in high demand by market.	institutions leading to a 51% increase in student numbers 2. Increase in Faculty by 30% and no of faculty members with masters doubled. 3. 675 members of existing faculty sent for PhD. And Masters abroad. 4. 35% female enrollment completed 5. 50% of curriculum update with focus on subjects in high demand by the market. 6. Accommodation in dormitories for 20000 females 7. Restructuring of MOHE and universities, development and implementation of financial and M&E systems, and quality assurance systems completed.

Program 4. Capacity Development to Accelerate NAPWA Implementation – (Gender mainstreamed in decision making in ministries and capacity of MOWA built.)

| Program Budget: 30 | 1. Program Management Unit and Working Groups for the implementation of the 6 activities established and operational (100%)
2. Mechanisms, strategy and accountabilities for training of 2,000 ministry and local government staff finalized (100%)
3. Mechanisms/arrangement to oversee gender policy research grants established (100%) | 1. 60 % of Framework / plan for MOWA's organizational reform finalized and implemented.
2. 20% trainings for targeted government staff completed.
3. Pilot projects funded and implemented (5%).
4. List of research priorities adopted.
5. Public education and awareness raising strategy developed. | 1. Framework/plan for MOWA's organizational reform finalized and implemented (100%)
2. Trainings for targeted government staff completed (100%)
3. Pilot projects funded and implemented (25)
4. Priority gender policy researches conducted (30)
5. Provinces covered by public educational and advocacy (34) |

Budget by Program USD Millions	Expected Results		
	Immediate Term (6- months)	Immediate Term (12 months)	Short Term (3 years)
	4. Public education and awareness raising strategy developed (70%)
5. Macro gender indicators finalized (100%)	6. Policy on incorporation of gender in the mandate and work systems of the Cabinet Committee on Social and Cultural Affairs adopted and implemented.
7. Oversight Committee for Gender Equality established and functional.
8. Annual government report on gender completed.	6. High level oversight mechanisms for compliance and monitoring processes functional (100%)
	Program 5. Human Resources for Health. – (3306 new people trained and entering professions; 4680 health workers receive in-service training to required standard; 10,000 new volunteer community health workers trained and 3.7M school students as Family Health Workers. Key institutional development is undertaken to build capacity to continue on with the activities.)
Program Budget: 194	1) Contracts for NGOs and Institutions to develop curricula and undertake training, and to manage projects like Medical Council and Health Complaints Offices awarded.
2) Expertise into MoPH to undertake institutional development projects, such as HR Database upgrade, Professional councils, IHSS, Hospitals and Transparency Working Group contracted.
3) Develop ground rules jointly with MoE for the operation of the FHW Program.
4) Advertise for training courses through IHSS.	1) Institutions develop curricula for degrees in Bio-medical engineering, medical technology, environmental health, and students solicited.
2) 13 Curriculum development workshops held for some of the medical specialties.
3) Training programs begin in provinces for IHSS courses: community nurses, midwives, psycho-social counselors, and physical therapists.
4) Training begins of Community Health Workers and Teachers who will train student Family Health Workers.	1) All IHSS courses are completed and planned numbers of health workers trained (3000).
2) Medical Council and Health Complaints Offices established and functioning.
3) Administrative staff (HR and Finance/Procurement) in PHOs and hospitals and Central Office, manage activities according to criteria established in training programs (4680).
4) 2nd year of Degree courses completed (306 students).
5) FHW Pilot program in 800 schools complete and program rolled out to all teacher training.
6) 10,000 Community Health Workers trained.
	Total Cluster Budget: US$1,882 billion

Inteqal is a process consisting of two phases

- Assessment of conditions in a province or set of provinces allowing for Inteqal to begin.
- Implementation of Inteqal, requiring achievement of certain milestones in the province subject to Inteqal in the areas of:
  - *Security* (establishment of capable Afghanistan National Security Forces (ANSF) to defend the independence, sovereignty, and territorial integrity of Afghanistan against internal and external threats and to ensure internal security, public order, and law enforcement);
  - *Governance* (ensuring government efficiency through administrative reform; transparent, fair and merit-based recruitment and appraisal systems within the Afghan civil service and creation of an efficient Afghan judicial system);
  - *Development* (following a nation-wide approach to development, based on the principle of equitable development, aimed at decreasing inequalities throughout the country, and at providing a sense of fairness and inclusion).

Assessment/Initiation and Implementation Phases of Inteqal:

Phase 1: Assessment/Initiation:

- *Assessment of Security:* Will include: the state of the local insurgency, violence trends, freedom of movement and security of the populace; ANSF operational effectiveness and institutional capacity; availability of adequate enablers and capabilities; provincial/national command and control relationships; ISAF/ANSF command and control relationships; and provincial Afghan civil/military coordination.
- *Assessment of Governance:* Will include: public confidence in government performance at the sub-national level, including government capacity to provide minimum services; basic rule of law; security enablers established and functioning with a dedicated dispute resolution mechanism; basic public administration structures established and functioning; implementation of the new pay and grading systems; fulfillment of the government structure (Tashkeel); operational and leadership capacity in the provinces and districts; and an inclusive representational balance across provincial structures and institutions.
- *Assessment of Development:* Will include: Existence of foundations for attracting private sector investment; local engagement in development initiatives; development of economic infrastructure; development programs are aligned with national priorities and provide reasonable attention to all development sectors; level of integration of Provincial Reconstruction Team (PRT) assistance with government planning and priorities; and improved program development in key ministries to deliver basic services.

Phase 2: Implementation: Implementation of the Inteqal process will take place in four stages:

Stage One:

Milestones: Civilian Lead for PRT; PRT fully coordinates with Provincial Development Committees; ANSF partnering ratios are reduced.

Achievements in the formatting of this section?

- *Area of Security:* ANSF maintain the lead for operations with ISAF moving from a supporting role, and remaining a partner providing robust support and enablers.
- *Area of Governance and Development:* The PRT leadership will change from military to civilian.

Stage Two:

Milestones: A province is able to provide adequate justice and public services; PRTs become Provincial and District Support Teams; ISAF focuses on mentoring and liaising with Afghanistan National Security Forces.

- *Achievements in the area of Security*: While continuing to further develop the capabilities and capacities of the ANSF, ISAF transitions from partnering to mentoring and liaison.
- *Achievements in the Area of Governance and Development:* The selected province shows that it is capable of providing justice and public services to the population.

Stage Three:

Milestones: Local institutions enhance service delivery capacity; International community funding channeled primarily through the central budget; Progressive SAF (P) OMLTs reduction.

- *Achievements in the Area of Security:* ISAF (P) OMLTs continue supporting activities to increase the capabilities of the ANSF with teams progressively reduced in size and capability commensurate with the enabling capability that the Afghanistan National Security Forces have developed.
- *Achievements in the Area of Governance and Development:* Local institutionsexhibit sufficient technical capacity to plan, design, implement, and monitor a more comprehensive range of service delivery, including rule of law, while ensuring adequate accountability and transparency.

Stage Four:

Milestone: Complete Afghan ownership of security, governance, and development.

- *Achievements in the Area of Security:* The ANSF is able to conduct operations independently, and its capabilities and capacity have developed to the point where ISAF provides minimal advisory and mentoring support. ISAF provides institutional training oversight to assist the ANSF in developing a self-sustaining capability. During transition, to maintain stability in Afghanistan and the region, a lasting strategic partnership between Afghanistan and its international partners will be deepened and further expanded.
- *Achievements in the Areas of Governance and Development:* At this stage, governance is effective and development resides under full Afghan ownership. The population is increasingly confident in government institutions and in their ability to provide services and equal access to justice and local resources. While the international community continues to commit to long-term support through the core budget and national programs, the Provincial and District Support Teams has exhausted its raison *d'être* and hands its functions over to the Government of Afghanistan.

RECONCILIATION AND REINTEGRATION THROUGH A NEW PEACE INITIATIVE

The Afghanistan Peace and Reintegration Program (APRP) has been developed on the basis of the recommendations of the 1600 delegates to the June 2010 *Consultative Peace Jirga*. The program will be led by the High Peace Council, comprised of state and non-state actors. It will be implemented by the Joint Secretariat, under the direction of the Chief Executive Officer. Provincial and district governors will play a pivotal role in organizing the support of the line ministries in local peace and reintegration processes. This will be accomplished with the support and inclusion of political, tribal, and religious leaders, as well as informal local governance institutions. The APRP requires strong civilian-military cooperation and coordination to achieve success. Moreover, the efforts of the Afghan government will be supported by the international community to achieve a durable peace. The program is based on a broad strategic vision led by Afghan men and women for a peaceful, stable and prosperous Afghanistan. The United Nations and International Security Assistance Force will coordinate international community support behind the leadership of the Government of Afghanistan.

Afghan men and women will be seated on the High Peace Council, and Afghan women, victims, and civil society groups will play a vital role in monitoring the peace and reintegration process; providing advice to the Government on how to promote peace that benefits all Afghan citizens and ensuring that all opinions can be expressed and all voices heard. The APRP will also support the role of victims and civil society groups in promoting constructive debate, building conflict management and grievance resolution capacity, leading advocacy for rights of all, and ensuring inclusive processes.

The Government will promote a strategy with three pillars. The first is the strengthening of security and civilian institutions of governance to promote peace and reintegration. The second is the facilitation of political conditions and support to the Afghan people to establish an enduring and just peace. The third is the enhancement of national, regional, and international support and consensus to foster peace and stability. Efforts are split between two broad categories that will operate simultaneously:

1. *Peace and Reintegration at tactical and operational levels*: There are various layers of ex-combatants that need to be reintegrated; they will each require different packages and approaches. At the tactical level, reintegration efforts focus on foot soldiers, groups, and local leaders who form the bulk of the insurgency.
2. *Strategic Reconciliation:* Efforts at the strategic level focus on the leadership of the insurgency: this is a complex and highly sensitive issue that requires a broader approach. The package of support for this level may include: addressing the problems of sanctuaries, measures for outreach, and removal from the UN sanction list, ensuring that insurgent leaders break their ties with *Al-Qaida*, and securing political accommodation or potential exile in a third country.

APRP Objectives – The over-arching goal of the Afghanistan Peace and Reconciliation Program is to promote peace through a political approach. It will encourage regional and international cooperation, create the political and judicial conditions for peace and reconciliation, and encourage combatant foot soldiers and commanders - previously siding with armed opposition and extremist groups - to renounce violence and terrorism, and to join a constructive process of reintegration and peace. It will have three basic "pillars": *Security Pillar* – Security for villages and districts participating in the APRP will be provided mainly by the Afghanistan National Security Forces supported by ISAF/Coalition Forces, and by strengthening the police. The Ministry of Interior's Public Protection Force, which guards against the creation of militias and other illegally armed groups outside control of Government control will be an option, where necessary.

- *Governance, Rule of Law and Human Rights Pillar* – The APRP will be administered with a high degreeof transparency and professionalism. In order to ensure the protection of human rights, the APRP will be open, transparent, and compliant with the Afghan Constitution.
- *Social and Economic Development Pillar* – A National Community Recovery Program will be developed as a component of the National Solidarity Program III, with additional training, facilitation and operational guidelines for conflict affected areas. The National Rural Access Program will also benefit the communities where reintegration occurs, with employment and vocational training opportunities offered through infrastructure projects in priority districts. Both programs will be funded from the Afghan Reconstruction Trust Fund.

Process, Activities, and Expected Results

The APRP is a flexible and simple umbrella framework for funding reconciliation and national and local peace and reintegration activities from the Peace and Reintegration Trust Fund. The program delegates to the Afghan people, in Government and civil society, the central leadership role in building peace in their country.

Three-Stage Process – The APRP proposes a three-stage peace and reintegration process presented below with program outputs for each stage.

- *Stage One – Social Outreach, Confidence- Building, and Negotiation*: Provincial and district leaders will conduct outreach to individuals and their communities who demonstrate their intent to join the peace process and will facilitate confidence-building activities, negotiations, and grievance resolution among the Government, communities, victims, and ex-combatants as necessary. The means for achieving this may include: peacebuilding capacity development and disseminating information about the program.
- *Stage Two – Demobilization*: Those who join the peace process will be demobilized through a social and political process that begins with an initial assessment, vetting, weapons management, and registration. Immediate humanitarian assistance may be provided, if necessary.
- *Stage Three – Consolidation of Peace*: Following the political and security processes of the first two stages, a standard needs assessment tailored to the requirements of the APRP will be used to assist communities, districts and provinces to select from a "menu of conflict recovery options." Not all options will be available to every community, due to the challenges of access, capacity and security, and the diverse needs of different communities.
- The "menu of options" includes but is not limited to: improving access to basic services, civic education, literacy, technical and vocational education/training, and employment. Other options include: the Community Recovery Program, an Agricultural Conservation Corps, a Public Works Corps, and also integration into the Afghanistan National Security Forces.

APRP Scale and Scope – Immediate priority provinces for introduction of the program are Helmand, Kandahar, Nangarhar, Khost, Baghlan, Badghis, Kunduz, and Herat. However, the program is flexible and will respond to emerging opportunities in any province, depending on the availability of resources and capacity.

Institutional and Organizational Development – The Joint Secretariat will be managed by a CEO, with the assistance of three Deputy CEOs for administration and logistics; program delivery; and local conflict resolution and reconciliation. The existing capacity of the *Peace through Strength* (PTS) and *Disarmament of Illegal Armed Groups* (DIAG) programs will be utilized to support APRP, and a consolidated organizational structure will soon emerge.

Technical Assistance Requirements – The Joint Secretariat will require immediate technical assistance to stand up the APRP. Two senior advisers to the deputy CEOs for peacebuilding and reintegration will be required for one year to advise on policy development, planning guidelines, quality control of Government plans, and budgets, and oversight of execution. One technical adviser for change management will be required to assist the process of assessing, planning, and merging DIAG and PTS structures into the national and sub-national peace and reintegration structure. A team of two advisers from the Ministry of Finance Capacity and Technical Assistance Program (CTAP) will be required to assist the Joint Secretariat to establish the national organization, determine the *Tashkeel* and program staff, and to evaluate long-term national and sub-national technical assistance requirements in the line ministries and provincial and district government offices.

Trust Fund and APRP Management Arrangements – Funding will be released to line ministries, provincial, district, and community governance mechanisms, and to civil society groups. The CEO of the Joint Secretariat will scrutinize and approve implementation plans and budgets.

The Peace and Reintegration Trust Fund will consist of three windows: a Ministry of Finance special account, a Bare Trust, and a UNDP window. Donors will be able to specify the activities under the APRP that they are willing to fund. The Afghan Government will ensure the effective implementation of these specifications.

Estimated Budget -- The proposed budget reflects the structure of the APRP and amounts to nearly $784 million for a five-year period (see table one below). It is designed to reintegrate up to 36,000 ex-combatants and will reach 4,000 communities in 220 districts of 22 provinces in Afghanistan.

Timetable – The APRP's aggressive timeline reflects the Government's ambition to promote a political approach to peace and reintegration, and to assert transition to full sovereignty and management of national political and security affairs by the Afghan Government and people.

Managing Information – The Joint Secretariat will design a standardized assessment form for the demobilization process to gather basic demographic data, including details on education levels and employment skills, and experience from individuals as they enter the process. This information will be gathered by the APRP provincial technical teams and entered into the Reintegration Tracking and Monitoring Database, managed by the APRP Joint Secretariat.

Financial Management Action Plan – The proposed Presidential Decree on expedited fund release will specify that the modifications apply only to the APRP. Procedures will be agreed and established for modified disbursement and commitment controls, and modified procurement procedures within budget ceilings of US$1million, US$500,000, and budgets and transactions less than US$250,000. The Joint Secretariat will issue a policy to executing ministries and governors on the use of budgets and special accounts, especially with regard to financial management standards, eligibility for participation in the program, and prohibitions on the use of cash to resolve local grievances.

Appraisal – The APRP integrates lessons and best practices from past Disarmament, Demobilization, and Reintegration and peacebuilding efforts in Afghanistan and around the world. Information management and confidence-building activities are key to meeting the challenges associated with reintegration.

APRP Action Plan – The action plan included in Volume II of the *ANDS Prioritization and Implementation Plan* outlines the Government's comprehensive approach to delivering peace and reintegration based on the recommendations of the *Consultative Peace Jirga*.

Table 1. Afghanistan Peace and Reconciliation Program Budget

S/NO	Description	Total Cost
1	Program Cost	
1.2	Phase One: Activities for Social Outreach, Negotiation, and Confidence Building	$ 32,310,000
1.3	Phase Two: Activities to deliver Demobilization	$ 149,267,100
1.4	Phase Three: Activities to consolidate Peace and to support Community Recovery	$ 510,931,000
1.5	Presidential Discretionary Peace and Reconciliation Fund	$ 50,000,000
2	Program Management and Operation Cost	$ 41,443,611
	Total Cost	$ 783,951,711

CURBING THE TRADE AND HARMFUL EFFECTS OF NARCOTICS

Counter-narcotics (CN) is among the most pivotal issues in Afghanistan. Much has been written about the direct impact narcotics cultivation and trade has had on security, governance, corruption, the economy, social issues, and, not least, Afghanistan's standing in the international community and its relations with its neighbors. The Ministry of Counter-Narcotics is as a member of the Government's Agriculture and Rural Development Cluster. However, it is imperative that CN, as a cross-cutting issue, is integrated into the four other clusters – the Governance, Economic and Infrastructure Development, Human Resource Development, and Security Clusters. CN's integration into these clusters carries three main action points based on an Afghan perspective:

First, the Government, with support from its international and national partners, needs to review, integrate, and implement a more effective, coherent, and pragmatic National Drug Control Strategy (NDCS) to address narcotics issues comprehensively and in a sustainable manner.

Second, the Ministry of Counter-Narcotics is mandated to coordinate NDCS implementation efforts through clearly-defined partnership roles and responsibilities, along with line ministries, sub-national administration, and the international community, through a series of consultations during and following the Kabul Conference.

Third, while counter-narcotics efforts have, in the past, been hindered by various external and internal factors (many of which have not been collectively addressed by CN implementers), the Kabul Conference provides an opportunity to introduce an Afghan CN perspective viewed as a *"new beginning"* in Afghanistan's transition away from narcotics production and trade towards alternative and sustainable livelihoods.

How does the CN *new beginning* initiative reflect the Afghan perspective? There are five points that deserve serious consideration and understanding by both the Government and international community.

1. The CN *new beginning* initiative is an Afghan-led, nationwide effort that is Afghan-owned and Afghan implemented. With full respect for Afghanistan's integrity as a sovereign country, the *new beginning* perspective recognizes that Afghanistan is willing and capable of dismantling the illegal economy that has spread its tentacles into almost every sector of Afghan society, and which has profound negative effects on neighboring countries and beyond.
2. CN, as a cross-cutting issue, is a development agenda priority in Afghanistan. Without serious integration and concerted actions – implemented within the national priority program formulation, implementation, monitoring and evaluation modalities for all Government clusters – overall Afghanistan development efforts will remain locked in limbo. While the National Drug Control Strategy and CN law prioritize CN in the development agenda, CN can no longer remain simply a policy on paper. CN policy must translate into positive actions, implemented by line ministries and sub-national administration with support from the international community.
3. CN will initiate a positive *new beginning* with the national review of the NDCS before the end of 2010, in accordance with Afghan law. Line ministries, sub-national administration, civil society, and the private sector must collectively join this review with a high level of commitment and dedication, as the NDCS is integral to Afghanistan's broader stabilization efforts.
4. CN must be mainstreamed into National Priority Programs implemented at all levels of Afghan governance. These programs should be aligned with the following CN strategic priorities of the Government of Afghanistan: (i) Stepping up the effective disruption of the drugs trade by targeting traffickers and their supporters; (ii) Facilitating the strengthening and diversification of legal rural livelihoods, with a particular focus on the needs of communities that abandon illicit cultivation; (iii) Ensuring the reduction of demand for illicit drugs and the treatment of drug users; and (iv) In support of these three priorities, ensuring the required strengthening of institutions both at the central Government level and in the provinces.
5. To ensure that NDCS policies and CN crosscutting initiatives are integrated into priority programs for all Government Clusters, the Ministry of Counter-Narcotics proposes that a CN budget allocation be provided to National Priority Programs. This allocation would enable CN activities to be made available in the respective National Priority Programs, subject to MoF implementation and monitoring guidelines. This allocation will also facilitate CN mainstreaming as a cross-cutting strategy, while remaining an Afghan-owned effort with Afghan officials taking the lead for program responsibility.

Some expected CN results from the strategy adopted by the CN *new beginning* initiative:

- Tangible and sustainable steps towards dismantling the poppy economy that affects larger stabilization efforts and broad-based development in Afghanistan.
- The sustained willingness of rural farmers and communities not to revert to or engage in illicit poppy activities through the provision of: (i) alternative livelihood options from farm to markets, (ii) appropriate human and physical infrastructure, and (iii) access to credit and land.

- Improvements in Afghanistan's security and the rule of law through the establishment of transparent, clean, effective and accountable CN-related governance mechanisms with achievable targets.

Finally, the imperative for a long-term CN commitment, rather than short-term CN expediency, should be discussed and agreed upon. There is an asymmetry between the expectations of Afghanistan and those of the international community for rapid results to address the illegal opium economy. But the reality is a timeline that may take one to two decades before the opium economy diminishes dramatically. Effective CN efforts require inevitably a combination of the Government's Five Clusters in action – with the proper sequencing and coordination of their new generation of National Priority Programs. This will take considerable time, as well as sustained financial commitment and political will. Collectively, let us start the counter-narcotics *new beginning* today.

EXPANDING REGIONAL COOPERATION

In the past several years, through the joint efforts of Afghanistan and its regional and wider international partners, important advances have been made to combat international terrorism, increase stability, combat the drugs trade, enhance regional economic cooperation, and address Afghan refugee issues. However, much work remains to secure a stable and prosperous Afghanistan.

The Kabul International Conference on Afghanistan will encourage our neighbors and wider regional partners to seek a coordinated and united approach to regional cooperation on the following four themes: Security, Counter- Narcotics, Refugees/Internally Displaced Persons, and Economic Cooperation.

Security

Success in defeating international terrorism requires increased regional efforts and continued international support. The Kabul Conference seeks the support of regional partners to:

- Firmly commit to forbid the use of their territories against their neighbors; Ensure greater inter-security agency coordination and intelligence sharing; Identify and eliminate terrorist sanctuaries and support bases; and Disrupt terrorist financial networks.
- Enhance cross-border cooperation, with a view to strengthening border controls to prevent the movement of terrorists and extremists; and Establish regionally integrated border management mechanisms to allow for interagency cooperation (e.g., border police, counter narcotics police, customs) along Afghanistan's borders.
- Support the reintegration and reconciliation program agreed at the January 2010 London Conference, which recognizes the need for a political solution to the crisis facing the region and as presented at the June 2010 *Consultative Peace Jirga*.

Illicit Drugs

Important progress has been made in curbing the trade in illicit narcotics, particularly in controlling the borders between the Governments of Afghanistan, the Islamic Republic of Iran, and Pakistan. Improved precursor controls have also been instituted in the wider region. Building on this progress, regional and international partners at the Kabul Conference are requested to lend their support in the following pivotal areas:

- Further strengthen and expand regional cooperation between relevant national law-enforcement agencies to prevent drug trafficking through enhanced border management, the control of precursor chemicals, and the sharing of intelligence.
- In accordance with the principle of shared responsibility, increase and expand regional cooperation in other areas covered by the Rainbow Strategy, such as the prevention and treatment of drug use and the promotion of alternative livelihoods.
- Encourage a greater role by transit countries to prevent trafficking of chemical precursors entering Afghanistan and for drug consuming countries to reduce their demand.
- Facilitate the identification of other issues related to drug trafficking and control to be addressed through regional cooperation.

Return and Reintegration of Afghan Refugees and Internally Displaced People (IDPs)

The Government of Afghanistan remains determined to ensure the completion of a successful repatriation process for Afghan refugees. It continues to work towards the full implementation of the Seventh Pillar of the *Afghan National Development Strategy* concerning refugees, returnees and IDPs. Afghanistan recognizes the effects of population movements and seeks the sustained support of the international community and regional neighbors in the following areas:

- Strengthen the capacity of relevant Afghan ministries dealing with repatriation and to assist them to establish better coordination with their counterparts in the region.
- Support a conducive Afghan environment that retains returning Afghan refugees by fostering job opportunities and the provision of basic needs, such as land, water, electricity, shelter, health-care, and general education.
- Facilitate progress towards the goal of sustainable refugee reintegration, as envisaged by the tripartite arrangements for voluntary repatriation with the Islamic Republics of Iran and Pakistan.

Regional Economic Cooperation

The Government of Afghanistan attaches specific importance to regional economic cooperation, as the key Afghan enabler for increasing prosperity, improving the welfare of the people, enhancing confidence and understanding between governments, and building peace and stability in the region. The Kabul Conference will, therefore, seek further regional and international support to:

- The implementation of the following regional projects: (i) Central Asia - South Asia Energy Market (CASAREM) initiative; (ii) Turkmenistan, Afghanistan, Pakistan and India (TAPI) natural gas pipeline project; and (iii) Construction of the Shirkhan Bander to Herat; Kandahar to Spin Boldak; and Jalalabad to Torkham railway lines.
- Strengthen border management cooperation to ensure a united approach to address crosscutting issues, such as strengthening trade facilitation; customs clearance harmonisation; environmental protection; and encouraging regular and deeper dialogue on border security and management with regional neighbors.
- Agreement on a coordination mechanism between nine key regional bodies (ECO, SAARC, SCO, OIC, CAREC, OSCE, UNESCAP, GCC, CICA) to ensure a coherent approach and plan for harmonizing regional initiatives with a strong Afghan component.
- Encourage regional bodies and neighboring countries to coordinate their regional initiatives through the recently established Center for Regional Cooperation (CRC) at the Afghanistan Ministry of Foreign Affairs.
- Expedite the conclusion of the Afghanistan - Pakistan Trade and Transit Agreement (APTTA) for the benefit of the wider region, with the aim of signing an agreement in the near future.
- Expedite the agreed deliverables from the third Regional Economic Cooperation Conference (RECCA III), held in May 2009 in Islamabad. Encourage and support the Government of Afghanistan to present concrete programs at RECCA IV in the following areas: sustainable natural resources development and management; national and regional employment support; transfer and access to energy; creation of modern transport infrastructure; facilitate the growth of regional trade and transit; and intra-regional investment in the extraction industries.
- Facilitate dialogue on labor migration between countries in the region (especially Gulf Cooperation Council countries) and the Government of Afghanistan to better regulate labor flows and to increase receptiveness to an Afghan work force.

Conclusion

The Kabul International Conference on Afghanistan provides an ideal opportunity for regional neighbors, regional organizations, and other international partners to:

- Re-confirm their commitment to regional cooperation at the London Conference and to help deliver concrete outcomes in the four thematic areas identified above.
- Coordinate activities to reduce overlap or duplication of efforts.
- Support the implementation of regional- oriented programs and initiatives for the benefit of citizens in the wider region.

- Further facilitate Afghan migrant workers who contribute to the economies of countries in the region.

MEETING RESOURCE REQUIREMENTS AND MEASURING FOR RESULTS

Budgets for each of the National Priority Programs are included in the Intended Results and Budget Matrices in this volume, as well as further elaborated in Volume II. Based on consultation with donors, the Government of Afghanistan estimates that approximately $10 billion will be available to support core socio-economic development initiatives over the coming three years, with additional resources available to support current governance and security sector strengthening priorities. The Government has stated its desire that the international community direct 80% of its total socio-economic development assistance in support of its fifteen socio-economic development National Priority Programs. In this regard, an overall budget ceiling of $8 billion was assigned, with the Agriculture and Rural Development Cluster accounting for around 26% of the total (US$2.8 billion), the Human Resource Development Cluster around 25% (US$1.9 billion), and Economic and Infrastructure Development Cluster around 49% (US$3.8 billion). These funds were judged to be incremental and could be added to existing high- performing programs with committed funds and additional absorptive capacity. Draft budgets for the Economics and Social Development and Governance Clusters National Priority Programs are outlined in the Intended Results and Budget Matrices in this volume, as well as further elaborated in Volume II. In addition, the projected budget for the Afghanistan Peace and Reconciliation Program is nearly US$800 million.

On the subject of monitoring and evaluation, even the best of plans are ineffectual if their implementation cannot be tracked with technical rigor. A major weakness of ANDS monitoring and evaluation efforts has been delays in defining a mechanism for monitoring and evaluation of the outcomes in sectors and ministry levels. Additionally, a lack of robust data systems has hampered effective monitoring.

Through the introduction of cluster groupings of ministries and development of this *ANDS Prioritization and Implementation Plan*, monitoring and evaluation is given renewed emphasis. Intended results – in the form of both outcomes and outputs – have been defined for all National Priority Programs individually, and in some cases for clusters as a whole. The total number of intended results has been kept manageable, and each are elaborated in *easy-toreview* matrices, allowing for the monitoring of different program components that contribute to the achievement of specific program and cluster outcomes and outputs. Moreover, full program results frameworks will be prepared following detailed assessments, design, and costing of the new National Priority Programs, and these will be connected to the national budget process and the ANDS results-based management system, initiated one year ago (as introduced in the *First Annual ANDS Report 2008/09*) to inform decision-making.

The Ministry of Economy is chiefly responsible for coordinating monitoring and evaluation, with the Central Statistics Organization responsible for data collection. While the Central Statistics Office will supply data, the Ministry of Economy will serve as the chief data-analyzer for generating monitoring reports and proposing corrective actions, with support from the Ministry of Finance.

Data generation for monitoring will occur on two levels. The initial basic level involves the collection of data from responsible implementing ministries and agencies through their normal operations in support of program monitoring indicators. It draws on monthly progress reporting by all ministries and agencies employing standardized reporting formats. At the second level, the Central Statistics Organization will collect data directly through various channels, including multi-purpose household surveys (e.g., the National Risk and Vulnerability Assessment), other surveys, standard reporting tools targeting various respondents, and an administrative statistical system. The Government will utilize the data to inform discussions and decision-making in the Cluster Coordination Committee, Cabinet, and Joint Coordination and Monitoring Board and its various Standing Committees and working groups.

The data will be further used to guide ministries and agencies about various aspects of ANDS implementation and future planning.

The Government of Afghanistan is committed to achieving greater transparency and accountability for its performance; it will systematically review the matrices of intended results contained in this *ANDS Prioritization and Implementation Plan* at six month intervals through semi-annual and annual conferences. These rigorous technical reviews will be undertaken with an aim to identify gaps in implementation and to propose necessary corrective actions, in consultation with key Government, Parliament, civil society, and private sector partners. Only through such a carefully planned and organized monitoring and coordination process can the understanding of what *makes a successful program* be realized, allowing for further National Priority Programs to be identified or existing programs to be scaled-up in subsequent years.

EFFECTIVE OFF-BUDGET DEVELOPMENT FINANCE

As a key milestone towards more effective implementation, the Government of Afghanistan and its development partners agreed at the London Conference, held in January, to work together to increase assistance through the Government's central budget to 50% over the next two years. This commitment represents a critical shift in financing for development, increasing the ability of Afghans to deliver Afghan-led, effective and cost-efficient National Priority Programs. Through its Financial and Economic Reform Program detailed in Volume II, the Government is fulfilling its respective commitments to its partners to strengthen the capacity of Government to effectively design and implement programming, while demonstrating the highest standards of transparency and accountability in the management of its finances. It is also setting out closely related economic reforms that demonstrate the Government's commitment to a stable, sustainable, and strong economy to provide an effective framework for improving development outcomes.

Off-budget programs will, nevertheless, remain a key part of the development portfolio for the foreseeable future. The Government recognizes that the capacity of Government channels to absorb assistance is limited – and some of its development partners also have legal impediments to on-budget assistance. It is, therefore, a priority for the Government that the effectiveness of off-budget development assistance also improves.

To ensure that all development activities undertaken directly contribute to shared development goals, the Government and its international partners have agreed to observe seven key principles, based on the *Paris Declaration of Aid Effectiveness*, for off-budget programs. Specific criteria to fulfill these principles are set out in the 2010 "Operational Guide: Criteria for Effective Off-Budget Development Finance", contained in Volume II. In particular, international partners must ensure that all off-budget programs are designed, reported on regularly, and evaluated with meaningful input by the Government, respond directly to Afghan priorities, and are in full accordance with Afghan laws.

For every off-budget program supported, international partners should seek to ensure sustainability and to build both private and public Afghan capacities. Externally funded, international partner-led programs that comply with these principles will be certified by the Ministry of Finance and presented in the Government of Afghanistan's comprehensive national budget. This budget will serve Afghan citizens and their international partners as a primary tool for development planning and advancing Afghan development policy priorities, giving a more comprehensive picture of development activities and their costs in Afghanistan.

CONCLUSION: AFGHAN PRIORITIES FOR THE AFGHAN PEOPLE

The Kabul International Conference on Afghanistan represents a turning point in Afghanistan's journey from conflict and aid dependence to peace, justice, and equitable development led by Afghan citizens. The Government and the People of Afghanistan understand the urgency and enormity of the tasks that lie ahead to bring security and stability through capable and accountable security forces; to create the conditions for peace, reconciliation, and justice for all; to build relations with their neighbors; to extract the country's natural resources in an ecologically-sensitive manner for the benefit of all citizens; to improve public sector capacity to deliver services to Afghans; and to manage public finances responsibly and effectively. We recognize that peace and security are not possible without progress in justice, governance, and development across the entire country.

The *Afghanistan National Development Strategy Prioritization and Implementation Plan* offers an ambitious yet pragmatic approach to tackle the country's seemingly intractable issues. It places people at the center of Government policies and programs. Its preparation brought together the Government, civil society, and their international partners in a collaborative way to forge a united response to Afghan challenges. With the introduction of the National Priority Programs presented in this action plan, the Government renews its commitment to the People of Afghanistan in their quest to achieve a prosperous future. With deep appreciation for the enormous sacrifices made to support their country's difficult transition to stability and inclusive governance, all Afghans embrace a common destiny with those who have shared the burden of helping Afghanistan return to its position in the community of nations.

KABUL CONFERENCE PREPARATIONS

Herat Governance Cluster Ministerial Retreat (24-26 June 2010).

Bamyan Economic and Social Development Cluster Ministerial Retreat (22-24 May 2010).

Map of Islamic Republic of Afghanistan.

End Notes

[1] The *"Faces of Hope"* Photographic Essay in support of the Kabul Conference, financed by the Government of Afghanistan, can be viewed at http://www.afghanistanfacesofhope.com.
[2] More robust estimation of revenue impacts will require development of the LEFMA and a supporting macroeconomic model.

In: Afghanistan National Development Strategies and Plans
Editor: Jennifer L. Brown

ISBN: 978-1-61209-637-7
© 2011 Nova Science Publishers, Inc.

Chapter 3

NATIONAL JUSTICE SECTOR STRATEGY

Islamic Republic of Afghanistan
Afghanistan National Development Strategy

FOREWORD

In the name of Allah, the most Merciful, the most Compassionate

Six and a half years ago, the people of Afghanistan and the international community joined hands to liberate Afghanistan from the grip of international terrorism and to begin the journey of rebuilding a nation from a past of violence, destruction and terror. We have come a long way in this shared journey.

In a few short years, as a result of the partnership between Afghanistan and the international community, we were able to create a new, democratic Constitution, embracing the freedom of speech and equal rights for women. Afghans voted in their first-ever presidential elections and elected a new parliament. Today close to five million Afghan refugees have returned home, one of the largest movements of people to their homeland in history.

Thousands of schools have been built, welcoming over six million boys and girls, the highest level ever for Afghanistan. Hundreds of health clinics have been established boosting our basic health coverage from a depressing 9 percent six years ago to over 85 percent today. Access to diagnostic and curative services has increased from almost none in 2002 to more than forty percent. We have rehabilitated 12,200 km of roads, over the past six years. Our rapid economic growth, with double digit growth almost every year, has led to higher income and better living conditions for our people. With a developing road network and a state-of-the-art communications infrastructure, Afghanistan is better placed to serve as an economic land-bridge in our region.

These achievements would not have been possible without the unwavering support of the international community and the strong determination of the Afghan people. I hasten to point out that our achievements must not distract us from the enormity of the tasks that are still ahead. The threat of terrorism and the menace of narcotics are still affecting Afghanistan and the broader region and hampering our development. Our progress is still undermined by the betrayal of public trust by some functionaries of the state and uncoordinated and inefficient aid delivery mechanisms. Strengthening national and sub-national governance and rebuilding our judiciary are also among our most difficult tasks.

To meet these challenges, I am pleased to present Afghanistan's National Development Strategy (ANDS) This strategy has been completed after two years of hard work and extensive consultations around the country. As an Afghan-owned blueprint for the development of Afghanistan in all spheres of human endeavor, the ANDS will serve as our nation's Poverty Reduction Strategy Paper. I am confident that the ANDS will help us in achieving the Afghanistan Compact benchmarks and Millennium Development Goals. I also consider this document as our roadmap for the long-desired objective of Afghanization, as we transition towards less reliance on aid and an increase in self- sustaining economic growth.

I thank the international community for their invaluable support. With this Afghan-owned strategy, I ask all of our partners to fully support our national development efforts. I am strongly encouraged to see the participation of the Afghan people and appreciate the efforts of all those in the international community and Afghan society who have contributed to the development of this strategy. Finally, I thank the members of the Oversight Committee and the ANDS Secretariat for the preparation of this document.

Hamid Karzai
President of the Islamic Republic of Afghanistan

ACKNOWLEDGMENTS

In the name of Allah, the most Merciful, the most Compassionate

The Afghanistan National Development Strategy (ANDS) could not have been developed without the generous contribution of many individuals and organizations. The ANDS was finalized under the guidance of the Oversight Committee, appointed by HE President Hamid Karzai and chaired by H.E. Professor Ishaq Nadiri, Senior Economic Advisor to the President and Chair of the ANDS Oversight Committee. The committee included: H.E. Rangeen Dadfar Spanta, Minister of Foreign Affairs; Anwar-ul-Haq Ahady, Minister of Finance; H.E. Jalil Shams, Minister of Economy; H.E. Sarwar Danish, Minister of Justice; H.E. Haneef Atmar,

Minister of Education; H.E. Amin Farhang, Minister of Commerce; and H.E. Zalmai Rassoul, National Security Advisor.

We would like to sincerely thank the First Vice-President and Chair of the Economic Council, H.E. Ahmad Zia Massoud. Special thanks are also due to H.E. Hedayat Amin Arsala, Senior Minister and H.E. Waheedulah Shahrani, Deputy Minister of Finance and the Ministry of Finance team. In addition, we would like to thank the Supreme Court, the National Assembly, Government Ministries and Agencies, Provincial Authorities, Afghan Embassies abroad, national Commissions, the Office of the President, Civil Society Organizations, and International Community.

All Ministers, deputy ministers and their focal points, religious leaders, tribal elders, civil society leaders, all Ambassadors and representatives of the international community in Afghanistan; and all Afghan citizens. National and international agencies participated actively in the ANDS consultations. Their contributions, comments and suggestions strengthened the sectoral strategies, ensuring their practical implementation. Thanks are also due to the Ministry of Rural Rehabilitation for their significant contributions to the subnational consultations. Special thanks are further due to the Presidents Advisors, Daud Saba and Noorullah Delawari for their contributions, as well as Mahmoud Saikal for his inputs. We are also indebted to the Provincial Governors and their staff for their contributions, support and hospitality to the ANDS preparations.

Special thanks to Wahidullah Waissi, ANDS/PRS Development Process Manager, for his invaluable contribution and for the efforts of his team of young Afghan professionals who dedicated themselves tirelessly to completing the I-ANDS, Afghanistan Compact and the full ANDS in consultation with both national and international partners. The Sector Coordinators included Rahatullah Naeem, Farzana Rashid Rahimi, Shakir Majeedi, Attaullah Asim, Mohammad Ismail Rahimi, Zalmai Allawdin, Hedayatullah Ashrafi, Shukria Kazemi, Saifurahman Ahmadzai, and; the Sub-National Consultations Team consisted of Mohammad Yousuf Ghaznavi, Mohammad Fahim Mehry, Shahenshah Sherzai, Hekmatullah Latifi, Sayed Rohani and Osman Fahim; and Prof. Malik Sharaf, Naim Hamdard, Saleem Alkozai, Mir Ahmad Tayeb Waizy, Sayed Shah Aminzai, Khwaga Kakar and Mohammad Kazim, and thanking Nematullah Bizhan from his special contribution from the JCMB Secretariat. We are also indebted to the many national and international advisers who supported this effort. In particular, we would like to thank Zlatko Hurtic, Paul O'Brien, Jim Robertson, Barnett Rubin, and Ameerah Haq.

Finally, I would like to thank all who contributed towards this endeavor in preparation of the first Afghanistan National Development Strategy, a milestone in country's history and a national commitment towards economic growth and poverty reduction in Afghanistan.

Adib Farhadi,
Director, Afghanistan National Development Strategy, and
Joint Coordination and Monitoring Board Secretariat

ABBREVIATIONS

AC	Afghanistan Compact
AGO	Attorney General's Office
AIHRC	Afghan Independent Human Rights Commission
ANDS	Afghanistan National Development Strategy
ARTF	Afghanistan Reconstruction Trust Fund
CJTF	Criminal Justice Task Force
CPD	Central Prisons Department
GIAAC	General Independent Administration of Anti-Corruption Commission
IBA	Independent Bar Association
IINLTC	Independent National Legal Training Center
MDG	Millennium Development Goals
MOF	Ministry of Finance
MOHE	Ministry of Higher Education
MOI	Ministry of Interior
MOJ	Ministry of Justice
MOWA	Ministry of Women's Affairs
NAPWA	National Action Plan for the Women of Afghanistan
NDS	National Directorate of Security
NJP	National Justice Program
NJSS	National Justice Sector Strategy
PIU	Program Implementation Unit
PJCM	Provincial Justice Coordination Mechanism
POC	Program Oversight Committee
SC	Supreme Court
TDR	Traditional (or informal) Dispute Resolution
UNAMA	United Nations Assistance Mission to Afghanistan
UNCAC	United Nations Convention Against Corruption
VCA	Vulnerability to Corruption Assessments
MRRD	Ministry of Rural Rehabilitation and Development

GLOSSARY

Holy Qur'an	The holy book of Muslims
Laws of Allah	God's Orders
Traditions of the Prophet (S.A.W.)	Sunnah(h) of the prophet (S.A.W)
Shari'a	Islamic Laws
Daira-yi '-Adalat	Circle of Justice
Wolesi Jirga	Lower House of Parliament
Meshrano Jirgas	Upper House of Parliament
Stage courses	Induction courses
Taqnin	Legislative Drafting Department
Huquq	Departments of Rights

Jirgas   Traditional Afghan gatherings
Shuras   Traditional councils

"And the Firmament (sky) has He raised high, and He has set up the Balance of Justice in order that you may not transgress due balance. So establish weight with justice and fall not short in the balance"

(Qur'an 55:7-9).

EXECUTIVE SUMMARY

Over the last six years, the Supreme Court (SC), Ministry of Justice (MOJ) and Attorney General's Office (AGO) have worked assiduously to lay solid foundations for the sustainable development of the justice sector. The National Justice Sector Strategy (NJSS) is designed to enhance performance, integrity, transparency, efficiency and independence of justice institutions.

The NJSS is based on a vision of an Islamic society in which an impartial, fair and accessible justice system delivers safety and security for life, religion, property, family and reputation with respect for liberty, equality before the law and access to justice for all.

NJSS builds upon prior reform efforts and in particular the individual strategies of the SC, MOJ and AGO.

A. The Conceptual Framework

NJSS is guided by a systems approach; that is, it seeks to strengthen the justice sector comprehensively, building and strengthening the institutions and systems that guide their relationships. The NJSS addresses the Justice and Rule of Law Benchmarks of the Afghanistan National Development Strategy (ANDS) in three fundamental goals:

Goal 1 – Improved institutional capacity to deliver sustainable justice services;

Goal 2 – Improved coordination and integration within the justice system and with other state institutions; and

Goal 3 – Improved quality of justice services.

B. Implementation

The National Justice Program (NJP) will implement the NJSS. Funding for implementation will come from a variety of sources, including the Ministry of Finance and international donors (using both bilateral and multilateral mechanisms) Implementation will be managed by an inter-institutional Steering Committee, assisted by a Program Support Unit(s).

INTRODUCTION

The Islamic Republic of Afghanistan presents the National Justice Sector Strategy (NJSS) for the development and strengthening of the rule of law and the justice sector institutions over the next five years. It reflects the values, traditions and Islamic culture of the Afghan people. It integrates the institutional strategies of the Supreme Court (SC), Ministry of Justice (MOJ) and Attorney General's Office (AGO), and recognizes the Government's constitutional obligations to adhere to international legal commitments and human rights standards. Finally, the NJSS demonstrates that Afghanistan's justice sector will need the support of the international community in order to realize its goals and aspirations.

C. Vision

The Government's vision for justice is of an Islamic society in which an impartial, fair and accessible justice system delivers safety and security for life, religion, property, family and reputation; with respect for liberty, equality before the law and access to justice for all.

D. Guiding Islamic Values

Justice in Afghanistan is dispensed according to the laws of Allah and the traditions of the Prophet (S .A.W.) as enshrined in the provisions of the Constitution. Justice must be provided in the most remote parts of the country and must be dispensed by justice sector institutions. This strategy's core values are derived from the higher goals of Islam, and the purposes for which Allah bestowed upon all men, women and children the sacred and undeniable rights and responsibilities in the Shari'a of equality before the law and access to justice for all. Achieving justice is therefore the main objective of the justice sector institutions. As the ninth century Islamic scholar, Ibn Qutayba, wrote: *There can be no government without an army, No army without money, No money without prosperity, And no prosperity without justice and good administration.*

The challenge for the Government and the justice institutions is to entrench these visions of justice, values, standards of conduct and performance into the justice system.

E. The Afghanistan Compact and the Afghanistan National Development Strategy (ANDS)

The Afghanistan Compact provides the framework for international engagement with Afghanistan for the next five years in three areas of activity: security, governance (including human rights and rule of law), social and economic development and cross-cutting areas such as counter narcotics, gender equity and anti-corruption. The Compact and the ANDS commit the Government to achieve several 'high level' benchmarks by the end of 2010 (1391) The ANDS provides the strategy and mechanisms for achieving the Compact's benchmarks as agreed upon by the Government and the international community.

Rule of Law Benchmarks of the Compact are as follows:

1). By the end of 2010 (1391), the legal framework required under the constitution, including civil, criminal and commercial laws, will be put in place, distributed to all judicial and legislative institutions and made available to the public.
2). By the end of 2010 (1391), justice institutions will be fully functional and operational in each province of Afghanistan, and the average time to resolve contract disputes will be reduced as much as possible.
3). A review and reform of oversight procedures relating to corruption, lack of due process and miscarriage of justice will be initiated by end of 2006 (1387) and fully implemented by end of 2010 (1391); by end 2010 (1391), reforms will strengthen the professionalism, credibility and integrity of key institutions of the justice system (the Ministry of Justice, the Judiciary, the Attorney-General's Office, the Ministry of the Interior and the National Directorate of Security).
4). By end 2010 (1391), justice infrastructure will be rehabilitated; and prisons will have separate facilities for women and juveniles.

Other justice-related benchmarks in the Compact have direct or indirect impact on the justice institutions and justice sector strategy-making. These include the benchmarks on Counter-Narcotics, Land Registration, Human Rights, Anti-Corruption, Public Administration Reform, Gender and Parliament.

APPROACH TO THE STRATEGY

At the July 2007 (1386) Afghanistan Rule of Law Conference in Rome, the Government, the justice institutions and the international community agreed on measures to improve coordination and set realistic and achievable goals for justice sector reform. The Rome Conference Conclusions and Joint Recommendations re-energized the justice sector strategy-making process, and resulted in pledges of new resources to the justice sector.

F. Systems Approach to Strategic Planning

This strategy provides a systems approach to planning and programming to ensure adequate and sustained coordination, focus and integration within justice sector. The systems approach recognizes that the justice system is comprised of several institutions that are accountable, interdependent and independent.

Its objectives and goals are stated broadly and holistically, in order to capture all elements and issues which are relevant for the re-building of the country's legal system. In addition, the strategy takes an access to justice and rights-based approach. Access to justice in this context is defined as the ability of people, particularly those from disadvantaged groups, to seek and obtain a remedy for grievances through the justice system, in accordance with the Constitution and international human rights principles and standards. Access to justice contemplates: (1) The availability of legal protection under the Constitution, laws, and regulations, and Islamic jurisprudence and traditional practices that are consistent with such protection; (2) The capacity to seek a legal remedy through legal awareness, legal counsel and formal and informal justice services; and, (3) The availability of an effective remedy through effective adjudication and due process in judicial proceedings, with enforcement through police and prisons with judicial, governmental and civil society oversight.

The strategy's premise is that productivity and professional excellence in the justice system can be primarily measured by the level of demand the system generates and sustains. Demand depends in part on access to justice (including access to services, laws and service providers), and in part on the accessibility and credibility of justice institutions (which are, in turn, dependent on the functionality, impartiality, professionalism, integrity, and infrastructure of justice institutions) While it is imperative that the Government creates and maintains an equitable system of justice throughout the country, it is important to note that many Afghan citizens use informal and traditional community- based dispute resolution mechanisms to resolve a range of disputes. This situation exists even though these mechanisms are not always easily accessible to women and children.

G. Structure of the Strategy

The strategy is divided into three goals. These goals represent the sector-wide changes or results that the strategy seeks to achieve as follows:

Goal 1 - Improved institutional capacity to deliver sustainable justice services focuses on improved functionality, competence and professionalism of the justice institutions that will enhance credibility and improve institutional arrangements for service delivery. It focuses on four main areas; administrative structure and information/operating systems, human resources development (including remuneration and professional education), and institutional and professional integrity, and infrastructure, transportation and equipment needs. This goal also integrates cross-cutting issues of gender, counter-narcotics, international cooperation and anti-corruption as well as special topics including national security, and counter terrorism and transitional justice.

Goal 2 - Improved coordination and integration within the justice system and with other state institutions focuses on linkages between critical areas of support necessary for the proper functioning of justice institutions that includes the legislative process, support for legal education and training as well as partner institutions in government and civil society.

Goal 3 - Improved Quality of Justice focuses on processes and practices in the justice institutions that will facilitate citizens' access to quality justice services. Specifically, it will address issues related to the availability of basic legal information to access quality justice by victims, witnesses, accused persons, civil litigants and other constituents of the justice system. Goal 3 is divided into three sections: criminal justice, civil justice and access to justice. Some of the key topics covered under this goal include reform of and coordination among criminal justice actors, streamlining of civil justice procedures and improved case management, improved standards of judicial education and training, the establishment of the

Bar Association and a legal aid system throughout the country, and legal awareness and also to draft a policy for determining necessary principles and benchmarks for the decisions of Jirgas and councils. *(for more details please see Annex I Policy actions Matrix)*

Rule of Law and Justice Institutions

The strategy's goals are aimed at improving access to justice and service delivery across the justice sector, in particular by the Supreme Court, the Ministry of Justice, the Attorney General's Office and the National Legal Training Center. These justice institutions, though either independent or independent in their functions, depend on each other and are jointly accountable to the public. Each justice institution is separately administered by its own administration and has its own property, staff and budgets. To achieve the goals of this strategy, each justice institution must be fully functional and competent.

1. The Supreme Court

The judicial power is an independent organ of the Islamic Republic of Afghanistan, comprising the Supreme Court, Courts of Appeal, and Primary Courts, which carry out their duties in accordance with the law and separate from the legislative and executive powers.

The SC operates as the highest judicial organ, dominating the judicial power.

Pursuant to Article 120 of the Constitution, the authority of the judicial power includes consideration of all cases filed by real or legal persons, including the state, as plaintiffs or defendants, before the court in accordance with the provisions of the law.

Pursuant to Article 121 of the Constitution, the SC has the authority to review the laws, legislative decrees, international treaties as well as international conventions for their compliance with the Constitution and the interpretation of these laws at the request of the government or courts, accordance to the provisions of laws.

Pursuant to Article 122 of the Constitution, no law shall under any circumstances exclude any case or area from the jurisdiction of the judicial organ as defined in chapter seven and submit it to another authority.

The Supreme Court and other relevant courts shall, according to the law, take appropriate action in order to protect the fundamental rights of citizens and resolve their legal disputes in a fair and transparent manner and to ensure justice through an independent, useful and effective judiciary system.

The SC acts as a final court of appeal. Its constitutional mandate is to resolve legal disputes in a fair and transparent manner, and to ensure justice through an independent, honest, and effective judicial system.

Thus, the Supreme Court heading the judicial power shall regulate the judicial system consisting of the high council (composed of members of the Supreme Court), five final divisions, 34 appeals courts and 408 primary courts and employing 6126 judicial and administrative staff including 1700 judges.

2. The Ministry of Justice

The Ministry of Justice has extensive responsibilities that include arrangement of drafts of Laws and Decrees of the President's Office, printing and disseminating of Legislative

Documents, protection of property and material interests of the State and when need arises taking legal actions against those liable, protecting the rights of property, employment, family and all other civil rights of citizens based on their complaints, and taking measures towards enforcing judgments issued by courts on civil rights disputes and raising public legal awareness.

In addition, The Ministry of Justice regulates and manages the activities related to Prisons, Detention Centers and Juvenile Rehabilitation Centers throughout the country.

The Ministry of Justice carries out its activities in accordance with the Constitution, Law on main organizational structure of the State and other Legislative documents of the country. The Ministry of Justice also has other duties which include dissemination of registered trade marks and advertisements on documents registration in the official Gazette, and expressing an opinion on congruence of legal and international treaties, compacts, and international trade agreements with the country's Laws is another aspect of the ministry's activities.

The MOJ also provides legal advice to the government and international institutions, registers political parties and social organizations, and licenses advocates practicing in courts. The MOJ has 11 departments and in general it has 7180 staff including 1971 professionals, 4000 prisons personals and 1209 service providers. The MOJ has departments in provincial centers and offices in 365 districts of the country.

The Central Prisons Department (CPD), with about 5,000 personnel is the largest department of the MOJ, which was transferred from the Ministry of Interior in 2003.

In accordance with the Advocates Law, the MOJ is further required to assist with the establishment of an independent bar association and ensure availability of legal aid in criminal cases to indigents.

3. The Attorney General's Office

In general, The Attorney-General's Office has four deputy Attorneys and there are 23 Departments in the Capital, 34 Appellate Departments in provinces, 365 Primary Attorney's Offices in districts and communities, 45 Military Attorney's Departments, 38 Attorneys Departments of The National Security's Presidency, and has 2500 attorneys and 2000 administrative staff throughout Afghanistan. In accordance with the article 134 of the Constitution and based on Laws, Attorney's Office investigates crimes and takes legal action against the accused in the courts, Attorney General's Office is part of the Executive branch and is independent in its work. During investigations, Attorneys act as impartial persons, while investigating. They monitor the activities of the police and other agencies, and guide them. Deputy Attorney General's Office monitor judgments of the appellate and boards (divans) of the Supreme Court, based on this duty the Attorney Generals Office has direct responsibility over all 34 provincial and more than 365 district offices throughout the country. Attorney General's Office has specialized sections to carry out its investigation and legal prosecution activities against crimes for internal and external security, military, police, financial crimes, administrative corruption and counter narcotics .For comprehensive and objective investigation of cases, especially administrative corruption crimes, there is a need to establish and equip a Criminal Technical Office with its related equipment and tools for finding evidence and signs of crimes during investigations. In addition, based on all Laws of the country, the Attorney Generals Office has duty to monitor implementation of Laws, decrees and sanctions of the Council of Ministers and internal regulations of departments, and monitor detention sites and enforcement of sentences and for enhancement of public legal education level, it publishes and disseminates "Tsarenwal" Gazette, "Tsarenwal" magazine, decisions of the Attorney general's Office's high Council and for the strengthening of this process. The Office needs to establish and functionalize its printing house with all relevant printing equipment.

4. The Independent National Legal Training Center

The Independent National Legal Training Center (INLTC) is the newest of the governmental judicial institutions and was established by Presidential Decree on 9 June, 2007. It is responsible for the induction training (the stages) for the other governmental judicial institutions, all of which are actively represented on the Board of Directors of the INLTC. The Center has a broad presidential mandate and is responsible for enhancing the knowledge and education of the legal profession of Afghanistan. Currently the Board of Directors is focused on increasing the knowledge and skills of the new recruits to the Supreme Court, the Attorney General's Office and the Ministry of Justice through the stage process.

5. Other Justice-Related Institutions

Other justice-related institutions are the proposed Independent Bar Association (IBA) In addition, the following institutions interact with the justice system: Ministry of Interior (Police); National Directorate of Security (NDS); Parliament (Wolesi and Meshrano Jirgas); Ministry of Higher Education; traditional (or informal) dispute resolution mechanisms (TDR); Ministry of Women's Affairs; General Independent Anti-Corruption and Anti-Bribery Commission (GIACC); Afghan Independent Human Rights Commission (AIHRC); media organizations; civil society organizations including professional organizations (judges and prosecutors associations), legal aid providers , Competent institutions for informal dispute resolution and the public.

These institutions have justice-related mandates and functions. By including the Ministry of Interior (police) and the NDS (as foreseen in the Afghanistan Compact's *Rule of Law Benchmarks*) this strategy covers parts of the security, coercive and law enforcement aspects of the rule of law. It also addresses the benchmark requirement to review and reform miscarriages of justices and lack of due process. Parliament's role in the justice sector relates to legislation, the legislative process and law reform while addressing the benchmark requirement to put in place the legal framework and disseminate laws. The Ministry of Higher Education's role addresses the human resource needs for appropriately qualified legal professionals, while also satisfying the benchmark requirement to reform and strengthen professionalism. The role of informal dispute resolution mechanism is that with handling individuals' disputes in cases other than criminal, it will reduce the load of work in the Courts. Meanwhile, it will save the litigants' time and money and brings settlement among parties.

The institutions that make up the justice system provide support to each other and act as the necessary balance and counterweight. They operate in the larger governmental and social environment in which the rule of law is upheld. This balance is essential if the weight of justice is not to fall short as mandated by the Holy Qur'an, which states: *"So establish weight with justice and fall not short in the balance."* [1]

6. *International Assistance and the Provincial Justice Coordination Mechanism*

Essential direct and technical assistance from international and bilateral donors has lacked a structured coordination mechanism with a presence in the provinces. The Provincial Justice Coordination Mechanism (PJCM), approved at the July 2007 Rome Conference by stakeholders and donors, will fill this gap. The PJCM will help improve the delivery of justice assistance in the provinces consistent with this strategy and the National Justice Program. PJCM will focus on coordinating donor actions to adhere to three strategic goals: (1) To facilitate the comprehensive and consistent reform of justice systems in the major cities; (2) To ensure comprehensive regional assessments of formal and informal justice systems in each PJCM area; and (3) To expand justice programming by identifying and helping to target future justice assistance to the district level and more remote provinces. UNAMA will provide supervision of the PJCM, which is funded by donors, and UNAMA. The PJCM will become operational in winter 2008 (last quarter 1386).

GOAL 1: IMPROVED INSTITUTIONAL CAPACITY TO DELIVER SUSTAINABLE JUSTICE SERVICES

H. Current State Analysis

Since 2001, significant achievements have been made in the capacity of the justice institutions to deliver services to the public. Yet even with many successes, deficiencies and challenges persist and work remains to be done.

The institutions experience difficulty in recruiting and retaining qualified professionals particularly in the provinces and districts. Nearly two out of every five judges appointed have not completed the "Stage" course induction training before taking office. A large proportion of judges and 80 percent of provincial prosecutors are not graduates of a law or Shari'a faculty.

A large proportion of judges, prosecutors and MOJ professionals work in provinces and districts without basic legal resources, such as appropriate Afghan laws, manuals and published works. While there has been considerable construction and rehabilitation of infrastructure in the past six years, the majority of buildings in the justice sector, including prisons, need repair or rehabilitation. Indeed, many justice professionals work in areas where there are no dedicated justice buildings or facilities, and are forced to operate in extreme crowding or in spaces inadequate for their mandated duties. In addition to infrastructure challenges, transportation and communication remains inadequate. For example, the AGO does not have a single vehicle in 26 provinces to transport prosecutors to courts or crime scenes or to bring witnesses and victims to hearings.

Salaries for judges and prosecutors and other justice professionals are low. Though there have been improvements in paying salaries on time, they are still sometimes paid late. The capacity to effectively manage human resources, finances and the assets of justice institutions remains weak. This affects in particular procurement and asset management.

Poor personal safety combined with low salaries makes justice officials prone to bribery and corruption. Corruption also thrives where there is a lack of clarity regarding appointment processes, career progression and transfers. A lack of credible mechanisms to enforce standards and codes of conduct governing accountability, discipline and ethics and lack of attention to and control over quality of services also contributes to a culture of impunity. Corruption and low morale can be found throughout the justice sector which results in a lack of confidence and credibility among the public.

Justice is a key concern for the National Anti-Corruption Strategy. The NJSS will support the implementation of the National Anti-Corruption Strategy by creating a legal and institutional framework that is sufficiently robust to reduce corruption in the justice sector.

I. Institutional Reform, Restructuring, Management, Information and Processes

1. Expected Results

Within five years the justice institutions will:

a) *Be structured, managed and staffed according to processes that improve efficiency and enhance performance;*
b) *Have strengthened their management, leadership and administrative capacity;*
c) *Have established program management units for development planning, analysis and implementation;*
d) *Have established and/or enhanced specialized capacity to prosecute and adjudicate cases involving cross-cutting issues in counter narcotics, violence against women, corruption, as well as juvenile justice;*
e) *Have a particular policy on the traditional dispute resolution mechanism;*
f) *Have Established a judicial service commission to evaluate the judiciary and make recommendations for necessary improvements; and*
g) *Have established translation and publication units in every justice institution*

2. Strategies to Achieve Expected Results

To enhance capacity to deliver services, the justice institutions' structure and management must enable them to fulfill their mandates. Good organizational design is a critical prerequisite for implementing increased pay and grading, improving work and security conditions and enhancing professional and career development. It is also necessary for the streamlining of internal processes and the achievement of higher performance standards. *(for details please see Annex I Policy actions Matrix)*

a) Administrative restructuring

Consistent with implementation considerations, reorganizing the justice institutions will initially focus on head quarters and the eight major provinces. Organizational re-design of the justice institutions aims to ensure efficient and cost effective delivery of justice services. Where necessary, organizational changes will be codified into law.

Deployment of human resources should be prioritized based on public need and staff merit. It is recognized that prioritization will require difficult choices, for which significant analytical preparation is needed. To ensure effective administrative restructuring the SC, MOJ, and AGO will:

- Conduct administrative restructuring assessments of their organizations aimed at identifying sustainable staffing levels and space needs;
- Implement new administrative structures in phases; initially at headquarters, then in the regional centers, and finally extending to all provinces and districts; and
- Train and develop capacity of staff in their new roles and according to new structures, involving the Civil Service Commission's Leadership Development Program in developing capacity training for change management.

Information systems and flows form a critical component of organizational design and structure. Areas of priority for information systems are human resources management, procurement, finance and pay roll. Establishing information technology in each institution including databases and revised records keeping practices in human resources and payroll are a prerequisite to pay and grading reform, determining appropriate staffing strength and performance levels. Departments within each institution responsible for keeping records and managing information will be among the first to be reformed to prepare the rest of the organization for reform.

b) Management and leadership

To better enable the justice institutions to fulfill their respective mandates and functions, professional management and quality leadership is required. Each institution will analyze and, in consultation with its stakeholders, develop recommendations for improving organizational leadership. The institutions will formalize the recommendations in new policies and procedures, which will in turn be communicated to managers via new operations manuals. Such measures may take the form of management support units, as has been outlined in the Strategy of the Supreme Court. As envisioned by the SC, the unit will increase administrative capacity and efficiency, helping to modernize operational procedures, support training programs, increase the use of technology, and establish proper procedures for the management of court records. Ensuring that administrative processes are understandable, transparent, and efficient may require revision of existing regulations. The Supreme Court in particular intends to appoint a committee to review and modernize existing regulations relating to court regulation.

c) Program management

The justice institutions will establish dedicated units to create and implement development strategies, and to assist in donor relations. The units will play an important role in the implementation of the National Justice Program (NJP) Because the Afghanistan Reconstruction Trust Fund (ARTF) will likely be one funding mechanism used for the NJP, the units should be designed and structured in accordance with the ARTF's Justice Sector Reform Project requirements.

d) Specialized criminal justice capacity

This strategy pays particular attention to the investigation and prosecution of cases involving narcotics, gender (violence against women), corruption, and juveniles. The justice system will benefit from specialization in each of these cross-cutting areas. Specialization will be achieved through training of judges, prosecutors and other professionals, and through appropriate institutional arrangements.

(1) Narcotics

The Criminal Justice Task Force (CJTF) is a specialized counter narcotics joint effort of several institutions. Despite significant progress in improving law enforcement interdiction and prosecution of drug traffickers, the CJTF lacks an effective presence in key geographic areas. The strategy aims to expand the geographic reach and effectiveness of the CJTF. To that end, the justice institutions will continue cooperating to:

- Improve the CJTF's capacity to address sentencing and treatment options for drug users and addicts,
- Link counter-narcotics efforts to the government's anti-corruption strategy by increasing investigation and prosecution of public officials associated with the drug trade; and
- Cooperate with regional governments in combating trafficking and narcotics money laundering.

(2) Violence against Women

Through the National Action Plan for Women, the Government has committed itself to eliminating violence against women. The three justice institutions play an important role in the implementation of the National Action Plan and have adopted a five-level approach that will require:

- Each justice institution to take a firm stand against violence against women, which will include strong leadership to communicate and raise awareness about the criminality of violence in general and violence against women in particular;
- Improving the investigation and prosecution of domestic disturbances to ensure that the rights of women and other vulnerable groups are protected;
- Reviewing laws and practices to identify those that are discriminatory to women, and recommending needed reforms;
- Increasing the number of justice professionals with specialized training in investigating and prosecuting violence against women, with a particular focus on techniques for effective and sensitive interviewing of victims and witnesses; and
- Developing the necessary infrastructure and referral mechanisms to ensure safety and security of female victims of violence.

(3) Corruption

The justice institutions will collaborate and coordinate in order to assist with the execution of the Government's Anti-Corruption Strategy. To this end the justice institutions will:

- Identify all laws that need to be harmonized with international anti-corruption standards, including the United Nations Convention Against Corruption (UNCAC), and will develop a plan for completing the harmonization;
- Support the creation of a well equipped and resourced, specialized anti-corruption department in the AGO to investigate and prosecute corruption;
- Ensure that judges and prosecutors gain international exposure to anti-corruption best practices in other countries; and
- Develop and provide specialized training on the detection, investigation, prosecution and trial of corruption.

(4) Juvenile Justice

The juvenile justice system will be improved by:

- Developing regulations, protocols, and manuals to implement the Juvenile Justice Code and international norms and standards on juvenile justice;
- Developing a common approach to re-integration of juveniles with their families, in cooperation with the Ministry of Social Affairs;
- Increasing the number of justice social service professionals with specialized training in juvenile issues; and
- Improving and expanding juvenile justice facilities and programs throughout the country, with a special attention to non-custodial measures such as community-based interventions.

e) Judicial service commission

An independent advisory commission, composed of up to five eminently qualified persons, will evaluate the judiciary and make recommendations for necessary improvements. Areas of inquiry by this commission will be judicial pay, conditions of employment, qualifications for appointment to judicial office, standards for appointment and transfer, judicial conduct and enforcement procedures, and reform of court practices. Having an independent commission making recommendations, after providing an opportunity for public and stakeholder input, will enhance objectivity, credibility, and the prospect of the adoption of its recommendations by Afghan institutions and the receipt of necessary support from international donors. The Judicial Service Commission will have an operating life of one year, with an option for an extension of an additional six months.

f) Translation and publication unit

Many of the laws of Afghanistan have been translated and made available in hardcopy and electronic form, and are also available on websites. However, written educational and training materials for more effective legal and judicial education, both at the university level and in continuing legal and judicial education programs, are urgently needed. One of the most serious education problems of the past 30 years has been the absence of books and other written materials for judges to study to increase their learning and knowledge. Since these materials do not exist in adequate numbers in original form in Dari, translation is required, at least for the foreseeable future. An abundance of written judicial and legal education materials exist in international languages, and if the capacity exists to translate those materials, the information gap will diminish. Lack of books and training materials in the justice sector requires the establishment of a translation unit of highly qualified translators, including individuals with native Dari and Pashto skills, all of whom must be proficient in English (and some proficient in Arabic, Urdu, and other languages as well) These translators will translate documents from English and other languages to Dari and Pashto. The translated documents will then be published for distribution to judges and court personnel to raise their judicial knowledge and skills.

J. Human Resource Development and Salaries

Human resource development strategies aim to establish a more professional and better-performing justice sector workforce. The strategies focus on vocational education, capacity development of administrative staff, recruitment, appointment and career development, salaries and benefits, job descriptions and classifications.

1. Expected results

Within five years, the justice institutions will:

a) *Have recruited and promoted justice professionals on merit, based on established policies and procedures, including meeting the target of 30% of the professional staff being female;*
b) *Be paying their professional and other staff recruited on merit according to increased salary and grading scales; and*
c) *Have developed and implemented institutional arrangements for vocational training of judges and prosecutors, as well as for continuing legal education.*

2. Strategies to Achieve Expected Results

a) Recruiting and Promotion
To recruit qualified graduates, the justice institutions will:

- Establish transparent, objective and merit-based recruitment and promotion policies;
- Adopt selection criteria requiring minimum levels of academic qualifications and professional experience;
- Monitor graduates after appointment to ensure that satisfactory progress is maintained through subsequent levels of induction and vocational training;
- Develop and put in place a program of continuous professional development consisting of practical on-the-job experience and mentoring by experienced personnel;
- Develop and implement special access programs to overcome obstacles women experience in attending or being selected for legal education and training; and
- In conjunction with the Civil Service Commission, develop and implement a policy specifically for recruitment and promotion of women.

b) Salaries

Salaries in the justice sector must be increased if the most capable people are to be recruited and retained, and if progress is to be made in the battle against corruption. The justice institutions will:

- Implement new pay and grading systems; and
- Deploy at least 50 percent of all justice professionals recruited under new pay and grading schemes to the provinces.

c) Vocational Training

Vocational training of justice professionals is essential to justice reform. The justice institutions will:

- Evaluate university curricula to determine preparedness of law and Shari'a graduates for justice office, and also for service as government legal officers;
- Evaluate existing justice training programs, in order to determine the extent to which such programs have enhanced justice competence and capacity;
- Assess and define vocational training requirements for judges and prosecutors, incorporating lessons learned and best practices identified during evaluation exercises;
- Design and implement training for educators at the INLTC and justice Stage courses;
- Forge closer ties between legal educators at universities and elsewhere with foreign institutions and experts in vocational legal training and adult learning methods;
- Develop capacity of the INLTC, and finalize arrangements for the justice institutions' use of INLTC or other facilities for training purposes;
- Develop plans for improving access to vocational education and continuing legal education, with particular focus on delivering training programs in regional facilities, so as to increase the participation of provincial judges, prosecutors and graduates, and in particular women in training and stage courses;
- Produce, publish, and disseminate manuals and other written reference resources for judges, prosecutors and other legal professionals; and
- Develop and implement plans for training justice professionals who do not have the formal qualifications required for the positions they currently occupy.

K. Information Systems and Processes

1. Expected results

Within five years, the justice institutions will:

a) *Have mapped in detail the processes linking all justice institutions, and have streamlined them to improve information systems and business processes, with the aim of reducing delays in processing of cases, administrative costs and vulnerability to corruption.*

L. Strategies to Achieve Expected Results

If new job descriptions, roles, reporting and management structures are to function effectively, the operational functions of the justice institutions must be clearly understood and intelligently designed. Mapping, review and redesign of processes and practices will be conducted at the same time as organizational restructuring to improve or eliminate processes that cause delays, unnecessarily increase costs, or provide opportunities for corruption. The justice institutions will assess their procedures and develop recommendations in the following phases:

- Assess current institutional processes and practices to identify gaps and design improvements, with a particular focus on eliminating delay; unnecessary cost, opportunities for corruption;
- Assess the information and communications gaps between headquarters and provincial offices within each justice institution, and design improvements to eliminate such gaps;
- Assess the information and communications gaps among justice institutions at the national and sub-national levels, and design improvements to eliminate such gaps;
- Improve processes for managing and storing information, and begin introducing new technology options for electronic information systems;
- Develop a recruitment and remuneration strategy to attract qualified information technology professionals to operate and maintain new electronic information systems that are introduced at the justice institutions; and
- Establish a clear communications strategy that explains new procedures and technology to justice sector officials who will be responsible for implementing and working with information systems, and train the justice sector work force on newly introduced technology.

M. Professional Integrity and Institutional Transparency

1. Expected Results

To improve both integrity within justice institutions and enforcement of public integrity laws to combat corruption, within five years the justice institutions will:

a) ave determined their vulnerabilities to corruption and established policies and procedures to eliminate such vulnerabilities;
b) Have published and disseminated codes of ethics and professional standards at the provincial level;
c) Have trained 60 percent of all judges and prosecutors on their respective ethics codes Have arranged for curricula at university and Stage courses to incorporate ethics training;
d) Have worked in cooperation with the Independent Bar Association to put in place enforcement, oversight and disciplinary mechanisms, like ethics panels;

e) *Have established an easily accessible and functioning public complaints system in at least eight major provincial capitals with clear processes for handling complaints.*

2. Strategies to Achieve Expected Results

All of the justice institutions are driven by a common goal to improve professionalism, integrity and credibility. The objective is to create accountable and transparent institutions, which is a precondition to public confidence in the justice sector. To achieve this objective, the institutions have identified a number of common priorities, strategies, programs and techniques.

- Ethics and disciplinary procedures must be established through amendment and promulgation of laws and regulations, as well as consideration of the use of integrity testing and severe enforcement of asset reporting. The implementation of the UN Convention Against Corruption may add other methods of administrative monitoring of unjust enrichment of legal professionals;
- Ensuring the personal security of judges in particular, and other justice professionals;
- Enabling the full implementation and growth of professional associations, such as *the Afghan Prosecutors' Association.*

a. Vulnerability Assessments

To identify weaknesses in administration, the justice institutions will conduct vulnerability to corruption assessments (VCA) The VCA should produce a set of recommendations that can be incorporated into a plan of action for combating corruption. The institutions will establish units to oversee and monitor the implementation of these action plans and policies, and will incorporate the findings of the VCA into other institutional development efforts, including in particular ethics training for staff and establishment of a public complaints system.

b. Ethics Codes, Training, and Enforcement

The professional ethics of judges, prosecutors and lawyers need certainty in definition and enforcement. Each institution is drafting or has completed its respective code for ethics. This strategy calls for finalization, dissemination and implementation of harmonized ethics codes in cooperation with the Independent Bar Association. The justice institutions will:

- Establish ethics and integrity units that will develop training material for the codes of ethics and will coordinate training. The units will also serve to provide confidential advisory services to guide justice professionals facing ethical issues;
- Establish enforcement (disciplinary) bodies in the three justice institutions to investigate, prosecute, and adjudicate claims of violations of proper ethical and professional conduct. The mechanisms will include appropriate rules to protect the rights of justice professionals accused of such violations. The Strategy of the Supreme Court envisage that the remit of existing inspection tours will be expanded to include training on the judicial code of ethics;
- Establish procedures to enable lawyers, prosecutors and judges to make confidential complaints relating to corruption, unprofessional conduct or breaches of ethics.

c) Public Complaints System

The justice institutions will:

- Launch a pilot public complaints mechanism in select provinces for court users that will involve representatives from all criminal justice institutions and the Afghan Independent Human Rights Commission;
- Incorporate lessons learned from the pilot program in the creation of a national public complaints system;
- In designing the pilot and nationwide public complaints systems, pay particular attention to ensuring access to the system by illiterate complainants and vulnerable groups, including women; and
- Launch a nationwide campaign to inform and engage the public on issues of judicial standards and conduct.

N. Infrastructure, Transportation and Equipment

Competent professionals without infrastructure, transportation and equipment have limited capacity to deliver justice. Justice infrastructures are the service centers of justice. The development of justice human resources must be accompanied by justice infrastructure, and the necessary tools (legislative and physical) with which to work.

1. Expected Results

Within five years the justice institutions will:

a) *Complete an inventory of all infrastructure and transportation assets;*
b) *Establish a comprehensive nationwide (regional, provincial and sub- provincial levels) infrastructure development plan with standardized design, prioritized and sequenced for Supreme Court, MOJ and A GO.*
c) *Develop training materials and programs for maintaining and managing facilities, transportation and equipment;*
d) *Construct new Supreme Court Building in Kabul; as well as new MOJ and AGO headquarters facilities;*
e) *Constructed or rehabilitated justice infrastructure, including offices, courts, prisons, and juvenile rehabilitation centers in all provinces;*
f) *Construct and maintain residences for judges; and*
g) *Have sufficient transportation assets to provide justice services throughout the country.*

2. Strategies to Achieve Expected Results

The strategy aims to concentrate on providing resources and infrastructure in areas where demand is the greatest.

a) Inventory

Before planning or construction of new facilities, justice institutions must assess their infrastructure needs. A pre-condition to any such assessment is a comprehensive understanding of the number of existing assets and their state of repair. To this end, the justice institutions will conduct a comprehensive inventory of all infrastructure assets, including detention centers and prisons, indicating location, age, state of repair, and ownership status.

b) Infrastructure Development Plans

Each justice institution will prepare an infrastructure development plan and timetable including construction of headquarters and centers at provincial and sub-provincial levels; as well as a transportation acquisition and deployment plan to address needs identified in the inventory. Such plans should be built on the experiences of the last six years; incorporating lessons learned and best practices, with particular emphasis on standardizing designs to increase efficiency. Moreover, the plans should prioritize construction timetables so as to achieve the maximum cost/benefit ratio. Infrastructure development for courts and offices will be informed by the need to expand the formal justice system throughout the country. Efforts will be made to continue integrating justice facilities where appropriate to reduce costs, facilitate access, expedite processes and improve security. The plans will forecast maintenance cost for new construction and rehabilitation to facilitate future budget projections.

c) Asset Management

Development of capacity to acquire, maintain, and manage assets is a critical component to this strategy. The justice institutions will establish dedicated units of trained and qualified personnel to fulfill this need.

d) New Headquarters

New headquarters for each of the three justice institutions will be constructed in Kabul. The headquarters will be designed with sufficient spare capacity to accommodate future need.

e) Construction and/or Rehabilitation of Existing Infrastructure

Buildings need to be constructed or rehabilitated to be ready for the deployment of qualified professionals in areas of greatest demand. Priority in construction and renovation should be given to the busiest courts, prosecutors and MOJ offices, as determined by reported caseloads.

To make a significant impact on the need in the first five years of strategy implementation, at least 20 courthouses should be constructed, and 40 buildings should be renovated each year.

Priority will be given to constructing: firstly, secure and safe provincial prison/detention centers; secondly, juvenile rehabilitation centers; and finally, transitional housing and shelters for women and children victims of violence.[2]

f) Residences for Provincial Judges

Construction of official residences for judges will enhance security and provide an incentive for qualified justice professionals to transfer to provincial posts.

g) Transportation

Transportation allows justice professionals to expand the reach of their services. The justice institutions will acquire vehicles for use by justice professionals in the performance of their duties. Priority will be given to equipping those areas where there are no permanent courts and other justice facilities.

GOAL NO. 2: IMPROVED COORDINATION AND INTEGRATION WITHIN THE JUSTICE SYSTEM AND WITH OTHER STATE INSTITUTIONS

O. Current State Analysis

1. Enhancing Cooperation in the Legislative Process

Prior to Parliament's inauguration in December 2005, the Government passed laws through approval by the Cabinet following review and finalization by Taqnin. The MOJ then published the laws in the official Gazette and distributed them to national and provincial institutions and made them available to the public. The MOJ also indexed the laws and posted them on its website (www.moj.gov.af).

Since December 2005, the Parliament has been also proposing and drafting legislation, and must approve all legislation however originated. While the legislative process is now enriched by the involvement of the two houses of the Parliament, it has also slowed down the process of passing laws. As a result, key pieces of legislation await consideration and approval by the Parliament. Further, more than 700 legislative documents must be reviewed to ensure their compliance with the new Constitution and about 10 new laws alone must be drafted and enacted in order for Afghanistan to comply with its international legal obligations. The review and enactment of these laws are required to ensure that the legal framework, including civil, criminal and commercial laws, will be put in place. These requirements are in addition to the laws required by various agencies to fulfill their mandates and the fact that the Parliament may wish to consider laws passed by the executive authorities between 2001 and 2005 – the period beginning with the establishment of the Interim Authority and the establishment of the Parliament. In short, there is need for the approval of a large number of laws.

2. Poor quality legal translation

The legislative process is also often delayed due to lack of professional legal translators and the lack of access to legal material in Afghanistan's official languages. Further, long delays in drafting and passing legislation have been attributed to language limitations of international experts, limited technical drafting capacity of legislators and legislative staff, and lack of explanatory notes accompanying laws presented for passage. Legal translators are needed to ensure that the legislative process may make best use of international resources and expert advice.

3. Inadequate level of higher legal education

Similarly, the capacity of staff of the justice institutions has suffered due to lack of adequate legal education and training. University legal education provides the foundation for the development of capable and professional justice sector actors. The long years of war have severely compromised the ability of universities to provide proper education to students, many of whom have joined the justice institutions after graduation. Further, due to lack of sufficient supply of graduates, the justice institutions have been forced to hire under-qualified staff. For instance, 80 percent of prosecutors in provinces are without university qualifications, and two out of five judges have not completed Stage training before assuming judicial appointments.

The lack of access to the latest materials has also limited Afghan professors' opportunities to develop Afghan Legal scholarship. Over the last five years, support has been disproportionately focused on Kabul University's Faculty of Law and Political Science at the expense of similar faculties in the rest of the country. Extending the curriculum and other reforms and changes to date to all universities in the country needs to be expedited. There remains much to be done to improve infrastructure and facilities, especially library and technology resources in Kabul University and at other universities. The division between the faculties of Shari'a and Law and Political Science has meant that there is a lack of core subjects common to both. There is a need for greater harmonization of curricula so that graduates of both faculties have knowledge of common foundational legal subjects. Further, consideration should be given to establish post-graduate masters program in law. The Independent National Legal Training Centre (INLTC) was established by a presidential decree in 2007 to enhance legal and professional knowledge of the staff of the judicial institutions and graduates of the faculties of law and Shari'a, and for continuing legal education. The INLTC is an independent institution. All justice institutions and the Ministry of Higher Education are represented on the INLTC board and are already using it to conduct training. The INLTC provides a single institutional approach to coordinate all remedial and vocational training.

4. Uncoordinated professional training

The last 5 years have witnessed an explosion in remedial vocational training offered by a variety of donor implementers agencies with little systemization and less coordination. Up until 2006, it was not uncommon for the senior management of the institution not to be aware of the training being conducted. Complaints have been made regarding the usefulness of the training. Further, providing training without improving the working conditions in which the newly trained professional is expected to deploy the new skills may even be wasteful. To address some of these concerns, the government requires a coordinated approach to training justice sector personnel. Currently, materials used for training are being compiled and uploaded onto a website www.afghanistantranslation.com. This and the INLTC as a central facility for continuing legal education and training will ensure greater coordination of all training.

P. Legislative Processes

1. Legislative Processes: Expected Results

Within five years,

a) The MOJ and Parliament will increase cooperation to strengthen and enhance the efficiency of the legislative process and clear the current backlog of legislation; and systems will be improved so as to ensure increased efficiency and the prevention of future backlogs;

b) Taqnin will be strengthened through reforms and restructuring to enable it to more effectively carry out its legislative duties;

c) Translation capacity of the justice institutions will be enhanced and regular English language classes will be provided to relevant staff so that they can communicate and make use of legal resources in English;

d) Taqnin will review the provisions of all submitted drafts and revisions from the perspectives of international human rights instruments applicable to Afghanistan;

e) MOJ will ensure timely publication and distribution of laws to all state institutions and ensure their availability to the public;

f) Relevant institutions will conduct a comprehensive and gender oriented review and prioritization of civil, criminal, and commercial laws that are required to be enacted or amended to complete the legal framework required by the Constitution;

g) All laws will be fully harmonized with the implementation requirements of the United Nations Convention Against Corruption, and other applicable international treaties and conventions, including the:
International Covenant on Civil and Political Rights, and the Optional Protocol;
Convention on the Elimination of All Forms of Discrimination against Women;
United Nations Convention against Transnational Organized Crime;
International Convention on the Elimination of All Forms of Racial Discrimination; and
International Covenant on Economic, Social and Cultural Rights.

h) By 2009 (1388), the new criminal procedure code will be enacted and published, and for its implementation training with written commentary will be provided to all legal professionals, as well as community legal education for citizens;

By 2010 (1389), all laws, regulations, and other legal instruments will be compiled, indexed, uploaded and maintained on government websites, will be published and distributed to state institutions at all levels, and will be made available to the people nationwide; and

All government agencies and ministries will have improved technical capacity to draft and propose non-discriminatory legislative and regulatory instruments.

2. Legislative Processes: Strategies to Achieve Expected Results

a) Removing Back-Logs, Eliminating Delays and Keeping Legislative Agenda on Schedule

The Government and Parliament shall conduct a comprehensive review of the legislative process, clarifying where necessary the roles and responsibilities of the relevant authorities as follow:

- The review will include assessments of areas where delays are occurring in passing legislation, and the reasons for the legislative backlog;

- Based on the findings of the review the Government and Parliament will develop procedures for clearing the backlog of legislation and review classification of legislation for agenda setting; and
- Practice manuals will be developed to improve awareness of the legislative process, including the mechanism for agenda setting and tracking of legislation.

b) Enhance Capacity of Taqnin

Efforts will be made to ensure that Taqnin and the relevant Standing Committees of the two houses of the Parliament have a smooth exchange of information on draft legislations. To improve Taqnin's capacity to review and revise draft and current laws, the MOJ with relevant national and international partners will:

- Conduct regular trainings for all professional staff of the Taqnin in, among others subjects, legislative drafting and provide them with study-tours and scholarships abroad to get comparative experience in legislative drafting;
- Establish a well-equipped legal resource center within the Taqnin to improve its access to national and international legal materials and resources; and
- Review Taqnin's organizational structure (Tashkeel) and, if necessary, make changes to meet its expanding legislative and advisory demands.

c) Enhance Technical and Translation Resources of the Taqnin

Since draft laws are usually drafted within Government ministries and agencies, with the assistance of international partners, Taqnin experts will conduct courses in cooperation with the INLTC to train and assist other government institutions to streamline the legislative drafting process. To enhance the technical and translation capacity of the Taqnin, the MOJ with the assistance and support of the SC and AGO will:

- Establish one or more training facilities for translation and will engage in cooperative arrangements with the international community to develop Afghan legal translation capacity for Taqnin, Parliament, SC, and AGO;
- Establish one or more facilities and recruit qualified language instructors in English and other languages to develop Afghan language trainers' competency in legal translation and interpretation;
- Publish a compilation of legal terminologies in Dari, Pashtu and English to ensure consistency and expedite high quality translation;
- Consider potential strategic partnerships with the Ministry of Foreign Affairs and Kabul University's Language Training Institute; and
- Support a shared long term goal to increase the English-language capacity of the three justice institutions to allow access to internationally-available materials.

d) Improve Publications and Dissemination of Laws and Regulations

The MOJ will develop publications capacity to disseminate and distribute legislation and legal instruments throughout Afghanistan. The MOJ will also develop its printing capability (either in- house and/or through out-sourcing) and build the necessary logistics and supply management needed to distribute legislation nationwide. This strategy has three components to be carried out by the MOJ:

- Ascertain the government printing requirements for legislation, and determine sustainability of printing all government legal and legislative documents;
- Assess the adequacy of current distribution practices and resources with recommendations for improvement; and
- Develop a detailed plan and costing of printing and distribution resource requirements, including staffing.

Q. Legal Education and Training

1. Legal Education and Training: Expected Results

Within five years:

a) A harmonized core curriculum for both Shari'a and Law faculties will be completed and launched;
b) A masters' program in law will be developed;
c) All new entry level prosecutors, judges and government lawyers will have legal qualifications from universities or other institutions of higher education and have completed Stage (induction) vocational training offered in coordination with the INLTC;
d) Afghan law professors and law students will have access to legal scholarship materials and resources and will have updated and modern (including technological) research and teaching facilities in all university law and Shari'a faculties;
e) The percentage of female professors and female students will be raised to 30 percent at faculties of Law and Shari'a, and provide them necessary facilities and remedial courses as necessary; and
f) Formal arrangements and procedures for partnerships, scholarships and other linkages with foreign academic and vocational training institutions will be concluded and operational.
g) INLTC will have expanded its activities to fulfill its duties under the Presidential decree and, in addition to conducting the judicial stages, will have developed, in consultation with the justice institutions:
   - Curricula and promoted continuous education for judges, prosecutors and legal officers; and
   - A national law library and legal archive for legal research.

2. Legal Education and Training: Strategies to Achieve Expected Results

The strategy for legal education and training is informed by the sector strategy of the Ministry of Higher Education. The justice institutions aim to transition from a professional workforce of mixed qualified and lay judges and prosecutors to a fully legally qualified workforce. Remedial legal education will continue to be provided to raise the competence of under-qualified officials.

a) Developing Law and Shari'a Faculties

A twofold strategy will be used by the Ministry of Higher Education and Kabul University, in collaboration with the INLTC and justice institutions, to further develop the curricula of the faculties of Shari'a and Law as follows:

- Completing the development of the new curriculum of the faculties of Law and Political Sciences and Shari'a in Kabul University in collaboration with relevant faculties of other universities in the country; and
- Developing core curricular subjects for both Shari'a and Law and Political Science faculties.

b) Enhancing Law Teachers' Capacity

To improve the capacity of Law teachers and students, the justice institutions will work with the Ministry of Higher Education and the INLTC to:

- Upgrade resources and facilities at the faculties of Law and Shari'a at Kabul University to improve the knowledge base of academics and students;
- Introduce the changes to other faculties of Law and Shari'a throughout the country;
- Design and implement a new post-graduate masters program in law in accordance with the strategy of the Ministry of Higher Education;
- Carry out student development by establishing and sustaining law journals;
- Develop internship programs for law students and career advisory services, including job fairs and other activities designed to introduce students to the practice of law; and
- Link academic staff of the faculties of Law and Political Sciences and Shari'a with similar international academics to expose them to international best practices and international peers.

c) Participation of Women in the Legal Profession

Consistent with the National Action Plan for the Women of Afghanistan (NAPWA) and the Ministry of Higher Education's strategy, the participation of women students and teachers in both Law and Shari'a faculties will be increased through:

- Development of incentive mechanisms, such as foundation courses for women and providing female dormitories for women coming from provinces;
- Designing and implementation of affirmative action programs by SC, MOJ, AGO and Ministry of Higher Education to encourage women's entry into and retention in the legal profession, including a special Stage for women judges, prosecutors, lawyers, and special remedial training programs; and
- Creating linkages of formal legal education to career development for government legal professionals.

Capacity of future Afghan academics and vocational trainers will be enhanced by exposure to foreign professionals, legal education and legal institutions in other countries.

The justice institutions will implement this strategy by:

- Exploring relationships with a view to technical and exchange partnerships with foreign legal training establishments – for example, in France and in Egypt.
- Developing a policy of academic and vocational exchanges to secure and promote scholarships and exhibitions/fellowships for promising Afghan legal professionals, in conjunction with the Ministry of Higher Education, and the justice institutions. Special attention will be paid to provide opportunities for women to participate in study abroad.

d) Establishing Institutional Capacity for Legal Research

To improve and enhance the knowledge of the legal system, the justice institutions will create mechanisms to establish institutional capacity for legal research. In particular, the MOJ will expand its library while the INLTC will establish a modern library with internet research capabilities to provide facilities to legal professionals and the public to conduct legal research. Further, examples and best practices in other countries will be taken into consideration to provide legal research facilities in provincial capitals.

(For detail please see Annex I Policy actions Matrix)

GOAL 3: IMPROVED QUALITY OF JUSTICE

This goal seeks to improve processes and practices in the justice institutions, and will facilitate citizens' access to quality justice services. Victims, witnesses, accused persons, civil litigants and other constituents of the justice system should also have sufficient knowledge of basic legal information to access quality justice.

R. Criminal Justice

1. Summary of the Current State of Criminal Justice

Since 2001, the criminal justice system has made tremendous progress. Some of the major achievements include: reconstituting the AGO, promulgation of an interim criminal procedure code, police law and counter-narcotics law, creating the Criminal Justice Task Force (CJTF) to combat narcotics, specialized and on-the-job training for judges, prosecutors and defense attorneys, reestablishing the induction "Stage" vocational courses for judges and prosecutors, reforms in prisons and juvenile rehabilitation centers, and the Ministry of Interior. The Ministry of Interior/Attorney General's Office Commission has been established to facilitate and implement police-prosecutor collaboration and coordination in investigations. At least ten non-profit organizations now provide legal services for the defense of indigent suspects and accused persons.

In spite of these achievements, however, many challenges remain. One major challenge is the lack of clarity about the roles and responsibilities of and among the institutions, and the relatively weak coordination mechanisms between them. Another challenge is the many cases of arbitrary and illegal pre and post trial detention. Many Afghans are detained without charge others are detained in violation of mandatory statutory timelines requiring release if they are exceeded, while many more remain incarcerated after their sentence has been completed. Women, in particular, are detained and prosecuted for alleged offenses like "home escape" that are not provided for in the Penal Code. A further challenge is that the detection, investigative and prosecution tactics most often utilized by police and prosecutors tend to rely on illegal confessions and police reports as the principle evidence produced before the court against the accused person. In addition, the applicable criminal procedures, including advisement of rights, provision of counsel to the indigent and defense presence and questioning of investigation witnesses and experts, are in many cases not followed in trials. Most importantly, in most cases the accused person is not represented by counsel.

Given this situation, the key challenge for the justice institutions is how to put in place an effective, fair and efficient criminal justice system with the limited resources available that puts the people involved -- men, women, and juveniles as suspects, accused, victims, and witnesses -- at the centre of the process.

2. Criminal Justice System: Expected Results

Within five years

a) ***Protection of the Rights of the Accused:*** No suspects or accused persons will be in detention or incarceration without lawful charge and being informed of the charges against them, and never without authorization of a competent authority.

b) ***Administrative Reform and Transparent Process:*** The SC, MOJ, AGO, police and NDS will take necessary measures to implement information management systems to better coordinate their functions and activities. This will include strengthening and fully integrating case management, tracking, and operating system with efficient reporting components deployed in at least eight major provinces;

c) ***Full Implementation of Juvenile Justice Reform:*** Juvenile Justice Code implementation will have resulted in regulations being promulgated and applied, juvenile justice professionals being trained in all justice institutions and juvenile justice facilities in at least eight major provinces;

d) ***Sentencing Reform:*** A comprehensive review of sentencing laws and policies will have been completed and recommendations for improving penal and sentencing system prioritized;

e) ***Victim/Witness Protection and Enhanced Security:*** Efficient and effective systems will be in place for protecting and assisting victims and witnesses, and managing evidence, in at least eight major provinces; and

f) ***Media Access and Public Information:*** Effective public awareness campaigns will have been conducted across the country to improve the knowledge of victims, witnesses, defendants, and the general public regarding their rights and responsibilities and how to access the criminal justice system.

3. Criminal Justice System: Strategies to Achieve Expected Results

Victims of crime, witnesses, suspects, accused, civil litigants, or simply ordinary citizens need to know which governmental agencies are responsible for protecting their safety and their constitutional rights. This strategy aims to build a criminal justice system that will be accessible to all citizens equally and fairly; and function reliably, promptly, and honestly. In order to achieve this goal, the quality of justice provided by the Government of the Islamic Republic of Afghanistan must be improved in specific ways.

a) Necessary Preconditions for Provision of Access to Quality Justice

A professional and competent prosecution and judiciary will:

- Provide the necessary laws and legal instruments effectively to conduct trials and deliver justice;
- Publish and disseminate the criminal laws and procedures, and prosecutorial and judicial practices and procedures, including specific information regarding individual cases;
- Provide professional development of the prosecution and judiciary by improved and comprehensive "stage" courses and continuing professional education through specialized training of experienced judges, prosecutors and attorneys;
- Develop administrative tools to clear the backlog of cases and increase efficiency with improved case management systems (both manual and automated) and improved training for judges, court officials and prosecutors in investigative, trial, and appellate case management;
- Improve oversight and monitoring of case management to ensure that crime is promptly investigated, accused are provided with prompt and fair trials, convicted persons serve their lawful sentences, and are released when their sentence is served.
- Increase public access to trials of criminal cases by ensuring that judges and prosecutors comply with the Constitutional requirements for public proceedings.

b) A Coordinated and Well-Structured Criminal Justice System

To provide for greater coordination within the criminal justice system overall, the justice institutions will:

- Improve policy and operational coordination by expanding formal inter-institutional coordination mechanisms such as the joint MOI-AGO Commission at national and sub-national levels;
- Strengthen and integrate centralized criminal justice information and management systems at all levels.
- Develop and adopt standard operating procedures to standardize operational practices within and between justice institutions.

c) A Victim and Witness - Sensitive Approach

To further the protection of the individual within the justice process, justice institutions will adopt a victim and witness-sensitive approach to improve public confidence in the system. This approach includes:

- Reviewing and reforming Afghan criminal procedure, to incorporate modern victim/witness protection and support practices and to facilitate victim and witnesses in coming forward and giving evidence;
- Establishing a special division at the AGO to support victims and witnesses, and to provide information and assistance;
- Encourage the establishment of nongovernmental organizations engaged in the support of and assistance to victims of crime and vulnerable witness;
- Assisting, in particular, victims of crimes of violence (including domestic violence), through collaboration by the AGO with the Ministry of Women's Affairs and the MOI to provide security during all phases of the process;

d) Increased Public Confidence in Criminal Justice Institutions

The SC, MOJ, and AGO will develop the following capacity to increase public confidence in the justice system:

- Support and protect witnesses and victims of crime throughout the criminal justice process. The AGO and the police, in particular, will support shelters and safe houses for victims of domestic violence and other serious offenses;
- Encourage press coverage of justice proceedings, public attendance at those proceedings, and general public understanding of the process at each stage of such proceedings. The justice institutions should encourage and participate in the development of outreach programs within civil society including curriculum for public education at all levels.
- Provide timely and regular public notice of judicial proceedings and widely disseminate the results of those proceedings;

4. Sentencing and Corrections[3]

The SC, MOJ, and AGO, with the support of the MOI, and the National Directorate of Security will develop corrections policies for male and female adults and for juvenile detainees and convicted offenders. Such policies will incorporate international standards for the treatment of prisoners and maintenance of humane conditions of confinement.

a) Detention, Juvenile Rehabilitation and Prisons Reform

To build upon the successes in corrections over the past six years, the following actions will be undertaken to achieve reform. Led by MOJ, the justice institutions will:

- Conduct a comprehensive survey and assessment to determine the frequency of detainees being held unlawfully without charge or indictment;
- Conduct a comprehensive survey and assessment to determine the frequency of convicts who remain incarcerated unlawfully after having served the entirety of their prison sentence;
- Implement inter-institutional policies that will prevent unlawful detention;
- Classify and segregate prisoners according to appropriate risk and security factors;
- Review and improve regulations and standard operating procedures governing the treatment of prisons and the maintenance of human conditions of confinement;

- Train corrections professionals on prison regulations and standard operating procedures. In addition, establish a monitoring and evaluating system for implementation of those procedures;
- Assist and support the Afghan Independent Human Rights Commission to fully enable it to report on prison conditions and the humane treatment of prisoners;
- Conclude protocols and arrangements with Ministry of Social Affairs to provide appropriate assistance to offenders from the early stages of their confinement through to their re-integration into society;
- Strengthen prisoner rehabilitation programs throughout the prison system; and
- Develop and implement policies and regulations to optimize the use of Open and Closed Centers with the aim to promote an effective rehabilitation of children in conflict with the law regardless of their charges, and with special attention to non-custodial measures such as community based interventions.

b) Non-Custodial Sentencing and Penal Reform

The justice institutions as coordinated by MOJ with other stakeholders[4] will examine options for longer-term penal reform alternatives to detention and imprisonment. In the interim, existing alternatives to prison will be enhanced as follows:

- Establish simplified sentencing guidelines for minor offenses;
- Develop new options and improve existing mechanism for enforcement of non-custodial sentences; include systematic collection of fines, confiscation of assets, non-custodial supervision, and court ordered destruction of contraband such as narcotics;
- Develop appropriate and Constitutional methods, in addition to the public appropriations process, to fund justice operations (particularly courts and legal aid), and to create and finance a victim's compensation system; and
- Develop a program to implement the provisions of the Juvenile Code on noncustodial sentences for juveniles.

S. Civil Justice

Improving access to quality civil justice requires making the courts and MOJ easier to use for litigants and witnesses, with particular concern for:

- Illiterate persons, the poor, women, and others with disabilities who need judicial resolution of civil disputes;
- Providing simplified access to the courts for citizens wishing to challenge the exercise of authority by government agencies;
- Providing simplified access to courts for citizens seeking resolution by simplification of legal documentation. Such documentation is critical to the exercise of a citizen's constitutional rights from birth, to identity, to marriage and beyond.
- To organize and regulate decisions of informal justice mechanism through drafting a policy and determining rules and principles governing the decisions.

1. Summary of Current State of Civil Justice

The Justice Sector in Afghanistan has made significant progress in civil justice over the past six years. In addition to the passage of major commercial legislation and the training of judges and Huquq officers, a new case management system (ACAS) has been developed for the courts to administer criminal and civil cases. More than 300 judges have completed at least one of a number of special training courses on civil and commercial law since 2003. Various legal identification document reforms have been completed, most notably a new marriage certificate approved by the Supreme Court.

Challenges in the civil justice system include the complexity of the system for users, the length of the process before a judgment is rendered and the difficulty in enforcing judgments. The most significant challenge for the justice institutions in the delivery of civil justice is how to provide civil justice dispute resolution and documentation services in a cost effective, fair and sustainable manner.

2. Civil Justice System: Expected Results

Within five years:

a) *Implementation of Administration Reform:* The Supreme Court will implement a more efficient court case administration and management and updated regulations will be introduced in the eight major regions. (In particular land, commercial and family cases will be easier to file, litigate, track, and enforce);

b) *Reforming the Traditional Dispute Resolution Mechanisms:* The government will develop a policy to reform the traditional dispute resolution mechanisms;

c) *Updating of Laws, Practice and Procedures:* Laws, judicial practices and practices for enforcing judgments will be updated and standardized to conform fully with Constitutional requirements and international commitments;

d) *Simplification of Processes:* Simplified processes for production, certification, storage and dissemination of documents for legal identity and entitlement, including deeds, birth and death certificates, marriage contracts and certificates will be promulgated by the courts and Government; and

e) *Commercial Courts:* The commercial court system will be expanded, modernized and staffed with adequately trained judges and ancillary service providers such as bailiffs and receivers.

3. Civil Justice System Strategies to Achieve Expected Results

The SC and the MOJ will:

- Strengthen and simplify the respective roles of the Huquq and Courts through development of regulations and greater public awareness;
- Establish mechanisms to enable the efficient and effective transfer of files, evidence, responsibility, and decision-making authority between the Huquq and primary courts by:
  - Clearly defining the transfer of authority and responsibility for custody of files; and

- Simplifying the protocol system for efficient daily relations between the Courts and MOJ, and between justice institutions and other agencies.
- Improve mechanisms to promptly enforce judgments to maintain confidence in the formal civil justice system.

a) Judicial Case Administration Reform

The Supreme Court will reform its courts' case administration system by:

- Strengthening and updating its case management and filing system;
- Developing a pilot computerized database based on the paper-based system, as the system strengthens;
- Simplifying operating procedures for case intake, management and disposition to ease access to the process for all citizens;
- Investigating the feasibility of deploying mobile courts in areas where there is currently no effective judicial presence.

b) Court Case Administration: Commercial Courts

The Law of Organization of Courts mandates that primary commercial courts be established in every provincial centre. Currently, primary commercial courts function in only two of the eight zones in the country, namely Kabul and Mazar. The Supreme Court will therefore implement the law in two phases:

- The first phase will introduce six additional commercial courts, one in each of the remaining zones;
- The second phase will increase the number and capacity of qualified commercial court judges with specialization in the areas of banking, energy, corporate and bankruptcy law. In addition, the courts will develop practical and efficient procedures for resolving small commercial claims.

c) Court Case Administration: Land Disputes

The SC and the MOJ will develop the capacity of the courts to resolve land disputes through the following steps that will facilitate the formalization of rights to and over land:

- The Supreme Court will develop judicial capacity in property dispute resolution and increase the number of judges trained in this area, initially in the eight major regions and thereafter in other provinces;
- The Courts and MOJ will encourage *jirgas* and *shuras* to record decisions in disputes related to land to facilitate the formal resolution of land disputes;
- The MOJ will improve the capacity of its Government Cases Department to litigate cases involving government land through training and improved procedures.

d) Court Case Administration: Family Courts

Strategies for improving the competence of family courts shall include:

- the development of judicial procedures to address the special needs of families and family disputes, including preserving the property and inheritance rights of women and children;
- The Government including representatives from the Ministry for Women's Affairs and interested national and international stakeholders will review the provisions of civil procedure and the civil code relating to divorce, child custody, and conditions for marriage to eliminate bias and discrimination against women as provided by the Constitutional and international standards and conventions applicable to Afghanistan.

e) Civil Processes and Procedures

1) Dispute resolution by the courts. The courts will:

- Review the civil justice process including the Civil Procedure Code with a view to simplification, gender sensitization and modernization;
- Modernize the *Law on Obtaining Rights* (enforcement of judgment procedure) that may necessitate some changes in civil procedure that takes into consideration the article 22 of the Constitution (equality before law).

2) Disputes Resolution outside the Court

1) Formal Dispute resolution by the Huquq department of MOJ, it will:
   - Enhance its capacity to conciliate and mediate private disputes through training and the production of manuals on conciliation and mediation;
   - Expand its conciliation and mediation services;
   - Increase its presence and performance in provinces and districts in close relationship with recruitment and infrastructure development.
2) Informal Dispute Resolution

Traditional (Informal) dispute resolution mechanism is one of the ways of access to justice. This mechanism, which is known as Jirga and council, has a historical background in Afghanistan and currently people refer to this system to handle their disputes. At the same time, informal justice has caused to violate individuals' rights also; so, in order to respect rights, litigants should abide by some standards and principles while proceeding their cases; it means, proceeding a case through council should take place with the agreement of litigants without any kind of discrimination and should not be criminal issues and decisions of Jirgas/councils should not be inconsistent with Islam, Constitution and Human Rights.

To better utilize the informal justice mechanism, the Supreme Court, Attorney General's Office and Ministry of Justice, as coordinator, will assess the informal justice mechanism and by drafting a policy, they will determine the priorities of using this mechanism. These priorities are consisted of the followings:

- To widely conduct public legal awareness programs to explain working framework, limitations and standards that should be abided by in the informal justice mechanism proceeding;

- To provide manual explaining standards fair proceeding, constitution principles, Islamic Rights and International Human Rights for decision makers of Jirga and councils.
- To collect information about balance and way individuals have access to the Jirga and council with gender recognition.
- Besides Jirga and council, other institutions like provincial council, district council, local development council and council of religious leaders are also permitted to handle informal disputes resolution.
- To assess decisions of Jirga and council so that should not be inconsistent with Islam, Human Rights and Constitution.

f) Enforcement of Judgments

The MOJ will, in conjunction with Parliament:

- Update the *Law on Obtaining Rights* to enhance and streamline processes for enforcement of judgments. Enforcement procedures need to include, among other methods, a mechanism for freezing bank accounts and conducting post-judgment discovery of assets;
- Assess how the law is currently applied, including the roles played by the MOJ and other relevant authorities with a view to increasing efficiency.

g) Legal Documentation

The courts and the Government will provide a critical public service of legal documentation, certification and authentication and seek to improve these services as follows:

- The Government will assess these services to provide increased value and greater access to legal identity documents for citizens;
- The courts will standardize and index legal identification documents and procedures, including:
  - Simplifying the process of certifying and registering such documents;
  - Developing special services specifically to help non-literate users access legal identity documentation;
  - Establishing a sex and age disaggregated pilot electronic storage and retrieval system.
- Justice institutions will coordinate and collaborate in producing, printing, and disseminating all public documents, forms and other instruments required, issued by or registered with justice institutions to be easily available to the public in at least eight major provinces.

h) Commercial Courts

Published and accessible judicial decisions, consistent and predictable judicial decision making, enforcement of judgments, and the availability of ancillary service providers, such as bailiffs and receivers, either require creation or strengthening. In addition, Afghan commercial court judges do not receive the necessary training or acquire the necessary commercial expertise to adequately deal with the myriad of commercial transactions and potential legal disputes that may come before the commercial courts. An assessment of the commercial courts system has been completed, and training programs for commercial courts judges will commence in the coming weeks. However Article 45 of the Law of the Organization and Authority of the Courts of the Islamic Republic of Afghanistan provides for the establishment of a commercial court in every province. Currently, only four commercial courts are functioning in Afghanistan, including two courts located in the national capital. Accordingly, as the first phase, six additional commercial courts will be constructed and professionally staffed in order for the Afghan commercial courts to begin functioning with the efficiency, transparency, and predictability required by the international private sector.

T. Legal Aid and Legal Awareness

Access to justice information, materials and advice is integral to citizens' proper use of the criminal and civil justice system.

1. Summary of Current State of Legal Aid and Awareness

A variety of legal aid and legal awareness programs have emerged since 2001. There are now at least 170 legal aid lawyers working for approximately ten legal aid organizations. Moreover, a department of legal aid provides legal aid in criminal cases through 19 staff lawyers. Pursuant to the new Advocates Law, this department is in the process of being transferred from the SC to the MOJ. Legal awareness programs and supporting systems – such as shelters for victims of domestic violence – are a welcome development. The creation of Family Response Units at the Ministry of Interior to facilitate and encourage intake and reporting of crimes against women and children are among the proactive developments in improving community based policing and legal awareness. The recently enacted *Advocates Law* demonstrates the government's commitment to improving access to justice by expanding legal aid and establishing a independent bar association.

Despite these achievements, much remains to be done. Legal aid organizations, though active in 20 of the 34 provinces represent only a small fraction of those accused of crimes. The Family Response Units experience difficulty recruiting women police officers and other qualified staff. There are too few shelters for women victims. The legal aid system needs to include civil representation to ensure that women and children's economic and social rights are protected as required by the Shari'a, constitutional and international human rights law. The challenge for the justice institutions is to provide access to justice for indigent, vulnerable and disadvantaged persons.

2. Legal Aid and Awareness: Expected Results

Within five years, the justice institutions in conjunction with other justice-related institutions, such as the Ministry of Women's Affairs, Afghan Independent Human Rights commission and civil society will:

a) *Establish a fully operational Independent Bar Association (IBA);*
b) *Establish a comprehensive administrative system for legal aid, with special attention to ensuring women's access to legal aid;*

c) Fully establish a unit in the MOJ responsible for monitoring human rights across the Government;

d) Continue and expand current legal awareness and legal literacy programs alongside expansion of resources and deployment of personnel. This will include development of legal awareness programs on:
- rights and responsibilities of the women, men and the justice institutions, and
- how the formal justice system works for Afghan citizens;

3. Legal Aid and Legal Awareness: Strategies to Achieve Expected Results

a) Establishing the Independent Bar Association

As required by the *Advocates Law*, the MOJ will support the establishment of the Bar Association within three months of the December 2007 (1386) enactment of that law to enhance the professionalism, competence, and credibility of the legal profession. The MOJ, with the support of international partners, will provide interim support to the Bar Association during its inception as follows:

- Drafting provisional by-laws, which will include provisions for the IBA's organizational structure and operating procedures;
- Helping to develop accreditation procedures, licensing requirements, and a code of professional conduct for members;
- Enhancing awareness of the *Advocates Law*, and encouraging unregistered advocates, especially those living in the provinces, to register.

b) Establishing the Legal Aid System

To implement the *Advocates Law*, the MOJ will establish a legal aid system to provide legal representation for indigent defendants in all provinces. This will require the MOJ to:

- Review existing legal aid needs assessments, consult with national and international partners involved in legal aid, and evaluate and select the most suitable legal aid system for the country;
- Coordinate with the Ministry of Higher Education to ensure the supply of qualified defense lawyers;
- Implement public awareness campaigns to promote legal aid services as they become available throughout the country. The campaigns will especially target justice officials emphasizing the key role of defense lawyers in the justice system.

c) Establishing a Human Rights Unit in the MOJ

Despite recent progress in efforts to promote human rights throughout the country, many problems remain. Protection of the human rights of individuals remains weak. Poor governance, insufficient government compliance with legal rules, and widespread lack of transparency endanger human rights. To promote consistent protection of human rights and the rule of law, the MOJ will establish a human rights unit, which will be responsible for monitoring human rights across the government.

d) Coordinating Legal Awareness Programs and linking them with Institutional Presence

The MOJ will develop and coordinate a legal awareness strategy by:

- Identifying those who use the justice system and the particular access to justice needs of each user;
- Improving legal awareness by tailoring messages to the intended audience using all appropriate national and local media;
- Providing low-cost or free legal services to indigent defendants;
- Bringing justice institutions to the people by making information available about locations of justice institutions to improve access.

The legal awareness program will:

- Be designed to reach illiterate or semi-literate persons, using various means of communication, such as radio and television broadcasts, educational movies, billboards, and workshops;
- Target local elders involved in informal dispute resolution to raise their legal awareness;
- Provide Afghans with information pertaining to their legal rights and obligations and with an emphasis on human rights, particularly as they pertain to women and children;
- Publish important decisions and directions from the courts, AGO and Ministry of Justice;
- Be regularly monitored and evaluated for effectiveness and coverage.

e) Transitional Justice

The Government's Action Plan for Peace, Reconciliation and Justice in Afghanistan acknowledges that any mechanism for building peace and justice must be carried out with the active and meaningful participation of all national stakeholders, including the justice institutions. In relevant sections, the Action Plan for Peace and Reconciliation requires:

- Development of an inclusive strategy for the general reform of the justice sector (judges, prosecutors, police, corrections and defense counsel), to ensure the establishment of a fair and effective justice system and to prevent patterns of human rights abuses of the past from being repeated;
- Draft legislation on the recommended truth-seeking mechanism to be presented to the National Assembly;
- Appropriate measures be taken to implement the objectives contained in the Action Plan; and
- Conditions for fair and effective justice procedures be established in accordance with the principles of the sacred religion of Islam, international law and transitional justice.

The justice institutions are fully committed to peace, justice and reconciliation. The justice institutions in general and the MOJ in particular will take measurable steps, including developing specialized capacity, to implement the Action Plan for Peace and Reconciliation as follows:

- Screening applicants during the recruitment and appointment process for judges, prosecutors and MOJ professionals for prior abuses of human rights; and providing oversight and interpretation of the law concerning appointments to public office;
- Assisting other agencies and civil society organizations, notably Afghanistan Independent Human Rights Commission, in the collection and preservation of evidence of past and or continuing abuses;
- Assisting victims of abuse to access their rights in the justice system;
- Assisting, where appropriate, investigations and prosecutions being conducted outside Afghanistan on abuses committed in Afghanistan or by Afghans; and
- Drafting legislative documents, as necessary

End Notes

[1] Surat- Ar Rahman - Verse 9.
[2] Many of these are outlined in greater detail in the National Action Plan for Women in Afghanistan (NAPWA), which the institutions will implement.
[3] Overhauling the detention and sentencing system will necessarily take time and may be beyond the timeframe of this strategy.
[4] Ministry of Finance, Ministry of Interior and National Directorate of Security.

CHAPTER SOURCES

Chapter 1 - This is an edited, reformatted and augmented version of a Islamic Republic of an Afghanistan, National Develoment Strategy publication, for 2008-2013.

Chapter 2 - This is an edited, reformatted and augmented version of a Kabul International Conference on Afghanistan publication, dated July 20, 2010.

Chapter 3 - This is an edited, reformatted and augmented version of a Islamic Republic of Afghanistan, National Justice Sector publication, dated 2008.

INDEX

A

abatement, 28, 187
abuse, 157, 159, 163, 415
accessibility, 137, 138, 380
accommodation, 360
accountability, 28, 58, 64, 73, 76, 77, 78, 79, 138, 140, 181, 182, 185, 189, 192, 193, 195, 204, 205, 211, 238, 239, 244, 247, 256, 268, 313, 315, 320, 321, 324, 326, 327, 330, 334, 337, 346, 358, 369, 387
accounting, 98, 99, 128, 161, 170, 205, 245, 275, 319, 368
accreditation, 23, 24, 139, 144, 148, 244, 261, 264, 294, 413
ADC, 4, 128
adjustment, 162
administrative support, 226, 227, 279
adult learning, 392
adult literacy, 147
adults, 142, 243, 406
advancement, 184
advancements, 151
adverse effects, 55
advertisements, 384
advocacy, 140, 153, 175, 184, 267, 278, 355, 359
affirmative action, 79, 87, 147, 281, 402
age, 47, 122, 135, 144, 155, 160, 220, 285, 287, 294, 305, 306, 396, 411
agencies, 3, 13, 18, 19, 29, 33, 48, 73, 89, 92, 93, 95, 99, 104, 106, 108, 113, 128, 137, 140, 152, 153, 167, 173, 176, 180, 182, 183, 188, 191, 192, 193, 194, 197, 198, 202, 207, 212, 216, 232, 236, 243, 251, 257, 260, 266, 278, 314, 316, 327, 332, 333, 337, 366, 369, 377, 384, 397, 398, 399, 400, 405, 407, 409, 415
aggression, 71
agricultural exports, 64

agricultural producers, 95
agricultural sector, 221
agriculture, 15, 19, 25, 36, 38, 40, 43, 44, 45, 50, 54, 60, 61, 65, 66, 95, 105, 108, 109, 110, 111, 113, 114, 115, 119, 150, 158, 171, 176, 199, 202, 220, 223, 224, 264, 269, 270, 298, 316, 344, 345
AIDS, 5
Air Force, 71, 279
air quality, 119, 172, 250, 287
airports, 21, 61, 116, 117, 118, 168, 250, 252, 288
alternative energy, 345
animal disease, 270
anthropology, 152
antigen, 220, 297
apex, 212
appointment process, 386, 415
appointments, 79, 87, 217, 331, 334, 398, 415
appraisals, 28
appropriations, 205, 325, 407
aquifers, 21, 102, 104, 105, 106
arbitration, 92, 239
ARDS, 4
Argentina, 132
armed forces, 224
armed groups, 17, 67, 68, 69, 70, 71, 360
arrests, 76, 87
articulation, 145
Asia, 87, 88, 171, 178, 179, 322
aspiration, 321
assessment, 14, 40, 59, 69, 80, 104, 139, 144, 145, 162, 186, 187, 188, 197, 209, 212, 222, 233, 234, 237, 248, 252, 276, 293, 317, 324, 336, 348, 354, 355, 361, 362, 396, 406, 412
assessment procedures, 145
assets, 20, 25, 27, 45, 49, 52, 66, 84, 87, 93, 97, 99, 100, 104, 109, 111, 113, 117, 128, 130, 155, 161, 184, 240, 291, 301, 320, 330, 345, 346, 386, 395, 396, 407, 411

asylum, 166, 276
asymmetry, 365
athletes, 266
audit, 58, 97, 170, 192, 205, 245, 246, 249, 253, 329, 330
audits, 93, 204, 240, 329, 330, 346
authentication, 411
authorities, 21, 32, 35, 72, 87, 103, 118, 145, 175, 176, 187, 277, 278, 316, 320, 327, 333, 341, 342, 344, 397, 399, 411
authority, 9, 22, 23, 92, 94, 105, 110, 111, 115, 118, 121, 125, 147, 154, 176, 181, 209, 239, 242, 251, 266, 326, 383, 404, 407, 408
automate, 123, 259
autonomy, 137, 148, 177, 251, 264
avoidance, 66, 223
awareness, 18, 24, 27, 28, 76, 82, 83, 86, 89, 121, 138, 153, 162, 170, 172, 182, 187, 209, 229, 230, 233, 236, 242, 248, 267, 272, 275, 276, 315, 328, 336, 337, 338, 353, 355, 356, 382, 383, 384, 389, 400, 410, 412, 413, 414

B

background information, 134
balanced budget, 62
ban, 168, 169
Bangladesh, 181
bank failure, 64
banking, 64, 93, 122, 161, 240, 409
banking sector, 122
bankruptcy, 409
banks, 64, 161, 240, 241, 275
barriers, 24, 93, 136, 170, 178, 188, 197
base, 22, 24, 45, 61, 64, 87, 111, 115, 127, 128, 146, 152, 174, 187, 254, 312, 338, 402
basic competencies, 149, 265
basic education, 146, 243, 350, 351, 354
basic needs, 41, 44, 366
basic services, 22, 25, 35, 46, 108, 127, 130, 199, 201, 219, 253, 289, 344, 357, 361
batteries, 96
BCG vaccine, 135
Beijing, 5, 183
benchmarks, 2, 9, 13, 14, 17, 23, 32, 69, 77, 81, 96, 112, 120, 125, 142, 147, 164, 183, 188, 190, 195, 210, 211, 216, 233, 262, 282, 330, 376, 380, 381, 383
beneficiaries, 175, 184, 228, 289, 291, 297, 306, 347, 349, 350
benefits, 14, 19, 26, 27, 28, 51, 53, 55, 91, 93, 101, 105, 107, 131, 132, 134, 154, 160, 165, 173, 178, 183, 190, 198, 205, 226, 227, 245, 248, 311, 315, 318, 331, 340, 350, 359, 391

beverages, 54
bias, 87, 410
biodiversity, 28, 187
births, 135, 136, 220, 297
blindness, 138
blueprint, 2, 305, 376
bonding, 253
bonds, 236
border control, 71, 73, 76, 365
border crossing, 76
border security, 75, 367
Bosnia, 195
bounds, 86
breakdown, 305
breast feeding, 138
breeding, 181
broadcast media, 152
browsing, 123
budget allocation, 47, 60, 61, 185, 364
budget deficit, 54
budget line, 196
budgetary resources, 98, 110, 192
building code, 126
bureaucracy, 121
business environment, 49, 50, 119, 289
business processes, 285, 392
businesses, 10, 13, 98, 101, 174, 225, 242, 246, 250, 299, 303

C

Cabinet, 32, 148, 186, 207, 210, 211, 229, 230, 239, 319, 321, 331, 332, 333, 343, 356, 369, 397
cable television, 151
cables, 120
caliber, 151
campaigns, 74, 226, 227, 228, 236, 238, 404, 413
canals, 7
candidates, 233, 332
CAP, 127
capacity building, 15, 23, 26, 39, 71, 76, 78, 79, 90, 107, 133, 158, 159, 160, 161, 162, 168, 169, 171, 177, 179, 182, 185, 195, 215, 216, 224, 226, 227, 234, 239, 243, 250, 251, 252, 254, 257, 274, 275, 288, 329, 332, 334
capital expenditure, 206
career development, 147, 233, 387, 391, 402
cash, 154, 158, 159, 160, 173, 180, 181, 240, 273, 274, 346, 362
cash crops, 180, 181
cashmere, 94
cation, 244, 295
CBNRM, 309, 347
CBS, 294

Index 419

CDC, 112, 128, 137
Census, 48, 77, 80, 231, 282
Central Asia, 5, 7, 12, 100, 114, 118, 177, 178, 179, 241, 367
central bank, 63, 64
certificate, 243, 408
certification, 124, 139, 243, 244, 408, 411
challenges, vii, 2, 8, 9, 12, 14, 17, 24, 27, 35, 53, 55, 56, 62, 67, 75, 76, 77, 79, 85, 110, 127, 136, 144, 154, 163, 178, 192, 193, 199, 200, 209, 221, 222, 225, 306, 312, 313, 315, 322, 324, 326, 328, 344, 350, 361, 362, 370, 376, 386, 403
Chamber of Commerce, 309
charities, 86
checks and balances, 253, 334
chemical, 318, 366
chemicals, 366
Chief Justice, 9
child labor, 47, 156, 275
child mortality, 138
childhood, 138
children, 10, 23, 46, 47, 49, 83, 85, 130, 135, 138, 140, 142, 143, 144, 146, 155, 156, 157, 158, 163, 164, 167, 172, 173, 190, 220, 236, 237, 238, 271, 273, 278, 294, 297, 300, 306, 354, 380, 382, 396, 407, 410, 412, 414
Chile, 132
China, 11, 12, 114, 177
circulation, 130
CIS, 5, 162
cities, 11, 22, 23, 26, 33, 44, 47, 49, 104, 120, 125, 126, 128, 130, 163, 169, 176, 241, 253, 254, 255, 258, 287, 386
citizens, vii, 8, 16, 17, 25, 28, 30, 41, 44, 64, 67, 87, 109, 120, 122, 142, 192, 211, 236, 259, 282, 285, 311, 315, 323, 326, 327, 359, 367, 370, 382, 383, 384, 405, 407
City, 126, 127, 129, 254
civic education programs, 337
civil law, 81
civil rights, 384
civil servants, 58, 87, 129, 154, 160, 228, 331, 332, 346
civil service, 87, 137, 184, 192, 251, 280, 281, 315, 327, 331, 332, 349, 357
civil society, 3, 14, 17, 26, 28, 29, 30, 32, 33, 51, 77, 79, 80, 84, 88, 92, 94, 112, 120, 124, 157, 182, 183, 189, 191, 192, 193, 199, 200, 201, 208, 214, 235, 239, 243, 246, 285, 303, 311, 313, 314, 316, 318, 322, 330, 331, 338, 345, 350, 359, 360, 362, 364, 369, 370, 377, 382, 385, 406, 412, 415

clarity, 386, 403
classes, 142, 273, 354, 399
classification, 400
classroom, 146
classroom environment, 146
clean energy, 96
clients, 11, 79, 344
climate, 59, 315, 340
closure, 186
clustering, 316, 346
clusters, 128, 313, 314, 319, 322, 346, 363, 364, 368
CNS, 288
coal, 20, 96, 97, 100, 101, 132
coherence, 77, 128, 210
collaboration, 105, 106, 139, 191, 248, 351, 402, 403, 406
collateral, 68, 129, 159
collateral damage, 68
colleges, 150, 257, 262, 332
commerce, 123, 168, 244
commercial, 10, 11, 12, 20, 25, 33, 64, 84, 92, 93, 95, 97, 101, 104, 108, 109, 112, 113, 114, 117, 120, 129, 133, 150, 167, 176, 222, 224, 240, 245, 246, 302, 322, 335, 347, 381, 397, 399, 408, 409, 411
commercial bank, 10, 93, 240
commercial ties, 95
commodity, 305
Commonwealth of Independent States, 5
communication, 19, 35, 117, 119, 149, 162, 174, 184, 192, 196, 272, 275, 283, 288, 292, 386, 414
communities, 16, 22, 30, 32, 33, 34, 39, 69, 70, 78, 108, 110, 111, 112, 113, 115, 118, 123, 129, 133, 137, 145, 146, 163, 164, 167, 170, 171, 175, 177, 180, 184, 197, 205, 228, 251, 278, 280, 283, 299, 312, 316, 318, 322, 337, 339, 340, 344, 345, 346, 349, 360, 361, 뺌362, 364, 384
Community Based Natural Resource Management, 247, 269
community service, 337
community support, 359
compensation, 407
competition, 68, 122, 141, 177, 245, 303
competitiveness, 61, 63, 94, 145, 201, 316, 340
compilation, 235, 400
complement, 212, 224
complexity, 408
compliance, 21, 93, 104, 116, 167, 171, 197, 219, 242, 250, 287, 351, 356, 383, 397, 413
composition, 67, 72
compounds, 41

computation, 40
computer, 23, 168, 170, 172
computer skills, 172
computer systems, 23
computing, 170
concessional terms, 195
conciliation, 410
conference, 278, 306, 313
confessions, 404
confinement, 406, 407
conflict, vii, 8, 9, 12, 16, 21, 26, 33, 39, 44, 45, 47, 56, 83, 85, 140, 153, 157, 158, 159, 163, 165, 195, 200, 208, 209, 212, 223, 226, 227, 237, 238, 267, 271, 272, 273, 274, 317, 321, 345, 359, 360, 361, 370, 407
conflict prevention, 226, 227
conflict resolution, 153, 267, 361
congruence, 384
connectivity, 21, 109, 115, 119, 120, 249, 251, 287, 341
consensus, 13, 30, 34, 327, 360
conservation, 28, 126, 168, 187, 267, 269
consolidation, 182
constituents, 312, 382, 403
Constitution, 1, 72, 77, 79, 81, 86, 90, 146, 151, 154, 183, 218, 230, 237, 281, 285, 306, 317, 360, 375, 380, 381, 383, 384, 397, 399, 410, 411
construction, 20, 49, 50, 54, 64, 82, 86, 95, 99, 100, 101, 109, 112, 117, 121, 126, 129, 130, 132, 134, 148, 150, 266, 294, 306, 316, 331, 334, 339, 340, 346, 353, 354, 355, 386, 396
Consumer Price Index, 52
consumer protection, 122, 245
consumers, 19, 22, 93, 96, 100, 141, 242, 286, 293
consumption, 21, 39, 40, 41, 42, 43, 44, 45, 46, 61, 155, 158, 180, 214, 216
contamination, 104
cooking, 96, 167
cooperation, 23, 30, 67, 69, 72, 73, 75, 76, 83, 88, 90, 91, 95, 105, 107, 123, 159, 170, 173, 175, 177, 178, 179, 180, 184, 188, 190, 192, 194, 195, 197, 206, 209, 212, 224, 234, 240, 271, 273, 274, 276, 305, 311, 313, 318, 351, 359, 360, 365, 367, 382, 390, 393, 394, 399, 400
copper, 11, 20, 64, 118, 120, 132, 343
cost, vii, 8, 13, 20, 21, 24, 41, 61, 81, 84, 92, 96, 98, 100, 101, 110, 115, 121, 129, 130, 132, 138, 139, 140, 160, 190, 196, 202, 205, 207, 225, 239, 242, 251, 274, 282, 286, 288, 316, 332, 335, 340, 369, 387, 393, 396, 408, 414
cost of living, 160, 225
Council of Ministers, 29, 207, 384
counsel, 382, 404, 414

counseling, 138
course content, 145
covering, 10, 46, 102, 108, 150, 151, 197, 219, 235, 258, 290, 291, 302, 314
CPI, 48
creativity, 151
credit market, 63
creditors, 63
crimes, 72, 73, 74, 123, 237, 384, 406, 412
criminal activity, 68, 72
criminal investigations, 235
criminal justice system, 84, 238, 403, 404, 405
criminality, 389
critical infrastructure, 115, 315, 340
critical thinking, 146
criticism, 84
crop, 45, 50, 112, 115, 270
crop insurance, 50, 270
crop production, 112, 115
crops, 50, 76, 109, 168, 171, 344
cultivation, 13, 16, 35, 50, 58, 68, 70, 109, 110, 111, 113, 129, 168, 173, 179, 180, 181, 220, 227, 228, 248, 256, 270, 280, 299, 318, 363, 364
cultural heritage, 151, 187, 267, 296
cultural values, 209
culture, 15, 18, 24, 35, 139, 151, 152, 170, 220, 259, 322, 337, 380, 387
currency, 10, 54
current limit, 312
curricula, 144, 170, 262, 264, 352, 355, 356, 392, 393, 398, 402
curriculum, 18, 86, 89, 123, 124, 142, 143, 145, 146, 147, 170, 234, 257, 262, 266, 285, 294, 295, 317, 351, 355, 398, 401, 402, 406
curriculum development, 262
customer service, 290
customers, 64
cycles, 201, 209

D

danger, 58, 133
data analysis, 212
data center, 122
data collection, 40, 48, 107, 175, 185, 212, 214, 252, 319, 368
database, 131, 154, 161, 215, 268, 274, 275, 347, 409
deaths, 70, 135, 136, 227, 280, 297
debt service, 217
decentralization, 23, 77, 115
decision makers, 184, 204, 411
decision-making process, 183
deconcentration, 331

defendants, 383, 404, 413, 414
deficiencies, 386
deficiency, 5, 24, 135, 138
deficit, 62
deforestation, 101, 159
degradation, 109
delegates, 359, 360
democracy, 29, 78, 85, 153, 222, 267, 321, 326, 352
democratic elections, 9
democratization, 191
demographic data, 362
demonstrations, 58
denial, 159
Denmark, 166
deposits, 11, 20, 64, 132
deprivation, 43
depth, 30, 39, 140, 216, 222, 306
destiny, 370
destruction, vii, 1, 8, 50, 143, 145, 375, 407
detainees, 406
detection, 168, 182, 220, 390, 404
detention, 72, 157, 237, 238, 271, 284, 337, 384, 396, 404, 406, 407, 415
developing countries, 345
developing nations, 49
development assistance, 13, 195, 196, 197, 209, 312, 319, 320, 329, 368, 370
development policy, 370
devolution, 21, 22, 111, 125, 177, 251
dialogues, 257
diesel fuel, 97, 121
dignity, 312, 321
diplomacy, 73
diplomatic efforts, 170
direct action, 180
direct cost, 23
direct investment, 52, 57
disability, 33, 46, 47, 157, 158, 160, 221, 273, 274
disaster, 26, 50, 72, 79, 113, 154, 156, 157, 161, 162, 164, 165, 171, 173, 230, 270, 275, 276, 281, 301, 337
disbursement, 261, 349, 362
discharges, 81
discrimination, 26, 78, 410
diseases, 24, 135, 138, 261
dispersion, 53
displaced persons, 166, 221
displacement, 26, 27, 49, 163, 164, 165
disposition, 409
distance learning, 146
distortions, 190
distress, 166

distribution, 8, 26, 48, 50, 53, 59, 99, 100, 123, 145, 150, 158, 159, 173, 225, 241, 246, 247, 248, 271, 272, 273, 315, 340, 348, 391, 399, 401
diversification, 45, 50, 80, 96, 113, 115, 318, 364
diversity, 15, 90, 106, 147, 224, 269
divestiture, 99
division of labor, 67
doctors, 16, 35, 46, 49, 149
domestic investment, 57, 216
domestic markets, 174
domestic violence, 406, 412
donations, 85, 89
donors, 17, 18, 26, 28, 29, 48, 49, 65, 73, 90, 95, 99, 102, 104, 107, 115, 116, 127, 139, 140, 150, 152, 154, 173, 174, 181, 185, 186, 188, 189, 190, 191, 193, 194, 196, 197, 198, 199, 200, 201, 204, 208, 209, 222, 223, 224, 225, 239, 240, 307, 314, 319, 320, 323, 325, 368, 379, 386, 390
draft, 83, 99, 123, 126, 128, 235, 256, 293, 302, 333, 383, 399, 400
drainage, 106, 130, 249, 250, 253, 287
drawing, 167, 181, 253
drinking water, 10, 11, 16, 35, 102, 103, 104, 106, 109, 110, 113, 125, 127, 219, 258, 290, 291, 293, 298, 343, 347, 349
drought, 21, 26, 60, 106, 163
drug abuse, 163
drug addict, 157, 163, 173
drug smuggling, 73, 228
drug trafficking, 68, 70, 76, 227, 228, 280, 366
drugs, 27, 72, 74, 78, 79, 87, 138, 163, 170, 171, 178, 179, 180, 181, 198, 229, 253, 318, 364, 365
dual task, 107
due process, 381, 382, 385
duopoly, 120

E

early warning, 162, 270, 275
East Asia, 19
e-commerce, 122
economic activity, 49, 53, 55, 81, 92, 116, 120, 178, 241, 248, 256, 302, 303, 312, 345
economic cooperation, 19, 75, 365, 366
economic development, vii, 12, 13, 15, 18, 19, 21, 51, 64, 66, 68, 75, 76, 81, 85, 90, 92, 94, 101, 125, 163, 178, 215, 218, 221, 222, 223, 224, 239, 243, 245, 246, 311, 313, 314, 316, 319, 330, 331, 339, 350, 368, 380
economic efficiency, 60
economic growth, vii, 1, 2, 3, 12, 13, 14, 17, 29, 45, 51, 52, 53, 54, 57, 60, 66, 90, 91, 96, 115, 116,

125, 132, 134, 142, 146, 151, 157, 162, 177, 188, 190, 201, 203, 205, 207, 222, 223, 224, 245, 269, 303, 311, 317, 321, 322, 323, 344, 345, 346, 350, 351, 375, 376, 377
economic growth rate, 54, 57
economic incentives, 130, 181
economic performance, 52
economic policy, 344
economic reform, 12, 190, 369
economic reforms, 190, 369
economic status, 141
economics, 8, 257, 264
economies of scale, 125, 316
education reform, 87
education/training, 142
educational institutions, 143, 234, 332
educational services, 23
educational system, 10, 150
educationally disadvantaged, 332
educators, 392
e-Government, 123
Egypt, 403
elaboration, 160
elders, 3, 7, 49, 274, 377, 414
election, 9, 331
electricity, 16, 20, 35, 46, 50, 59, 63, 91, 96, 97, 98, 99, 100, 101, 103, 110, 121, 125, 130, 149, 224, 241, 247, 286, 298, 343, 366
emergency, 26, 71, 72, 104, 107, 113, 138, 161, 162, 175, 270, 275
emergency preparedness, 175, 270
emergency response, 71, 162, 275
employability, 317, 351
employees, 93, 150, 160, 172, 242, 323
employers, 23, 49, 148, 242
employment, 10, 12, 16, 20, 22, 24, 25, 27, 38, 44, 49, 51, 53, 54, 58, 60, 61, 65, 66, 76, 81, 95, 101, 108, 109, 113, 116, 118, 119, 125, 127, 131, 133, 134, 149, 153, 156, 159, 163, 166, 167, 169, 171, 172, 188, 191, 194, 202, 221, 223, 225, 244, 265, 272, 277, 278, 298, 300, 303, 305, 312, 313, 316, 322, 339, 340, 345, 347, 348, 351, 360, 361, 362, 367, 384, 390
employment growth, 65, 66, 223
employment opportunities, 16, 20, 22, 24, 25, 44, 53, 61, 66, 76, 101, 108, 113, 118, 125, 131, 134, 153, 159, 172, 223, 265, 277, 339, 351
empowerment, 17, 171, 296, 321
EMS, 310
encouragement, 28, 125, 187, 269
encryption, 122
energy, 5, 15, 19, 20, 36, 50, 61, 66, 95, 96, 97, 98, 99, 100, 101, 102, 118, 126, 133, 149, 156, 157, 167, 178, 216, 218, 223, 224, 246, 247, 248, 249, 269, 286, 300, 306, 313, 316, 340, 341, 345, 349, 350, 367, 409
energy consumption, 126, 156, 216, 300
energy efficiency, 248
energy supply, 99, 341
enforcement, 12, 17, 60, 77, 79, 83, 117, 167, 168, 170, 182, 187, 237, 238, 251, 252, 253, 366, 382, 384, 390, 393, 394, 407, 410, 411
engineering, 255, 264, 293, 327, 356
enrollment, 27, 142, 183, 317, 350, 351, 355
enrollment rates, 142
entrepreneurs, 59, 114, 129
environmental awareness, 187
environmental conditions, 167
environmental factors, 138
environmental impact, 169, 171, 188
environmental issues, 247, 261
environmental management, 15, 27, 28, 177, 187
environmental protection, 127, 172, 187, 352, 367
Environmental Protection Agency, 6, 187
environmental regulations, 174
environmental resources, 125
environmental standards, 168
environmental sustainability, 103, 321
equal opportunity, 294
equality, viii, 27, 82, 191, 199, 379, 380, 410
equilibrium, 56, 58, 59
equipment, 17, 21, 82, 83, 84, 101, 104, 112, 116, 120, 132, 146, 148, 150, 152, 160, 161, 162, 173, 233, 276, 284, 288, 327, 336, 382, 384, 395
equity, 10, 35, 77, 129, 136, 140, 145, 146, 160, 172, 183, 184, 201, 306, 312, 321, 350
erosion, 258
ethical issues, 394
ethical standards, 81, 262, 264
ethics, 78, 82, 84, 238, 387, 393, 394
ethnicity, 141
EU, 4
Europe, 7, 162, 177, 179
European Commission, 4, 44
European Union, 4
evidence, 15, 16, 25, 26, 39, 122, 138, 139, 163, 211, 325, 384, 404, 406, 408, 415
examinations, 263
exchange rate, 10, 41, 55, 63, 305
execution, 53, 59, 60, 61, 82, 110, 147, 193, 201, 203, 241, 306, 314, 319, 323, 324, 325, 327, 329, 333, 334, 351, 361, 389
executive power, 383
exercise, 29, 33, 85, 86, 140, 166, 175, 189, 216, 222, 281, 334, 407

exile, 26, 163, 165, 360
expanded trade, 178
expenditure policy, 61
expenditures, 28, 52, 60, 61, 62, 70, 74, 183, 185, 189, 192, 201, 205, 213, 226, 227, 279, 325, 329
expertise, 172, 181, 184, 198, 411
exploitation, 64, 100, 131, 132, 133, 134, 178, 246, 315, 339, 340
explosives, 69
export market, 94, 95, 316
exporters, 94
exports, 64, 93, 94, 112, 171, 217, 268, 345
exposure, 145, 390, 403
external shocks, 60
extraction, 20, 102, 131, 133, 134, 255, 322, 367
extreme poverty, vii, 8, 39, 47, 222, 225, 344
extremists, 12, 17, 68, 365

F

FAA, 289
facilitators, 33
factories, 64, 98, 101
fairness, 357
faith, 75
families, 10, 26, 40, 44, 45, 47, 49, 99, 110, 126, 154, 155, 157, 158, 159, 160, 163, 175, 273, 274, 317, 343, 390, 410
family income, 47
family planning, 49, 135, 138
farmers, 108, 109, 110, 111, 112, 113, 115, 125, 192, 316, 322, 346, 348, 364
FDI, 4, 64
fencing, 194
fertilizers, 270
fiber, 259, 292, 343
filters, 151
financial, 10, 12, 13, 18, 19, 24, 25, 53, 58, 59, 62, 63, 64, 65, 66, 69, 71, 76, 91, 92, 93, 99, 108, 109, 110, 114, 115, 122, 123, 127, 129, 133, 136, 140, 142, 152, 159, 169, 182, 185, 189, 192, 196, 212, 213, 223, 226, 227, 240, 254, 262, 270, 272, 277, 299, 314, 315, 322, 323, 324, 325, 326, 329, 333, 340, 351, 355, 362, 365, 384
financial crimes, 384
financial distress, 24, 136
financial institutions, 64, 299
financial markets, 92
financial resources, 12, 13, 19, 53, 62, 140, 189
financial sector, 59, 63, 64, 92, 240
financial support, 69, 123, 185, 277
financial system, 91, 92

fiscal policy, 53, 60, 62, 63, 206
fisheries, 105, 106
flexibility, 60, 193, 246
floods, 50, 163
flowers, 94
food, 25, 39, 40, 41, 42, 43, 44, 45, 46, 50, 51, 54, 68, 88, 102, 108, 110, 111, 112, 113, 115, 125, 126, 138, 155, 158, 159, 199, 225, 268, 272, 273, 344, 345
food intake, 39, 43
food safety, 268
food security, 25, 50, 88, 102, 108, 110, 111, 112, 113, 115, 345
force, 54, 67, 68, 70, 72, 74, 76, 83, 121, 151, 180, 187, 217, 226, 227, 235, 280, 312, 328, 367, 393
forecasting, 71, 313, 323, 341
foreign aid, 327, 350
foreign assistance, 52, 53, 54, 56, 61, 62, 68, 194, 314
foreign direct investment, 57, 131
foreign exchange, 63, 64, 93
foreign firms, 19
foreign investment, 91
foreign policy, 73
formal education, 149, 153, 262, 267, 294, 350, 351
formal sector, 81, 84, 245, 303
formation, 35, 87, 106, 122
formula, 160
foundations, viii, 91, 246, 322, 351, 357, 379
France, 166, 403
free market economy, 85
freedom, vii, 1, 8, 85, 153, 357, 375
freezing, 411
fuel efficiency, 119
fuel prices, 51, 305
funding, 19, 22, 24, 65, 68, 80, 86, 95, 101, 112, 115, 117, 136, 140, 141, 148, 160, 181, 193, 195, 196, 202, 203, 204, 206, 248, 252, 264, 288, 306, 307, 325, 354, 358, 360, 388
funds, 13, 17, 20, 22, 28, 63, 67, 71, 76, 93, 98, 110, 112, 118, 123, 127, 140, 141, 148, 150, 156, 159, 170, 174, 189, 192, 193, 194, 195, 196, 204, 205, 246, 250, 306, 315, 319, 323, 325, 326, 329, 368

G

GDP, 4, 48, 52, 53, 54, 56, 57, 60, 61, 62, 64, 91, 109, 125, 191, 205, 216, 217, 302, 306, 329, 339
GDP per capita, 54
gender balance, 263
gender equality, 15, 27, 78, 177, 183, 184, 188

gender equity, vii, 8, 146, 147, 183, 184, 380
gender gap, 44
gender inequality, 17, 42, 77
gender-sensitive, 171
general education, 150, 366
geography, 147
geology, 134, 257, 264
global demand, 181
global economy, 60, 116
God, 378
goods and services, 90, 92, 93, 94, 125, 193, 216, 224
government budget, 56
government policy, 213, 327
government revenues, 19, 20, 131, 134, 169
grading, 7, 79, 147, 186, 233, 357, 387, 388, 391, 392
grants, 28, 52, 62, 195, 197, 347, 349, 355
grass, 29
grassroots, 33, 39, 222
grazing, 44
grids, 96, 100, 101
Gross Domestic Product, 4
groundwater, 102, 105, 106, 107, 257
growth, 1, 13, 18, 19, 22, 25, 26, 39, 40, 47, 48, 49, 51, 52, 53, 54, 55, 56, 57, 58, 59, 60, 61, 63, 66, 81, 85, 91, 92, 96, 98, 109, 113, 114, 116, 121, 122, 125, 137, 138, 139, 140, 143, 147, 149, 150, 157, 174, 179, 185, 198, 200, 208, 213, 222, 223, 225, 305, 312, 313, 315, 316, 317, 322, 339, 340, 341, 345, 346, 347, 348, 367, 375, 394
growth rate, 48, 53, 54, 55, 57, 59, 185
guidance, 2, 20, 29, 122, 186, 207, 213, 273, 313, 376
guidelines, 69, 128, 139, 162, 204, 335, 348, 355, 360, 361, 364, 407
guiding principles, 77

H

harassment, 76
harmonization, 32, 178, 189, 192, 194, 204, 390, 398
harmony, 161
harvesting, 107
health, vii, 1, 5, 8, 10, 24, 27, 36, 40, 46, 47, 48, 49, 50, 61, 66, 95, 105, 108, 109, 113, 119, 129, 130, 131, 134, 135, 136, 137, 138, 139, 140, 141, 150, 158, 163, 166, 167, 168, 172, 173, 175, 176, 187, 190, 199, 215, 220, 223, 242, 245, 260, 261, 277, 296, 297, 306, 312, 317, 350, 351, 353, 356, 366, 375
health care, 10, 134, 135, 136, 137, 138, 139, 140, 141, 175, 176, 260, 261, 277, 296, 297, 317
health care system, 138, 261
health condition, 167
health education, 317
health services, 5, 24, 49, 95, 109, 131, 135, 136, 138, 140, 190, 296, 306, 312
health status, 24, 135
hepatitis, 297
hepatitis d, 297
high school, 144, 145
higher education, 18, 23, 86, 89, 143, 144, 145, 146, 148, 149, 244, 264, 266, 295, 317, 350, 351, 353, 354, 401
Highlands, 38, 43
highways, 11, 116, 227, 249, 286, 287
HIPC, 4, 195, 197, 201, 203, 206
hiring, 79, 81, 264
history, vii, 1, 3, 8, 24, 152, 339, 375, 377
HIV, 4, 5, 135, 138, 172, 220, 261
HIV/AIDS, 135, 138
home ownership, 45
homes, 26, 49, 127, 129, 162, 163
hospitality, 3, 377
host, 123, 164, 175, 278
House, 8, 378
household income, 44, 45, 171, 345
housing, 23, 126, 128, 129, 131, 163, 172, 173, 175, 254, 277, 278, 290, 396
hub, 12, 19, 94, 177, 178, 212, 254
human capital, 49, 61, 78, 115, 157, 201
human condition, 406
human development, 151
Human Development Report, 12
human health, 138
human resource development, 139, 350
human resources, 21, 67, 104, 205, 232, 233, 316, 350, 353, 382, 386, 387, 388, 395
human right, 17, 33, 77, 78, 79, 80, 83, 85, 90, 111, 163, 164, 188, 191, 199, 215, 218, 222, 224, 238, 283, 315, 326, 328, 337, 338, 360, 380, 381, 399, 412, 413, 414, 415
human rights, 17, 33, 77, 78, 79, 80, 83, 85, 90, 111, 163, 164, 188, 191, 199, 215, 218, 222, 224, 238, 283, 315, 326, 328, 337, 338, 360, 380, 381, 399, 412, 413, 414, 415
hydrocarbons, 20, 99, 131, 134, 178, 293, 341
hydroelectric power, 105
hygiene, 113, 130, 138, 146

I

ideal, 367
identification, 93, 130, 242, 314, 319, 346, 349, 366, 408, 411
identity, 407, 408, 411

illiteracy, vii, 8, 9, 27, 121, 183
imbalances, 206
IMF, 5, 203, 214, 215, 329
immunization, 135, 190, 261
immunodeficiency, 4
impact assessment, 167, 215
import substitution, 339
imported products, 63
imports, 64, 93, 99, 100, 115, 171, 268, 315, 340
imprisonment, 407
improvements, 24, 27, 61, 78, 90, 100, 105, 108, 109, 117, 125, 130, 135, 139, 154, 183, 210, 224, 252, 323, 338, 340, 344, 350, 386, 387, 390, 393
inauguration, 397
incarceration, 404
incidence, 39, 42, 46, 53, 135, 155, 158, 190, 216, 220
income, 1, 25, 27, 39, 40, 44, 45, 46, 47, 49, 50, 61, 107, 111, 129, 171, 175, 181, 183, 192, 214, 248, 298, 375
income support, 25, 111
income tax, 61
increased access, 22, 103, 125, 127, 302
independence, viii, 67, 143, 151, 153, 315, 322, 328, 337, 340, 352, 357, 379
Independence, 330
India, 101, 179, 264, 367
individuals, 2, 30, 86, 87, 149, 157, 158, 159, 160, 163, 186, 273, 274, 277, 305, 333, 361, 362, 376, 385, 391, 410, 411, 413
induction, 385, 386, 391, 401, 403
industries, 19, 54, 64, 94, 108, 180, 310, 312, 313, 315, 340, 341, 367
industry, vii, 8, 12, 13, 17, 51, 54, 56, 58, 66, 68, 70, 94, 95, 96, 115, 120, 122, 133, 179, 188, 192, 223, 224, 244, 339, 340, 341
inequality, 39, 42, 43, 44, 157, 214
inequity, 45, 138, 177
infant mortality, 47, 50, 135, 157, 297, 300
infants, 135
inflation, 10, 48, 55, 63, 92, 305, 306
informal sector, 53, 303
information sharing, 197, 235
information technology, 82, 388, 393
ingredients, 53
inheritance, vii, 8, 159, 184, 410
injuries, 119
insecurity, 13, 16, 24, 33, 43, 44, 45, 55, 56, 60, 76, 86, 125, 138, 155, 179, 203, 209, 344, 345
inspections, 168, 248, 251
institution building, 106, 185
institutional change, 20

institutional infrastructure, 12, 229
institutional reforms, 267, 339
insulation, 60
insurgency, 357, 360
integration, 29, 39, 62, 80, 84, 108, 156, 164, 174, 177, 193, 201, 202, 269, 273, 300, 305, 312, 319, 340, 357, 361, 363, 364, 379, 381, 382, 390, 407
integrity, viii, 72, 75, 80, 115, 181, 182, 247, 256, 262, 264, 268, 284, 326, 327, 331, 352, 357, 364, 379, 381, 382, 393, 394
intellectual property, 122
intellectual property rights, 122
intelligence, 75, 179, 181, 228, 318, 365, 366
interdependence, 111, 208
interest rates, 63, 129
interference, 75, 76, 241
internal processes, 387
internally displaced, 15, 26, 47, 108, 163, 164, 318
International Covenant on Civil and Political Rights, 399
International Covenant on Economic, Social and Cultural Rights, 399
international financial institutions, 63
international investment, 133
international law, 73, 414
International Monetary Fund, 5, 202
international relations, 73, 87
international standards, 75, 76, 83, 117, 218, 251, 252, 288, 329, 331, 406, 410
international terrorism, 1, 365, 375
international trade, 178, 384
internship, 402
interoperability, 122
intervention, 27, 35, 129, 171
intimidation, 145
inventors, 151
investment, 11, 12, 13, 19, 20, 21, 27, 52, 53, 57, 59, 60, 61, 66, 73, 78, 81, 91, 92, 94, 95, 98, 99, 100, 102, 104, 105, 108, 116, 118, 122, 123, 124, 125, 126, 129, 131, 132, 133, 134, 149, 174, 176, 178, 181, 188, 195, 219, 221, 223, 224, 269, 289, 292, 302, 312, 322, 339, 340, 344, 367
investments, 11, 18, 21, 22, 39, 50, 63, 64, 65, 66, 90, 95, 98, 100, 102, 104, 106, 110, 118, 119, 122, 123, 125, 126, 133, 149, 165, 191, 195, 223, 224, 244, 253, 312, 313
investors, 13, 19, 59, 91, 94, 95, 98, 101, 123, 129, 188, 240, 242
IPO, 330
Iran, 10, 26, 114, 162, 163, 164, 166, 173, 175, 264, 276, 278, 279, 301, 302, 318, 366

irrigation, 7, 10, 21, 50, 61, 66, 94, 98, 102, 103, 104, 105, 106, 107, 108, 109, 111, 112, 113, 115, 168, 219, 223, 258, 269, 270, 291, 299, 306, 316, 322, 344, 345, 347, 349
Islam, 85, 86, 118, 191, 380, 410, 411, 414
Islamabad, 367
Islamic law, 264
Islamic society, viii, 82, 379, 380
Islamic state, 51
isolation, 95, 212, 224
issues, 13, 15, 16, 17, 27, 28, 31, 32, 33, 35, 49, 59, 68, 71, 75, 79, 83, 84, 87, 88, 90, 92, 98, 107, 122, 124, 131, 139, 140, 142, 149, 154, 170, 172, 173, 177, 187, 188, 193, 196, 198, 199, 205, 215, 222, 224, 226, 229, 235, 236, 237, 239, 248, 254, 260, 261, 266, 267, 270, 272, 277, 313, 318, 323, 325, 338, 350, 363, 365, 366, 367, 370, 381, 382, 387, 390, 395, 410

J

Jirga, 7, 8, 9, 178, 179, 228, 305, 317, 323, 359, 362, 365, 378, 410, 411
job creation, vii, 101, 202, 311, 316, 321, 322, 323, 345
job insecurity, 44, 47
job training, 288
jobless, 49
judicial power, 383
judiciary, 2, 69, 79, 81, 87, 217, 281, 326, 376, 383, 387, 390, 405
jurisdiction, 27, 122, 383
just society, 75
juvenile justice, 387, 390, 404
juveniles, 381, 389, 390, 404, 407

K

kerosene, 96
kill, 277
kindergartens, 10, 155, 158, 274

L

labor force, 54, 60, 194, 312, 350, 353
labor market, 49, 271, 350
lack of confidence, 387
land acquisition, 251
land tenure, 126, 254, 276
landscape, vii, 8
language skills, 168
languages, 264, 390, 397, 400
law enforcement, 68, 69, 74, 76, 84, 357, 385, 389
laws, 12, 19, 64, 70, 71, 78, 81, 83, 91, 92, 93, 103, 106, 128, 168, 172, 174, 192, 233, 235, 237, 239, 240, 245, 248, 252, 257, 259, 261, 262, 264, 268, 269, 272, 290, 302, 315, 317, 327, 328, 330, 333, 335, 336, 370, 380, 381, 382, 383, 385, 386, 389, 390, 393, 394, 397, 399, 400, 404, 405, 413
laws and regulations, 12, 64, 78, 93, 172, 192, 245, 268, 269, 272, 327, 394
lawyers, 93, 235, 240, 394, 401, 402, 412, 413
lead, 18, 48, 66, 74, 76, 86, 91, 92, 105, 115, 124, 125, 129, 134, 147, 156, 178, 184, 185, 191, 195, 199, 206, 317, 325, 358, 364
leadership, 27, 72, 78, 88, 107, 121, 124, 139, 149, 153, 180, 182, 184, 189, 208, 266, 267, 311, 312, 314, 317, 321, 322, 326, 328, 332, 339, 357, 358, 359, 360, 387, 388, 389
leadership development, 317, 332
learners, 142
learning, 142, 144, 145, 146, 147, 264, 294, 352, 353, 354, 390
learning disabilities, 146
learning environment, 146
legal protection, 9, 130, 165, 225, 381
legislation, 8, 19, 24, 29, 83, 84, 87, 90, 91, 99, 105, 106, 122, 123, 124, 131, 133, 137, 149, 152, 153, 154, 155, 161, 162, 169, 170, 173, 197, 207, 216, 239, 241, 250, 252, 253, 268, 275, 330, 333, 336, 341, 342, 385, 397, 399, 400, 401, 408, 414
lending, 64, 73, 93, 129, 195, 240, 246
level of education, 43, 45
liberty, viii, 82, 379, 380
librarians, 145
life expectancy, 108, 155
lifetime, 65
light, 169
light rail, 169
liquid fuels, 97, 99
liquidate, 329
liquidity, 63
literacy, 18, 40, 44, 45, 49, 89, 123, 142, 143, 144, 145, 146, 149, 150, 153, 159, 168, 191, 192, 262, 263, 267, 272, 277, 317, 350, 351, 353, 361, 413
literacy rates, 144, 263
litigation, 84
livestock, 44, 45, 50, 109, 112, 115, 158, 159, 271, 276, 305
living conditions, 1, 169, 344, 375
loan guarantees, 128
loans, 44, 129, 159, 176
lobbying, 239
local authorities, 35, 44
local conditions, 16

Index

local government, 17, 68, 77, 87, 88, 128, 184, 192, 315, 327, 334, 353, 355
logistics, 118, 137, 361, 400
loyalty, 312

M

machinery, 201, 212
macroeconomic environment, 92
macroeconomic management, 66, 223
macroeconomic policies, 52, 66, 223
macroeconomic policy, 59
Madrasas, 86, 89
magnitude, vii, 8, 222
maiming, 145
major issues, 49
majority, 17, 26, 40, 43, 44, 48, 51, 73, 98, 144, 163, 195, 350, 386
malaria, 135, 261
malnutrition, 24, 50, 135, 138
man, 41, 111, 138, 167, 233, 280, 347
man-made disasters, 111
manufacturing, 54, 64, 94, 129
mapping, 80, 129, 137, 166, 175, 215, 252, 253, 255, 282, 331, 334, 353, 354
market access, 22, 117
market economy, 9, 13, 90, 321
market-based economy, 18, 20
marketing, 25, 109, 110
marriage, 155, 236, 407, 408, 410
married women, 135
mass, 26, 163, 184
mass communication, 184
materials, 20, 129, 132, 144, 145, 146, 236, 239, 249, 264, 336, 390, 395, 398, 400, 401, 412
matrix, 16, 112, 246, 347
matter, iv, 102
MCP, 332, 333
measles, 220, 261, 297
measurement, 41, 211, 214
media, 11, 15, 16, 24, 33, 74, 86, 151, 152, 153, 170, 184, 213, 220, 267, 274, 296, 338, 385, 414
mediation, 92, 239, 273, 410
medical, 141, 163, 356
medical care, 163
medicine, 46
melt, 104
membership, 124, 171, 179, 207, 244
mental health, 138, 337
mentally ill persons, 157
mentoring, 184, 244, 332, 337, 358, 359, 391
mentoring program, 184
merit-based appointments, 280
messages, 414

methodology, 348
middle class, 14
Middle East, 12, 19, 177, 178, 340
migrants, 127
migration, 26, 27, 44, 47, 163, 164, 166, 173, 178, 179, 195, 278, 302, 319, 367
military, 13, 17, 67, 71, 72, 73, 74, 75, 154, 158, 160, 181, 223, 312, 318, 357, 358, 359, 384
military courts, 74
militias, 17, 73, 360
mineral resources, 12, 20, 114, 131, 133, 149, 315, 339, 340
Ministry of Education, 6, 123, 147, 150, 243, 306, 337
minorities, 157
minority groups, 142, 151
minors, 163
miscarriage, 381
miscarriages, 385
mission, 9, 239
missions, 70, 139, 226, 279
misuse, 181, 324, 327
mobile phone, 22, 121, 124, 219, 292, 344
models, 237, 243, 264, 335
modernization, 103, 160, 161, 162, 410
modifications, 352, 362
modules, 352
monetary policy, 54, 56, 59, 63, 64
money laundering, 78, 389
monopoly, 19
moral imperative, 311
morale, 338, 387
morbidity, 138
mortality, 24, 27, 108, 134, 135, 136, 156, 184, 191, 220, 297
mortality rate, 135, 136, 220, 297
motivation, 144, 190
movement restrictions, 120
multidimensional, 47
multimedia, 123
museums, 24, 152, 153, 296
music, 266, 267
Muslims, 8, 85, 378
mutual respect, 76

N

NAP, 351
narcotic, 18, 88
narcotics, vii, 2, 5, 8, 9, 12, 13, 15, 17, 27, 39, 51, 59, 61, 67, 68, 70, 73, 74, 75, 76, 105, 111, 119, 150, 167, 168, 170, 172, 177, 179, 180, 181, 182, 188, 192, 215, 223, 248, 254, 256, 260,

262, 267, 270, 277, 318, 344, 363, 365, 366, 376, 380, 382, 384, 387, 389, 403, 407
national identity, 79, 230, 282
national income, 48
national interests, 67, 71, 72, 73
national parks, 255
national policy, 29, 80, 203, 244, 322
national product, 108
national security, 17, 24, 67, 68, 71, 72, 73, 75, 76, 87, 223, 382
National Security Council, 71, 72
national strategy, 15, 70
National Survey, 217
natural disaster, 10, 45, 46, 47, 71, 110, 155, 156, 157, 159, 161, 163, 270, 272, 301
natural disasters, 10, 45, 46, 47, 71, 110, 155, 156, 161, 163, 270, 272
natural gas, 64, 97, 100, 101, 241, 249, 255, 367
natural resource management, 28, 187, 258
natural resources, 19, 22, 53, 66, 76, 94, 102, 109, 115, 131, 132, 133, 155, 168, 174, 176, 202, 223, 242, 293, 345, 347, 367, 370
needy, 10, 85, 254
negative consequences, 26, 162
negative effects, 364
neglect, 96, 326
Netherlands, 166
next generation, 179
NGOs, 16, 23, 26, 30, 33, 48, 51, 94, 110, 112, 128, 130, 140, 141, 154, 157, 159, 160, 174, 184, 193, 194, 196, 197, 211, 213, 223, 271, 273, 274, 303, 307, 354, 356
nickel, 20, 132
normative acts, 259
North Atlantic Treaty Organization (NATO), 67, 69, 74, 181, 272, 273
Norway, 166
nuisance, 174, 242
nurses, 356
nutrition, 24, 47, 134, 136, 138, 140, 172
nutritional status, 115

O

objectivity, 390
obstacles, 27, 64, 68, 69, 97, 110, 163, 184, 211, 213, 237, 391
offenders, 83, 237, 238, 406, 407
Official Development Assistance, 7, 189, 193
officials, 16, 68, 70, 71, 73, 76, 78, 87, 88, 170, 230, 238, 266, 283, 315, 327, 330, 364, 386, 393, 402, 405, 413
oil, 20, 49, 60, 97, 98, 99, 100, 101, 132, 133, 134, 247, 255

old age, 275, 301
olive oil, 94
on-the-job training, 244, 403
open spaces, 23, 131
openness, 77
operating costs, 245, 313
operating system, 382, 404
Operation Enduring Freedom, 7, 69
operations, 17, 19, 20, 25, 60, 64, 68, 69, 73, 74, 75, 76, 93, 95, 96, 97, 98, 99, 100, 101, 114, 121, 133, 134, 141, 150, 158, 167, 176, 181, 199, 208, 212, 218, 223, 239, 246, 248, 249, 276, 282, 286, 303, 315, 323, 330, 338, 358, 359, 369, 388, 407
opportunities, 19, 22, 23, 25, 27, 50, 51, 54, 74, 79, 84, 85, 92, 94, 95, 98, 111, 112, 117, 125, 131, 133, 134, 142, 153, 156, 159, 163, 166, 168, 169, 173, 174, 175, 177, 178, 180, 183, 184, 188, 190, 241, 246, 248, 267, 272, 274, 300, 312, 313, 317, 321, 323, 339, 340, 350, 351, 352, 360, 361, 366, 393, 398, 403
optimism, 9, 305
organ, 33, 81, 383
Organization for Economic Cooperation and Development, 7
organize, 87, 103, 115, 407
organs, 82
OSCE, 7, 179, 367
outreach, 34, 130, 240, 285, 334, 338, 360, 361, 406
outreach programs, 285, 406
outsourcing, 100, 243
overlap, 190, 367
oversight, 17, 19, 20, 31, 71, 77, 79, 82, 84, 87, 96, 97, 167, 183, 188, 206, 210, 211, 212, 243, 284, 315, 327, 330, 331, 332, 337, 344, 346, 351, 356, 359, 361, 381, 382, 393, 405, 415
ownership, 15, 28, 29, 30, 45, 68, 69, 90, 171, 184, 189, 190, 196, 204, 224, 317, 320, 325, 329, 351, 358, 359, 396

P

Pacific, 87, 88, 171
Pakistan, 10, 26, 75, 101, 114, 162, 163, 164, 166, 173, 175, 179, 239, 245, 264, 276, 278, 279, 301, 302, 305, 318, 342, 366, 367
parallel, 17, 47, 77, 131, 193, 195, 210, 244, 324
parents, 144, 237, 271
Paris Club, 63, 195, 197
parity, 333
Parliament, 152, 313, 319, 321, 333, 369, 378, 381, 385, 397, 399, 400, 411
participants, 184
pasture, 44, 174, 276

pastures, 274
payroll, 160, 161, 275, 388
peace, vii, viii, 8, 12, 27, 67, 71, 73, 80, 83, 85, 152, 153, 154, 165, 198, 209, 267, 311, 312, 318, 321, 328, 337, 338, 352, 359, 360, 361, 362, 367, 370, 414, 415
peace process, 361
penalties, 252, 253
pension reforms, 49, 156, 158, 160
pensioners, 10, 155, 161, 275
per capita expenditure, 41
per capita income, 51, 66, 190, 223
percentile, 181
performance appraisal, 333
permit, 59, 128, 190, 241, 255
personal communication, 120
persons with disabilities, 142, 300
Peru, 132
petroleum, 64, 167
physical therapist, 356
piracy, 122
plants, 112, 247
platform, 173, 242
platinum, 20, 132
playing, 56
police, 10, 17, 68, 72, 73, 82, 90, 167, 227, 235, 238, 312, 328, 336, 360, 365, 382, 384, 385, 403, 404, 406, 412, 414
policy issues, 213, 243
policy makers, 48, 88, 247
policy making, 20, 26, 27, 39, 48, 71, 133, 161, 208, 216
policy options, 343
policy reform, 22, 84, 120
policy responses, 165, 166
polio, 135, 261, 297
political parties, 384
politics, 26
pollution, 28, 138, 168, 187, 287
popular support, 73
population, 10, 11, 13, 22, 24, 25, 36, 41, 42, 43, 45, 46, 49, 51, 53, 54, 60, 61, 68, 84, 96, 103, 109, 110, 125, 126, 127, 134, 135, 136, 140, 141, 143, 144, 145, 155, 156, 157, 163, 164, 165, 166, 173, 176, 212, 216, 217, 219, 220, 221, 225, 274, 278, 292, 293, 297, 298, 300, 306, 315, 326, 328, 331, 332, 333, 334, 335, 336, 337, 338, 341, 343, 344, 345, 350, 351, 358, 359, 366
population density, 127
population growth, 13, 49, 110
porous borders, 192
portfolio, 97, 191, 320, 334, 369

portfolio management, 334
poultry, 112
poverty alleviation, 34, 115
poverty line, 39, 41, 42, 44, 46, 47, 51, 53, 126, 155, 212, 214, 216, 225, 299, 343
poverty reduction, 3, 13, 15, 16, 17, 18, 22, 25, 29, 33, 40, 47, 48, 49, 50, 51, 54, 58, 66, 81, 85, 86, 88, 89, 91, 101, 105, 108, 111, 116, 118, 146, 154, 163, 188, 189, 190, 191, 205, 206, 207, 210, 213, 214, 221, 222, 223, 305, 377
poverty trap, 44
power generation, 50, 59, 94, 100, 224, 241, 248, 315, 340
power plants, 101, 132
pragmatism, 312
precious minerals, 64
precipitation, 102
predictability, 63, 193, 209, 412
pregnancy, 155
preparation, iv, 2, 3, 32, 33, 34, 51, 61, 65, 97, 107, 160, 173, 174, 294, 319, 342, 343, 347, 370, 376, 377, 388
preparedness, 26, 50, 79, 106, 154, 156, 157, 161, 162, 164, 165, 171, 173, 230, 270, 275, 276, 281, 301, 337, 392
preschool, 23
preservation, 28, 49, 130, 187, 267, 415
President, 2, 3, 9, 29, 32, 71, 91, 121, 149, 154, 177, 186, 207, 208, 211, 229, 230, 231, 232, 241, 246, 252, 253, 306, 307, 312, 376, 377, 383
presidential authority, 269
prevention, 28, 138, 172, 187, 275, 366, 399
price index, 288
price stability, 48, 63
primary school, 40, 43, 44, 45, 49, 142, 144, 146, 294, 305, 306
primary school age children, 305
primary school enrollment, 43, 45, 49
principles, 8, 14, 33, 35, 47, 81, 90, 120, 165, 166, 189, 190, 191, 200, 201, 224, 242, 276, 301, 320, 325, 370, 381, 383, 407, 410, 411, 414
prisoners, 237, 406, 407
prisons, 83, 284, 337, 381, 382, 384, 386, 395, 396, 403, 406
private banks, 129
private education, 150
private firms, 25, 100, 101, 114, 133
private investment, 12, 13, 19, 20, 25, 57, 59, 60, 91, 92, 94, 95, 96, 98, 100, 107, 114, 118, 123, 125, 129, 131, 169, 176, 177, 224, 315, 340
private sector investment, 11, 12, 19, 20, 22, 23, 25, 59, 66, 90, 95, 96, 100, 102, 114, 119, 124, 127, 176, 177, 218, 223, 246, 302, 322, 346, 357

privatization, 93, 130, 241, 274
probability, 170
problem solving, 212
process indicators, 215
producers, 93, 113, 129
production technology, 345
productive capacity, 21
professional development, 82, 391, 405
professional management, 192, 241, 388
professionalism, 74, 284, 360, 381, 382, 385, 394, 413
professionals, 3, 81, 82, 83, 86, 97, 139, 147, 148, 149, 169, 183, 184, 233, 234, 236, 238, 264, 284, 350, 377, 384, 385, 386, 389, 390, 391, 392, 393, 394, 395, 396, 397, 399, 402, 403, 404, 407, 415
profit, 24, 25, 33, 136, 137, 139, 140, 141, 403
profitability, 171
program staff, 362
programming, 24, 45, 111, 138, 153, 191, 206, 258, 266, 314, 318, 327, 351, 369, 381, 386
progress reports, 51, 214, 338
project, 14, 21, 28, 44, 53, 61, 100, 105, 106, 107, 126, 129, 132, 133, 149, 160, 161, 167, 171, 173, 174, 178, 182, 184, 190, 193, 196, 205, 209, 215, 241, 244, 250, 257, 271, 272, 273, 274, 277, 288, 307, 314, 320, 323, 325, 329, 343, 344, 347, 367
property rights, 59, 121, 128, 159
prosperity, vii, 8, 73, 75, 177, 198, 222, 305, 312, 321, 366, 380
protected areas, 171, 255
protection, vii, 10, 15, 19, 24, 26, 28, 36, 39, 40, 45, 47, 48, 49, 50, 53, 66, 68, 72, 76, 80, 90, 102, 106, 111, 122, 136, 153, 154, 155, 156, 157, 159, 160, 163, 164, 165, 166, 175, 176, 180, 187, 201, 215, 220, 223, 242, 258, 268, 272, 273, 274, 275, 277, 287, 301, 311, 321, 337, 343, 360, 382, 384, 405, 406, 413
PST, 334
public administration, 16, 35, 50, 58, 77, 79, 147, 182, 192, 196, 247, 256, 260, 268, 301, 315, 327, 332, 357
public administration reforms, 147, 192, 197
public affairs, 28, 184
public awareness, 18, 74, 85, 89, 130, 138, 151, 162, 172, 237, 276, 337, 404, 408, 413
public broadcasting, 24, 153
public education, 150, 285, 355, 406
public expenditures, 61, 203
public figures, 79
public finance, 61, 194, 313, 326, 327, 370
public health, 15, 19, 24, 103, 105, 138, 140, 172

public investment, 52, 57, 130, 224, 313
public life, 184
public officials, 389
public policy, 16, 29, 30, 313
public resources, 127, 182, 327
public sector, 13, 15, 17, 19, 21, 25, 60, 77, 78, 79, 80, 87, 90, 93, 96, 100, 101, 114, 119, 121, 122, 124, 129, 133, 139, 141, 144, 150, 169, 176, 185, 205, 222, 224, 245, 252, 256, 280, 327, 328, 370
public support, 155, 197
public welfare, 72
public-private partnerships, 243
publishing, 239, 282
purchasing power, 129

Q

qualifications, 23, 49, 82, 144, 148, 263, 353, 390, 391, 392, 398, 401
quality assurance, 110, 147, 148, 261, 351, 355
quality control, 137, 361
quality of life, 25, 61, 102, 108, 153, 187, 267
quality of service, 260, 387
quality standards, 139, 243
questioning, 151, 404

R

radicalization, 337
radio, 24, 33, 151, 152, 153, 267, 414
rangeland, 113, 316, 345
rate of return, 166, 205
ratification, 87
raw materials, 92
real terms, 48, 185
realism, 314, 325
reality, 365
recognition, 65, 122, 209, 352, 411
recommendations, iv, 73, 78, 123, 139, 186, 204, 232, 233, 234, 235, 237, 238, 241, 259, 270, 272, 305, 321, 330, 359, 362, 387, 388, 390, 393, 394, 401, 404
reconciliation, 81, 83, 85, 128, 312, 317, 337, 338, 360, 361, 365, 370, 415
reconstruction, vii, 8, 52, 54, 60, 69, 71, 76, 119, 129, 133, 190, 194, 195, 196, 197, 203, 209, 222, 250, 253, 352
recovery, 22, 23, 85, 98, 100, 101, 113, 125, 129, 130, 152, 153, 198, 286, 312, 314, 335, 345, 361
recovery plan, 335
recreation, 153
recruiting, 139, 233, 386, 412

Reform, 4, 5, 6, 34, 67, 69, 74, 77, 79, 89, 92, 93, 132, 139, 148, 157, 186, 207, 226, 227, 228, 231, 243, 252, 254, 311, 316, 326, 330, 331, 333, 339, 369, 381, 387, 388, 404, 406, 407, 408, 409
refugees, 1, 9, 10, 15, 26, 27, 34, 47, 108, 127, 162, 163, 164, 165, 174, 175, 176, 178, 221, 276, 277, 301, 318, 366, 375
regeneration, 25, 108, 112, 220, 299
regional cooperation, 9, 15, 27, 39, 67, 168, 174, 177, 178, 179, 188, 201, 215, 223, 247, 256, 261, 267, 269, 318, 323, 365, 366, 367
regional facilities, 392
regional problem, 318
Registry, 6, 230, 259
regulations, 23, 26, 71, 72, 91, 94, 99, 106, 128, 134, 137, 168, 178, 218, 235, 243, 248, 250, 251, 252, 253, 254, 256, 259, 271, 287, 289, 333, 336, 382, 384, 388, 390, 399, 404, 406, 407, 408
regulatory agencies, 20, 98
regulatory bodies, 149
regulatory framework, 11, 19, 20, 22, 92, 97, 99, 102, 109, 117, 118, 119, 123, 127, 133, 169, 176, 177, 182, 221, 239, 250, 256, 260, 261, 292, 296, 299, 322, 333, 342
rehabilitation, 11, 21, 23, 24, 86, 97, 99, 100, 103, 104, 106, 107, 108, 112, 116, 117, 126, 129, 130, 143, 144, 159, 161, 164, 170, 172, 173, 249, 250, 258, 261, 273, 314, 386, 395, 396, 403, 407
rehabilitation program, 24, 107, 258, 407
relative size, 299
relatives, 159, 167
relevance, 79, 145, 350
relief, 195, 197
religion, viii, 71, 72, 82, 85, 86, 379, 380, 414
REM, 306
remittances, 91, 125, 164, 319
renewable energy, 97, 98, 167, 247
rent, 44, 45, 46, 129, 192, 194
rent subsidies, 129
repair, 267, 386, 396
reputation, viii, 73, 82, 379, 380
requirements, 15, 30, 43, 46, 63, 71, 82, 94, 105, 106, 112, 118, 121, 129, 169, 186, 197, 201, 202, 206, 214, 215, 216, 242, 250, 268, 287, 312, 336, 361, 362, 388, 392, 397, 399, 401, 405, 408, 413
research facilities, 234, 403
reserves, 132, 217, 255, 268
resolution, 18, 83, 93, 94, 122, 201, 357, 359, 361, 382, 385, 387, 407, 408, 409, 410, 411, 414

resource allocation, 15, 19, 34, 35, 39, 53, 93, 193, 205, 206
resource management, 21, 82, 102, 103, 108, 113, 182, 189, 260, 290
resource utilization, 205
response, 13, 50, 72, 79, 87, 113, 127, 154, 156, 157, 161, 162, 164, 165, 174, 230, 236, 237, 243, 270, 272, 275, 276, 281, 301, 322, 350, 370
response capacity, 157
responsiveness, 123, 225
restoration, 28, 111, 150, 187, 267
restrictions, 94
restructuring, 20, 26, 84, 99, 147, 159, 160, 186, 218, 286, 333, 387, 388, 393, 399
retail, 54, 123
retirement, 160, 355
revenue, 18, 23, 60, 69, 74, 81, 93, 122, 128, 178, 192, 202, 205, 219, 242, 246, 254, 292, 293, 303, 312, 319, 321, 322, 327, 329, 332, 339, 341, 342, 343, 374
risk, 19, 26, 49, 50, 53, 63, 81, 104, 110, 117, 146, 154, 155, 157, 158, 159, 161, 162, 163, 173, 194, 196, 205, 209, 240, 246, 273, 275, 276, 329, 330, 344, 406
risk factors, 146
risk management, 26, 157, 159, 205, 209, 240, 344
risks, 13, 50, 60, 64, 138, 154, 155, 161, 162, 200, 205, 209, 240, 276, 314, 323, 324, 325
risk-taking, 246
river basins, 21, 103, 105, 107, 168, 177
river flows, 107
roots, 29, 192
routes, 44
routines, 130
rubrics, 331
rule of law, 45, 56, 61, 68, 71, 72, 75, 77, 78, 81, 83, 89, 90, 92, 179, 181, 183, 199, 201, 222, 224, 315, 317, 326, 327, 337, 357, 358, 365, 380, 385, 413
rules, 160, 259, 326, 331, 356, 394, 407, 413
runoff, 102, 104
rural areas, 22, 24, 44, 45, 59, 95, 96, 101, 103, 109, 112, 113, 114, 115, 116, 117, 119, 120, 135, 136, 144, 146, 156, 240, 248, 282, 286, 340, 344, 345
rural development, 15, 25, 50, 58, 61, 65, 66, 99, 108, 109, 112, 114, 125, 133, 171, 223, 345
rural people, 43, 258
rural population, 10, 43, 53, 55, 103, 108, 109, 110, 298
rural poverty, 43, 44, 50, 111, 158

S

safe haven, 10, 75
safe havens, 75
safety, viii, 47, 50, 70, 82, 97, 100, 101, 117, 137, 149, 155, 167, 168, 177, 228, 233, 242, 251, 280, 343, 379, 380, 386, 389, 405
sanctions, 336, 384
sanctuaries, 255, 318, 360, 365
savings, 140, 216, 251
scaling, 306, 315, 316, 340, 348
scarce resources, 48
scholarship, 398, 401
school, 1, 8, 10, 18, 23, 35, 45, 47, 49, 85, 86, 89, 103, 105, 112, 123, 130, 134, 138, 142, 143, 144, 145, 146, 147, 155, 158, 170, 173, 175, 191, 243, 262, 263, 265, 273, 274, 293, 294, 306, 312, 317, 349, 350, 351, 353, 354, 356, 375
school enrollment, 45, 312
science, 134, 145, 152, 234, 264, 275, 295
SCO, 6, 168, 179, 367
scope, 19, 91, 92, 95, 101, 114, 147, 150, 168, 179, 325
seasonality, 53, 155
secondary education, 23, 143, 146, 147, 149, 150, 190, 261, 262, 317, 354
secondary information, 212
secondary school students, 145
secondary schools, 124, 142, 262, 263, 294, 354
secondary teachers, 262
securities, 64
security assistance, 14, 65, 67
security forces, 17, 67, 74, 75, 76, 223, 370
security services, 16, 35
seed, 29, 109, 344
self employment, 270
sellers, 139
seminars, 266
Senate, 8
sensitivity, 16, 33, 181, 200, 209, 212
sensitization, 410
sentencing, 237, 238, 389, 404, 407, 415
sequencing, 35, 201, 202, 305, 365
service industries, 129, 340
service provider, 122, 149, 250, 272, 350, 382, 384, 408, 411
service quality, 24, 25, 136, 139, 167
settlement policy, 23
settlements, 22, 23, 44, 122, 126, 127, 128, 129, 131, 175, 253, 254, 289
sewage, 50
sex, 184, 185, 263, 265, 411
Shanghai Cooperation Organization, 6, 118, 179
shape, 34
Sharia, 8, 81, 89, 234
sheep, 112
shelter, 22, 68, 125, 126, 127, 131, 173, 219, 254, 290, 343, 366
shock, 42
shortage, 44, 120, 133, 144, 145, 146
short-term interest rate, 64
signals, 227
signs, 384
silver, 20, 132
skilled workers, 124
skills training, 25, 111, 265, 317
small businesses, 50
smoking, 138
smuggling, 167
social acceptance, 28, 184
social contract, 90, 224
social costs, 188
social development, 18, 51, 102, 165, 176, 178, 181, 182, 187, 188, 199, 246, 317, 321
social environment, 138, 340, 385
social exclusion, 313
social expenditure, 61
social fabric, 67
social group, 34
social housing, 343
social indicator, 306
social inequalities, 45
social justice, 157
social organization, 384
social programs, 50
social responsibility, 246
social services, 10, 27, 109, 119, 131, 141, 166, 175, 222, 312
social support, 26, 154, 156, 157, 158, 159, 173
social welfare, 8
social workers, 160
society, 2, 8, 20, 24, 25, 26, 28, 30, 33, 42, 51, 55, 67, 68, 73, 75, 77, 82, 84, 85, 94, 96, 108, 111, 140, 150, 151, 153, 156, 162, 170, 173, 176, 183, 184, 191, 192, 220, 243, 246, 273, 300, 303, 305, 306, 317, 321, 340, 343, 350, 359, 364, 376, 407
software, 170
solid waste, 130
solidarity, 18, 26, 85
solution, 59, 75, 239, 312, 365
Somalia, 181
South Asia, 5, 6, 12, 19, 42, 100, 171, 172, 177, 178, 179, 306, 340, 367
South Asian Association for Regional Cooperation, 6

sovereignty, 72, 73, 227, 313, 352, 357, 362
Soviet Union, 162
spare capacity, 396
specialization, 80, 389, 409
specifications, 362
speech, 1, 151, 375
spending, 47, 48, 49, 50, 65, 74, 140, 189, 193, 196, 206, 210, 213, 227, 305, 325, 329
spin, 133
Spring, 41, 46, 155, 299, 305
stability, vii, 8, 10, 12, 13, 15, 17, 48, 53, 54, 55, 59, 60, 62, 63, 67, 69, 71, 72, 73, 74, 75, 76, 84, 92, 131, 155, 157, 162, 163, 165, 177, 179, 191, 201, 204, 206, 209, 210, 312, 316, 321, 322, 323, 350, 352, 359, 360, 365, 367, 370
stabilization, 73, 107, 199, 203, 209, 316, 340, 364
staff members, 169
staffing, 249, 344, 388, 401
stakeholders, 16, 29, 32, 80, 83, 84, 124, 128, 141, 187, 193, 196, 200, 201, 204, 214, 222, 233, 235, 242, 243, 250, 305, 307, 322, 386, 388, 410, 414
standard of living, 60, 66
standardization, 23, 148, 149
state, vii, 1, 2, 8, 9, 12, 13, 17, 18, 19, 20, 24, 25, 27, 34, 56, 66, 77, 79, 91, 93, 95, 96, 97, 99, 103, 109, 114, 133, 148, 151, 170, 176, 180, 181, 209, 222, 240, 315, 328, 357, 359, 375, 376, 379, 382, 383, 396, 399
states, 41, 86, 90, 142, 180, 200, 287, 385
statistics, 108, 185, 212, 214, 263, 265, 266
statutes, 81, 335
stomach, 41
storage, 21, 102, 105, 162, 236, 241, 322, 348, 408, 411
stoves, 167
strategic planning, 139, 153, 267, 333
stress, 161, 222
structural reforms, 315, 320, 327
structure, 30, 31, 51, 81, 105, 128, 136, 148, 168, 211, 227, 249, 250, 255, 275, 277, 296, 341, 357, 361, 362, 382, 384, 387, 388, 400, 413
structuring, 332
student development, 402
style, 146
subscribers, 11, 19
subsidy, 129, 254, 290
subsistence, 110
sugar beet, 94
suicide, 158
supervision, 32, 139, 161, 177, 213, 252, 344, 386, 407
supply chain, 113

support services, 265, 269
Supreme Council, 6, 103, 106
Supreme Court, viii, 3, 9, 74, 78, 81, 183, 284, 326, 377, 378, 379, 380, 383, 384, 385, 388, 394, 395, 408, 409, 410
surplus, 70, 228, 302
surveillance, 113, 138, 261
survey design, 40
survivors, 157, 158, 160
sustainability, 18, 52, 54, 59, 60, 62, 63, 66, 74, 89, 100, 101, 149, 160, 166, 195, 196, 201, 205, 206, 223, 246, 255, 316, 320, 327, 328, 329, 337, 344, 346, 370, 401
sustainable development, viii, 20, 67, 76, 105, 107, 131, 132, 191, 198, 221, 379
sustainable economic growth, 12, 127, 133, 322, 350
sustainable growth, 111, 190, 268, 297
sweat, 129
Sweden, 166
Switzerland, 166
synchronization, 209
synthesis, 313

T

tactics, 404
Tajikistan, 11, 97, 114, 116, 177, 241, 264
Taliban, vii, 8, 9, 13, 67, 68
Tanzania, 132
target, 15, 24, 25, 51, 60, 113, 128, 140, 142, 151, 157, 158, 184, 186, 192, 200, 218, 228, 284, 286, 299, 327, 334, 337, 348, 386, 391, 413
tariff, 92, 93, 239, 249, 288
tariff rates, 92
tax base, 60, 123, 329
tax collection, 191, 329
tax deduction, 246
tax policy, 61
tax system, 128, 191, 242
taxation, 98, 122, 131
taxes, 23, 123, 128, 134, 161, 174, 242, 275, 289, 341
taxis, 247
teacher training, 10, 23, 143, 146, 262, 351, 356
teachers, 10, 16, 18, 35, 85, 89, 142, 143, 144, 145, 146, 149, 158, 262, 264, 293, 294, 352, 353, 354, 402
teams, 162, 180, 196, 197, 275, 305, 358, 362
technical assistance, 28, 89, 94, 108, 154, 181, 184, 185, 186, 194, 195, 197, 205, 224, 234, 247, 277, 361, 386
technical support, 25, 114, 184, 186, 283
techniques, 257, 298, 389, 394
technologies, 61, 91, 97, 115, 269

technology, 27, 134, 137, 149, 152, 162, 171, 178, 356, 388, 393, 398
technology transfer, 171
telecommunications, 11, 19, 22, 64, 94, 96, 114, 115, 119, 120, 121, 124, 176, 224, 292, 312, 343
telecommunications services, 176
telephone, 22, 120
television stations, 151
tempo, 302
tenants, 130
tension, 179
tensions, 27, 166, 205
tenure, 22, 23, 87, 111, 126, 128, 129, 131, 221, 253, 289
term plans, 229
terminals, 250, 287
territorial, 72, 75, 352, 357
territory, 20, 132
terrorism, 2, 27, 67, 71, 72, 73, 75, 145, 179, 188, 198, 226, 227, 318, 360, 376, 382
terrorist activities, 179
terrorist groups, 26, 75
terrorist organization, 318
terrorists, 10, 12, 17, 145, 365
tertiary education, 142, 143, 144, 145, 150, 221
testing, 139, 262, 394
textbooks, 145, 263
thoughts, 151
threats, 12, 67, 70, 72, 74, 145, 168, 198, 357
time frame, 28, 205
tobacco, 54
total revenue, 60
tourism, 130
tourmaline, 20, 132
TPA, 302
trade, 11, 12, 18, 19, 22, 27, 45, 50, 52, 54, 73, 76, 78, 79, 87, 91, 92, 93, 94, 101, 114, 116, 117, 122, 125, 148, 167, 169, 174, 177, 178, 179, 180, 181, 188, 192, 212, 221, 229, 239, 253, 289, 315, 318, 322, 340, 363, 364, 365, 366, 367, 384, 389
trade agreement, 93, 179
trade policy, 19
trade preference, 181
traditional practices, 382
traditions, 120, 157, 380
trafficking, 68, 72, 73, 75, 76, 157, 178, 180, 318, 366, 389
training programs, 27, 73, 93, 145, 186, 238, 336, 337, 352, 356, 388, 392, 402, 412
transaction costs, 193
transactions, 64, 83, 92, 122, 123, 362, 411

transformation, 9, 12, 25, 96, 124, 143, 224, 225, 227, 345
translation, 139, 387, 390, 397, 400
transmission, 50, 99, 100, 118, 120, 150, 167, 241, 247, 248
transparency, viii, 64, 76, 79, 93, 119, 122, 140, 167, 172, 174, 181, 182, 191, 193, 206, 211, 238, 240, 247, 251, 256, 268, 313, 315, 324, 327, 329, 330, 331, 358, 360, 369, 379, 412, 413
transpiration, 253
transport, 15, 21, 22, 50, 60, 83, 105, 115, 116, 117, 118, 119, 130, 150, 167, 169, 174, 178, 218, 224, 246, 250, 251, 252, 287, 288, 289, 313, 315, 336, 340, 341, 345, 367, 386
transport costs, 345
transportation, 11, 19, 21, 24, 54, 66, 83, 84, 115, 116, 117, 118, 119, 130, 136, 137, 223, 224, 233, 245, 250, 251, 284, 288, 340, 382, 386, 395, 396
transportation infrastructure, 24, 66, 136, 223, 224, 245
treaties, 183, 383, 384, 399
treatment, 27, 74, 138, 172, 177, 180, 205, 261, 297, 318, 364, 366, 389, 406, 407
trial, 235, 238, 331, 390, 404, 405
trust fund, 28, 196, 205
Trust Fund, 4, 5, 6, 62, 180, 193, 205, 329, 360, 362, 378, 388
tuberculosis, 135
Turkmenistan, 116, 367

U

unemployment rate, 47, 53, 54, 149, 225, 350
UNHCR, 7, 10, 26, 166, 276, 277, 278, 279
unification, 106
United, 7, 27, 152, 153, 166, 179, 211, 359, 378, 390, 399
United Kingdom, 166
United Nations (UN), 7, 12, 14, 27, 32, 76, 140, 152, 153, 164, 179, 211, 213, 214, 271, 359, 360, 378, 390, 394, 399
United States, 7
universities, 23, 49, 142, 143, 144, 145, 148, 170, 184, 233, 257, 264, 295, 350, 354, 355, 392, 398, 401, 402
updating, 146, 185, 236, 330, 409
urban, 11, 22, 23, 34, 39, 42, 43, 44, 45, 46, 47, 48, 49, 50, 59, 81, 96, 102, 103, 104, 105, 106, 117, 118, 119, 125, 126, 127, 128, 129, 130, 131, 144, 145, 146, 156, 168, 169, 173, 187, 190, 219, 249, 250, 253, 254, 255, 257, 282, 286, 287, 289, 290, 291, 300, 305, 316, 339, 340, 341, 342, 343

urban areas, 22, 23, 43, 45, 46, 49, 81, 96, 102, 103, 104, 125, 126, 127, 128, 146, 190, 282, 286, 287, 289, 290, 291, 300, 343
urban population, 11, 42, 43, 44, 103, 126, 341, 343
urban schools, 144, 145
urbanization, 11, 22, 125, 127, 128, 255
Uzbekistan, 116

V

vaccine, 135, 138, 220
vacuum, 18
validation, 341
variations, 60
vehicles, 96, 117, 167, 168, 247, 321, 350, 397
Vice President, 124
victims, 10, 26, 50, 68, 72, 83, 154, 155, 157, 158, 159, 173, 237, 238, 272, 273, 274, 359, 361, 382, 386, 389, 396, 404, 406, 412, 415
violence, 1, 27, 50, 68, 76, 125, 155, 157, 173, 184, 209, 237, 273, 314, 318, 357, 360, 375, 387, 389, 396, 406
vision, viii, 14, 18, 30, 39, 66, 69, 77, 78, 82, 86, 90, 96, 102, 108, 115, 119, 120, 125, 131, 141, 144, 151, 163, 177, 187, 188, 191, 199, 321, 339, 359, 379, 380
visions, 380
vocational education, 23, 24, 84, 142, 143, 145, 148, 149, 150, 220, 243, 244, 261, 265, 295, 317, 351, 353, 361, 391, 392
vocational training, 16, 19, 23, 35, 82, 83, 93, 142, 143, 145, 148, 150, 169, 175, 234, 284, 337, 360, 391, 392, 398, 401
volatility, 54, 63
voters, 9, 79
vulnerability, 16, 22, 27, 33, 39, 42, 45, 47, 50, 53, 110, 113, 117, 140, 154, 156, 157, 161, 173, 184, 189, 192, 200, 214, 270, 272, 285, 306, 392, 394
vulnerable people, 23, 108, 113

W

wages, 27, 44, 160, 183, 251
walking, 135, 220, 297
war, vii, 8, 10, 24, 26, 68, 96, 103, 116, 154, 155, 157, 158, 159, 160, 190, 273, 274, 398
waste, 96, 100, 101, 102, 123, 130, 138, 169
waste management, 102, 130, 169
wastewater, 106
water, 8, 11, 12, 21, 23, 36, 40, 46, 50, 60, 61, 66, 68, 94, 98, 102, 103, 104, 105, 106, 107, 108, 109, 112, 113, 115, 119, 125, 126, 127, 130, 133, 134, 138, 149, 167, 168, 169, 172, 174, 175, 178, 219, 220, 221, 223, 224, 245, 253, 255, 256, 257, 258, 269, 277, 289, 290, 291, 293, 298, 299, 306, 316, 340, 344, 345, 347, 366
water quality, 21, 102, 104
water resources, 21, 98, 102, 103, 104, 105, 106, 107, 168, 219, 224, 255, 257, 258, 291, 293, 344, 345
water supplies, 21, 103, 104, 138
watershed, 268
weakness, 161, 170, 319, 368
wealth, vii, 8, 268, 297, 339
weapons, 361
web, 130, 259, 291
websites, 120, 122, 232, 259, 390, 399
welfare, 17, 39, 73, 78, 113, 154, 166, 192, 197, 215, 296, 305, 366
well-being, 108, 151, 317
wells, 7, 21, 112
Western Europe, 340
wetlands, 255, 268
WHO, 172
wholesale, 54
wildlife, 113
windows, 362
wires, 120
withdrawal, 76
witnesses, 237, 238, 382, 386, 389, 403, 404, 405, 406, 407
women managers, 184
wood, 96
work activities, 49
work environment, 184
workers, 24, 44, 49, 96, 100, 132, 135, 136, 137, 138, 139, 159, 167, 172, 194, 272, 273, 317, 349, 356, 368
workforce, 53, 66, 79, 80, 87, 139, 142, 174, 223, 280, 391, 401
working conditions, 315, 327, 398
working groups, 32, 184, 208, 249, 320, 326, 369
workplace, 76
World Bank, 7, 17, 43, 59, 78, 148, 181, 202, 203, 214, 303, 305, 306
World Trade Organization (WTO), 7, 93, 121, 179

Y

yield, 209, 215, 244
young adults, 144, 317, 351
young people, 9, 24, 79, 151, 153, 243, 267
young women, 153, 267

Z

Zimbabwe, 181
zinc, 20, 132